The Entrepreneurial Manager

IN THE SMALL BUSINESS

The
Entrepreneurial
Manager
IN THE SMALL BUSINESS

TEXT, READINGS, AND CASES

WILLIAM NAUMES

Clark University

Addison-Wesley Publishing Company

Reading, Massachusetts
Menlo Park, California ▪ London ▪ Amsterdam
Don Mills, Ontario ▪ Sydney

ISBN 0-201-05201-6
ABCDEFGHIJK-MA-798

Preface

This text is directed to managers who prefer to chart their own course in the business world. The entrepreneur who desires to test all his or her skills in a highly personalized structure is the subject of the text, cases, and readings presented here.

A primary assumption of this text is that the reader has already acquired a background of knowledge in the functional areas of business administration. We will attempt to build on that foundation to enable beginning entrepreneurs to develop and maintain their own operations.

The text is not directed toward any specific functional area. Rather, it emphasizes *management* of all aspects of the small firm. This emphasis, however, includes the entrepreneurial manager who might also anticipate direct involvement with new or small businesses through various service-oriented functions.

Although the text is not functionally oriented, some of the cases and readings center on specific functional problems (i.e., finance, marketing, production, operations). As such, cases are drawn from a wide spectrum of business areas. Manufacturing firms, financially oriented institutions, service organizations, and commercial firms are all represented.

Typically, business texts have not been oriented toward entrepreneurial managers. They have been primarily oriented toward professional, functionally oriented managers.

Typically, we know much more about professional managers than entrepreneurs. We can not only identify professionals, but we also know how to recruit, train, and motivate them. At best, we can only identify entrepreneurial managers.

The blame for this failing, if indeed it is one, belongs at least in part to schools of business. Most schools of business or administration have placed primary emphasis on developing professional, functionally oriented administrators. The perceived, current demand is from large organizations. These large organizations say they need competent managers to serve primarily as specialists within given functions. The objective is to make students proficient in the use of various kinds of analytical tools, both quantitative and qualitative. Little effort is made to develop creativity or entrepreneurial spirit.

Until recently, this may well have been a reasonable strategy for educational institutions. Supply of personnel had been maintained at reasonable levels consistent with demand. Over the last several years, however, a subtle shift has occurred in the environment leading several schools to question the wisdom of this strategy. These changes occurred from two separate directions at approximately the same time.

Entrepreneurs are a scarce and valuable commodity. They provide a vital link in the evolution and revolution of business forms and ideas in our society. Too often they have been pictured as shady operators on the used car lot. This is due in great part to their being misunderstood by society as a whole and educators in particular. Instead of ostracizing them as mavericks, threats to the status quo, we should try to understand them and bring them into the mainstream of business life.

Entrepreneurs must be shown how to use current ideas and practices presented in business education. The management function is a combination of intellectual, social, and political approaches. The key in presenting these approaches to entrepreneurs is to educate them in their uses without inhibiting the iconoclastic goals essential to their progress. We must develop their analytical skills while preserving their entrepreneurial natures. Basically, we must show them how to overcome the more standardized problems with available management techniques and tools while using their own, unique skills to overcome nonprogrammable problems.

The various materials presented in this text are designed to help entrepreneurial managers forcast both programmable and nonprogrammable problems. The book also provides methods for solving both types of problems building on the natural instincts embodied in the type of person who treads the entrepreneurial path.

Part I of the book is composed of two portions. The text portion is designed to present general, introductory comments on the various issues outlined in the chapters. Problems, opportunities, and methods of overcoming the former and taking advantage of the latter are briefly described in these sections. The readings expand on these general areas of discussion. They provide both descriptive and prescriptive comments to supplement the text material.

Part II is composed of cases which have been selected to provide practice to potential entrepreneurs in evaluating and solving problems they are likely to face. Although there are specific problems presented in the cases, they should be treated merely as symptoms of much broader based issues.

The material presented in this book has been reviewed by many people, either directly or through discussion. I particularly want to express my gratitude to John Bonge, Arnold Cooper, and Karl Vesper for providing editorial comments on a draft version of this text. Also, I want to thank my wife, Peggy, for noting potential problems of style, grammar, and content and suggesting changes for the final version of the book. She also suffered through typing large portions of the draft and final manuscripts.

Keith Nave, my editor, demonstrated great restraint and confidence in bearing with me through the various rewrites of the book.

Of at least equal importance is the inspiration provided by one of my professors at Stanford. Frank Shallenberger presented me with motivation and insight into the world of the entrepreneur. His early involvement in teaching small business and entrepreneurship has provided the impetus for similar courses throughout the country. More important, he has provided the stimulus for many students to try their hand at venture management.

It is to Frank Shallenberger that this book is dedicated.

Worcester, Massachusetts   *W.N.*
June 1978

Contents

3/Financing for the Small Business

4/Entrepreneurial Planning

5/Control in the Small Business

6/Environmental Forces

7/Developing Organizations and Implementing Entrepreneurial Decisions

PART II/CASES

Part I
TEXT
AND
READINGS

1
The Entrepreneur
in
Modern
Organizations

Introduction

Much has been written recently describing how to be successful in entrepreneurial ventures. In this book the emphasis will be on small business and the role it plays in society and the economy. Increasingly, students are becoming aware of the importance of small business. Large corporations don't spring up overnight; their origins can always be traced to some entrepreneur who had an idea of a different way to perform a function needed by others. The key issue that develops is whether entrepreneurs will reap the rewards of their own ideas, or whether it will be others who will benefit from these initial efforts.

Entrepreneurial managers are found throughout society, in both large and small organizations. Their roles are not restricted to profit-oriented organizations. They can be found in public as well as private ventures. They are not bound by sex, religion, race, or age. An understanding of the diversity of entrepreneurs and their impact on society has intensified the need for discussing the factors that lead to their success and failure.

This book does not provide a cookbook approach to helping the entrepreneur succeed. The comments, readings, and cases won't provide a checklist of things to do. If that were all that was presented, it would add little to the entrepreneur's basic store of knowledge. Also, it probably would not be used by actual entrepreneurs, given their basic value system and personality profile. Entrepreneurial managers do not want to be confined by tedious lists and regulations. The very traits admired in entrepreneurs tend to be stifled by the approach taken by many educators and consultants.

The approach taken here will be to explore the role of the entrepreneur in our society, to understand the methods typically used for developing new ideas and implementing those ideas in a complex society. Some of the pitfalls faced by entrepreneurs will be discussed. Methods which have been used by other entrepreneurs to overcome these pitfalls will be presented throughout the book. The key factor will be the spotting and development of entrepreneurial traits, rather than the confinement of these traits. Guidelines and tools will be presented at various stages to assist the entrepreneur in implementing his or her ideas. The guidelines will be general enough to permit flexibility in implementation. I emphasize that they are not designed as procedures to be followed strictly if failure is to be avoided. Rather, they are flexible methods that should be adapted to individual circumstances in a way that best fits the individual.

The Role of the Entrepreneurial Manager

Entrepreneurial managers do more than just start new, small business organizations. Their function in our society is more varied and valuable than that: they also serve as innovators. They should be among the prime challengers of the status quo. They are also risk takers in a society that is generally averse to risky situations. Basically, entrepreneurial managers shake up present values and ideas and lead the rest of society to question current directions.

A question that arises, however, is whether the entrepreneurs can perform this questioning role effectively, given the increasing complexity of our modern economy and society. Questioning based on ignorance or misinformation could be counterproductive or disruptive. Many of the comments presented in later chapters are designed to provide entrepreneurial managers with a realistic format for exploring avenues of questioning current problems. Methods for evaluating the environment as well as developing potential solutions are also presented in a manner designed to provide entrepreneurs maximum freedom of thought and action. The planning model presented in Chapter 4 is designed to provide the format for balanced decision making by entrepreneurs.

Developing the Entrepreneurial Manager

A key criticism that is often leveled at entrepreneurial managers is that they are unable to implement changes in a business setting. Entrepreneurs are frequently able to think of new ways to meet untapped demand. The problem arises when these new ideas run into typical business problems, both in small businesses and in large ones. Fortunately, a group of potential entrepreneurs is now being developed to overcome this problem. This new pool of talent has emerged as a result of certain changes which have taken place in our society.

The first change was a shift in values of many (though not a majority) students in business schools. An increasing number of students didn't particularly want to work for large, established corporations. The advantages of security offered by large organizations had to be weighed against the likelihood of becoming lost in the bureaucracy of the organization. Also, these students believed that they would have to give up both their individuality and their creativity in order to specialize and implement corporate-wide goals and objectives.

These students were searching for alternative methods of using their business-school educations. They found, however, that few of the school programs were designed to help them find outlets in small business. Typical recruiting, like the educational process, was geared toward large, profit-oriented organizations. Students quickly found that career service groups in business schools could not help them find jobs with small business organizations. These students thus had to find positions on their own.

When the students got out into the "real world," moreover, they found that they were ill-prepared to handle the kinds of problems encountered by many small businesses. The behavioral problems they faced involved close personal relations, not the broad organizational schemes frequently discussed in courses. The financial problems could not be solved with the complex approaches discussed in school. Large-scale financing was inappropriate for the relatively minor needs of the small business. These, and other experiences, were extremely frustrating to both the former students and their new employers. Where the students tried to form companies of their own, the frustration was even greater. The feedback to the schools concerning these problems also tended to be faster and more intense. Initially, however, there were relatively few such occurrences.

As time progressed, during the late sixties, more students asked for courses directly relevant to their needs and values. This led to one, or at most a few, courses being offered to these students. The basic objective of most business-school programs was still to develop professional administrators.

Only recently have well-rounded programs been designed and implemented to develop entrepreneurial managers in schools of business. The programs, most of which are too new to be evaluated yet, typically combine course work with field-work experience. Both types of work are designed to replicate problems experienced by small businesses. It is still not known whether this process stimulates or inhibits entrepreneurial development.

The key to this program is a well-integrated program of experiences. The course work provides the theory and background information. The field work, typically in the form of consulting to troubled small businesses, provides actual insights into what goes wrong when trying to implement those theories. This model corresponds to the structure of this text. The first part of the book provides the model for analysis and decision making. The cases provide the vehicle for applying the theories presented in earlier courses as well as the material in the first part of this book.

Entrepreneurs in Large Organizations

The type of entrepreneurial program discussed above is designed primarily to develop the skills required to run successful small businesses. Recently, however, some large businesses have begun seeking to enlist entrepreneurs for their own organizations. As the external environment changes more rapidly, large organizations are realizing that traditional management techniques cannot keep pace. They had hoped, at least initially, that entrepreneurial managers, trained in traditional techniques, could provide the relevant risk acceptance and innovations necessary to discover new opportunities.

At the same time, increasing emphasis has been placed on entrepreneurial actions by noted students of management. Peter Drucker emphasized the key role of the modern entrepreneur in an article for *Harvard Business Review*. He says that management theory has long assumed that "entrepreneurship and innovation lie outside the management scope."[1] The role of management was to utilize efficiently the vast resources of complex organizations. The role of the entrepreneur was to present professional managers with new inventions when they were needed to adapt to changes in the environment. Drucker goes on to state that this assumption must be changed. The rapid environmental changes taking place require that "entrepreneurial innovation will become the very heart and core of management."[2]

Ansoff supports this view in his belief that only those managers who possess an entrepreneurial spirit are able to "anticipate both problems and opportunities."[3] Firms directed by this type of manager do not wait to react to the actions of others. They constantly search for new opportunities in their environment.

Basically, the large organizations were looking for people to shake up the internal environment in a methodical, professional manner. At first, however, it was difficult to find entrepreneurial individuals. And then, after finding them, it was just as difficult to convince them that there was a place for them in large, modern corporations.

At first, entrepreneurial managers were used primarily to head up new, small operations. These operations were typically in high-risk areas or industries. The initial investments were not astronomical, but were usually large enough that the top managers wanted to protect their investments. After enough exposure to these entrepreneurial managers, some organizations began to realize that they could be useful in the main organization as well.

To repeat what was stated earlier, coping with rapidly changing environments required the skills of new and different managers. The standard forms of analysis and budgeting procedures do not necessarily permit managers to react quickly enough. As a result, large organizations have begun using entrepreneurial managers for this purpose. The top managers of the pioneering organizations who have taken this step are hoping that they will be able to find and keep this type of manager. The top managers are also hoping that the entrepreneurs will be able to shake their organizations without toppling them.

In the process of using entrepreneurial managers in this manner, organizations are legitimizing the status of this kind of manager. As Harold Leavitt pointed out in a speech given in 1967, entrepreneurs have not always been presented in the best light. All too often, they have been pictured as hucksters in flashy clothes, selling dubious gold stocks or snake oil. The incorporation of entrepreneurs into the mainstream of American economic life has helped to erase that image. Further successful use of entrepreneurial managers in similar enterprises will lead to acceptance of entrepreneurs. Moreover, this will lead to an increased demand for well-trained entrepreneurial managers. Since business schools have been adept at satisfying the demands of large organizations, they will surely find it worthwhile to develop entrepreneurial programs that will meet the demand of their best clients. This, also, will further legitimize the position of the entrepreneurial manager in our society.

Text Focus

The primary focus of this book, however, is the role of the entrepreneurial manager in the small business environment. There are currently estimated to be eight million business organizations operating in the U.S. economy. Well over seven million of these are legitimately classified as small businesses, no matter whose definition is used. They account for close to half the goods, services, and employment generated by the private sector.

The importance of this sector demands the major emphasis of this book. It is in this sector that entrepreneurs are felt first. The impact of entrepreneurs on any given organization is greater in the small business, simply because they comprise a greater portion of the management in the small business. Entrepreneurs rarely possess the decision-making authority in large organizations that they possess in small organizations. It is to enhance that decision-making capacity that the material in the remainder of this text is aimed.

Specific sections will present discussions of several functions crucial to entrepreneurial success. Issues related to venture initiation will lead to different forms of venture capital and funding.

A planning format appropriate to entrepreneurial ventures is presented to provide the basis for sound decision making. A valid control system is inherent in any realistic planning process. Entrepreneurial ventures don't necessarily have the historical data typical of larger organizations. This requires adapting control methods to specific problems found in the entrepreneurial venture.

Planning does not rely strictly on internal factors, however. Market opportunities develop from the external environment. Constraints and opportunities in that environment are explored in Chapter 6. Regulation, technology, the economy, and social forces in general are discussed to note the effects they have on entrepreneurs and their ventures.

The text and readings end with a discussion of problems associated with implementing entrepreneurial decisions. Particularly, the fit between the factors presented earlier and the organization is highlighted. Typical stages of organizational growth are presented.

The cases presented after the text and readings are designed to present examples of how entrepreneurs have reacted to various pressures. The purpose of these cases is to help potential entrepreneurs develop the ability to analyze and solve problems in general. The cases presented should be regarded as opportunities to develop general skills as opposed to lessons in how to cope with specific issues.

Summary

We have seen that the entrepreneur has held an important position in our society. Entrepreneurs can be found in all walks of life and in most areas of endeavor. Their roles are not restricted to small, profit-oriented business enterprises; they also serve as innovators and risk takers in our society.

Problems arise when entrepreneurs seek programs designed to train them for positions in small and large organizations. Traditionally, business education is designed to produce functionally oriented administrators. Changes in the values and career goals of students have led to different ways of thinking about traditional education programs. As these students have filtered out into the economy, they have become more accepted in the society as a whole. This acceptance has led to a legitimization of their role and an increased demand for this type of manager. Hopefully, this will lead in turn to the development of more and better conceived programs for the development of entrepreneurial managers.

The remainder of this book is designed to present a combination of text, readings, and cases to expand the creativity of entrepreneurial managers. The various factors are not meant to confine decisions of entrepreneurs. Rather, the objectives are to provide entrepreneurs with the means to implement and develop these basic traits leading to their increased demand.

Topical areas such as financing, planning, and controlling organizations are designed to demonstrate common pitfalls. Some general methods of overcoming these problem areas are also presented. Other key problem areas in the internal and external environment are discussed as well. The case studies are designed to present the basis for class discussion and analysis. They are not designed to provide either good or bad examples of entrepreneurial practice. They should be used to show how other entrepreneurs have approached real problems and opportunities. Students should be encouraged to develop their own analyses of the environment as well as methods of taking advantage of, or overcoming, the environment. In this manner, students will be able to advance their own position as entrepreneurial managers. Further, they will aid in the development of the entrepreneur in our society as a whole.

Readings

The three readings following this chapter present a general discussion of the characteristics and roles of entrepreneurs in modern society. Patrick Liles explores studies designed to discover which traits are typically found, or lacking, in successful entrepreneurs. Particularly, he notes that external stimuli may be just as important as particular internal traits. Being in the right place at the right time with the proper resources leads to entrepreneurial ventures, at least at the outset. These environmental factors help to set the entrepreneur apart from other managers, as Liles notes.

Craig Lundberg supports this notion in his article, "On the Usefulness of Organizational Rascals." Entrepreneurs are necessary for all organizations, if these organizations are to adapt to an increasingly complex society. Lundberg emphasizes the role of the entrepreneur, regardless of organizational setting, as a stimulus for change. He says the entrepreneur provides the organization with an ability to take a proactive as opposed to reactive role relative to its environment.

Arnold Cooper, in "Incubator Organizations and Other Influences on Entrepreneurship," demonstrates that more than the entrepreneurial spirit and traits are necessary to increase one's chances of a successful venture. If the total environment provides a conducive atmosphere, as is found in several areas of the country, the development of entrepreneurial ventures is enhanced.

All these articles expand on the position taken in this book. Entrepreneurs are not necessarily born. All of us have the potential for taking the proactive role. Much depends on the position of the individual when confronted with an entrepreneurial activity. Success after the initial stage, however, requires a well-formulated decision process. It is this process that is expanded in succeeding chapters and in the cases.

REFERENCES

1. Peter F. Drucker, Management's new role, *Harvard Business Review* (Nov.-Dec. 1969), p. 50.

2. Ibid., p. 52.

3. H. Igor Ansoff, *Corporate Strategy* (New York: McGraw-Hill, 1965), p. 208.

Who Are the Entrepreneurs?

Patrick R. Liles

It's a game not everyone can play, but more people should be aware of this career alternative.

Most American businessmen have at some time in their careers thought about starting their own company. Some have envisioned their own enterprise as an avenue to personal wealth through large capital gains. To them, there is a beautiful formula for financial success: *(1) start a small company, preferably in a glamour industry; (2) generate rapid growth in sales and profits; (3) then sell out either to the public or to some large acquisitive conglomerate.*

Others have seen their own company as an opportunity to do what they really wanted to do: to get close to a sport by developing a ski area, or to reduce a new technology to practical use. Still others have sought an escape from stultifying large-company constraints, politics, or career impasses. In their dreams, their own venture would be a means to gain the top position in a business.

Despite dreams, wishful thinking, and even plans, few people actually take the step of trying to start a company. Why is this? Is there a special breed of man which is particularly inclined to become an entrepreneur? Are there special characteristics or conditions which stimulate entrepreneurial activities?

The basic questions we are asking here are classic ones: Are entrepreneurs born or are they made? If they can be made, what are the ingredients? I have reached the conclusions that, given a degree of ambition and ability not uncommon to many individuals, certain kinds of experiences and situational conditions—rather than personality or ego—are the major determinants of whether or not an individual becomes an entrepreneur.

If we examine some of the attitudes in the subculture of American businessmen we find that there are significant connotations to starting a company as a career alternative. Almost everyone gets a glow—a tingle—at the idea of being an entrepreneur. To men in their thirties and forties the idea of starting a company means "free enterprise" and "opportunity," as reflected in Horatio Alger stories. In value terms of the younger generation, starting a company is a way to "do your own thing." For such businessmen and for many business school students, starting a successful

Patrick R. Liles, "Who are the Entrepreneurs?" pp. 5–14, *MSU Business Topics,* Winter 1974. Reprinted by permission of the publisher, Division of Research, Graduate School of Business Administration, Michigan State University.

Patrick R. Liles is on the faculty of the Graduate School of Business Administration, Harvard University.

company is a very attractive idea, yet only rarely do they seem to consider it a serious alternative. When a possible opportunity presents itself, there is somehow too little time to investigate it properly and too little time to determine whether or not the idea really makes sense. Thus, it appears that *most* would-be entrepreneurs stop before they get started. Unfortunately, there is very little information on people who have had ideas about starting companies but never seriously pursued them.

We might think that we already know a lot about the entrepreneurs themselves—those who actually go ahead and start companies. Yet, do we really? We find that there are people who think of entrepreneurs being formed by school systems and child raising,[1] by rejecting fathers,[2] or by the business environment.[3] However, efforts to measure and predict entrepreneurial potential are, at best, still in the development stages.[4]

Perhaps one of the best broad-based studies on entrepreneurs was carried out by Orvis F. Collins and David G. Moore at Michigan State University in 1964. Using a series of personal interviews and psychological tests, they reached a number of rather unsettling conclusions regarding people who start their own company:

> Throughout the preceding analysis, obviously we have been having difficulty deciding whether the entrepreneur is essentially a "reject" of our organizational society who, instead of becoming a hobo, criminal, or professor, makes his adjustment by starting his own business; or whether he is a man who is positively attracted to succeed in it. We have, perhaps without intention, regarded him as a reject.
>
> Entrepreneurs are men who have failed in the traditional and highly structured roles available to them in the society. In this . . . entrepreneurs are not unique. What is unique about them is that they found an outlet for their creativity by making out of an undifferentiated mass of circumstances a creation uniquely their own: a business firm.
>
> The men who travel the entrepreneurial way are, taken on balance, not remarkably likeable people. This, too, is understandable. As any one of them might say in the vernacular of the world of the entrepreneur, "Nice guys don't win."[5]

Several small-sample studies at Harvard and MIT have yielded results different from the Collins and Moore study.[6] Entrepreneurs were found not to be failures. Instead "most of the founders had experienced a generally higher than average level of success in their previous employment. Several had established outstanding records of achievement."[7] These entrepreneurs seemed more typical of the successful, hard-charging, young business executive or engineer than a reject figure.[8]

One possible explanation, of course, is that people in Michigan are very different from those in New England. It might be more helpful, however, if we categorized in some detail: (1) the kinds of business which are used in studies of small business fatality rates and in the Collins and Moore study, and (2) the kinds of business which might be started as alternatives to professional management or engineering careers. The survey-type studies are comprehensive in that they essentially look at *all* companies which are started within a particular period of time. This includes a wide range of business ventures: dry cleaners, retail shops, electronics manufacturers, computer software firms, gas stations, and so forth. Each of these is used in the computation of a wide range of statistics about the rise and demise of new companies. There should be no reason to doubt the aggregate figures or the results of in-depth studies made of these situations. The Collins and Moore study looked at 110 manufacturing firms started between 1945 and 1958 in Michigan but made no further distinctions as to the nature of the business, size, or potential.

If we consider kinds of ventures which might be of interest to a professional manager or an engineer, the vast majority of the enterprises started each year (and, therefore, the bulk of those considered in large, broad-based studies) would not be included. A dry cleaning establishment or a small metal fabricating shop is not the basis for the dreams of these people. From their perspective (and therefore the perspective of this article), we should label this subcategory of small business as *marginal firms*.

That leaves us with the task of considering the kinds of venture situations which are potentially attractive career alternatives. The first, which I have labeled the *high-potential venture*, is the company which "is started with the intention that the venture grow rapidly in sales and profits and become a large corporation."[9] In its planning stage the high-potential venture is the extreme of personal economic opportunity, the entrepreneur's big dream: such as Polaroid, Digital Equipment, Scientific Data System, Cartridge Television, Viatron, and so on.

Another type of enterprise, less obvious than the high-potential venture, also holds a strong interest for many would-be entrepreneurs. This type of venture we might call the *attractive small company*. In contrast to the high-potential venture, the attractive small company is not intended to become a large corporation, probably will never have a public market for its stock, and will not be attractive to most venture capital investors. However, in contrast to the marginal firms, attractive small companies can provide salaries of $40,000 to $80,000 per year, perquisites (company car, country club memberships, travel, and so forth) to its owner/managers, and often flexibility in life-style such as working hours, kinds of projects and tasks pursued, or geographical location. In this subcategory we find such businesses as consulting and other service firms and some specialized manufacturers.

Both the high-potential venture and the attractive small company are interesting beyond the scope of the benefits they may provide to their founder/owners. In the high-potential venture we find the genesis of the major corporations of the future and, therefore, the source of a growing number of jobs and other contributions to the economy. The attractive small companies provide less spectacular but stable inputs of a similar nature. Both of these kinds of companies must gain and maintain their position by providing competitive discomfort to the existing corporate giants through innovation, flexibility, and efficiency.

The marginal firms, on the other hand, provide support for their owners/employers but frequently at a lower level than might be obtained by employment if they could or would work elsewhere. However, these people are not likely to seek employment elsewhere because of their difficulties in functioning in larger and more structured organizations.[10]

Without question, some of the businessmen and engineers who start high-potential ventures or attractive small companies *are* compulsive entrepreneurs. They cannot function effectively in a large organization. They must be their own boss and they may have known this all their lives. It may seem as if they could have behaved in no other way. But what about the others who started companies? What about the entrepreneurs who are basically well-adjusted people and who had given little previous thought, if any, to the idea of their own company? How did these people happen to become entrepreneurs although most were already successful in the pursuit of a more conventional career? What factors play a leading role in determining who becomes an entrepreneur? Which factors might be largely fortuitous and which might be controlled by the individual?

A BASIC PREREQUISITE:
ACHIEVEMENT MOTIVATION

Not all people are inclined to take on significantly more than they have to. A high-potential venture or an attractive small company is usually recognized as requiring a tremendous amount of determined effort and commitment. These kinds of activities are not attempted unless an individual is willing to expend more effort and energy than would be required in a more conventional career.

People high in achievement motivation are the people who strive to make things happen—in the laboratory, on the production floor, in the sales office, in the classroom.[11] Obviously this factor alone is insufficient to determine who starts companies and who does not. But it is a beginning. People without this kind of orientation are unresponsive to the other influences which might encourage starting a venture. However, people with achievement motivation together with other influencing factors may become entrepreneurs.

Achievement motivation can be developed.[12] It would appear unlikely, however, that someone would try to develop achievement motivation in himself in order to start a high-potential venture or an attractive small company. One would expect that it would take a highly achievement-motivated person to want to start either of these kinds of enterprises in the first place.

A DISQUALIFYING INFLUENCE:
SOCIAL SELF-IMAGE

The majority of people trying to do exceptionally well in their careers never seriously consider starting a company. Even among the professional managers or career businessmen the number is small. This is not to say that many of these people would not gladly *be* successful entrepreneurs in their own companies. They are unwilling, however, to take what they see as a backward or downward step necessary to achieve that success.

An acquaintance of the author's, a Yale graduate, has described the effect of his college experience on his own thinking about his career:

> It all came clear one night when I was arguing and describing how Charlie had not been able to go to college, but instead after working in a restaurant had bought a second-hand dump truck. That's when it dawned on me that *because* I went to college I could *never* buy a second-hand dump truck, not even a brand new one with someone else to drive it. When I ran across an old friend, I could not afford to explain that I was the owner of a dump truck. No, I was "with" the ABC Corporation. Not necessary to explain that they are the largest producers of this and that in the world. I was "with" them, and my friend was "with" someone just like them.

Because of recent increasing sentiments favoring personal independence and relevance, we might expect to find in the future a greater general public acceptance of entrepreneurial activities and, therefore, to discover less and less of a conflict between this kind of a career and a person's social self-image. In this sense, it may be becoming easier for someone to decide to strike out on his own than it has been in the past. Perhaps we shall come to the point where becoming an entrepreneur is recognized as a socially legitimate, and even attractive, career alternative.

INFLUENCE ON ENTREPRENEURIAL CAREERS

For the person who has achievement motivation and whose social self-image is not in conflict with starting a company, there are two kinds of conditions which become critical: (1) how *ready* he sees himself for undertaking such a venture, and (2) how many *distractions* or *obligations* he sees holding him back.

The reader will note that what an individual does depends upon how he perceives a situation rather than upon what the situation actually is. This is particularly critical in considering a person's readiness or his restraints because there is no way for anyone to make direct, objective measurements of these characteristics. Instead, a personal assessment of readiness or restraints is going to be a combination of knowledge, insight, judgment, and personal values.

Readiness

In terms of his decision to initiate a company and to try to run it successfully, a person's own assessment of how ready he is probably is a good approximation of how ready he really is. One would not likely find a runner expecting to run a four-minute mile without having some objectively valid reasons behind those expectations. Similarly, an individual who believes that he is ready to start a company is probably reaching that decision from some background of experience, exposure, special skills, and industry knowledge. This is not to say that some people do not try to initiate businesses when they are totally unprepared. It would imply, however, that in most of such instances the individual himself knows very well that the odds are against his being able to make a go of it.

It might be useful to think of an individual's readiness in terms of levels of specific and general self-confidence. Specific self-confidence in this context represents an individual's feeling of mastery over the kinds of tasks and problems he would expect to encounter in starting a company and making it successful. General self-confidence would be his feeling of well-being and his universal assurance that he can accomplish things.

What people learn through a variety of business and related experience accumulates over time. Most people learn relatively more and learn relatively more rapidly early in their careers when much of what they do and see is new to them. And although the relative rate of learning may diminish over time, the cumulative effect is an increasingly competent individual. The evolution of a person's readiness as reflected in his specific self-confidence to master various elements of a venture is depicted graphically in Fig. 1.

General self-confidence, which is necessary for someone to want to try something new, is an elusive idea. Most people can identify in their own lives those periods when they were confident and up for doing big, new things. They can also recall other times when they were anxious, and uncertain—unwilling to get away from the sure and the known. Given the high degree of uncertainty for most people in starting a company, a high level of general self-confidence is necessary for them to be willing to try.

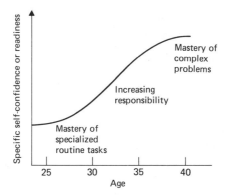

Fig. 1 Readiness to Start a Venture.

Restraints

Perhaps the most effective restraint on someone who otherwise might start a company is his continuing success and satisfaction in pursuing his present job. Why should anyone want to change if things are going well? Especially with the passage of time, increasing seniority for such people means a larger salary, greater responsibilities, and greater benefits. In addition, an individual develops a personal power base within an organization: key knowledge and skills, confidence and loyalty of associates, and so forth, which enables him to assert himself and to be effective. At some point, even in the face of a grave disappointment or disenchantment with the company, it becomes almost prohibitively "expensive" to resign and pursue another career direction.

A would-be entrepreneur's freedom to break away and start a company also becomes hindered by financial and other obligations typical of the U.S. male life-cycle development between the ages of twenty-five and forty years. A man gets married, buys a house, and starts to raise a family. He may immediately incur a sizable mortgage and heavy real estate taxes. With children he acquires the cost burdens for their future education. In addition, he assumes responsibility for his family in the event of his death or disability. These immediate and future costs tie him to a schedule of direct expense payments, a plan for savings, and the costs of insurance.

In addition, the usual pattern is for expenditures on living expenses to rise as a person receives promotions and increases in salary. He now has two cars instead of one, a larger house, and takes more expensive vacations. These costs, closely following if not sometimes overtaking income, as a practical matter are only adjustable upward. And until the children have finished school, it is unusual to find sufficient funds for anything approaching financial flexibility.

Other commitments created by marriage and families may do as much to restrict the freedom and flexibility of would-be entrepreneurs as do his financial obligations. Few women marry with the intention of becoming nurses and housecleaners for absentee husbands. Moreover, personal relationships among people take time, including even the minimum of spoken communication, the ritual of certain courtesies, and the recreational activities people pursue together. And some part of evenings, weekends, and holidays are expected by the family to be devoted to these activities. The family life-cycle experience usually creates an increasing time requirement upon the husband until the children go away to school. As small children begin to lose physical dependence upon their mothers, the role of the father increases in both depth and scope. In the wisdom of everyday life, "This is the time when the children need a father."

Two other interesting phenomena frequently appear as part of the male career life cycle. The first is an evolution of values as the family, especially children, enters into his thinking. Their security is related to his career security and, therefore, his career security becomes more important to him. The time spent with wife and children is more than the minimal to satisfy physical or emotional obligations, but is is a part of a change in the importance he places on what he does—a transition from preoccupation with a career to a realization of new interests in his life. The other aspect, closely related to a change of values, is a change of pace. The drive and physical and emotional energy expended by so many young executives in pursuit of a career do not lend themselves to the pursuit of many other interests. Perceived at the office, Joe at the age of forty is slowing down. Perceived by his wife, Joe is beginning to live. Perceived by himself, Joe is just doing other things—not necessarily enjoying himself more than when he was hotly pursuing his career interests, but enjoying himself in other ways.

For starting a company, an individual's self-perceived *effective capacity* can be derived from a combination of readiness and freedom from restraints and distractions. The results, depicted graphically in Fig. 2, show that effective capacity for starting a company typically increases with age between 25 and 30 as the individual learns rapidly from his early experiences. As a person grows older, however, this trend is modified and then reversed as the marginal learning experience becomes less, and the influences of successful employment plus family-related interests and obligations are incurred. If we identify a certain level of capacity as being necessary for a person to be able to act, we can define a certain period—a *free choice period*—when the individual sees himself as able to act. During this period the capability, the self-confidence, and the career commitment on balance can be more of an influence than are his economic or emotional commitments and interests in other areas.

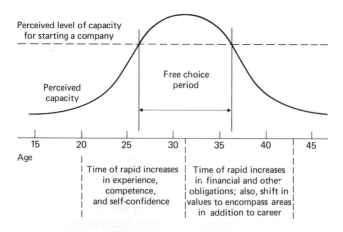

Fig. 2 The Free Choice Period for the Would-Be Entrepreneur.

Precipitating Events

For some people, the combination of circumstances is such that they never attain sufficient capacity to start a company. They never reach a free choice period. Their other commitments become too large before they reach a point where they could strike out on their own. On the other hand, there probably are thousands and thousands of people who pass through a period when they could choose to start a company (when they have sufficient capabilities and few restraints) but they don't do it. It would appear that most people need something more: something to help break established ties, to create resolve, and something specific to pursue.

Three additional kinds of conditions appear to be major influences on decisions to start ventures. The first, *deterioration of job satisfaction*, disposes the individual to consider seriously other career alternatives. The second, *identifying a new venture opportunity*, helps to focus upon what might otherwise be a largely undefined possibility. The third, *encouragement to start a company*, helps an individual make what becomes a very subjective decision.

Dissatisfaction. This element—a negative outlook on his present and future job situation—appears to have a strong influence on the would-be entrepreneur. Relative to his expectations, something disturbs him. A budget for product development is cut back, the right promotion or salary increase does not occur, an addition to his staff is denied. Although entrepreneurs will cite such specific events or unfulfilled expectations as the triggering event which brought them to leave, the reasons usually are more complex. The last straw is but one of a number of disquieting and disappointing incidents which occurred over time and which produced a general feeling of dissatisfaction and, perhaps, resentment.

Job dissatisfaction—for whatever reasons—is not an unusual condition. Changing jobs in most instances is the easiest and more common occurrence. Frequently, it is the opportunity of another job that triggers a critical assessment of one's current employment situation. The transition from one job to another is relatively quick, and its results—at least in the short term—are predictable. In addition, it usually achieves direct use of special skills and knowledge accumulated in prior positions. The unusual thing is when an individual instead of expressing his objections in the conventional way by changing jobs, elects to start a company.

Identifying a new venture opportunity. Opportunities for new ventures, like most other opportunities, usually emerge over time instead of suddenly appearing. In a technical area, an individual may find or learn of a solution to a particular kind of problem and see the potential for using this approach in areas where it has not been applied before. Or in dealing with his employer's suppliers, he may identify key features of purchased products or services which he believes he can handle better, or at less cost, than others in the business. Or he may discover that there are needs for particular products or services that no one else supplies.

An individual in any part of a business enterprise may see potential opportunities for new ventures related to areas in which he is active. The alternative of starting a company becomes possible only when an individual perceives the basis for a viable enterprise and can see himself playing a major role in it. Whether or not a person interprets a situation as an opportunity is determined to a large degree by his perception of his own ability to take advantage of it.

Encouragement and support. Today when most middle managers or engineers begin to think of leaving their jobs they never *seriously* consider the possibility of starting a company. Unlike the established training programs and junior positions created by major corporations, there are no recognized patterns or channels for getting into one's own business. A few individuals have the special insights from their fathers' having been entrepreneurs, but the majority do not. For many, any substantial encouragement or help in the direction of becoming an entrepreneur is happenstance or luck.

Inputs which expand an individual's thinking about starting a company may range from an encouraging word to assistance with a detailed plan and analysis. It may be offered in a casual way or directed toward achieving some specific objective of the helper. In any case, it frequently plays a significant initial role.

One source of support comes from other individuals who share in the feelings of job dissatisfaction and would like to join in pursuing a venture or to become part of a team that undertakes such an effort. These people may represent a logical combination of diverse talents and personalities needed to overcome the problems and inertia of getting the venture started and continuing it as a profitable operation. Moreover, they may be known to each other and therefore represent a degree of certainty about how specific tasks will get done. But at the outset, a key role for these people and for others outside the immediate founder group can be to provide psychological support and encouragement. At the initial stage, momentum for the venture originates from talking it up, proposing different ways to solve the problems of starting, and giving helpful criticism to each other.

A wife's reaction to the idea of starting a company usually is a major influence upon how long and how seriously an individual considers starting a company. Eventually, she will be directly affected. Her husband's happiness, her life-style and the family's financial future are at stake. I have seen wives who have responded with extreme anxiety at the prospect of their husband's starting a company, and I have seen those who have become a key part of the new venture. At either extreme the wife's role is critical.

Another source of support emerges from people to whom the would-be entrepreneur goes for help: potential suppliers, lawyers, bankers, other entrepreneurs, government officials, and so forth. These people can help an individual clarify his own thinking. They can assist in clarifying some of the specific uncertainties associated with starting the venture and can indicate their potential role in providing future information, assistance, or service should the venture be actively pursued. The existence of this kind of readily available help is part of the process of transforming an individual idea into a realistic alternative. If these sources of help are not apparent, then real and imagined problems of getting a venture going may appear insurmountable.

What about Risk?
Up to this point we have not dealt with risk as a factor *per se*. Entrepreneurs, in fact, have been described as people who *like* to take risks. (I believe the entrepreneurs I know would describe such people as fools.) There is more than a little difference between the person who likes risk and the person who finds risk to be a challenge. Risk

covers a multitude of areas, all of which impinge in most instances upon entrepreneurial decisions.

Only when an individual considers starting a company as a serious alternative does his perception of risk become a key factor. Risk in this context has three elements: (1) the perceived "odds" of various good and bad events occurring, (2) the perceived consequences of these events, and (3) the perceived seriousness of these consequences. It should be noted that all three aspects of risk are subjective. The individual's assessment of the risk is what influences his decision.

When an individual is in a free choice stage of his career, and when he is considering starting a company as a specific alternative, the perceived risks in a situation will influence whether or not he goes ahead with it. Below are briefly described four critical risk areas.

Financial risk. The problem most people would think of first is whether or not they can afford to work with little or no salary for a period of several months to several years while the venture is getting started. This is particularly significant for the successful young executive or engineer who has improved his standard of living as he received promotions and salary increases. What would happen to the family budget without the monthly paycheck? How many families are willing to take a severe cutback in their living expenditures?

But this is more a question of financial *sacrifice* than financial *risk*. In most new venture operations the individual will put a significant portion of his savings or other financial resources at stake. This money *is* risked and will in all likelihood be lost if the venture fails. The entrepreneur *may* also be required to sign personally on company obligations which far exceed his personal net worth. When such obligations significantly exceed the tangible net worth of the company, the individual exposes himself to the extreme condition of financial risk: personal bankruptcy.

Career risk. A question raised by most would-be entrepreneurs is whether or not they will be able to find a job should they experience a failure in their own company. Obviously many people who are unsuccessful in their own firms *do* get jobs afterward with major corporations. The question, of course, is how difficult is it to get such a job and how will an employer look upon this kind of prospective employee?

Family risks. As already mentioned, the requirements of starting a new venture frequently consume the energies, emotions, and time of the entrepreneur. As a result, he has little to give elsewhere, and his other commitments suffer. Entrepreneurs who are married, and especially those with children, expose their families, at best, to the risks of an incomplete family experience and, at worst, to permanent emotional scars from inattention, quarreling, and bitterness.

The psychic risk. An entrepreneurial effort by an individual has special features which subject a person to high psychic risk. First, everyone, including the entrepreneur himself, identifies the venture with one or two men. The company *is* these people. In addition, the magnitude of effort required to start a venture has given those activities priority over everything else in their lives—family, friends, and other interests. The greater the commitment, the more the identification with the venture is internalized.

If an individual fails, the experience can be shattering. In addressing the causes of a venture's failure, the entrepreneur himself is always one of the reasons. He planned poorly, he executed poorly, he followed through poorly, or in some way he did not allow sufficient margin for the unexpected. If an individual concludes that his failure in a particular effort was because of an inherent incapacity or inadequacy, he has lost his self-confidence. *The* risk to an individual is the risk of losing his self-confidence. The individual without self-confidence loses not only his abilities to function effectively in his career or profession but also loses his ability to deal effectively in his personal life. Moreover, once begun, such a process gains momentum and tends to whirl into a relentless downward spiral.

Summary and Conclusions

We have examined the entrepreneur who is involved in substantial ventures and have considered what we found in light of traditional thinking that he is a special type of individual—somehow an unusual and uncommon man—a man apart. It probably is true that very successful entrepreneurs *become* men apart. But, at the beginning, when they make the decision to start an entrepreneurial career, they are in most respects very much like many other ambitious, striving individuals. It appears, moreover, that the entrepreneurial interests for those who elect that path are more a function of *external* differences than internal ones—more the result of practical readiness and cost/income constraints than of individual psychology or personality. This is not to suggest that starting a successful company is a game that anyone can play. It is, however, a statement that far more people could become entrepreneurs than ever do, and that the inclination of people to move in this direction could be increased by an increased awareness and recognition of this as a career alternative.

REFERENCES

1. William F. Whyte and Robert R. Braun, Heroes, homework, and industrial growth, *Columbia Journal of World Business*, Spring 1966.

2. Manfred F.R. Kets de Vries, The entrepreneur as catalyst of economic and cultural change (Ph.D. diss., Harvard Graduate School of Business Administration, 1970).

3. Arnold C. Cooper, Entrepreneurial environment, *Industrial Research*, Sept. 1970.

4. Michael Palmer, The application of psychological testing to entrepreneurial potential, *California Management Review*, Spring 1971.

5. Orvis F. Collins and David G. Moore with Darab B. Unwalla, *The Enterprising Man* (East Lansing, Mich.: Division of Research, Graduate School of Business Administration, Michigan State University, 1964), pp. 241, 243, 244.

6. Herbert A. Wainer, The spin-off of technology from government sponsored research laboratories: Lincoln Laboratory (M.A. thesis, Massachusetts Institute of Technology, 1965); Paul V. Teplitz, Spin-off enterprises from a large government sponsored laboratory (M.A. thesis, Massachusetts Institute of Technology, 1965); and Patrick R. Liles, The use of outside help in starting high-potential ventures (DBA diss., Harvard Graduate School of Business Administration, 1970).

7. Liles, The use of outside help.

8. Walter Guzzardi, Jr., *The Young Executives* (New York: The New American Library, 1964).

9. Liles, The use of outside help.

10. Collins, Moore, and Unwalla, *Enterprising Man.*

11. David C. McClelland, Business drive and national achievement, *Harvard Business Review*, July-August 1962.

12. David C. McClelland, Achievement motivation can be developed, *Harvard Business Review*, Nov.-Dec. 1965.

On the Usefulness
of Organizational Rascals

Craig C. Lundberg

Are rascals—the "kooks", the unusual, even the dangerous—important additions to the ranks of modern organizations?

I believe so and in the following I shall propose that organizations set out to deliberately adopt and nurture persons (rascals) who have the potential to change them. Since, by the common customs of organizational life, this is minor heresy, let me outline the argument in advance.

It is commonplace and true that we live in a world of change. Organizations, particularly economic ones, are the major vehicles for initiating and supporting most of the significant changes in our society. Yet, paradoxically, organizations as we know them today are among the most conservative and stable of society's elements. As the bureaucratic form has become widespread and coupled with a corps of "professional" managers, organizations themselves have become one of the most resistant of structures. Yet society's dependence, even need for change, is tied to the capacity of organizations to change themselves. Now it is apparent that organizations will change given some minimal capacity when some stimulus for change exists. Such stimuli are either external, as in a competitive market, altered legislation, or the person of a consultant, and so on, or "internal." To date, internal sources of stimuli have been relatively neglected, with the result that those that are designed into an organization tend to be well controlled or simply lack much punch. Needed, I am arguing, are members whose personality and role set them apart from others and who furnish a source of constant stimulation for organizational development and change.

The Business Quarterly, Winter 1969, pp. 7–13. Reprinted with permission.

THE PARADOX OF CHANGE
FOR ORGANIZATIONS

Most of the key issues for today's executives revolve around the intelligent promotion and management of change. Scientific, technological, and social advances are legion, yet the means to efficiently, economically, and justly utilize them continue to obstruct progress. The major means for utilization is the organization, that crucible of multiple resources that orders and patterns individual as well as societal existence. I suggest that a lot of the difficulty in living with change today is simply that organizations themselves have become dysfunctionally resistant to internal adaption; that is, they do not operate as effectively as they might in the initiation, transmission, or enhancement of change because they themselves are relatively unchangeable. Organizations are caught in a dilemma: to achieve efficiencies and economies with large scale and complex components requires stable, standardized structures and quite a lot of internal controls, yet to foster innovation, acquire growth, diversity, or renewal requires structural adaptiveness and flexibility of organization.

The internal environments of modern, large organizations (the prevalent type, to be sure) are rampant with mechanisms which result in an overriding conformity and acquiescence on the part of their staffs. I refer to mechanisms such as policies, procedures and rules, budgets, appraisal systems, supervisory practices—the host of control devices referred to as "channels and red tape." Management itself is becoming more and more highly trained, to the point where we have idealized the professional manager as someone well adapted, "cool," with technical competence—an "organization man" no less. What this means, of course, is that management is becoming relatively obedient, passive, and reactive. While these trends occur, we, perhaps subconsciously knowing better, decry the disappearance of risk takers, power and achievement-driven men. To recapitulate: training, formal and informal, operates to constrict freedom of thought and action, to reduce the variety of persons, and to reduce individual autonomy. Hence organizations are peopled more and more with "commissars," whose mission is to insure conformity to existing ways, to the image that is current.

OF IMAGES AND CHANGE STRATEGIES

The emphasis on internal conformity and the dilemma that puts organizations in vis-à-vis the management of change has alarmed thoughtful practitioners and observers for some time. Efforts at offsetting or otherwise altering the situation have been fostered; they are roughly of two types: altering the executive's image of himself (and hopefully altering his practice) and devising and incorporating into organizations a variety of nonpersonal change strategies.

Several new images of the executive are being promulgated to counteract the commissar one. Worthy of note are the efforts at bringing formerly secondary aspects of the executive role to the front and of highlighting them as the major functions for the future. One line of reasoning is as follows: human resources are the critical organizational resources, especially those loosely referred to as leadership. The development of executive leadership, therefore, is crucial and one of the primary responsibilities of incumbent executives. Thus an image of the executive as a teacher follows.[1] A somewhat complementary image is promoted by C. West Churchman:

... in the future management will have to become research minded. Good management of the future will have to rely on a sound research base. We are beginning to realize that we shall not be able to solve all the problems of organizational planning for at least several centuries, if ever. The problems are too big for a blueprint theory. This means that the successful manager will have to view his job as not only to earn money, i.e., to maximize profit, but also to learn more about how his organization and the environment function. The successful manager will have to consider himself a researcher...[2]

Paralleling the reorientation of the executive's image of himself have been numerous advancements in implementing change in organizations through strategies other than affecting the personnel. Here efforts at altering the nature or combination of tasks (e.g., job enlargement), the revamping of technology (e.g., computerization), and the modification of structure (e.g., project and matrix organizations) have been focused upon. These strategies of course exploit our preferences for dealing with ideas or things rather than with people (which would mean ourselves).

Let me be clear that new images and new change strategies are useful and no doubt needed. My argument is that they may be necessary but not sufficient for the production of viable internal organizational changes. It appears as if these developments function best to support and develop change, not to continuously prompt it.

A CYCLE OF RENEWAL

To focus our attention once again on the stimuli for internal change, we can ask who unleashes vigorous efforts of renewal. Where do the sparks inciting change come from?

If we examine social units over time, whether persons, groups, or organizations, we can discern them moving through a cycle of renewal. Typically the first phase of the cycle represents some sort of relative equilibrium, a time when habits have taken over. Organizational members then are prone to experience staleness and various sorts of impasses. After a while a second phase begins, this one characterized by spreading monotony and boredom. Sometimes it slips unretrievably, deepening for some members into frustration or even despair. This second phase, if interrupted in time, then becomes a fertile ground for the third phase—the insemination of a new focus, usually in the form of an invitation or challenge. This focus sparks the ambitious, talented, or progressive organization members, provoking a fascination, calling forth their energies and competencies. When a sufficient fascination exists, the fourth phase occurs. Here the whole organization's resources are tapped, mobilized, and channeled in a wide-spread change program, one that produces programs, structures, and practices that transcend previous ones. The concrete manifestations of these phases are familiar enough. However, we have tended to see the first and second phases, as well as the focus of the third, most often as "problems," not viewing them as natural events. Also we tend to perceive mostly external or formally instigated problems. Assured that these will go on occurring, our attention returns to the issue of internal stimuli.

BEYOND COMMISSARS TOWARD CATALYSTS

I propose that large, complex, modern organizations badly need to make a deliberate, calculated investment in a form of human resource that can offset or counteract the complacency and conservatism of trained professional managers and the multiple formal and informal forces which pressure for conformity. If we, in the natural cycle of renewal, require from time to time foci which stimulate, fascinate, "turn us on," why not intentionally spice our organizations with persons capable of this? Let me put this melodramatically: we need "specialists" who, when the organizational doldrums set in, would create dissatisfaction, shatter our rigidities, even foster subversion. Useful, I argue, are persons known to be rogues, gurus, authenticators, and entrepreneurs Mark II! Perhaps it would be useful to briefly indicate what each of these roles is.

A *rogue* is a free-roving adventurer, often manifesting a streak of lawlessness. He tends to operate outside of contemporary structures, violating on occasion the old boundaries of time, place, conscience, and probability. The rogue, as one of his advocates has noted, is "the man of many devices, constantly exploring, probing the environment—learning."[3] Little appreciated is the rogue's frequent use of the frontiers of technology and other innovation in his struggles against being swept up in the establishment.

An *authenticator* is the person who values candidness and truth, who is unafraid to "say it like it is." He relishes being "connected or engaged" with others, but doesn't hold back his feelings toward or reactions to these others. He often is embarrassing to ordinary folk, for he is self-disclosing, often very much in tune to the pattern and flow of sentiment, and passionately seeking greater awareness. The authenticator, in a word, is transparent.

The *entrepreneur Mark II* is Professor H. J. Leavitt's label for a white-hatted entrepreneur, not the shady, corrupt kind, rather a promoter, operator, developer, man with connections.[4] He is, to be sure, usually self-centered and biased toward expediency. His specialty is getting people to swallow things—anything, searching relentlessly for new angles, new openings, new opportunities, for new "marriages." While his activities are often looked down upon, they are surprisingly socially functional, for the entrepreneur Mark II is primarily the archetype of a bridge builder or mediator, whether between society and technology or science or knowledge. He is the out-and-out highly charped promoter.

Gurus are persons who live with vividness and serenity, unfettered by the "games people play." The guru experiences more and more fully than normal individuals. He is in touch with himself in all dimensions; enlightenment from himself and liberation from himself and his culture exemplify him. Gurus invite others to full experiencing of self and worldly things without being captive of either.

Each one of these rascals has the quality to provide fascination for the rest of us. When we or our organizations need, in the cycle of renewal, stimulation, encountering or confronting these roles can "turn us on." Clearly they pose invitation or challenge by just being there. When stale, bored, or frustrated, encountering a rogue, authenticator, entrepreneur Mark II, or a guru charges us to either be different from or like them in some way. Often their very presence is encouraging; we feel that becoming more than we are, or different than we are, is once again possible. They, by example or directly, encourage us to stretch our imaginations and create discontent with the status quo in ourselves and our situations. They sometimes simply confirm our humanness, rekindling aspirations and fostering independence. At minimum these anticommissars spark curiousity or produce wonder in us. In short, when we most need it, they provide the stimulus to "get with it" or at least to reexamine.

Traditionally, of course, society as well as organizations isolate, negatively sanction, disenfranchise, damn, and otherwise attempt to drive out these roles. They are potentially potent foes of the familiar, and we so far have unquestionably feared they might corrupt, breed dissent, tempt us from the status quo. This is all so, but to put it positively, these four roles can help free us from the pressures of social conformity, strengthen our individual autonomies, and promote engagement with the normally unthinkable, unlovable, unfeelingable.

The existence of rascals will have many consequences, only some of which can be hinted at here. The patterns of sponsorship and the practices of personnel counseling will have to be altered as well as to take seriously the notions of organizational and professional allegiance as opposed to only organizational loyalty. Rewarding rascals will be tricky, perhaps management will be prompted to become more conscious of nonformal rewards. Consciously counterbalancing rascals with conservatives will be another consequence. Protecting rascals will probably require the wider use of mechanisms not widespread today, such as appraisal by top management in addition to immediate supervision and more extensive motivational practices. Clearly the various team approaches to management would less likely suppress the existence of rascals.

CONCLUDING COMMENT

In this paper I have suggested that the roles of guru, rogue, entrepreneur Mark II, and authenticator be incorporated, protected, and rewarded. The argument has been that vital, self-renewing organizations require internal as well as external sources of stimulus in the cycle of renewal, that the four roles elaborated are functional as internal stimulus sources, and hence their existence should not be left to chance. While the impact of these four roles can be thwarted or nullified, recent developments in the executive image, in organization forms, and above all in the personal and interpersonal change mechanisms such as sensitivity training, suggest organizations are now ready to tolerate and even exploit these organizationally uncommon persons.

REFERENCES

1. A cogent, if detailed, presentation of this reasoning can be found in Harry Levinson, *The Exceptional Executive* (Cambridge: Harvard University Press, 1968).

2. C. West Churchman, New frontiers to conquer—the research challenge, from a seminar at Indiana University, 1967.

3. George B. Leonard, *Education and Ecstasy* (New York: Delacorte Press, 1968), p. 90.

4. See Harold J. Leavitt, Entrepreneurs, Mark II, *In Search of Leaders,* American Association for Higher Education, 1967.

Incubator Organizations and Other Influences on Entrepreneurship

A. C. Cooper
Purdue University

This paper first considers the possible impact on regional economic development of new growth-oriented firms. Factors influencing the birth of these firms are then examined, with particular emphasis given to the role of incubator organizations and such regional factors as the presence of an "entrepreneurial environment" and the availability of venture capital. Policies which might stimulate the birth of such firms are then considered.

The typical new business in America is a small retail or service business, oriented toward a local market and with limited prospects for growth or even survival. Although these firms may be important in the aggregate and are certainly important to those involved, they are unlikely to contribute significantly to regional economic development. The problems of the many marginal small businesses sometimes overshadow the more substantial contributions of soundly based, growth-oriented small firms.

The potential economic impact from the establishment of new growth-oriented businesses is suggested by two studies of high-technology firms.

1. In Palo Alto, 250 new high-technology firms founded during the decade of the 1960s were studied by Cooper and Bruno in mid-1973 to determine their patterns of development.[1] At that time, when the median firm was seven years old, only 24 percent had discontinued. Of the 250 companies, 27 had sales exceeding $5 million and 20 had sales exceeding $10 million. These new firms have played a major role in making the Palo Alto area a world leader in such growth technologies as integrated circuits.

2. Earlier studies by Roberts of more than 200 high-technology firms in the Boston area also showed the economic impact of growth-oriented new firms.[2] After four to five years, the median company had annual sales of $1.5 million. After the same length of time, only about 20 percent of the firms had discontinued. The aggregate employment provided by the spin-off firms exceeded within a few years that of the university laboratories and individual industrial firms from which the spin-offs had come.

Proceedings of Project ISEED, Summer 1975. Published by Project ISEED, Ltd., The Center for Venture Management, Suite 508, 207 E. Buffalo Street, Milwaukee, WI 53202, U.S.A.

These are only two studies, both related to high-technology firms. We might wish for more extensive studies, relating to a wide range of growth-oriented new firms. However, we can note that almost every major firm now in existence can be traced to small beginnings. From the viewpoint of regional economic development, new independent firms broaden the economic base, lessening the reliance upon a few employers. They also provide not only jobs, but also corporate headquarters, with opportunities for professional employees who can think in terms of lifetime commitments to the region.

Births of growth-oriented companies seem to vary widely from time to time and place to place. We can observe that particular regions sometimes have large numbers of new firms founded, often associated with the same industry. Examples are semi-conductor firms in the Palo Alto area, mobile-home manufacturers in Elkhart, Indiana, and new chemical firms in Buffalo. Sometimes a period of high entrepreneurial activity will subside. Thus, many of the major industries of the American Midwest are relatively mature, tracing their origins to entrepreneurship in the earlier part of the century.

What causes new, growth-oriented firms to be founded at particular times and places? There appear to be three broad influences: (1) the entrepreneur himself, including the many aspects of his background that affect his motivations, his perceptions, and his skills and knowledge; (2) the established organization for which the founder had previously been working, which might be termed an "incubator organization"; (3) various environmental factors, many of them regional in nature. They interact in a variety of ways to create a climate more or less favorable to the founding of new firms.

The characteristics of the individual entrepreneur are being examined in depth by many people in many different countries. It is undoubtedly true that many people, probably most, lack the combination of energy, drive to achieve, and knowledge necessary to establish a growth-oriented business. However, I believe that in industrialized areas there is a substantial pool of potential entrepreneurs. Whether particular qualified people will take the step of starting a new firm depends upon the characteristics of the organizations for which they work and the environmental "climate" for entrepreneurship.

All of the available research shows that entrepreneurs tend to start new firms where they are already living and working. It is the nature of the established organizations already within a region which influence whether entrepreneurship occurs and the nature of the businesses which are founded. This is particularly true with growth-oriented businesses, whose competitive positions are so dependent upon the knowledge and skills of the founders. Thus, most new growth-oriented firms tend to serve the same general market or utilize the same general technology as the parent organization.

The nature of the business of the parent organization, the way it is organized, and the extent to which it frustrates or satisfies its best employees all bear upon whether it is a "good incubator" or "bad incubator" in the sense of spinning off growth-oriented entrepreneurs.

A number of environmental factors interact to create a regional climate more or less favorable to entrepreneurship. It seems clear that climates can change over time and that, to some extent, past entrepreneurship makes future entrepreneurship more likely. The decision to found a business is affected by the entrepreneur's perceptions of risks and rewards and his knowledge of individuals and institutions which might provide help and advice. Past entrepreneurship creates what might be termed an "entrepreneurial environment," in which the prospective founder is surrounded by examples and enveloped in knowledge about the process. The extent to which the act of starting a business seems credible, as compared to a "step into the unknown," depends upon the degree to which an entrepreneurial environment exists in a region.

The availability of venture capital is also an important factor. Salary levels, taxation rates, and the availability of stock options determine the extent to which entrepreneurs can save the needed "seed capital." For external sources of venture capital, the founder must search out those individuals or institutions who would find his particular venture appealing. If there is a history of successful entrepreneurship in a region, local wealth is created through investing in new firms; individuals and institutions develop skill and confidence in their abilities to invest in and assist new firms. Well-developed communication channels develop, such that the prospective entrepreneur, although not assured of backing for his venture, can at least make contact with investors who make a practice of investing in venture situations.

Past entrepreneurship also generates experienced founders who, after they have sold their firms or fought with their cofounders and left the business, often turn to entrepreneurship again. Past entrepreneurship also generates within a region many small, growth-oriented firms. These firms make excellent incubators, hiring and training the next generation of entrepreneurs. These small firms also provide consultant opportunities for founders who are trying to support their families while getting businesses started. Thus, past entrepreneurship creates a climate making future entrepreneurship more likely.

What might be done to stimulate the birth of growth-oriented firms in industrialized areas which lack entrepreneurship? No single action is likely to transform a region, but a number of actions might improve the climate. The characteristics of the established organizations in a region seem to be critical, since they attract potential entrepreneurs to a region (or keep them there); they help them to acquire the needed technical, market, and managerial knowledge; and they provide the satisfactions and frustrations which may provide motivation. It is interesting to speculate about whether a region could develop a self-supporting incubator organization, which would have as one of its objectives the nurturing of growth-oriented entrepreneurs. It would have to be involved in developing technologies which give promise of having substantial commercial potential. It might employ some people on a full-time basis, and also provide supporting services and advice to entrepreneurs just getting started.

In efforts to attract branch facilities of large companies, consideration might be given to the extent to which they would be good incubators. Unusual incentives might be offered to attract R & D laboratories and ventures which offer a toehold in developing technologies.

It is also interesting to speculate about what could be done in a region to create some of the features of an entrepreneurial environment. Courses and short conferences directed at the prospective growth-oriented entrepreneur may help to convey needed knowledge, to provide contacts, and to make the act of starting a business seem more credible to the would-be founder.

It may not be feasible or desirable to create large regional pools of venture capital. However, there is probably a real need to provide organized assistance to prospective founders in developing and improving their plans and in helping them to make contact with suitable venture capital sources. In some instances "seed money" to assist them in investigating their ideas may be desirable. Groups of civic-minded businessmen, bankers, university people, and experienced entrepreneurs might be organized to provide such assistance, possibly in conjunction with the entrepreneurship conferences described above. These groups also could provide communication channels to major sources of venture capital located in the region or elsewhere.

The birth of a single growth-oriented firm is the culmination of a sequence of events and the result of a multitude of factors, not all of which are clearly understood. Despite our limited knowledge, programs directed toward stimulating the birth and development of growth-oriented firms seem to be unusually promising as a method of stimulating regional economic development.

REFERENCES

1. A. Bruno and A. Cooper, Patterns of development for new technologically-based firms (unpublished working paper, Krannert Graduate School of Industrial Administration, Purdue University, West Lafayette, Indiana, 1975).

2. E. Roberts, Influences upon performance of new technical enterprises, in *Technical Entrepreneurship: A symposium*, eds. A. Cooper and J. Komives (Milwaukee: The Center For Venture Management, 1972).

Suggestions for Further Reading

Henderson, C. What the future holds for small business. *Nation's Business* 64: 25-26 + 8 (March 1976).

McManus, G. J. In business, the big and the small need each other. *Iron Age* 214: 41-42 (Sept. 16, 1974).

Sheridan, J. H. Is there still room for the little guy? *Industry Week* 186: 30-31 + (Sept. 15, 1975).

Waite, D. Economic significance of small firms. *Journal of Industrial Economics* 21: 154-165 (April 1973).

Weimer, G. Key to corporate survival: understand the little guy. *Iron Age* 217: 31-32 (June 11, 1976).

White, W. L. What will determine the future of small business? *Journal of Small Business Management* 14: 1-5 (July 1976).

2
Starting a New
Enterprise

Introduction

Entrepreneurial spirit is a key ingredient in starting a new enterprise. The text and readings in the first chapter have described those qualities commonly attributed to that spirit. This is not enough to assure success, however.

It may well be true that venture capitalists would rather have a mediocre idea combined with a top management team than a top idea coupled with a mediocre team. Given their total preferences, however, venture capitalists would rather support a well thought out, good idea being implemented by a top management group.

The introductory phase of the development of an organization frequently is critical to the long-run viability of the enterprise. If the entrepreneur can plan effectively to overcome the problems that typically occur during the start-up phase, the organization has a much higher probability of surviving long enough to be able to reach maturity. The purpose of this chapter is to discuss the problems found at the outset of a new enterprise. We will also present some methods of overcoming these problems.

Opportunity Analysis

A key ingredient for a new enterprise is a match between market potential and entrepreneurial interest. There are many areas of unfilled consumer demand. There are still products and services that are not being supplied to a willing public. It may be that the public has not even perceived the need for the particular product. The demand for the new product may be artificially created, such as that for most deodorant products. It may also be the result of the introduction of another product, as when the development of complex automotive systems led to the need for well-trained mechanics to keep these machines operating efficiently. Independent diagnostic centers have sprung up throughout the country to evaluate the work done by service centers. Many of these diagnostic centers are run by entrepreneurs.

Opportunities can come from other sources, as well. It has frequently been bemoaned that all the relevant innovations have been invented. Even if this were true, which is highly unlikely, there are still opportunities that can be developed from existing innovations. The large electronics firms that developed the technology and market for electronic calculators realized that other markets might exist for applications of the same technology. Several of those firms decided to apply electronic miniaturization to the watch industry. This has proven to be an extremely successful adaptation of a technological breakthrough to a market other than that originally intended. The Swiss watch industry has learned that competition may come from totally unexpected sources. What proved to be an opportunity for the firms in the semiconductor industry turned out to be an unforeseen threat to firms in the traditional watch industry.

Essentially, opportunity analysis involves the process of matching resources available to the entrepreneur with alternative courses of action provided by the environment. There has to be more than a simple match of physical resources with external opportunities, however. There has to be a commitment on the part of the entrepreneur to a particular direction if the proposed enterprise is to have any chance at success. Any new enterprise requires a wholehearted commitment of the time and efforts of the entrepreneur, particularly at the outset, to guide it past the various obstacles facing it. This became clear to Tap Pryor in the Sea Life Park case included in this text. There were many points in time when Tap, the entrepreneur leading Sea Life Park, could have gracefully backed out of the enterprise. Instead, he continued to press on with his project. It was only after the enterprise had been initiated that he allowed himself to transfer his energies to another, more personal, enterprise, that of completing his education. He had been totally committed to the concept of developing a marine research facility and exhibition park in Hawaii. This commitment kept him going, through early failures, until he finally was able to provide financing and construction of his project. Possibly, however, he left the organization too early. He may not have been willing to immerse himself totally in the entrepreneurial project to the extent typically necessary for success.

External Entrepreneurial Support

While demand for a product or service and commitment to a project are necessary factors for successful ventures, they are not sufficient. As Cooper discussed in his study of entrepreneurial ventures, an environment conducive to new ventures should also be available to the potential entrepreneur.[1] Sources of external support for financing, technology, management, and productive capacity should be readily accessible. The success of many new ventures located near areas such as the San Francisco peninsula and the Route 128 complex around Boston is due, in great part, to the proximity of the previously mentioned resources. The mere fact that there are other entrepreneurs in the vicinity who have succeeded at new venture initiation draws entrepreneurs to the area and encourages potential entrepreneurs already in the area. As Cooper pointed out in his study, past entrepreneurial success seems to generate imitators.

Particularly, successive entrepreneurs can draw from the knowledge of previous successes and failures. If they have made the effort to study their predecessors, they can develop an understanding of management requirements in the various functional areas. Problems in marketing, finance, production, accounting, etc., revolve around lack of expertise in solving problems effectively in those areas. Where there has been built up a body of practical knowledge in handling typical problems among entrepreneurs in a locality, the probability of recurring mistakes is lessened.

Word of entrepreneurial success spreads throughout the financial community. The realization that there is money to be made by backing new enterprises helps to provide sources for more entrepreneurial ventures. Those successful entrepreneurs also provide a potential source of capital. The successful entrepreneurs are frequently sympathetic to other new ventures. They may even be looking for new ventures in which to participate as a managerial as well as financial outlet. Other financial resources become aware of the potential for profit in new ventures. As more resources gather, a formal network of venture financing takes shape. Standard financial institutions set up departments to handle business generated by entrepreneurs. The Small Business Administration is likely to follow suit with its own assistance. Large investment-oriented institutions, such as insurance companies, seek out investment opportunities in these success-oriented areas.

Ancillary services also appear in such areas. Experts offering advice and counseling find a ready demand for their services. Accountants, tax experts, lawyers, and consultants specializing in new ventures and small businesses follow the concentration of entrepreneurs. This further assures that new ventures will be more successful in the future. Management skills are further enhanced.

These advisors understand the typical problems present in starting a new enterprise. They help entrepreneurs overcome many of the initial stumbling blocks to successful new venture initiation. One area, in particular, in which expert advice could be of great help is in the preparation of a prospectus for financing purposes. Few entrepreneurs are proficient enough in the financial area to be able to prepare a balanced prospectus likely to attract venture financing. They simply have not had enough experience to be able to generate this kind of document easily. Consultants can offer this service at a reasonable cost, however. These experts understand the type of information desired by financial institutions. They also know how to present that information in a manner designed to show the new venture in its best possible light. A new venture that knows how to approach sources of capital is more likely to receive a fair hearing from those sources.

Another area providing a source of trouble to successful new venture initiation is knowing how much capital to seek at the outset. One of the most common problems faced by entrepreneurs is lack of adequate capital or cash flow. This problem is discussed further in the readings and is graphically illustrated in several of the cases. Tap Pryor, in the Sea Life Park case, found at several points that he had to seek extra capital to continue his attempts to get his venture started. He was taking a high-risk approach to his new venture. He succeeded because he was persistent, faced a friendly environment, and, to some extent, was lucky.

The Casa Madrid case is a good example of a group that has sought expertise in venture capital formation. The general partners included in their group a member who had prior knowledge of the venture capital process as well as an understanding of how to prepare an appealing, yet informative prospectus. They were able to present their project to potential investors in the best possible light for the partnership. They had been attracted to the Houston area because of the successes enjoyed by other entrepreneurs in developing other real estate ventures. They have experienced much the same kind of environment described by Cooper.

Financing and cash flow are not the only problems faced by new enterprises, however. Entrepreneurs seeking to start new enterprises are faced with a broad range of management problems. Particularly, the combination of marketing and technological expertise tends to follow entrepreneurial success quickly. Many of the successful new enterprises in the previously mentioned regions have, in fact, been based on technological innovations. Since most entrepreneurs start their careers by trying to provide a new product or service, or provide that product in a novel manner, technology and marketing tend to be the focus for new enterprises.

As was stated earlier, however, successful ventures must be based on more than the personal belief of the need for the product or service. In both the Boston and the Palo Alto experiences, it was seen that, once again, familiarity with success breeds more success. Technological innovation has led to spin-offs from established companies. These spin-offs have led to other innovations and even more new enterprises. The newer entrepreneurs are able to build their ideas, and firms, on past successes. They are also able to draw on the large talent pool already existing in the area. Further, this talent is more likely to risk leaving relatively secure positions for the high risk of new enterprises; once again, because they have seen what can result from these innovations. Moreover, the risks associated with the ensuing new ventures are more controlled and readily assessed.

This ability to draw on the talent pool adds to the success quotient of the new enterprises. Unworkable ideas are exposed by outside consultation. Marginal ideas are improved through technology. Good ideas are made marketable by people experienced with past success. The Shalco case series presented at the end of the book describes how a firm was able to feed on its own internally generated success and expertise. In the Shalco series, the entrepreneurs were first encouraged by the success of other technological innovations. The firm was able to call upon the resources of some faculty at a prestigious university. The entrepreneurs made some mistakes in their initial efforts, however. They attempted to use the experience gained from their early attempts to build an even greater success after divesting their first enterprise.

Organizing for Success

The presence of the various forms of expertise discussed above does not assure its proper use, however. The new enterprise has to be effectively organized if it is to make proper use of that expertise. All too often, entrepreneurs fail to take advantage of outside help in running their organizations. The firm is typically built around the entrepreneur. All decisions are intended to be made by one person. While the entrepreneur may well best understand the direction the firm is supposed to take, this does not mean that he or she possesses the necessary experience to be able to make good decisions in all management areas.

Small businesses, moreover, are faced with a problem not found in large organizations. They simply cannot afford specialists in all the functional areas. This means that the available managers have to be able to fill in all the managerial gaps. The Bryn Mawr National Bank case provides a good example of this problem. The three top executives provide the primary managerial expertise for the bank. Their responsibilities go much further than their titles would imply. Also, there is a great deal of overlap in their positions, although it is unclear that they truly understand the degree and complexity of overlap.

In the Vail Industries case, the comments of the president show that he understands the problems of developing the organization. At Vail, the officers have been trained to perform each others' functions. They are capable of covering for one another in the event of absence for any reason. This type of planning is uncommon for a small business. It should be noted, however, that Vail has been in operation for some time. The president of the firm is trying to plan for a new growth phase for the firm. The managers had also had time to become accustomed to the various operations of the firm. An entrepreneur starting a new enterprise does not usually have this advantage.

The organization should be designed with a relatively long run point of view. The purpose of the entrepreneur is to plan for the future of the firm. The entrepreneur should limit personal participation at the early stages of the enterprise to those areas for which he or she is best suited. Other managers should be brought in to fill areas not covered by the expertise of the entrepreneur. If necessary, multi-faceted managers can be found to fill more than one function. Any manager who is considering working in a small business atmosphere should be prepared to accept this kind of generalist flexibility due to the nature of this type of organization.

The form of any organization must be structured to fit the style and values of those managers currently working within it. Structure must be flexible. Entrepreneurs should realize that the form the organization takes will change as the firm grows and develops. This development process will be expanded on in Chapter 7.

Many new enterprises try to limit the size of the organization at the outset to conserve resources, however. This can lead to suboptimal short-term savings. Lack of sufficient expertise in critical areas may lead to increased costs, lost sales, and general inefficiencies. This course of action may require greater resources at the outset, but will probably lead to more effective use of those resources as well as give the new enterprise a higher assurance of success.

Planning the New Enterprise

All the factors previously discussed help to comprise the planning process for new venture initiation. The purpose of planning is to detail the direction in which the new firm is going. Moreover, it should provide the new organization with an understanding of how it is to progress in that direction. It provides coordination for all managers in implementing the mission and ideas of the entrepreneur.

A well-formulated plan also demonstrates to the external environment that more than random thoughts or entrepreneurial desires have gone into the new project. It frequently shows to the venture capitalist or potential investor that the entrepreneur has the managerial skills necessary to succeed.

The plan should combine a definition of actions to be followed in all the functional areas. The marketing segment should supply guides demonstrating not only what specific market segments are to be attacked, but also the method for securing those markets. Tap Pryor, in the Sea Life Park case, clearly shows that he expects to pursue the tourists who are in Hawaii for more than two days as his primary market. The local population is considered a secondary market only. He then details how he expects tour packagers to provide access to that primary market.

A production plan should detail the actions required to produce the product or provide the service of the new enterprise. Tap Pryor details the timing necessary to be certain that all facilities will be ready when the first customers come through the gates at Sea Life Park. Timing is frequently the critical element in this segment of the plan.

Management controls are also key factors in the overall plan. Controls provide a method for evaluating the effectiveness of the operation. Inclusion of controls in the actual plan shows managers and investors alike what the benchmarks are to be and how they are to be measured. The most common forms of controls are accounting tools. Although management controls are based on historical data, their primary purpose is to provide information useful for adapting the plan to a changing environment.

A financial plan, in many respects, ties the whole plan together. This segment should combine the best aspects of cash flow, balance, and income statements. It is designed to show when the enterprise will need funds. It then shows how and where these funds are to be generated. It also demonstrates the expected return to potential investors as well as the risk of failure. Information from the three previous segments is necessary to prepare a thorough and realistic financial plan. Many of the cases mentioned to this point, including Sea Life Park, demonstrate the effectiveness of a well-prepared financial plan. Caution has to be given to the investor, however, to question the source of the financial data. Tap Pryor provided many of the statements included in the Sea Life Park case and these statements present many inconsistencies. Financial plans also change over time. Possibly this is due to new inputs which help to prepare more realistic projections. They may simply be presented, however, to provide the new project in its best light.

Organizational Forms

The combination of actions, projections, missions, objectives, and plans discussed to this point all help to determine what specific organizational form the new enterprise should take. At times, regulations may provide the greatest constraints on organizational form. Many industries and services follow traditional forms. Real estate, as an example, has frequently opted for syndication and partnership forms.

The different legal forms offer varying advantages in the areas of liability, taxation, and decision-making freedom. They also provide constraints on actions, financing, and expansion. The entrepreneur has to choose that form that provides the best fit for all these constraints and advantages. There is never a perfect form. As is typical with any planning process, what is realistically sought is an acceptable fit, not necessarily an unrealistically optimal solution.

It is not the intent of this section to present the pros and cons of each of the various forms from sole proprietorship through a publicly traded corporate form. That is discussed, to some extent, in the readings at the end of this, and subsequent, chapters. It is graphically presented in many of the cases, including Casa Madrid, Ltd.

Summary

The formative stages of an entrepreneurial organization are frequently the most crucial. The actions taken at this stage provide the basis for the eventual success or failure of the venture.

It is at this stage that entrepreneurial ideas are fleshed out for presentation to those individuals and groups interested in helping to implement the ideas. What everyone is looking for here is whether entrepreneurial spirit can be combined with effective action. Good ideas are not sufficient to assure success. A well-balanced management team headed by a committed entrepreneur is also necessary to pursue the ideas.

The managerial track record of the organization is only one method of evaluating the potential effectiveness of the new venture. The entrepreneurs' ability to organize effectively, given the constraints of operating a small company, is another method for evaluation. Also, the balance and thoroughness of plans generated by the potential managers goes a long way toward evaluation of overall ability.

A part of the venture-initiation process includes an evaluation of opportunities and resources available in the external environment. A given geographic or market area may seem to provide a tempting target for exploitation. If support resources, such as capital, technology, and managerial expertise are not readily available, however, potential for successful implementation may be seriously impaired.

Much of the discussion presented in this chapter has been involved with new, small enterprises. While many new enterprises are formed from existing, often larger, firms, these frequently have greater resources from which they can draw. The ability to tap management expertise and financial resources of a large parent lessen significantly the problems of initiating new enterprises. It is for this reason that emphasis has been placed on developing new ventures by independent entrepreneurs.

It should also be noted that the same guidelines presented here for initiating totally new ventures also apply to acquisition of an existing operation. Where an entrepreneur desires to purchase an ongoing firm, the operation must be adapted to match the values and purposes of the entrepreneur. The same guidelines apply to this form of new venture since the entrepreneur usually intends to alter its operations radically.

Readings

The readings at the end of Chapter 2 describe various aspects and problems associated with starting entrepreneurial ventures. As has been noted earlier, new ventures develop from a variety of sources and reasons.

The first article, by Patricia Tichenor, is titled simply "Starting a Business." This article prescribes some general characteristics of new ventures and their initiators. Also further references for help in starting new ventures are presented. Some of these references, particularly literature produced by the Small Business Administration (SBA) can be quite informative. Some of these materials can be found among the readings in this text. The problem with this and the other references discussed is not the lack of material available, but its overabundance. Much of it is irrelevant for most entrepreneurs. Specifically, much of the SBA literature is geared toward presenting nuts-and-bolts details for inexperienced entrepreneurs. It is designed for people who have no formal business training or education. There are some sources within the SBA designed for the more sophisticated entrepreneur, however. Also, the SBA can provide access to the other forms of information and resources mentioned in the Tichenor article. This is frequently of greater assistance to the entrepreneur, particularly at the idea-generation and formulation stages.

The aptly titled article by Leonard Smollen, "Corporate Activities in Venture Formation," describes some of the recent attempts in this area. As we have noted, entrepreneurial activities are not limited to small businesses. New venture initiation provides many benefits for larger organizations. A symbiotic relationship can be developed between businesses in the large and small sectors. This is not easily implemented, however. Organizational inertia is difficult to overcome. Personalities may clash. Objectives may not be clearly defined or mutually acceptable. The forms that corporate entrepreneurial activities may take, and their problems, are outlined in this article.

The final article, "The Illusion of Owning a Business" by Frederick Copeland, describes the travails of typical entrepreneurs. Particularly, Copeland notes that entrepreneurs rarely find the total independence they desire simply by starting their own business.

Essentially, the three articles present a listing of various issues and problem areas encountered by entrepreneurs. They provide, along with the text in Chapter 2, the basis for the latter portions of the text. The first two chapters have described in general terms many problem areas faced by entrepreneurs. The later chapters will explore these areas in greater depth. They will also provide methods of solving problems or keeping them from occurring.

REFERENCES

1. Arnold C. Cooper, Entrepreneurial environment, *Industrial Research* (Sept. 1970), pp. 74-76.

Starting a Business

Patricia Tichenor

Every article or book you'll ever read on starting a business will preach the same line: "Hard Work—High Risk—You Too Will Suffer—The Path Is Fraught With Dangers!" You can almost picture the businessmen authors, hands folded piously, gravely intoning the deadly sins of entrepreneurship: Ignorance, Laziness, Under-capitalization . . .

If you're seriously thinking about starting your own business, be prepared for lots of sermonizing, irritating advice—mostly from the gospel according to Horatio Alger. Every agency, from the Small Business Administration to the corner bank, will hand you this rags to riches philosophy. They can't help it; they're products of an earlier era. The dash and bravura of today's younger entrepreneurs has not yet penetrated the corridors of these agencies.

Don't discount the advice, though. Their programs work and their advice may save your neck. With their help, you may be one of the two out of ten business starters who make it—and maybe you won't even have to work 16 hours a day to do it.

What is the key to success in a new business? How do you finance one? And what all do you need to consider before—and after—starting a business? Maybe the following discussion—you could call it "advice"—will answer some of your questions.

Q. What's the key element in the success of your new business?

A. You. All the money in the world won't save your business if you're not qualified to run it. While all experts agree that you—the owner/manager—must be qualified, they don't agree on what "qualified" means.

The Small Business Administration lists ten personality traits you should possess to be successful: initiative, positive attitude toward others, leadership, ability to handle responsibility, strong organizing ability, industriousness, decisiveness, sincerity, perseverance, and great physical energy. Of course, if everyone currently running a business who does not have all these traits were to quit work tomorrow, the economy would fall apart. Virtues don't fully explain why some entrepreneurs succeed and others don't.

The J.K. Lasser Tax Institute suggests that the better you are at managing, the more qualified you are as a businessman: "Some businesses," they say, "fail because of a lack of capital, but most failures result from a lack of some management know-how." So read a management textbook and you've got it? Maybe, but Franklin J. Dickson, author of an excellent book for small businessmen, says management inexperience accounts for only 18 percent of unqualified owners. He breaks down management-related failures as follows:

Inexperience in field	9%
Inexperience in management	18%
Unbalanced experience	20%
Incompetence	45%
Neglect	3%
Fraud	2%
Disaster	1%
Other	2%

The dictionary defines an incompetent as one who cannot manage his own affairs. Unbalanced experience indicates that you're good at some facets of business but lousy at others. If Dickson's numbers are right, then if you can handle your affairs and have industry experience, you've a 92 percent chance of making it, right? No. Bank casebooks are full of stories about competent, experienced managers for large corporations who failed at running businesses of their own.

Probably the most sensible assessment of the qualified entrepreneur comes from Louis Allen, president of the Chase Manhattan Capital Corporation. In essence, he says the people who will win—even if they make mistakes—are those who (1) understand the gravity of what they are doing, (2) are motivated enough to stick things out, and (3) know their business.

By understanding the gravity he means realizing that this thing will burn up years of your life (and youth), and that it will drastically affect the lives of others. People you hire, people you yell at, people you like, people you play favorites with, people you influence, people you fire—all will be changed by you. You could make or break the spirits of these people. Your failure can put them on unemployment lists. Your success can assure their financial and even emotional security all their lives. That's not small.

Motivation is sticking to your job even when things aren't going so well and people are criticizing you for mismanaging your business.

As for knowing your business, Allen, like Dickson, insists that you've got to have specialized experience before you can run a business. How much experience depends on the scope of your effort. If you're starting a manuscript-typing service, knowing how to type is probably enough experience. But if you want to get something like stereo-component manufacturing, working several years for one of your future competitors is the only way to get the know-how you need.

Q. Where's the money going to come from?

A. Before you answer that, first find out how much you need. And this amount can range from less than $1,000 to more than $100,000. Here's where those advice agencies come in handy, and the best of these is probably a good bank. Of course, the catch is in the word "good." Choose your bank carefully. Find out if it is interested in your line of business (some specialized banks won't be). Then find out if any federal or state laws limit its lending ability (some banks are forbidden by law to make long-term loans). Does the bank have vault services; are its officers accessible when you want to talk to them; are its deposits insured; are its charges for collecting out-of-town checks in your range; will it willingly give you information you need on customers or trade contacts? Perhaps a small banker, who like you is a small business-man, will be your best bet. But maybe a large bank will have better rates or will have a special small business department. Compare. There are other factors for choosing a banker, so naturally there are books and articles that can help you do it.

You may not want a loan in the beginning, but do get friendly with your chosen banker. He will be an invaluable source of advice—like suggesting ways to save money by buying on discount; like warning you that depending on a few big customers could put you in a bad cash-flow squeeze; like showing you how lots of little customers will add to your capital needs by increasing your credit-extension requirements: like all sorts of things you haven't thought of.

But if you're not far enough along in your thinking or self-education, a banker's advice could be too advanced for you. Get your initial business background from the library and the Small Business Administration. Two useful books are *How To Run a Small Business* by J.K. Lasser Tax Institute (New York: McGraw Hill, 1963) and *Successful Management of the Small and Medium Sized Business* by Franklin J. Dickson (New York: Prentice-Hall, 1971).

The library also has dozens of directories. Here you can get the names of suppliers and wholesalers, shippers and delivery services, printers and advertising agencies—services that will be essential to your business. Contacting these businesses will provide you with most of the facts and figures you will need for calculating start-up costs and operating expenses. Be sure you dig deeply for this information, however. For example, if you're setting up a design firm you might save considerably on your start-up estimate if you talk to a carpenter and a lumber company rather than a drafting-board manufacturer.

Besides general books and directories, the library may have books on your specific business. Ask. Of course, the more unusual your business, the less likely it is that someone has written a book on it. In New York City there is a new School of Holography. Since few people have seen a holograph or know what they are (three-dimensional photographs made by laser beams), you can be sure the proprietor didn't learn his business from the New York Public Library (although he may have learned his holography there).

The library has one other thing you'll need: the address of the nearest Small Business Administration field office. The SBA is the best place to start if you are totally naive about business. It publishes an extensive and excellent series of Management Aids, most of which are free. Everything from patent procedures to using census data to choosing the legal structure for your firm to. . . . And then there are numerous bibliographies and guides for specific businesses from pet shops to wholesaling. The field office will have counselors who can help you draw up your cash plan and operating ratios. The SBA will also have names and addresses of bankers and venture capital firms interested in helping new businesses, including the names of firms interested in helping minority entrepreneurs. These firms, many of which are licensed by the SBA as Small Business Investment Corporations (SBICs), are particularly good sources of practical, although not always free, advice.

Now then, how much money or capital do you need? After talking to all these sources you'll have a pretty good idea and will be able to draw up a cash plan. Essentially this plan will include your start-up costs, your monthly operating expenses for however long it will take you to break even, and your expected income from sales or fees. This last should determine the first two, not the other way around. Too many new businessmen figure out how much they think they should spend and then calculate how much they will *have* to sell or charge to survive. That's backwards. Start with what you *can* sell based on conditions in your area (or the nation) and then figure what you need to spend to get to that figure.

To do this, operating ratios given you by your banker or the SBA can be important. For example, a florist shop in a certain city can be expected to net $30,000 in sales a year. The SBA calculates that (assuming an owner salary) 41.3 percent or $12,390 of that should go for operating expenses and 46.8 percent or $14,040 for buying goods to sell. Ratios have never been compiled for all types of businesses, but you and your banker might be able to come up with some rough ratios. Using them will force you to budget carefully even before you begin, and may save you some grief later.

Having worked out your money needs and imagined all possible contingencies (strikes, fires, unusual competition), double what you think you need. Murphy's Law ("if something can go wrong, it will") is especially applicable to new businesses. How big is safe? Experts disagree. If you do not have enough capital, you may be unable to afford enough employees, invest in proper equipment, maintain enough supplies or inventory, take advantage of creditor discounts or give customers credit. Undercapitalization (after manager incompetence) is a major cause of business failures.

On the other hand, overcapitalization can cause unnecessary interest costs, extra tax burden, and depression in value of securities on your company. Besides, it's a wasted reserve—a checking account draws no interest.

Q. But where *does* the money come from?

A. There are three ways to raise capital: (1) investment by you and others in the business; (2) borrowing; (3) retaining profits (that is, plowing them back into the business each year). Obviously this last won't help you for a while. As for the first two, here are some rough rules of thumb. Investment—the money you and your friends put up—should cover the start-up costs or soon-to-be "fixed assets" of your new firm. Ideally this money should also cover the initial operating expenses, too.

Borrowing can open all sorts of trouble or be the only way to insure covering your cash-flow needs. Loans can come from so many sources it's hard to list them all: banks, industrial banking firms, small-loan companies, factoring companies, insurance firms, equipment manufacturers, wholesalers, the Small Business Administration, SBICs, even the GI Bill. So shop around.

You won't get into trouble if the loan helps you to cut costs or increase profits by more than the interest rate. But using loans to extricate yourself from difficulty (and then just *hoping* your sales go up enough to cover the interest) is generally fatal. Don't be overly afraid of borrowing, however. Skimping on money for your business is poor thinking. You have to spend money to make it. If you or your employees don't have the equipment or time they need to do a good job, you'll go under eventually. Nobody can make something out of nothing.

Q. What else should I consider when starting a business?

A. After poor management and undercapitalization, the third biggest cause of business failure is poor location. So choose it carefully. This is true whether you sell goods, offer a service, or run a manufacturing plant. Selecting a location depends on more than just parking facilities (although some businessmen think that's all there is to it). For instance, is the community you're interested in receptive to your business? (Some towns or neighborhoods won't support art galleries.) Is there adequate transportation—for employees *and* goods? Can you get the kinds of employees you need? (Don't locate a technical publishing firm in a town with few educational resources.) If your location is unusual, will the people you need move to your area? (Usually no, unless your salary is very, very good and local cultural and educational facilities are superb.) Will the local blue-collar labor supply be adequate? Are there good local advertising media? Are rents and taxes reasonable? Etc. There's more to a community than parking lots. Having chosen a town, then exercise the same care in choosing a neighborhood and a building.

Q. Then what?

A. Then nothing. You've got you, your money, and a good location. You're all set to start your business. Of course, *after* you start then you'll have to cope with keeping and using good accounting records; tax management; hiring, training, and paying personnel; preventing employee and customer frauds; buying insurance; operating the front office; buying advertising; selling. All of which means—right— back to the library, banker, SBA, SBIC, or whatever. But maybe there'll come a day when you sit, hands folded piously in front of you, telling some young college graduate how hard it is to start a business, how hard he'll have to work at it—like 12 or 16 hours a day, how eight out of ten new businesses fail within ten years.

Corporate Activities in Venture Formation

Leonard E. Smollen
Institute for New Enterprise Development

There is an increasing interest in corporate venturing as a means of growth and diversification. The hoped-for results from such venturing and the principal approaches to venture formation that United States corporations have tried and are trying, are described and discussed. Included in this is the development of ventures within a firm (internal venture management) and external venture formation through corporate venture capital, sponsored spin-offs and joint ventures. Some observations are made on corporate practices and attitudes that help or impede these venturing activities.

Proceedings of Project ISEED, Summer 1975. Published by Project ISEED, Ltd., The Center for Venture Management, Suite 508, 207 E. Buffalo Street, Milwaukee, WI 53202, U.S.A.

There is a growing interest on the part of many United States corporations in various ways of forming, financing, and managing successful new ventures to achieve corporate growth and diversification. Part of this interest stems, no doubt, from the reduced attraction of acquisitions because of the increased opposition of the United States government to acquisitions by the larger corporations; the changes in accounting and tax rules that restrict pooling of interest accounting; low price-earnings ratios; and the failure of many acquisitions to live up to corporate expectations.

Corporate venturing activities are an attempt to overcome the barriers to innovation that are inherent in the operating practices, priorities, and organizational structure of large companies. There is by no means agreement as to the best way for a corporation to engage in venture activities. And corporations have experimented with one or more of the approaches to be described.

POTENTIAL BENEFITS OF CORPORATE VENTURING
Corporate venture-formation activities can be external (e.g., venture capital, spin-offs, joint ventures) and involve relationships and investments with entrepreneurs and firms outside of the corporation. Or the corporation's venture activities can be internal and based on some form of entrepreneurial venture management within the corporation.

Corporations seek the following kinds of results from both internal and external venturing activities:

- Controlled, diversified growth consistent with corporate objectives
- Long-term capital gain
- A window into new technologies and markets
- An improved corporate image
- Creation of an entrepreneurial atmosphere within the corporation
- Increased effectiveness in turning R & D into commercial products
- Attraction and retention of talented entrepreneurial employees

The corporation may also expect one or more of the following additional results from an external venturing program:

- Nurturing of future acquisition candidates that might be acquired early enough to avoid antitrust issues
- Opportunities for later stage investments in ventures initially seed-financed by the corporation
- Opportunities to spin-off and realize a gain from unused technology that has too small or different a market for the corporation but could be successfully exploited by an independent venture.

APPROACHES TO CORPORATE VENTURING

Corporate Venture Capital
Corporate venture capital involves the corporation investing in small companies conceived and managed by independent entrepreneurs. Some corporations do this themselves and others use an outside venture capitalist who is responsive to the corporation's diversification and growth objectives. Although corporations may

think that they will supply more (e.g., management assistance) than just financing to the company, capable entrepreneurs are not likely to want or need much corporate help. Those entrepreneurs who do need help might be better off not financed.

Some corporations have done extremely well with venture investments. Fairchild Camera and Instrument provided the seed capital to start Fairchild Semiconductors and later exercised an option to purchase the remainder of its outstanding stock. Fairchild Semiconductors' sales are now over $150 million. On the other hand, some corporations have not been successful in venture capital and have dropped the activity.

For some corporations, the grooming and nurturing of future acquisition candidates is the primary motivation for their venture capital activities. General Electric's venture capital arm, Business Development Services, Inc., follows this philosophy and makes investments in small companies whose markets and products are related to or of interest to GE.

It is difficult to know how many corporations are currently involved in venture capital because some prefer a low profile for their activities. An examination of a listing of venture capital organizations indicates that about twenty U.S. corporations list themselves as active in venture capital.[1] Undoubtedly, there are more. Those listed include General Electric, Exxon, Johnson and Johnson, Xerox, Singer, Dow, FMC and Sperry and Hutchinson.

Sponsored Spin-Offs

In 1969, Roberts[2] pointed out that the 32 independent spin-offs from one corporation in the Boston area had sales that exceed their erstwhile parent. The sponsored spin-off is a way for a corporation to have a "piece of the action" in such spin-off companies and retain some ties with its entrepreneurially minded employees. In the sponsored spin-off the corporation receives an equity position in a company launched by its employees in return for some corporate technology and, in some cases, initial capital.

GE is an example of a company seeking minority stock positions for supplying technology from its R & D center to companies that would be launched by entrepreneurs spun out of GE and financed by outside investors. EG&G, Teradyne, and Unitrode are high-technology companies in the Boston area that have taken equity positions in spin-off companies in return for both capital and technology. In these deals, the sponsor corporation usually has the right, at some future time, to buy all or a significant part of the entrepreneur's stock. The purchase price is generally based on both future earnings and earnings growth.

In any such deal, the entrepreneur's potential capital gain should be significant enough to make his total commitment to the spin-off worthwhile. In one spin-out situation observed by the author, this was not so. The sponsor's stock purchase conditions were such that it was highly unlikely that the entrepreneurs could achieve a gain commensurate with their commitment of time and effort. As a result the venture failed to attract the best people to it, and this was undoubtedly a factor in its subsequent failure.

Recently, one corporation has experimented with a variant of the spin-off approach that I call the "big pay-off." In this approach, the corporation supplies the technology, the capital, and the entrepreneurs to start a spin-off venture. Some of the initial capital may also be furnished by outside investors. The entrepreneurs receive no stock in the spin-off but will receive a very big bonus (e.g., $1-2 million) if the venture achieves certain agreed-upon profit and return-on-investment performance. There can be certain tax advantages to the sponsoring corporation in this approach.

Joint Ventures

Joint ventures combine the resources of two or more companies to implement a venture that no one of them could do alone. Sometimes this will be accomplished through a new joint venture company and other times through a contractual agreement. Often joint ventures involve a foreign and a United States company, one of which has the technology and the other, the marketing resources. Another common joint venture involves two or more United States corporations with a common interest in a capital-intensive venture.

Most of the above sorts of joint ventures involve large corporations. Of perhaps more interest here are those joint ventures that involve a large and a smaller corporation ($50 million sales or less) in the development and commercialization of a product or process. This joint venture can combine the entrepreneurial skills and high-technology capabilities of the smaller firm with the marketing, manufacturing, and capital resources of the larger one. It should be a very effective way to develop new growth ventures. But it is not easy to do. The disparity in size of the venturing corporations results in differences in outlook that can be difficult to resolve—particularly when the larger brings so much more power to the partnership. A current example of this kind of joint venture is the Tyco-Mobil venture to develop efficient solar cells.

Internal Venture Management

Internal venture management involves the stimulation of entrepreneurial activity and successful innovation within the corporate environment to the end of developing products that can make substantial contributions to profits.

The particular form of organization (venture department, task force, or subsidiary) used for internal venture management depends on the management style and objectives of a company.[3] However, more important to successful venturing than the particular organizational form used to implement it, are the corporate attitudes and practices in regard to entrepreneurship and venturing. The corporation must give an entrepreneurially minded individual (often called a "hero" or "product champion") responsibility, resources, and authority to develop a venture. To the maximum extent possible he should feel like an independent entrepreneur. His compensations and rewards should be tied to his profit and loss performance. But many companies do not provide this kind of special compensation program because of the resentment it engenders in other managers.

One problem in internal venturing is the tendency of many corporate executives to lose confidence in a venture that changes its direction or misses its scheduled milestones. But if there is any certainty about a venture, it is that it will change its direction and not meet its schedule. Corporate entrepreneurs should be able to make rational changes in a venture's direction or schedule without losing credibility and support. After all, this is the freedom accorded to the independent entrepreneur. Another obstacle to internal venturing is the emphasis on short-term goals and profits that restricts the resources available to new venture managers.

Corporations active in internal venture management include Minnesota Mining and Manufacturing (3M), Dow, Dupont, Union Carbide, General Foods, and W. R. Grace. Of these, 3M has had one of the most successful programs of internal venture management operation. In no small measure this is due to the fact that its top executives were once themselves venture managers or "product champions" and appreciate the problems, opportunities, and approaches required in internal venture management. Also, 3M allows the internal company entrepreneur to seek financial and other support from many departments of the company. This practice is important and tends to simulate the conditions faced by the independent entrepreneur who, if turned down by one venture capitalist or banker, will go to another and another. Finally, 3M's employees know from prior example that successful internal entrepreneurism is a path that can lead to recognition and top executive position.

CLOSURE
It is not clear which of the above forms of corporate venturing will work best for any one corporation. But it is clear that *any* kind of successful corporate venturing will require an ability to attract, retain and identify capable entrepreneurs who can build a core team and take advantage of a technical opportunity. It is in this area that a corporation should direct its attention; results will follow.

REFERENCES
1. S. Rubel, *Guide to Venture Capital Sources* (Chicago: Capital Publishing Corp., 1974).
2. E. Roberts, What it takes to be an entrepreneur...and hang on to one, *Innovation* 7 (1969), pp. 46-52.
3. F. Cook, Venture management as new way to grow, *Innovation* 25 (Oct. 1971), pp. 28-37.

The Illusion of Owning a Business

Frederick W. Copeland

As an elder business executive, I am approached from time to time by young men who are emerging from educational or military training and want advice on the selection of a career.

Today's young man is no worshiper of Horatio Alger. He has watched his father carrying an increasing load of worry as he rose in prominence — always fussing about taxes, inflation, labor, and rising costs. The son's goal is simple and specific; he likes to think of himself with a wife and a couple of kids, a small house, a secondhand station wagon, a trailer, a boat, and a pair of skis. He already has definite plans for his weekends and his annual vacations. An income of $8000 a year will suit him perfectly, and he is much more interested in reaching that point as rapidly as possible than in shooting for $100,000 a year eventually.

He does not care particularly how he earns his $8000, and he expects to work hard. But he has one very specific reservation: "I am not going to spend my life taking orders from someone else or licking boots to get a salary raise. I am going to own my own business and work for myself."

Admittedly, there is no more satisfied businessman than he who owns and operates his own established and profitable business. He has the fun of making all the decisions and of keeping all the rewards of success. He does not have to defer to the orders or moods of others, and he can exercise his own whims and moods as he sees fit. He can sleep late in the morning if he is tired and go fishing when the fish are biting. He can take out all the profits currently or leave them in the business for future growth. Within reason, he can have tax-free luxuries by charging the business with club dues, home entertaining, and trips to New York, Florida, and even Europe. And, of course, the business is charged with the purchase and upkeep of his Cadillac.

When you meet this lucky man, however, and he brags about the joys of independence, you will find it interesting to draw him out on the subject of his early history. Unless he inherited the business he will be proud of the hardships and narrow escapes he suffered before he got his head above water. He will tell you how he, and usually his wife, worked twelve hours a day, seven days a week, because they could not afford to hire a stenographer, bookkeeper, or janitor; how he did not take a vacation until he was fifty; how, on various occasions, he was down to his last dollar and had to bluff his creditors or get a prepayment from a customer. And as you listen to his life story, you will recognize that his success is the result of a combination of special skill, shrewdness, willingness to gamble, hard work, personal sacrifice, and usually some luck.

Ordinarily this businessman has all his eggs in one basket: all his personal capital is invested in his business. On paper he is a wealthy man, but little of his wealth is in liquid form. What will happen to his estate if he dies? The inheritance tax people will put a high value on his company holdings, but there will not be enough cash to pay the tax. Should he sell the business while the going is good? How about straddling the issue by selling a portion of the business for cash? No, that would mean sharing ownership with a stranger and losing most of the fun. How about gradually transfering ownership to his son, so that there will be no inheritance tax? Is his son capable of carrying on the management? Suppose he conveyed ownership to his son; would his son get greedy and crowd the old man out?

If he is a manufacturer, he is always afraid that a competitor will outdesign him, steal his best man, or start a price war, and he has the constant dread of arriving at the shop some morning and finding a union picket at the gate. The personally owned company is usually too small to be diversified in products and personnel, one hard bump in the form of a lawsuit, a bad account, or the loss of a key man can do irreparable damage.

This successful man represents not more than one per cent of the men who started their own businesses when he did. It is my best guess that out of 100 starters 40 fall by the wayside and 59 become hopelessly locked into a marginal situation, with all resources tied up in the struggle to survive, with a net profit lower than the wages they could earn outside, and with absolutely no escape because they cannot sell out. Statistics show that, in 1955, 65 percent of the total business failures were for amounts of $25,000 or less; 56 percent of the total failures were companies five years old or less. Dun & Bradstreet reports that 90 percent of all failures are attributable to inexperience and poor management.

Disregard for odds and complete confidence in one's self have produced many of our greatest successes. But every young man who wants to go into business for himself should appraise himself as a candidate for the one percent to survive. What has he to offer that is new or better? Has he special talents, special know-how, a new invention or service, or more capital than the average competitor? Has he the most important qualification of all, a willingness to work harder than anyone else? A man who is working for himself without limitation of hours or personal sacrifice can run circles around any operation that relies on paid help, particularly if it is unionized. But he must forget the eight-hour day, the forty-hour week, and the annual vacation. When he stops work, his income stops unless he hires a substitute. Most small operations have their busiest day on Saturday, and the owner uses Sunday to catch up on his correspondence, bookkeeping, inventorying, and maintenance chores. The successful self-employed man invariably works harder and worries more than the man on a salary. His wife and children make corresponding sacrifices of family unity and continuity; they never know whether their man will be home or in a mood to enjoy family activities.

If you are burning with an inspiration to invent a new product or service, it would be a great pity not to give it a good try. But do not overlook the time and loss element. You must first develop the product or service to your own satisfaction; next, demonstrate it to the satisfaction of the trade; next, make the public aware of its virtues; and finally, arrange that the willing buyer can get prompt delivery and service. In the meantime you must eat.

This brings us to the critical subject of capital. After the war several young men came to me saying, "I have saved up $10,000 and want to go into business for myself. What do you suggest as an activity?" They assumed that this amount of money had a tremendous impact. They expected to make a living wage at once, get a good return on their capital, and run a steadily growing business. Their faces fell when I suggested, in all seriousness, a filling station, a hamburger stand, a laundromat, a radio-repair sevice unit, or a vending machine route. They wanted something where they could hire someone else to do the leg work.

I explained that every man has two assets, his services and his capital. His services, whether he is working for himself or for an employer, have an open-market value (probably $350 per month for an inexperienced man with a college degree). The return to be expected from capital depends on the risk: 6 percent would be good if he wanted safety. Why should he expect more income unless he developed a special skill or took greater chances?

I told each man not to expect that his college degree or recent knowledge of the humanities will give any immediate edge over the high-school graduate who has already been on the job for four years; that comes later when he has caught up in applied knowledge. I explained that with few expections it takes money to make money in business. Someone has to put up the money for equipment, inventory, and operating expenses before there is a dollar of income. Even a free-lance commission salesman must finance his living and travel expense until he builds up an income.

The young men showed me advertisements from the Business Opportunity columns of the newspaper: "Good Business for Sale—$10,000"; also, "Want Partner in Profitable Business — $10,000 Investment." I asked, "What kind of going business do you think you can get for $10,000? Remember that your money must cover both purchase price and working capital. If it is a store or a manufacturing operation, you would be lucky to turn your capital three times a year (unless working on credit). With capital of $10,000 you might expect annual sales of $30,000 to $50,000, and a net profit of $5,000, before a salary for yourself and taxes. Now take the case of the man who is advertising for a partner with $10,000. If he had a good thing, he would not have to appeal to strangers. Selecting a partner is almost as delicate an operation as choosing a wife."

Probably the easiest and quickest way to become an independent businessman is to be a commission salesman or manufacturer's agent. You are given a sample kit, a price book, some order blanks, and a pat on the back. You are completely on your own and you sink or swim on your own. You do not have to tie up any capital in inventory or accounts receivable; neither do you get any salary or expense account. It stands to reason, however, that no one is going to give a very hot item or an established territory to an inexperienced salesman.

Some young men seem to think that if they have a new idea and good character they can borrow their starting money from a bank or from the Small Business Administration without collateral. They do not understand that any new venture is a gamble and that the lending institutions cannot see any merit in a transaction in which they stand to lose 100 percent or at best get their money back plus a small interest. Private moneylenders are not interested in advancing money to set up a business; the antiusury laws will not allow a rate of interest commensurate with the risk. Beware of any individual who offers to lend you capital at the legal rate of interest plus outside considerations such as a commission on sales or management fee.

I personally would rather see a young man work for someone else for ten years until he has learned the business and matured in his judgment. Then he can evaluate his own talents and the cost of getting started on his own. I hate to watch some fine young man start his career with a blind stab at a hopeless venture, and then, after sweating it out for five years, have to give up and look for a job. The personnel manager of the employing company asks him, "In what category do you classify yourself: design, production, sales, accounting, administrative?" The young man has to reply, "I have been the president of a company with three employees. I have a smattering of all functions but cannot say I am expert at any of them." How can the personnel manager place him? The general experience is valuable, but he cannot put the young man in a job above more experienced men and he cannot start him at the bottom because he is too old or cannot live on a learner's pay.

Everything I have said, so far, has been negative and discouraging to a young man contemplating starting a business of his own. I admit that in most cases my advice is: "Drop the idea of self-employment. Get yourself a job with a good-sized company and invest your money in A. T. & T. stock. If you have a yen to be an inventor, get a job as a designer; if you have already invented some gadget, turn it over to a large manufacturer on a royalty basis. If you want to be a merchandiser, get a job with Sears, Roebuck. If you think you like manufacturing, try to get a job with some company in the $5 million to $10 million class, large enough to be solid, small enough to be personal. If you aim to be on your own eventually in insurance or real estate, spend some years under a first-class operator. Let someone else pay for your training and your living expenses."

If you are completely vague about a career, go to some company that is expanding in an expanding industry and say, "I want a job in this company. I will do anything, go anywhere, and accept any pay you care to give me." In an expanding company there is likely to be more rotation and upgrading. I caution against starting with a small and young company, regardless of the charm of companionship, the early assumption of responsibility, and the dream of being in on the ground floor of what may someday grow rapidly in size. When, without special ability or experience, you start a new job, you are gambling on your ability to make good. If there is a chance that your employer will fail and go out of business, regardless of your ability, you are pyramiding the odds against you. In a small company there are few openings at the top and these are closely held by the owners.

Generalizations are always dangerous because they can be refuted by exceptions. You may be the exception. If you have guts and determination and no silly scruples against long hours, dirty hands, and waiting on customers over the counter, you may be able to get into some service operation without much capital and without having to wait to get a living wage. Don't sneer at the small service operation. If you can learn that business and make good at it you can expand indefinitely and eventually break into the big league. If you have enough capital to live on for two or three years, you should be able to set yourself up in some commission-selling operation that will snowball into a profitable business if you work hard on it. If you have substantial capital, say $50,000, you might buy a hardware store, where the assets are all in solid inventory and the momentum should carry the business until you learn how to run it.

There are always a few cases of brilliant young men who have had rapid and phenomenal success. Such men have an uncanny sense of timing and opportunity. They gamble cheerfully with their own and other people's money and start a second gamble before they know the results of the first one. After the war one young veteran, in complete disregard of my sincere advice, used his $10,000 as a down payment and with government financing built a $100,000 apartment house. With his profit and government financing he undertook to build ten G.I. homes, which he sold before completion. Now he is a big operator.

Another young man secured a government development contract for a scientific product, on a cost-plus basis. He did not make much profit on the transaction, but the contract financed him in building a staff and equipping a plant with which he now makes products of his own. Another man brashly contracted to buy a $100,000 business with $10,000 down (every cent he had in the world), agreeing to pay the balance out of future earnings. Another paid $5000 for an option to buy a piece of property at $200,000; he turned around and sold it to a third party for $250,000. In all of these cases the individual gambled to the limit and would have been cleaned out if there had been any setback. We do not hear of those who gambled and lost.

Suggestions for Further Reading

Butrick, F. M. Buy a small business for next to nothing. *Financial Executive* 44: 22-26 (Feb. 1976).

Hanan, M. Venturing corporations—think small to stay strong. *Harvard Business Review* 54: 139-148 (May 1976).

Minihan, M. J. Persistent inflation: its effect on small business. *Journal of Small Business Management* 14: 32-35 (July 1976).

Rassam, C. Small is beautiful. *International Management* 31: 41-44 (April 1976).

Robertson, J. Helping the little guy. *Electronic News* 21: 18 (March 29, 1976).

SBA report: management tips help small firms to grow. *Nations Business* 60: 12 (June 1972).

Wood, G. Breeding small firms. *Director* 26: 385-387 (Sept. 1973).

3
Financing for the
Small Business

Introduction

Financing often presents a significant problem for entrepreneurs. Traditional methods and markets are not always available for small enterprises. Even in the best of times, investors can usually find traditional alternatives to new venture financing. They perceive these alternatives as involving lower risk, if only because they understand them better. This provides serious obstacles to small ventures acquiring sufficient outside capital. When demand for capital is intense, as it frequently has been in recent years, the small business sector is all but shut off from the financing it needs.

This means that the small business entrepreneur either has to start off with sufficient internally generated funds or learn how to live a hand-to-mouth existence. Since most entrepreneurs are not born with the proverbial "silver spoon" in their mouths, living in a constant state of financial undernourishment becomes a fact of life. Understanding and applying this state of nature is the first step in being able to plan for the long-run stability of the small business enterprise.

This may seem to be a contradictory set of statements. Stability and uncertainty do not normally go hand in hand. The physical scientists usually refer to this state of nature as unstable equilibrium. This is analogous to balancing a coin on its edge. So long as it is not disturbed, it remains upright. The slightest breeze will send it toppling over, however. This is the position in which most small business ventures find themselves. If everything goes smoothly, the firm manages to stay upright. Any unforeseen occurrences, and the firm collapses. These occurrences could include everything from internal factors such as strikes and bungling to external factors such as increased competition or something as prosaic as a recession. Frequently, the natural occurrence, including prolonged bad weather, provides the nudge required to push the firm from its state of unstable equilibrium. Poor timing of funds, needs, and demand expectations, as occurs in the Sea Life Park B and C cases, exemplifies these problems.

This does not mean that small businesses have to starve to death, however. There are sources of funds available from various sources, both internal and external to the firm, that are frequently not considered by entrepreneurs.

Financing the New Venture

Clearly, the most difficult organization to try to fund adequately is the new venture. By definition, the organization does not have a proven track record on which it can base a claim for investor confidence. It is forced to trade on the reputation of the entrepreneur or group supporting the new organization for much of its status. The quality of the product or service offered is frequently of secondary importance.

It was noted earlier that potential investors prefer an exceptional management team to an exceptional product. Obviously, a combination of the two provides the best of all worlds. In the absence of this ideal, however, the competence of the entrepreneur is critical. Recently, a venture capital group on the West Coast was approached by a small group of entrepreneurs who wanted to expand their small, but prosperous, service-oriented company. The group lacked basic financial skills. They had, however, succeeded in differentiating their product in a unique manner. Moreover, their knowledge of personal skills as well as the basic demand patterns of their particular industry was enough to convince the venture capitalists that the entrepreneurs offered a fair likelihood of success. After a minimum of negotiations, the venture capital group agreed to support the entrepreneurs both with funds and financial expertise. It was clearly felt that the technical skills of finance could be obtained easily. What was difficult to gain was the expertise in that particular industry.

If, however, the entrepreneurs had been able to demonstrate technical expertise in finance as well, they would probably have been able to strike a better deal with the investors. Although they were able to attract external financing, they had to pay a high price because they lacked a balanced background. Also, it took quite a bit of time for them to find the right investment avenues for their particular needs. It then took more time to develop an acceptable prospectus to present to the potential investors. This timing factor could have proved more costly than the financing agreement. There existed other organizations with similar expansion plans at the same time. Our entrepreneurs could have found themselves at a competitive disadvantage if they had come out with their service too late. Fortunately for them, the other groups experienced similar delays in financing. Also, our group of entrepreneurs possessed a greater amount of expertise in the industry than competing enterprises. This provided the competitive edge. The critical factors that led the venture capital group to provide funds for the enterprise turned out to be the difference between a highly successful venture and another statistic in the long list of entrepreneurial failures.

Sources of Venture Capital

The sources available to the new, small venture are, typically, quite limited. Most funds are generated from the personal funds of the entrepreneur and his or her family and close associates. There is little or no financial leverage involved in this type of arrangement. The personal exposure and risk are extremely high. High personal exposure makes it difficult for the entrepreneur to use these qualities on which his or her success must depend. The entrepreneur could lose the ability to evaluate or accept risk in an objective manner, particularly where the funds being used are those of family or close friends.

Another source of funds for the new venture is venture capital operations. The definition and details involved in this form of financing are described in the articles at the end of this chapter. What is more interesting is the availability—or lack of it—regarding venture capital. This source tends to be highly concentrated in a few metropolitan centers. Because entrepreneurial ventures are not nearly as concentrated as the venture capitalists, the entrepreneur usually must go to the capital centers to seek out investors. Areas such as Boston, New York, the San Francisco Bay area, and Dallas-Ft. Worth-Houston provide high concentrations of venture capital.

Venture capitalists, as previously discussed, prefer qualified entrepreneurs to totally innovative ideas. They also frequently desire a mixture of fixed-return obligations and equity involvement. The problem, from the entrepreneur's view, is to end up with the proportion of debt and equity participation most beneficial to the objectives of the new venture.

If return on capital is relatively long term in nature, and short-term cash flow is critical, equity participation may be preferred. In this manner, payments of interest or principal on loans will not have to divert scarce cash flow. Conversely, if control is a critical requirement, then the entrepreneur may press for a higher proportion of debt obligations. This may restrict cash flow, but it may also remove a psychological block from the entrepreneur, who frequently feels the need to have a totally free hand in the decision-making process.

Finding a venture capital group whose objectives concerning investment mix are consistent with the entrepreneur's objectives will probably not be an easy task. The entrepreneur must usually approach more than one venture capitalist or group as described in the readings. If this is inconsistent with the timing requirements of the venture, the entrepreneur must consider the relevant priorities involved and determine which objectives are most important. Basically, the entrepreneur must decide whether the time lost seeking a better financing package is worth the better fit with financing objectives. The entrepreneur must also consider the probability of obtaining the ideal financing package. This is a classic case of decision making amid conditions of uncertainty.

The capability for flexibility is available from the venture capitalists. This is not true, however, concerning another potential source of funds—the Small Business Administration. The SBA offers loan guarantees to operations that meet specific qualifications outlined in the readings. These funds are strictly in the form of debt capital, however. This enhances the control aspects for the entrepreneur, but it also presents a cash-flow problem.

It also presents an interesting disadvantage to a normal bank loan. Since the loan is guaranteed by the SBA, at least partially, some banks frequently are far less diligent in policing these loans. Although this may at first seem beneficial to entrepreneurs, who usually prefer more flexibility in their actions, banks can provide valuable counseling and management assistance. But banks, knowing they can recoup most of their losses in the event of default, place a low priority on assistance to firms that have this type of loan.

The SBA, however, will provide financial counseling assistance to organizations in their programs. This would seem to balance the negative aspect noted above. But the SBA frequently does not stress this form of assistance until the entrepreneur experiences trouble, which is often too late. Then, by the time that the SBA consultants can get together with the entrepreneurs, the damage that has been done is frequently too great to overcome. This factor seriously detracts from the benefits offered by the SBA consulting service.

New, small ventures are able to get some capital from the banking community, as well. For the very small enterprise, a requirement for bank capital frequently rests upon the personal, as well as organizational, guarantee of the loan by the entrepreneur. Once again, we see that the personal exposure of the entrepreneur is heightened. This can, similarly, inhibit the natural decision-making tendencies of the entrepreneur.

The cost of capital for the new, small venture is frequently quite high from bank sources. The banks view these operations as both risky and expensive to fund. There are less overall talent and resources available to the organization, adding to the risk. Also, other things being equal, the cost of maintaining a loan is relatively fixed and, therefore, is cheaper per dollar loaned for large loans than for small loans. These factors all help to explain the reluctance of banks to loan funds to new, small ventures.

New, large, entrepreneurial ventures often find that many sources of funds are available to them that are unavailable to the new small venture. Banks are frequently more willing to make loans to the larger firms, for the obverse of the reasons above. Also, the larger firms frequently have more equity capital available to them at the outset. This further decreases the financial risk to the bank since there are more total assets to protect the bank's investment. In the Sea Life Park (A) case, this point is well demonstrated. That organization found a welcome at the local banks because the venture capital package is able to support bank loans.

The large venture also is frequently able to go to the traditional capital markets for financing. Both equity and money markets are willing to risk venture financing where the offerings are large enough to provide at least the potential for a secondary market. This, moreover, is one of the major reasons why the traditional capital markets are closed to the new, small venture.

Another source of funds that has been traditionally friendly to larger venture organizations has been the insurance companies. A small portion of the cash flow generated by these institutions has found its way into venture capital. While the portion may be small, the volume is quite large. This source of capital is becoming increasingly available to smaller organizations.

The larger insurance companies still typically restrict venture financing to packages in excess of $500,000. Some, however, are going below that level. Nevertheless, most still feel that the risks and costs associated with smaller financing packages simply outweigh the potential returns. This source of funds is never likely to find its way to the very small firms. The added availability to new, small ventures of the size of Sea Life Park (although they did not participate in that particular venture) provides a greater degree of flexibility to new entrepreneurs. What is even more promising is the increased willingness of this new source of venture capital to tailor the financing package to the needs of the individual entrepreneurs. Various financial instruments are now being accepted by the insurance-venture groups. Some of these instruments even show signs of innovativeness, a trait not traditionally found in the conservative insurance industry.

An even more exciting source of funds for new ventures is demonstrated by the interest large, mature corporations are placing in entrepreneurial activities. An increasing number of companies are allocating a portion of their resources to new ventures that do not fit within the confines of their traditional areas of expertise. Moreover, the criteria for evaluating these investments are quite different from those used in standard, internal investments. The venture-investment criteria combine higher potential return with a realization of much higher risk than would be acceptable from other corporate investments. The venture investments are also expected to be longer term in nature. The evaluation is based on long-term expected payoffs instead of the traditional short-term evaluation process.

Financing Expansion Plans

Once the organization has been able to demonstrate that it is a viable institution, financing for added projects becomes somewhat simpler. Many sources are still closed to the small business, but a proven track record does open some of the doors enough to enable the entrepreneur to present plans and needs.

The ongoing venture usually experiences a need for funds to finance expansion. At that point when the entrepreneur has to decide whether to maintain the status quo or expand operations, the availability of adequate financing is critical. If the entrepreneur has gone this far, personal and organizational commitment to expansion is usually present. There is also, in all probability, at least a perceived market for the organization's product or service.

That perceived market frequently determines what types of financing are most appropriate and available. Ventures involving the use of capital assets can frequently generate substantial funds through the use of debt instruments. Those where an expanded service is to be offered, or where risks would drive reasonable debt rates too high, often require some form of equity instrument.

Since the organization has already experienced some degree of success (expansion, after all, implies a given base), entrepreneurs find it somewhat easier to justify requests for funds. Unlike new ventures, ongoing ventures have financial records to draw on to demonstrate strength and stability. In particular, questions referring to liquidity, ability to pay interest and a portion of principal, are of interest to lenders.

Lenders of growth capital like to see a net-asset position that has grown with the organization. This indicates that the organization has used its own retained earnings to finance previous expansion. It also shows that the entrepreneur and owners have demonstrated a willingness to commit their own capital to the enterprise. This is in contradiction to those owners who try to recoup their own investment, through dividends or salaries, at a fast pace. It also denotes an excess of assets that do not have a prior claim from senior creditors, making reclamation of loan funds more assured. Other ratios can be calculated with a greater degree of certainty, as well. Lenders may realize that past performance regarding financing goals does not necessarily imply future actions. This past performance, however, does provide a basis for some degree of confidence in the future actions of entrepreneurs. As we have seen from some of the readings in the early chapters, the motives and characteristics of entrepreneurs have often been held suspect. Past records connoting a degree of financial responsibility help to allay fears of being taken by some fast-talking, manipulating entrepreneur.

More important, however, is the proof of the earning ability of the organization. The entrepreneur seeking growth funds is able to develop statements showing that the product or service has generated demand and, therefore, revenues. Since the entrepreneur has survived to the point where expansion is now a possibility, financial records usually show that revenues have exceeded normal operating expenses, as well. These past earnings provide potential investors with something more tangible than theoretical forecasts from which to extrapolate future returns for the entrepreneurial organization.

This latter point is very important to equity investors in growth organizations. They are not only investing in the promises of an entrepreneur, but also in the past performance of a tested product and organization. Equity markets, therefore, are much more receptive to offerings from ongoing small ventures. The details and methodology of securing funds from the equity market for venture purposes are well documented in the readings and cases. A serious question that the entrepreneur has to answer while considering this source of capital involves the degree of control by his or her own value system. The timing of equity offerings is critical and sometimes beyond the control of the entrepreneur. Equity markets have cycled between ready acceptance of such offerings and total rejection of any such offerings, including all points between these two ends of the market spectrum.

Typically, much of the stock of the organization is either directly or indirectly controlled by the entrepreneur. A formal offering, even if it is a private placement, often necessitates relinquishing control over some of the stock in the company. Many entrepreneurs feel that their creativity is inhibited if they do not have total control over their organizations. This can lead to, at least in their minds, constraints on entrepreneurial actions.

The question of what is an acceptable degree of control can, therefore, be a serious problem. Legal control frequently means more than 50 percent ownership of voting stock. In most organizations, however, effective control can be exercised with far less than a majority of the voting stock. The larger the amount of stock outstanding, the smaller proportion of stock required for operating control. Also, the higher the value of the stock outstanding, the easier it is for an entrepreneur to maintain operating control with less than a majority of the voting stock.

A tactic that has been used successfully by some entrepreneurs in need of capital is to use nonvoting, equity participation. In this manner, the entrepreneur can hold much or all of the voting stock while gaining access to equity capital. This form of equity, however, is less valuable than voting stock unless extra inducements are offered. These inducements might include a prior call on common dividends, priority standing on liquidation assets available to common stock, or first preference when voting stock becomes available to the public. In either event, this form of common stock is used only when necessary for gaining venture capital in difficult situations.

Nontraditional Sources of Funds

The discussion to this point has been concerned with traditional sources of growth funds. These are other sources of funds available to entrepreneurs which, although frequently not advantageous for long-term investments, may serve to ease financing needs in the short run.

One method, which is actually a traditional source of funds in the garment industry, involves factoring of receivables. This essentially means that a firm sells its accounts receivable to another firm, usually specialists in factoring. The factor buys the receivables, at a discount, and is then responsible for collecting these amounts. There are several types of arrangements available under this form of financing. The factor may choose to buy all of the receivables a firm may have at any time. If so, the discount is usually fairly steep, often as much as 20 percent of the total amount. The factoring arrangement may also allow the factor to select a previously agreed-upon percentage of the accounts, or only those accounts recently incurred. Under these arrangements, terms may approach short-term, risk-oriented, bank loans.

Factoring arrangements can be made on either a temporary or permanent basis, as in the garment industry. The advantage to factoring is that working capital is not tied up in receivables. A disadvantage involves the psychological effect on suppliers and customers. In those industries where factoring is not a traditional method of financing, a firm which resorts to it is often considered to be in poor health. It is frequently perceived to be the last, legitimate, source of funds available to a firm in poor health.

Suppliers may be hesitant to supply credit to a firm that is known to be factoring its receivables. Many firms try to stretch their payables while factoring receivables to gain maximum benefit from the combined "float." Customers, moreover, frequently resent having their bills sold to another organization. Since factoring firms make their money by getting early payment of the receivables, they are often more zealous in their collection procedures. For these reasons, factoring should be approached with caution by firms in industries where it is not viewed as a traditional, and acceptable, method of financing.

Floor-financing arrangements, as found among automobile dealers, are a variation of secured, short-term loans. Swane Motors, one of the cases in this book, uses this method of financing. A bank loans money with particular vehicles pledged as collateral. When that vehicle is sold, the loan is theoretically repaid. Since a relatively constant (except for seasonal fluctuations) level of stock is kept on hand, loans are always outstanding under this type of arrangement.

Other methods of financing can be lumped under the general term of interbusiness transfers. For various reasons, one firm may be willing to extend credit either directly or indirectly to another firm. Customers may loan funds or prepay for goods or services, where sources of supply may be a critical issue.

Suppliers, moreover, may also be willing to extend extraordinary credit to key customers. A firm wishing to expand its operations may be able to approach its suppliers for funds. Agreements may require long-term supply commitments. The decision usually involves a break-even analysis concerning the costs of the supply contract versus the benefits of the credit arrangement. The oil industry provides an example of such an arrangement. Petroleum refiners frequently provide loans to valued independent dealers to fund renovation and expansion projects.

Other forms of financing between businesses may include various forms of balance-sheet transactions. Accounts payable may be stretched out. Accounts receivable may also be accelerated. Customers may supply vital resources to their suppliers (this was common during the period of severe resource shortages in 1974). Suppliers, on the other hand, may advance goods on consignment, so that the goods do not have to be paid for until sold. Machinery may be loaned or sold to another firm at advantageous terms.

All of these forms of financing are usually short term in nature. They usually require some form of power on the part of the borrowing firm. Entrepreneurs intent on expansion through the use of inter-business transfers should consider whether they can provide the right kind of incentive to either suppliers or customers to convince them to provide assistance.

Summary

The source of funds for entrepreneurs seeking to start or expand ventures is surprisingly large. Constraints on size and source of financing frequently rest on the risk entailed in the use of capital. New ventures are more limited in the sources of funds available to them. New ventures have to rely on the perceptions of potential investors concerning the future prospects of relatively untested ideas or managers. Established ventures seeking funds for expansion at least have some history of achievement on which to base their claim for funding.

Traditional sources of funds include the capital and equity markets. Each source is seeking an investment opportunity with just the right degree of risk, timing, industry, and background in which to place its funds.

Nontraditional sources of funds may also be used to provide money for expansion. These are typically used to finance short-term needs. Caution has to be followed in using many nontraditional sources due to the varied reception by suppliers and customers of some of these methods.

The key to selecting the right mix of funding sources essentially rests with the values of the entrepreneur in charge of the organization. Acceptance of risk as well as desire for control on the part of the entrepreneur may provide greater constraints than the marketplace for venture capital. Technical considerations should not be the only considerations when selecting from the various traditional and nontraditional sources of financing.

Readings

The readings for Chapter 3 provide insight into general and specific problems in funding new ventures or expanding older small businesses. These readings vary from a more general discussion presented by Liles to specific criteria necessary for venture-capital initiation proposed by the SBA article. They vary from prescriptive discussions of entrepreneurial financing to descriptions of actual instances of an entrepreneur seeking to fund a new venture.

The article by Patrick Liles, "Conventional Wisdom and Practical Problems in the Financial Requirements of New Ventures," adds to the comments presented in the text concerning sources of funds for new ventures. Particularly, Liles reinforces the concept that entrepreneurial ventures are frequently forced to live on a "shoe-string." Ideally, entrepreneurs should secure adequate financing from the outset. This may be difficult, or impossible, especially for the inexperienced entrepreneur. Liles points to reasons for these difficulties and problems. They need not be insurmountable, however.

The *Forbes* article points to a new, overlooked source of financing. Some large corporations are now providing seed money to new or expanding ventures. Also, individual investors within these corporations can be approached for funds. Frequently, funding for new ventures comes from several different sources. The *Business Week* article provides a graphic example of the lengths that one entrepreneur went to in order to secure adequate funding for his new venture. He wanted to be sure his organization wasn't in the shoestring category described in the Liles article.

The final article, "The ABC's of Borrowing," prepared by the SBA staff, is a prescriptive source of advice on how to prepare to find funds. Specific types of information sought by prospective investors are outlined. Similarly, types of capital available to entrepreneurs are defined. The article concludes with questions that should be answered by the entrepreneur before approaching financing sources.

The readings, as a group, discuss the problems and methods of securing financing for new and expanding ventures. Financing has to be considered in the context of a total plan for the organization. The next chapter discusses the format for planning in the small business within which the financing decision can be made.

Conventional Wisdom
and Practical Problems
in the Financial Requirements
of New Ventures

Patrick Liles
Harvard Business School

The initial financing of the entrepreneur's venture is a complex interaction of his needs, expectations, lifestyle, management ability, and several other expected and unexpected factors. In this paper, these factors and the many problems that might occur are explored in light of United States and international new venture financing. In the presentation, Dr. Liles defines many of the critical stages in financing a new venture and presents alternatives. Throughout the paper, the nature of the entrepreneur, his or her attitudes and motivations, are discussed.

Anyone who wants to start a new company in the United States today can readily learn a lot about the financial requirements of a new enterprise. In financial planning for a venture and in his quest for funds, the would-be entrepreneur can get helpful advice from any number of knowledgeable individuals, from seminars and from a spate of practical literature on the problems of starting new companies. My intention is to examine three closely related dictums of conventional wisdom which are frequently offered by entrepreneurs as guides to those who are pondering the financial aspects of starting their own companies. I would like also to explore some of the common sense and practical problems which lie behind this advice.

To better understand these basic generalizations, it will be helpful to identify the kinds of situations which over time have prompted entrepreneurs to formulate these rules of thumb. We shall also probe to determine when conventional wisdom seems most appropriate and when it appears to have some serious limitations. Finally, we shall attempt—and here I want to proceed with utmost caution—to consider the usefulness of this conventional wisdom as it might apply to some aspects of venture financing outside the United States.

Before proceeding, however, it would be useful to set some boundaries and give some focus to the kinds of new venture situations being considered. First, none of this discussion is intended to deal with the many marginal retail and service ventures which are established each year largely as an individual's alternative to a marginal job or unemployment. Nor is there any intention to consider the attractive small

Proceedings of Project ISEED, Summer 1975. Published by Project ISEED, Ltd., The Center for Venture Management, Suite 508, 207 E. Buffalo Street, Milwaukee, WI 53202, U.S.A.

companies which become financially rewarding to the individuals directly involved in them but which are not sufficiently large or permanent enough to interest outside equity financing. Instead, the conventional wisdom to be discussed here relates to what has been called high-potential ventures—that is, companies which were started with the intention that they grow rapidly in sales and profits and become large corporations. The successful companies among these ventures will at some future date become major forces in domestic and world economies.

In discussions of the financial requirements of starting a company, the would-be entrepreneur is repeatedly given the advice, "Learn to do things on a shoestring." The basic common sense that lies behind this observation is that much of the time during the early start-up period of a new venture, money is extremely scarce. And even after money becomes available, there are far more needs and perceived opportunities than could possibly be funded. Moreover, of those uses of funds which appear essential and which promise to contribute the most to the development of the venture, some will inevitably prove unproductive. In starting a business, the approach of doing things on a shoestring is a fundamental law of financial survival.

Doing things on a shoestring is unquestionably a necessity until outside financing is received. Even when outside funds are scheduled to be invested early in the venture, entrepreneurs are caught during a period when they must use friendly money—that is, their own funds plus money from friends and family. While they are getting together the elements of the business and describing what the venture is all about to potential investors, they are eating away at limited funds which cannot be replenished by those supplying it.

Raising outside money is also an uncertain business. There are significant advantages for the potential investor to delay in making up his mind. It is better for him to wait and see how some of the uncertainties in the venture resolve themselves before giving a commitment. One of the senior men in the Boston venture capital community has observed that if he finds it difficult to evaluate a start-up situation, his decision is to wait six months. Then if the company is still alive, it merits his further consideration.

In some industries it is possible for a well-executed and lucky shoestring operation to carry the venture from its inception to a point of substantial development. This may be attempted either because the entrepreneur wishes to retain maximum equity or because outside funds for the venture are simply unavailable. For whatever reasons, the absolute necessity of a shoestring operation to keep the company financially viable may become prolonged.

Although an easy concept to understand for people who have no choice, there are some practical problems which frequently occur. Learning to do things on a shoestring is particularly difficult for the entrepreneur who has spent most of his working life in a large corporate, government, or university research environment. By the very nature of his work, he is accustomed to improvising. But he is accustomed to doing his improvisations with a vast backup of expensive equipment and personnel. In such institutions, selection and purchase of equipment are made on the basis of long-term requirements which provide some economic justification for quality and quantity. By contrast, new venture situations must make do with very little.

Another kind of problem also appears because of changes in going from corporate life into a venture operated on a shoestring. The poor equipment, bad appearance, and inconvenient location of the entrepreneur's new work environment in most situations reflects a loss of position and prestige which the entrepreneur finds in conflict with his self-image. Doing things on a shoestring usually means a decrease in salary as well and that in turn means a reduction in living standard. For some, being president of a struggling little company does not fully compensate for these losses. Most people would readily shift into the position of the successful entrepreneur with his modern office, company car and handsome salary. But they find the prospect of several years of living on a shoestring and a great deal of uncertainty regarding the final outcome of their efforts not at all attractive. As a forty-year-old engineer once responded to a proposed shoestring approach for his venture, "But I just couldn't do it that way. I am simply accustomed to much better than that."

The would-be entrepreneur who fails to understand or to accept the shoestring requirement for initiating a venture plans to purchase new equipment, lease modern facilities in an attractive location which is also convenient to his home, and maintain his current salary level. He anticipates immediate hiring of a number of qualified people to assure that the initial work of the venture is done correctly and on schedule. This is not to say that he has any intention of being reckless or careless. It is only his wish to "do things right" according to the standards which he has known in the past.

As one might imagine, this approach is rarely anticipated by anyone putting up a sizable amount of his own money to finance the venture. It is almost as rare to find outside investors other than the public willing to back this approach with their funds. When the serious would-be entrepreneur repeatedly finds resistance to this plan for high levels of expenditure, he usually revises them downward toward a shoestring approach. But the will to go this way requires more than good intentions. Unless the entrepreneur has some natural inclination toward such things as scrounging up low-rent space and finding equipment for sale at distress prices, his initial attempts at shoestring efforts will be unproductive. Exposure to this phenomenon has led to the effective development of some of these kinds of entrepreneurial skills among some of the groups providing financing and assistance to new venture situations.

Other problems occur with a shoestring approach when the entrepreneur and his backers fail to perceive that for a high-potential venture a policy of minimum expenditures is a short-term strategy of necessity and not a viable condition over the longer term. Inevitably, there are seriously damaging effects from severe financial constraints if pursued indefinitely. Failure to hire additional people can cause critical tasks to be neglected or require key people to allocate their time ineffectively. It may not be initially possible, for example, to hire a draftsman to document all design changes. But over time, this omission produces serious problems and inefficiencies in production and servicing. Similarly, using the creator of a technical product to troubleshoot on the production line means that he is unavailable to give critical sales assistance in the field. The shoestring strategy which initially serves well to conserve cash also sows the seeds of longer term problems which at some point can no longer be ignored.

Low salaries and wages may initially be an acceptable policy over several months or a year. At some point, however, good people begin to perceive their personal opportunity losses and to move on the other employers who are willing to be more competitive.

A low salary level for the entrepreneur is a special class of problem. First, in a shoestring effort it is difficult for him to take a salary more competitive in the market-place than the salaries he pays to others in the venture. Both debt and equity investors give careful scrutiny to what the entrepreneur draws out of the venture, the former because of the liquidity drain and the latter in fear that the entrepreneur might become content before the venture had provided a return to the outside investors. Yet a low salary for the entrepreneur can be particularly dysfunctional to the company because of the additional strain it makes on his personal life if he is married and has a family. During the start-up period, the entrepreneur, like the young doctor, dentist, or lawyer, is frequently absent from his home and has little time for his family. But for the entrepreneur the problem is more acute. He can never get away from the problems of the company entirely. Because he is usually older than his intern counterparts, his family is likely to be more developed and the demands are greater for a higher level of income. Allowing the financial pressure at home to continue for significant lengths of time can create family discord and strife which distracts if not disables the entrepreneur's attention to the business.

Most of the basic uncertainties and potential financial problems in starting new companies appear to be universal. In most other countries, sources of risk capital are even more conservative and less numerous than here. It would seem, therefore, that a strategy aimed at carefully constraining cash outflows in a new venture would be at least as necessary abroad as in the United States. One question this raises, however, is to what extent in other countries do those individuals best able to create high-potential ventures find the financial and other sacrifices of a shoestring operation to be personally unacceptable? Are the problems and effects of making the change as great or greater than for American entrepreneurs?

In purely economic terms some of the problems for the individual in trying to operate on a shoestring would have to be less in countries with more extensive social-service programs such as health care, unemployment programs, and public transportation. In these countries one could get along with less and live in reasonable security and comfort. But more significant, perhaps, are noneconomic factors. In the United States there are few strong traditions in most aspects of life, including career patterns. Many people spend their entire working lives in one company, but each year many thousands of others change jobs and go to work for other companies. In this atmosphere of change, it is easier in a social context for someone to try something very different. In fact, in parts of California and Massachusetts the scenario of an individual trying to start a high-potential venture has happened so frequently that in those areas it is no longer considered so unusual.

In societies which have more traditional patterns of career development, it must be very difficult for an educated person to take what is perceived by himself and those about him as a step downward. From a position of respect and likely continued advancement, a would-be entrepreneur must move out—not only into something different but into something which requires compromise and sacrifice because of financial constraints. Viewed in this way, the conditions of getting things done on a shoestring could be prohibitive to many people.

A second wise observation which has evolved from the experiences of those involved in new ventures is "Be sure to raise enough money at the beginning." The fundamental common sense underlying this advice is that first it is very difficult to know how much money it will take to start a company and secondly, the consequences of running out of money are most severe. In scrambling to assemble resources and to make them function as a profit-making enterprise, there are many things which defy systematic forecasting and projections. Even when things are done on a shoestring during the start-up period of a new venture, money manages to slip away with alarming ease and extreme difficulty is experienced in getting income to cover this drain. Almost all of the unknowns and uncertainties in whatever form have a way of translating themselves into negative cash flows. Individuals who have started their own companies point out that compared to their original expectations things turned out to cost three times as much and to take twice as long or to cost twice as much and to take four times as long.

The first problem of the would-be entrepreneur is the question, "What is enough?" The fact of the matter is that in most industries there is no chance of a rapidly growing company ever reaching the point where it can generate enough cash internally to finance its requirements for working capital and the equity portion of fixed assets. However, it can be possible for a company to reduce its growth rate and survive without external financing if it can reach a point in operations above cash break-even. Enough money for a venture to reach cash break-even means that the company has enough money to achieve independent financial viability. For operations which are not able to reach this point, however, having enough money at the outset means having sufficient funds to assure that the business can reach a point where its record of performance and progress will attract additional investment from outside the company.

Cynics will say that not raising enough money is a favorite excuse of entrepreneurs who had a poor idea in the first place or who executed good ideas poorly. In such situations any additional money put into the venture would have meant additional losses. But in other situations which have difficulties the concept of the venture has been sound and most of management's efforts have been well directed. The problems just turned out to be greater than expected and the costs to be in excess of the funds available.

Yet the uncertainties and unpredictables should not be surprising if one considers that for the entrepreneur many things he must do are for him first-time efforts. When a sales engineer, for example, tries to develop a marketing strategy, create a new product, form a distribution system, and establish production operations, he is inevitably doing things which are beyond his prior experience. His situation is further complicated because somehow many of these tasks must be done at the same time. A potential customer wants to see a record of proven product performance before he installs the new company's product as part of his production equipment. But proven product performance requires that someone use the product under regular operating conditions. At the same time service for the new equipment must be available. But without evidence that a number of units will soon be in place, it is difficult to find service organizations willing to learn the care of the equipment. When difficulties are encountered in one area, they create difficulties in other areas and during the start-up period, these interrelated and interdependent tasks seem to go on forever. At the same time, with the exception of the entrepreneur, the problems of the small new firm are low in everyone's sense of priorities.

Running out of money creates problems for anyone but for the entrepreneur and his company the effects are particularly acute. Typically the unexpected events which cause excessive cash outflows also require the entrepreneur's full-time attention as well as more funds to correct the situation. But the process of raising additional funds also requires large commitments of the entrepreneur's time, especially when the unanticipated problems are still unresolved. And as the demands of these two activities on the entrepreneur's time continue, other tasks become neglected. It is this combination of conditions which has created absolute havoc in the early history of so many new venture situations.

To raise additional money under distress conditions requires that the original grand scheme of the venture still be convincing. It also requires that evidence be given to show that the venture can extract itself from its current predicament and that no other unexpected calamities are likely to occur. Because of what has happened, there is inevitably some doubt cast over the venture and the entrepreneur.

If the inflow of additional funds is delayed significantly, a venture begins to become an entirely different investment situation for the venture capitalist. His normal orientation is to find opportunities where his money will make major contributions to developing a profitable business. As a new venture situation becomes overextended with banks and trade creditors, however, money to be injected by the venture capitalist into the business has in fact already been spent. The creditors now stand ready to pounce upon newly acquired liquid assets. Much of any new funds therefore would be used to maintain solvency rather than to develop or expand activities of the firm. For many new ventures this condition prevents the inflow of any additional money. Even when overextension does not preclude obtaining additional funds on some basis, it requires additional negotiations, agreements, and still further delays.

The question of how much money should be invested at a given point in time is one of the issues resolved between the entrepreneur and his financial backers. Neither party wants the entrepreneur to waste his time in coming back for additional funds just because some of the tasks turn out to be somewhat more difficult and require a little more time and money than was originally anticipated. The financial people, however, want to be sure that they are not making a large commitment when a smaller amount of money invested initially could clarify some of their key uncertainties about the business concept, the entrepreneur, and the industry. The entrepreneur, on the other hand, prefers to have greater flexibility to move on to the next stage or into some variation of the original plan even if the initial efforts do not produce the desired results.

In practice, the major problem for those who have been successful in raising a sizable amount of money is that they no longer believed it necessary to continue doing things on a shoestring even when that approach is the most appropriate one for most of its activities. In this country it has been amazing and appalling how fast several new companies with large amounts of initial capaital raised from the public have spent tens of millions of dollars in just a few months but failed to establish viable companies.

Not only were funds spent rapidly, but they were spent without regard for some of the basic concepts of financial strategy. Without prior testing and without adequate controls, any number of new products were developed all at one time for a variety of different markets. The resulting chaos and disaster were inevitable. Also, large investments were made in low-return assets such as buildings and land when adequate and much less expensive facilities were available. The idea of doing things right, which has been described as an alternative to doing things on a shoestring, was transformed into the approach of doing things in a needlessly extravagant style, hardly justifiable for any company at any stage in its development.

In the experience of many venture situations in the United States, another major problem is that the venture and the original sources of funds are a poor match for each other in the first place. The moment of truth does not become obvious until the venture needs more money. Some venture capital investors, especially individuals, have a very limited capacity for making these kinds of investments. Even when they would like to follow up with additional funds, they are financially unable to do so. And unless a new source of money has the time and interest to investigate thoroughly how the venture got into its predicament, it cannot risk investing in a distress situation.

Some entrepreneurs find that their original investors are not in a position to understand the nature of the venture's difficulties or its prospects for recovery and ultimate success. This may be due to their lack of competence in certain areas or to the entrepreneur's poor communication with them. Those who keep quiet or try to play down problems seriously undermine the confidence of their financial backers. Nothing is more frightening to an investor than bad news that comes as a complete surprise.

Until recently the problems of a poor match between venture and investor were probably far greater in the United States than anywhere else in the world. Things started in the early '60s when great numbers of inexperienced venture capitalists began getting together with an even larger number of budding entrepreneurs for about ten years of frenzied activity. From time to time the public was invited to participate. At first it was almost difficult for entrepreneurs not to get enough money at the beginning because funds for second and third round financing were easily available. Legal restraints regarding alternative investments of idle funds prompted some SBICs to make venture deals to obtain current income. Even when serious problems began to develop in some of the publicly held venture capital portfolios, additional funds had to be committed to prevent showing disastrous performance—an earlier version of what is now occurring with some of the publicly held REITs in this country.

Reactions in the industry were severe and costly. Some of the venture capital companies sold what was left of their portfolios and ceased making venture investments. For some of the promising venture situations, the problems of getting additional money were insurmountable. But the shakeout left a far more sophisticated group of venture investors. And the new entrepreneurs seem to have a greater awareness of the problems of continuing funding requirements. People now are not in as much of a hurry. Fewer are thinking of venture investing as a way to quick money. Entrepreneurs and venture capitalists are looking for relationships that make sense over the longer term.

The third bit of conventional wisdom from entrepreneurs is "Keep as much of the equity as possible." Perhaps not surprisingly those who would supply capital to new ventures have some almost diametrically opposing advice. They argue that it is better to own part of a very large company than to own all of a very small one.

Equity, like cash, has a way of slipping away at a rapid rate from the very beginning. In the process of assembling resources for the venture, the entrepreneur finds that help is needed from a number of other people. For example, getting a particular individual to join the venture is critical to obtaining key selling skills or a finder makes a contribution by providing introductions to people in the financial community. With little funds at the outset, the entrepreneur's major incentive and reward for these individuals is frequently equity participation in the venture. Before he even gets into negotiations for raising money, a number of these kinds of payments have already diminished his ownership. By the time the company has gone through several financings, the entrepreneur is left with such a small part of the company that he feels it was not worth all the trouble and hardly worth the effort to continue. Or, he may feel that although he has come out well, he should have come out a lot better.

Some entrepreneurs are disappointed at the equity they are able to retain because they initially fail to realize the fundamental basis of financial reward for being an entrepreneur. To the one that puts it all together belongs the value which remains after all the others have been paid at going market rates. In determining how much equity is to be distributed, the naive entrepreneur evaluates his time and efforts the same way he evaluates the time and money inputs of others. With this outlook he quickly gives away far more of the company than is necessary and without realizing it.

Early dissipation of equity creates problems for potential investors as well as for the entrepreneur. It is very much in their interests that the entrepreneur keeps enough ownership in the company to maintain his interest and commitment to the venture's success. On making their assessments of the situation, the outside investors must consider the effects of their initial and any subsequent financings. To have to make a series of investments which would cause too great a dilution of the entrepreneur's ownership would be self-defeating.

In trying to maximize his equity ownership when raising money for a venture, there are two key dimensions for the entrepreneur: the source which provides the financing and the posture he assumes in negotiations. Of these, the most significant step is locating the source of capital which places a high value on the company. Different venture capitalists place very different values on the same situation because they have different expectations and different levels of confidence about the venture's eventual outcome. Within the same financial community, a $300,000 investment from one group may demand 40 percent of the equity, whereas the same deal would require only 20 percent of the company if financed by another group. In a so-called hot new issues market, a public offering for $300,000 might be done for 10 percent of the company.

Problems can and do result from an entrepreneur's seeking to maximize his ownership position, however. First of all, what mathematically is the best arrangement at one point in time in purely financial terms may not be best over the longer term. A venture investor may overvalue a situation because he doesn't really understand it—a condition that can prove difficult if problems develop and additional funds are required. Or he may not have sufficient financial staying power to see the venture through additional fundings. Or he may not be able to provide some of the help and assistance which the entrepreneur needs and could obtain from other investors. In trying to optimize his chances for the venture's success and the value of his position, the entrepreneur's best choice is not necessarily the cheapest money.

Other difficulties can occur if the entrepreneur and the investor are not careful about how far the investigations go without some clear understanding of the basic price and terms of the deal if the decision is made to invest. On one hand, the investor is expending time and money to carry out an investigation. He has to examine and analyze the venture's potential as reflected in the entrepreneur, the industry, the markets, and so on. He will not make the effort if he believes that there are going to be prolonged negotiations on price after he has completed his study. He will be even more concerned if he finds that he is not alone in his investigations but that others are also going through a similarly expensive inquiry and the entrepreneur will possibly be in the position of taking his choice to get the best deal.

From the entrepreneur's point of view, however, more is at stake than just price. The venture capitalist's proclivity to take his time means that during the period of investigation—which may take three weeks to six months—the venture continues to incur costs but without sufficient financial means to proceed with its essential tasks. For the entrepreneur to enter the investigation stage with a single source of capital puts him in a poor negotiating position not only regarding price or other conditions of the agreement but also in terms of what the venture is like if afterwards it must be another investor.

To raise money successfully from outside investors, the entrepreneur must offer an attractive incentive. The venture capitalist would like to be in on a situation where he has a reasonable chance of not losing all of his investment and a reasonable chance of making several to many times his investment over the next 5 to 10 years. But the investor is not unaware of the lesser financial inputs and the high potential gains of the entrepreneur. Insofar as he can challenge the entrepreneur's right to whatever value remains after others have received compensation, he can make a case for a still greater share of the equity. Where the entrepreneur brings the entire venture and the investor has little to contribute other than money, the entrepreneur is in a position to negotiate from strength. If the money sources are likely to make significant inputs of time and advisory help in addition to their investment, they have participated in the entrepreneurial process and can more easily justify rewards for that kind of effort.

Some entrepreneurs have not been able to raise money for their venture because they were simply unwilling to give up any more of their company. At some point, potential investors become concerned about what they see as unreasonable selfishness. Honest, different expectations can sometimes be incorporated into a sliding scale or payback feature in the agreement.

Because most venture capital financings require multiple inputs of money, the results of original negotiations are rarely, in any sense, the final outcome. A lesson learned by many entrepreneurs and venture capitalists is that advantage in negotiations shifts back and forth between the parties involved. The entrepreneur who forces a hard bargain today is likely to be asking for more money tomorrow. The venture capitalist who takes advantage of the principals in one situation may have a portfolio company with poorly motivated management. In the long-term kinds of relationships created in venture capital investing, it is rare for there to be just one winner or just one loser.

In a number of countries other than the United States, the question of equity ownership has a very different position in the context of small-business ventures. Far fewer opportunities exist for an outside investor to realize a return on his investment either in the form of a public offering or from the sale of his ownership to some larger company. The situation is similar to what happens in this country when a venture loses its momentum and potential for growth and falls into a viable but stagnant operation of around a million dollars in sales. In addition, in some countries less rigorous audit practices and less serious pursuit of tax revenues by the government preclude accurate information about the venture's operations and leave the outside investor in an even less meaningful position. Unless accompanied by family or other noneconomic ties, outside equity ownership in small situations simply has no value.

One result of these conditions is that private sector venture capital is available in many countries only in the form of very high cost debt from banking institutions or individuals. As would be expected, the lender must consider the total credit position of the borrower with the results that financing for new venture activities is more open to people of means. The enterprising individual wishing to proceed is able to keep all of the equity, but operates an extreme shoestring-level company with only limited and tightly controlled debt money available.

To the Rescue?

Forbes

If the capital squeeze gets worse, direct investing by pension funds may well have to fill the gap.

A few years ago all you needed was a fancy name and an idea. The public wanted new issues—any new issues—and Wall Street obliged. Today some of those hot new issues are bankrupt, and others are selling at three times earnings. A new issue is as popular with investors now as *The Washington Post* is in the White House.

Because you can't sell new issues, venture capital, too, has dried up. What do the venture capital people do with the company once it is successfully launched? Without a new-issue market, how do they cash in?

Forbes, July 1, 1974, p. 52. Reprinted with permission.

Would-be entrepreneurs are complaining that they are suffering because venture capital is in hiding. Is there no way out of this sad state of affairs—short of a new bull market?

A glimmer of hope. It comes from, of all places, that home of the first-tier stocks, the investment department of the Trust and Investment division of Morgan Guaranty Trust Co. of New York. The Morgan is definitely not going into the venture capital business. That's too risky for its pension fund and other fiduciary clients. But Morgan is beginning to get its feet wet in the second stage, the stage where new companies need refinancing or expansion capital.

What Morgan's investment department does is put up equity capital or other front money, then help arrange both long-term loans and bank financing, which can be supported by the additional equity capital.

The man in charge of this project is Gilbert Butler, 37, an intense man with a fast mind for numbers, who heads Morgan's specialized investment portfolio. "As long as bond and equity markets aren't doing the job," says Butler, "we feel we ought to try."

As we said, don't go to Butler with your promising invention or your hot new idea. He's not a venture capitalist. "We are looking," he explains, "for firms with at least $7 million and less than $50 million in net worth, and with an earnings and dividends record. Companies of this size often have had to resort heavily to short-term bank borrowings in the past two years. These companies need to tap the securities markets to avoid getting top heavy with short-term debt."

Butler's criteria are tough ones. He is only interested in companies that are earning 13 percent to 15 percent on their equity capital. "What's the point of lending money to a company that is earning a 9 percent return when money costs you 12 percent and up?" he asks.

A few years ago, investment bankers would be camped in the waiting rooms of such corporations. But not today. There are few places today for smaller companies to raise long-term capital. If a company meets his standards, Butler can structure a deal for it in several ways, all involving a degree of risk on Morgan's part—and commensurate potential rewards.

1. The bank as trustee can arrange to buy property and lease it to the company, with the residual value of the assets accruing to the *investor*. This way, the bank gets both a lease deal and a participation.

2. Where farm or timberland is involved, Morgan can make a deal whereby it, as subordinated lender, will share in the appreciation in the value of the property.

3. Morgan can make a subordinated loan, taking part of its reward in the form of a percentage of the sales growth resulting from the loan—a so-called sales override.

4. Morgan can finance a new subsidiary of the company, with the lender sharing in the subsidiary's profits or in its ownership.

5. Morgan can take income bonds, where the interest rate may run as high as 15 percent but need only be paid if earned.

6. In the more common deal, Morgan actually takes common stock in the company or a combination of stock and subordinated loans.

What good is equity if there is not much of a market for stock in these smallish companies? Butler gets around this by arranging to take a "put," which gives Morgan the right to sell the stock back to the company either at a preset price/earnings ratio or at book value. The bank thus shares in the increased profit or assets that result from its financing.

When a package involves both common stock and debt, the borrower gets a break in that the lending rate on the debt is usually fixed a point or two below prime; this minimizes the cash burden on the young company.

"Once the equity and long-term loan base has been established," Butler says, "then the company can borrow short term from the banks." Enter conflict-of-interest problems: Morgan insists that any such borrowing be done from a bank other than Morgan; this saves the bank from being both an owner and a lender.

Butler won't talk about any specific deals: "These are all private and a number involve privately held companies. I can only say that we have lent to lumber companies, agricultural companies, real estate developers, mining, retail trade—all kinds of companies. Most of our participations have been in the $3-million-to-$5-million range, although right now we are doing a larger deal for a California agri-business firm with a net worth of around $100 million."

WILL IT CATCH ON?

Will Morgan start a trend with this kind of deal making? Will the bank trust companies fill a vacuum that a dying Wall Street has all but abandoned? This remains to be seen. Not every bank has Morgan's resources and know-how; others will want to wait and see how Morgan makes out. Also, there are some complex problems—for example, how to properly and frequently value letter stock and other nonmarketable illiquid assets.

At any rate, Morgan is beginning to make an intelligent effort to fill a serious gap in the U.S.' capital-raising and capital-allocating apparatus. It may also help companies to remain private without sacrificing growth; and events of the past few years have shown that going *public* is a mixed blessing.

Who says all trust departments are stodgy and unimaginative?

An Adventure in Raising Venture Capital

George Hirsch

George Hirsch's search is a case study on finding backers for a new magazine.

George Hirsch, ex-publisher of *New York* magazine, has the easy lope of a long-distance runner, and, in fact, he has even been known to finish in the middle of the pack in the 26-mile Boston marathon. A few weeks ago Hirsch finished first in another kind of marathon—a cross-country search for money to launch a magazine called *New Times*. The prize was astonishingly better than a silver statue: A $2.7-million pledge of working capital from the nation's bluest blue-chip investors, ranging from American Express Co. to the small business investment companies linked with Bank of America, First National Bank of Boston, and three other leading banks.

At a time when venture capital is seeking far more glamorous and less risky businesses than magazine publishing, Hirsch ferreted out 17 prospects and convinced more than half of them that his new biweekly "news-magazine" makes sense. At the closing a month ago, "it was a scene to behold," says Hirsch, as all the venture-capital specialists gathered in one room, with Hirsch chipping down their individual shares from, say, $300,000 to $200,000 because—as Hirsch puts it—"I need only $1.7-million, not $2.7-million, to start with."

While the six-month fund-raising job had some stumbles, there were some comic-serious moments too. Hirsch brought along Jimmy Breslin, one of the star contributors to his forthcoming magazine, to a sedate lunch at Morgan, Stanley & Co., one of whose partners, Richard Fisher, is a personal friend of Hirsch and investment adviser for *New Times*. The hosts apologized for the absence of cocktails, noting that nonalcoholic lunches had been the tradition since the days of J. P. Morgan. To which Breslin, in a grumpy, loud voice, replied: "I'd rather be broke."

"Targeted" audience. The 38-year-old Hirsch is the first to pose all the questions that doubters raise about magazines: "Isn't there already too much to read? In a television era, will magazine advertising decline? What effect will the postal increases have on magazines?" But he answers just as readily by explaining the "targeted audience" he hopes to offer advertisers. "Our average reader will be college-educated, well-read, between 18 and 34 years of age, professional, urban, and on his way up with a big discretionary income that he will spend on vacations, books, wardrobe, and other entertainment and leisure-time activities."

Business Week, April 14, 1973, pp. 92-96. Reprinted with permission.

In his magazine, Hirsch hopes to combine the newsiness of a *Time* or *Newsweek* with the sprightly, personal "new journalism" that often appears in *Harper's* and *Atlantic*. Besides Breslin, his contributors will include Pete Hamill, Studs Terkel, Joe McGuinness, Larry King, and Pulitzer Prize winners J. Anthony Lukas and Mike Royko. Hirsch claims that no other magazine is filling the role that he envisions for *New Times*.

While he would get an argument from *Time* and *Newsweek*—and even from *Harper's* and *Atlantic*, both of which are putting a stronger accent on contemporary issues—no one can fault Hirsch's ability to sell his concept. As one New York venture capital specialist says admiringly: "With the death of *Life, Look*, and the old *Saturday Evening Post* and reports of troubles at *Saturday Review* and other magazines, the investment climate is even more bearish than usual on new magazines. George provides a rare casebook on how to do it right."

Split on direction. Hirsch framed his fund-raising strategy late in 1971 after leaving *New York* in the wake of a behind-the-scenes power struggle with editor and cofounder Clay Felker. Hirsch says he wanted to keep *New York* circulation more oriented to the city itself, while Felker was shooting—mistakenly in Hirsch's view—for a substantial national audience.

In financing strategy, Hirsch decided to depart radically from the scheme used to launch *New York* six years ago. That project had been the pet of a small group of largely Wall Street and New York City big names—John Loeb, Armand Erpf, and Edgar Bronfman. For *New Times* (a name which he got from a friend and which also is the title of a Soviet English-language weekly), Hirsch focused mainly on private institutions.

"Personal investors tend to invest for ego reasons, status, or to gain a political voice," he claims. "Because this is going to be a national magazine, I also wanted to spread the financing around, so that no one investor or one part of the country dominates." At the same time, he refused financing offers from several large Wall Street houses, preferring instead to handle the whole deal himself, from legal aspects (his father was a New York lawyer) to stock certificates.

Hirsch discussed his idea of a news-magazine with more than 300 media and advertising executives. Then last August he personally wrote most of a detailed, 175-page business proposal to show potential investors. He figured that his magazine would move into the black in its third year. Circulation is projected to start at 100,000 and go up "depending strictly on the economics," says Hirsch—"in others words, we will not be building circulation for the sake of circulation, but in terms of renewal rates, revenue per copy from both newsstand and subscription sales, and the acquisition costs of new subscriptions." To lighten the burden on advertisers and help refine the circulation, readers will pay higher-than-average subscription rates that may run from $.31 to $.46 per copy, depending on results of four test mailings.

"The key is leverage," Hirsch says. "As you raise your circulation and ad rates and lower your cost per thousand of audience reached, much more comes back to the magazine." At 100,000 circulation and roughly $12.50 per thousand, for instance, Hirsch projects the break-even point at 35 pages of ads per issue. At 150,000 circulation and $12.33 per thousand, break-even is 24 pages; and at 250,000 or $12.10 per thousand, only 10 pages.

Dragging his foot. Hirsch planned to kick off his fund drive right after Labor Day. "Then came trouble," he recalls with a visible twinge. A jogger who likes to run an hour or more a day, Hirsch was taking his Labor Day constitutional when a cab shot out of a sidestreet and knocked him flat, tearing several ligaments in his foot.

The next morning, after a trip to the hospital, Hirsch ignored the pain and hobbled to his first big luncheon meeting. "That was a mistake," he says. "My foot was still swelling, and for 72 hours after that, I had to keep it in ice." For the next two months, he struggled around on crutches—"on and off planes, in and out of cabs. It was a mess." To make matters worse, says Fisher, "the first prospects we called all had the same reaction: 'You guys have a tough sell ahead of you.' Yet some of these same people finally ended up as investors."

The first investor was Pioneer Ventures Co. "The thing that impressed me," says James Niven, a Pioneer partner, "was that George's ideas were not overly ambitious. When the new people at *Saturday Review* claim they can raise circulation from 750,000 to 4-million, that does not make economic sense. But George started with a low base, had reasonable projections, checked out very well with the people we talked to, and never varied in his original proposal."

Yet Niven admits to a few early doubts. "I grew up in the film business"—as the son of actor David Niven—"and I know the problems of trying to predict what's going to appeal to the public." So before coming aboard, Niven made one condition: "I told George he had to raise all the money before he would get our final commitment. If he raised only half and wanted to move ahead on a shoestring, then he had to count us out."

A setback. To help provide more momentum, Hirsch was banking on Gunwyn Ventures Co., a Princeton (N. J.) company with a strong name in the venture capital field. "They were quite interested," recalls Hirsch, "then on a Sunday evening—what became a very Black Sunday—I had a call from one of the partners, who said they had decided against coming in."

Says Gunwyn partner Peter Danforth: "Even under the best of conditions, publishing ventures are always difficult to decide on. It's like backing a new consumer disposable product. You allocate 80 percent of your initial dollars to a big ad campaign, and once that's gone, what do you have left if the product doesn't go? Despite all the respect we had for George and the way he handled himself, we just had too many doubts." One of the biggest: a three-year wait for profits. "In an industrial venture," says Danforth, "you have the same big upfront requirement, but you turn your capital faster, so you know sooner."

When Gunwyn fell through, Hirsch started worrying. "Short of not raising the money you need," he claims, "the worst thing that can happen to you in the venture capital market is getting what they call a 'shopped-around' look. Everyone talks to everyone else in this field, and once you get turned down a few times, word spreads fast." Shortly after the Gunwyn decision, for instance, Hirsch called a prospect in California. "It was my first contact with him," he recalls, "and even before I could describe the magazine, the guy said, 'Oh yeah, you're that marathon runner who got run over by a cab.' "

Waiting it out. Where Hirsch finally made a sale, the negotiations regularly dragged on for months. Last November, for instance, he telephoned James Rawlings, a vice-president for the Bank of America SBIC in Los Angeles. "At first," Rawlings concedes, "I wasn't at all interested. I told George if he had a business plan, to shoot it along. But then when I saw his credentials and the contributing editors he had lined up, I got a little intrigued."

Hirsch and Rawlings met five times in the next two months—once in Los Angeles and four times in New York. During one two-day session, they spent 20 hours poring over details. When they were not meeting or telephoning each other, Rawlings was often talking with one of the nearly 40 sources that he checked.

By the time Hirsch finally had his commitments and completed last month's closing, he claims he ended up with far more than a fat bank balance. "This kind of experience," he says of the fund raising, "forces you to advance your thinking to an extraordinary degree. At this stage today," he adds with some relief and satisfaction, "we have gone as far as we possibly can without actually putting out a magazine. In many ways, all this is even tougher than publishing itself."

The ABC's of Borrowing

Revised by Members of The Staff, Financial Assistance, Small Business Administration, Washington, D.C.

Summary. *Some small businessmen cannot understand why a lending institution refuses to lend them money. Others have no trouble getting funds, but they are surprised to find strings attached to their loans. Such owner-managers fail to realize that banks and other lenders have to operate by certain principles just as do other types of business.*

This Aid discusses the following fundamentals of borrowing: (1) credit worthiness, (2) kinds of loans, (3) amount of money needed, (4) collateral, (5) loan restrictions and limitations, (6) the loan application, and (7) standards which the lender uses to evaluate the application. The SBA form is used to illustrate suggestions for filling out a loan application.

Courtesy of the Small Business Administration.

Inexperience with borrowing procedures often creates resentment and bitterness. The stories of three small businessmen illustrate this point.

"I'll never trade here again," Bill Smith* said when his bank refused to grant him a loan. "I'd like to let you have it, Bill," the banker said, "but your firm isn't earning enough to meet your current obligations." Mr. Smith was unaware of a vital financial fact, namely, that lending institutions have to be certain that the borrower's business can repay the loan.

Tom Jones lost his temper when the bank refused him a loan because he did not know what kind or how much money he needed. "We hesitate to lend," the banker said, "to businessmen with such vague ideas of what and how much they need."

John Williams' case was somewhat different. He didn't explode until after he got the loan. When the papers were ready to sign, he realized that the loan agreement put certain limitations on his business activities. "You can't dictate to me," he said and walked out of the bank. What he didn't realize was that the limitations were for his good as well as for the bank's protection.

Knowledge of the financial facts of business life could have saved all three men the embarrassment of losing their tempers. Even more important, such information would have helped them to borrow money at a time when their businesses needed it badly.

This *Aid* is designed to give the highlights of what is involved in sound business borrowing. It should be helpful to those who have little or no experience with borrowing. More experienced businessmen should find it useful in re-evaluating their borrowing operations.

IS YOUR FIRM CREDIT WORTHY?

The ability to obtain money when you need it is as necessary to the operation of your business as is a good location or the right equipment, reliable sources of supplies and materials, or an adequate labor force. Before a bank or any other lending agency will lend you money, the loaning officer must feel satisfied with the answers to the five following questions;

1. What sort of person are you, the prospective borrower? By all odds, the character of the borrower comes first. Next is his ability to manage his business.

2. What are you going to do with the money? The answer to this question will determine the type of loan—short or long term. Money to be used for the purchase of seasonal inventory will require quicker repayment than money used to buy fixed assets.

3. When and how do you plan to pay it back? Your banker's judgment as to your business ability and the type of loan will be a deciding factor in the answer to this question.

4. Is the cushion in the loan large enough? In other words, does the amount requested make suitable allowance for unexpected developments? The banker decides

---

*All names in *Aids* are disguised.

this question on the basis of your financial statement which sets forth the condition of your business and/or on the collateral pledge.

5. What is the outlook for business in general and for your business particularly?

Adequate Financial Data Is a "Must"
The banker wants to make loans to businesses which are solvent, profitable, and growing. The two basic financial statements he uses to determine those conditions are the balance sheet and profit-and-loss statement. The former is the major yardstick for solvency and the latter for profits. A continuous series of these two statements over a period of time is the principal device for measuring financial stability and growth potential.

In interviewing loan applicants and in studying their records, the banker is especially interested in the following facts and figures.

General information: Are the books and records up-to-date and in good condition? What is the condition of accounts payable? Of notes payable? What are the salaries of the owner-manager and other company officers? Are all taxes being paid currently? What is the order backlog? What is the number of employees? What is the insurance coverage?

Accounts receivable: Are there indications that some of the accounts receivable have already been pledged to another creditor? What is the accounts receivable turnover? Is the accounts receivable total weakened because many customers are far behind in their payments? Has a large enough reserve been set up to cover doubtful accounts? How much do the largest accounts owe and what percentage of your total accounts does this amount represent?

Inventories: Is merchandise in good shape or will it have to be marked down? How much raw material is on hand? How much work is in process? How much of the inventory is finished goods?

Is there any obsolete inventory? Has an excessive amount of inventory been consigned to customers? Is inventory turnover in line with the turnover for other businesses in the same industry? Or is money being tied up too long in inventory?

Fixed assets: What is the type, age, and condition of the equipment? What are the depreciation policies? What are the details of mortgages or conditional sales contracts? What are the future acquisition plans?

WHAT KIND OF MONEY?
When you set out to borrow money for your firm, it is important to know the kind of money you need from a bank or other lending institution. There are three kinds of money: short-term money, term money, and equity capital.

Keep in mind that the purpose for which the funds are to be used is an important factor in deciding the kind of money needed. But even so, deciding what kind of money to use is not always easy. It is sometimes complicated by the fact that you may be using some of various kinds of money at the same time and for identical purposes.

Keep in mind that a very important distinction between the types of money is the source of repayment. Generally, short-term loans are repaid from the liquidation of current assets which they have financed. Long-term loans are usually repaid from earnings.

Short-Term Bank Loans
You can use short-term bank loans for purposes such as financing accounts receivable for, say, 30 to 60 days. Or you can use them for purposes that take longer to pay off—such as for building a seasonal inventory over a period of five to six months. Usually, lenders expect short-term loans to be repaid after their purposes have been served: for example, accounts receivable loans, when the outstanding accounts have been paid by the borrower's customers, and inventory loans, when the inventory has been converted into salable merchandise.

Banks grant such money either on your general credit reputation with an unsecured loan or on a secured loan—against collateral.

The *unsecured loan* is the most frequently used form of bank credit for short-term purposes. You do not have to put up collateral because the bank relies on your credit reputation.

The *secured loan* involves a pledge of some or all of your assets. The bank requires security as a protection for its depositors against the risks that are involved even in business situations where the chances of success are good.

Term Borrowing
Term borrowing provides money you plan to pay back over a fairly long time. Some people break it down into two forms: (1) intermediate—loans longer than one year but less than five years, and (2) long-term—loans for more than five years.

However, for your purpose of matching the kind of money to the needs of your company, think of term borrowing as a kind of money which you probably will pay back in periodic installments from earnings.

Equity Capital
Some people confuse term borrowing and equity (or investment) capital. Yet there is a big difference. You don't have to repay equity money. It is money you get by selling a part interest in your business.

You take people into your company who are willing to risk their money in it. They are interested in potential income rather than in an immediate return on their investment.

HOW MUCH MONEY?
The amount of money you need to borrow depends on the purpose for which you need funds. Figuring the amount of money required for business construction, conversion, or expansion—term loans or equity capital—is relatively easy. Equipment manufacturers, architects, and builders will readily supply you with cost estimates. On the other hand, the amount of working capital you need depends upon the type of business you're in. While rule-of-thumb ratios may be helpful as a starting point, a detailed projection of sources and uses of funds over some future period of time—usually for 12 months—is a better approach. In this way, the characteristics of the particular situation can be taken into account. Such a projection is developed through the combination of a predicted budget and a cash forecast.

The budget is based on recent operating experience plus your best judgment of performance during the coming period. The cash forecast is your estimates of cash receipts and disbursements during the budget period. Thus, the budget and the cash forecast together represent your plan for meeting your working capital requirements.

To plan your working capital requirements, it is important to know the "cash flow" which your business will generate. This involves simply a consideration of all elements of cash receipts and disbursements at the time they occur. These elements are listed in the profit-and-loss statement which has been adapted to show cash flow in Table 1. They should be projected for each month. Note that it shows "Bank Loans To Be Obtained" as well as "Bank Loans To Be Repaid."

Table 1. P&L Statement Adapted to Show Cash Flow

The profit and loss statement elements listed below have been adapted to show cash flow. Note that it shows "Bank Loans To Be Obtained" as well as "Bank Loans To Be Repaid." The P and L statement should be projected for each month of the year.

Monthly operations

Net sales	$_____
Less: Material used	_____
Direct labor	_____
Other manufacturing expense	_____
Cost of goods sold	$_____
Gross profit	$_____
Less: Sales expense	_____
General and administrative expense	_____
Operating profit	$_____

Cash flow

Cash balance (beginning)	$_____
Receipts from receivables	
Total available cash	$_____
Less disbursements	
Trade payables	_____
Direct labor	_____
Other mfging expense	_____
Sales expense	_____
General and administrative expense	_____
Fixed asset additions	_____
Bank loans to be repaid	_____
Total disbursements	$_____
Indicated cash shortage	$_____
Bank loans to be obtained	$_____
Cash balance (ending)	$_____
Materials purchased	$_____
Month-end position	
Accounts receivable	$_____
Inventory	$_____
Accounts payable	$_____
Bank loans payable	$_____

WHAT KIND OF COLLATERAL?

Sometimes, your signature is the only security the bank needs when making a loan. At other times, the bank requires additional assurance that the money will be repaid. The kind and amount of security depends on the bank and on the borrower's situation.

If the loan required cannot be justified by the borrower's financial statements alone, a pledge of security may bridge the gap. The types of security are: endorsers, co-makers, and guarantors; assignment of leases; trust receipts and floor planning; chattel mortgages; real estate; accounts receivables; savings accounts; life insurance policies; and stocks and bonds. In a substantial number of states where the Uniform Commercial Code has been enacted, paperwork for recording loan transactions will be greatly simplified.

Endorsers, Co-makers, and Guarantors

Borrowers often get other people to sign a note in order to bolster their own credit. These *endorsers* are contingently liable for the note they sign. If the borrower fails to pay up, the bank expects the endorser to make the note good. Sometimes, the endorser may be asked to pledge assets or securities that he owns.

A *co-maker* is one who creates an obligation jointly with the borrower. In such cases, the bank can collect directly from either the maker or the co-maker.

A *guarantor* is one who guarantees the payment of a note by signing a guaranty commitment. Both private and government lenders often require guarantees from officers of corporations in order to assure continuity of effective management. Sometimes, a manufacturer will act as guarantor for one of his customers.

Assignment of Leases

The assigned lease as security is similar to the guarantee. It is used, for example, in some franchise situations.

The bank lends the money on a building and takes a mortgage. Then the lease, which the dealer and the parent franchise company work out, is assigned so that the bank automatically receives the rent payments. In this manner, the bank is guaranteed repayment of the loan.

Warehouse Receipts

Banks also take commodities as security by lending money on a warehouse receipt. Such a receipt is usually delivered directly to the bank and shows that the merchandise used as security either has been placed in a public warehouse or has been left on your premises under the control of one of your employees who is bonded (as in field warehousing). Such loans are generally made on staple or standard merchandise which can be readily marketed. The typical warehouse receipt loan is for a percentage of the estimated value of the goods used as security.

Trust Receipts and Floor Planning

Merchandise, such as automobiles, appliances, and boats, has to be displayed to be sold. The only way many small marketers can afford such displays is by borrowing money. Such loans are often secured by a note and a trust receipt.

This trust receipt is the legal paper for floor planning. It is used for serial-numbered merchandise. When you sign one, you (1) acknowledge receipt of the merchandise, (2) agree to keep the merchandise in trust for the bank, and (3) promise to pay the bank as you sell the goods.

Chattel Mortgages

If you buy equipment such as a cash register or a delivery truck, you may want to get a chattel mortgage loan. You give the bank a lien on the equipment you are buying.

The bank also evaluates the present and future market value of the equipment being used to secure the loan. How rapidly will it depreciate? Does the borrower have the necessary fire, theft, property damage, and public liability insurance on the equipment? The banker has to be sure that the borrower protects the equipment.

Real Estate

Real estate is another form of collateral for long-term loans. When taking a real estate mortgage, the bank finds out: (1) the location of the real estate, (2) its physical condition, (3) its foreclosure value, and (4) the amount of insurance carried on the property.

Accounts Receivable

Many banks lend money on accounts receivable. In effect, you are counting on your customers to pay your note.

The bank may take accounts receivable on a notification or a *nonnotification* plan. Under the *notification* plan, the purchaser of the goods is informed by the bank that his account has been assigned to it and he is asked to pay the bank. Under the *nonnotification* plan, the borrower's customers continue to pay him the sums due on their accounts and he pays the bank.

Savings Accounts

Sometimes, you might get a loan by assigning to the bank a savings account. In such cases, the bank gets an assignment from you and keeps your passbook. If you assign an account in another bank as collateral, the lending bank asks the other bank to mark its records to show that the account is held as collateral.

Life Insurance

Another kind of collateral is life insurance. Banks will lend up to the cash value of a life insurance policy. You have to assign the policy to the bank.

If the policy is on the life of an executive of a small corporation, corporate resolutions must be made authorizing the assignment. Most insurance companies allow you to sign the policy back to the original beneficiary when the assignment to the bank ends.

Some people like to use life insurance as collateral rather than borrow directly from insurance companies. One reason is that a bank loan is often more convenient to obtain and usually may be obtained at a lower interest rate.

Stocks and Bonds

If you use stocks and bonds as collateral, they must be marketable. As a protection against market declines and possible expenses of liquidation, banks usually lend no more than 75 percent of the market value of high grade stock. On Federal Government or municipal bonds, they may be willing to lend 90 percent or more of their market value.

The bank may ask the borrower for additional security or payment whenever the market value of the stocks or bonds drops below the bank's required margin.

WHAT ARE THE LENDER'S RULES?

Lending institutions are not just interested in loan repayments. They are also interested in borrowers with healthy profit-making businesses. Therefore, whether or not collateral is required for a loan, they set loan limitations and restrictions to protect themselves against unnecessary risk and at the same time against poor management practices by their borrowers. Often some owner-managers consider loan limitations a burden.

Yet others feel that such limitations also offer an opportunity for improving their management techniques.

Especially in making long-term loans, the borrower as well as the lender should be thinking of: (1) the net earning power of the borrowing company, (2) the capability of its management, (3) the long-range prospects of the company, and (4) the long-range prospects of the industry of which the company is a part. Such factors often mean that limitations increase as the duration of the loan increases.

WHAT KINDS OF LIMITATIONS?

The kinds of limitations which an owner-manager finds set upon his company depend, to a great extent, on his company. If his company is a good risk, he should have only minimum limitations. A poor risk, of course, is different. Its limitations should be greater than those of a stronger company.

Look now for a few moments at the kinds of limitations and restrictions which the lender may set. Knowing what they are can help you see how they affect your operations.

The limitations which you will usually run into when you borrow money are:

1. Repayment terms.

2. Pledging or the use of security.

3. Periodic reporting.

A loan agreement, as you may already know, is a tailor-made document covering, or referring to, all the terms and conditions of the loan. With it, the lender does two things: (1) protects his position as a creditor (he wants to keep that position in as well a protected state as it was on the date the loan was made) and (2) assures himself of repayment according to the terms.

The lender reasons that the borrower's business should *generate enough funds* to repay the loan while taking care of other needs. He considers that cash inflow should be great enough to do this without hurting the working capital of the borrower.

Covenants—Negative and Positive

The actual restrictions in a loan agreement come under a section known as covenants. Negative covenants are things which the borrower may not do without prior approval from the lender. Some examples are: further additions to the borrower's total debt, nonpledge to others of the borrower's assets, and issuance of dividends in excess of the terms of the loan agreement.

On the other hand, positive covenants spell out things which the borrower must do. Some examples are: (1) maintenance of a minimum net working capital, (2) carrying of adequate insurance, (3) repaying the loan according to the terms of the agreement, and (4) supplying the lender with financial statements and reports.

Overall, however, loan agreements may be amended from time to time and exceptions made. Certain provisions may be waived from one year to the next with the consent of the lender.

You Can Negotiate

Next time you go to borrow money, thresh out the lending terms before you sign. It is good practice no matter how badly you may need the money. Ask to see the papers in advance of the loan closing. Legitimate lenders are glad to cooperate.

Chances are that the lender may "give" some on the terms. Keep in mind also that, while you're mulling over the terms, you may want to get the advice of your associates and outside advisors. In short, try to get terms which you know your company can live with. Remember, however, that once the terms have been agreed upon and the loan is made (or authorized as in the case of SBA), you are bound by them.

THE LOAN APPLICATION

Now you have read about the various aspects of the lending process and are ready to apply for a loan. Banks and other private lending institutions, as well as the Small Business Administration, require a loan application on which you list certain information about your business.

For purposes of explaining a loan application, this *Aid* uses the Small Business Administration's application for a small loan. (SBA Form 6B)—one for $25,000 or less. The SBA form is more detailed than most bank forms. The bank has the advantage of prior knowledge of the applicant and his activities. Since SBA does not have such knowledge, its form is more detailed. Moreover, the longer maturities of SBA loans ordinarily will necessitate more knowledge about the applicant.

Before you get to the point of filling out a loan application, you should have talked with an SBA representative, or perhaps your accountant or banker, to make sure that your business is eligible for an SBA loan. Because of public policy, SBA cannot make certain types of loans. Nor can it make loans under certain conditions. For example, if you can get a loan on reasonable terms from a bank, SBA cannot lend you money. The owner-manager is also not eligible for an SBA loan if he can get funds by selling assets which his company does not need in order to grow. (For other examples, see Table 2.)

When the SBA representative gives you a loan application, you will notice that most of its sections ("Application for Loan"—SBA Form 6B) are self-explanatory. However, some applicants have trouble with certain sections because they do not know where to go to get the necessary information. Section 3—"Collateral Offered" is an example. A company's books should show the net value of assets such as business real estate and business machinery and equipment. "Net" means what you paid for such assets less depreciation.

If an owner-manager's records do not contain detailed information on business collateral, such as real estate and machinery and equipment, he sometimes can get it from his Federal income tax returns. Reviewing the depreciation which he has taken for tax purposes on such collateral can be helpful in arriving at the value of these assets.

Table 2. Situations which Make a Business Ineligible for a SBA Loan

The Small Business Administration cannot lend money in the following situations:

• If the company can get money on reasonable terms:

1. From a financial institution.
2. By selling assets which it does not need in order to grow.
3. By the owner's using, without undue personal hardship, his personal credit or resources of his partners or principal stockholders.
4. By selling a portion of ownership in the company through a public offering or a private placing of its securities.
5. From other Government agencies which provide credit specifically for the applicant's type of business or for the purpose of the required financing.
6. From other known sources of credit.

• If the direct or indirect purpose or result of granting a loan would be to:

1. Pay off a creditor or creditors of the applicant who are inadequately secured and in a position to sustain a loss.
2. Provide funds for distribution or payment to the owner, partners, or shareholders.
3. Replenish working capital funds previously used to pay the owner, partners, or shareholders.

• If the applicant's purpose in applying for a loan is to effect a change in ownership of the business; however, under certain circumstances, loans may be authorized for this purpose, if the result would be to aid in the sound development of a small business or to keep it in operation.

• If the loan would provide or free funds for speculation in any kind of property, real or personal, tangible or intangible.

• If the applicant is a charitable organization, social agency, society, or other nonprofit enterprise; however, a loan may be considered for a cooperative if it carries on a business activity and the purpose of the activity is to obtain financial benefit for its members in the operation of their otherwise eligible small business concerns.

• If the purpose of the loan is to finance the construction, acquisition, conversion, or operation of recreational or amusement facilities, unless the facilities contribute to the health or general well-being of the public.

• If the applicant is a newspaper, magazine, radio broadcasting or television broadcasting company, or similar enterprise.

• If any of the gross income of the applicant (or of any of its principal owners) is derived from gambling activities.

• If the loan is to provide funds to an enterprise primarily engaged in the business of lending or investments or to provide funds to any otherwise eligible enterprise for the purpose of financing investments not related or essential to the enterprise.

• If the purpose of the loan is to finance the acquisition, construction, improvement, or operation of real property that is, or is to be, held primarily for sale or investment.

• If the effect of granting of the financial assistance will be to encourage monopoly or will be inconsistent with the accepted standards of the American system of free competitive enterprise.

• If the loan would be used to relocate a business for other than sound business purposes.

If you are a good manager, you should have your books balanced monthly. However, some businesses prepare balance sheets less regularly. In filling out Section 7—"Balance Sheet as of _____, 19, Fiscal Year Ends _____" of the SBA loan application, remember that you must show the condition of your business within 60 days of the date on your loan application. It is best to get expert advice when working up such vital information. Your accountant or banker will be able to help you.

Again, if your records do not show the details necessary for working up profit and loss statements, your Federal income tax returns (Schedule C of Form 1040, if your business is a sole proprietorship or a partnership) may be useful in getting together facts for Section 8 of the SBA loan application. This Section asks for "Condensed Comparative Statements of Sales, Profits or Loss, etc." You fill in the blocks appropriate to your form of business organization—corporation, partnership, or proprietorship—and attach detailed profit-and-loss statements.

Insurance
SBA also needs information about the kinds of insurance a company carries. The owner-manager gives these facts by listing various insurance policies. If you place all your insurance with one agent or broker, you can get this information from him.

Personal Finances
SBA also must know something about the personal financial condition of the applicant. Among the types of information are: personal cash position; source of income including salary and personal investments; stocks, bonds, real estate, and other property owned in the applicant's own name; personal debts including installment credit payments, life insurance premiums, and so forth.

EVALUATING THE APPLICATION
Once you have supplied the necessary information, the next step in the borrowing process is the evaluation of your application. Whether the processing officer is in a bank or in SBA, he considers the same kinds of things when determining whether to grant or refuse the loan. The SBA loan processor looks for:

1. The borrower's debt-paying record to suppliers, banks, home mortgage holders, and other creditors.
2. The ratio of the borrower's debt to his net worth.
3. The past earnings of the company.
4. The value and condition of the collateral which the borrower offers for security.

The SBA loan processor also looks for: (1) the borrower's management ability, (2) the borrower's character, and (3) the future prospects of the borrower's business.

FOR FURTHER INFORMATION
Readers who wish to explore further the subject of borrowing may be interested in the references indicated below. This list is necessarily brief and selective.

The following *Management Aids for Small Manufacturers* are available free from the Washington, D.C., and field offices of Small Business Administration:

1. Is your cash supply adequate?—MA174.

2. Financial audits: a tool for better management—MA176.

The following *Small Marketers Aids* are available free from the Washington, D.C., and field offices of Small Business Administration:

1. Controlling cash in small retail and service firms—SMA110.

2. Accounting services for small service firms—SMA126.

3. Analyze your records to reduce costs—SMA130.

The following *Small Business Management Series* booklets published by SBA can be bought from the Superintendent of Documents, Washington, D.C. 20402.

1. *A Handbook of Small Business Finance*, SBMS No. 15.

2. *Guides for Profit Planning*. SBMS No. 25.

Suggestions for Further Reading

Baron, T. Smaller company's struggle for investment dollars. *Public Relations Journal* 32: 30-31 + (April 1976).

Chapman, C. H. Small business financial model. *Management Accounting* 57: 20-22 + (July 1975).

Leonard, G. L. Financing a small business. *CA Magazine* 109: 52-54 (Sept. 1976).

Munder, B. How smaller companies are tackling their financial problems. *Management Review* 64: 36-38 (June 1975).

Osborn, R. C. Supply of equity capital by the SBICs. *Quarterly Review of Economics and Business* 13: 68-86 (Spring, 1973).

Pace, E. A., and F. Collins. Bankers-accountants-financial statements: their relationship to small-business loan decisions. *Journal of Small Business Management* 14: 16-22 (Oct. 1976).

4
Entrepreneurial
Planning

Introduction

Much has been written in recent years about the purpose and necessity of planning in business. Most studies and discussions center on the planning process, either as it should in theory be carried on or as it is in fact carried on in organizations such as the *Fortune* 500 or some other aggregation of corporate giants.

Planning isn't only for the large firm, however. Often, because of the constant demand for limited resources, planning in the small business can spell the difference between failure and success.

Frequently, entrepreneurs enter business with an ill-defined concept of a product or service to offer an equally ill-defined market segment. Planning, both short and long range, is designed to refine these ill-defined directions into a consistent, feasible, and acceptable set of actions. These actions must be based on a well-defined set of objectives, however.

As can be seen in Fig. 1, objectives and actions can't be formed in a vacuum. A thorough analysis of the total environment, both internal and external, must be made to ensure the feasibility of the plan. As is also demonstrated by the exhibit, the values of key people, as well as external factors in the environment, are important inputs into the determination of objectives for the firm. This assumes that the entrepreneur has already considered what his or her values are, as well as what are the values of key people who must be called on to help with implementing the plan.

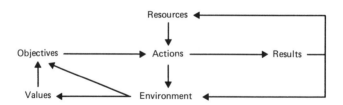

Fig. 1 Strategy Formation (From Frank T. Paine and William Naumes, *Strategy and Policy Formation: An Integrative Approach* (Philadelphia: W.B. Saunders Company, 1974), p. 13.)

Similarly, the figure demonstrates that a well-rounded action plan is based on a thorough understanding of the resources available to the firm as well as external opportunities and constraints. Those new enterprises that succeed are typically ones that have explored the marketplace and developed a product or service that matches an unfilled need. Moreover, they have found a market where they are not at a disadvantage due to their small size. Frequently, they try to use the size factor as an added strength against larger, potential competitors. The small firm often has greater flexibility to tailor its product or service to the direct needs of a particular market segment. The management in the Bryn Mawr National Bank case viewed their size as a potential asset in their market. They tried to generate a friendly, neighborhood bank image in contrast to the formality of their large competitors.

The Role of Objectives

Planning is a future results-oriented process. If people within the firm do not understand what results are expected, then they cannot be faulted for not using the resources of the firm in the most advantageous manner. The basic purpose of objectives is to show everyone associated with the firm what the primary direction of the firm is. This helps to direct the efforts of key people within the firm toward attaining results consistent with those objectives.

Along with this purpose, objectives are also designed to be used as a tool for evaluating the performance of people within the firm. If objectives are well defined *and* communicated to people inside the firm, everybody understands what targets to aim for. Results, both long and short run, can then be compared to objectives to see who is efficient and who is not effective within the firm. Those people who have helped in either beating or failing to meet objectives can be singled out for further explanations regarding their performance. Discussions of this sort provide valuable inputs into the objective-setting and planning process.

Since the situations usually facing an entrepreneur involve changes in current direction or new venture initiation, properly defined objectives become more critical. They provide the primary method of defining the future direction of the enterprise for other interested parties. Well-defined objectives also provide constraints for future actions. The defined objectives, therefore, provide a coordinating function as well as the basis for evaluation.

The investors in the Sea Life Park (B) case are questioning the lack of specific objectives. They are unsure of Tap Pryor's priorities concerning the general objectives that are presented.

Discussion of results can be used to further refine objectives that have been found to be unrealistic for whatever reason. Objectives should be both challenging and realistic if they are to be effective. If they are set too high, frustration usually results. If they are set too low, incentive for achievement is usually lacking. In either case, the effectiveness of objectives is lost.

Walking the rather narrow boundaries set up by the previous constraints would seem to be difficult. On the one hand, objectives are designed to be an incentive for good work. On the other, they are supposed to spotlight people or areas which could be trouble spots for the firm. One situation calls for broadly worded objectives allowing for freedom of action. The other calls for tightly defined goals against which specific results can be tested and compared.

A method suggested for overcoming these apparent contradictions is to set forth levels of objectives with different priorities. An overall objective should be set forth rating the primary direction of the firm. This primary objective should be an easily recognized, quantifiable goal such as earnings growth. Secondary objectives can then be used to place constraints on the methods of reaching that primary objective. For the small firm, examples of secondary objectives would include control of the organization, quality of service or product, sales growth, market segment, etc.

The use of this two-tier system of objectives presents the aggressive manager with an understanding of the overall direction of the firm. Subordinates are also given guidance as to the latitude they have in achieving that overall objective. Venture capitalists are provided with greater inputs to evaluate investment potential and fit.

The Action Plan

Once objectives are determined and communicated to the rest of the organization, an action plan must be developed to achieve those objectives. The action plan is designed to show people within the firm specifically how and what is expected of them in the future.

The action plan should note what resources are required, at what stages, to ensure the success of the overall plan. It should define the market the firm has targeted for its product or service. This is particularly true for the small business. It can ill afford to test-market products or services extensively in the manner of large corporations. Resources cannot be wasted on trial-and-error efforts to find market and product fits. Also, since the ability to react rapidly is considered a strength of small firms, wasting time eliminates a critical advantage over larger firms.

The action plan should also contain an outline of the role of key people in the firm in using these resources to attack that market. The responsibility and authority of key personnel must be specified in detail if the action plan is to be effective. This further states that entrepreneurs must have determined what degree of delegation they are willing to accept to achieve their objectives. As we shall see later, this can often be a traumatic experience for those entrepreneurial managers who have decided to start their own business because they want to be their own boss. This entrepreneurial spirit has to be tempered, at least to some degree, to ensure the success of the plan.

Other key factors to be included in the action plan are the location and timing of all these events. People in the organization should be able to tell where and when they are supposed to bear the responsibility for carrying out their role in the firm.

What we see, therefore, is that the action plan is designed to answer the following questions:

1. What is to be done?
2. Who will do it?
3. When will they do it?
4. Where will they do it?
5. What resources are necessary for the task?

Functional Planning

The previously stated questions are clearly action oriented. They usually depend on other actions, people, and resources. Plans, however, are frequently stated in terms of functional issues. We frequently hear managers speak of the marketing plan or the financial plan. This can lead to a narrow view of the planning process.

Functional plans are necessary, however. The problem that entrepreneurs face is that they often have to fulfill both the specialist and the integrative roles within the enterprise. Developing functional plans fleshes out the overall direction of the enterprise. It helps to assure that the appropriate amount of detail is developed for the plan. Essentially, this exercise forces the entrepreneur to see the trees within the forest.

The process of integrating the various functional plans further helps to note what reactions might occur when an action is taken in any given area. In the Passport Dinner Club case, Mr. Keene's decision to sign up a limited number of restaurants for his service limited his potential consumer audience. This then helped to describe what type of advertising campaign would be most effective in reaching this audience. This further affected the potential return on investment of the enterprise. The initial move had been based on a cursory analysis, almost a "gut-feel" decision process, partly based on timing considerations.

Essentially, a decision was made without due consideration for the interactive effects. A lack of in-depth planning in the various functional areas led to a hasty decision being made which may drastically alter the long-term direction of the enterprise. Detailing how actions are to be implemented in finance, accounting, production, marketing, or management areas would help to show what requirements are necessary from each of the other areas. Typically, this leads to an interactive process where plans are revised until all aspects of the overall strategy are internally consistent.

Importance of Timing

A key factor in the total plan is the timing associated with both objectives and actions. Crucial to a clear statement of objectives is an understanding of the time element involved in achieving those objectives. Realistic benchmarks have to be provided so that everyone in the firm knows when he or she is expected to reach a particular goal.

Likewise, a realistic appraisal of the time necessary to implement an action is necessary if the plan is to be successful. All too often, potentially successful ideas are crushed because an entrepreneur rushed into a commitment of scarce resources without stopping to see how long it would take to implement various parts of the plan. What typically happens, as we saw in Chapter 3, is that the firm unnecessarily ties up people and money in actions that could have waited until later.

The two owners in the Passport Dinner Club case provide a classic example of timing problems during implementation of their strategy. They underestimated the time and effort necessary to start the operation. This forced them to put back the original introduction of their service to a point where they might well miss what they consider to be their peak selling season. They have also incurred costs that they had not expected. They are starting to run out of funds at the end of the case. This means that they will have to either increase the investment in the enterprise, alter the action plan, change their objectives, or develop some combination of these factors.

A firm also frequently shows competition its plans prematurely by pushing ahead on all fronts. A more ordered set of actions can be used to hide strengths and direction of the firm until it is best able to take advantage of opportunities.

Proper use of timing isn't only a defensive move, however. It can, and should, be used offensively. The entrepreneur should design his plan to be timed to beat competition to the market. The first competitor into a market has the problem of opening that market. However, he or she also frequently gains the advantage of becoming associated with that market, service, or product in the minds of the consumer.

The key to initial timing is the ability to spot an unfilled need, find products or services to fill that need, and present it to the consumer faster and more effectively than anyone else. Successful entrepreneurs, therefore, have to combine the aggressiveness for which they are noted with the precision that is more commonly associated with the professional manager. The proper use of management-science techniques such as PERT and Critical Path Method should be encouraged to sharpen the decision-making ability of the entrepreneur.

Use of these tools requires the kinds of analysis discussed early in this chapter. Entrepreneurial managers must know what kinds of resources will be at their disposal to plan for effective implementation of plans. Entrepreneurs must also understand what potential threats may appear in the external environment to alter the ability to take advantage of existing opportunities. Once again, we see that knowledge, as far as practical, of the total environment is necessary to decide the most effective timing of actions.

Evaluation of Alternatives

We usually think of evaluation as considering whether a particular course of action is acceptable according to some set of criteria. This procedure may be effective when grading papers. The planning process, however, usually involves constantly refining plans to match the environment, both internal and external.

A typical scenario would follow this path: A set of objectives is formulated consistent with the values of the entrepreneur. A check with other key individuals might come up with conflicts, either major or minor. If necessary, the stated objectives are changed to account for these conflicts.

The revised set of objectives is then evaluated for consistency with the external environment. If no problems are perceived outside the firm, the objectives can be accepted. If external constraints are found, such as moral, ethical, and political objections, then the objectives may have to be further refined to fit with the external environment.

Once the objectives are made to fit with the total environment, the action plan must be formed in such a way that it is feasible and acceptable. At this stage, the actions designed to achieve the objectives are evaluated to determine if resources are potentially available to implement these actions. If it can be shown that resources are not available to implement a part of the plan, that portion would be changed to accommodate the realities of the internal environment. This frequently affects the small firm to a greater degree than the large firm. The small firm can not afford to hire management and technical expertise to perform specific functions. The small firm also finds it more difficult to find funds for expansion (or survival) than the large firm. This leads to a further refinement of the action plan pursued by the entrepreneur.

Tap Pryor, in the Sea Life Park case, went through just this sort of process. His initial objective was to start a marine research institute. He quickly found that, for various reasons, this was infeasible. He then altered his action plan to include founding a marine tourist exhibit, operated by an outside agency, to fund the institute. When he could not find an outside agency to perform this function, he changed his objectives to include the exhibit as part of his own overall strategy. He ended up having to start and operate both enterprises to meet his primary objective of marine research.

Entrepreneurial managers, and their firms, do not operate in a vacuum, however. Their plans have to be both consistent with and feasible within the constraints placed by the external environment. It makes little sense for a small firm to enter a market segment dominated by big competitors. Similarly, the firm that comes up with a product, then searches for a need to match that product, finds it more difficult to sell that product than if the need were determined first. All too often, entrepreneurs become so convinced of the importance of their product or service that they fail to place the potential-demand factor in its proper perspective.

The economists tell us that unless demand and supply are in equilibrium, somebody will lose. Where improper planning takes place, the entrepreneur is usually the loser. If the entrepreneur overestimates demand, excessive resources are committed to the project, leading to an actual loss of funds. As noted earlier, the small business can afford such losses less than larger firms. If the entrepreneur underestimates demand—often considered a fortuitous occurrence—an opportunity is lost: the firm could have gained added revenues, and hopefully profits, if it had matched production with demand.

All of these factors affect the feasibility of the action plan, often leading to compromise and refinement of the plan. What the entrepreneur is finally presented with is not an evaluation of one particualr decision but, more typically, several alternatives from which to select the most acceptable portions, taking into consideration all aspects of the environment affecting the plan.

What we can see is that there are three general criteria for evaluating alternative plans. First, the plan should be internally consistent. Any conflicts within the objectives should be defined. Priorities should be spelled out. Also actions should be designed to achieve results consistent with objectives.

Second, the plan should be feasible. The objectives, and particularly the action plan, should have a reasonable chance of success. The actions outlined in the plan should match both the resources available within the firm and the constraints and opportunities facing the firm from the external environment.

Finally, the plan has to be acceptable to the key people within the firm. The plan has to deal with factors such as the degree of acceptable risk, as well as the value systems appropriate to the key decision makers. The potential outcomes must be shown to match with the desires of the entrepreneur and his or her subordinates.

This demonstrates that planning is not simply an intellectual process. The entrepreneur must consider the social, political, and ethical climate when preparing an effective plan. If the plan can't be sold to the people necessary to implement it, however, the plan is virtually worthless. Consideration must be given to the practical aspects of implementing plans.

Summary

The planning process is designed to provide direction and detail to the enterprise. Small or new businesses need this as much as or more than large businesses. The small business is faced with limited internal resources. It must utilize these resources as effectively as possible. It frequently can't afford the slack often found in large organizations.

Strategic plans demonstrate the direction being followed by the entire organization. They include both objectives and actions designed to achieve that direction. The objectives provide a method for coordination, control, and evaluation as well as overall direction.

The action phase of the plan provides the detail for implementing the strategy. Through the various functional areas included in the action plan, all people directly related to the enterprise are made to understand the requirements necessary to achieve the stated objectives. Interaction between various areas, resources, and managers is also brought forth by the action plan.

The various parts of the strategy should be feasible as well as consistent. Objectives should have a reasonable chance of being reached. Actions should make sense relative to the resources available to the enterprise, as well as to the constraints and opportunities posed by the external environment.

The planning process is not just a theoretical process, however. Plans have to be implemented at some point. This requires acceptance by various constituents, including managers and customers. The overall strategy should be acceptable to these various constituent groups.

This chapter is designed to provide the framework for developing plans for small and new enterprises. The text points out the general concepts to be considered in planning for the enterprise. The following readings develop, in greater detail, the costs and benefits of the factors discussed in general terms above. Pitfalls frequently encountered by entrepreneurs while using (or failing to use) planning techniques are spotlighted. Some methods of avoiding these pitfalls are also discussed. Combining these more specific analyses and recommendations with the general-planning format presented above should aid the manager to plan for growth and success instead of just hoping for it.

Readings

The readings presented in this chapter further explore the problems planning poses for small businesses. The comments presented in the text are designed to provide a general overview of planning for the new or small venture. George Steiner's article, "Approaches to Long Range Planning for Small Business," further describes the various parts of the plan for effective operations. He demonstrates how the planning process expands in relation to the size of the organization. He then demonstrates a planning outline as carried out by a small business.

Steven Wheelright provides an in-depth view of planning as it was carried out in three small businesses. From this descriptive research, Wheelright prescribes a general method for selecting a planning process appropriate to a particular small business.

The final article, "Breaking the Barriers to Small Business Planning," was prepared by Roger Golde for the SBA. In this article, Golde discusses typical problems encountered by entrepreneurs in developing balanced organizational plans. Some of these problems are based in the psyche of the entrepreneur. Others are due to lack of resources available to small businesses. Golde then prescribes methods to overcome these problems.

The text provides a general framework for planning in the small business. The readings then provide depth to this framework. They also describe methods frequently used to overcome problems of planning in small businesses, where one or only a few people are responsible for planning. We can see that all these sources note that planning provides direction and control for the entrepreneurial organization.

Approaches to Long-Range Planning for Small Business

George A. Steiner

The author presents some new thoughts on long-range planning designed specifically to assist the small businessman.

There is little doubt that the great majority of small businesses do little, if any, long-range planning. While the virtues of long-range planning have been rather well "sold" to most of the large corporations, the job still remains to be done among the small business community.

Expansion of long-range planning among smaller enterprises can best proceed upon two platforms.

1. The small businessman must be convinced that long-range planning is worthwhile, and he must develop a genuine desire for it.

2. He must adopt methods and principles suitable to his situation.

The essence of long-range planning is thinking systematically about the future and making current decisions on that basis. Implicit in this concept is the idea of examining future consequences of present decisions, as well as choosing bases for making current decisions from among future alternative courses of action. Long-range planning, therefore, is not without current impact.[1]

Every businessman thinks ahead. But what is new in long-range planning today is looking ahead in a methodical, organized, and conscious fashion. Managers have found that the formalization of the long-range planning process produces better results.

This new concept of long-range planning does not imply an exhaustive inquiry into the future. The process actually used in a company should merely be adapted to the particular circumstances existing in the company.

The typical small businessman is likely to give one or more of the following responses when asked why he does so little (or no) long-range planning:

- That's for big companies, not me.
- Why should I? I'm doing O.K.
- You can't forecast the future, so how can you do long-range planning?
- I am in a cash squeeze, and that's all I can think about now.
- It's too complicated.
- My business is simple, and I know what the problems are.

© 1967 by the Regents of the University of California. Reprinted from *California Management Review,* volume X, number 1, pp. 3 to 16, by permission of the Regents.

- I can do all the planning I need in my head. Anyway, I don't want to discuss my plans with anyone. Why give someone a chance to find out and lose my competitive advantage?

The average small businessman is faced with many barriers to long-range planning. He is pressed for time. He has most of the problems of an executive in a medium-size company, but must solve them without helpers. He is constantly fighting "brush fires," and, as anyone who has followed business planning knows, these pressures drive out long-range planning. He is a man of action and has a habit of doing things by himself. Typically, the small businessman keeps his ideas, plans, and intentions secret. He is reluctant to discuss plans which may not materialize because he does not want to be thought foolish or inept.[2]

Finally, although the literature on long-range planning is increasing, most of it is not very helpful to the small businessman. He needs detailed guides to tell him how to go about long-range planning which are not easy to find.

Yet none of these obstacles can justify a businessman's avoiding systematic long-range planning.

The matter of forecasting the future seems to bother many businessmen. Of course, no one can foresee the future. Forecasting, however, is making a judgment about the future on the basis of present knowledge. The more accurate the forecast, the better a plan will be, but planning can be effective even if a forecast is not too accurate at first. Whether they realize it or not, all businessmen forecast. The only difference is how well they do it. If a manager, for example, decides not to purchase a new machine, he is in effect forecasting that his profits will not be increased in the future by the purchase.

The meanings of forecasting and planning are confused in the minds of some businessmen. Forecasting is not planning, but only a part of it. Planning is determining what a manager wants in the future and developing methods to achieve it. Forecasting may tell which type of environment can be expected; planning will determine how to take advantage of it or, if it is inhospitable, how to prevent it from taking advantage of the firm.

Answers to some of the other reasons given for failure to plan ahead are obvious. If long-range planning is important, a businessman simply must and can find the time to do it. Actually, long-range planning is simpler than many businessmen imagine. The businessman who rejects planning for the future because he is doing so well today could not be more misguided. Products as well as production methods are growing obsolete faster, and customers are becoming more fickle. Prosperity today is no assurance of tomorrow's profits.

Long-range planning is essential for a small as well as a large business for no other reason than that it permits them to take better advantage of the opportunities which lie in the future and to forestall the threats which it contains. This is the essence of entrepreneurship. Long-range planning should stimulate this function. Only a few small businesses have the financial reserves to cover the unexpected loss that occurs when they must shift from dependence on a single obsolete product or a few major customers. Yet this sort of crisis may be avoided by recognizing that it can happen and taking early action to avoid it. And there are other advantages to long-range planning for a small businessman. For example, he will find banks and other sources of cash much more willing to finance his needs if he has a well-designed long-range plan. He may be able to "go public" much more easily and without fear of losing his business. And he can be sure of perpetuating his business beyond his retirement.

Before discussing a variety of possible approaches to long-range planning, it is useful to set forth a simple conceptual frame of reference for types of business plans and steps in their development. Fig 1 is a simplified sketch of different types of plans needed in a business. It also shows the general flow of action in the process of planning.

Two important facts should be mentioned before discussing Fig. 1:

- A very large number of companies doing long-range planning have systems that fit this model.
- The structure is exceedingly flexible and can be adapted to just about any size of business, style of management, type of business, or stage in the development of organized planning.

So long as a manager is really interested in long-range planning, this conceptual model can be used with any magnitude of resources, and it can be applied equally well to a very small and a very large enterprise.

To the left of the chart are the fundamental premises that go into any planning effort. First are the basic purposes of the firm, usually expressed in broad terms. Many companies have only recently written out their basic purposes, but it is not necessary to put them on paper so long as businessmen think about them, for they are the starting point in long-range planning. Of major significance, too, are the values, ideas, and philosophies which a businessman holds. These, of course, permeate all he does and are major determinants of all the decisions he makes. For example, a businessman who is working to enlarge a small business will go about his long-range planning in a far different manner from one who wishes to work alone to invent new products in his own small laboratory.

Planning also must be based on an assessment of the future environment, both within and outside the firm. The possible number of elements to be examined is very great, and the art of long-range planning involves an ability to choose those which are of major importance to the firm.

Upon these bases the over-all objectives, strategies, and policies of the firm can be set forth. They can be few in number or many. They can concern any element of the business. The more concrete they are, however, the better the plans are likely to be. The time dimensions of objectives, strategies, and policies extend from the immediate future to the infinite. For example, a firm may set as its objective to be the top quality producer of microelectronic products in the industry. This has no time limit. On the other hand, the objective to hire a chief engineer by next month has a short time dimension.

Medium-range plans cover a fixed time dimension set by a manager. A large number of smaller companies consider two years to be a suitable period for meidum-range plans. Four- and five-year plans are more frequent among larger companies. In this kind of plan one finds more expectations placed on such parts of the business as sales, profits, finance, production, research, and facilities.

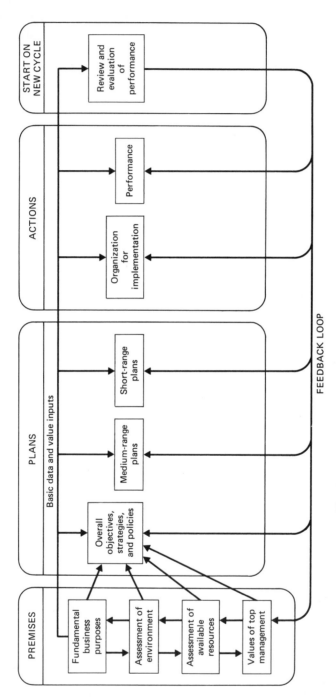

Fig. 1   The Structure and Process of Planning for a Business.

The short-range plans usually apply to quarterly or monthly cash budgets, raw material purchase schedules, production schedules, and shipment schedules.

To the right of the diagram are actions needed to complete the process, assuring that arrangements are made to operate on the basis of plans and then reviewing and assessing performance during and after operations.

Operational versus analytical steps in planning. Analytical steps have been set up as the preferred procedures in all problem solving. They take the following basic form for business planning:

- Establish objectives.
- Prepare basic premises.
- Determine alternative courses of action to achieve objectives.
- Examine different alternative courses of action.
- Choose alternatives to be followed.
- Put the plan into action.
- Review plans periodically.

These steps are implicit in Fig. 1 and are fundamental in all effective planning. But a businessman may not follow this sequence at all. The sequence of operational steps in planning may be much different from the analytical steps. For example, it is rare to find a planning program proceeding from one step to the next without retracing or overlapping. A tentative goal found too high or too low may be changed after examining various alternative courses of action to achieve it.

In the following sections a number of operational steps for planning are presented. While they differ markedly, they will be more easily performed if both the conceptual model of planning structures and the analytical steps are kept in mind. But precisely what sequence is followed and what depth of analysis is employed will depend on many considerations: type and size of business, nature of top management, available help, nature of problems facing the business, and whether long-range planning is just beginning or has been in operation for some time.

The following suggestions begin with simple and conclude with complex methods—which need not be mutually exclusive. All of them can be incorporated into advanced, sophisticated systems, and all have actually been used with success by small businessmen.

Asking questions. Columella is as correct today as he was centuries ago when he said, "The important part of every business is to know what ought to be done." But this is not as easy as it sounds. Consider the case of the small businessman whose sales grew rapidly but whose receivables did not turn over quickly enough to finance his current needs. He had to borrow, but, because he was not well established he had to pay high interest rates for his loan, and this wiped out his profit. This man was not asking the right questions.

A survey of over one hundred small manufacturers concluded that "the hardest part of planning seems to be getting started."[3] A simple way to get started in long-range planning is by asking some basic questions. A good place to begin is with objectives. It is most naive to say, "Our objective is to make a profit—period." Of course it is, but maximizing profit involves answering questions such as:

- What business am I in?
- What is my place in the industry?
- What customers am I serving? Where is my market?
- What is my company image to my major customers?
- What business do I want to be in five years from now?
- What are my specific goals for profit improvement?
- Need I have plans for product improvement? If so, what?
- What is my greatest strength? Am I using it well?
- What is my greatest problem? How am I to solve it?
- What share of the market do I want? Next month? Next year?
- Are my personnel policies acceptable to employees?
- How can I finance growth?

For those small businessmen who are preparing such lists and are answering the questions, this is one excellent way to get started down the path of systematic and useful long-range planning.

It is readily apparent how a decision about any one of these questions can have an important impact on most of the others. What is most useful is to get at the major issues, think about them continuously, and set up specific plans of action.

Key to success. Every business, both large and small, will succeed or fail depending on a limited and variable number of strategic factors. The best way to get started in long-range planning is to try to discover those few strategic factors which will be responsible for future success. Since finance is such a critical factor to most small businessmen, this area is traditionally the prime subject of analysis for them as well as for scholars who are interested in small business problems.

But other factors may be just as important strategically. Imagination may be the strategic factor responsible for the success of a toy company or an advertising firm. Quality may be the strategic factor responsible for the success of a company making components for a complicated aerospace product. Cost control and cost reduction may be the strategic factors responsible for success of a company producing standard metal stampings for an automobile manufacturer.

Strategic factors like these should come to light in a comprehensive long-range planning program. But if no such program exists, a small businessman may start his long-range planning simply by drawing up a list of possible strategic factors which may be responsible for his future success. Once the pertinent ones are identified, they should, of course, be the subject of deep thought and appropriate action.

Check-off lists. Some firms use so-called check-off lists to guide their planning. These lists cover important elements of planning such as sales and marketing, research and development, products, land and property, personnel, organization, finance, and competition. The list of questions in Table 1 concerning the addition of new products

Table 1. A New Product Check-off List

Relationship to present operations

- Does the product fall within the manufacturing and processing know-how of the company?
- Will the product benefit by the present research and engineering activities of the company?
- Does the profit fit into the lines now handled by our sales organization? Will it permit more efficient utilization of our present sales organization?

Character of the product

- Will the product capitalize on the engineering strength of the company?
- Is there a reasonable volume potential?
- Can the product maintain a high degree of distinctiveness in comparison with competing products?
- Will the product contribute to the company's reputation?

Commercial considerations

- Is the product necessary or desirable in maintaining completeness of line?
- Does the inclusion of this product in the line have any effect on the other lines?
- Will it strengthen our position with distributors?
- Will the company name be of aid in marketing the product?

illustrates this approach. For many of the questions absolute measurement is difficult, if not impossible; simple ratings, therefore, are usually given for each question, such as: "excellent," "good," "average," "poor," "unsatisfactory."

Simplified master planning. Questions like those in Table 1 are helpful, but more systematization is desirable. Roger A. Golde, a small business consultant, has devised a form to help the small businessman organize his planning (Tables 2 and 3).[4]

Table 2. Master Planning Form

Item	Change		Comment
	Next year	Year after next	
Research & Development			
Products			
Product Mix			
Service			
Supplies			
Suppliers			
Inventory			
Subcontracts			
Storage & Handling			
Quality Control			

Table 2. cont'd.

Item	Change		Comment
	Next year	Year after next	
Space			
Leasehold Improvements			
Equipment			
Employees			
Fringe Benefits			
Customers			
Sales Outlets			
Terms of Sale			
Pricing			
Transportation			
Advertising			
Promotion			
Packaging			
Market Research			
Financing			
Insurance			
Investments			
Management Reports			
Management Procedures			
Management Organization			
Governmental Environment			
Economic Environment			
Industrial Environment			
Competition			
Community Environment			

Instructions: All changes are estimated in relation to the preceding year.

If a quantitative change is anticipated—i.e., change in size or amount—use the following symbols: L = large, M = medium, and S = small. Quantitative changes are assumed to be increases unless preceded by a minus sign.

If a qualitative change is anticipated, use the following symbols: l = large, m = medium, s = small.

Note that the notions of small, medium, and large changes are obviously subjective and will vary with the person using the form.

In general, a small change denotes some sort of minimum level of change which is thought important enough to make note of. Most of the expected changes will probably fall in the medium category, indicating significant change of some magnitude. The large category will usually be reserved for unusual changes of striking impact.

The notion of qualitative changes may need some clarification. This category of change would cover such items as a change in customer mix (which might or might not result in an increased number of customers). Using a new source of supply for raw materials and changing the media allocation of the advertising budget would also be examples of qualitative changes.

Source: Roger A. Golde, *Harvard Business Review* **XXIV**: 5 (Sept.–Oct. 1964), 151 f.

Table 3. Hypothetical Completed Master Planning Form

Item	Change		Comment
	Next year	**Year after next**	
Research & Development	Mm	—S	Start development of new altimeter for executive planes.
Products		Ss	First sales of new altimeter.
Product Mix			
Service		s	Slightly different for private planes.
Supplies		s	Needed for new altimeter.
Suppliers			
Inventory			
Subcontracts		S	Most of subassemblies will be subcontracted.
Storage & Handling			
Quality Control			
Space		S	Little bit of production space for new altimeter.
Leasehold Improvements	M		Need for dust-free area.
Equipment	S		New test equipment.
Employees	S		Couple of technicians for development work.
Fringe Benefits			
Customers		sS	Plan to hit owners of executive planes.
Sales Outlets		Mm	Will need more sales representatives rather than own sales force.
Terms of Sale			
Pricing			
Transportation			
Advertising		—M	Not so effective to private owners.
Promotion		m	Will switch to more demonstrations and trade shows.
Packaging			
Market Research	S		Informal poll of private owners known by company.
Financing	S		Additional working capital for production.
Insurance			
Investments			
Management Reports		1	Need for simple product costing system.
Etc.			Etc.

Source: Roger A. Golde, *Harvard Business Review* XXIV: 5 (Sept.–Oct. 1964), 151 f.

A manager-owner can work with Golde's form at odd moments, informally, with or without help. This form has the great virtue of getting at the major elements of success or failure of a firm. Working with it will raise questions and encourage decisions. For many small businessmen, starting with comparatively abstract goals and strategies is difficult. The practical approach of Golde, however, should eventually lead them to a better understanding of objectives and strategies.

Selecting concrete key objectives. Not all objective setting need be abstract. An approach developed by Dr. Gunther Klaus, a small business management consultant, is concrete, pragmatic, and leads directly into systematic planning. He begins with a framework for decision which is illustrated in Table 4. This particular exhibit concerns sales objectives, but it could also be used for profit. The assumption here is that, if sales are considered first, the profit objectives will follow in logical fashion.

Table 4. Sales Objectives

Area	First year	Second year	Third year	Fourth year	Fifth year
Product					
Modification					
New Products					
Joint Ventures					
New Markets					
Acquisition					
Totals					→ BEGIN HERE

Klaus begins with an objective for sales as far in the future as it is practicable for the small businessman to contemplate, in this case five years. The question is, What dollar volume of sales do I want five years from now? When that question is answered, it naturally raises a great many more. One immediate question is whether the present product line will permit the achievement of that objective. If not, a number of other questions arise: Can the target be met by product modifications? If so, which ones? If not, what new products can be produced? If this will not permit target achievement, should a joint venture be considered? Penetration of new markets? Acquisitions? Dealing with these questions opens up a "decision-tree" with many other branches. What manpower will be needed? What financing will be required? What will my costs be? Must some employees be sent to an executive training program to get prepared to assume larger responsibilities?

This approach, like the preceding ones, is quite adaptable to different conditions and sizes of businesses.

The planning gap. A modification of this approach is to identify the so-called planning gap.[5] This calls for the establishment of tentative sales goals and the forecasting of current momentum, or what present and anticipated lines of business will produce in the future. The difference, as shown in Fig. 2, is the planning gap. The issue is, How will the gap be filled? (Similar charts can be drawn for profits, costs,

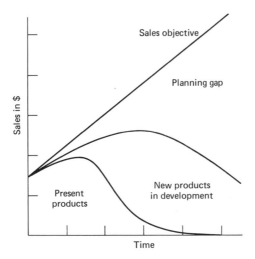

Fig. 2 The Planning Gap.

personnel, floor space, etc.) Asking and answering this question leads to the same sort of analysis as that discussed above.

Return on investment. Another approach is to concentrate on the return on investment calculation for a firm. The elements of this calculation are shown in Fig. 3. As in the previous approach, a return on investment objective can be tentatively established for selected time periods. The analysis then begins by probing (in a fashion similar to that described above) what is necessary to achieve the objective. This approach is flexible in dealing with both short- and long-range factors in business life.

For many years, this has been the approach of the planning and control program of E. I. du Pont de Nemours & Company. It is, of course, usable by a small company as well. But a small company would find (as does Du Pont) the approach more useful when accompanied by other elements of planning noted in Fig. 1.

Break-even analysis. The break-even point for a business is that point in production at which sales volume equals costs—at that point there is neither a profit nor a loss. Figure 4 shows a break-even analysis. A simple formula will also yield the break-even point:

$$\text{Break-even} = \frac{\text{Fixed costs}}{100\% - (\text{Variable costs}/\text{Sales})}$$

The break-even analysis is a powerful tool to answer puzzling questions such as: What is the impact on profit if fixed costs rise 10 percent and sales decline by 10 percent? Or if variable costs increase by 15 percent and volume drops by 14 percent?

This is a simple method to get at some major issues important in company planning. If break-even analysis is used to ask a widening range of questions, as illustrated above, it can be the starting point for a long-range planning program.

Economists have criticized this tool because they rightly claim that cost curves are curves and not linear as drawn on the chart. Furthermore, the technique assumes

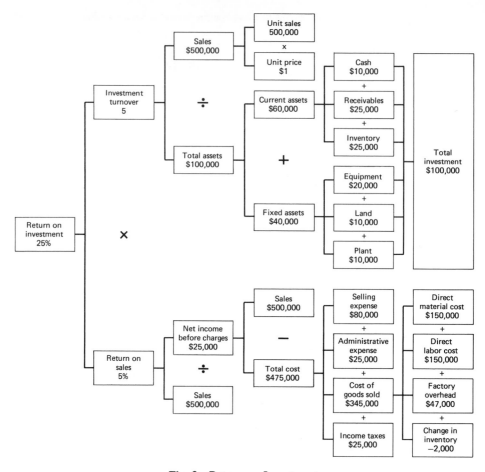

Fig. 3   Return on Investment.

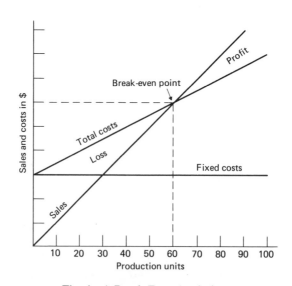

Fig. 4   A Break-Even Analysis.

many things that may not be true; for instance, that productivity remains the same over time, or that fixed and variable costs can be separated. This is not the place to argue the merits of such criticisms. It is in point here to observe, however, that within a "range of relevance," the functions of a break-even chart are rather linear. For many companies within a range of 10 to 15 percent on either side of the break-even line, an assumed linear relationship can be approximated closely enough to form a solid basis for planning. Hence this is a useful short- and long-range planning tool. Its value does, however, decrease the longer the time span covered and the wider the ranges of output are.

Standard accounting statements. Standard accounting statements are excellent bases for developing long-range planning. They can be very simple for a very small enterprise or developed in complex detail in a comprehensive planning program.

In a simple approach, and one which is indispensable to proper management in small as well as large enterprises, cash forecasts are prepared. What is involved is the identification and forecast of all important future sources and uses of cash available to the enterprise. Table 5 gives an elementary arrangement of items to be forecast to

Table 5. Five-Year Forecast of Cash Sources and Needs for a Small Business

Item	First year	Second year	Third year	Fourth year	Fifth year
Cash Sources:					
Opening balance					
Revenue from sales					
Depreciation					
Borrowing on facilities					
Borrowing on inventory and receivables					
Total cash sources					
Cash Expenditures:					
Direct labor costs					
Materials purchase					
Payments to subcontractors					
New machinery and tools					
Increases in inventory					
Increases in receivables					
Increases in operating cash					
Payments on loans					
Factory burden					
Officers' salaries					
Selling costs					
Taxes:					
Employer's share of Social Security					
Local property					
Income					
Total cash disbursements					
Net cash change					

determine net cash flows. A number of different formats are contained in Schabacker's *Cash Planning in Small Manufacturing Companies*.[6] Most commercial banks have developed cash-flow forms which are available to businessmen. These forms can be used to forecast cash flows for any period of time chosen—daily, weekly, monthly, quarterly, or over a number of years.

The revenue-expense forecast can also be used as a beginning point for long-range planning. Table 6 shows a simple revenue-expense forecast format. Here the task is to identify and forecast all important elements of cost and revenues. The difference will show profit or loss, and this in turn will provide the basis upon which simple or sophisticated rates of return on investment may be calculated. Revenue-expense forecasts can and should be prepared for each important product of an enterprise as well as for the enterprise as a whole. Revenue-expense forecasts for individual products should at least extend over the major part of the life span of the product.

An important feature of the revenue-expense forecast is that when depreciation is added to net profit the result is cash gain from operations. As noted in Table 6, this does not, however, represent net cash flow. So, when simple revenue-expense forecasts are used in planning they should be accompanied by cash-flow analyses.

Complete balance sheets and profit and loss statements constitute a more complicated basis for developing long-range planning. When a company gets to the point where it can develop such documents for the length of time for which organized future planning is done, it has demonstrated high capability for planning. Consequently, the

Table 6. Five-Year Revenue-Expense Projection for a Small Business

Item	First year	Second year	Third year	Fourth year	Fifth year
Sales revenues:					
Product A					
Product B					
Operating expenses:					
Direct labor					
Overhead					
Materials					
Selling expenses					
Depreciation					
Total					
Nonrecurring expenses					
Total operating expenses					
Interest and loan amortization					
Net profit before taxes					
Taxes					
Net profit after taxes					
Cash gain from operations (net profit after taxes plus depreciation reserve)					

company might just as well develop a more comprehensive formal long-range planning program in which these documents are included as parts.

As companies grow in size and experience with organized long-range planning, it becomes possible and desirable to have a more complete planning program than those discussed up to this point. The shape of the planning program follows more closely the conceptual model presented in Fig. 1 and results in a comprehensive set of objectives and plans covering all major parts of the business.

Here is a brief description of an actual comprehensive planning program. This five-year plan was prepared by the president and his four major department heads, who worked evenings and weekends to complete it. The firm had less than $2,000,000 annual sales and about one hundred employees at the time the plan was prepared.

Corporate Long-Range Plan for Magnetic Design, Inc.

I. Corporate Purposes: the fundamental purposes of MDI. Two basic purposes are given, which is about standard. The four modifiers, however, are a little unusual.

    A. Two prime objectives of MDI are:
- To improve earnings through productive effort primarily applied (but not limited) to the manufacture of magnetic devices and power supply equipment.
- To conduct the business in a manner that is constructive, honorable, and mutually profitable for stockholders, employees, customers, suppliers, and the general community.

    B. These objectives are amplified further:
- To earn a reasonable return on investment with due regard to the interests of customers, employees, vendors.
- To expand sales while increasing profits.
- To support the military effort of the United States by producing top quality products.
- To grow at a steady rate.

    C. Departmental purposes: Administration, marketing, production and engineering, and finance. It is a little unusual for departmental purposes to be specified at this point in a plan; they are usually blended into specific goals set for their operations. Following are the objectives of the production and engineering department:
- Manufacture and design quality products with cost and delivery schedules which will be attractive to prospective customers.
- Stay alert to developments that promise new and improved company products.

II. Basic Corporate Five- and Ten-Year Sales and Profit Objectives:

    A. The five-year annual sales and profit objectives are:

	Sales	Pretax Profits	Pretax (%) Profit	Federal Tax	Posttax (%) Profit
First year					
Second year			[Specified in dollars		
Third year			and percentages.]		
Fourth year					
Fifth year					

    B. The ten-year sales and profit objectives are:
- After taxes, sales will be $5,000,000 and earnings will be $750,000.

III. Basic Premises: forecasts of future markets, technology, competition, and evaluations of internal strengths and weaknesses. A framework of premises, with illustrations from the MDI plan, follows:

A. External projections and forecasts:
   - Survey of general business conditions, including Gross National Product forecast.
   - Survey of the market for company products, based upon general economic conditions for industrial products and estimates of government spending for company products.
   - Forecast of company sales based on the above two forecasts. (MDI made forecasts for each of the next five years. Since the company is in the Midwest, government spending for its products in the Midwest was estimated. Included were the Department of Defense, the National Aeronautics and Space Administration, and the Federal Aviation Agency.)

B. Competition: Because competition is keen for most companies, objective estimates of its strength are important. After looking at what its major competition was likely to do, the firm looked at itself.

   - Several advantages have placed MDI several years in advance of competition in the magnetic devices equipment field. These are cryogenic magnets for commercial applications and high reliability power supplies for long-endurance military application.
   - However, in order to realize fully the growth commensurate with the above advantages, several weaknesses must be overcome by developing an ability to construct crystals as well as developing more sophisticated test procedures.

C. Internal examination of the past and projections: Analyses of various parts of the enterprise, e.g.
   - Product line analysis:
     a. Product(s) performance (i.e., sales volume, profit margin, etc.).
     b. Customer class served.
     c. Comparison with major competitors' product(s).
     d. Comparison with substitutes and complementary performance.
     e. Possibilities for product improvement.
     f. Suggestions with regard to new products.
   - Market analysis:
     a. Important factors in projected sales changes: product success; marketing organization; advertising; and competitive pressures.
     b. New markets to be penetrated (i.e., geographical areas and customer classes).
   - Financial analysis:
     a. Profit position.
     b. Working capital.
     c. Cash position.
     d. Impact of financial policy on market price per share.
     e. Prospects for future financing.
   - Production analysis:
     a. Plant and equipment (maintenance and depreciation).
     b. Productive capacity and productivity.
     c. Percent of capacity utilized.
     d. Suggestions for: productivity improvements; cost reduction; utilizing excess capacity; and planning expansion.
   - Technical analysis:
     a. Research and development performance.
     b. Suggestions for improving research and development effectiveness.

- Employees:
  - a. Employment and future needs.
  - b. Technical manpower deficiencies.
  - c. Appraisal of employee attitudes.
- Facilities:
  - a. Evaluation of current facilities to meet new business.
  - b. Machine replacement policy and needs.

IV. Basic Objectives, Policies, and Strategies: This covers every important area of the business, but most companies concentrate on A through F of the following:

A. Profits.

B. Sales.

C. Finance.

D. Marketing.

E. Capital additions.

F. Production.

G. Research.

H. Engineering.

I. Personnel.

J. Acquisitions.

K. Organization.

L. Long-range planning.

This list can be expanded. As noted elsewhere, the more concrete the specification here can be, the easier it usually is to implement the plans. It is especially important for a small businessman to know precisely what he is seeking and the method to be employed to get there. For example, MDI marketing objectives were set forth as follows:

- Increase sales of magnetic devices 100 percent in the next five years. Increase sales of power supply equipment 200 percent during the next five years.
- Increase the total volume of industrial sales from today's 25 percent to 50 percent of total sales at the end of five years.
- Penetrate the western market to the point where the company will control 10 percent of it at the end of five years.
- Enter the foreign market within five years by a licensing agreement, a joint venture, or manufacturing facility.

For each of these objectives, the company prepared a detailed series of strategies ranging from a strategy to "sell custom designs directly to prime contractors in geographic regions where their main plants are located" to details such as special services to selected specified customers, training programs for employees, and top management meetings with customers.

Further strategies which might be included in this section of the plan, with special regard to marketing, are organization, use of dealers, possibility of distributing products manufactured by others, salesmen's compensation plans, and pricing policy.

Drawing a proper line of demarcation between the strategic plans and the detailed operational plans is difficult. Ideally, the two blend together in a continuous line. This was the case with MDI, where those making the strategic plan also were the ones to implement it.

V. Detailed Medium-Range Plans: more detailed plans growing out of the above. For MDI these plans were developed for each of the succeeding five years:

A. *Pro forma* balance sheet, yearly.

B. Income statement, yearly.

C. Capital expenditure schedule, yearly.

D. Unit production schedule for major products, yearly.

E. Employment schedule, yearly.

F. Detailed schedule to acquire within three years a company with design capability in solid state magnetic devices.

VI. One-Year Plans: the next year's budgets. The first year's budgets for items A through N were, in the aggregate, the same for the first year of the five-year plan, but broken into quarterly time periods. In addition, MDI had other budgets, principally purchasing schedules for major components and raw materials and typical detailed administrative budgets covering such things as travel and telephone.

Comprehensive planning in decentralized companies. When divisions are established as profit centers, a new dimension is added to the planning process. At first, long-range planning is usually done for the entire company by the central office. But once the process is established the central office usually concentrates on over-all company objectives, strategies, and policies and leaves the detailed medium- and short-range planning to the individual divisions, reserving only the right of review and approval. Sometimes the divisional plans are aggregated into one composite company plan. The structure and substance of the plans parallel that given for MDI.

Help for the chief executive. One of the major problems of the chief executive in doing long-range planning is getting adequate help. It is important for the manager-owner of a very small enterprise, as well as the president of a medium-sized business and the chief executive of a large one, to recognize that help is available. Each needs only to understand what is available and to learn how to use it.

His own staff is a prime resource. A manager always can do the planning himself—almost obligatory for a very small firm. As firms grow larger, however, it becomes impossible. Growth leads to staff help. Methods which have been employed in using staff successfully are:

• The chief executive can conduct a freewheeling "think" session to get long-range planning started. Many companies take their top executives away from daily routine to some spa to engage in thinking and planning about the future and conduct these sessions as part of a well-entrenched planning program. These sessions are useful to get the process started.

• The chief executive can first prepare objectives for the firm and then ask each functional manager to prepare plans for his own area of responsibility.

• The chief executive can ask each functional manager to tell him what his plans are for the future and then develop over-all objectives and strategies on the basis of them. Or, to initiate the process, he can ask each functional officer what he thinks ought to be done by the firm to get long-range planning under way.

• The chief executive can assign to one functional officer the job of starting planning. This man can monitor the process in progress.

• The chief executive can get together with his functional officers to form a committee to prepare strategic over-all as well as working plans for his company. This is what MDI did. As the number of employees increases, there may be great advantage to this method. A committee can offset some traits of chief executives, such as the desire for one-man authoritative control, making snap judgments, preoccupation with short- at the expense of long-run planning, and secretiveness which hurts the firm more than it helps it. Committees of this sort bring to the front different points of view, which is usually healthy. Better communications are promoted, and individuals are likely to feel more intimately associated with the prospects and problems of the firm.

- When a firm gets larger it may be able to afford one person or a small staff to devote full time to planning. Such a staff is especially useful in decentralized, divisionalized companies. The staff coordinates work of the central headquarters' functional officers in the development of over-all firm objectives and strategies, aids the divisions in improving their planning capabilities, and helps the central headquarters management review plans. Sometimes the director of such a staff serves as the secretary to a corporate planning committee.

Outside sources of help are available, including consultants for all the major problems of the firm. These are well known and need no further analysis here. One of the most neglected sources of help, particularly for the small businessman, is his board of directors. Small businessmen should think seriously about the advantages of placing on their board one or more individuals with talents that can be used in actually performing long-range planning or advising the president about the use of outside consultants.

Summary. Many small businessmen do not engage in effective long-range planning because they are puzzled about how to begin the process and execute it so that its values exceed its costs. Many of these approaches have been tested by small, as well as large, firms, and they have been found operational and valuable in doing effective long-range planning.

REFERENCES

This article is based on a chapter from a book edited by Professor Irving Pfeffer, entitled *Financial Aspects of Profit Planning for Small Business,* to be published later this year.

1. For a fuller definition of long-range planning, see my The critical role of top management in long-range planning, *Arizona Review* XV:4 (April 1966); and my long-range planning: concept and implementation, *Financial Executive* XXXIV:7 (July 1966), 54-61.

2. For a profile of the successful small businessman, see Orvis F. Collins, David G. Moore, and Darab B. Unwalla, *The Enterprising Man* (East Lansing, Mich.: Bureau of Business and Economic Research, Graduate School of Business Administration, Michigan State University, 1964).

3. Delbert C. Hastings, *The Place of Forecasting in Basic Planning for Small Business* (Minneapolis: University of Minnesota Press, 1961), p. 23.

4. Roger A. Golde, Practical planning for small business, *Harvard Business Review* XXIV:5 (Sept.-Oct. 1964), 151 f.

5. See my Making long-range company planning pay off, *California Management Review* IV:2 (Winter 1963), 28-41.

6. Joseph C. Schabacker, *Cash Planning in Small Manufacturing Companies, Small Business Administration* (Washington, D.C.: U.S. Government Printing Office, 1960).

Strategic Planning in the Small Business

The procedure in three corporations

Steven C. Wheelwright

The importance and value of strategic planning is often discussed in management seminars and publications. However, few of the details of how a firm might approach the task of strategic planning have been investigated in a research setting. Taking the importance of strategy as given, this article considers some of the important characteristics of strategy and summarizes the findings of a recent research program on strategy at the Stanford Business School. The author then reports on the application of these research findings to three small but growing companies in order to develop strategies for them. Finally, the factors that should be considered, as a company develops its own approach to strategic planning, are summarized.

There are few industries in the world today where a company can achieve satisfactory profitability simply by meeting its competition head-on. This is particularly true for small, growth-oriented firms; companies of this kind usually achieve success by developing an approach that gives them some competitive advantage in meeting the needs of the market. The development of such an approach, most often referred to as "a strategy," has been the subject of considerable discussion during recent years.

The reason for the tremendous interest in corporate strategy and strategic planning is twofold: first, managers realize that a good strategy greatly enhances the likelihood of a firm's success; second, a body of research results has been developed that can help a company to formulate a strategy and then evaluate it to determine how good it is.

Taking the importance of strategy as given, this article considers some of the important characteristics of strategy, summarizes the findings of a recent research program on strategy, reports on the application of these research findings to three small but growing companies in order to develop strategies for them, and finally summarizes those factors that should be considered as a company develops its own approach to strategic planning.

Business Horizons, vol. 4, Aug. 1971, pp. 51–58. Copyright, 1971 by the Foundation for the School of Business at Indiana University. Reprinted by permission.

Mr. Wheelwright, a faculty member of the Harvard Business School, spent the 1970–1971 academic year at INSEAD (the International Institute of Business Administration) in Fontainebleau, France.

CHARACTERISTICS OF STRATEGY
The first aspect of corporate strategy that is of major importance is the identification of a set of criteria that can be used to evaluate a strategy. While the most accurate evaluation can be given only after the firm has followed a strategy for some time, this is of only minimal value to the firm planning a new strategy. What is needed is some method for evaluating corporate strategy before it is implemented.

The best approach available today for making such an evaluation is to use a set of questions regarding the strategy. A variety of questions have been suggested;[1] most of these relate to one of four basic areas:

- How well does the strategy fit with corporate objectives and purposes?
- How well does the strategy fit with the company's environment?
- How well does the strategy fit with the company's resources?
- How committed is the corporate management to the strategy?

Questions along the lines of the first three are based on the notion that a good strategy effectively matches the firm's resources with the opportunities and realities of the market in order to accomplish the goals of the firm. The assumption is that matching or fitting the strategy to the specific situation will result in a unique (differentiated) approach that will lead to the development of some kind of competitive advantage. The fourth question relates to how well (and how rapidly) the firm will be able to adopt the desired strategy, since the greater the commitment to the strategy, the more likely the company will follow it successfully.

A second aspect of strategy and strategic planning that is of major importance is the purpose it is to serve in a company. Since corporate situations vary widely, the role of strategic planning in the success of the firm also varies widely. At least three major purposes can be aided through the development of a strategy: the need for specialized skills and resources within the firm can be identified and defined; corporate activity can be focused and coordinated; and a standard can be established against which future performance can be compared.

RECENT RESEARCH
Identification of the specific purpose of strategy in a given firm is particularly important to the selection and development of an effective procedure for strategic planning. Recent literature on strategic planning has suggested a number of procedures that a firm might follow in preparing a strategy.[2] Since these procedures vary widely, one would expect that the resulting strategies would also vary.

In order to study the effect of various factors, especially the strategic planning procedure, on corporate strategy a program of research was carried out over a two-year period at the Stanford Graduate School of Business.[3] This research consisted of three phases.

The first phase of the program was strictly exploratory. Using two time-shared computer terminals, a number of business managers enrolled in the nine-week Stanford Executive Program (summer, 1968) were asked to use a computer program to help develop a strategy for a situation described in a business policy case. This interactive computer program acted like a consultant, probing the businessman (student) with questions to help him formulate and improve his strategy. The results of this part of the program showed that those who used the computer program developed much more creative and unusual strategies; in most cases, they felt that their strategies were improved significantly through use of the computer program.

Because the initial research was only exploratory, the second phase aimed at developing a controlled experiment that could effectively test the impact of an interactive computer program on strategies. This work, carried out by McKinney, not only tested a research methodology for examining some of the factors relevant to strategic planning, but also compared two complementary procedures for strategic planning recommended by Cannon.[4]

McKinney's work produced four major findings. *First*, it showed that the experimental methodology he devised was suitable for examining strategic planning. *Second*, by using the two procedures in sequence, as recommended by Cannon, students developed significantly better strategies than when using either of them separately. *Third*, the first procedure recommended by Cannon (referred to as opportunity oriented) led to better strategies than those developed without following one of these set procedures. *Fourth*, the second procedure (referred to as tactically oriented) resulted in strategies that were inferior to those developed without following one of these set procedures.

Because the results of the second phase of the research showed that some procedures for strategic planning can be better than no set procedure and that some can be worse, it was decided that a natural third phase of the research program would be to examine at least two different procedures for strategic planning in more detail.[5] To help in identifying the important factors in this phase of the research, the simple model shown in Fig. 1 was developed. This model indicates that the final strategy depends not only on the procedure that is followed, but also on the strategic planner (his background, bias, and so on), the strategic task (the company's situation), and the general environment (the urgency and motivation for strategic planning, for example). While these factors overlap somewhat, they do present a scheme that is useful in designing research and in determining what type of approach would be best for a specific company to adopt.

Fig. 1   A Model of Strategic Planning.

The third phase of this research began by identifying two general classes of procedures for strategic planning—the synoptic and incremental. These two were chosen because a number of examples of each can readily be found in the strategic planning literature.

Procedures that are synoptic in nature emphasize setting corporate objectives, generating a range of alternative strategies, and then using the stated objectives to evaluate these alternatives and select the best one. This type of procedure focuses on examining the entire range of possible strategies for the company and selecting the one that will best accomplish a stated set of objectives.[6]

Incremental procedures, on the other hand, generally consist of identifying the firm's existing strategy, examining the strengths and weaknesses of the firm, and the threats and opportunities of the environment (particularly competition), and then improving the existing strategy.[7] Thus the incremental approach does not seek a comprehensive analysis of alternative strategies as does the synoptic approach, nor does it involve explicit specification of corporate objectives at the outset.

The methodology used in testing these two classes of procedures was developed by McKinney.[8] The results of this phase of research were indeed striking. *First*, it was found that even though the strategies developed using the synoptic approach were more creative (distinctive) than those developed using the incremental approach, the incremental prepared strategies were better—over-all—than those prepared with the synoptic procedure. *Second*, it was found that the strategic planner, the strategic task, and the environment in which the planning took place each had an impact on the relative effectiveness of the synoptic and incremental procedures for preparing strategy.

Those planners who were "quantitative" in their general problem-solving orientation (such as engineers and mathematicians) preferred the synoptic approach and thought it was most effective. Planners who were "nonquantitative" preferred the incremental approach.

Three different strategic planning tasks (three different corporate situations) were assigned. The company that was most successful and could follow a wide range of alternatives was handled best by planners using the synoptic approach; the company with the least amount of flexibility in its options was handled best by planners using the incremental approach.

The two aspects of the general planning environment that were examined were the motivation for planning and possible carry-over effects from the synoptic to the incremental approach. It was found that planning done in a supportive atmosphere produced a much better strategy than planning in a nonsupportive atmosphere. There was no carry-over effect, indicating that using the synoptic and then the incremental approach is generally no better than using the incremental approach alone.

Since the results of this three-phase research program were very significant, the researchers felt the need to interpret these findings in terms of how they might apply to the practicing manager. This was one by helping three small, growth-oriented firms to each develop a procedure for strategic planning and a strategy through application of these experimental results. (This was not a controlled experiment; it was simply an attempt to apply what had been learned.)

STRATEGY IN THREE FIRMS

The three companies in which these results were implemented included a new enterprise in the computer peripheral equipment industry, a prominent firm in the urban planning field, and a well-established firm in the yearbook printing industry. Each of these will be discussed in turn by first describing the firm's situation in terms of the factors identified in the figure, then describing the procedure for strategic planning that was used in each situation, and, finally, reviewing the effectiveness of each of these.

Computer Peripheral Company (Company A)

This company was in its first year of operation at the time the author became involved in the development of a procedure for strategic planning. The company had been started by two "quantitatively" oriented members of a graduate business school faculty who were interested in meeting some of the needs of the unsophisticated users of computers. Thus the orientation of those involved in strategic planning for this firm was quantitative.

In terms of the general environment, the principals in the company were well aware of the need for developing a strategy to guide them in decision making, especially since they did not yet have an established set of operating procedures which could serve as a basis for most of their short-term decisions. The strategic task facing this company was indeed mixed in nature, since its managers could follow a wide range of alternative strategies; the risk of corporate failure, however, was very high because of the competitive nature of the industry.

The first steps taken by Company A in developing a procedure for strategic planning were essentially synoptic in nature. They focused on trying to state a set of objectives for the firm and formulating some alternative strategies that could accomplish these objectives. While several ideas were generated during this phase, it soon became apparent that the range of alternatives had to be narrowed considerably in order to move forward in the strategic planning process.

This narrowing was achieved, first, by using the objectives to determine what alternatives were acceptable. Second, pressing problems were examined to decide what some of the subparts of the strategy would be, for example, what type of production facility to have, what type of marketing sales force to employ, and so on. The approach of making decisions on a subject of a strategy before the composite strategy has been stated would normally be risky, since it could easily lead to suboptimization in one area that would not fit into the over-all strategy at some later point in time. This did not seem to be a major problem in this case, however, because the company had examined a range of alternatives and these were still fresh in their minds as they began to make these decisions.

In the case of Company A, the major focus of the strategic planning process (after the initial search for alternatives) was the development of a strategic plan that could serve as a guide to action. This purpose was effectively accomplished in initiating the subparts of the strategy in such a way that they could be a guide in making the important decisions that the company faced.

Urban Planning Firm (Company B)

Unlike Company A, the urban planning company that was involved in this study had been operating for about eight years and enjoyed a solid reputation in the urban planning market. The firm had been built around the abilities of two men, each recognized in the industry for his skill in architectural design and urban planning. The president of the firm, who was professionally the better known of the two founders, was definitely "qualitative" in his approach, but had been very successful in his handling of the company's financial affairs, as well as in directing several of their consulting projects.

Company B had grown rapidly during the two years preceding this study and was close to doing $1 million in annual sales. The general environment was one in which strategy was little known in the terms generally used in business. The firm chose to focus on strategic planning at this point because their recent growth had fully utilized their existing financial resources, and they recognized that they would either have to severely limit their growth or look for other financing. The second alternative would obviously commit the founders to staying with the company for some years, and they were not certain they wanted to make such a commitment.

The strategic task facing the company provided a wide range of alternatives, each of which appeared likely to be successful, but each of which would leave the founders in a very different position in three to five years. Thus personal objectives were extremely important in the selection of a strategy for the company.

The first step in the strategic planning process was to specify a suitable set of objectives for the firm, which the principals could agree on. The background of the planners seemed to suggest that an incremental approach would be best. However, a synoptic approach (starting with objectives) was used because of the importance of objectives in this situation and because the firm recognized the need for a major decision on strategy rather than a mere modification of existing strategy.

The firm identified a number of important objectives during this first phase; these were grouped into four areas so that the impact of various strategies on them could be more easily evaluated. It was particularly important at this stage of the planning to keep the process moving so that it would not get bogged down in attempts to resolve minor differences in the objectives.

Once the relevant objectives had been identified, it was possible to evaluate and compare a number of alternative strategies in terms of how well they accomplished the four major objectives. After some lengthy discussion and additional investigations, the company was able to agree on a strategy that would meet the majority of the firm's objectives without overly constraining the principals who were involved.

Thus the major focus of strategic planning in Company B was to select a strategy which would ensure the continued success of the firm and be acceptable to the two founders of the company. Finding such a strategy was of critical importance in order to get the commitment of the entire firm to that strategy so that it could be effectively followed, and so that the decisions that were to be made in the next several months would be made in a consistent manner.

Printing Company (Company C)

The third company for which a strategy was developed as a part of this study was a family-owned printing firm. This company had originally been founded by two brothers. For approximately twenty years, the older brother had been president and in charge of sales, and the younger brother had been in charge of production.

About three years before the study was made, the older brother left the firm (selling his half to his brother) to become an administrator in a nearby university. Thus the younger brother suddenly became president and owner of the entire company. This man was knowledgeable in the production aspects of the business and systematic in his analysis of problems, but he felt somewhat unsure of himself in the sales area and as chief executive.

The company was quite aware of technological advancements being made in the industry and anxious to take advantage of them. The firm enjoyed a good reputation for quality in their geographical region, but had recently felt their position slipping somewhat as other firms seemed to be advancing more rapidly than they were. The management team (composed of five people) seemed to be convinced of the need for strategic planning but were uncertain of the procedure they should follow.

In terms of the strategic task involved, the company was anxious to maintain its position of prominence. There appeared to be at least two or three alternative strategies they could follow in order to do that. It was apparent from the start that a major shift in strategy did not seem feasible or attractive; rather, what was needed was a sharpening of strategy and a rounding out of some of the areas overlooked in the past.

An incremental approach to strategic planning appeared to be the most appropriate. Therefore, the first step was to examine what the company's strategy had been in the past. The management team of Company C spent three days (away from the office) examining their strengths and weaknesses, and the opportunities and challenges in the environment. Eventually, the team came up with a revised strategy. This strategy was stated both in simple prose and as a series of actions that were to be taken. Since many of these actions were spread out over time and since it was felt that other actions would have to be added as the strategy was adopted, the management team decided to hold a monthly planning meeting to evaluate their progress in implementing the strategy and to define these additional actions.

Thus in Company C, the major purpose of the strategy was to strengthen the corporation's position by focusing management attention on those actions required to implement the strategy. In addition, management was provided with a broader base on which to relate its many day-to-day decisions.

THE PLANNING PROCEDURE

A general approach for selecting and implementing a strategic planning procedure in a firm can now be suggested. Because of the complexity of most situations, the exact planning procedure that will work best is difficult if not impossible to specify beforehand. Nevertheless, it is possible to suggest some guidelines that will usually lead to the utilization of an effective procedure.

The first step in selecting a strategic planning procedure is to specify and define the three major variables that are relevant: the planners, the environment, and the strategic situation. Some of the factors that are important to each of these variables are listed in Table 1.

The second step in selecting a procedure is to identify the major purpose of strategic planning within the firm in question. The most common purposes are to:

- Develop a strategy that will lead the firm to a strong competitive position.

- Focus and coordinate corporate activity on those areas that are most important.

- Establish criteria that can be used to guide decision making and to evaluate performance.

Rather than merely saying that all of these purposes are important in a specific situation (which would be of little value in selecting a planning procedure), it is important to state the one main objective of strategic planning in the situation in question.

Table 1. Important Variables in Strategic Planning

The Planners

Their background
Their orientation in problem-solving situations
Their roles in the company (managers, professionals, owners,
and so on)

The Environment

The factors prompting the development of a strategy
The motivation of the planners
The urgency in completing the task

The Strategic Situation

The range of alternatives available to the company
The company's current competitive position
The range of alternatives the company might be willing to consider

Once the above two steps have been taken, the strategic planning procedure can be selected. The aim is to select a procedure somewhere between the incremental and the synoptic that will fit the company involved and will best help its managers to achieve their purpose.

Once a procedure has been selected, the major task of implementing it can be undertaken. The first phase of implementation is to assign responsibility for preparing, recording, and communicating the corporate strategy to the appropriate members of the management team. Obviously, the chief executive officer must take over-all responsibility for strategic planning.

The second phase is to start the task of strategic planning and to keep moving. This requires keeping the major purpose in mind so that if things start to slow down on a minor point, the chief executive can get them moving onto a more important part of the task. Staying on the move also requires that the planners be somewhat flexible in the procedure they are following so that, as unforeseen difficulties arise, they can make the necessary adjustments.

The final phase of strategic planning is to get the strategy in written form so that it can be communicated to others and easily be referred to. The plan is not complete until it is in writing.

In order to ensure that the company adopts the strategy which it develops, it is important that the written strategy be translated into a series of specific actions so that the completion of these actions can be measured. This evaluation of adoption of the strategy will be most effective if the firm establishes a series of periodic planning meetings (monthly or quarterly) to review progress in the adoption of the strategy and to solve special problems as they may arise.

The importance and value of strategic planning is often discussed in management seminars and publications. However, few of the details of how a firm might approach the task of strategic planning have been investigated in a research setting. This article describes how the recent program of research on strategic planning conducted at the Stanford Business School has been related to three corporate situations. The procedures used in these three situations and the general approach for selecting and implementing a strategic planning procedure are intended to help the small, growth-oriented firm achieve satisfactory profitability.

REFERENCES

1. See Edmund P. Learned and others, *Business Policy: Text and Cases* (Homewood, Ill.: Irwin, 1965); George W. McKinney III, An experimental study of the effects of systematic approaches on strategic planning, unpublished Ph.D. dissertation, Stanford University Graduate School of Business, August 1969; Seymour Tilles, How to evaluate corporate strategy, *Harvard Business Review* XLI (July-Aug. 1963), pp. 111-121; and S. C. Wheelwright, An analysis of strategic planning as a creative problem solving process, unpublished Ph.D. dissertation, Stanford University Graduate School of Business, June, 1970.

2. See H. Igor Ansoff, *Corporate Strategy* (New York: McGraw-Hill, 1965); J. Thomas Cannon, *Business Strategy and Policy* (New York: Harcourt, Brace & World, 1968); Frank F. Gilmore and Richard G. Brandenburg, Anatomy of corporate planning, *Harvard Business Review* XL (Nov.-Dec. 1962), pp. 61-69; Robert L. Katz, Cases and concepts in corporate strategy, Stanford University Graduate School of Business, unpublished, 1967; Robert F. Stewart, *A Framework for Business Planning* (Long-Range Planning Report No. 162; Menlo Park, Calif.: Stanford Research Institute, 1963); George A. Steiner, Long-range planning: concept and implementation, *Financial Executive* XXXIV (July 1966), pp. 54-61.

3. Henry B. Eyring, Edwin V. W. Zschau, George W. McKinney, and Steven C. Wheelwright, Research in methods for formulating and analyzing changes in a corporate strategy: progress report no. 1, Stanford University Graduate School of Business, unpublished, 1968; McKinney, An experimental study of the effects of systematic approaches on strategic planning; and Wheelwright, An analysis of strategic planning as a creative problem solving process.

4. McKinney, An experimental study of the effects of systematic approaches on strategic planning, Cannon, *Business Strategy and Policy.*

5. Wheelwright, An analysis of strategic planning as a creative problem solving process.

6. Alan R. Eagle, *Analytical Approaches in Planning* (Long-Range Planning Report No. 238; Menlo Park, Calif.: Stanford Research Institute, 1965); Ansoff, *Corporate Strategy*; Cannon, *Business Strategy and Policy*; and Steiner, Long-range planning: concept and implementation.

7. Robert L. Katz, Cases and concepts in corporate strategy, Stanford University Graduate School of Business, unpublished, 1967; Edmund P. Learned and others, *Business Policy: Text and Cases* (Homewood, Ill.: Irwin, 1965); Robert F. Stewart, *A Framework for Business Planning* (Long-Range Planning Report No. 162; Menlo Park, Calif.); Organized entrepreneurship: a network of tasks that produce a coherent chain of reasoning, Stanford Research Institute, unpublished, 1969; and Eyring and others, Research in methods for formulating and analyzing changes in a corporate strategy: progress report no. 1.

8. McKinney, An experimental study of the effects of systematic approaches on strategic planning.

Breaking the Barriers to Small Business Planning

Roger A. Golde

President, Golde Management Services, Cambridge, Massachusetts

Summary. *Most small manufacturers do not use long-range planning even though they could gain much from it. Planning can, for example, help owner-managers to provide lead time for necessary actions and to use resources effectively. With such benefits in the offing, why do small business owners neglect this management tool?*

In many instances, certain barriers get between owner-managers and long-range planning. Some do not plan because of fear of the future or because of the inexactness of the future. Others fail to think systematically about where their companies may be two or three years hence because of the lack of proper time and place for planning or because of the lack of planning knowledge.

This Aid *discusses these barriers to small business planning and offers suggestions for overcoming them.*

Many small business owners feel that they are doing enough planning when they use short-run sales forecasts, expense budgets, and other short-range planning tools. They shrug off the idea of long-range planning by saying, "That's for big companies."

Such owner-managers couldn't be more mistaken. Because of the rapid rate of change in today's world, present production methods may be totally inadequate next year or the year after next. Or present products may be dead or dying a few years from now.

In either case, which small company will have the best chance of survival—the one whose owner-manager neglects planning because he is busy with today's crises? Or the one whose owner-manager tries to plan ahead?

Small companies need to plan as thoroughly if not more thoroughly than large ones. Few small firms have enough resources to overcome their future problems with aggressive financial force. Few can afford to underwrite the loss that can occur while adjusting to an unexpected change when they depend on a single product or on a few key customers.

Essentially, *long-range planning is the process of systematically and consciously thinking about the future of an enterprise as an integrated whole.* It, therefore, is a vital tool for competing effectively and for trying to reduce future crises.

Courtesy of the Small Business Administration.

BENEFITS FROM LONG-RANGE PLANNING

When an owner-manager systematically thinks about the future of his company, he stands to gain certain benefits. The planning process helps him: to provide lead time for necessary actions; to make decisions where there are long-term effects; to use resources efficiently; and to improve current operations.

• *Lead Time.* Doing things in business takes time. The owner-manager must anticipate not only the changes that his business will need but also the time required to make these changes.

For example, if you expect that one of your products will become obsolete, you probably couldn't think of trying to develop a new product, produce it, and market it in only 30 days' time. You know that a development project for a new product may take 1 or 2 years, or longer. Therefore, you start early—while the product destined for obsolescence is still marketable—to develop its replacement.

Other examples of business activity that require lead time are: building a new plant; beefing up a sales force; and putting together a promotional program. With specific plans for such activities, you can see what actions will be needed and provide the lead time for getting them done on schedule.

• *Long-Term Effects.* Planning helps make decisions where there are long-term effects. Many management decisions involve investments, that is, expenditures of time, effort, or money in the present in order to achieve benefits over a number of years in the future. As automation and mechanization increase, the number of investment decisions is also increasing. If money is to be spent on a machine that will last for five years, it is vital to think about the five-year future of your business to be sure the purchase is really justified. Mistakes in investment policy are costly and difficult to rectify.

• *Efficient Use of Resources.* Planning can help you provide for the efficient use of your company's resources—an especially vital area when they are scarce. When money, personnel, or facilities are limited, you have to be careful in using them.

You have to make choices as to *what* will be done as well as to *when* it will be done. You have to consider alternatives and weigh their impact on the prosperity of your whole company. Planning is necessary if the best choices are to be made.

When you look at long-range planning as a matter of choices, it is an extension of an ordinary activity, such as scheduling a day's production. There you have to decide which orders should be first. Similarly, in planning for next year, the year after next, and so on, you have to decide what activities are most important. Then you have to schedule these activities in a way that produces the best possible results per dollar of expense.

• *Improved Operations.* Another benefit which you may get from planning is improved current operations. Because planning often involves making periodic evaluations of the company *as a whole*, it can show up areas which need improvement.

For example, you might discover that your salesmen spend too much time selling the product with the lowest profit margin. Or you might find that a slight cut in your cost of raw materials could increase profits more than the increase which could be made by hiring another salesman.

BARRIERS BLOCK PLANNING

Even though they are aware of the advantages of long-range planning, many small business owners fail to do it. In fact, most small companies do little, if any, long-range planning.

Why do most owner-managers neglect trying to look ahead—in an orderly and detailed fashion—for at least two years? Life being what it is, certain barriers tend to discourage them from planning.

Among these barriers which block attempts at long-range planning are: fear, inexactness, changeability, lack of proper time and place, and lack of planning knowledge.

OVERCOMING THE BARRIERS

Recognizing that such barriers exist is an important step in overcoming them and moving along toward some long-range planning. Keep in mind also that only one of the five barriers may by itself be enough to impede planning in a small company. For example, the barrier which blocks one owner's planning efforts may be the inexactness-of-two-years-from-now while fear-of-the-future is the barrier which bothers another.

• *Fear.* Even though most people don't talk about it, fear is a barrier to many kinds of activity. It is especially a roadblock to planning, and it may be the biggest hurdle for most owner-managers.

Fear, for example, causes some owner-managers to feel that careful thought about the future of their companies will bring to light a host of trouble. "I've got enough worries without trying to cross bridges ahead of time," is a normal reaction.

Somehow it seems easier to live with vague apprehensions about a fuzzy future than it does with reasoned expectations. When the owner-manager has no clear description of the problems *and opportunities*, he tends to feel that his company can get by with token measures.

Yet such token solutions are often just "whistling in the dark." They remind one of the story of the executive who snapped his fingers as he paced up and down outside his plant. Asked what he was doing, he replied, "I'm keeping away the lions."

"But there are no lions around here," an observer said.

The executive nodded, smiled, and proclaimed, "Then it looks as though I'm doing a good job, doesn't it?"

A ridiculous story, perhaps, but it does show what can happen when a person doesn't recognize fear for what it is. Fear is a natural reaction. Realizing this fact is important in overcoming fear as a barrier to planning. The events, the problems, and the opportunities of the future cannot be taken care of with a snap of the fingers. They have to be faced. And the real fear which the owner-manager should have is that of facing the future without a plan—without a set of alternatives to choose from when a possible event occurs.

• *Inexactness.* Another barrier to the planning process is inexactness. One small business owner sums up this barrier by saying, "Planning is so inexact that it doesn't seem worth doing. No matter how carefully I plan, things often do not work out according to the plan."

And what he says is true—to an extent. Planning is an uncertain thing because, among other reasons, the future is uncertain.

However, the important fact is to realize that business operates in a world where certainty is impossible but where probability is sufficient to govern action. Essentially businessmen are bettors, trying *to find out the best way to play the odds.* The job is to make the best possible decision *before* a series of uncertain events, not after.

One way of illustrating long-range planning is to look at a die which carries the numbers "1 through 6." When you roll this die, the probability of any one number—for example, 4—coming up is only 1 out of 6.

Now suppose that you find a special die. Upon scrutinizing this die you find that the number "4" is on five of its sides and the numbr "2" is on the sixth side. When you roll this die, the probability is that the "4" will come up 5 times out of 6. However, you are not surprised if the number "2" comes up instead of a "4." In the long run, it is bound to happen 1 out of 6 times.

The important thing in this example is taking time to learn the odds—to determine what is likely to happen. And so it is in business. The problem is getting some idea of the odds. For example, what are the odds that more customers will need your type of product two years from now? Ten years from now?

You formulate that idea by planning—by developing a description of what will probably happen. Then you plan what you want to happen within the framework of those odds. If your plans do not materialize, does that necessarily mean you should not have made them? Does it mean you should not have taken the time to examine your company and its environment in order to discover how best to bet on its future?

• *Changeability.* Often small businessmen complain that plans and goals change too frequently to make planning worthwhile. "I no sooner make a plan than something happens, and I have to modify it. Or I have to make a completely new plan."

Of course, this can be a serious problem. However, the solution lies in the frequency and flexibility with which you plan, rather than in the rejection of planning altogether.

If the situation changes rapidly in your company, review your long-range plans periodically—and alter your original project to the changing situations. Perhaps you should not try to plan five years ahead but only one or two years in the future.

However, in most small businesses, the time scale of events demands that you look ahead at least a year or two. Rare is the industry where some significant change does not occur within a period of one or two years. It is also hard to find the company in which certain necessary projects do not require a year or more to be completed.

Part of overcoming the barrier of changeability lies in flexibility. Make flexible plans. Do not plan for one narrow set of possibilities. Rather, consider how you might alter plans if a change materializes. For example, in thinking about building a new plant you should consider: (1) What would I do if the demand for my product turns out to be substantially less than I expected? (2) What would I do if the demand turns out to be much greater than I had predicted?

• *Lack of Time and Place.* Many small business owners say that the lack of proper time and place is an obstacle to planning. Quite often, however, this statement is just a way of avoiding a task which they do not really want to do.

Then, too, it is easy to let planning slide when you are busy. Many owner-managers do not plan because they feel that they cannot be spared from daily operations—from the day-to-day crises. They tend to forget that their plants and sales forces operate successfully when they are out sick for several days.

Like many other vital aspects of management, the owner-manager has to make a conscious effort to find the time and place for planning. In the normal run of affairs, the time for planning just will not turn up by itself.

Special conditions are needed for planning. You also need some peace and quiet—some protection from continual interruptions.

Some owner-managers create an environment for their planning by doing it in the evening at the office or on Saturday. The president of one small company rents an office at the other end of town and uses it to get away from the daily crises of the plant.

Setting a schedule for planning is another way to help get it done. For example, you might decide to spend one hour every Wednesday evening on planning. Or you might set aside every other Saturday morning for thinking about your company's future.

• *Lack of Knowledge.* Lack of planning knowledge can be a most serious barrier to planning. Even when the owner-manager has a proper time and place, he must have some idea of how to go about planning in order to do it effectively.

One common approach to planning contains three steps: (1) set goals and objectives, (2) develop plans to achieve the goals, and (3) assess progress toward the objectives. Yet this approach is often confusing to the owner-manager who has never tried to plan.

Essentially, the important thing about planning in small business is getting started.

GETTING STARTED

If you've never planned, start by getting a *complete* picture of your operations. You may know some of the details individually, but the chances are you need more information to get the complete picture.

• *Five Written Statements.* Here's the type of information you need to stimulate your planning thought.

1. A brief description of your company's present practices in all important areas such as products, purchasing, storage, quality control, labor relations, training, sales outlets, advertising, and research and development.
2. A brief description of your present management procedures, reports, and organization (including informal job descriptions along with an organization chart).
3. A list of the main factors exterior to your firm which affect your company the most. Areas to be considered include government, the national economy, your competition, the community in which you do business, scientific advances, and overseas markets.
4. A list of the changes you expect in any of these factors in the next few years.
5. A list of the main strengths and weaknesses of your present operation (based on items 1 through 4).

It is essential that you write down your thinking because (1) getting something on paper is at the heart of any formalized kind of planning, (2) writing things down clarifies your own thought. Written plans are also helpful in conveying your ideas to others who will play a part in implementing them.

You probably noticed that several of the five items above refer to your business as it now exists. Planning for the future starts with the present. You have to have a clear idea of where you are before you can think about where you want to go. Only then can you select a few specific goals to work toward.

• *The Right Frame of Mind.* In trying to get started, remember that the *right frame of mind* is important. Most of the barriers to planning stem from one basic situation: Planning represents a vastly different type of activity and approach from the one you use in the day-to-day management of your company. Because long-range planning is so different from dealing with daily brush fires, the owner-manager needs to make a conscious effort to plan on a formal basis. Otherwise proper planning will not get done.

The owner-manager's attitude is important. It can make or break planning. In order to plan effectively, your attitude should be one that is unafraid of discovering what the present state of your business really is. It should also be one that is not afraid of trying to learn what the future might bring.

Such an attitude can help you to clarify problems and plot solutions. And once you have developed possible solutions, following through on your plans is largely a matter of management—of doing what is needed at the proper time. Keep in mind that a very important part of making plans work is reviewing periodically performance against plans.

Suggestions for Further Reading

Carrington, J. H., and J. M. Aurelio. Survival tactics for the small business. *Business Horizons* 19: 13-24 (Feb. 1976).

Four M's of business success. *Director* 27: 32 (Jan. 1975).

Goetz, B. E. Management of risk in small new enterprises. *SAM Advanced Management Journal* 38: 21-27 (Jan. 1973).

Hlavacek, J. D., *et al.* Tie small business technology to marketing power. *Harvard Business Review* 55: 106-116 (Jan. 1977).

Kick, R. C., Jr. Profit-planning and control system (PPCS) for the small firm. *Journal of Small Business Management* 14: 8-15 (Oct. 1976).

Role of the chief executive in a small corporation. *Paperboard Packaging* 61: 88 (Sept. 1976).

Tower, J. Plan to help small business solve its problems. *Nations Business* 61: 34-36 (Feb. 1976).

Woodward, H. N. Management strategies for small companies. *Harvard Business Review* 54: 113-121 (Jan. 1976).

5
Control in the
Small Business

Introduction

The control process in large organizations has been discussed extensively in the business literature. All functional areas present solutions to issues of control. The analytical tools and requirements of these large-scale control processes may not be appropriate for the small firm, however.

Historical data are, quite often, absent in the new or small enterprise. Sophisticated, quantitative analytic techniques used frequently in large organizations may not be worthwhile for the very occasional usage required in the small firm. This does not mean, however, that all control techniques are inappropriate for entrepreneurial purposes. Interestingly, many chief executives of large corporations feel that effective use of control techniques will foster entrepreneurial spirit. Kirby Warren wrote that a broad interpretation and use of control "could best develop a sense of true entrepreneurial responsibility in subordinates."[1]

The control process is usually concerned with evaluation of short-term results versus projections and plans. It can be equally effective for evaluating long-range plans, as well. The control process also frequently utilizes historical accounting data. The accuracy and effective use of this type of data have recently been questioned by revelations of fraud and mismanagement. Clearly, what was once considered a relatively consistent method for evaluation is only as efficient as the people implementing the process.

This is both a positive and a negative factor for the small organization. Entrepreneurs usually oversee all aspects of the new or small enterprise. There is less likelihood of hiding relevant information from the entrepreneurs because of their personal control of all phases of operations. The necessity of overseeing all aspects of the organization makes it more difficult to properly evaluate all results, however. Rarely is one person capable of understanding the nuances of all functional areas. This means that entrepreneurs must still rely on the verbal explanations of subordinates or outside consultants for evaluation of results in areas outside of their own personal expertise. If not, they run the risk of completely misreading the information that may be available from both internal and external sources.

Ineffective use of such information can negate a well-formulated strategy. As was discussed in the last chapter, planning has to be more than an intellectual process. Proper control techniques can assist in assuring efficient implementation of these plans.

Control Aspects of Planning

Proper formation of plans makes it easier to evaluate performance of those individuals charged with implementing the plan. Since entrepreneurs are typically concerned with implementing new types of strategies and changes, many standard forms of controls are felt to be inappropriate, for their purposes.

As discussed in Chapter 4, the development of a well-rounded strategy can provide benchmarks for the evaluation of future results. The strategy is typically made up of various levels of detail. Top managers should be considering the overall effects of strategic decisions. Evaluation at this level should be concerned with the manner in which short-range and long-range actions tie together to produce consistent results. Other layers of management or employees are more concerned with determining the budgets associated with various actions. These budgets should contain enough detail that personnel other than the planner, who is usually the individual entrepreneur, have a clear idea of what actions are required at what time. Also, all personnel involved with implementation of the plan should know what resources are required at the various stages of the plan. In this manner, everyone should have a clear idea not only of what results are expected at various times, but also what support they should expect.

This is actually somewhat easier in the small organization. There are not a large number of organizational layers present. The people who have to use the data are those who are also gathering it. This insures ready access to control information. It also presents a danger, however. The effectiveness of a system of checks and balances for which management controls were designed is decreased due to most people in a small organization having to evaluate themselves, at least to some extent.

Large firms as well as small firms are always seeking methods to increase responsibility at lower levels of the organization. The concept of decentralization in large firms has been developed to further this process. This has helped to foster the use of entrepreneurs in large organizations. Initially, it was felt that decentralization within the large firm would bring about increased flexibility. As Warren states, "by granting them 'entrepreneurial' authority, it was hoped they would assume a sense of entrepreneurial responsibility."[2] This attempt at forcing entrepreneurial spirit has not been overly successful, however. Many firms, as has been noted earlier, have found it much simpler to search for managers who are already entrepreneurially oriented and place them in charge of growth-oriented divisions with appropriate authority and responsibility.

There is a serious question whether entrepreneurs, running their own organizations, are willing to delegate sufficient authority to encourage subordinates in a similar manner. Decentralization in the large or small firm is simply a method of defining a control process consistent with a desire for delegating authority and responsibility to lower levels. It requires an effective evaluative format consistent with the planning process.

Evaluation and Control

Specifically, good planning aids evaluation through the following control techniques. The first advantage is that variances between budgets and actual results can be readily checked. Obviously, this requires not only detailed budgets and plans, but also well-kept records of up-to-date events and actions. Attention to this kind of detail can help small businesses to overcome problems before they become serious. It can also be an aid in taking advantage of opportunities not previously recognized. All too often we speak of the traps leading to failure. We forget that there are times when entrepreneurs do not foresee the degree of acceptance of a product or service. This can lead to their not being able to take advantage of this demand and subsequently losing control of a potentially profitable market segment.

Objective setting, as discussed earlier, is a key factor in the planning process. This involves more than the general directions, or long-range goals, however. Secondary objectives should be clearly defined to provide criteria for evaluating short-term actions. The secondary objectives should be designed so that they form the basis for specific policy decisions in both the long and the short term. These policies, from a control viewpoint, would include guides for the various functional areas.

Production should have some guidance concerning the trade-offs between quality and costs. Accounting should be able to define allowable variances from budgets for other areas. Marketing should be given guides concerning priorities for different products or product lines. Engineering should be provided with an understanding of its role and the direction its efforts should take concerning development of new products and cost reduction of present products. This list could be carried on to all areas in greater detail, but the concept should be clear. Objectives, and the planning process in general, are designed to provide direction as well as evaluation guides for all areas of the firm. Entrepreneurial managers use planning to transmit their own ideas and values to others in the firm.

The use of secondary objectives to define short-term priorities can provide dangers as well as direction. There is always the potential that, in the minds of subordinates, the secondary objectives may become primary. This can lead to sub-optimization on the part of units within any organization, large or small. Even worse, some methods of evaluation may lead to subordinates placing their own advancement before the best long-term interests of the firm. Steve Kerr has presented an interesting discussion on the potentially dysfunctional aspects of using short-term evaluation methods to measure long-term objectives.[3]

Entrepreneurs may be pressured to follow similar behavioral patterns due to expectations of venture capitalists and other external supporters. The external environment, in this culture, expects rapid results from any enterprise. We are not noted for our patience and willingness to take on long-run commitments without substantial, positive results being shown throughout the enterprise. This factor can lead entrepreneurs, normally impatient individuals anyway, to press for immediate results. These results may come at the expense of long-term success. The managers in the Passport Dinner Club case could develop strategies to produce positive short-term results. They could plan to develop specific segments of the market that eliminate long-run expansion potential. They could also rush the enterprise into operation without a suitable product to offer the public. Consumers may be led to believe they can expect more from their purchase than the Club can provide. While this may well lead to high sales in the short run, it may also lead to disastrous long-term results. The firm may lose customers' goodwill at the very least. It could also have legal action taken against it by regulatory authorities such as has happened to other, similar, organizations for false or misleading advertising. This could lead to imprisonment of the individuals and to closing of the organization, if fraud can be proven.

Behavioral Aspects of Control

Whatever methods are used for control purposes, they must, in the long run, at least appear equitable to those being evaluated. This is one reason why targets should be clearly stated to all those within the organization. They should also be accepted by these "significant others" in the organization.

Entrepreneurs usually have a clear view of their own goals and objectives. That does not mean that they are able to communicate their ideas to others, either inside or outside the organization. As noted earlier, it was demonstrated in the Sea Life Park (B) case that several stockholders were still questioning Tap Pryor's motives shortly before the Park was supposed to open. It had taken that long before the stockholders realized that there was a potential conflict between Tap's research interests and their objectives of securing a reasonable return on their investment from the marine exhibit.

In this instance, there was a perceived conflict between the objectives of a group of owners and the entrepreneur. The owners began to question whether there was any effective control mechanism to assure that their investment would be protected.

In the final analysis, only the top executive who is, in our cases, the leading entrepreneur can give these assurances. The Liberty Bell Furniture cases demonstrate this point clearly. The President of Liberty Bell is projecting an image of competition to most people within his relevant environment. That environment is relying on him to control his organization and see that it operates within the regulatory and legal framework set forth by society. The President has developed a method to overcome these regulations. Without his acceptance of societal norms, the only control procedure that is effective is the judicial system. Even this is questioned in this case, however. The President feels that the most that will happen to him is a minor fine and a soft slap on the wrist. He feels that, since he has been able to get away with his behavior for some time, he will continue to be able to do so. He perceives that his aberrant behavior has been reinforced. Therefore, he will continue with this behavior.

Entrepreneurs also have a preconceived idea of how their plans should be implemented. This carries with it a concept of evaluation and control. As with all strategies, this may not be viewed as the best way to achieve a particular end.

As was stated earlier, the final, evaluative criteria for new strategies involve their acceptability to the critical constituency groups. Typically, what happens is that a process of give and take occurs until all are willing to accept the final decision. Some, or all, of the constituents may be unhappy about the final decision. On balance, however, they feel that the result is the best they can expect. Also, they feel that it is acceptable. No one constituent or group is perceived as gaining at the expense of another. In behavioral terms, the various constituents have reached a balance of interests. They perceive that this is the best result that can be expected. Also, they accept the final decision only so long as they believe that the decision will be implemented in a manner that is consistent with the agreed-upon strategy and expected results.

The last point brings into focus an informal method of controls frequently found in organizations. Anyone who has worked in an assembly line or job shop where output depends on individual speed has seen this process in operation. The relevant, informal groups typically determine the approrpriate work pace for their group. Anyone who exceeds that pace is subtly or not so subtly informed of what is considered an appropriate work pace. If the excessive pace is continued, the group will find ways to "punish" the person behaving in this manner. This frequently takes the form of ostracism or verbal abuse. It may also take the form of physical abuse, if the group feels especially threatened by the unwanted behavior.

The only way to overcome this group behavior is to convince the leaders of the group that the previously accepted norm is no longer appropriate. Entrepreneurs are usually faced with this problem, both inside and outside the organization. They are trying to convince subordinates, competitors, and consumers that there is either a better product or process available. The entrepreneur in the Prescription Services (B) case found that the competitors had banded together to fight the threat of a new form of selling technique. The competition had not accepted the need for change and was retaliating by using their buying strength to get suppliers to embargo the firm.

The same can hold within the firm, as well. Subordinates must be convinced that the new strategy is effective if they are to respond positively. They must perceive that the strategy will benefit them in some manner. This may take the form of expected delegation of responsibility, as demonstrated by the Allen Personnel case, or of improved production techniques, as in the Shalco case series. In any event, the need and process for change has to be accepted by the relevant constitutent groups. If it is not accepted, the groups will perform their own, internal control process to try and stop the change from being implemented. This may be extremely difficult to detect, moreover. The question now becomes one of developing countercontrol methods to detect these and other blocks to successful implementation of strategic change and entrepreneurial actions.

Quantitative Control Methods

Entrepreneurs have to develop formal methods for determining if actions are being implemented properly. Many managers of small businesses take the approach that if there is any money left after paying all bills at the end of the year, the operations have been successful. This is pretty late, however, to find out if the enterprise has been either a success or a failure. The managers would like to know as soon as possible that something is wrong so that remedial action could be instituted.

The accounting profession has developed several methods for detailing poor performance. In most instances, a measure of standard costs and revenues must exist to provide an appropriate yardstick for actual performance. Standard costs are projected for the relevant accounting or evaluation period. This period is analogous to the short run of the economist. It should be that period of time over which changes cannot be made in the cost of production, or in demand.

In many of the cases presented in this book, the various entrepreneurs have prepared projections of expected costs and revenues. In very few of these cases, however, have these same entrepreneurs tried to determine why the projections have not been met or possibly why they have been exceeded. Often the projections fail to consider critical timing considerations. The totals may balance over the course of the year, but if, as usually happens, expenses predate income, the firm may find itself in a short-term cash-flow bind. This could cause the venture to fail before it is able to reach the projected break-even point. Sea Life Park finds itself facing these problems in the (C) case.

The three usual reasons for variances occurring are associated with volume, price, and cost. If the volume of production or sales differs from projections, this will cause a variance in both expenses and revenues regardless of any other differences. This in itself does not necessarily explain all variances, however.

The firm may end up charging a different price than originally anticipated. Tap Pryor eventually changed his pricing policy for Sea Life Park. This resulted in revenues different from those projected. Similarly, changes in the cost of materials and labor may result in variances in projected expenses.

Unfortunately for the entrepreneur, more than one of these effects may be occurring at the same time. The drop in prices charged for annual passes to Sea Life Park led, in part, to an increase in sales. The increased demand more than offset declines in revenues caused by lower prices (which the economists would applaud since total revenues have increased due to an elastic fit between prices and demand). In the same case, costs have risen due to later-than-expected opening of the park. Also, construction costs were greater than expected, leading to higher depreciation figures.

If Tap Pryor simply looks at the overall profit figures, he may be misled as to the reasons for variances from projections. This could lead him to develop suboptimal or even incorrect decisions to counter the variances. The specific methods that have been developed to determine the precise reason or reasons for the types of variances discussed are presented in most standard accounting texts.[4] The details of these methods are beyond the scope of this text, as noted in the preface.

Information and Control

Information must be present and available for any of these control processes to be effective. Entrepreneurs should have properly analyzed the external environment to understand the views of consumers and competitors. Entrepreneurs also should have a thorough understanding of the expectations of subordinates and other managers within the enterprise. This particular kind of information flow must be two-way, however. The objectives of the entrepreneur have to be communicated in a clear and consistent manner to all those constituent groups.

Once this factor has been accounted for, information has to be provided to evaluate whether these objectives are being achieved. This requires an efficient accounting system. The advent of the computer has simplified the task of aggregating information for relevant managers. Use of the computer also helps to distill the available information such that entrepreneurs will not be completely overwhelmed with paper. Fortunately, inexpensive computer facilities are now available to small businesses. These systems have been designed to meet the needs of small businesses, as well.

The information-flow process frequently provides the integrative force within the organization. It permits the linking-pin process, to use Likert's phrase, between the entrepreneur and the environment. The views and actions of the entrepreneur can be made more consistent. To perform this task, however, information must be generated quickly from all the various functions. It must clearly reflect current trends in operations. The trend to point-of-purchase information systems, exemplified by the electronic cash register systems, is moving to this end. These types of systems combine various functions. They provide sales, inventory, pricing, and revenue data to upper-level managers on a continuous basis. This allows entrepreneurs to adapt to changes in the environment rapidly. Since flexibility has long been a strong point of entrepreneurs, this should be viewed as an opportunity rather than a threat. Certainly, large organizations will benefit from the added information flow, as well. The small firm should be able to adapt to the added information much more rapidly, while the large firm may get smothered in it. Information is only as good as the people using it. If the entrepreneurs are willing to adapt aggressively to the added inputs, they will certainly succeed over the slower moving, professional administrators who are bound by the constraints of their larger organizaitons. Once again, we can see that the flexibility of the entrepreneurial venture, one of the major strengths, can be increased through effective management.

Summary

If planning provides direction for the new or small enterprise, control provides the means to assure effective implementation. The control process is of particular importance in entrepreneurial organizations. These types of enterprises usually are involved with new or changed strategies. This increases the chance that problems will occur in the implementation of the strategy.

An effective control process begins with a well-defined set of objectives. This provides the overall direction for the enterprise to follow. It also provides a set of benchmarks against which future actions and results can be measured.

This assists entrepreneurs in explaining their desires to all the relevant constituent groups, as well. The various groups are interested in different rewards and aspects of the enterprise. The control process should be designed to coordinate these diverse interests to achieve the aims of the entrepreneur. This also allows entrepreneurs to evaluate performance in areas outside their own areas of expertise.

The control process requires effective communication within all areas of the enterprise. The different functional areas should be set up such that information flows freely to and from the entrepreneurs. This forces the entrepreneur to analyze the interaction between the various areas. It also forces the entrepreneur to consider what behavioral factors may be involved in implementing actions and information flows.

Too often, entrepreneurs are interested only in their own personal objectives and areas of expertise. Others, both inside and outside of the organization, may feel that these interests are too one-sided. The analysis necessary for effective control can help entrepreneurs to note these imbalances and restore equity, or at least the perception of balance, to the system. This should, therefore, lead to the acceptance of the need for change. The agent for that change, the entrepreneur, will then find the task that much easier.

The control process is made up of formal and informal methods and procedures. The formal procedures developed by quantitative and behavioral scientists should always consider the potential effects on the informal group. This informal-group structure, if ignored, can impede or destroy the plans of even the most effective entrepreneurs.

The control process relies on an effective information-flow procedure. The entire process must be integrated into an analysis of both the internal and external environment. One of the greatest comparative advantages often ascribed to entrepreneurs is their flexibility. Without information and control, they will find it difficult to utilize that flexibility effectively and adapt more quickly and more efficiently than larger organizations.

Readings

The following readings present an overall view of problems and solutions to control issues in various entrepreneurial ventures. The article by Jeffrey Susbauer, "Intracorporate Entrepreneurial Programs in American Industrial Enterprise," traces the problems encountered by large organizations in fostering entrepreneurial programs. The important point noted by Susbauer is that many forms of standard controls prove too constraining for entrepreneurs.

In "Control Methods for Small Business" Donald Reddington relates the control process to the planning process in the small business. Control, as Reddington notes, "provides the communication channel between the decision-making process and operational results."

The two articles on audits and forecasting discuss the necessity of being able to predict and evaluate potential and actual flaws in entrepreneurial plans. B. LaSalle Woelfel, in the article "Financial Audits: A Tool for Better Management," prepared for the SBA, describes how this process has helped small businesses in general, and six in particular. The auditing process is necessary if forecasts are to be properly evaluated.

Harvey Quitel in "Budgeting and Forecasting" demonstrates the various benefits of combining these two areas into the planning process to provide effective direction for the firm.

The final article, "Is Your Cash Supply Adequate?", was prepared by Jack H. Feller, Jr. for the SBA. He provides a detailed method for developing and evaluating income and outflows within a small business. The purpose, he notes, is to help the entrepreneur control growth within the firm.

Essentially, the four articles discuss problem areas associated with the control process when applied to entrepreneurial organizations. The text has noted the necessity for control if planning is to be effective. The readings provide methods for implementing these methods in entrepreneurial organizations.

REFERENCES

1. E. Kirby Warren, *Long Range Planning: The Executive Viewpoint* (Englewood Cliffs, N.J.: Prentice-Hall, 1966), p. 63.

2. Ibid., p. 67.

3. See Steven Kerr, On the folly of rewarding A while hoping for B, *Academy of Management Journal* 18:769-783 (Dec. 1975).

4. For example, see R.N. Anthony, J. Dearden, and R.F. Vancil, *Management Control Systems: Text, Cases and Readings* (Homewood, Ill.: Irwin, 1972).

Intracorporate Entrepreneurship Programs in American Industrial Enterprise

Jeffrey C. Susbauer

The Cleveland State University

This paper looks at intracorporate entrepreneurship program (ICEP) practices in 210 U.S. industrial corporations. The survey summary notes characteristics of such programs, both formal and informal, as well as attempts to highlight and evaluate corporate practices in this area. The paper also explores the factors prompting ICEP development in the U.S. and summarizes the observations of the corporations surveyed about the success and failure of programs.

INTRODUCTION

Evidence suggests that creative abilities are frequently stifled by organizations. Organizational inflexibility and disregard for new innovations/inventions/technology are often cited as one of the prime reasons for the "push" to entrepreneurship. Those who manage organizations, large and small, are neither ignorant nor oblivious to the advantages of retention of skilled innovative employees through mechanisms permitting them to fully utilize and develop their creative ideas within the framework and to the advantage of the existing organization.

This paper summarizes the results of a 1971-1972 survey conducted to evaluate the nature and extent of such practices in American industrial corporations. Though the survey results are now three years old, indications from follow-on contacts and other subsequent research lead to the conclusion that the basic philosophy has remained unchanged though many firms have cut back their efforts in this area due to the uncertain state of the economy.

INTRACORPORATE ENTREPRENEURSHIP DEFINED

An intracorporate entrepreneurship program, or ICEP, is an organization resource commitment which allows company members to act with the same kind of spirit, freedom, and commitment that typify the small, new enterprise.

"Venture management" and an ICEP are substantially the same. They differ primarily in the application and degree of commitment exerted in establishing the program. Venture management is defined as a *formal* establishment of an ICEP; all

Proceedings of Project ISEED, Summer 1975. Published by Project ISEED, Ltd., The Center for Venture Management, Suite 508, 207 E. Buffalo Street, Milwaukee, WI 53202, U.S.A.

venture management is an ICEP, but not all ICEPs can be classified as venture management.

Such programs typically manifest characteristics which enable them to be categorized into two classifications: formal and informal. A *formal* intracorporate entrepreneurship program is an explicit commitment of resources to elicit entrepreneurial behavior within the organization boundaries. *Informal* programs, conversely, are implicit philosophies of internal growth. In both types, the organization is committed to the internal development of new ideas, products, processes, and inventions that may fall outside the scope of present corporate activities. When such ideas are generated, a procedure is available to the innovator to bring the idea before decision makers for recognition and evaluation. However, in the informal program, the commitment is less stable, generally lacks corporate policy sanction, and the firm may withdraw from the commitment more easily than under more formalized structures.

EMPIRICAL EVIDENCE OF INTRACORPORATE ENTREPRENEURSHIP PRACTICES

The research reported here was conducted among 1000 American industrial corporations, drawing a stratified random sample of 250 of the *Fortune* top 1000 firms in America, and 750 other firms of lesser size selected for industry dispersion and comparison with the *Fortune*-listed corporations. Seventy-seven companies responded, and 133 of the smaller firms replied. Of the 210 total respondents, 145, or 69 percent, reported initiation of either formal or informal programs of intracorporate entrepreneurship.

Space does not permit a detailed examination of the respondent company results, but a summary is provided below (see Table 1).

1. ICEP program development is a relatively recent practice, with few companies establishing ICEPs prior to 1965, and the majority establishing programs between 1966 and 1971.

2. Company size and age apparently have little casual effect on the timing of starting an ICEP, but different industries appear to have developed program initiation patterns that seem to be nonaccidental.

3. Older large corporations have adopted ICEPs, but they did so later than some of their younger competitors. In the process, they devoted less resources to their programs, usually adopted informal programs rather than formal programs, and are generally less-well satisfied with the results of their programs than others in their size group if they initiated only an informal program.

4. The most dynamic and successful ICEP activity probably can be found in the more recently-founded large enterprises. Such companies are more likely to establish formal programs than any other class of firm surveyed, and have shown a tendency to adopt ICEPs earlier in their history than any other class of firm studied.

5. Smaller firms established for some years can be considered prime candidates for the infusion of new growth strategies like ICEP. The available data also suggest that they are the slowest to adopt ICEPs.

6. Smaller firms established more recently approximate clearly their larger counterparts in ICEP establishment rates. In some industries, they tend to lead their

Table 1. Profile of Respondent Company Reports of Intracorporate Entrepreneurship Programs by Industry Group Classification and Size of Company

Group number	Industry group classification	Total number All respondents	Small company respondents[2] reporting programs					Large company respondents[1] reporting programs				
			Total number	Formal only	Informal only	Both formal & informal	No program	Total number	Formal only	Informal only	Both formal & informal	No program
1	Instruments	39	33	6	3	12	12	6	0	0	3	3
2	Machinery	18	12	3	3	0	6	6	3	0	0	3
3	ADPE	24	12	0	4	0	8	12	4	8	0	0
4	Controls	25	15	1	5	6	3	10	5	4	0	1
5	Chemicals	8	2	2	0	0	0	6	6	0	0	0
6	Components	16	16	8	4	0	4	0	0	0	0	0
7	Aerospace	15	9	0	3	0	6	6	3	0	0	3
8	Specialty R&D	42	31	6	10	8	7	11	5	4	2	0
9	Misc. Mfg.	23	3	0	0	0	3	20	5	5	4	6
	Totals	210	133	26	32	26	49	77	31	21	9	16
	Percentage		100%	19%	24%	19%	38%	100%	40%	27%	12%	21%

1. Large companies are survey respondents from the *Fortune* 1000 list; they have annual sales in excess of $50 million.
2. Small companies are survey respondents with annual sales less than $50 million.

more bureaucratic cousins, and the rationale for this idiosyncrasy can be traced to a desire to grow at the expense of their slower-moving competition.

7. The companies that are most satisfied with ICEPs are the larger firms that have instituted formal programs. Smaller companies are not dissatisfied with their programs generally, but the strength of their satisfaction and the percentage of firms willing to enthusiastically endorse their programs are less than for large companies. Companies of all sizes are not nearly as impressed with the results of their ICEPs if they have established only informal programs.

8. Newer firms, both large and small, probably have the least need to establish ICEPs of all organizations. However, ther appears to be a distinct tendency for such firms, particularly the larger ones, to view this as sound business practice and they have indicated a very high willingness to invest in these programs.

FACTORS PROMPTING INITIATION OF ICEPs
Research and inquiry into the innovation process suggest that most organizations have more creative people and ideas than can be effectively handled by their current organizational frameworks. Bureaucratic organization forms tend to stifle natural creativity and frustrate the prospective innovator. As a consequence of these factors, it is interesting to note the reasons given by firms with ICEPs surveyed, ranked in frequency of response, citing why they had established either informal or formal programs:

1. A desire to broaden the enterprise base by promotion of internal, rather than external, growth sources.
2. Response to other companies within their own industry having initiated similar programs.
3. To cope with rapidly changing technological advances and to get new products "on stream" faster.
4. To develop and market new products with a perceived commercial potential invented by employees, but falling outside the existing scope of company activities.
5. To attract, retain, and compensate creative talent and creative work.
6. To consolidate activities after rapid growth, which can lead to increasing bureaucratization and lessened efficiency in transmitting ideas to the marketplace.
7. Reorganization to overcome technological obsolescence.
8. A desire to create a spirit of internal competition among organization members.

SUCCESS OF INTRACORPORATE ENTREPRENEURSHIP PROGRAMS
As noted above, such programs are a relatively recent phenomenon in American industrial practice, though new product committees, R & D activities, and suggestion systems have been in existence for decades. Many organizations—particularly those which initiated programs in the late 1960s—felt that it was premature to discuss their endeavors in this area in terms of success or failure.

The majority, however, unhesitatingly felt that their attempt to create entrepreneurially vital activities in their organization had met with more success than

Table 2. Profile of Intracorporate Entrepreneurship Programs by Year Interval Program Started and Type of Program

Group number	Industry group classification	Pre-1960 Formal	Pre-1960 Informal	1960–65 Formal	1960–65 Informal	1966–71 Formal	1966–71 Informal	Totals Formal	Totals Informal	Total small cos.	Total large cos.	Total all cos.
1	Instruments	3	6	6	3	12	9	21	18	33	6	39
2	Machinery	0	0	3	3	3	0	6	3	12	6	18
3	ADPE	4	0	0	8	0	4	4	12	12	12	24
4	Controls	2	0	3	7	7	8	12	15	15	10	25
5	Chemicals	2	0	4	0	2	0	8	0	2	6	8
6	Components	0	0	0	0	8	4	8	4	16	0	16
7	Aerospace	3	0	0	3	0	0	3	3	9	6	15
8	Specialty R & D	0	4	10	14	11	6	21	24	31	11	42
9	Misc. Mfg.	3	2	4	4	2	3	9	9	3	20	23
	Totals	17	12	30	42	45	34	92	88	133	77	210

failure. Of all respondent companies with programs, 70 percent felt this way. Companies which had initiated only formal programs felt more positive toward their programs (87 percent) than companies which had initiated informal programs, regardless of the size of the company, and a greater percentage of larger companies felt that their efforts were successful than smaller companies (82 percent to 63 percent).

Success, of course, can be measured in many ways, depending upon the objectives of the program and its evolutionary development. Among the indicators of success mentioned by the respondent companies, return on investment, reduction in turnover of key employees included in the program, and new product developments headed the list.

Not all companies are happy with ICEPs. Several companies reported having started an ICEP in the early 1960s, only to drop the program in the late sixties. Some respondents, primarily smaller, considered the very notion of a formalized program to foster innovative entrepreneurial activity an anomaly in itself.

Importantly, though tables from the study have purposely been constructed to protect anonymity of respondents, a clear trend emerged in 1971 and later to reduce ICEP commitments in hard economic times, thus confirming a seemingly standard American management practice to cut back on the "frills" during recessionary periods (see Table 2).

CONCLUSION

Can entrepreneurship exist and survive in the large corporation? Can ICEPs survive bureaucratic structures? Is there a viable corporate entrepreneurial phenomenon in American society? The evidence from this survey suggests the questions can be tentatively answered in the affirmative—if the corporation *wants to*, it can do these things. The evidence is far from conclusive, based on performance and action since the survey was taken, that the corporation is *willing* to do this, except in very limited instances, with real formal commitments for the long term.

Intracorporate entrepreneurship programs are neither necessary nor sufficient conditions for revitalizing organizations or keeping vital organizations lively. But they do appear to be a means of self-renewal and growth that are too important to ignore.

NOTES

1. Research reported in this paper was supported by grants from the Center for Venture Management and Cleveland State University. It is fully reported in a research monograph, Intracorporate entrepreneurship programs in American industry (Bureau of Business Research, Cleveland State University, 1973).

Control Methods
for Small Business

Donald A. Reddington

The accountant's goal should be to create and maintain a profitable environment for small as well as large businesses.

To meet the requirements of a highly competitive market, the functions of management have become more sophisticated and demanding. If the owner of a small business desires to survive and prosper in his marketplace, he must adapt to this changing environment. He must develop a flexible management policy that will provide methods to control his business.

Control is the measuring of performance against a plan and the taking of corrective actions necessary to ensure that the objectives of the business are accomplished. It should reflect the nature and needs of the organization concerned. The essentials of good control are:

1. Prompt detection of deviations from objectives.
2. Flexibility in execution.
3. Benefits exceeding their cost.
4. Understanding.
5. Assurance of corrective action.

Basically, two kinds of controls have been established to accomplish these requirements. Accounting controls are mainly concerned with safeguarding assets and ensuring the reliability of financial records. Administrative controls relate to operational efficiency and managerial policies. In this article, attention is primarily given to questions that small-business owners may raise pertaining to administrative controls.

ACCOUNTING SYSTEM

Why are accounting records needed? If an operation is to be successful, adequate and accurate accounting records are a necessity. When a business is not provided an accurate and timely record of its activities, it is operating blindly and the chances of success are limited.

What is the purpose of a good accounting system? A good system provides information on the present status as well as past activities of a business and makes available information necessary for planning operations. A good accounting system contributes to the safeguarding of assets, provides a measure of performance and

---

Management Accounting/September 1973, pp. 15–17, 26. Reprinted with permission.

financial condition, facilitates establishment of credit lines, and enables a comparison of results with those of competition.[1]

What kind of accounting system is most appropriate for a small business? The most efficient accounting system will be determined by the size of the organization, the type of organization, and the kind of business.

The success of a system's design is determined by its ability to economically satisfy the needs and requirements of management. In design, a good accounting system should be:

1. As simple and direct as possible without sacrificing any essential records.

2. Able to produce current information in a form readily available.

3. Useful as a working tool and not as a scrapbook.

4. Tailored to meet specific requirements.

5. Economical in operations to avoid duplication and excessive effort.

6. Equipped with internal checks to ensure that information generated is correct.

The design considerations for an accounting system should include an evaluation of various alternatives: (1) manual systems that include ledger accounting, "write it once" systems, or ledgerless accounting; (2) electric accounting machines; (3) electronic accounting machines or mini-computers; and (4) computer time-sharing services.

The proper training of accounting personnel must be a major consideration. A system is only as good as it is operated. Finally, the information generated must be utilized for its intended purpose.

BUDGETARY CONTROL
What good can a budget do? The small businessman may be unaware that budgetary control is an effective and essential aid to sound business management. A small business still must have a sound policy of budgetary control. The elements that create a foundation for a budgetary control system are that management:

1. Provides a definite business objective.

2. Indicates variance between budgeted and actual results.

3. Assigns responsibility to each segment of the business.

4. Regulates expenditures and prevents waste.

5. Measures performance of policies.

6. Provides a method of predicting cash flow requirements.

7. Develops the need for a system that is integrated with accounting and reporting requirements.[2]

Management's opposition to budgetary control is frequently due to lack of knowledge and understanding. Thus, the accountant has an obligation to educate the small business owners in the effectiveness and value of budgetary control. An effective system of budgetary control should include an evaluation of internal and external factors. Internal factors should include: (1) establishment of objectives; (2) issuance of directives concerning responsibility; (3) assignment of costs as variable, fixed, or programmed; (4) allocation of resources; and (5) documentation and dissemination of information. External factors should include: (1) knowledge of competitor's strengths and weaknesses, (2) knowledge of market conditions as shown through key business indicators, and (3) knowledge of market position.

ANALYSIS OF OPERATIONS

The owner of every small business needs to have a clear idea of his firm's position. Is it making a profit? If so, how much? If not, should it be making a profit? Should its profit be greater? Are costs out of line? At what sales volume does the profit really begin? The proper utilization of break-even analysis provides the answers to these questions and an easy method to predict the impact of a specific decision related to operations. Break-even analysis involves the interrelationships of several variables such as sales volume, margin, and fixed and variable costs. The utlization of break-even analysis permits the owner of a small business to know at a glance whether each day has paid its way and to identify the products that were responsible for the net result.

The specific uses of break-even analysis as a management aid are:

1. Budgetary control.
2. Improvement of volume and mix of sales.
3. Profit control.
4. Pricing policy.
5. Wage determination.
6. Merchandising policies.
7. Assessment of capitalization and expansion.[3]

Break-even analysis provides management with a valuable tool, but its success is contingent upon the adequacy of the accounting system. Thus, the interrelationship of the control methods become more evident.

Another method of operational analysis is the utilization of trends and business ratios; financial information in these forms can be more easily understood and employed. If computed consistently and continuously over a period of time, the results may be used to identify changing conditions of trends with respect to performance. Results of a particular business may be compared with published industry averages as a standard.

The accountants should inform management of the merits and application of operational analysis through the utilization of break-even analysis trends, and business ratios. This facet of the control function is a sound detection device that allows management to be alerted to potential problems.

COST CONTROL

When the attention of management is focused on the profit picture, emphasis is usually directed toward an increase in sales volume. However, the effect on profit can be insignificant if costs and sales volume were to increase at similar rates. The subject of cost control is often neglected and the accountant must ensure it is given proper consideration by the small business owner.

The basic objective of cost control or good expense management is profitable spending for desired results and not merely for the reduction of expenses. Methods for the achievement of that objective are constructive and consistent cost consciousness, timely financial reporting and organization of operations, and assignment of responsibility with delegation of authority. Some aids for attaining cost control objectives are the expenditure budget, an adequate and accurate accounting system, operating ratios, and method studies. Once again the interfacial effect of control methods becomes apparent. The accomplishment of one control depends upon the adequacy of another.

INVENTORY CONTROL

The problems related to inventory are numerous—the solution often proves to be a system of inventory control. Through efficient inventory control, management can maintain a well-balanced stock which will satisfy customer requests, bring greater profits, make purchasing more effective, and minimize the investment in inventory. The mere application of a system of inventory control will not achieve these objectives. Management must perform a careful analysis and interpretation of data generated from the information system, such as the monthly sales forecast, to control stock movement. Thus, the combination of data and sound judgment provides the essentials for inventory control.

Some noncontrollable and semicontrollable conditions that should be considered in determining the policies for inventory control are seasonal stock items and sales promotions, lead time required for vendors and production, safety allowance to prevent out-of-stock items, and inventory carrying costs.[4]

The possible applications of inventory control are as numerous as the needs of business. However, the basic concepts for design of an inventory control system remain fairly standard: (1) nature of business, (2) determination of goals, (3) identification and measurement of uncertainties, (4) development and implementation of the system, and (5) follow-up with revision. A general inventory control system for a small business stratifies inventory items into two groups, high unit cost with low quantity and low unit cost with high quantity. Perpetual inventory records are maintained for high value items to control inventory movement. The low value items are controlled by bin cards, traveling requisitions, or observation. A specific system can be developed by the application of these concepts to the particular business.

CREDIT AND COLLECTION CONTROL

Credit may be defined as the offer of goods or services in exchange for the promise to pay a specific amount at a specified future time. The primary objectives of a sound credit policy generally include an increase in total sales volume, the development of goodwill, the minimization of related costs, and an increase in profits.[5]

Credit Granting

The advantages and disadvantages associated with the granting of credit privileges are numerous, and management should be informed of them.

Advantages

1. Credit sales are easier to make than cash sales.
2. Customers pay less attention to prices.

3. Customers have a tendency to buy more.

4. Customers become steadier due to convenience and accommodation.

5. Customers have a tendency to be interested in higher quality merchandise.

6. Customer are permitted to buy things they could not otherwise afford.

Disadvantages

1. Working capital is tied up, and costs are introduced that relate to credit investigations, maintaining accounts, billing customer, and collecting payments. These costs may result in borrowing of money and paying interest.

2. Credit may cause customers to overestimate their ability to pay in the future.

3. Uncollectible accounts are inevitable.

4. Refusal of credit may cause ill will and loss of sales.

5. Customers are more inclined to abuse the privileges of returning goods and having goods sent out on approval.

6. Credit requires merchandise to be priced sufficiently high to cover additional costs attributed to repossession, recondition, and resale.

Policy Development

Another question that should be considered is: How sound is the credit policy? A definite policy must be developed as one of the basic operating principles. The development of a credit policy arises from one of four fundamental policy types:

1. Liberal credit granting as well as liberal treatment in collections.

3. Liberal credit granting pursued by strict collections.

3. Strict credit granting followed by liberal collection treatment.

4. Strict credit granting as well as strict treatment in collections.

The principles of the policy selected must provide a measure of control. The questions to be used in evaluating the related controls are:

1. *Question:* Are new credit customers investigated thoroughly and selected carefully?
   Control: Evaluate the number of new accounts opened monthly. How many credit applications were refused?

2. *Question:* Are credit terms explained and credit limits established for new accounts?
   Control: Analyze limit checks, ratio of customer turnovers, ratio of credit sales to total sales, and changes in volume of credit sales.

3. *Question:* Are collections pursued systematically?
   Control: Review monthly statements and aging of receivables; analyze collection percentage.

4. *Question:* Has the responsibility of enforcing credit policy been delegated?
   Control: Activities related to credit manager should be assigned to one individual.

5. *Question:* Are personnel aware of the credit policy?
   Control: Give an orientation program for new personnel and a sales training program for old employees.

Collection Procedure

The sequel to the establishment of a sound credit policy is adequate control procedures for collections. Most businesses face difficulty with collections at one time or another. Thus, a collection system is needed that performs a systematic and tactful operation and improves the timing of collections. A business does not want to create ill will nor does it wish to be taken for granted.

The fundamentals for prompt collections are:

1. Use tact and avoid high-pressure techniques.
2. Prevent accounts from exceeding credit limits.
3. Keep customers available to make new purchases by having prompt collections.
4. Keep informed of each account that is past due or beyond its credit limit.
5. Never allow debtors to take their time to pay or it will be harder to collect.

The collection process should be planned so execution is orderly and regular. The series of steps and applications is:

Step	*Application*
1. Remind customer	1. Monthly statement
2. Request response	2. Telephone call or personal visit
3. Insist on payment	3. Collection letter
4. Final action	4. Legal action

The owner of a small business should have methods available to control collection activities. Techniques for control, applied on a monthly basis, would include changes in accounts receivable balances, collection percentage, accounts receivable turnover, changes in volume of collections, number and amount of delinquent accounts, aging of accounts receivable, and write-offs of bad debts.

TAX AND ESTATE PLANNING

The owners of small businesses frequently lack knowledge of taxes and, as a result, fail to provide an adequate program of tax planning. The accountant should be concerned with the education of management in matters that relate to taxation and alert to recognize a tax problem.

If an owner dies, a business must be provided with continuity so operations may continue. Accordingly, estate planning should be included in the realm of the accountant's concern for small businesses. As a measure for adequacy of continuity, estate planning should:

1. Assure that funds are immediately available to meet the requirements of tax, indebtedness, and administrative expenses.
2. Provide heirs with sufficient income and an equitable distribution of property.
3. Enable an advantageous disposition of the business if the heirs do not take it over.
4. Put heirs in a sound financial situation of they assume the business.
5. Stabilize the credit of the business.
6. Eliminate uncertainties for employees and, thus, maintain good relations.[6]

CONCLUSION

Control is vital because it provides the communication channel between the decision-making process and operational results. The various aspects of control should be sufficiently familiar to the accountant to alert him to the existence of a problem or to provide answers to management's inquiries.

The accountant's goal should be to create and maintain a profitable environment for management. Therefore, the accountant should strive to attain a more professional relationship with management. His part should include roles as an initiator, an advisor, and an analyst. Thus, the accountant must be aware of management's functions so he can be alerted to related problems and take the appropriate corrective action.

REFERENCES

1. H. Earl Sangstor, *Suggested Management Guides,* Small Business Administration, 1962, p. 43.
2. Ibid., p. 44.
3. Ibid., p. 44.
4. Ibid., p. 45.
5. Ibid., pp. 111–124.
6. Ibid., p. 169.

Financial Audits:
A Tool for Better
Management

B. LaSalle Woelfel

C.P.A., and Executive Vice President, St. Edward's University, Austin, Texas

Summary. *In providing a professional opinion about the fairness of a company's financial statements, financial audits help to show up weaknesses in management. Thus they are a tool which owner-managers can use for locating and correcting problems in their small companies.*

This Aid discusses this management tool by presenting the experiences of six small companies. In each, the financial audit played an important role in helping to improve management.

The primary function of the financial audit is to provide the owner-manager and other interested persons, such as key executives, creditors, and stockholders, with a professional opinion about the fairness of his company's financial statements. Such an examination of a company's financial records focuses attention on areas which require management improvement.

The questions which the accountant asks when he makes a financial audit are designed to ascertain whether there are financial deficiencies. Some of them are: Does your firm have an organization chart which shows clearly to whom each individual in your company reports? Are employees in a position of trust—those who handle cash receipts and disbursements—bonded? Are all inventories reviewed periodically and controlled by you or another responsible person? Are purchase invoices paid within the discount period?

The financial audit may also be expanded into areas of management service. In such an expanded audit, additional questions, such as the following, would be asked: Does the owner-manager check periodically to see that all machines are used to the best advantage? Are decisions which are of a routine nature delegated to subordinates so that the owner-manager can concentrate on important matters?

These and other questions were asked in the audits of the six small companies whose case histories follow. The owner-managers of these firms used their audits to improve their management practices. Their experience may suggest areas into which you might want to check.

SAFEGUARDING ASSETS

An independent audit of Tom Mapper's* small company showed that he had not provided the control procedures necessary to safeguard his company's assets. The reason was that, being in business only a few years, he had concentrated all his efforts on production and sales.

Lacking internal control procedures, Mr. Mapper's company was exposed to unnecessary risks. For example, the audit revealed that the company's bank statement had not been reconciled with the company's books for the five months prior to the audit.

Fortunately, Mr. Mapper's employees were honest. Nevertheless, he had run the risk of overdrawing his account. It so happened that he thought he had $540 more than he actually had. This bookkeeping error was revealed only when a reconciliation was made.

To correct this and other weaknesses, the accountant who made the audit urged Mr. Mapper to adopt the following techniques of internal control:

1. Organize his recordkeeping so that only qualified personnel would be responsible for recording financial and statistical data.

2. Assign duties so that no one person would be in complete control of an entire transaction which involved handling cash or other assets.

3. Make sure that his recordkeeping system gave him or another key executive control—a yes or no—over transactions.

---

*All names in *Aids* are disguised.

In adopting these recommendations, Mr. Mapper did not have to hire any new employees. Several had to be retrained, however, in order to do the job in an efficient and economical manner.

IMPROVED CONTROL OF CASH

When the accounts of Streeting and Company were audited, Mr. Streeting learned that his accounting procedures did not provide adequately for the control of cash. This laxity was practically an invitation to his employees to be careless and even dishonest. To plug this possible leak, the accountant offered several recommendations.

First, Mr. Streeting should adopt methods which would get his cash under control immediately. To protect cash receipts, he was advised: (1) to separate the handling of cash from the recording of cash receipts (for example, the cashier should not be the same person as the bookkeeper); and (2) to deposit *all* cash receipts daily.

To control cash disbursements, the auditor advised Mr. Streeting: (1) to adopt the voucher system for all cash payments; (2) to make cash disbursements by prenumbered checks written on safety paper on a check-writing machine; (3) to make one person responsible for preparing vouchers and checks and another for okaying them; and (4) to set up a petty cash fund so that small cash disbursements could be made only after proper authorization.

The auditor also insisted that Mr. Streeting, or someone other than the person responsible for the recordkeeping, prepare the monthly reconciliation of the company's bank statement. Thus a double check on cash receipts would be provided.

Finally, Mr. Streeting agreed to arrange for periodic surprise audits. This procedure was suggested after the independent auditor discovered that Mr. Streeting's bookkeeper had pocketed a cash payment of $85 which a customer had paid on his account.

The bookkeeper concealed his theft by not crediting the customer's account; in the next accounting period, he credited the account with a payment from a second customer—a practice called lapping. Surprise audits would discourage such practices.

RELEASING CAPITAL

Another owner-manager, Bill Polman, found additional working capital as a result of an audit. It showed that he had approximately $28,000 tied up in excessive inventory.

This fact was brought to light when the outside accountant supervised the inventory count. The count confirmed the existence of a declining rate of inventory turnover.

An analysis of purchasing and inventory control procedures led Mr. Polman to set up a centralized purchasing department. To run it, he hired an experienced purchasing agent who standardized certain parts which went into the product. Thus the assistant reduced the company's investment in materials. Mr. Polman also found that he could discontinue the manufacture of several slow-moving product lines which had lost their profit-making potential according to the auditor's cost studies.

Finally, with the help of the accountant, Mr. Polman installed a standard cost system. As a result, he was able to keep track of six important manufacturing costs by reading reports and asking the following questions:

Are *raw materials* being *purchased* at prices above or below standard prices? Are *raw materials* being used in *production* in amounts more than or less than allowed by standard?

Is *labor* being *paid* for at rates above or below standard? Is *labor* being used in *production* in amounts more than or less than allowed by standard?

Were actual manufacturing *overhead expenses* more than or less than the budget allowed at standard hours for work performed? Was there idle *plant capacity*; or was the plant used in excess of standard capacity?

IMPROVED MANAGEMENT

Another example of the benefits which an owner-manager can get from an independent audit is shown in the experience of The Associates Company which was operated by three partners. When the company was 10 months old, they decided they were not making the progress they had hoped for.

Upon the advice of an accountant, who was experienced in their type of business, they learned that you cannot operate a business on "hope." Rather, profit planning requires the establishment of an approximate profit goal based on the factors which contribute to it.

The accountant urged the partners to use a profit-planning tool called Cost-Volume-Profit Analysis. It would help them to work with the four variable factors which contribute to profit-making: (1) sales volume, (2) sales price, (3) sales mix, and (4) costs. The one he worked out for them is shown on page 156.

In all five situations, variable costs are kept the same to make the example easier to follow. Notice that the best profit-making situation is "B" in whcih the number of units sold remains the same but the selling price is increased by 10 percent. The worst profit-making situation is "E" in which the number of units sold remains the same but the selling price is decreased by 10 percent.

Such a Cost-Volume-Profit Analysis chart allows the owner-manager to see what will happen to profits under certain conditions. Thus, he can work out realistic profit goals and make plans to achieve them.

The partners also adopted a budgetary system which helped tighten control over revenue and expenses. Each month, their accountant prepares a budget report which the partners use to isolate and correct trouble spots.

PLANNING FOR GROWTH

John Halton, another owner-manager, came up with a solution to a difficult financial problem after he had an outside accountant conduct a financial audit. Periodic deficiencies of cash were making it increasingly difficult for Mr. Halton's expanding company to pay its current bills on time. Even though sales and production were constantly increasing, Mr. Halton was unable to tell from month to month whether he could pay for raw materials, labor, and other expenses.

This constant lack of cash was the result of poor financial planning, the audit showed. Mr. Halton corrected it by setting up a cash budget to spell out cash requirements. His cash budget, which was prepared by his own accountant for November and December is shown in the box on page 157 of this *Aid*.

Cost-Volume-Profit Analysis for The Associates Company

Situation A = actual (normal) volume		Situation D = 10 percent decrease in volume; no change in price			
Situation B = 10 percent price increase; no change in volume					
Situation C = 10 percent increase in volume; no change in price		Situation E = 10 percent decrease in price; no change in volume			

	A	B	C	D	E
Sales					
1,000 units $4.00	$4,000				
1,000 units $4.40		$4,400			
1,100 units $4.00			$4,400		
900 units $4.00				$3,600	
1,000 units $3.60					$3,600
Variable Costs					
1,000 units $2.00	$2,000				
1,000 units $2.00		$2,000			
1,100 units $2.00			$2,200		
900 units $2.00				$1,800	
1,000 units $2.00					$2,000
Marginal income	$2,000	$2,400	$2,200	$1,800	$1,600
Fixed costs	1,000	1,000	1,000	1,000	1,000
Net income	$1,000	$1,400	$1,200	$800	$600
Net profit rate	25%	31.8%	27.3%	22.2%	16.6%
Break-even sales [(Fixed costs divided by marginal income) × sales]	$2,000	$1,833	$2,000	$2,000	$2,250
Profit on investment of $10,000 in company	10%	14%	12%	8%	6%

This budget helps Mr. Halton to determine the amount of cash he expects to flow into and out of his business each month. If his budget forecast shows a cash deficiency, he arranges for a bank loan.

After Mr. Halton got his short-term cash problem under control, he began to think about the long-run possibilities of his business. The long-range plan which he and the accountant developed included seven steps:

1. Define the basic philosophy of the business (in Mr. Halton's case, making quality metal products and growing with the economy).
2. Determine and rank objectives and profit goals.
3. Set up programs and plans to attain these goals.
4. Reorganize administrative functions in order to carry out programs and plans.
5. Train present employees and hire additional qualified ones as needed to achieve programs and plans.
6. Provide employees with the facilities necessary for doing their work.
7. Supply the operating and capital funds necessary for achieving objectives.

DECIDING THE ORDER OF ACTION

The last story also deals with growth but in a small company whose owner-manager, John Site, has learned that orderly expansion can be a way of life. He tries to reach the following growth objectives in his five-year-old company: (1) increased earning power, (2) increased assets, and (3) improvement in trade position.

In making long-range plans for these goals, Mr. Site has learned certain ground rules, such as deciding on how to finance expansion. He can get funds from internal sources, such as profits retained in his business, or from external sources, such as a loan. Over the years, audits have helped him decide that the best method for him is plowing profits back into the business.

Another ground rule which Mr. Site learned is deciding which part of an expansion program should come first. He planned to add new product lines, to replace machinery and equipment, and to build a new plant.

To determine which he should do first, Mr. Site uses the following tests:

1. Which proposal promises the best rate of return on capital invested (anticipated profit divided by capital employed)?

2. Which proposal will most quickly recover through total cash flow (profits plus depreciation) the capital outlay?

In this manner, he is able to plan, administer, and control his expansion program. Thus in an orderly way he turns plans into assets on his company's balance sheet.

Mr. Halton's Cash Budget
(For November and December)

	November	December
Cash sales	$10,000	$12,000
Collections on accounts receivable	20,000	25,000
Other cash receipts	2,000	2,000
Total	$32,000	$39,000
Payments for merchandise	$10,000	$12,000
Payments for expenses	15,000	16,000
Other cash payments	1,000	1,000
Total	$26,000	$29,000
Cash increase (decrease) for month	$6,000	$10,000
Cash balance at start of month	4,000	10,000
Cash forwarded to succeeding month	$10,000	$20,000

THE STARTING POINT

In thinking about how you might use the experiences you've just read about, keep in mind that the financial audit can well be the starting point for improving operations as well as financial management. Often trouble spots which a financial audit shows up are merely symptoms of management weaknesses, for example, buying more inventory than is needed or continuing to carry a product that is no longer profitable.

You will want to look behind the figures to see what is involved in sales, production, plant maintenance, and so on. Such an examination can be helpful to correcting the source of the trouble.

Budgeting and Forecasting

Harvey B. Quitel, CPA

INTRODUCTION—THE NEED FOR DIRECTION

A *Time* magazine article in 1966 reported: "Today, the President does not consider the budget just a report on spending or an accounting of his stewardship, as it once was, but a powerful tool for controlling the whole government and a potent instrument for manipulating the economy."

Whether we speak of organizations the size of the U.S. Government, giant corporations, medium size companies, or the so-called small business, one thing is prevalent—the need for direction. The toll taken on small businesses since the late sixties indicates that planning and control are just as critical to small concerns as to larger organizations and institutions.

During the "good times," from World War II until the late sixties, running a successful and profitable small business seemed to be a cinch, almost automatic. Management of many small businesses made money in spite of themselves. But along came the days of reckoning, and the rough and unpredictable economy separated the men from the boys. Many small companies had no direction, no plan of action, no coordination of activities, no means of controlling operations. As a result, many were forced out of business.

There is probably no need to further stress the importance, necessity, and benefits of an efficient system of budgets and forecasts in small businesses to the financially-oriented readers of this periodical. What should be stressed, however, is the tremendous gap between the theoretical and practical approach to the problem of budget installation and operation.

The incorporation and operation of a budgetary system for purposes of planning and control is probably made more difficult in smaller companies than in larger ones because of two very important factors:

1. Availability of necessary funds and trained personnel in smaller businesses is usually less than in larger ones.
2. A lesser degree of sophisticated financial thinking among top and middle management of smaller businesses than in larger ones.

SELLING THE CONCEPT—THE CRITICAL TASK

The most critical and difficult task of a chief financial officer of a small organization is that of selling the budgeting and forecasting concept. The chief financial officer must convince top and middle management of the need for direction; the need to plan and control the future of the business in order to maximize profits, achieve growth-oriented goals, and in some cases merely to survive.

Long-term profit maximizing is the primary goal of successful management. Other objectives, such as growth, and responsibilities, such as to employees and

Pennsylvania CPA Spokesman, October, 1972, pp. 12–14. Reprinted with permission.

customers, often are emphasized, but long-run profits are essential for survival. Budgeting and forecasting help plot the future profit course. Budgets are formal expressions of managerial plans. They are targets that encompass all phases of operations—sales, production, engineering, distribution, and financing.

Budgeting is too often considered to be a mechanical exercise; however, the budgetary system relies more on the human elements than accounting techniques. The success of the system depends upon its acceptance by the personnel who are affected by the budgets. Attitudes ideally should be sympathetic, cooperative, and cost conscious.

Budgets focus attention on departmental responsibility. The natural reaction to restriction, control, and criticism is resistance and self-defense. The job of education and selling is extremely important. Many managers feel budgets represent a penny-pinching, negative pressure. They do not accept the idea that, properly utilized, the budgetary system is a tool for establishing standards of performance, for providing motivation, for gauging results, and for aiding management to advance towards its objectives. The budget technique in itself is free of emotion; its administration, however, is often packed with trouble. A major function of the budget is to communicate the various motivations that already exist among management so that everyone can see, understand, and coordinate the goals and drives of the company.

The importance of the human aspects cannot be overemphasized. Without a thoroughly educated and cooperative management group at all levels of responsibility, budgets are a drain on the funds of the business and are a hindrance instead of a help to efficient operations. A budgetary program per se is not a remedy for weak managerial talent, faulty organization, or a poor information system.

A system of budgets and forecasts for small businesses need not be as elaborate as those used by some larger corporations or as outlined in certain financial textbooks, but some planning and control is useful to any size business. Many managers claim their businesses or particular responsibilities make budgets impractical for them. Yet one can nearly always find at least some companies in the same industry that use budgets. Such companies are usually among the industry leaders and they regard budgets as indispensable aids. The point is that managers and businessmen must grapple with uncertainties with or without budgets and forecasts. Budgeting makes the grappling more effective, and the benefits from budgeting nearly always exceed the costs. This picture is very difficult to present to certain businessmen who still believe that only selling and production people contribute to profits.

BUDGETARY SYSTEMS—AN OVERVIEW
Budgets are basically forecasted financial statements which may span a period of one year or less, and in cases of capital budgeting for plant and product changes up to ten years or more. To assure communication and agreement of corporate goals, an organization should ideally have a master budget which would consist of two major units: (a) an operating budget and (b) a financial budget.

The operating budget should include the sales forecast or budget, the production budget, and various operating expense budgets. The financial budget should consist of the cash budget, budgeted balance sheet, and budgeted statement of sources and disposition of funds.

Long-term budgets, often called capital or facilities budgets, are not directly part of the operational and financial budgets but should always be considered as part of the master plan.

The most important aspect of making a budgetary system work is the analysis—the comparisons of planned performance with actual performance. Too many times this after-the-fact analysis is not given the attention it should receive.

The investigation of budget variances and deviations should be the line manager's responsibility. The controller or some other high ranking financial manager should also be directly involved, but the actual preparation of the various cost center budgets and review of variances should be the ultimate responsibility of the individual responsible for the cost center.

Ineffective budgetary systems are characterized by the failure of management to develop and use budgets to the fullest potential. Specifically, budgets are many times used only for planning purposes. The real benefits from budgeting lie in the quick investigation of deviations and the subsequent corrective action. Budgets should not be prepared if they are to be ignored or improperly applied.

Accounting formalizes plans by expressing them in the language of figures as budgets. It formalizes control by performance reports, which compare results with plans and spotlight exceptions. These reports spur investigation of exceptions and then operations are brought into conformity with the plans or the plans are revised. This is an example of management by exception, which means that the executive's attention and effort are concentrated on the important deviations from expected results. Such a system reflects the needs of management who want their attention directed to unusual situations and who do not want to be bothered about the smoothly running phases of operations.

Well conceived plans incorporate enough flexibility or discretion so that the manager may feel free to seize any unforeseen opportunities to improve efficiency or effectiveness. It is very important to realize that the definition of control as conformity to plans does not mean the management should rigidly and blindly adhere to a pre-existing plan when unfolding events indicate the desirability of actions which were not specifically thought of in the original plan.

SALES FORECASTS—THE STARTING POINT

The sales forecast is the starting point for the preparation of budgets. Just as accounting and financial people have the reputation of being negative, conservative, and pessimistic personalities; sales and marketing people have the reputation of being positive thinking, optimistic types. Management should beware of unreasonably high sales forecasts and projections. It seems that the closer in time projections get to becoming actual results, the smaller become the sales forecasts. Incurrence of cost naturally correlates with production activity. Activity, in turn, depends on expected sales. The sales forecast is the foundation for putting in writing the entire business plan.

The term "sales forecast" is sometimes distinguished from "sales budget" in that the forecast is considered to be an estimate or prediction which may or may not become the budget depending on whether management accepts the figures as being realistic and objective. Preparation of a sales budget or forecast which is attainable and realistic is a critical point in the budgetary process.

There are many variables which must be considered in establishing accurate forecasts. Some of the more important considerations are past sales statistics; general economic and industry conditions; market research studies; pricing policies; competition; advertising and sales promotion; quantity and quality of sales force; production capacity; seasonal variations; and relative productive profitability.

An effective aid to accurate forecasting is to approach the same goal by several methods; each acting as a check on the others. For example, a company may have the entire sales force, as a group, come up with a prediction for a particular period. At the same time, sales management may prepare a forecast independently using a more or less statistical approach involving trend, cycle projection, and correlation analysis. Finally, all top officers including production and financial officers may use their experience and knowledge to project sales on the basis of group opinion. This type of joint involvement by a large group of responsible and pertinent people should help zero in on a set of realistic figures which are so very important to the system. An accurate and meaningful end result is very much worth the effort.

PROBLEMS OF BUDGETING—DEBATABLE QUESTIONS

The key point of this article is that budgeting, which should theoretically be considered as an important and necessary management tool for small businesses as well as large, is crammed with practical problems. The reason for most of the practical problems is that budgeting rests on principles which have more in common with concepts of human relationships than with rules of accounting. The financial executive probably faces his greatest challenge in his attempts at educating and selling budgeting theory and concepts to his management associates.

Many pertinent questions and problems, most of which have no definite clear-cut answers, must be dealt with using all of the executive's prior training, experience, education, and resources. For example:

• Should two sets of budgets be employed—a "liberal" one for lower level use and a "conservative" one for use by higher level management?

Perhaps the justification for using a conservative or "safe" budget is that it provides a more secure basis for corporate planning, especially with respect to cash availability. On the other hand, advocates of a more liberal approach to the subject prefer a "reach" or "stretch" budget which is designed to induce incentive and possibly to apply pressure to the responsible people. However, somewhere between the two extremes of liberal and conservative is a desirable type of budget which could be labeled "most likely to happen."

• Should the budget be considered a guarantee of performance; does meeting the budget automatically indicate that a good job has been done and does missing it indicate poor performance?

It must be realized that because of many unforeseeable and unpredictable variables which are beyond the control of the responsible persons, actual results which are better, equal to, or worse than the budget cannot be conclusive evidence of the quality of the managerial job performed. Appraisal of performance against budget requires sound judgment and good common sense.

• Should the budget be revised during the year?

Pros and cons on this question most likely would depend on which level of management is answering. Generally, top level management would prefer more rigidity in the system once all the pains have been taken to prepare a realistic budget. Lower level management tends to prefer more flexibility during the period depending on changing circumstances.

- Should incentives be in the form of cash or other tangible compensation?

Proponents of a cash incentive program for meeting or bettering the budget use the analogy of piecework as an effective incentive for workers. They claim that nothing works like money. The fallacies and problems of this reasoning are numerous. For example, the task of setting a completely fair and acceptable budget for this purpose is almost impossible considering the unforeseeable changes in operating conditions. Also, the tendency of a foreman, supervisor, or manager emphasizing budget performance to the detriment of necessary action becomes a distinct possibility.

Arguments supporting both yes and no answers to these questions and others could well be the subjects of many lengthy debates.

CONCLUSION

Perhaps a summary of thoughts for consideration by management of small businesses for purposes of establishing a budgetary system on a sound foundation could be reduced to the following:

1. Establish the system as a means of setting standards of performance, gauging actual results of operations, and guiding management to proper decisions and achievement of goals.

2. Make it well known that the system is not a pressure device to coerce personnel into greater efforts and performance.

3. Integrate the budget system with the overall corporate philosophy and plan. The budget is not the plan; it is the statement of the plan in the language of numbers.

4. Establish the meaning of control; then be sure it is exercised. The budget should not be considered untouchable but neither should it be taken lightly. Managers should be made to understand that budgets will help them control their particular responsibilities.

5. The system must operate within a clear-cut organizational structure. The budget mechanics should be simple and based on common sense accounting which is more oriented to business than bookkeeping.

6. A relentless and continuous selling and educating campaign must be carried out by the top financial people. Active participation in the program by top management must be insured in order to succeed.

Is Your Cash Supply Adequate?

Jack H. Feller, Jr.

Managing Partner, J. H. Feller and Associates, San Rafael, California

Summary. *The amount of cash necessary for financial health and growth varies according to types of businesses and with individual companies. This Aid suggests some of the ways owner-managers can determine whether they have an adequate cash supply.*

The amount of cash can be determined only by careful analysis of the business. To assure an adequate cash supply, the owner-manager needs records on which to prepare meaningful forecasts and reasonable budgets.

Only then can he control and conserve cash so that it will be available at the right time. Only then will he know whether his business will generate sufficient cash or whether he will need to borrow. Included is an adapted budget form which should be helpful in planning for, and keeping track of, the cash supply.

"How much cash does my business need?" is a question which often troubles owner-managers of small manufacturing companies. And rightly so because cash is the fuel which is necessary for operating the business.

The amount of cash which a company needs for profitable operation depends on the company itself because cash requirements vary according to the type of business. The amount which would be an adequate cash supply for one company may well be too small for another.

In thinking about cash needs, many managers use an old rule of thumb. It says that usually a company's cash balance should be equal to at least *one-fourth* of the company's *current debts*. However, if you operate blindly on this rule you may run into trouble.

Another method for determining cash needs is to compare industry ratios and statement studies, offered by trade publications, with your company's finances. But keep in mind that these ratios and statement studies are averages and should not be relied on solely when determining your own company's needs.

Companies have individual requirements and goals which have to be considered in order to ensure profitable operation. You'll need to make your judgment on facts which you can get from your past financial records.

After you have these facts, you'll need to: (1) decide whether your cash supply *was* adequate in the past, (2) estimate your future cash needs, and (3) take effective steps to control and conserve your cash for those future needs.

Courtesy of the Small Business Administration.

TWO KINDS OF CASH

An adequate cash supply for your company should be one which enables you to pay your current operating costs on time and to provide for future expansion costs. Thus you need to think about and provide cash for two kinds of costs.

First, you have to have *working cash*. Funds you use to buy raw materials, to pay wages, and to pay other day-to-day business expenses fall in this category. For most companies, they come from daily receipts—that is, from cash sales and payments of accounts receivable.

Second, you have to have cash for *capital* expenditures—additions to, as well as replacements of, fixed assets such as your plant, equipment, and tools. Such cash may come from either a long-term loan or from daily receipts in excess of working cash requirements. If the latter source is used, it may be necessary to withhold the distribution of profits in the form of cash until enough cash is accumulated to meet the capital requirements.

An owner-manager should have a firm understanding of which portions of his cash he is going to use as capital cash and which as working cash. In his thinking, he should keep them separate. He should realize that cash on hand and in the bank must first be set aside for outstanding obligations. The cash that remains may be used for new capital expenditures if the business warrants them.

A company's cash supply is the amount of money on deposit at the bank. (It also includes undeposited receipts and readily convertible securities such as U.S. bonds and notes.) Except in highly seasonal businesses or in extraordinary situations, it should take care of requirements for working cash. But, a company's cash by itself is not profit because there may be large unpaid debts which can eat up a large checking account balance.

On the other hand, profit—a good net income—cannot be used for additional working cash if it has been distributed to its owners and is no longer available for expenditure. Profit is an importat goal, and you should keep it in mind constantly. However, don't let preoccupation with profit block your vision so that capital cash is not available for growth and expansion.

In providing an adequate cash supply, you should also think of: (1) possible future increases in operating costs because expanded sales will mean bigger bills for labor and raw materials, for example, and (2) possible future increases in your capital expenditures when you have outgrown your present plant and equipment.

PLANNING YOUR CASH SUPPLY

Your planning for an adequate cash supply should be done in three phases: (1) make a forecast, or estimate, of your future sales; (2) set up an operating budget based on your sales estimate; and (3) make a cash budget to show the amount of funds needed in order to carry on your operations.

Besides your basic books on account, the kinds of records you will usually need are: (1) sales records, (2) production cost records, and (3) monthly cash statements. These records help you determine the business (or cash) cycle in your company—how much money comes in from sales, how much goes out for raw materials, and so on. You use these records to provide you with information about your cash needs based on anticipated sales.

Estimate Sales

Sales are the starting point in forecasting the future needs of your business. You make a careful estimate of your sales expectations. You base this estimate on your company's past performance as described in your financial records.

Keep in mind that the past is just a yardstick and does not take into account growth or any plans for expansion. So along with the facts from your records, take into consideration any expected changes in your business. For example, if your sales have increased by 5 percent each year for the past three or four years, you'd expect them to increase 5 percent next year if conditions stay the same. In making sales forecasts, you'll want to try to include some margin for unforeseeable events. For example, what happens if sales drop off 20 percent in the slack season rather than the 10 percent which is normal for your operation?

When you have an estimate of your total sales volume for next year, break it down by months. You'll need monthly figures when you determine what is an adequate cash supply.

Operating Budgets

Once you have an estimate of your sales volume, you can set up a production budget. This budget will project the selling, manufacturing, and overhead costs based on your estimated sales.

In developing an operating budget, you start with your estimated monthly sales figures for the next 6 or 12 months. Figure how much each activity of your business will cost in order to make your expected sales goal. Your records of past expenses will serve as a guide. For example, if you spent $40,000 last year for the raw materials necessary to do $100,000 in sales and expect to do $110,000 in sales this year, you would need to budget $44,000 for raw material—an increase of 10 percent in both sales and raw materials.

You then set a figure for other cash needs, such as labor, overhead, and selling expenses.

Some owner-managers find the advice of their keymen and foremen valuable when they work up operating budgets. These supervisors, for example, help to see that details about their departments are not overlooked.

Prepare a Cash Budget

After you have your operating budget, you are ready to work up a cash budget. It is a plan which shows the cash receipts you expect to take in during a certain period and the expenditures you expect to make during that time. These figures should be on a monthly basis. Prepare a detailed forecast of the amount of cash you expect to take in and spend month-by-month to cover one year.

Some owner-managers who have never budgeted find it easier to start with a 6-months budget. They then use their experience from the first 6 months when developing the budget for the second 6 months. It is also a good idea to make a skeleton forecast for an additional 12 months. In this manner, you will have a plan for the next two years.

In preparing your cash budget, you use figures from your sales forecast and your operating budget. If you've never prepared a cash budget, Table 1 has been adapted for helping you to provide for adequate cash of both types—capital cash and working cash. This *Aid* deals mainly with the latter.

Table 1. Cash Budget (for three months, ending March 31, 19__)

	January		February		March	
Expected Cash Receipts:	Budget	Actual	Budget	Actual	Budget	Actual
1. Cash sales						
2. Collections on accounts receivable						
3. Other income						
4. Total cash receipts						
Expected Cash Payments:						
5. Raw materials						
6. Payroll						
7. Other factory expenses (including maintenance)						
8. Advertising						
9. Selling expense						
10. Administrative expense (including salary of owner-manager)						
11. New plant and equipment						
12. Other payments (taxes, including estimated income tax; repayment of loans; interest; etc.)						
13. Total cash payments						
14. **Expected Cash Balance** at beginning of the month						
15. Cash increase or decrease (item 4 minus item 13)						
16. Expected cash balance at end of month (item 14 plus item 15)						
17. Desired working cash balance						
18. Short-term loans needed (item 17 minus item 16, if item 17 is larger)						
19. Cash available for dividends, capital cash expenditures, and/or short-term investments (item 16 minus item 17, if item 16 is larger than item 17)						
Capital Cash:						
20. Cash available (item 19 after deducting dividends, etc.)						
21. Desired capital cash (item 11, new plant equipment)						
22. Long-term loans needed (item 21 less item 20, if item 21 is larger than item 20)						

CONTROL AND CONSERVE

After you have set up your cash budget, your task will be that of seeing that your company operates within it. If your budget estimates are good, the necessary amount of cash will be available at the right time.

Therefore, the owner-manager must see that his company lives within its sales, production, and cash budgets. At the same time, he must make sure of his supply of cash by seeing that his customers pay their bills promptly and by safeguarding funds after he receives them.

Company procedures should safeguard assets, especially those which are easily negotiable. Only you, or employees to whom you delegate spending authority, should be able to spend cash.

Control procedures should cover every expense item from purchasing to payroll checks. There should be a reasonable explanation for any sizable difference between actual and budgeted expenditure. Where there is, budgets should be adjusted and adhered to.

One of the most obvious ways of safeguarding your company's money is the separation of your personal funds from those of your business. Let your company pay you a salary and show that amount as an administrative expense item in your company's budget and accounting records. Then use a separate bank account for your salary and personal expenses. In paying themselves a bonus, good managers wait until the end of the year and draw from the profits which are left after the needs of their businesses are taken care of.

You may want to keep in mind also that the owner-manager's salary can offer a way to improve the cash position, especially in a fairly new company. By timing the drawing of his pay, he can sometimes keep his cash balance high on critical days in the month. For example, if you pay for raw materials on the first of the month, you may want to draw your salary check around the 15th after funds have come in from several of your slow paying customers.

Your methods for assuring an adequate cash supply should also cover credit which you give your customers. The owner-manager who allows customers to fall behind in their payments creates a drain on his cash balance. In effect, he is financing them when he cannot afford it.

If your need for cash is great around the first of the month, your credit policies should encourage customers to pay you near that time. Offering a discount for prompt payment, in many cases, enables a company to keep its money turning and thus operate with smaller cash balances.

Purchasing offers another way to save money. Teach your people to buy raw materials and other items at the best price. In delegating purchasing, make one person responsible. Thus you can avoid the waste which sometimes occurs when several persons buy items and none knows what the other is doing. Inventory and materials control are important in reducing confusion and duplication.

OVERCOMING TEMPORARY DEFICIENCIES

Even though you plan and control cash, there may be times when income from sales may not be great enough to cover your current bills. The problem: adjusting to a temporarily weak cash supply.

Sometimes you may be able to adjust by rearranging your billing cycle and by tightening your credit limits. At other times, you may need to arrange a short-term loan at your bank.

Usually, it is easier to do such borrowing when you plan for it. When you know ahead that your cash balance will be low at certain times of the year, discuss it with your banker and thus prepare him ahead of time.

A BASIS FOR GROWTH

Finally, maintaining an adequate cash supply is a basis for growth. Many owner-managers realize that it is good business not to distribute all their profits. They plow a large part of profits into expanding the business by using them for capital expenditures such as new machines and equipment.

In order to develop surplus cash which can be reinvested to provide additional profits, a company must, first of all, take in enough to pay its bills including periods when little, or no, money comes in from sales, for example, in a seasonal type of business. When such needs are provided for, the owner-manager can plan for growth.

He may wait until the end of the year to invest surplus cash in a new piece of equipment, for example. Or he may siphon some of it off during the year. Items 20, 21, and 22 in the sample budget in Table 1 of this *Aid* are for your use in planning for, and keeping track of, such capital expense items.

Sometimes a business does not generate surplus cash fast enough so the owner-manager has to get his capital cash by long-term borrowing. He finds that it is easier to get such loans when he has maintained an adequate supply of working cash— one that enables him to build a reputation for paying his bills on time. Such a reputation makes a favorable impression with bankers, especially when they see that the owner-manager has built it by planning his cash supply.

Regardless of how you manage the details of your company's growth, keep in mind that an adequate cash supply is vital to expansion. Plan to keep close watch on your cash position. Inspect it periodically—every week, two weeks, every month— according to the best time for your business. In this manner, you can make sure that cash is coming in, as you expected, and being used, as you planned.

Suggestions for Further Reading

Brown, J. Designing an accounting system for a small business. *Management Accounting* 56: 27-30 (June 1975).

Buerke, E. A. Small-business accountant. *Management Accounting* 54:51-52 (Nov. 1972).

Drews, A. L. Bookkeeping for a small business. *Management Accounting* 57: 33-34 + (Oct. 1975).

How can small firms put cash to work? *Industry Week* 189: 60-61 (April 26, 1976).

Penick, W. C. Small business tax reform. *Journal of Accountancy* 141: 86-89 (Jan. 1976).

Rhoads, J. L. Tax considerations for small business. *Management Accounting* 56: 20-24 (Jan. 1975).

Todd, J. T. Small Business control systems in a dynamic environment. *Small business Management* 14: 1-7 (Oct. 1976).

Welsh, J. A., and J. F. White. Keeping score in business: an accounting primer for entrepreneurs. *Journal of Small Business Management* 14: 29-40 (Oct. 1976).

6
Environmental
Forces

Introduction

An article in a recent edition of a small-town newspaper discussed the effects on small businesses of a large rise in the cost of insurance. The article related incidents from actual situations. The conclusion to be reached by many would be that small businesses are much more restricted in their ability to adapt to such external factors as insurance-rate increases than are large firms.

In the definition of perfect competition used in economic theory, the individual firm has no measurable effect on its external environment. Basically, the external environment is treated as totally external; it is a "given" that can only be reacted to but never affected.

There are few people who believe that the concept of perfect competition actually exists. In many instances, however, small firms fit the model of perfect competition much more closely than large firms. Small firms are frequently in the position of having to react to environmental factors. Large firms, in contrast, often have the ability to affect, if not shape, their environment.

Small firms also are more likely to be confined to a particular region. Sales, promotion, services, personnel, and other factors are frequently related to the immediate environment. This environment may not necessarily reflect aggregate conditions of the nation as a whole. In periods of economic recession, some regions of the country are prosperous. Similarly, in periods of prosperity, there are usually pockets of recession. Within the region where the small business operates, the environment may possibly even be affected by the firm.

Economic Factors

Entrepreneurs often feel that they are at the mercy of an economic environment that is beyond their control. They feel that since their organizations are small and cannot affect the economy, they need not consider the economy in forming plans for the future. This kind of fallacious reasoning can lead to haphazard results such as those experienced by many new, small firms in the electronics industry. Many entrepreneurs started their own firms in the latter 1960s only to run into a recession that reduced the need for outside suppliers on the part of the large electronics firms. Many of the firms that survived the recession failed to foresee the upswing in the economy, and were unable to take full advantage of improved demand once it occurred.

As stated earlier, not all sectors of the economy are affected equally by national economic factors. Conditions in some geographic regions may run counter to national trends either on a consistent or a haphazard basis. The entrepreneur must understand the basis for the strength or weakness of the local economy in order to predict future trends for the region. A regional economy based on the manufacture of luxury goods will probably be adversely affected by a recession. An entrepreneur seeking to form or expand a venture catering to those manufacturers would not find a declining economy a very hospitable environment. A firm supplying goods or services to manufacturers of automobile replacement parts may find that same declining economy a fortuitous time to start or expand operations. The auto replacement parts industry is usually considered an example of a counter cyclical industry. Its fortunes react opposite to the economy as a whole. There are still other industries that react independently of the economy. Some goods, salt being an example, are in demand during all phases of economic activity.

The task for the entrepreneur in planning new or expanded ventures is to determine the proper time frame appropriate for his actions. That time frame should then be matched, as much as possible, to economic trends in the relevant environment in which the entrepreneur expects to operate.

Tap Pryor, the entrepreneurial force behind the Sea Life Park venture, realized that Hawaii was in a period of long-term economic growth. This was his relevant economic region. He felt confident of the overall success of the venture. He failed, however, to note precisely the short-term, seasonal fluctuations in the economy. He had not allowed sufficient slack in his plans to open the park and, as a result, lost part of the tourist season because of a late opening. This led to serious cash-flow problems during the first year of operations.

Seasonal factors of demand are common occurrences in many industries other than tourism. In most instances, these factors are fairly well known. What often has to be determined is the severity of the fluctuations caused by these seasonal factors. These seasonal fluctuations can aggravate broader-based economic trends. Entrepreneurs, therefore, have to time their ventures so that the various economic forecasts provide an environment that is amenable to expansion or initiation of the ventures.

Technological Factors

It has been said that the rate of technological advance is increasing at an increasing rate. The question of the ability of society to adapt to these changes has been discussed in both general and technical literature. In much of the general literature it has been assumed that large corporations are coming to control this source of change and that through that control they are becoming an even more dominant force in our economy.

The advantage that large organizations have in controlling technological change is their size and the amount of resources they have available to apply to research and development. This same advantage, however, turns out to be one of the major factors that has held them back from taking advantage of change. The sheer size of these firms gives them an inertia that makes it difficult to adapt to change rapidly.

Small firms, on the other hand, are not burdened with this inertia. Entrepreneurs possessing an appropriate tolerance for risk are often the most likely to apply the resources available to them to the new technological advances. As the readings have noted, people do still invent their way to wealth and fame. Entrepreneurs do not have to be inventors to be successful, however. They simply have to be able to present the inventor with the resources necessary to match the product with potential customers.

There are large numbers of inventors who are interested more in developing new ideas than in developing market strategies. The key is for the entrepreneur to be available with the right package for promoting the idea. This requires a knowledge of a particular field of technology. It also requires perseverance and a degree of luck.

The key is that the entrepreneur must be able to forecast technological advances in a relevant field. Potential future advances, not just the current state of technology, must be anticipated. Unfortunately, this means that the entrepreneur must keep track of seemingly unrelated technological advances. Many an entrepreneur has developed a strategy for a technological advance only to find it become obsolete by a technological development in another field.

Recent developments in the watch industry bear out this problem. The traditional manufacturers have lost a sizable share of their market to the manufacturers of integrated circuits. Firms like Texas Instruments have applied advances in solid-state electronics to produce accurate, inexpensive watches that have proven extremely popular with consumers. Firms like Timex have been slow to realize the threat that this seemingly unrelated innovation poses for the industry. Many industry analysts feel that a complete restructuring of the industry is taking place.

The ability to match technological advances with potential markets has been an entrepreneurial trait of long standing in our society. The small business is more flexible in its ability to take advantage of innovation. It is this flexibility, coupled with the entrepreneur's risk-taking capacity, that has led to the development of many new products in the face of heavy competition from large, entrenched organizations. This combination has frequently provided the vitality necessary to maintain the economy on a forward track.

Social Factors

Economic changes are frequently the result of changes in the values of society. An ability to forecast social trends can aid the entrepreneur in forecasting economic trends as well. More important, however, is that entrepreneurs may be the members of the business community most likely to be able to interpret the true direction of social values. The socialization process that goes on in large organizations works against anything but conservatism among managers in the upper level decision-making ranks. This ability to interpret, or possibly predict, social change may help to explain why entrepreneurs have provided successful innovations in large as well as small business, as discussed previously.

The entrepreneur typically has less of a stake in the status quo. Frequently, fewer resources are tied up in assets devoted to long-term production of potentially obsolete services or products. This decreases inhibitions and prejudice concerning new directions and demands on the part of society.

Another advantage in being able to predict social change lies in the areas of regulation and legislation. Social and economic changes usually result in formal, legislative changes. Those entrepreneurs who can predict how social trends are likely to show up as governmental regulations are far less likely to waste resources in nonproductive efforts.

Problems relating to regulation are becoming increasingly important, moreover. This particular type of nonproductive effort cannot be totally eliminated. The spread of governmental paperwork required of business is pretty much unavoidable. The ability to predict and understand regulatory trends can lessen the impact of these factors.

Those people who were able to predict the enactment of antipollution legislation from observing subtle changes in values concerning the environment could have made decisions based on these predictions during the start-up of new ventures. The prediction of antipollution legislation prompted some entrepreneurs to develop methods of satisfying the regulations in advance of their passage. They were able to take advantage of a new market demand by understanding the relationship between social and legal changes in society. Moreover, they were willing to take advantage of that knowledge.

Competitive Factors

Thus various factors combine to help define the competitive environment in which a firm must operate. Frequently, the difference between an entrepreneur and an administrator is the view taken of that environment. One source notes that "some managers dominate the organization, seek bold opportunities and quickly decide to enlarge their empire."[1] This characterizes the entrepreneur. The entrepreneur views the environment as presenting opportunities for new or expanded ventures. The administrator, on the other hand, views these same environmental characteristics as providing constraints on decision-making ability. The administrator takes a reactive role to the competitive environment, whereas the entrepreneur takes a proactive role.

An understanding of the manner in which these environmental forces relate to each other can help entrepreneurs in planning successful ventures. Recently, the oil industry has been viewed as highly concentrated, with little competition between the dominant firms. There are segments of the industry where competition is fierce, however. This competition still takes the form of pricing and service, particularly at the local level.

The automobile industry, on the other hand, takes great pains to maintain an air of competition. General Motors even competes within itself to maintain this posture. Regardless of these gestures, however, few people seriously believe that American Motors provides a serious threat to the long-run viability of General Motors. The simple fact that the long-run market share enjoyed by General Motors has remained remarkably stable over the years belies the competitive posture of the industry.

In both types of situations, however, there may be significant opportunities for the entrepreneur. General Motors, because of its size, finds it inefficient to produce vehicles for relatively small markets. This leaves the way open for a firm to produce Checker cars as cabs, primarily, but also as private transportation vehicles. Checker found its niche as a producer and filled a demand, even if it was a relatively limited one.

There is frequently an unfilled market niche waiting to be found in most industries. The task of the entrepreneur is to find that niche and provide the appropriate product or service in a manner that gives the firm a comparative advantage over potential competitors. In many instances, that advantage involves a lower price. The first firm into a given market has the opportunity to derive significant experience in that industry. This experience can lead to cost reductions which will allow that firm to provide its product at a competitive price and still earn a profit. The electronics industry understands this concept well. Innovations in solid-state electronics provide the first firm that introduces a product or service with the opportunity to slide down the experience curve the fastest. Any firm trying to catch that firm must make extraordinary expenditures to make up for lost time.

Price is not the only form of competitive advantage, however. Technology itself may be an advantage. That organization maintaining sole possession of a form of technology, whether in the product or in a process, can create an artificial barrier to competition. Polaroid Corporation has relied on this form of advantage throughout its corporate lifespan.

Service, brand loyalty, brand proliferation, and advertising also provide forms of comparative advantage. Not all are appropriate for any given market, however.

Another task of the entrepreneur is to find that mix of factors that will give the venture an edge over present or potential competition.

Forecasting Trends

None of these factors mentioned above changes spontaneously. The reason why many organizations fail to anticipate these changes is that managers view change as a disrupting influence. They fear that change is another challenge to their position in a relatively stable bureaucracy. The organization provides the professional administrator with anonymity and strength through numbers. Environmental changes that threaten the stability of the organization tend to be opposed by professional administrators.

Traditionally, a strength attributed to the entrepreneur has been a willingness to take advantage of environmental changes. The entrepreneur possesses no great loyalty to an organization. Frequently, quite the opposite is true. The entrepreneur views entrenched bureaucracy as a potential enemy. The ability to adapt to environmental change, therefore, provides a comparative advantage to entrepreneurs and small businesses.

The major problem faced by the entrepreneur is to know early enough when changes are taking place. This requires a knowledge of the various forecasting techniques available in modern society.

Economic-forecasting methods are both numerous and readily available. While not totally reliable, they do give reasonably accurate estimations of broad-based directions in the economy. Some even help to predict turning points in specific subsectors of the economy, as well as general economic trends. The Index of Leading Indicators, for example, is helpful as a predictor of general economic conditions. Indicators such as the number of housing permits issued can also be used to predict trends in specific industries, in this case housing and construction. They can also be used to predict events in related industries such as home furnishings and heavy appliances.

Broad-based technological indices are also becoming more readily available. They attempt to aggregate innovation for society as a whole. Better indicators, however, are simple relationships of the number of innovations, as related in trade journals, since these would be specific to a particular industry.

Legislative trends are far easier to predict. Given the proclivity for politicians to talk almost any issue to death, new laws and regulations can frequently be predicted well in advance.

The area where forecasting is much more difficult is the social area. Value shifts are slow, and often quite subtle. Some institutions, such as the University of Michigan, are attempting to provide such indicators. That school currently has developed an index of consumer confidence and attitudes to assist the business community in predicting overall demand. Social values, however, are the most difficult to predict at present. This is unfortunate in that values are frequently leading indicators in the other key areas discussed above. This is the one area where entrepreneurs appear to have an edge over other managers. The entrepreneurs seem to be able to sense changes in social values earlier than most individuals. It could be, as noted above, that they are simply less fearful of social change than others, and are more willing to view change as an opportunity rather than a threat.

Availability of Resources

A factor that is not often considered critical by entrepreneurs seeking to start new ventures is the availability of resources. Since the entrepreneur feels that the resource requirements of the new, frequently small, venture are relatively inconsequential, there is no need to consider this a problem. Unfortunately, resources are a potential barrier to entry in some industries.

Many large firms use their control of resources as a means of decreasing competition in an industry. Through such control, they can legitimately protect their dominance by shifting profits from one level of the organization to another. An integrated firm can afford to charge all users of its resources, including its own manufacturing or sales divisions, a high price in the face of low consumer demand. The vertically integrated firm can make profits on any or all of the parts of the distribution process.

Few small firms are endowed with this luxury, however. For this reason, the entrepreneur must be certain that resources are available in the quantity and at a price which gives at least a probability of success. This often means treating the suppliers fairly as well as being treated fairly by them. The Vail Industries case presents a prime example of a situation where a small venture and its large suppliers existed amicably by treating each other in this manner. In periods of slack demand, Vail continued to accept as much product from its suppliers as it could possibly absorb. Vail did not try to play one supplier off against another simply to gain a temporary price advantage. This treatment was repaid during the period of the paper shortages of 1973-1974. Its major suppliers continued to provide Vail with its fair share of raw paper. Often Vail was able to secure scarce goods for valued customers when all other sources proved futile. The Vail situation demonstrates the necessity for securing and maintaining stable sources of supply.

Summary

The external environment provides the greatest source of opportunities for entrepreneurs. They do not view the environment as a threat, but as a means to ensure the success of new or expanding ventures. The critical factor is a balanced knowledge of the various factors facing the entrepreneur.

Environmental factors are often considered separate and discrete from each other. They are highly related, however. Changes in social values frequently show up later as economic and legislative changes. An ability to forecast trends in any of these areas can provide the entrepreneur with the comparative advantage that often spells the difference between success and failure.

Knowledge of the important, relevant factors in the environment can help to assure a stable source of supply for the entrepreneur as well. Resource availability is not guaranteed simply by asking for it. This is often the critical factor used by large organizations to maintain their own dominant positions.

The ability to integrate an understanding of these various factors is essential to good planning. Those entrepreneurs who realize this have overcome one of the biggest barriers to the success of new ventures.

Readings

As we noted, the external environment provides both opportunities and constraints for enterpreneurs. In the Forbes article, leading off this set of readings, it is noted that all the opportunities have not yet been taken. The article relates how six entrepreneurs perceived unfilled needs in the environment and proceeded to provide products or services to fill those needs.

Albert Shapero, in his article "Entrepreneurship and Economic Development," explores in depth the interaction between entrepreneurial ventures and the economies of localized regions. He traces the phases, similar to Cooper's, of the development of the infrastructure within a region designed to foster successful new ventures. This is important since too often we think only of the national impact of large business. As Shapero, and the text, note, small businesses frequently have at least as great an impact on their own local economy and society.

In the final article, Frank McGee discusses the relationship between "Small Business Enterprise and Governmental Decision Making." As was noted in the text at various points, government regulation is becoming a pervasive influence in all sectors of our economy. McGee notes the many opportunities open to entrepreneurs who are able to predict and adapt to changes in that sector of the environment. Frequently, small firms feel the effects of government actions more strongly than large firms because of the relative impact of these actions compared to their size. This apparent size constraint can be turned into an opportunity since taking advantage of opportunities also has a relatively large impact on the small firm, as noted by McGee.

The articles echo the statement of the text material that the impact of environmental factors should be considered by entrepreneurs during the planning process. Of equal importance, however, is the plea that government, in particular, consider the impact of regulation and legislation on small as well as large business.

REFERENCES
1. Paine, F.T., and W. Naumes, *Strategy and Policy Formation: An Integrative Approach* (Philadelphia: Saunders, 1974), p. 50.

Americans Still Invent Their Way to Wealth

Forbes

The independent inventor is an endangered species. But here are six live ones.

Remember that traditional American type, the ruggedly individualistic inventor-tinkerer? The basement scientist who helped propel the U.S. into world industrial leadership? Men like Edison, Westinghouse, and Bell?

The day of the truly important basement breakthrough is largely past. But the tradition lingers. On the following pages, Forbes talks with half a dozen men who refused to quit and finally made big money through their own inventions.

The odds are stacked against one man working alone. It takes big money to produce something worthy of patenting; the rough *average* is $500,000. No wonder that 80 percent of the nation's 115,047 patent applications last year were assigned to corporations and the Government.

Assuming the loner gets his patent, he now faces the do-or-die step. He must convince someone, usually a disinterested corporation, to make and market his brainstorm. The roadblocks are formidable—legal expenses, corporate resistance to NIH ideas (not-invented-here) and a shortage of venture capital. Plus the 250 invention-marketing firms, often staffed by con artists who merely make big promises and collect big fees (around $100 million a year).

Those who survive are the few who prove to be inventor-entrepreneurs. For the key to success, as our six case studies illustrate, is not how good is the invention, but how good a businessman is the inventor. The inventor must show a corporation how his invention would work in the marketplace as well as the laboratory. Or he must start his own company, where there is more risk, but also a chance for more reward. As four of our six can testify, a big capital gain is better than a little royalty any day.

Disturbing thought: Three of the six inventors *Forbes* found worth highlighting are not *Yankee* tinkerers; they were born abroad and immigrated. Why so? Nobody really knows, but can it be that more and more of us prefer a secure career to the risks of doing our own thing? Is that old spirit of rugged individualism getting ragged? Or does it take a foreigner to realize the unique opportunities in America?

BRAIN DRAINEE

"Call me anything you want," says Dr. Narinder Kapany: scientist, entrepreneur, executive, rancher, artist. But if you pin him down, he prefers to answer to his first love, inventor.

Kapany, a 46-year-old Sikh from India, now toils in one of the technology companies in "silicon gulch," south of San Francisco. Among other things, Kapany

Forbes, August 1, 1974, pp. 46–49. Reprinted with permission.

is the father of fiber optics technology. This involves the passing of light over flexible fibers for image transmission. He spawned the concept as a graduate student at London's Imperial College of Science & Technology in the early fifties. Fiber optics has since yielded a multitude of applications like medical devices for peering into body organs, and promises many more in the future.

Kapany had left New Delhi in 1951 to learn advanced optics, planning to return home to make optical instruments. But once abroad, one thing led to another.

During five years of research at the Illinois Institute of Technology in the mid-fifties, Kapany found that many of his ideas were being shelved outside his laboratory. So he decided to become a doer as well as a thinker. He went west in 1958 to raise money, founded Optics Technology Inc. and took it public in 1967.

Optics Technology marketed a wide range of products: the first flexible tubes for seeing around corners, laser devices for eye surgery, optical filters and other gadgets that Kapany brainstormed and often patented. In 1972 he resigned as chairman.

Now that he has gone on to other projects like teaching at Stanford, tending his ranch and sculpting, Kapany recalls the Sixties as the ideal era for the inventor-entrepreneur. "Venture capital was really venturesome, and in the high-technology field you were walking on water." Alas, he says, the days are now gone when you could put out a press release and then watch the money pour in.

Today the road for the independent inventor is rough. Kapany doesn't blame the bankers for spurning start-ups while stocks sell below book value. He can understand why corporate chiefs are reluctant to embark on the risks of investing in, tooling, and inventorying an innovation in these uncertain times. "But," says the Sikh, who wears a turban as well as paisley shirts, "it's a terrible loss to the country not to create a climate where inventions can be helped to grow."

Kapany has recently set up a small organization to help cultivate a climate for successful invention. He presides over privately owned, Palo Alto-based Kaptron, which turns out invention prototypes for corporate clients in areas of social need such as solar energy and pollution control. Kapany owns 80 percent of Kaptron.

Kapany's humanism shows in his sculpture. One evening in his lab, he saw the potential for art in the inner workings of the little black boxes of fiber optics instruments. Now an exhibition of his lighted glass and plastic constructions is on world tour.

Kapany considers inventing serious business. He calls it juggling mental inventories to produce an answer to technical problems. Inventors, he says, work in jigsaw-puzzle fashion.

Kapany didn't think much of the self-made business back when he was a technician in the laboratory. But how he respects the entrepreneur—and the American way of life. When he visits India today he carries a U.S. passport and is living proof to his countrymen that wearing a turban is no barrier to success here.

PLAYING AROUND
Ask your kids about Chatty Kathy, the talking doll, or Hot Wheels, the dinky racing car, and tell them about Jack Ryan, the inventor. He made a fortune from this child's play.

During the sixties, while consulting for toymaker Mattel Inc., Ryan and his engineers were turning out new product ideas that produced $100 million in toy sales annually. Royalties that he still collects on 95 percent of Mattel's line have made Ryan many times a millionaire.

At Raytheon Corp. in 1955 Jack Ryan was just another bright aerospace engineer out of Yale trying to get the Sparrow Missile off the drawing boards. While a project officer there, he invented a high-powered antenna, installed it in a crystal radio set and sold it by chance at a New York toy fair to Mattel's founders, Ruth and Elliot Handler. The Handlers lured him West to advise on product devlopment. It was goodbye missiles, hello Barbie Doll.

Today Ryan, a mischievous Peter Lorre look-alike, lives with some friendly college students in a huge Bel Air, Calif., estate once owned by silent screen star Warner Baxter. Gadgets abound. Dial the right phone—of the 150—and the lights go on, the garage doors open or the pool fills. There's even a chandelier-rigged tree house for entertaining "special guests."

Now that Mattel has fallen on hard times (*Forbes*, September 15, 1972), Ryan and his 15-man staff have turned to experimenting in optics, chemicals, and electronics. Invention now comes easily because he says it's an intuitive skill you develop like playing a smart game of tennis. To invent a cheap telephone-answering device, Ryan did Edison's work over again with modern tools. Says he: "If old Tom had had teflon, cellophane tape, and an oscilloscope, his recorder would have been a hell of a lot better.

Ryan invents to order for corporate clients. His simple rule: Make a sale before you invent. "If somebody tells you they want a black box that plays *Yankee Doodle*, blows smoke, and shows movies, give them a mock-up and they'll change their minds when they see what they asked for."

Once past the model stage, inventing for commercial success requires making a profit projection for every budding idea. Says Ryan: "Most idea men avoid financial poeple like a trip to the dentist, but invention starts with economics." One of the best types of invention, he says, is finding a way to make something better *and* cheaper.

Now that he has stopped working on toy projects, Ryan has a closet full of consumer products he wants to take to market: a talking movie cassette, a new bicycle brake, a home spot welder, a cheap instant photography kit, a redesigned typewriter.

To save fruitless knocking on company doors, he has devised a new marketing wrinkle: Go to the *retailer* first. He has found out the hard way that tooling and development costs discourage manufacturers from nurturing an invention. Reasons Ryan: "You erase all those fears if you get Sears behind your idea and let them sell it to industry."

Sound easy? Just try making a rubber baby doll stand on its head without wetting its pants. And then call Ryan at home in his castle. He's always looking for a new idea.

IT HAS TO BE USEFUL

Dr. Myron A. Coler practices what he teaches. As director of New York University's Creative Science Program, Coler lectures from experience. Some years ago he turned his knowledge of chemical engineering into practical inventions and ran a successful business based on them.

Professor Coler harbors no romantic nonsense about inventing. "One of the world's most brilliant inventions," he says, "are the luggage lockers in Grand Central

Station. They work day and night collecting coins, where once there was only empty space. You can't patent an idea like this any more than you can patent the design for the Sistine Chapel, but both are extremely useful to mankind."

Coler's useful products stemmed from consulting on the chemistry of materials. He earned his engineering Ph.D. at Columbia in 1937, worked on the Manhattan Project, and did wartime studies on using plastics to conserve metals. But it wasn't until the fifties that he showed that treated plastic had uses in electronics.

"Even if you invent, you have to innovate to make money," he says. To prove the point, he turned consulting into production and founded Markite Corp. in 1953 to turn out his precision potentiometers using a new conductive plastic covered by Coler patents.

A simple potentiometer controls the volume on a radio. Markite developed precision types that are used to convert the movements of aircraft controls into instrument signals. Markite went public on the strength of this product, and was later bought out by Geophysical Corp. of America for some $2.8 million. When GCA proved unable to develop commercial markets, Litton Industries bought the company. Coler figures about $100 million worth of the potentiometers have been sold on projects like the B-58 and the Apollo modules.

Good timing is crucial to selling inventions, says Coler. "Launching an idea the marekt isn't ready for is like putting out an employment ad for a jet pilot in ancient Babylon."

Dr. Coler is now back to his first love, inventing. "I have to think about it differently because the marketplace has changed," he notes. A current interest is in ways to harness energy more efficiently with coated heat exchangers. But he thinks nowadays you've got to be as inventive about marketing your idea as you are in dreaming it up. "Having a lump of something different," he says, explaining why most inventors go wrong, "isn't worth much. You really don't own anything until you can shape it into a useful form."

PROLIFIC BUREAUCRAT

Unless you know better, Jacob Rabinow, 64, might strike you as an unspectacular civil servant in just another government agency. At the National Bureau of Standards in Washington, D.C., he is chief of the Office of Invention & Innovation. But Rabinow is no mere paper-pusher. He has 206 patents to his credit and a slew of products in the marketplace.

Rabinow toils for the Government because he wants to, not because he has to. "Successful invention," he says, "made me independent." He returned to the Bureau of Standards in 1972 to become head of invention and engineering research and promote the cause of the independent inventor.

Electrical engineering was his student passion at New York's City College in the thirties, but Rabinow's inventions run the gamut: weapons devices, sorting machines, watch regulators, a high-fidelity phonograph, a computer disc file, reading machines and home-improvement gadgets. What encouraged his far-flung inventiveness? Two things, says Rabinow: curiosity and necessity.

He spent his childhood in the Ukraine, Siberia, and China, a refugee from the Bolsheviks. Rabinow and his immigrant mother landed in New York in 1921. He put himself through school selling hot dogs at Coney Island and building radios for friends. But as for making a living, who during the Depression needed future inventors? Young Jack got a job at the Bureau of Standards calibrating meters.

Then came World War II. Rabinow's first group of patented devices were safety catches for bombs. After the war, he recalls, "I had a boss who let me play," so he produced a spate of inventions. In the fifties he left the Government to form an engineering service firm that eventually manufactured Rabinow-designed reading machines. The company prospered. In 1962 Control Data bought him out for stock which he later sold for close to $1 million.

Numerous Rabinow inventions have been moneymakers. His magnetic particle clutches are used in computers, cars, and aircraft. General Time pays him $30,000 a year for his automatic watch regulator. Burroughs Corp. sold some $70 million worth of his letter-sorting machines, used by every major U.S. post office. Harman Kardon makes his phonograph arms.

Despite his own success, Rabinow worries about the survival of the independent inventor. He figures that in 1950, when he first started turning out inventions, half of the nation's inventors were independent. Today it's less than 20 percent and the ranks are thinning. He blames tight money and businessmen's reluctance to take long shots. He says his own productivity rose when he went into business for himself.

As spokesman for the National Inventors Council, Rabinow says he gets many sad letters from people who have spent their last buck and can't raise money on Wall Street. "Why should someone invest in crazy Rabinow's ideas when he can put his money in tax-free bonds?" Is there no hope, then? Yes, says Rabinow: "If you know someone rich and can put stars in his eyes."

Now that he's a civil servant again, Jack Rabinow is putting his energy into inventing for the public good. His latest project is the nonexploding bottle. Then there's the reading machine for the blind, a pressurized self-cleaning home, and. . . .

LEARNING BY STARVING

Nathan Zeppel spends his days thinking about pens: push-button clip pens, retractable fountain pens, dry-resistant marker pens, long-life ballpoint pens. "Wherever I go," he says, tapping his head, "I take my work with me."

Zeppel spent nine years in the fifties pounding the pavements of New York before making his first sale. At first, all he could say in English was, "all right." He literally starved. His friends called his inventing an obsession. Even the patent lawyer who helped support him lost faith and called him a screwball.

Born Nathan Zeppelovich in Latvia 59 years ago, Zeppel was hardened by adversity. During World War II, the Germans confiscated his furniture factory, killed his family and 19-year-old fiancee, and imprisoned him at Buchenwald for four years. "Hitler," he muses, "taught me how to starve." As with inventing, he says he was sustained by *belief* in survival. When liberated, he weighed 87 pounds.

Zeppel was inventing weapons for the Israeli army in Palestine when a visiting lawyer, impressed with his pen ideas, persuaded him to come to "the land of opportunity" in 1950. Only by then, there were already about 10,000 pen patents registered in Washington, including, from 1888, one for the original ball-point.

"Pen technology is simple," says Zeppel, "but Buckminster Fuller once told me that designing a new pen sounded harder than perfecting a new missile. It has got to be a certain length and diameter. It has to work 150,000 times in different positions, and be so simple a child can handle it. It has to be suitable for mass production, and the costs are critical because of the small profit margins.''

Zeppel finally sold a simple retractable clip ball-point to Columbia Pen and Pencil Co. and it was an immediate success. Major manufacturers had rejected it because it didn't fit their line, but little Columbia was eager to take a chance. The company still sells around 5 million of his pens a year.

After his first sale, Zeppel says he felt reborn. Schaeffer, now a division of Textron, hired him to set up shop in Ft. Madison, Iowa, to dream up new product ideas, which he did for three years. Schaeffer still manufactures his ''Reminder Clip'' pen that prevents inky pockets because you can't clip it in without retracting the point.

Living comfortably on royalties, he and his wife have settled in Santa Barbara, Calif., after scouting the Riviera, Florida, and Hawaii. The house has everything he wants—an ocean view and a basement workshop.

Zeppel says that success for the inventor comes when he sees things from the manufacturer's viewpoint. With his first sale, one producer told Zeppel that he had proved one man can be right and a whole industry wrong.

He says an inventor must never fall in love with his idea. ''The first thing I try to learn,'' says Zeppel, ''is what's wrong with it.'' He's applying that yardstick to such new ideas as a flat pen that doubles as a bookmark and a retractable fountain pen.

He is also contemplating another project—writing his autobiography. His motive? ''After what I've gone through, I feel like a man who has lived 700 years.'' He credits the fact that he's an immigrant—''not spoiled by abundance and comforts''—for some of his success. He says in clear, but accented, English: ''We are becoming a nation of spectators, and the only muscle we use is the one we sit on.'' That and the ones we use to push those 100-million Zeppel pens.

YOU CAN'T BE ONLY AN INVENTOR

''Mine is a happy story,'' says Howard Arneson, ''where none of the perils inventors worry about went wrong.''

Turning solemn, Arneson says, ''Inventors know I'm successful, so they bring their ideas to me. I feel so sorry for them. You can see in their faces that they are already spending their dreams. They are filled with dread that someone will steal their ideas.

''Then their faces drop when you ask if they've sold a device. They don't realize that the truth comes out when you try to sell a stranger.''

Howard Arneson, 53, grew up in suburban San Francisco so poor he didn't even think of college. But winning the California skeet-shooting championship also won him an appointment as a naval gunnery instructor. After the Navy, he worked on developing an emergency-vehicle light. ''It wasn't very successful,'' says Arneson, ''but it hooked me on inventing.''

His big break came when he went to work on a solution to the bane of every swimming pool owner, the leaves and other debris that constantly foul the water. He joined another inventor whose patents Arneson later licensed. Finally Arneson came up with a gadget consisting of a motor, some plastic, and two hoses to blow the refuse into a spot where it could be removed without laborious sweeping. Their original backer, a swimming pool manufacturer, dropped the invention because of production problems. Then Arneson got a new backer. In 1970 Castle & Cooke (*Forbes,* November 15, 1973), the big Hawaiian conglomerate, came along and bought them out for $7.3 million in stock—half of which went to Arneson.

One hundred twenty thousand Pool-Sweeps have been sold, and Arneson still runs the company for Castle & Cooke; it grosses $6.5 million a year and nets a fabulous $2 million a year.

Why did Arneson succeed where so many inventors fail? In a word: marketing. The necessity of selling and financing his invention kept him in touch with economically productive work rather than mere gadgeteering.

Arneson's favority invention is a dry-dock system that lifts his 36-foot racing boat completely out of the marina water. But Arneson is making no effort to sell the device. It is too expensive and too bulky and conflicts with California laws that forbid cleaning boats over water. In short, it is an invention without a market.

Entrepreneurship and Economic Development

Albert Shapero
University of Texas at Austin

In a major presentation at Project ISEED, Professor Shapero discussed major issues related to entrepreneurship and economic development. This paper is an expanded review based on that presentation.

Social and economic development have preoccupied the attention of a considerable portion of the political and intellectual world in the past three decades. For a variety of reasons, following World War II, there was a general awakening of people throughout the world to the thought that they might expect to escape the stagnation of a subsistence way of life. Increasing communications, travel, and education have made all people aware that in some parts of the world the inhabitants live in a manner that allows them to more fully realize their potentials.

As a consequence, for many political and humanitarian reasons, large efforts have gone into attempts to provide the things, conditions, and processes associated

Proceedings of Project ISEED, Summer 1975. Published by Project ISEED, Ltd., The Center for Venture Management, Suite 508, 207 E. Buffalo Street, Milwaukee, WI 53202, U.S.A.

with a high level of material (and sometimes social) well-being to those who do not have them. Many approaches have been proposed and attempted, ranging from highly elaborated, long-range plans covering all aspects of an economy to project-by-project attempts to supply one good thing at a time.

The record of accomplishment in economic development is very uneven, and not very successful. We find that we cannot readily ". . .generalize from the 'special case' of the advanced countries. . ." (Myint, 1971) to the underdeveloped countries or from one underdeveloped country to another. The theories propounded quite firmly in the first two decades folowing World War II are doing poorly. Furthermore, in the advanced countries that served as models and suppliers of resources for the development of others, there are now great dissatisfactions and doubts as to the desirability of what has been achieved.

The current economic retreat has acted like a receding tide. It has laid bare the limits of our rationality, and has shaken our faith in tricks and recipes for development. The outgoing tide has also uncovered great dissatisfactions, apocalyptic pessimisms, and what one writer has referred to as a civilizational malaise reflected in the inability of a civilization directed to material improvement to satisfy the human spirit (Heilbroner, 1974). A number of recent international conferences on food, the environment, population have witnessed the so-called underdeveloped world rushing toward a condition from which the developed countries are rushing away.

Is it possible to offer any hope for the utility of any kind of program of action in times like these? The theories and methods we have accepted are in doubt, and we are in the midst of a large reordering of values in the most advanced and powerful countries in the world. Nevertheless, I suggest the answer is "yes." I suggest that there is hope and a basis for optimism if we shift our attention to a level of consideration and activity located somewhere "in the middle," between the cosmic schemes of the central planners and the random actions of local authorities. I would even suggest that a shift in scale is now occurring, (so to say), "in nature."

We find that the 500 largest firms in the United States are not as profitable as the second 500, and that the top 1,000 are not as profitable as smaller firms. In the advanced countries of Europe, we are witnessing a recrudescence of regional identity. The Scots and Welsh are fiercely expressing their differentness, and so are the Bretons and the people of Languedoc. In the more developed countries there is a growing engagement with self-expression, and a willingness to trade many material benefits for a chance to control more of one's personal space. Young people increasingly want to avoid being a cipher in someone's organization or plan. Is this disintegration and a return to chaos? I suggest that it reflects a return of focus to a level where events are comprehensible, needs are not averaged away, and actions are more easily matched to perceived problems.

The subject of "entrepreneurship and regional development" is cast at the proper level for hope and success. It recognizes that all developmental efforts must be translated into the specific actions of nameable individuals located in specific geographic and cultural locations. This would seem to be a truism, but it is lost in the abstractions of theory and aggregated statistics. "Entrepreneurship" is at a level where action is quite feasible, and where useful local and national successes are more easily achieved.

What do we want from development? It is a question not answered very well in the voluminous literature on economic development. One official statement puts the aims of economic development as helping developing countries achieve a state in which the people have "... the material opportunities for using their talents, of living a full and happy life and steadily improving their lot" (Schumacher, 1973 quotes it). I imagine we could all agree with this general goal, but we would be hard put to picture the operational characteristics of such a condition. Further, if we identify the operational characteristics associated with such a condition, can we say that they are such that, once reached, the task is over? Must we aim at achieving some underlying process that continues to vary operationally as new, unknowable things occur in the future? What are the operational conditions and target characteristics that we want to achieve?

Some of the answers can be obtained from descriptions of lively communities and from comparisons of dynamic with stagnant communities. Jane Jacobs, the architectural writer and critic, provides us with some clues in her comparison of Manchester and Birmingham. Jacobs points out that in the days of Marx, Manchester was held up as the paragon of efficiency, the model of the future. At the same time, Birmingham "... was precisely the kind of city that seemed to have been outmoded by Manchester. ... Birmingham... has no specialty of the kind that made Manchester's economy so comprehensible. .... But as it turned out Manchester was not the city of the future and Birmingham was. . . . Manchester has acquired the efficiency of a company town. Birmingham had retained something different: a high rate of innovation. Indeed, Birmingham and London are the only two cities in Britain today that retain a significant capacity to create new work from their existing world. . . . (Jacobs, 1969).

The Jacobs description and other studies give us some descriptors of a dynamic community, region, economy, or society. We obtain a positive picture of a region or community denoted by: *creativity and innovativeness*—experimentation and invention in the economy, the arts, and the social-political sphere, *resilience*—the ability to respond to changes in the environment, *initiative taking*—a willingness to take risks in the economic and social marketplace, *diversity*.

A region or community with the foregoing conditions has a high likelihood of responding dynamically to setbacks and opportunities. Diversity makes a region relatively invulnerable to any single event or decision, while creativity and innovativeness provide a region with prospects for continuity. Taking an ecological approach to regional development, we find that there is stability in diversity, and that diversity is essential to survival. The Irish potato famine is a historical lesson in vulnerability from dependence on a single source of food. The history of the effects of technological changes in transportation and in textiles on various communities illustrates the vulnerability inherent in dependence on a single industry.

The negative consequences that result from lack of diversity can be illustrated by a community's dependence on a single major corporate division. The short-term apparent advantages gained from importing many jobs with a low level of industrial skill set a trap for a region, as can be attested to by examples such as the Mexican-American border program which in 10 years attracted some 450 American manufacturers through the bait of low-cost labor. Now that wages are improving (though still low by any standard) the companies are leaving for Central America, the

Far East, and Ireland where wages are lower yet. The last 18 months have witnessed a 30 percent decrease in employment in the area, and 25 to 40 percent of the in-migrant American plants have closed down, moved to other regions, or severely reduced their operations (*New York Times*, 26 May 1975).

Typically, a city, a regional or national development authority, or group launches an intensive campaign to attract large industrial plants in order to generate "jobs." It is assumed that to have more jobs is positive and good, and in an effort to attract jobs many kinds of concessions are offered to the industrial concerns being wooed; tax breaks, free or cheap land, long-term low-interest loans, buildings, highway construction, railroad spurs. In the process, the consequences of trying to obtain large plants are often overlooked. The consequences include a high probability that the effort will fail. One study made in the late 1950s found that in the United States at that time there were approximately 16,000 development organizations competing for 200 available corporation moves; the efforts cost well over $250 million. If the effort succeeds there is a high probability that the incoming company brings its managers and highly skilled workers from other areas, while the local area provides the low-cost, unskilled workers. A flow is set up in which the skilled, educated, professionally trained youth of the community leave for other cities while the unskilled youth of the community and the unskilled of other communities are attracted and retained. The result of an in-migrating company, attracted by cheap labor and low costs, can be to lower the net quality of the human resources of a community.

With a large in-migrant company comes an enlarged work force that sets up a demand for all of the services that cities provide their citizens; police, fire protection, education, waste disposal. The tax demand goes up, but the incoming company frequently has been given a tax concession and is freed from paying the taxes that its presence has generated.

Finally, the incoming company makes the community vulnerable. The community adjusts to the dominant source of jobs and income and becomes dependent on it. The vulnerability is made apparent when it is suddenly realized that decisions about the local plant are made by a distant, uninvolved management that can easily shift its plant to a lower cost region. Of course, managements are not eager to disrupt communities, and many corporations deliberately refuse to locate in a community where their decisions will have a disproportionate local effect.

To achieve diversity, innovativeness, and resilience, in short, the kind of dynamism ascribed by Jane Jacobs to Birmingham, brings us to "entrepreneurship." Entrepreneurship has recurringly intrigued economists, psychologists, historians, economic developers, and the general public. Jacobs, quoting a London journalist of the 1850s, writes: "It was always a peculiarity of Birmingham that small household trades existed which gave the inmates independence and often led—if the trade continued good—to competence or fortune." Jacobs goes on to state that many of these endeavors failed and that they did not constitute a majority of the city's industry. Nevertheless, Birmingham's peculiarity led to the development of a diverse, responsive, resilient capacity that serves the city 125 years later. The lesson of Manchester and Birmingham is that it is better to create the conditions for achieving 25 diverse enterprises with a payroll of $2,000,000 each than to attract a single corporate division with payroll of $50,000,000.

What do we mean by entrepreneurship? I am sure that this conference will hear many variations on definitions of entrepreneurship and the entrepreneur.[1] The terms are variously defined in the technical or academic literature (Shapero, 1971).

The term "entrepreneur" has been used and elaborated upon by a large variety of scholars, industrialists, and government officials since it was first introduced into the literature by Cantillon in 1775 (Schumpeter, 1965). The term has been used to designate the "economic agent who unites all means of production" (Say, 1821); the individual whose function is to carry out new combinations called enterprises (Schumpeter, 1934); the individual or group of individuals who undertakes "to initiate, maintain, or aggrandize a profit-oriented business unit for the production, or distribution of economic goods and services" (Cole, 1959): a risk taker (Drucker, 1965); an organization builder (Harbison & Myers, 1959); and even, in the eyes of one writer, the firm itself (Strauss, 1944). Although each of these designations is useful in terms of a general discussion of the individual and the function that has to do with innovative activities in the economic and social systems, we are concerned with the entrepreneur in a much more restricted sense.

For the purpose of my discussion the entrepreneur is defined as the person who starts ". . . business enterprises; furthermore, when we use the term entrepreneur, we mean the innovating entrepreneur who develops an ongoing business activity where none existed before" (Collins & Moore, 1964), or the person who is ". . . the active initiator of a new enterprise in the form of a new company. He plays a major role in starting the company and managing it, and usually has an important equity position in it" (Draheim et al., 1966).

In almost all of the definitions of entrepreneurship, there is agreement that we are talking about a kind of behavior that includes: (1) initiative taking, (2) the organizing or reorganizing of social/economic mechanisms to turn resources and situations to practical account, (3) the acceptance of risk of failure. A major resource, perhaps the prior and prime resource utilized by the entrepreneur, is himself; which may explain why entrepreneurs unhesitatingly opt for a role which can mean a seven-day week, 14-hour-a-day commitment. Very often the entrepreneur is also directly concerned with managing the enterprise he has initiated, but we should not conclude, as have some writers, that all managers are by definition entrepreneurs. Furthermore, we should not conclude that all inventors are entrepreneurs. We have some very well publicized examples of great inventors who have also been very successful entrepreneurs, such as Land of Polaroid and Beckman of Beckman Instruments, but these are exceptional men. More often than not, a great invention finds its way into public use through the actions of an entrepreneur who pries it loose from the possessive grasp of its creator in order to help it realize its potential in the market place. In most cases, the new enterprise is the invention and not the product or service that it is delivering.

If we perceive utility in entrepreneurial behavior, then for the purpose of regional development we are interested in what we might do to systematically develop, or capture it for our purposes. We want to know how new enterprises get started. We are interested in answering such questions as: Who starts new enterprises and under what conditions? Are there systematic patterns to be observed in the company formation process? In what ways does the company formation process vary by culture, country, industry, and region?

For the past several years, there has been a continuing and expanding exploration of the entrepreneurial event.[2] There has been a continuing effort to explicate and delineate the contextual, situational, social, and psychological factors that combine in the generation of that extraordinary act, the formation of a company or its intraorganizational or civic equivalent. The work, of necessity, has been multidisciplinary, drawing upon methods and materials from psychology, sociology, anthropology, economics, and business.

The explorations are still in process, but the picture is coming into some kind of focus. We know that the entrepreneurial event is overdetermined; that no single variable accounts for it, but we are beginning to know enough about the various factors that go into the entrepreneurial event to feel that we can do something about it.

From an engineering, as differentiated from a scientific, viewpoint we now have enough information to be able to interpolate, extrapolate, and design programs that have a fair chance of effecting company formations. Further, though most of our available data is from the U.S., we are beginning to accumulate data from other countries that tend to support the general conclusions reached from U.S. data.

THE COMPANY FORMATION PROCESS

Company formations vary greatly in many respects since each is the unique culmination of a process affected by the specific industry, place, and time period in which it occurs. However, when we examine a great many formations in terms of what triggered the initiative-taking actions, who took the initiative, and why the initiative was taken, a fairly general pattern emerges. The general pattern includes: *displacement* of the entrepreneur(s), and apparent *disposition to act*, examples or models that lend *credibility* to the act of company formation, and *available* resources (see Fig. 1).

Displacement

What leads to the initiative-taking behavior that results in a company formation? We find that most company formations are associated with some kind of displacement; some dislodgement from a comfortable or otherwise inertia-laden state of being. The most definitive displacements are those experienced by the political refugee and the individual who has been fired. They cannot choose not to act.

Each wave of political refugees has produced its own special history of company formations in the country of adoption; the *pied noir* in France, the East Germans in West Germany, the Cubans in Florida, the Indian emigres from Uganda. In the available studies of entrepreneurs there is explicit or implicit reference to the role of the refugees from political or religious persecution (two examples are Sayigh's study of the Lebanese entrepreneurs and Derossi's study of the Mexican entrepreneurs).

Displacements are both negative and positive, externally imposed or internally perceived, and it is often a combination of the negative and the positive that dislodges the potential entrepreneurs into the active, initiative-taking mode. The most appropriate way to look at the displacement is in terms of vectors or directed forces of varying strength operating on the individual at any time. Inertia is one of the vectors, acting like gravity. Inertia is associated with the present, the known, and the comfortable.

It takes some accumulation of force to displace an individual from the position in which he is established. It can be a purely negative, powerful displacement. It can be a combination of a very positive pull plus some negative push. We do know that

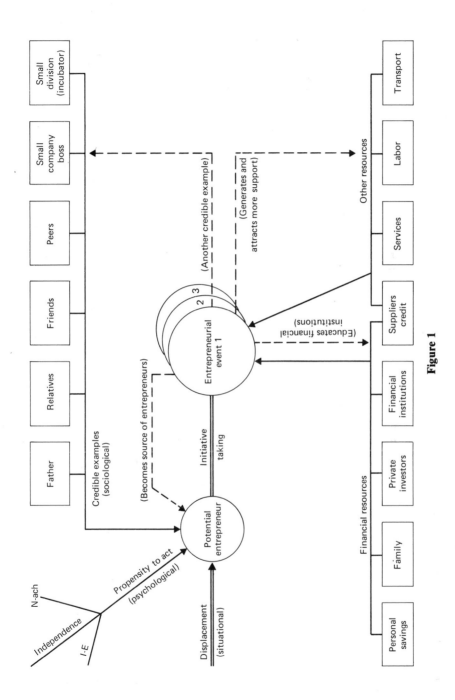

Figure 1

negative information is much more likely to lead to action than positive information. In studies of 109 company formations in Austin, Texas (technical companies, accounting firms, boat stores, high-fidelity equipment stores, advertising firms, publishing firms), we found that 65 percent of the influences leading to starting a new enterprise were identified as negative. The negative influences included: "getting fired," "boss sold the company," "organizational changes," "being transferred but did not want to leave the city," "no future," "didn't like the job." The positive influences, 28 percent of those given, primarily included the encouragement of peers and, more weightily, the encouragement of customers and backers. The remaining 7 percent were accounted for by being out-of-place or being between things.

Other studies of company formations have not explicitly examined them from the viewpoint of displacements, but many of the studies provide anecdotal support for the notion. Boswell, in his field study of small business in the United Kingdom, speaks of "the emigration of frustrated men from corporations" being a prime generator of new engineering and hosiery/knitwear firms. Carroll, in his study of Filipino manufacturing entrepreneurs, gives several examples of negative displacements; having one's taxi horse taken by the Japanese, losing one's job with the government because of the war, a family business argument, the closedown of a plant. The same kinds of incidents show up in entrepreneurship studies in Italy, Mexico, and the United States. Papanek (1962) writes of Pakistanis with exclusive import licenses suddenly forbidden to import who initiated new manufacturing enterprises.

Some displacements are internal to the entrepreneur. In many cases, the entrepreneur mentions a magic number like "40" or "50." "I realized that within three months I was going to be 40. It was now or never." Internally generated feelings of displacement occur often without reference to outside events. It is the result of an internal dialogue, fed by the outside world, but not responsive to it.

As already mentioned, some company formations occur when the potential company former is not "in-place" or is out-of-place. Such formations occur during a break in fixed life patterns. Having just finished school or been discharged from the military are frequent points of departure into company formation activity. There is one study of 22 exoffenders who started their own companies when paroled from prison; their particular example of break in life pattern (of 3500 parolees there were 30 self-employed at the time of the study) (Jansyn et al., 1969).

The amount of displacement required to move an individual into action must vary with various individual characteristics, and this has not been measured as yet. The refugee and the person who has been fired are unequivocally displaced, and don't have to weigh the pushing and pulling forces before moving. I suspect that the individual who is more likely to act, the one driven by a high need-for-achievement, the one whose locus-of-control is very internal, may subjectively be more prone to feelings of displacement and more ready to take action on a smaller amount of displacement than would others.

Disposition to Act

It seems tautological to say that initiative taking or the disposition to act must be related directly to whether or not the individual feels it is possible to affect events. In our very recent studies of company formations in the United States and in Italy, it was not surprising to find that entrepreneurs were measured to be far more Internal (that is, far more dependent on internal reinforcement; therefore, more self-reliant, desirous of independence and autonomy) than almost all of the groups reported by Rotter (1966), with the exception of Peace Corps volunteers (5.94). We also found that the Italian entrepreneurs had more internal scores than did U.S. entrepreneurs, with an average of 6.74 for the Americans and 6.06 for the Italians. Considering the generally negative bias toward the small company and its ownership in Italy as differentiated from the United States where small businessmen are fold heroes, the results are not surprising. The individual would have to be much more self-reliant in Italy to even imagine forming a company (Shapero et al., 1974).

A comparison of a sample of French graduate students with a similar sample of graduate students of business at the University of Texas on the basis of Rotter I-E scores showed both groups to be far more External than the company formers in both Italy and the United States, and the French students (I-E mean of 12.2) to be more External than the American students (I-E mean of 10.2). The very external scores of the business students are not surprising to anyone familiar with the ambience that typifies most business schools. In effect, business schools are academies for corporate management rather than for entrepreneurship. The difference between the French and American students compares with the sparseness of company formations in France as compared to the U.S.

In a study of the expectations of a cross-section of 375 business school students at the University of Texas, Borland, using Levenson's locus-of-control instrument,[3] found that students with higher expectancies of starting a company at some time had significantly higher belief in Internal control than those with moderate or low expectancy. Interestingly, the high and low expectancy groups did not differ significantly in nAch. Further, it was found that locus-of-control moderates the influence of nAch on expectancy of starting a company. Only among those with low belief in control by Chance (C) did students with a high nAch score have significantly higher expectancy of starting a company than those with lower nAch.

The anecdotal literature and some of the discussion found in studies of company formations support the notion that the company former is measurably more disposed to act than are his non-company-forming associates.

The biographies of company formers are replete with examples of initiative taking, inventing, active management in other's firms, previous company formations.

Credibility of the Act
The most important variable we have found associated with the company formation act has been the existence of credible models or examples for the potential company former. A potential entrepreneur must be able to conceive of himself starting a company, and credible examples make the conception possible.

The most prominent credible example is that provided by one's father or mother. In studies of company formations in the United States, the percentage of company formers found to have fathers/mothers who were independent (company owners, free professionals, independent artisans or farmers) ranges between 50-58 percent in a variety of industries and locations. This compares with a census count of less than 12 percent of the U.S. population listed as self-employed. In our Italian study the percentage was similar (56 percent). In Carroll's study of the Filipino entrepreneurs the percentage was 74 percent, and in Harris's study of Nigerian entrepreneurs the figure was almost 89 percent. Supporting the findings from the field studies, Borland's study of business students found that the variable most positively associated with whether the business students ever expected or desired to start a company was whether or not one's father had ever started a company. Not surprisingly, only one of the 75 girls in Borland's sample expected to start a company.

The credible model or example is not necessarily one that is consciously followed. In a study of technical entrepreneurs by Susbauer, he asked the entrepreneurs whose fathers had been independent if their fathers had been their models or had encouraged them to start a company. The usual answer was that their fathers told them never to start a company, and/or that their fathers had been unsuccessful; but the prevalence of independent fathers in the sample was remarkable.

Other credible examples include relatives, colleagues, and classmates. Frequently, we find that there has been precedent entrepreneurial action on the part of a brother, uncle, grandfather, classmate, or colleague. Often the remark is made derogatorily of a colleague, "If he can do it, I certainly can!" When a corporate vice-president breaks away to form a new company, this does not make the company formation act credible to his many subordinates. However, when a group of engineers, far down in the organizational line break away to form a company, their colleagues are much more likely to follow their example (Draheim et al.).

In Cooper's study of technical company formations in the San Francisco area, he found that new company formations were more likely to have originated from small corporate divisions than from large ones. Cooper calls the small divisions "incubators." A small firm provides a close view of the man who formed or headed the firms; a man who in many cases is very much like themselves. In the small organization contexts it becomes possible for the potential entrepreneur to see the role of company head as credible for himself.

Many of the entrepreneurs studied were found to have formed more than one company, and many had experienced previous business failures. Failures apparently do not shake the credibility of the company formation act, but may even reinforce the credibility of the act to the entrepreneur (as well as serving as a learning experience).

It is no accident that entrepreneurship is identified highly with certain ethnic groups: Jews, Lebanese, Ibos in Nigeria, Jains and Parsis in India. Today, each of these groups provides a large number of examples of the credibility of the act of starting a company to its members. The combination of credibility and displacement provides a very powerful impetus to company formations.

The Availability of Resources
Initiative taking, credible models, and the disposition to act are necessary but insufficient. The final required ingredient is resources. The company-forming entrepreneur must have or obtain the labor, materials, equipment, facilities required for the venture or must obtain them with his or other people's capital.

In times of readily available venture capital, the number of company formations goes up. In hard times, despite the displacement caused by job loss, the lack of available capital keeps the company formation rate from rising.

If private or public venture capital sources are not available for certain kinds of industries, companies, or entrepreneurs, fewer companies are formed or survive. Companies move from one city to another to take advantage of more responsive capital sources. The urban economist, Thompson, writes that the U.S. automobile industry moved from other areas of the country to Michigan in response to the urging of a single banker interested in automobiles who offered them financial support.

The great majority of the capital for new companies comes from the savings of the entrepreneur, those of his family and friends, and from personal bank loans. Personal and socially close sources accounted for 90 percent of the initial financing for the new ventures in our studies, and dominate all of the anecdotal literature. The rest of the capital comes primarily from private investors who regularly invest in ventures of many kinds.

New ventures almost never receive financial support from formal financial institutions. Banks are constrained to treat new company financing as "not bankable," though there are some exceptional examples of loan officers consciously making personal loans to individuals with little collateral for the purpose of starting companies. According to a recent NSF sponsored study in the United States, venture capital firms were found to make an average of 2.6 investments a year, less than 15 percent of them for new ventures. Since there are only something between 600 and 700 of these highly publicized firms in the U.S., they can only account for about 250 startups. Even adding in the SBICs, the special programs for minority entrepreneurship and various Federal programs, it is obvious that the role of the formal institutions is miniscule in the new company formation process in the U.S.

The process by which new or young companies actually get venture or almost-venture capital is not very well explained by the conventional literature on finance. Studies of the ways in which private venture capitalists and bank lending officials respond to the financial needs of new and young companies, particularly of those in new fields, suggest the existence of a process that is little understood in a systematic way. Furthermore, the studies make clear that the presence of a financial community that responds positively to new companies is a key factor in whether or not a region will generate, develop, and keep new enterprises (Shapero et al., 1969; Hoffman, 1972).

THE DEVELOPMENT OF AN INDUSTRIAL COMPLEX IN A REGION
The individual company formation process provides us with a basic element in constructing an understanding of how we might go about developing an industrial complex in a given locale. What we need is some idea of how the individual formations affect each other and how they eventually interact and link with the larger entities that may come into a region. We need to know something of the kind of environment or industrial ecology that elicits, attracts, and enhances the organizations that finally become the core of a dynamic region.

A number of studies of high-technology industrial complexes in the U.S. provide us with some useful clues as to the way the process has worked in the United States. The data suggest that the process may be directly applicable to other advanced countries, and may have utility for industrializing countries.

As previously mentioned, the individual technical company formation comes about as the result of the actions of a technical entrepreneur or group of technical entrepreneurs in response to some triggering event, or situation resulting from many interacting personal and environmental forces. Among the forces and factors leading to an individual company formation that play an important role is the presence in the area of at least one surviving technical company formation and the environmental conditions, if any, that contributed to its survival. Thus, the first formation affects the second, and the number of technical companies already formed in an area affects the probability of subsequent formations and their survival. Consequently, the technical company formation process in an area varies in rate and quality with the number and kinds of technical companies already in the area, and with the variations in the social and economic environment.

An analysis was made of U.S. counties with at least one technical company in 1968 that fell within the nonmetropolitan population ranges. (The initial sample consisted of 141 counties.) One result of the analysis was a convenient categorization of an area's technical company formation process into three phases denoted by the rate of technical company formation (Shapero, 1971). The phasing, though not universal, was noted in the majority of counties examined. The three phases were identified as follows (see Fig. 2):

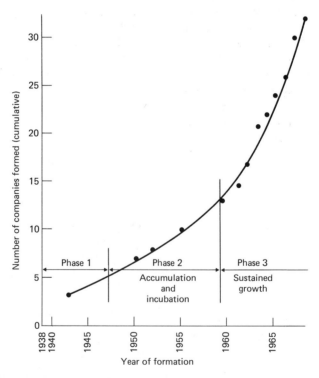

Fig. 2   The Three Phases in the Technical Company Formation Process in an Area, as Exemplified by Mercer County, New Jersey.

1. A period in which the first (one to four) technical companies are formed, as if by chance.

2. A period of accumulation and incubation in which technical companies are formed at a rate of approximately one per year.

3. A period of accelerated and sustained growth in which technical companies are formed at a rate of approximately two or more per year.

We made a further selection, from the initial 141 counties, of a sample of 22 counties that could provide a better basis for an analysis of the technical company formation process. This second sample consisted of counties that:

1. Had reached the third phase of accelerated and sustained growth, thereby providing data on the kinds and mix of technical company formations in each phase.

2. Were not suburban. Counties that are suburbs of major metropolitan areas do not experience the same technical company formation process found in other areas, since the proximity of large metropolitan areas changes the number and kinds of companies formed.

The First Phase—The First Company Formation
The first technical company formed in a local area can be considered as almost a random event. This is pointed out by the fact that over half of the counties in the U.S. had at least one technical company in 1968. The first company formations appear to be contrary to any rational explanation of an "economic man" making a calculated decision. In many instances, a single technical company forms and survives in an area for decades without the support of important services and without a susbsequent company formation.

Whether or not the first technical company in any area survives is related to a number of circumstances. It may be related to a more than average capability on the part of the founder-manager as a manager or as a technical professional. It may be related to whether or not the company has a product or service sufficiently salable and sufficiently unique to provide it with a temporary monopoly or quasi-monopoly in the marketplace. Finally, the first company survival is related to the company's ability to get financing and supporting services.

Its financing is often dependent upon the attitude, experience, and risk-taking propensity of the local banking community, or the company's ability to obtain enough trade credit and immediate sales to make it independent of local financial sources. The first company can be independent of the availability of supporting services in the area, so long as these services are not vital to its ability to perform, or so long as the company itself can carry out these services—even as marginal operations—without harming its price structure.

The first company formation process described above may be repeated with a second, third, or fourth company, each completely independent or even oblivious of the existence of any previous company. After the first few companies are formed and have survived, however, their existence in the community becomes a very definite factor in subsequent technical company formations. In many cases, the first companies formed become sources of entrepreneurs for subsequent company formations. The first companies enhance the credibility of the action of company formation within the community. As personal displacements occur and potential technical entrepreneurs are triggered to take action, the formation of a technical company is seen as a realistic and credible alternative because of the first companies' existence and visibility in the community.

The Second Phase—Accumulation and Incubation

As the number of technical companies formed in the community increases, the technical company formation process loses its random nature and enters a phase of accumulation and incubation. There is the beginning of a technical labor pool, the market for supporting services grows and begins to attract manufacturers' representatives, and the area gains warehousing of needed supplies. Supporting services are exchanged among the technical companies in the city, and local providers of professional services become "educated" to the special character and needs of highly technical industries.

During the second phase of development, an area often attracts a major corporate division that is engaged in high-technology industry. A large corporate division, added to the accumulating number of locally generated companies, provides considerable impetus to the creation of a local technical labor pool, the attraction of suppliers and services. The division then becomes another source of potential entrepreneurs.

Community factors play a contributory role in the overall development process, particularly during the second phase. The presence of a local university is an amenity that acts to attract and retain technical workers. Many corporations consider the presence of a university as one of their major location criteria for a technical division. Cultural amenities play a similar role to that of a university; theater, music, entertainment. Local facilities for education are highly important as a family attraction. All of these special attractions tend to create a community with an intellectual profile that tends to attract technical entrepreneurs and the key manpower resources they must collect around themselves.

Areas that have a high tourist attraction value (i.e., the "sunshine" states, coastal resorts, etc.) have an advantage in attracting and retaining potential entrepreneurs, technical professionals, and corporate divisions from other areas. Familiarity with an area resulting from many years of attracting tourists provides a "pull" on all kinds of industries, particularly on the "footloose" industries—those not tied to local natural resources or transportation services. High-technology companies are in the footloose category. The primary resource in a technical activity is the technical professional workforce. Given an attractive community as a location, the company experiences less trouble in bringing the necessary resources to the location.

The Third Phase—Sustained Growth

The number of technical companies accumulates in an area and a point is reached in which the technical company formation process begins to be self-sustaining. The number of technical company formations rises from one a year to two and more a year. Services formerly maintained as marginal operations within the companies are now spun-off to provide efficient services to a community of companies. The more companies in the community, the greater the number of spin-off sources, and the formation rate increases.

The time required to reach the third phase and the strength of its thrust is dependent on the way the earlier phases of technical company formation in a community have developed. The greater the variety of technical companies in the community, the greater the apparent strength of the third phase. When a community devleops as a technical industrial area clustered around a single specialty, the development is more limited. A single specialty area may create more jobs than other areas, but it is less resilient to shifts and variations in the marketplace.

MAKING IT HAPPEN

Can entrepreneurship be deliberately made to happen in a community? What can we affect in the process of eliciting and developing and even attracting entrepreneurial behavior in a community? What can be done to generate the entrepreneurial events that might be a key to the development of a self-sustaining, developmental process in a community and in a region?

The kinds of programs that might be undertaken to develop and bring entrepreneurship to bear on regional development are suggested by the data described above. Some of the elements that might be included in such programs include the following:

1. Actions to attract small and diverse companies to the region—new companies form more readily from small companies rather than large companies. It is intriguing to me to see lesser developed companies expending great efforts to attract large companies that deal with them on almost equal terms while ignoring smaller firms with experiences that are most relevant to the scale of operations of the country. Furthermore, smaller firms gain real advantage from small concessions, while larger firms must be given very large concessions. Smaller companies also generate entrepreneurs; as Cooper has shown, small corporate divisions are incubator organizations.

2. Programs to generate new company formations—It is possible to provide potential entrepreneurs with experiences that will make the company-forming act more credible to them. I do not include within this the many courses on business management that help the committed entrepreneur, but are not too effective in making the individual feel that the act is credible and, of course, supplying resources helps.

3. Programs to provide the industrial "ecology" that will enable new companies to form and survive—This can include: (a) Programs for educating the financial community in the risks and characteristics of new, small companies and in the requirements of different industries. (b) The development and fielding of substitutes for the various factors and services only available in very large, well-established communities. An example of the latter could be the governmental support for a network of excellent manufacturers' representatives as a substitute for the market opportunities of a larger community. (c) Special efforts to attract the kinds of support services to a community that make company startup less costly and company survival easier to achieve; machine shops, plating services, blueprinting, etc. (d) Transportation support is very useful in this regard, and communities have much experience in this sector.

REGIONAL DEVELOPMENT THROUGH ENTREPRENEURSHIP

Undertaking a program for the generation and encouragement of entrepreneurship does not guaranty the development of a region. We all know by now that development is a complex process and that a region or an economy is an open system in which old variables disappear forever and new ones appear to confound us. There is no single approach or technique that is both necessary and sufficient for regional development. However, there is no approach that offers the same potential for development offered by a program that includes a strong effort to develop entrepreneurship. No other kind of program offers the same kind of limited risk, social learning, cultural fit, potential diversity, and ability to deal with unexpected change that appears possible through a program for the generation and development of entrepreneurship.

Risk and Social Learning

The entrepreneurial event and the entrepreneur can be considered as renewable and growing resources. The role of the successful and growing enterprise is obvious, but the potentially positive effects of a failed enterprise (particularly the small enterprise) have really been ignored.

When an enterprise fails, it is seldom a net loss for the community or society in which it occurs, though it may be a tragic experience for the entrepreneur and those who have a financial stake in the venture. Each entrepreneurial event is a generator of social learning for the community, and can be a net gain for all concerned. The entrepreneur has learned. We frequently find that successful entrepreneurs have had failed ventures behind them. Henry Ford failed in business twice before his final success. All those who have been associated with the venture have learned; the employees, bankers, suppliers, lawyers, accountants, and customers. That the learning is not all negative is borne out by the fact that there is often a growing rate of enterprise formations in a region. In fact, the very evidence presented to you concerning the company formation process might well be described as a social learning process. Each company-former gains his credible example from the observed behavior of others including father, relatives, employer, and colleagues. Thus, each company formation, successful or not, is a potential generator of subsequent attempts to form ventures. (My colleague, Professor Neff, suggests that the liberalization of bankruptcy laws was a powerful institutionalization of the social learning process.)

If a community manages to retain those who were part of a failed entrepreneurial event and the capital that went into the event, there is almost no loss, for all is available in the community. This is one argument for encouraging local, regional, or national investment. It is one more way of making sure the resources remain within the country.

From the viewpoint of concerned public officials, particularly those in democratic countries, a program for the encouragement of entrepreneurial formations is a low-risk, high-potential-gain strategy. It removes the official/planner/political figure from a direct concern for the failure of specific enterprises, and shifts his attention and responsibility to the aggregate of failures and successes for the entire program. Unlike the large, expensive, long-term, highly-visible project, like the building of a major industrial plant, a program for generating entrepreneurial events distributes the economic and political risks over a larger and less visible number of discrete points. Furthermore, entrepreneurial events have a higher likelihood of producing some successes early in time and throughout the same time period that it takes to bring a single major project to a point where you even know if it will fail or succeed. In other words, the larger the number of entrepreneurial formations and by the very nature of the size of new ventures, the larger the probability of some successes and the lower is the potential loss in both resources and political coinage. Of course I am assuming some modicum of intelligence in developing the program on the basis of what has been learned about the company formation and survival process.

Cultural Fit
The entrepreneur, even when drawn from a minority or immigrant group, is part of the fabric of the culture in which he is found. The entrepreneur lives close to and is part of the culture of the country and region and locale. He is attuned to place and custom, and has an intimate awareness of what can and cannot be done with the local resources. Unlike the manager of an immigrant industrial plant, the local entrepreneur does not have to be "oriented"; taught how to understand the local natives, given language lessons, taught about the local customs.[4]

It is important to understand that the French entrepreneur is a very French product. Even more, a Breton or Languedoc entrepreneur, is a very concentrated expression of local outlooks, values, prejudices, conditions, traditions, needs, and capabilities. The local entrepreneur is more likely to bring to his efforts a special passion and devotion to locale that affects his willingness to "hang on," his desire to do something for the locale, and his willingness to forego the maximization of some particular economic variable that would require he relocate in some other area. When you consider the number of variables that enter into the determination of the success or failure of a particular business decision, it is plausible to say that the feelings of the entrepreneurs are a factor that may affect the outcome.

From the viewpoint of society, entrepreneurship provides operational expression to new idea, new structures, new products, new devices. Each entrepreneurial event is an action experiment, testing some new combination of resources and processes, some new approach to the environment. In the aggregate, entrepreneurial events provide society with a relatively low risk, low cost, actuarial approach to the problem of dealing with an unknown, onrushing future. Entrepreneurship provides a society and a region with a multiplicity of independent decision points, each responding to events in some unique way; each worrying away a piece of the total problem.

Take the example of the energy crisis; entrepreneurship cannot solve the energy problem. However, entrepreneurship, encouraged and supported, can find 10,000 ways to turn specific pieces of the problem to practical account. Consider further, if 10,000 entrepreneurial events are generated in an effort to profit or gain prestige or prevent disaster by lowering a small part of the energy demand or by substituting one form of energy for another or by inventing and marketing some new way of using existing energy, what might the energy crisis look like in one or two years time?

Governments and academics respond to cosmic questions with efforts to find the solutions. When they cannot find singular and comprehensive solutions (and there are few such solutions for large and complex problems), there is a sense of resignation, malaise, and a rise in the literature that speaks in apocalyptic terms of impending doom and the end of mankind. When the focus of attention is shifted to a level in which hundreds or thousands can perceive ways of doing something about pieces of the problem, hope is generated and creativity released.

I am sure there are problems that are not amenable to disaggregation, but I am also sure that they are much fewer than presently perceived by authorities of all kinds. We really do need a shift in the focus of our attention and efforts, and we really do need a new way of seeing the relationship between the center and regions. The role of the central planner must be to set outer limits and boundary conditions for national action, and to do everything in their power to generate and encourage independent and multiple decision-making units to form and act within the boundaries that have been set. The center is the only place where broad directions and constraints can be considered, but the center does a very poor job or fails technically, economically, and politically when it specifies solutions and actions in detail. Actions are always specific and local in their implementation, and it is the collectivity of local actions that aggregate in, to some, messy, overlapping and human way to change the shape of our problems and of our society.

As I pointed out earlier, Heilbroner crystallizes an expression of the pessimism and malaise that grips the main body of the intellectuals and professionals of the so-called developed world. He writes lucidly and movingly of the lack of empirical findings to support an optimistic view of the human prospect. For those of us who have studied entrepreneurship, pessimism is harder to maintain. We see a constant human effort to make something positive happen, to come to grips with situations, to refuse to accept defeat. In spite of all the problems that beset our economy and our political world, last year we witnessed more than 350,000 company formations in the United States (we suspect the number is really much higher), and the pace of company formations continues this year. To study entrepreneurial behavior is to be exposed to a deep underlying optimism, a deep commitment to the future on the part of individuals handling more variables each day than I have ever seen used in a computer game for business decision making.

In closing, I would like to quote from the lovely book by Schumacher, *Small is Beautiful:*

> What is the meaning of democracy, freedom, human dignity, standard of living, self-realization, fulfillment? Is it a matter of goods, or of people? Of course it is a matter of people. But people can be themselves only in small comprehensible groups. Therefore we must learn to think in terms of an articulated structure that can cope with a multiplicity of small-scale units. If economic thinking cannot grasp this it is useless. If it cannot get beyond its vast abstraction, the national income, the rate of growth, capital/output ratios, input-output analysis, labor mobility, capital accumulation; if it cannot get beyond all this and make contact with the human realities of poverty, frustration, alienation, despair, breakdown, crime, escapism, stress, congestion, ugliness, and spiritual death, then let us scrap economics and start afresh.

FOOTNOTES

1. "Entrepreneur" is a term, unfortunately, that suffers from diverse definitions in both the popular and technical literature. By origin it is a French term, but in France it tends to mean a businessman, particularly a construction contractor. In Germany the term becomes "unternehmer," which in English means undertaker, a rather funereal term.

2. I have coined the expression "entrepreneurial event" as a means of identifying the many kinds of venturesome creations that most of us intuitively identify as being entrepreneurial even though they do not fit in with classical definitions of entrepreneurship or cannot identify with some distinct, individual entrepreneur. I define the entrepreneurial event as being the result of the initiative-taking action of an individual or group in which resources are brought together or reorganized into some organizational entity that is relatively independent in disposing of its resources and returns and that has the opportunity to fail. Thus, a community theater group, a wholly owned subsidiary, and a new, independent government organization can all be considered to be entrepreneurial events.

3. The Levenson instrument gives recognition to the multidimensionality of locus-of-control and consists of three scales: Internal (I), which measures the extent to which a person believes he has control over his own life; Powerful Others (P), the extent to which one believes powerful others have control over his life; and, Chance (C), the extent to which someone believes luck, chance, or fate controls his life. Borland also administered Lynn's Achievement Motivation Questionnaire in order to examine the relationship of a measure of need for achievement (nAch) with intentions to start a company and the measure's interaction with locus-of-control.

4. The manager of the large enterprise is denationalized and becomes a participant in an international culture of managerhood. Place and local custom are artifacts to the manager of a large corporate division. He does not relate to the local scene except outside the dictates of his organization. The local scene is something to be coped with, and, if he is lucky and competent, tomorrow he will be promoted to another local scene and another until he escapes all local scenes by going to headquarters.

BIBLIOGRAPHY

Borland, Candace. *Locus of Control, Need for Achievement and Entrepreneurship.* PhD Dissertation, University of Texas at Austin, 1974.

Boswell, Jonathan. *The Rise and Decline of Small Firms.* London: Goerge Allen & Unwin, 1972.

Carrol, John J. *The Filipino Manufacturing Entreprenuer.* Ithaca, N.Y.: Cornell University Press, 1965.

Cole, Arthur H. *Business Enterprise in Its Social Setting.* Cambridge: Harvard University Press, 1959.

Collins, Orvis F., and David G. Moore. *The Organization Makers—A Behavioral Study of Independent Entrepreneurs.* New York: Meredith Corporation, 1970.

Cooper, Arnold C. Spin-offs and technical entrepreneurship. *IEEE Transactions of Engineering Management* V. EM-18 # 1, Feb. 1971.

Derossi, Flavia. *The Mexican Entrepreneur.* Paris: OECD, 1971.

Draheim, Krik, Richard P. Howell, and Albert Shapero. *The Development of a Potential Defense R&D Complex: A Study of Minneapolis-St. Paul.* Menlo Park, Calif.: Stanford Research Institute, 1966.

Drucker, Peter F. *The Age of Discontinuity—Guidelines to Our Changing Society.* New York: Harper & Row, 1965.

Harbison, F., and C.A. Myers. *Education, Manpower and Economic Growth.* New York: McGraw-Hill, 1964.

Heilbroner, Robert L. *An Inquiry into The Human Prospect.* New York: W.W. Norton & Company, 1974.

Hoffman, Cary A. *The Venture Capital Investment Process.* PhD Dissertation, The University of Texas at Austin, 1972.

Jacobs, Jane. *The Economy of Cities.* New York: Random House, 1969.

Jansyn, Leon, E. Kohlhof, C. Sadowski, and J. Toby. Ex-offenders as small businessmen: opportunities and obstacles. Final Report under Office of Manpower Contract, Project #27-4990, Rutgers University, July 1969.

Levenson, Hanna. Distinctions within the concept of internal-external control. *Proceedings, 80th Annual American Psychological Association Convention*, 1971, 261-262.

Myint, H. *Economic Theory and the Underdeveloped Countries.* New York: Oxford University Press, 1971.

Papanek, Gustav F. The development of entrepreneurship. *American Economic Review* 52, May 1962.

Rotter, Julian B. *Generalized Expectancies for Internal Versus External Control of Reinforcement.* Psychological Monographs, 1966, 80 (Whole No. 609).

Say, Jean-Baptiste. *A Treatise on Political Economy.* London, 1821.

Sayigh, Yusif A. *Entrepreneurs in Lebanon.* Cambridge, Mass: Harvard University Press, 1962.

Schumacher, E.F. *Small Is Beautiful.* London: Blond & Briggs, 1973.

Schumpeter, Joseph A. *The Theory of Economic Development.* Cambridge, Mass.: Harvard Economic Studies, Harvard University, 1934.

Schumpeter, Joseph A. *History of Economic Analysis.* New York: Oxford University Press, 1954.

Shapero, Albert, C. Hoffman, K.P. Draheim, and R.P. Howell. *The Role of the Financial Community in the Formation, Growth and Effectiveness of Technical Companies.* Austin, Texas: MDRI Press, 1969.

Shapero, Albert. *An Action Program for Entrepreneurship.* Austin, Texas: MDRI Press, 1971.

Shapero, Albert, Jorge Garcia-Bouze, Achille Ferrari. *Technical Entrepreneurship in Northern Italy.* Milano: IIMT, 1974.

Small Business Enterprise and Governmental Decision Making

Frank McGee

Assistant Professor of Public Administration, University of New Haven

The objective of this paper is to highlight clear-cut trends in the American economy and in government policy making which have had a profound impact on the very character of small business enterprise. In this light, the program priorities of the Small Business Administration will be questioned.

1. THE PUBLIC-PRIVATE PARTNERSHIP

As predicted by Robert Dahl and Charles Lindblom in their classic *Politics, Economics and Welfare*, published in 1953, big government and big business in the intervening years have created at an incredible rate a host of formal and informal arrangements to guarantee mass provision of goods and services to the vast majority of Americans in an effective manner at relatively low cost. John Kenneth Galbraith in his *New Industrial State* reaffirmed the significance of this trend. Big government has assumed the cost of high-risk research and development of complex, technological hardware such as aircraft which has allowed the aircraft manufacturers and the airlines to do business. The Federal interstate highway system has provided the "fixed stock" necessary for the high-speed "rolling stock" produced by the big auto-makers. Presently, the railroads are forging their own form of partnership with the Federal government in order to survive in the marketplace.

Government-by-contract with the private sector is *the* growth area in providing quality public goods and services. The success of the space program, the vitality of our national defense systems, the construction of our interstate highways depend upon government-by-contract.

At the local level, as pointed out by John Bollens and Henry Schmandt in their *The Metropolis*, the phenomenal growth of the suburbs in large measure has been possible only through flexible contract arrangements between town governments of a rural character and small-scale real estate developers, sewer contractors, and a miscellany of small subcontractors. Because of this arrangement, rural town governments have been able to respond quickly and effectively to rapid suburban growth in their midst. Practically every local government function from the automated processing of municipal records to public works was contracted out to small business.

Prepared for: North East Regional Conference of the American Institute for the Decision Sciences Workshop on Small Business, University of Massachusetts, Amherst, Mass., April 24, 1975. Reprinted with permission.

The need for greater numbers of able subcontractors for large Federal and state contracts, for small contractors in the area of government procurement as stressed by Senator William Proxmire in his *Can Small Business Survive?*, and for local government contractors and subcontractors is probably the most important area of small business enterprise in the country today.

2. ENTERPRISE IN TRANSITION: FUTURE SHOCK

The virtues of large-scale private and public organization have been well documented. Large-scale organizations can undertake complex tasks which are well beyond the means of small-scale enterprise or individual endeavor. As a form of rational calculation and control, hierarchical organization can tame an uncertain environment and assure sufficient predictability. Hierarchical organization which entails a clear-cut command structure, centralized authority, and a narrow span of control is the most prevalent form of organization in the United States. The virtues of predictability, stability, and security are highly esteemed. Philip Selznick in his *TVA and the Grassroots* describes the process of cooptation through which organizations take control of elements in their immediate environment which previously were outside their boundaries. Clearly the maturation process of organization illustrates the cooptation function. As an organization grows and becomes more successful, it no longer has to contract for most of its operational needs. These operations or functions can be coopted or provided in-house. These virtues of large-scale organization can also be serious vices. Stability and predictability are the enemies of creativity and adaptability. Alvin Toffler in his *Future Shock* points out the difficulties arising from telescoping change; that is, an environment transforming at an ever-increasing rate. Like many individuals, a hierarchical organization does not respond and adapt easily to its ever-changing environment. This is particularly true in government where, for example, there existed until recently a massive farm subsidy program in the face of impending and actual world-wide famine and food shortages, and where foreign policy and domestic regulation of energy monopolies were caught short in the face of the Arab oil embargo. Private industry is also far from immune. Recently, the auto-makers miscalculated and wrongly predicted consumer preference regarding large, energy-inefficient automobiles. Unfortunately, rapid adaptation and creativity are not characteristics of large-scale, hierarchical organization. On the other hand, small-scale enterprise is often very creative and venturesome. Ironically, small new ventures find it exceedingly difficult to break into markets already staked out by large-scale enterprise.

Raymond Vernon in his *Anatomy of a Metropolis* proposes that one crucial economic reason why large urban centers are so important and, therefore, worthy of massive infusions of Federal grants-in-aid for redevelopment purposes is that these central cities are the incubators of new ventures. Innovative enterprise starts out on a small scale, perhaps in a low-rent loft, and contracts out as much of its overall operation as possible until the worth of its new product or service has been established. Without this high-density garden of contractors, new, small-scale ventures would not be possible. This area of small business enterprise is extremely important in assuring that the American economic system be creative and adaptive in the face of rapid sociological and technological change. During the New Deal,

Franklin D. Roosevelt created the "alphabet soup" agencies such as the WPA to contend with massive economic problems, rather than giving the task to established Federal agencies who he felt would have been unresponsive and unimaginative in facing the crisis. For similar reasons, the Office of Economic Opportunity (OEO) was created in the 1960s to launch the War on Poverty instead of leaving the job to established Federal domestic agencies. In the private sector, small new ventures must have a reasonable opportunity to compete effectively in the marketplace. Inasmuch as this becomes increasingly difficult, then society will be more dependent on large-scale, established enterprise for innovation and adaptation to rapid change. To allow this condition to develop further would be most unwise.

3. THE SMALL, FAMILY RETAIL BUSINESS:
A GLARING ANACHRONISM

The most common image of small business enterprise is the "ma and pa" neighborhood retail store. The American public subscribes strongly to the small business ethos. The solid values of small business competition, rugged individualism and independence, and the legacy of Horatio Alger are held dear. However, it is folly to live this ethos in traditional terms by investing in a form of small business enterprise more suited for a less complicated period in history.

Ours is a mobile society. Small businesses claiming a small-neighborhood clientele or those holding a neighborhood monopoly based upon consumer immobility are inexorably passing from the scene. Highly organized retail chains and large-scale shopping malls have been steadily capturing the small independent's market. Operating with an extremely low overhead, the fortunate few independent retailers have been able to survive in a marginal way. Fast-food chains have devastated small-neighborhood restaurants and convenience-store chains have overwhelmed the small variety store.

Government policy has consciously and unconsciously encouraged the demise of small-neighborhood enterprise. Anthony Downs in his *Urban Problems and Prospects* indicates in a rigorous manner the economic impact of Federal and state highway right-of-way acquisition and construction on small-neighborhood businesses. Small retail operations relocated because of highway site acquisition have very often failed. Basil Zimmer in his *Rebuilding Cities: The Effects of Displacement and Relocation on Small Business* displays this sad record of neighborhood business failure due to the impact of government transportation policy. The Federal urban renewal program has likewise had a similar impact on small-neighborhood enterprise. Often, small-neighborhood retailers have been cut-off from a significant portion of their clientele because of the barrier of a new highway arterial. Often, the thinning of neighborhood densities or the change in the composition of people residing in a neighborhood due to urban renewal programming has seriously impaired or ruined small-neighborhood businesses without any government compensation for real business loss.

Municipal government policy too has weighed heavily against small neighborhood-based businesses. Local zoning ordinances often categorize small-neighborhood retailers as "nonconforming uses," meaning that no new business can operate the same type of enterprise on the site. Obviously, if a business' worth is based upon location and a particular neighborhood clientele, then restrictive zoning can destroy the market value of that business. More recently, small businessmen in strip commercial developments along urban arterials have been hurt by the growing numbers of large shopping malls. Local government policy, particularly zoning, has followed suit by restricting strip commercial uses in the name of better traffic flow, traffic safety, and urban blight elimination. In addition, local property tax breaks, concessions, or postponements are often available to large-scale local enterprise while small businesses continue to assume a still greater burden of local property taxation. Small retailers in municipalities are harder pressed all the time. They have state sales tax collection responsibilities, have to worry about income tax audits, and must face myriad local ordinance and licensing requirements. They face every day the specter of rising crime rates and are particularly vulnerable in this regard.

4. SMALL BUSINESS TRENDS AND THE SMALL BUSINESS ADMINISTRATION'S PRIORITIES

Small business enterprise is vital to the well-being of the American economy and is crucial in the provision of effective government services. The existence of small government contractors and subcontractors allows government to respond quickly and professionally to changing conditions and needs. New small business ventures provide much of the creativity and innovation that the economy must have to remain healthy. These new ventures must be allowed to enter the marketplace and grow and prosper if warranted.

Unquestionably, the role of small business enterprise has changed greatly in the overall political economy. Government policies have been fairly consistent in encouraging this change. The stress that government puts on its contract relations with small and large private enterprise, the emphasis it has placed on renewing large central cities to serve as incubators of new ventures, and the consistency of government policy in accelerating the demise of neighborhood-based retail businesses should be reflected in priorities set by the Small Business Administration in providing technical assistance to, and adequate financing for, small business enterprise in America. It is hoped that the SBA will stress programs aimed at providing investment capital and managerial assistance to struggling new ventures trying out innovations in manufacturing, distribution, and professional services. Identical stress should be given programs aimed at small contractors who provide important government services.

Certainly less emphasis should be given to programs geared to traditional small-neighborhood retailers whose role has diminished in importance in our ever-changing economy. By following this proposed priority scheme, SBA would be in line with the rest of government policy making.

Suggestions for Further Reading

Bruno, A. V. *et al.* Technology forecasting in small companies. *Sloan Management Review* 15: 49-63 (Fall, 1973).

Federal units to outline services to small businesses. *Commerce Today* 4: 17 (Sept. 16, 1974)

Small business watchdog with a bigger bite (House Small Business Committee). *National Business* 63:34-36 (May, 1975).

Small firms say they have unfair share of shortages. *Industry Week* 179: 17-18 (Dec. 24, 1973).

Small firms win some help from Congress: want more. *Industry Week* 188: 19-21 (Feb. 9, 1976).

Study seeks to cushion cost impact of pollution fight on small firms. *Commerce Today* 3: 10-11 (April 2, 1973).

Thieblot, A. J., Jr. How government chokes small business growth. *Nations Business* 64: 70-72 (May 1976).

Unnecessary government interference is costly to small business. *Air Conditioning, Heating and Refrigeration News* 137: 13+ (March 1, 1976).

Walsh, R. J., and L. R. Hess. Small company, EEOC, and test validation alternatives: do you know your options? *Personnel Journal* 53: 840-845 (Nov. 1974).

7
Developing Organizations and Implementing Entrepreneurial Decisions

Introduction

The generation of good ideas for new ventures is only the start of the entrepreneurial function. The text to this point has presented a discussion of problem areas inherent in getting those ideas from the formulation stage to successful implementation. This final hurdle, however, frequently turns out to be an insurmountable problem for entrepreneurs. This is the primary reason why venture capitalists prefer to see a superior entrepreneurial team with an average idea rather than an average team with a superior idea.

Many of the issues that develop during the implementation stage involve organizational and behavioral problems. Successful implementation requires attention to detail on the part of the agent responsible for this task. People, not machines, implement actions. This means that interpersonal relations within the organization must be refined to a high degree to ensure cooperation during implementation of key decisions. This stage of the decision process also requires attention to details concerning the various functional and environmental areas discussed to this point.

A key question revolves around the ability of entrepreneurial managers to adapt to this mode of behavior. Particularly as the organization grows and becomes more complex, an entrepreneur starts to lose touch with operations. This frequently is associated with a loss of control of the operations. In a struggle to maintain control, entrepreneurs fail to delegate responsibility and authority within the organization. This leads to loss of morale by subordinates. It also overtaxes the decision-making ability of the entrepreneur who expends most of his effort reacting to the environment instead of planning for it. As the organization grows, these problems grow at least as fast. Different stages of organizational growth provide different problems. The final problem faced by entrepreneurs during the growth cycle involves planning for succession by new managers.

Stages of Organizational Growth

Organizations follow standard patterns of growth. Each of the various stages presents different constraints to entrepreneurs intent on implementing action plans.

Typically, organizations start with one product or service offered in a tightly defined market area. The organization is highly centralized at this stage. The entrepreneurial manager at the helm of the organization usually performs many functions. The entrepreneur also takes an active part in making all decisions within the organization. The size of the organization necessitates a relatively loose structure. Specialization is a luxury that cannot be afforded. This type of structure is ideally suited for the generalist-oriented entrepreneur. Coordination and control are relatively simple functions at this stage of growth. The few managers who are involved in decision making frequently have previously agreed on the overall direction the organization is to take. This consonance of thought means that individual decisions are consistent internally. Also, given that these managers are usually located in the same area, frequently the same office, little time is wasted in seeking different opinions on a given decision. One manager need simply raise his or her voice to determine the views of fellow managers. Decisions can be made rapidly and with a high degree of consensus. This has often been described as the major advantage of small business, its ability to shift directions and resources rapidly. It lacks the inertia of large firms. It does not have large amounts of resources tied up in a particular way of doing something. These very strengths, however, can often provide the greatest constraints for the small business.

At the initial stage of growth, the small business lacks the resources to take advantage of multiple opportunities. Entrepreneurs whose organizations are in the early part of the growth cycle must choose their courses of action very carefully. Wrong decisions can frequently bring disaster to the fledgling organization. The large firm may be able to absorb one or more mistakes. This situation is made even worse by the lack of specialist advisors within the small business. Entrepreneurs must make decisions based on incomplete and often insufficient data. Fortunately, however, entrepreneurs have been imbued with the desire to make their own decisions with no constraints from an entrenched bureaucracy.

The lack of management depth provides another constraint on the small business. The lack of management depth means that all the members of the management group must oversee some area of operations. They then get bogged down in operating problems to the exclusion of long-range problems. This preoccupation with short-term, operating problems frequently robs the entrepreneur of the ability to take advantage of the flexibility that is the small firm's greatest strength. The ability to make rapid shifts in direction is diminished by the preoccupation with day-to-day operating problems.

Successful entrepreneurs are frequently those who find a way to make both kinds of decisions. They find the time to make both the tactical, operating decisions as well as the opportunity-oriented, strategic decisions. These entrepreneurs provide the impetus to proceed to the next stage of organizational growth.

The second stage of organizational growth typically finds the small business expanding into multiple market segments. This may take the form of multiple, but related, products in a single geographic market. It may also take the form of a single product expanding into multiple geographic markets.

With this growth, the pressure to concentrate on operating details becomes intense. Advancement into this stage of the growth cycle is frequently accomplished with few, if any, additions to management depth.

Entrepreneurs retain the ability to make rapid shifts in direction and resources because of the relatively lean management group. Coordination of managers is still relatively easy because of the small organizational size. These managers, however, find they have more responsibility within the organization. Operating problems proliferate simply because there are more people to supervise without a proportional increase in the number of supervisors. These operating problems frequently take on crisis proportions. This leads to the organization controlling the entrepreneur, as opposed to the entrepreneur controlling the organization.

This is the stage of growth where the entrepreneur should be considering plans for the future of the organization. Responsibility for operating decisions should be delegated to other managers. The traditional strengths of entrepreneurs—propensity for risk, iconoclasm, and high tolerance for ambiguity—are needed at this stage to maintain the viability of the firm. Instead, most entrepreneurs find their talents being buried under the weight of each new operating crisis.

The kinds of decisions encountered by the entrepreneur center around the feasibility of growth. Analysis of the demand for the product or service offered by the firm has to include the ability of both the internal and external environment to sustain growth. Demand may be demonstrable. The entrepreneur must decide whether the resources are available to take advantage of that demand.

This is the stage of the growth cycle where much larger firms may decide that the market is worthy of their own efforts. The entrepreneur must decide if strengths are present to offset the size advantage of potential competitors.

A strength that the entrepreneur has at this stage that might have been absent earlier is that financial resources are usually easier to obtain. The organization has a proven track record, as discussed earlier in the section on financing growth operations. The firm also has at least the start of a reputation on which it can build customer loyalty. If the entrepreneur decides, based on rational analysis of the total environment, that the cards are stacked against the firm, then plans must be made to successfully withdraw or limit operations in this area.

A decision in favor of growth carries its own implications for future plans. Particularly, the entrepreneur must plan for increasing management depth within the organization. The question of seeking and grooming a successor, at least for the top operating position, has to be considered at this time. The readings at the end of this chapter describe sources and methods of securing a successor for an entrepreneur. The key factor to be considered is the timing required for these moves, however. It takes a great deal of time simply to find an acceptable candidate as a successor. The founding entrepreneur must find a manager with whom he or she can work. More importantly, however, the entrepreneur must feel confident in trusting the future of the organization to the new manager. It is one thing to work with someone. It is quite another thing to have to abide totally by that person's decisions.

This latter point is one that frequently proves to be the greatest barrier to growth for the small firm. If the entrepreneur can overcome this barrier, the organization may be able to proceed to the next stage of the growth cycle. At this stage, product and market proliferation start to take place. New products introduced tend to be in areas related to the primary product offered by the firm. They are designed to take advantage of present strengths. The organization typically does not depart from proven areas of expertise to expand operations.

The cautious manager remains with a safe, consistent strategy for growth, or perhaps simply maintenance of position. This is the time when entrepreneurial fervor and iconoclasm are needed to shake organizations out of their conservatism and lethargy.

If the entrepreneur has remained in the organization, he or she needs the management depth provided for in the stage of growth discussed earlier. Without that depth, the entrepreneur will be innundated with operating problems. There will be no time available to develop innovative products. Neither will there be sufficient time to develop methods to attack new markets in a novel manner.

This is also the stage of the growth cycle where many of the firms now find themselves in our economy. The difference is that, for the most part, they have developed a bureaucracy that is more interested in security than growth. This is why many large firms are now seeking entrepreneurially oriented managers. They are needed to shake the organization out of its preconceived notions concerning direction and actions. If the entrepreneur is successful at redirecting the organization into a new growth strategy, it will in all likelihood proceed to the next stage of organizational growth.

The next stage in the growth cycle finds the firm offering multiple products in multiple markets. The structure usually switches to a decentralized form of decision making. Entrepreneurs are now needed throughout the organization, with renewed vigor at the divisional levels. Without their direction, the firm is likely to pass into the decline stage of the growth cycle.

Product development during these stages of growth is frequently dependent on perceived market conditions and fit with internal resources and values. The firm with excess capacity may try to find methods to sell more of their present product. This may lead to supplying other firms with private label products, as an example.

The same firm might also try to develop a product using the same type of production process, regardless of the fit of that product with the current marketing channels. Other firms may try to develop new products that fit with current market channels (possibly to make more efficient use of salesmen) regardless of fit with production expertise. It is beyond the scope of this text to note the different methods of developing all those avenues of growth. This is the purpose of texts dealing with marketing and operations management.

Some firms decide not to follow these courses of action, however. The entrepreneurs in these firms find their current resources match present demand. They find that they enjoy working in a firm that is relatively small. The size and fit with demand are sufficient for their needs and values. They make a conscious decision to restrain growth. Essentially, they demonstrate their independence once more by eschewing growth in a growth-oriented society.

The entrepreneur who starts the organization on the growth cycle is unlikely to stay with the firm throughout all stages of growth. There are too many wrong decisions that can be made along the way. Also, even if all the decisions are the right ones, there are environmental factors beyond the control of the entrepreneur that may cause the entrepreneur to leave the firm, either voluntarily or otherwise. The entrepreneur may also simply lose interest in the direction the organization is taking. It may be the product, the market, or simply the luster wearing off the adventure of being an innovator. At some point, even die-hard entrepreneurs have to retire. Bill Lear, of Lear Stereo and Lear Jet fame, has frequently stated that it is at this stage of the growth of his ventures that he prefers to step down from active management, for just these reasons.

Usually, however, entrepreneurs find that they can no longer perform all the functions within the firm themselves. There just is not enough time available to make all the decisions for the entire organization. Help is needed from other managers. The problem that faces entrepreneurs in this position is how to find those managers; how to select them; how to train them; and finally, and most important, how to work with them.

Expanding Management Talent

Entrepreneurs usually need help in the functional areas, particularly finance and accounting. Since, at the outset, a wide range of decisions is required from a small management group, successful entrepreneurs usually fit the mold of the generalist. Larger scale operations require expert decisions in all areas, however. Many entrepreneurs find it difficult to work with functional specialists. The entrepreneurs rebel at the necessity for adhering to rigor in the analytical process leading to decisions.

Understanding of the problems in adopting decision-making styles is a two-way street, however. Both the entrepreneur and the new, functional managers have to give a little to get along effectively. In the past, this has presented a great problem. Many of the best specialists have been trained as professional administrators by schools of business, as discussed in Chapter 1. The emergence of strong entrepreneurial programs at this source has improved the understanding of the problems inherent with functional specialists entering the world of the entrepreneur. Prospective managers are less likely to try to utilize standard, textbook solutions that may be inappropriate for small businesses.

The other major source of management talent is from the ranks of large businesses. Many managers tire of the regimen and lack of responsibility available in many large organizations. They seek what they perceive as the freedom and challenge of the small business. The process of matching up these managers with entrepreneurs seeking help can often be a haphazard affair. Word-of-mouth referrals through friends and associates frequently provide the major source of match-ups for this purpose.

There are several more efficient methods of finding likely candidates. Most of these sources provide services for both large and small businesses. Accountants, lawyers, and consultants often know who is available to fill what positions. Managers in large corporations frequently confide in these sources their desires to move to a smaller firm. These service-oriented firms are viewed as neutral sources of information. They are usually perceived as being discreet with any information given to them. A final source for management talent comes from the management-search firms, commonly referred to as headhunters. These are formal placement services for upper-level managers or firms seeking people to fill upper-level positions. They do not usually handle small-firm placements. They may be able to find suitable managers, however, since they do have wide contacts among management ranks. This source is usually expensive and, as stated earlier, may not be eager to serve small firms since repeat business is, for obvious reasons, infrequent.

The first problem frequently observed when a new manager is recruited from a large firm involves that manager's expectations concerning support functions. He or she has become used to being able to call on sophisticated analytical resources to assist in decision making. The small firm cannot call on large computer systems, staff experts in depth, consultants when necessary, or the financial resources available to most large firms. It takes a great deal of adjustment on the part of new managers to overcome this form of cultural shock.

The next problem faced by the transplant from large organizations involves the lack of role definition in small firms. A manager in a small firm frequently has to be a jack of all trades. As is demonstrated in the Vail Industries case, there is a great deal of overlap in the management functions. Everyone does a little bit of everything. Successful adaptation to this fluid type of organizational structure requires a high tolerance for ambiguity on the part of the new manager.

Another problem—unfortunately, the most common one—involves the founding entrepreneur. Any new manager has to be able to work with the existing personnel. But if the entrepreneur is unwilling to give up some degree of control or responsibility, the new manager will soon become disillusioned with the small firm. One reason for leaving the large organization was the constraints placed on the individual manager's decision-making authority. If similar constraints are found in the new position because of the entrepreneur's desire to maintain total control, the new manager may feel that the added responsibility simply is not worth the supposed freedom. Responsibility without attendant authority leads to frustration with the organizational structure.

The entrepreneur has to be willing to relinquish some authority, at least for operating decisions. The need for new management usually springs from the lack of management depth in key functional areas. Unless the entrepreneur is willing to listen to the specialist and take his or her advice, the situation will simply continue.

Failure to relinquish control will simply lead to a waste of time, effort, talent, and resources.

Summary

The book, to this point, has traced the development of entrepreneurial managers and their ventures from inception to implementation. Essentially, we have to come full circle back to the point where new ventures are conceived by existing or new entrepreneurs.

The characteristics of an effective entrepreneur have been presented. Specific traits have been attributed to entrepreneurs. These very traits have led many traditional members of the business community to distrust entrepreneurs. These same traits, however, may provide the key ingredients for continued rejuvenation of not only existing organizations but also the economy as a whole.

The United States' economy has developed into what is principally a service economy. It has been suggested that the two commodities we will be exporting most in the future are agriculture and ideas. Entrepreneurs may provide the largest pool of effective ideas available both now and in the future. Governmental policy has led to a greater acceptance and support of entrepreneurial ventures at the small business level. Large organizations are now starting to follow suit, although in a cautious manner. Top executives at these organizations are finding that entrepreneurial values can be harnessed effectively to achieve organizational growth objectives as well as the goals of the entrepreneur.

The key to effective use of these entrepreneurial values frequently lies in the proper matching of environmental factors with new venture ideas. Whereas many managers view the external environment as filled with constraints and risks, the entrepreneur views that same environment as presenting opportunities to satisfy personal objectives for change. Analyzing that environment in a rational manner is one area where entrepreneurs can exercise greater skill.

This combination of values and environmental inputs provides the basis for a sound planning process for entrepreneurs. The traditional problem encountered by entrepreneurs has been a lack of planning for the intitial stages of the new venture. While entrepreneurs need optimism to keep going in spite of lean times at early stages of venture initiation, this trait often blinds them to potential delays. Any delay at early stages may tax the limited resources available to entrepreneurs, particularly financial resources.

The planning process is designed to provide an effective matching of resources, opportunities, and values. The culmination of this match is a detailed action plan designed to achieve the objectives set for the organization.

The fit between action plan and objectives also provides a method for evaluating the overall effectiveness and feasibility of the new venture. While this is useful in itself, it further provides the basis for coordinating and controlling the new venture.

Benchmarks are provided, through this process, for the organization to follow. No single entrepreneur can implement ventures of the scope discussed in this book. Others have to be entrusted with at least part of the responsibility for the success of the venture. Coordination assures that all members of the organization are aiming for the same result. Control helps to evaluate the effectiveness of the plans and resulting actions by the various members and groups within the organization.

Proper control methods require effective internal information processes. This is viewed as wasted effort by many entrepreneurs. They see it as morbid interest in the past, while they are primarily concerned with the future. These data, if effectively gathered and analyzed, can provide up-to-date insight on the operation of the venture. This analysis can then be used to project reaction to future moves by the organization.

Organization design is often crucial throughout the planning and control process. The organization should be consistent with the long-term objectives of the entrepreneur and the backers of the new venture. Too often, entrepreneurs design the organization around their own values and desire for tight control. While this might be quite effective at the very early stages of the new venture, at some point decisions have to be made by others within the organization.

People, in the final analysis, have to implement the plans to form a new venture. People have different values and objectives for participating in any organization. Entrepreneurs must be sensitive to the varying needs of people within their organizations. The entrepreneurs have to plan for the future of all parts of the new venture, including their own role. The ability to step back from active participation in the organization is a trait that is rarely appreciated by entrepreneurs. This becomes exemplified by a failure to plan for an eventual successor at the top. This often proves disastrous to the long-run effectiveness of the venture.

The cases following this section are designed to provide insight into the development and operation of new and small ventures. The cases present examples of all the different issues brought out in the text and readings. They should be used to develop an understanding of the issues, as opposed to being used as examples of proper or improper entrepreneurial practice. They stress an analytical approach to solving the types of entrepreneurial problems presented in the readings and text.

Readings

The readings for Chapter 7 discuss various aspects associated with implementing entrepreneurial actions. In the first article, "The Development of Organization in the Entrepreneurial Concern" by Bernard Berry, the concept of structure following strategy is once again explored. Berry explores the problems facing organizations entering that awkward stage of growth when one person can no longer make all decisions effectively.

The size problem is also inherent in the article "Where Entrepreneurs Run into Trouble" from *Forbes*. Questions of product mix add another dimension to the organizational problems presented in the Berry article. Sophistication in the areas of marketing and product development is an added requirement often lacking in the entrepreneur.

The last two articles, "How to Find a Likely Successor" by Joseph Robinson and "Preparing for New Management" by F. Frederick Halstead, were prepared for the SBA. They provide practical solutions to searching for, selecting, and preparing for the transition to new management in the growing small firm.

The thrust of these articles expands on the point made in the text that plans have to be implemented by people. Planning is a social process. No one can expect to be able to run a one-person operation for all time. Changes in the environment require changes in the organization. This is usually reflected in changing management needs. We live in a dynamic environment. Entrepreneurs must be willing to adapt their plans, behavior, and organization to experience continued success.

The Development
of Organization
in the Entrepreneurial
Concern

Bernard Berry
Ashridge Management College

Central problems which face entrepreneurial concerns are how to cope with the succession of the founder; how to grow beyond the stage at which they can be controlled by one man and how to develop management expertise and an organization structure appropriate to subsequent stages of growth. This paper describes the characteristics of organization structure which may facilitate the transition from an entrepreneurial concern to a more formal business and discusses some of the problems which may be encountered. The conclusion is that movement to a more formal organization structure can be achieved successfully, provided that the entrepreneur is aware of at least some of the difficulties and takes steps to overcome them.

Entrepreneurial concerns play a vital part in filling many of the nooks and crannies of economic systems which are inclined to be ignored by larger firms. They tend, however, to face two basic problems. One is the much-discussed question of how they can remain in existence after the entrepreneur is no longer available to control his business; the other is how they can grow beyond the stage at which they can still remain under the personal control of one man, which may be vitally necessary if they are to provide an effective challenge to the market leaders in some sectors of advanced economies. Both of these difficulties revolve around the question of entrepreneurial succession and the development of management expertise within the firm. The normal solution to both problems is to introduce and develop an organized management structure for, as Stanley Davis has pointed out: "Men die, but organizations generally continue to exist beyond the life of their leaders".[1] This paper will describe some of the problems likely to be encountered in developing an organization structure in the entrepreneurial concern and will offer some suggestions on how they may be overcome.

THE CHOICE OF AN APPROPRIATE ORGANIZATION STRUCTURE
Research by social scientists into business organizations has involved many attempts to classify organizations into types. Certainly, people have very different ideas about the form an ideal work organization should take. Some, for example, consider that it

Proceedings of Project ISEED, Summer 1975. Published by Project ISEED, Ltd., The Center for Venture Management, Suite 508, 207 E. Buffalo Street, Milwaukee, WI 53202, U.S.A.

should involve a cluster of characteristics which may be termed bureaucratic. The principal features of this form of organization include:

1. a well-defined chain of command;
2. a formal system of rules and procedures;
3. a division of labor based on functional specialization;
4. personnel selection and promotion based on objective assessments of competence;
5. impersonality in relationships, with emphasis on role or position rather than individuality.

On the other hand, for others the ideal work organization should include such features as the following:

1. a flexible organization structure emphasizing lateral relationships;
2. participation and involvement in decision making together with openness in personal relationships;
3. authority derived from the task rather than personal authority or authority derived from hierarchical status;
4. emphasis on teamwork in relation to the whole task as against specialization.

Such organizations have been termed "organic" or "organismic."[2] Rather than regarding these two extreme forms of organization as unique alternatives it may be more useful to consider them as occupying opposite ends of a continuum between which lie a whole range of organizational possibilities.

The type of organization structure which should be adopted by the entrepreneurial concern will depend on such factors as the task involved, the technology with which it is pursued, and the markets served. Research carried out in small and medium sized firms in the British printing and building industries by the Ashridge Management Research Unit indicates that, other things being equal, firms with tasks most capable of being routinized and using mass production technology are more likely to be successful with the bureaucratic type of organization, whereas firms with more creative tasks, or ones which employ craft technologies or continuous flow, are more likely to achieve success with a more organic form of organization.[3] However, the organization structure initially adopted will almost certainly differ from that which might be regarded as ideal as there will be a need to take into account the personalities, needs, and values of those people already employed in the concern. What will probably be required will be a planned programme of change—usually requiring the advice and assistance of outside advisors—in order that the concern may develop over a period of time towards the most appropriate form of organization.

PROBLEMS LIKELY TO BE ENCOUNTERED IN THE DEVELOPMENT OF AN ORGANIZATION STRUCTURE

If the decision is taken that the business should attempt to grow beyond the stage at which it can still be controlled by one man, several problems may be anticipated. Some of these will stem from the pattern of expectations that people build up about how they should interact, and others will occur because of the personality characteristics of the entrepreneur and his team.

Any group of people in an unstructured or loosely structured situation will tend to develop relationships among themselves and thus develop their own "informal" group structure. Such informal relationships may be important in helping to satisfy the emotional needs of those concerned and may also be useful in helping the firm to carry out its task. It may be expected, however, that the introduction of an organization structure into a group with its own informal pattern of relationships will cause some problems for those concerned. Entrepreneurs, for example, usually tend to favor a pattern of exclusively informal communication contacts but such a pattern may be inappropriate or impossible with large numbers of employees. Employees may also be expected to be resentful if they no longer communicate directly with the owner of the firm.

Larger production runs may require technical knowledge which neither the owner nor anyone else in the firm possesses, or for the outside finance which may be on a scale which will demand the introduction of accounting procedures to achieve financial control. Such developments are likely to call for managers possessing the appropriate skills and knowledge to be recruited from outside and their introduction into the firm may precipitate further difficulties. The owner of a firm is—in the eyes of many of the employees concerned—the personification of it and where he has maintained a close personal supervision of the firm's activities, the appointment of managers from outside often leads to two separate, but distinct, problems. One is the need for the chief executive to withdraw from close personal contacts with operating departments and to rely on information reaching him on a more formalized basis. Such an adjustment may not be easy to make, but failure to achieve it can only result in inadequate utilization of the managers appointed from outside and a reduction in the effectiveness of the organizational structure, which will eventually restrict the growth of the firm. The other problem lies in the acceptance of managers recruited from outside by the established employees of the firm. As has already been pointed out, employees often obtain considerable satisfaction from their day-to-day contact with the owner of a business and may resent no longer dealing with him directly.

Another likely difficulty will be the question of management style in the business. Those individuals who have worked closely with entrepreneurs during the growth period of a firm are often prepared to accept and possibly welcome a more autocratic style of management than is usual in industry and commerce. The professional manager, on the other hand, will tend to demand a degree of autonomy and will resent interference in his sphere without just cause. Indeed, the personalities of entrepreneurs and their teams are such that Weinshall[4] has suggested that the introduction of an organization structure into an entrepreneurial concern can generally only be achieved by the replacement of the chief executive and many of his team. This somewhat extreme view is not shared by the present writer, but it has to be accepted that the provision of leadership to a group of professional managers will call for very different skills and methods than most entrepreneurs will be used to exercising. It is also probably the case that most entrepreneurs will be more likely to be effective in starting and building things up than they will be in managing larger organizations.

It is also generally accepted that there are some personality differences between entrepreneurs and managers.[5] McClelland, for example, has proposed that there is a strong relationship between the personal qualities associated with what he terms a high need for achievement (i.e., the desire to have full personal responsibility for results; the tendency to set challenging standards; the desire for "feedback" and to have rewards on the basis of performance) and successful entrepreneurship.)[6] Individuals with a high need for achievement tend to work extremely hard for long hours, enjoy innovating work, and rather than follow standard practices, like to study the requirements of each situation carefully and then meet its specific demands. They enjoy their work and are usually loath to retire from it. Although such personality factors may be extremely important and valuable during the early stages of the growth of a firm, paradoxically, they may lead to inefficiency and inflexibility in the enterprise at later stages of its development.

Entrepreneurs frequently regard more formal organizations with some suspicion. Typically, they regard flair and hunch as indispensable to success and tend to be skeptical of systematic or scientific procedures. They usually cherish their independence and are reluctant to see their enterprises grow beyond a certain size lest that independence be threatened.

The problems likely to be encountered in the transformation of a firm from a one-man concern to a more formal business enterprise, therefore, are considerable, but provided that the entrepreneur is aware of at least some of the difficulties and takes steps to overcome them, there seems to be no reason why the transition should not be accomplished. Clearly, many large businesses began as entrepreneurial concerns and have effected successful development. Nevertheless, the rate of failure among smaller companies is high[7] and the transition from entrepreneurial concern to large business is much more likely to be effective if it is carried out as a systematic program of organizational development.

Movement to a more formal organization structure may be accompanied by considerable regret and many of those concerned will look back with affection to the "good old days" of the period of early growth. Such a transition, however, should help to ensure that the enterprise founded by the entrepreneur will be more likely to continue after his demise and, in the long run, make it more effective in meeting the challenge of competition.

REFERENCES

1. Stanley M. Davis, Entrepreneurial succession, *Administrative Science Quarterly,* Vol. 13, No. 3 (Dec. 1968).

2. Tom Burns and G. M. Stalker, *The Management of Innovation* (London: Tavistock Publications, 1961).

3. Peter Lansley; Philip Sadler; and Terry Webb, Organization structure, management style and company performance, *Omega,* Vol. 11, No. 4 (1974).

4. Theodore D. Weinshall, *Application of Two Conceptual Schemes of Organizational Behavior in Case Study and General Organizational Research* (Berkhamsted, Hertfordshire, U.K.: Ashridge Management College, 1971).

5. See, for example: R. Lynn, Personality characteristics of a group of entrepreneurs, *Occupational Psychology,* Vol. 43 (1969).

6. See: D. C. McClelland et al., *The Achievement Motive* (New York: Appleton-Century Crofts, 1953).

7. Merrett Cyriax Associates, Dynamics of Small Firms, *Committee of Inquiry on Small Firms, Research Report No. 12.* (London: Her Majesty's Stationery Office, 1971).

Where Entrepreneurs
Run Into Trouble

Forbes

"Size problems?" asks Donald K. Clifford, Jr., 42, partner in New York's big McKinsey & Co. management consulting firm. "The giants run into them just as the start-up companies do. But the really difficult problems arise in the companies in between—the ones that are transforming themselves from small, probably privately held outfits into complex and highly organized, publicly owned giants. This is the area where the way you manage a company changes more rapidly than at any other phase of its life cycle, and the problems of being big grow out of this process."

The basic problem, Clifford says, is the explosive growth in the complexity of the business. "You are moving from a fairly simple mix of products, economics, and people to an elaborate one that can very easily run out of control. So you've got to have effective organizational staffing to cope with it. "When you're less than $20 million, what you really need is no structure at all. You have a sales force and a plant, and you communicate informally. Coordination and control are so easy. But there comes a time when you can't do it that way anymore, and you've got to set up an organizational structure to recreate what you had before." You've got to develop planning procedures and information systems, hire staff specialists—people to cope with the Cost of Living Council, the Justice Department, labor, security analysts.

The size of such transitional companies—Clifford calls them *threshold* companies—varies with the kind of business they're in, the kind of product they produce. They're rarely less than $5 million in sales and more likely $20 million and rarely more than $200 million. This is a sizable category. As against the roughly 700 giants with more than $200 million in sales, there are over 3,000 in the $20-million to $200-million range. (Compare this with 1.5 million units in the under $20-million category).

There is no reason a company *has* to cross that threshold, however. "There are a lot of companies in the $10-million-to-$50-million range that don't have to grow. Lovely little sinecures that probably perform very well. They can play for the long term. They can build a product that will last forever. They can run the business in the way they sense it ought to be run—in the interest of the family or that small group that controls it.

"Once you go public, you have no choice but to grow. It's not just the pressure of the stock market for performance. Once the business becomes complex and goes public, you have to grow in order to stimulate people inside the organization. You have to create ways of stimulating them—new products, new businesses, new geographic markets—and unless you're going to become static, you have to bring in a flow of good motivators."

Forbes, May 15, 1974, p. 73. Reprinted with permission.

Clifford specializes in the problems of such transitional companies. He says these transitional companies grow more rapidly in both sales and earnings than the largest industrials—on average, more than 20 percent faster. In part, this is because the 500 can't make major leaps by acquisitions; the transitionals often can. At the same time, their earnings are noticeably more erratic. Their product lines and market positions are narrower, so they're more vulnerable to cycles, and they're less conservatively financed. They're more highly leveraged, for one thing; they need more capital to finance their growth and they pay more to get it.

Their profit margins are also narrower, and they're getting still narrower because of the costs imposed by their growing complexity. "You don't have the dominant market share," Clifford says, "you're No. Two, Three, or Five in the market, so you don't have a chance to get the scale economies. One salesman sells a grocery store 50 percent of its coffee needs, another sells 10 percent, but their costs are the same. So what these 10 percent-share companies have got to be good at is profit-improvement work—cutting administrative expenses, product-line pruning, balance-sheet planning."

As a group, the transitional companies are both better and worse than they look. If they're doing well, they're generally doing extremely well, probably earning more on their investment even than the giants—"a distinctive product will always command major margins." But such companies can't afford to make moves that require large capital investments or heavy outlays on research and development—they don't have the capital; they have to be careful not to acquire beyond their ability to manage their acquisitions; and they have to learn to cut their losses quickly if a new product doesn't catch on. "Procter & Gamble doesn't have to worry too much if a new product falls on its face—it isn't going to kill them, but it *can* kill one of these companies. You've got to say, 'If we're not at 5 percent of the market by Aug. 1, we're out.'"

Such companies have some distinct advantages, however. Because they're small, they may be particularly attractive to entrepreneurs who want to sell out their companies. They can afford to cultivate markets too small to interest the giants. "You look for a niche where you can be a dominant force. You get 25 percent of a strong business, and you've got something." Such companies can also enter large markets and take as much as 5 percent without disrupting the market. Let a new company move into some area of the computer market International Business Machines has overlooked, and nothing much may happen. But if Sperry Rand's Univac does so, the reverberations are likely to shake the industry.

The thorniest problem for the threshold company, Clifford says, is the chief executive. Entrepreneurs are not especially adept at running complex organizations, and many of them have stagnated their companies by lacking enough sense to step aside in favor of an outsider. "Very few of these men want to grow with a company, to undertake the voyage through managerial change."

"People who start small businesses love to do everything themselves, but when it gets to be highly complex, there's not way. You need a different kind of guy. If the entrepreneur is smart, he sells out and starts again."

How to Find
a Likely Successor

Joseph A. Robinson

Principal, Joseph A. Robinson Associates, San Francisco, California

Summary. *A good man is hard to find, especially when the owner-manager of a small business goes outside to look for his own successor. There he must fish in a shrinking pool along with scouts who seek executive personnel for large organizations.*

To land a likely successor, the owner-manager must start recruiting early. Many candidates slip away to nibble at other lines. He should look for prospects in sources such as those discussed in this Aid *and "sell from strength." That is, he should emphasize the advantages which his small organization offers a top management man.*

When you think about your business a year from now, three years from now, five years from now, what do you think about? More capital? More competition? Or the more basic and really tough question of continued profitable survival?

Whenever Charlie Parsons* forced himself to look beyond the day-to-day problems of running the successful small manufacturing business which he had built around his own invention, one question troubled him more than any other. Charlie had no sons or nephews. His two key men were nearly his own age. The rest of his men were competent but certainly not top management talent.

Charlie's big question was just this: *How do I find and bring along* a backup and successor who can see that this company survives and prospers?

When he finally faced up to his situation, Charlie soon found that he was only a small part of a large problem all industry faces today. That problem is an increasing need for high-potential management candidates just when the supply is decreasing.

By digging into the problem Charlie developed a systematic approach which you may be able to adapt to your own situation. Here are his main conclusions:

1. You must have a good man coming along if your business is to survive.
2. Finding and attracting a good man to small business is not easy in today's market.
3. To compete you must plan carefully.
4. Small business can offer some special advantages.
5. Hunting for management talent is improving in the big league (top universities, technical institutes, and graduate business schools).
6. The minor league (noncampus scores) is probably still the best for small business.
7. Many sources exist, and each has its own advantages.

Courtesy of the Small Business Administration.
*All names in *Aids* are disguised.

YOU MUST RECRUIT TO SURVIVE
The man who creates and builds a business often finds it difficult, even painful, to think of leaving it. But leave he must, and if what he created is to live after him, he must plan for leaving.

Doing nothing until the last possible minute can bring disaster. Without a successor already on board, failure looms large. Financing arrangements can collapse, production can bog down, marketing can drift and falter.

A less obvious but no less important reason to have a good man coming along concerns change. You can have his help in meeting the demands of the changing times. Every day business becomes more complex, more competitive, more sophisticated. The wise manager counts on surviving by bringing in new blood, new ideas, new talent tuned to today's and tomorrow's problems.

GOOD MEN ARE HARD TO FIND
Charlie Parsons soon discovered that finding and attracting a good man to small business is not easy in today's mapower market. At least three factors contribute to the problem:

1. Supply and demand will probably be out of kilter until the mid-70s. The low birthrate of the 1930s simply cannot meet the demands generated by more and larger companies.

2. Large companies can afford to put lots of money and full-time professional talent into their efforts to get more than their share of the small supply.

3. The nature of modern education and training, especially at the graduate level, often works against small business. Theoretical problems, complex enough to challenge the student and interest his professor, usually relate to operations in large, complex organizations. In planning his future, the student thinks this is where the action is, sets his career sights accordingly.

CAREFUL PLANNING IS THE KEY
As soon as Charlie realized what he was up against, he turned to a friend, Ben Wilson. Ben was personnel manager for the local branch of a national company, and he had some experience in recruiting and hiring management trainees.

Ben suggested a couple of chapters on manpower planning and recruitment in a standard book on personnel administration. Charlie studied them and did some planning. He developed a checklist so he would know what he wanted to look for, what he had to offer, and how he would proceed. (You will find his checklist on Table 1 of this *Aid*).

First, Charlie had to think about his industry, project some obvious trends, and speculate about others—new technology, new materials, competition from other industries, mergers and acquisitions. Next he thought about his own company and its possible future growth and development. Here he tried to bracket between the most optimistic and the most pessimistic estimates, using all his past records instead of relying only on his memory.

Then he selected a range of company objectives which satisfied him and which he thought would appeal to a man he would want. This gave him some idea about the number of people and the organization structure his successor would have to handle.

Table 1. Checklist to Find a Successor

What is my industry?

Questions about your industry, such as those listed below, can be helpful in deciding the type of candidate you need. For example, if your industry is making rapid changes in technology, you may need a successor who has a scientific or an engineering background.

- What products does my industry make?
- What raw materials are used?
- What processes are used?
- What is the pace of technological change?
- What trends are being set by the leader companies in my industry?

What is my company?

Questions about your company can help you to estimate its growth and development.

- What research and development is my company doing?
- What research and development may be needed five years from now? Ten years from now?
- What is my company's sales position in my industry?
- What is my company's profit goal? How does it compare with profit in the industry?
- What are my company's weak points?
- What are its strong points?
- What technical skills are in the company?
- What management skills?
- What organization structure is used? Why?
- With what supervisory personnel does the owner-manager work?

What can my company offer?

To be a likely successor to the owner-manager, the candidate should be interested in growth. Moreover, a qualified prospect will want to know whether the tools for growth will be available to him.

- During this orientation period—before your departure—will the successor be given a free hand in hiring supervisory personnel?
- What authority will he have for replacing assistants who do not produce?
- What is the dollar limit he can spend without your approval?
- Will that dollar limit be greater in your absence?
- Does the company finance increases in sales volume with reserve funds? By short-term borrowing?
- What are the plans for financing the plant's expansion?
- Does the company budget and use cash flow projections?
- Is a line of bank credit available to supplement operating cash?
- What financial rewards can the candidate expect? Bonus? Part ownership?

What do we need?

Your answers to the questions about your industry, your company, and what it can offer should be helpful in determining the type of successor you need. For example, a company that is weak in sales promotion may need a top executive with experience in marketing.

- In what age range should the candidate be?
- What experience should he have?
- What formal education should he have?
- What technical training, if any, is needed?
- What kind of personality is needed?
- Are there any special problems which demand special skills?

Table 1. *cont'd.*

Where can we look?

Once you know the type of person you need, the problem comes down to looking at the source, or sources, which are most likely to provide that type of candidate. Will you recruit from:

- Friends and relatives of employees, business acquaintances?
- Local college faculties (especially business professors)?
- New young professionals?
- Advertising in trade papers and journals?
- State departments of employment?
- Armed forces dischargees?
- Graduate business schools and technical institutes?
- Executive recruiters (for special circumstances)?

This done, he listed the top management talent required to handle the projected organization and keep the company moving toward those objectives. He knew if he were to retire that month he would have to find a man who could start with all those talents. Charlie also knew that the more time he had to train and develop his replacement, the less talent and experience would be needed at the start.

Charlie had decided some time before that he wanted to retire in about seven or eight years. He felt two or three years would be enough for an experienced manager to learn the company and the industry. But he also felt that in seven or eight years he could easily train a not-so-experienced college graduate.

Charlie now had a good idea of what he wanted: a man with a few years' experience. His next step was to try to find and attract such a man.

SMALL BUSINESS HAS ADVANTAGES

As he began to think about how he could compete in this tough market, Charlie began to accumulate some ideas about what small business could offer an executive with a few year's experience. He decided to apply a principle he used successfully in selling his product against stiff competition—sell from strength. Here is his list of special opportunities small business can offer the high-potential man who wants and can handle them:

1. *The opportunity to become the top man.* Charlie emphasized this point even though it was seven or eight years in the future. He did not want to consider a man who would be satisfied with second place. People being what they are, you may have to try two or three men before you find the right one. To forestall misunderstanding, spell out the trial period—including the amount of severance pay—before hiring the new man. When the likely successor passes the trial period, he will want assurance about where he stands if the owner-manager decides to sell the business or dies suddenly.

2. *Intimate contact with the top man, his problems, and decisions.* After years of learning at second hand from books, case discussions, and professors, the young man embarking on his career hungers for some first-hand exposure to reality. Small business gives him the opportunity to be there when it happens. Communication with the top boss is direct, face-to-face. Problems appear, bloom, and stay conspicuously on stage until they are resolved, one way or another.

The man temperamentally suited to small business who has served his apprenticeship as a small cog in a large organization can be even more eager to work next to the top man than the new graduate. He knows the frustration of seeing only a small part of the total picture, of trying to understand his small role in the scheme of things, of fighting clogged communication channels up and down the line. He is ready to work in a small company "where the buck" stops at the top man or his immediate assistant.

3. *Direct responsibility as fast as it can be handled.* Young men these days want responsibility, and they want it fast. As they move up the ladder, they often report "no trouble with salary; but it's tough to get responsibilities." Interesting, challenging work and a sense of accomplishment head their list of characteristics for the ideal job.

If you understand this, *and are really willing to delegate,* you have an almost irresistible lure for the high-potential man. As you discover his interests and aptitudes, you can assess which of your responsibilities he can handle immediately and use this as a concrete example of what the future may hold.

One word of caution: if you are *not* willing to delegate some specific responsibility almost immediately; don't promise it. And don't hold too high hopes of getting the man you need, because you probably won't.

4. *Fast, flexible recognition and rewards for good performance.* As a small businessman, you can also offer immediate, substantial recognition and reward for good performance. Without having to worry about complicated executive incentive compensation pools, group appraisals, or a lockstep salary structure, you can promise and deliver fast action, man-to-man. Later, you may want to add an arrangement for him to buy part of or all of your interest in the business.

You have also the ability to tailor your rewards to your man's needs. The young, hard-driving executive may have some special family or personal situation where a little flexibility can accomplish much more than a corporate-wide incentive plan. For example, he may need a few extra days for combined business-vacation travel with the family or summer jobs for his children.

5. *Minimum disruption of personal and family life.* If you have been a long time building your business, you may not realize the advantage you have in offering a man a career with a stable personal and family life.

A one-location company gives him a chance to establish himself in the community. He can rear a family without the agony of repeatedly pulling up roots, changing schools, selling and buying a house, and being accepted by a new, strange community.

THE BIG LEAGUE HAS POSSIBILITIES

With these five strong selling points in hand, Charlie Parsons decided first to check out the big league—the top universities, technical institutes, and graduate business schools. Even though he had decided he needed a man with a few years' experience, he felt he could learn something about the market, and especially about what happened to their alumni in later years.

Immediately he learned that these larger institutions have formalized student placement bureaus. They also have more requests for men than they can possibly supply. To have a chance against such competition, you must start early in the school year, be prepared, and put yourself in the placement director's hands.

But Charlie came away feeling that if small business owners would use something like his checklist to plan and prepare, their chances to compete in the big league were better than he had expected. Here, he learned, are some of the reasons why small companies can appeal to business school graduates:

1. Many business school graduates are impatient with the prospect of being lost in a large company and are looking for "special situations" in small companies. This is especially true of those who have been in industry for a few years before they came back for their higher degree.

2. Once a man has taken a job with a large company, the glamor wears thin as he lives every day with the built-in irritants. High-potential men especially chafe at slow progress and resistance to change.

3. In other cases, they tire of the constant moving and family turmoil caused by it.

In effect, a man who has completed his first three to five years with a large company is often ripe for a small business. He has begun to look differently at his long-term career. Moreover, he can prospect for a better job with little risk through his alumni placement service.

In addition, your chances for a receptive hearing are good if you persist. More than half of these men change jobs during their first five years out of school.

THE MINOR LEAGUES STILL LOOK BEST
Satisfied with what he had learned about the big league, Charlie turned his attention to finding candidates from the minor league—noncampus sources closer to home. Some of these men may lack college training, but as Ben Wilson told Charlie Parsons, such candidates have advantageous strengths.

First, the noncampus candidate is older and more settled than the recent graduate. As a result, he knows pretty well what he likes and wants in his work. Moreover, his present and previous jobs give some clues about what he can do and will do.

In addition, the older man may have picked up specialized experience that can be used in your company. It may be a skill—such as numerical control—that your company lacks.

Another advantage, of course, is availability. He does not have to wait until after graduation as does the business school candidate. This fact means that you need not be tied to a once-a-year appearance on campus to be competitive.

However, there are disadvantages to using concampus sources. Some of them are:

• The possibility is greater in noncampus sources that candidates will be job-jumpers. Thus, they require more sifting, more paperwork, and more caution in selecting. The best men are less likely to change jobs because employers try to keep them satisfied with promotions and challenging assignments.

• Keep in mind that starting salaries increase with age and experience. Thus, mistakes in selection cost more at the higher starting responsibility level.

• Bringing in outsiders from any source may generate resentment from employees who feel they deserve promotion. Noncampus sources often provide applicants who are known to your employees. Unless it is obvious that no employee has the required qualifications, this resentment increases as higher level jobs are filled from outside the company.

With these advantages and limitations of the minor league, noncampus sources in mind, Charlie felt more confident about identifying and evaluating the sources most available to him.

NONCAMPUS SOURCES RUN THE GAMUT

Here are the principal sources which Charlie investigated and his conclusions about each:

Friends and relatives of employees, business acquaintances. This source must be handled with care, for obvious reasons, but it can be fruitful. Employees are less likely to be able to suggest top level talent than candidates for jobs at their own level, but a simple reminder that suggestions will be appreciated may develop some worthwhile leads.

Young public accountants and attorneys. Many professionally trained young men become disenchanted with their chosen profession and are ripe for the right opportunity in small business. Many of these young men can adapt easily to business management careers, and often their professional skill complements an area where the businessman is weakest.

Advertising in selected media. Trade journals, professional magazines, or technical publications reach a highly select audience and may deserve consideration. Returns from advertisements generally vary considerably in quality because many applicants risk the cost of a resume and stamp even if they are less than marginally qualified.

By the same token, screening resumes is a quick, inexpensive way to consider (at least superficially) a large number of applicants without any commitment. This is especially true if you use telephone calls for the preliminary screening of likely looking applicants.

Executive recruiters only for special needs. The fees which most reputable executive recruiters charge may not put them beyond practical reach for some small businesses. Sometimes the applicant pays. In any event, it may be worth the price to get a good man. Beware of the high-pressure operator who "guarantees" fast, infallible results. After all, you have to select your man. Reputable firms will be conservative in predicting results. Also they will carefully spell out their proposed arrangements and furnish client references for you to check.

Local college faculties, especially business professors. If there is a college in, or near, your community, it may have business professors who can help provide contacts. Over the years, they are in contact with a surprising number of former students and others who may be in the executive job market.

State departments of employment. Many states now have a specialized service for the man with professional and managerial qualifications. These services may be the point of entry for a capable man new to the area.

Men discharged from the armed services. Reserve officers (commissioned and noncommissioned) who may have been called back after starting successful civilian careers often decide they prefer not to return to where they once lived. You may be able to register your interest and requirements formally or informally with local military and veterans authorities and talk to some potential candidates this way.

MOST IMPORTANT—GET STARTED
In finding a likely successor, the first step—getting started—is often the toughest. When things are going well, it is easy for the owner-manager to say, "I've got plenty of time to pick a successor."

But as Charlie Parsons learned, finding someone to take your place can be a time-consuming job. If you're thinking of retiring in the next five years or so, you should be thinking also about a successor and about the action necessary to finding him.

Preparing for New Management

Written with the assistance of E. Frederick Halstead, Partner, Haskins & Sells, Miami, Florida

Summary.   *Sometimes a small company suffers when the owner-manager retires and turns the business over to a son, another relative, or a hired manager. Sales drop off, production lags, or finances become snarled because the owner-manager's special touch is lacking.*

Such loss of sales, production, or financial strength can be prevented by preparations which will enable the new manager to pick up where the departing one leaves off. The key is to make the specialized knowledge which the retiring owner-manager has accumulated over the years available to his successor.

This Aid *discusses the kind of information the new manager needs and suggests ways for making it available to him. If possible, the new manager should also be brought in early enough for the retiring owner-manager to coach him in getting the feel of the operation.*

After more than 35 years as an owner-manager, George Clipper* decided that he had had enough and retired. "I'm tired of putting out brush fires in that production shop," he said, "and arguing with my sales manager about rush orders." Furthermore, because he was spending more and more of his time on the business' financial affairs—a chore he had never liked—he decided to sell out.

Courtesy of the Small Business Administration.

*All names in *Aids* are disguised.

The price he got was enough for his retirement, but not as much as he had hoped to get. As the buyer saw it, "It's a sound company, Mr. Clipper, but so many things need to be done that it's not worth the price you ask."

Another small manufacturer, Ivan Macie, ran into a different problem when he retired. He put himself on a retirement salary and hired a manager to run the business. Mr. Macie coached him for about a month and left for a long vacation. After several emergency telephone calls from the new manager, Mr. Macie returned to the plant.

Several months later, he fired the manager because "he got things in such a mess" and hired a new one. The discharged manager's side of the story was "After he left town, I found that things were more confused than I had thought, mainly because he always carried everything in his head and there was no place I could go to find the facts I needed."

A third small manufacturer, Tom Buff, had no problem when he turned the business over to his son who had been active in it. Mr. Buff then went on a tour of Europe.

On the plane, Mr. Buff told his wife that it was a great satisfaction to be able to pass the business on to their son. She agreed, but back at the plant Mr. Buff, Junior, wasn't experiencing the same satisfaction. As the company's sales manager for several years, he felt that his knowledge of the business was good. However, he learned differently as he tried to solve some of the production and financial problems that cropped up.

Although each of the three owner-managers you've just read about went about his retirement in a different way, they had one thing in common. Each failed to prepare for the new management. And for each this failure was expensive.

The expense to Mr. Clipper was a lower selling price than he might have gotten. To Mr. Macie, the expense was anxiety and frustration in hiring and keeping tabs on new managers. In Mr. Buff's case, his son paid the expense. He had to learn the overall management by himself. "I can't call Naples and say, 'Look, Dad, what do I do about this bottleneck in the finishing room? All the spray equipment is on the blink.' "

MAKING KNOWLEDGE AVAILABLE

Many owner-managers are similar to the three you've just read about. Long experience has made them so familiar with the "ins and outs" of their companies that often they do not realize the amount of knowledge they carry around in their heads.

Often this knowledge comes from a lifetime of being the pivot around which others revolve, especially in a very small company. In many cases, when, and if, the owner-manager is withdrawn by sudden illness or death, the company falters. Because he failed to share his knowledge it may even fall apart, and his family suffers.

Thus one of the important tasks in preparing for new management is the owner-manager's making available to his successor the knowledge he has accumulated over the years. In the case of a son, or other relative, much, but not all of it, can be made available by his working closely with you for several years before you leave the business. If he is still attending school and is interested in running the business, he could gain experience by working there during summer vacations. Even then, it is a good idea to get the information on paper so the new manager can refer to it when the need arises.

TAKING INVENTORY OF THE INFORMATION

One way to create a reference source for a new manager is by making an inventory of the various kinds of information used to operate your company. Such an inventory gives the new manager a roadmap, so to speak. It should help him to avoid false starts and to steer around the barricades which employees may, consciously or unconsciously, throw in his way.

The task of making the inventory may also suggest things which should be done to improve the company before or immediately after your retirement. Such improvements might add to the asking price if you plan to sell the business, and they might ease the way for the new manager or your son and provide for more friendly family relationships.

The inventory should be on three kinds of information: (1) facts about the general administration of the company, (2) facts and figures about the company's finances, and (3) information about the operating and technical side.

Some of the details involved in these three kinds of information are listed in Tables 1, 2, and 3 of this *Aid*. They have been prepared as a starting point for your inventory. If you or your people are pressed for time, you may want to use outside professional help to make the inventory.

Table 1. Inventory of Facts about Administration

• *The Company's History.* Pull together the following kinds of facts: date organized, key founders, and major events—such as moving from a rented building to your own plant.

Assemble clippings of stories which newspapers, trade journals, and other publications carried about the company.

Also include brochures which you may have issued about new products, processes, sales personnel, and so on.

• *The Organization.* Make a chart showing the key spots and names of the persons presently holding them. Indicate the responsibility and authority clearly.

Write job descriptions for all key spots, including the owner-manager's.

Describe each key employee by listing his age, length of service with the company, jobs held and dates, a history of his earnings, his education, special training, and your evaluation of his potential. Identify his strong and weak points.

File, with the above items, copies of any reports of studies which your people or an outside consultant may have made on your organization.

• *Policies.* Set up a policy file including information on vacations, retirement plans, employee loans and advances, credit and selling terms, and so on. Often such policies are announced and kept up-to-date in letters or memoranda. If such is your case, copies can be put in this file.

• *Legal Matters.* List all patents, licenses, and royalty agreements and note where each formal document is filed.

List all employment and labor agreements, including the pertinent features and any change made in past years.

List all leases.

List contracts with suppliers and customers.

If your company has had law suits, list them and the outcome. Also list pending suits.

• *Outside Services.* Make a list and a brief description of outside professional people who work with your company, such as bankers, accountants, insurance agents, brokers, or representatives, advertising agencies, public relations men, and other consultants.

Table 2. Inventory of Operating and Technical Information

• *Marketing.* List your company's products or services and note briefly how each fares in customer acceptance, profitability, and your idea about each's future.

List the geographical areas in which each product is sold, the types of customers, and the five largest customers.

List your distribution channels.

Prepare a brief outline of your advertising program, including how it is coordinated with other selling efforts.

Describe briefly your programs for training new salesmen and keeping present ones up-to-date.

Describe briefly how prices are set for present and new products.

Prepare a brief description of your competitors, including a list of their products, the location and size of their plants, share of the market, pricing policies, and methods of distribution.

• *Production.* Make a list of your major pieces of equipment. Include a brief appraisal of the efficiency of the plant and equipment as you see it.

List product and manufacturing specifications (if applicable) and process procedures.

Make a list of all studies that have been made to improve layout, production flow, and quality control or to replace existing equipment. Assemble copies of the study reports.

Describe briefly how production is scheduled and controlled (orders on hand or for stock).

Describe the standards you use for measuring performance and comment on your methods for eliminating waste.

• *Purchasing.* Make lists about the following: (1) major materials purchased; (2) the name of each supplier and years of doing business with him and special reasons, if any, for doing business with these concerns; (3) present contracts and/or agreements with suppliers; and (4) procedures for buying, including the kind of approval required for various types of purchases.

• *Other Areas.* Some owner-managers may need to take inventory of their knowledge in special areas such as research and development, engineering, quality control, and traffic, to name several which may vary with the company.

Table 3. Inventory of Financial Facts

The following should be brought together when making an inventory of your company's financial information:

• Profit and loss statements for the past 10 years

• A copy of your most recent balance sheet.

• A copy of your most recent budget.

• A brief description of the company's working capital turnover trends, return on investment trends, operating ratios, and so on.

• A list of current bank accounts, including approximate average balances and the name of the bank employee who handles the accounts.

• A list of previous banking connections, indicating the line of credit and the bank officer who supplied it.

• A list of paid tax bills—Federal income, state, and local. Comment briefly on any problems.

• A list of insurance policies, including a description of coverage and premiums and the name of the agent, broker, or representative who services each policy.

• Copies of your financial and control reports with a notation about frequency of preparation and distribution.

• Copies of procedures or procedure manuals.

GOALS AND OBJECTIVES

When you have finished taking inventory of the various kinds of information, you will have, so to speak, a basic text which the new manager can use in learning about the company. However, you should go one step further and set down some information about the goals and objectives you hope to see the company reach before you retire. If you plan to turn the business over to a son or other relative, you may want to ask him to help with this planning.

Perhaps some of the goals and objectives will be a continuation of projects you started several years ago—for example, accumulating funds to replace a plant that will be noncompetitive in a few years. If so, you should back them up with profit-and-loss and cash-flow projections.

List such long-range goals in two parts: (1) the steps to be accomplished before you retire and (2) the steps to come after you leave. Include the first part in your financial projections for the next several years. Plan ahead as far as possible, but if the second set of steps is too far away, sketch them in broad outline. The new manager can fill in the details when the time comes.

SHARING THE MANAGEMENT

The new manager should be brought in as early as possible so he can learn from you. Letting him share the management while you are still around helps him to get the feel of your operation.

Such a warmup period can result in a smooth transition when you retire. Key customers, for example, will continue to receive their orders on time rather than suffering delays because the new manager—be he new owner, hired man, or your son—did not know how to overcome a production bottleneck or some other difficulty.

How soon you bring the new management in depends not only on your plans but also on the type of business, the new manager's experience and knowledge, and whether he is a relative or a hired outsider, to name a few things.

The transition may be gradual as in the case of a son who is already working in the business. You may want to start three, four, or even five years ahead of your retirement date so he can learn about all phases of the business while holding down his present job. Then, near the end of his training period, he will need only to train the replacement for his specialty—production, financial, sales, or whatever.

Money may be the determining factor in how soon to bring in a hired manager if your retirement plans call for this sort of arrangement. If you have to pay a five-figure salary to attract the right kind of man, you won't want him on board until you're about ready to leave. A high-salaried manager may need less time to orient himself because he brings considerable knowledge with him.

How soon also depends on the ability and makeup of the hired manager. An alert and aggressive manager, especially in the same field, may prefer only a few weeks coaching. He may feel that all he needs is the inventory of information you have compiled, the opportunity to ask questions, and the opportunity to observe how you and your top assistants operate.

If you plan to sell the business—to get completely out—then your action on sharing the management will be determined by the buyer. He may prefer to stay away until you are gone. And if he should want to come early and learn from you, the decision as to how early will be largely up to him.

Suggestions for Further Reading

Bennett, K. W. How to handle the pains of rapid company growth. *Iron Age* 219: 17-19 (Jan. 31, 1977).

Foxall, G. Need for general management in small firms. *Industrial Management:*19-21 (March 1976).

Gill, L. W. G. Manpower Planning in the smaller company. *Personnel Management* 5:39-41 + (Oct. 1973).

Holdsworth, R. Selection tips for small firm managers. *Personnel Management* 7:31-33 (March 1975).

Kroeger, C. V. Managerial development in the small firm. *California Management Review* 17: 41-47 (Fall, 1974).

Lawrence, S. Personnel in small firms (Bolton Report). *Personnel Management* 4: 24-27 + (Sept. 1972).

Most small companies misuse human resources. J. H. Cohn suggests: recruiting policies faulted. *Management Advisor* 9:9 (July 1972).

Rimler, G. W., and N. J. Humphreys. New employee and the small firm: some insights to modern personnel management. *Journal of Small Business Management* 14:22-27 (July 1976).

Part II
CASES

The Analysis of Cases

The previous discussions have presented a framework for analyzing problems and issues confronting an entrepreneur in a small business setting. Managerial decision making, however, is more than a theoretical process. A method for learning how to apply this theoretical process is through the analysis and solution of business cases.

The cases following this section represent actual situations that have confronted various entrepreneurs in small business settings. They describe the reaction of various managers to pressures and opportunities from both the internal and external environment. They are designed as the basis for class discussion and application of entrepreneurial processes to real-world situations.

The student should completely read through the cases at least once to become acquainted with the general issues and problems involved in each case. Later readings should focus on the specific problems and their potential solutions. It should be realized, however, that no case can ever include all the information necessary for such an analysis. Information on the general economy, demographics, and competition frequently has to be gathered from other sources. For those cases that are not disguised, where the actual name of the firm is used, even more information can frequently be gathered on the specific organization.

The primary method for analysis should follow the planning framework outlined in Chapter 4. Particularly, the values of the major participants should be explored thoroughly. The consistency of these values with the resources available to the firm, as well as constraints and opportunities present in the external environment, should be considered.

These relationships require an analysis of the market structure facing the entrepreneur. Competition, environmental trends, and customer wants and needs should all be analyzed.

The external environment only provides opportunities to those firms capable of taking advantage of these factors. Financial and nonfinancial resources must be analyzed to determine if there is a potential match with these opportunities.

In particular, the cases should be studied to determine strengths and weaknesses of the individual firms in their various functional areas. Financial, marketing, accounting, production, and management capabilities all enter into any such analysis. The organizations presented in the cases should be analyzed to determine if resources in these areas are either presently or potentially available.

Based on this analysis of the match of internal resources and values with external, environmental opportunities, an overall solution set should then be derived. Analyzing the problems is only half the typical case assignment. An action plan designed to take advantage of this strategic match should be developed. This plan should include both short- and long-run actions and commitment of resources designed to achieve the objectives initially set for the firm.

The action plan should be concerned with problems and methods involved with implementing the overall plan. The implementation should pay particular attention to the problems faced by small businesses. The plan should be consistent with entrepreneurial values. It should also be feasible relative to the total environment. The personnel, physical, and financial resource needs of any such plan must be demonstrated to be met in a feasible manner. Particularly, these resource requirements have to be met in the time frame provided by the plan. If the plan calls for detailed objectives being met in a specific time frame, the resources necessary to implement those plans should be available at the time required.

Essentially, the analysis should focus on internal strengths and weaknesses as well as external opportunities and threats. This analysis should provide the basis for a consistent, feasible, acceptable strategy for entrepreneurial action within the various firms outlined in the cases.

Sea Life Park (A) (Revised)

Sea Life Park, a new marine exhibit in Hawaii, planned to open its doors January 1, 1964. The Park was the product of the dream and creative effort of a young biologist, Taylor A. (Tap) Pryor, who first became interested in marine research while investigating the reaction of sharks to radiation at Enewitok as a Marine. Later based as a helicopter pilot in Hawaii, he came to realize that Hawaii offered unique opportunities for marine research—warm, beautifully clear waters, great depths close to shore, and an abundance of colorful and unusual marine life.

When he was released from the Marine Corps as a Captain in 1957, Pryor enrolled as a Ph.D. candidate in Marine Biology at the University of Hawaii. He continued to pursue his dream of a marine research institute and concluded that it could best be financed through establishment of a privately-owned marine exhibit, catering to the large numbers of visitors vacationing in Hawaii each year. He had located a piece of state-owned land ideally suited to his purpose, twelve miles from Waikiki on the northeast side of the island, where the winds and currents first strike the island, bringing an unlimited supply of clear and unpolluted water. He set about negotiating a lease on this land from the state of Hawaii for joint use for an exhibit and a research institute, with rentals from the privately-owned exhibit to be used to underwrite the research activities.

Pryor searched for a company to construct and operate the marine exhibit. His own interest was research, and the exhibit was only a means to this end. He was successful in persuading a major broadcasting firm to invest $12,000 in a feasibility study and engaged Stanford Research Institute to carry on the study. After studying the existing oceanariums on the mainland, SRI estimated that the cost of building a satisfactory marine exhibit in Hawaii would be $2,500,000. SRI also analyzed the tourist industry on the island and concluded that revenues would not be adequate to justify such an investment.

While the SRI study was under way, Pryor visited the oceanariums on the mainland and talked at great length with Dr. Kenneth Norris, curator at Marineland of the Pacific and Professor of Marine Biology at the University of California at Los Angeles. Together they concluded that with new design concepts and construction techniques, a far better oceanarium could be built for less money. Pryor discussed their ideas at length with Honolulu contractors with particular respect to engineering feasibility, architectural treatment, and cost.

In December 1962, Pryor related the progress of his concept to date:

> Well, we found that a much bigger and better marine exhibit, and perhaps one that would be a lot more interesting, could, in fact, be built around our ideas and the natural assets of the location. When the cost estimates began to come in from the contractors, they indicated that the exhibit could be built for a great deal less than SRI had determined based on

---

Reprinted from *Standard Business Cases 1969* with the permission of the Publishers, Stanford University Graduate School of Business, © 1969 by the Board of Trustees of the Leland Stanford Junior University.

existing oceanarium design. It began to look as though the construction could be done for perhaps $1,200,000, or less than half the cost used in the SRI report. This, of course, doubled the return on investment. I took this new information back to the broadcasting company, but by this time they had made their decision to drop it.

So in 1960 I was left with a very fat negative report, but, at the same time, a belief, backed up by scientists and cost data, that the exhibit could, in fact, be built successfully. I began to pursue this, looking for more funds and for a company to build the exhibit, still negotiating with the state on the land and still operating on the thesis that as far as I was concerned the exhibit was only the means to the end—the marine research installation. The research institute would have to be a part of the plan or I wasn't interested in pursuing it. I formed the Oceanics Foundation to present the plan to the state and negotiate for a lease on the land for research purposes, with permission to sublease the exhibit area to a company which I had not yet found, which would build and operate the oceanarium while I operated the research institute.

I visited all the companies operating oceanariums on the mainland, but they had quite different ideas from mine on what ought to be done, and they were not impressed with our plans and new designs. We parted ways after a while, and so it went from one place to another.

In the winter of 1960-1961, I met a businessman who looked at the SRI report, our plans and designs, the SRI data on tourism in the islands, some of the prospects that had come up and had been turned down, and so forth. He told me he knew nothing about oceanariums, but that it looked to him like a good plan and that he felt it could be made to work. He also showed me that I wouldn't have to seek an outside company to finance and operate the exhibit, but that I could form a company of my own and raise whatever capital was necessary to build and operate the exhibit if the prospective revenue were sufficiently attractive. Working together, we began to form the organization we now have, and the project has progressed from there.

In January 1962, we created a new company, Sea Life, Inc. We sold some stock in this company at $1 a share and brought in an initial investment of $50,000. This money enabled us to pursue the designs and complete the arrangements for getting the land, which was obtained from the state by September 1962. By that time we had actual contractors' estimates with a predicted maximum cost of $1,200,000 for constructing an oceanarium which would be the biggest in the world and which then looked to be not only as good as SRI had assumed originally, but perhaps a lot better.

I then went back to Stanford Research Institute in September and asked them to review the project on the basis of the increased size, higher quality, and lower construction cost of the exhibit. We just got their report a couple of months ago, in October, which stated that if we could keep the total investment down to a million and a half dollars we could earn on the financial plan they developed—$1,000,000 for construction and $700,000 for working capital and startup costs—about 8 percent for the investors the first year.

Then we took some time off to explore the potential of the research institute. I began with the belief that the marine research center would use the oceanarium facilities—the tanks and water and animals and catching and training facilities—for marine research purposes. But as I go around the country, partially seeking equity capital and partially on general promoting for this thing, I take the opportunity to drop in on a lot of companies that are just beginning to get interested in the marine world. As a result of the success of the Polaris missile and the new nuclear submarine, I find that a great many aerospace companies are now becoming greatly interested in the sea. They have some very sophisticated requirements. It looks like sea defense activities will have to go very deep now and there will be a tremendous requirement for sophisticated electronic equipment that will permit communications at great depths, that will allow navigation and detection and other deep water operations, that will permit complete observation of undersea weather and so forth at all depths and through vast areas.

There seems to be a very definite trend toward more industrial interest in the sea. They haven't begun to spend much money yet, but they recognize that the sea is a great, new, exciting, and untapped opportunity for profitable industrial and defense activity. And not only is there active industrial interest in the great depths, there is also latent interest in Hawaii as the logical place to accomplish marine research.

There is no single area of science offering greater opportunities for research or industrial exploitation than the sea. Its riches in minerals, food, chemicals, power, medicines, and biological knowledge are virtually unlimited. The oceans cover three-quarters of the earth's surface. There are more minerals and more living things in the ocean than on all the land areas. Miles of ocean floor are covered with manganese nodules and phosphates. The ocean is the only feasible source of protein for the world's exploding population. Yet we search for the ocean's food in the same way that early man hunted wild fruits and animals—with crude weapons, tradition, superstition—without cultivation, fertilization, breeding, fencing, or other techniques of modern agriculture. We know less about the floor of the ocean than we know about the surface of the moon. The ocean has a far greater potential than space and it is right at our doorstep, available for the taking.

The ocean is a vast, worldwide laboratory shared by every country. It holds a fantastic potential for joint peaceful research into man's future. And it holds an equal potential for conflict. Yet we spend 30 times as much on space research as we do on oceanic research. When the government realizes the limitless military and peacetime potential of the seas, a flood of research expenditures comparable to that now being spent in space will flow into industry. We expect the Institute and Sea Life to share in that endeavor.

The interest from industry began to put a new dimension on the other half of our project, the research side. We organized the Oceanics Institute as the research arm, and it looks like the Institute might go its own way very early as an added and separate project with its own facilities alongside the oceanarium exhibit. It can actually benefit the exhibit through the interest and prestige it will create, and also through the income it will generate. For example, the Institute can share the general overhead with the marine exhibit; for another, it can subcontract noninvestigative services to the staff of the oceanarium, such as maintenance, collection, training, administrative, and other functions normally required by a research institute. The research operation can also feed exciting new technology and new research discoveries into the exhibit; and finally, it might even provide new investment opportunities for the owners of the exhibit.

Well, this, in turn, puts a whole new light on the exhibit potential. It is impossible to project what this might mean to earnings of the oceanarium. It's one thing to analyze how many visitors come to Hawaii and how many of them might be brought out by the tour companies to the Park, what to charge them, and how much they might spend; but it's quite another thing to try to figure how many companies might use a research facility, how much they would pay, and how much this might result in income to the exhibit company alongside. But the concept adds, as one potential investor says, enough "sex" to the total picture that people begin to look at this thing as somewhat more exciting and our revenue projections as more realizable.

To give you an idea of what we have planned, we have 118 acres owned by the state of Hawaii, on lease to the Oceanics Foundation for 65 years, located about 12 miles from Waikiki or midpoint on the "short island tour" route. It's an excellent location from the standpoint of the tour industry. It's also the point on Oahu where the trade winds drive the currents into the islands, so we can pick up fresh, clear sea water to pump through our various facilities, 300,000 gallons an hour, for both exhibit and research purposes. It's a *beautiful* location. Of the 118 acres, about 50 acres are actually usuable. We arbitrarily decided that 20 of these would be used for exhibit purposes, 20 for research purposes, and 10 for those facilities that can be shared by the oceanarium and the research institute. About 10 acres of the 20 set aside for the oceanarium is for what we call Sea Life Park. The Park will be laid out quite differently from other oceanariums. Marineland of the Pacific, for example, has a tank three stories high with a grandstand on top. We pulled this tank apart into a series of different tanks of exhibits, each designed around something important and exciting that we want to show about the marine world. Each one is essentially a one-story building, but because they are designed for specific purposes, they seem to be a great deal more exciting than the bigger buildings used elsewhere.

We have laid the Park out in two halves. The first half is to show all that we can about the sea and its life, and the other half is to show all we can about man's role in the sea, which we think is perhaps even more exciting. The visitor to the Park comes over the hill from Waikiki, turns off, and drives up to the parking lot behind the Park. An 800-foot mountain rises up behind the 50 acres, a beautiful, high cliff. You enter through an admission gate and come out onto an Entrance Dock where you view the whole of the Park and all of the beautiful offshore area with the surf and cliffs and islands. You then walk across a gangway to our first exhibit, the Hawaiian Reef Tank. Under an opii-shaped roof, sort of a shell-shaped roof above you that shades most of the area, you see laid out in front of you a magnificent 70-foot wide pool of water. As you walk around this, the corridor begins to descend, the railing turns to glass, and you find yourself descending into the sea, through an all-glass corridor that spirals on down from the surface to the ocean floor below. It's only a one-story building, but you make a 16-foot descent spiraling twice around this tank. Inside the tank we will create a complete replica of offshore Hawaii. With fiberglass, we will build a huge lava flow coming out of the side of the pool—the lava bubbling up over the beach and arching across the water and coming up to form an island in the center. By shaping the tank in this manner and cutting the corridor into the lava formation, we will create a whole series of shelves and caves and variations in the sides—a limestone shelf, a coral reef, and a sandy shore with silt beds and so forth—all the features that you find in offshore Hawaii. It is very difficult to distinguish from the real thing. When this tank is filled we will be able to display all the offshore marine life of Hawaii except whales and propoise, which will go into other tanks. For the first time, an oceanarium can have all the invertebrate life, which is some 80 percent of the life offshore, in addition to the dramatically colorful fish of the Hawaiian waters. Anybody who makes this descent will know exactly what it is like to dive on a tropical reef.

You then come out at the base of this building through a fairly narrow exit and find yourself behind a solid wall of water. This water is falling into a shark pool where the sharks swim in and out to join you behind the waterfall. We try to give a highly realistic sense of participation in the marine world!

That's all we will do right now in this first half of the Park. We would also like to develop in the next three, five, seven years a simulated descent to 18,000 feet. We will put into this corridor all the sights and sounds of a descent to such great depths, and through another series of corridors the visitor will walk across the bottom of the Pacific and eventually emerge through another tank in which we are going to have an exhibit displaying the Great Barrier Reef of Australia in all its glory. In this way we will set up a cross-section of the Pacific from Hawaii to Australia using living models.

The other half of the Park will show as much as we can about science and man and the sea, about the colorful paths of men in the sea, particularly of Hawaii, and we will try to use various techniques to interpret what is happening in the marine world. In the first exhibit, the Ocean Science Theatre, we will use another large building with a 100-foot span roof, seating for 600 people, and an all-glass oceanarium tank. The tank will be 50 feet in diameter and 12 feet deep. From any seat you will be able to see above and below the water at the same time. Here we are going to put on a technically-oriented demonstration of all that is known about porpoise up to the minute you're watching.

There is great scientific interest in porpoises these days. As man begins to enter the sea, he has many things to learn about how to get along in what to him is a hostile environment. The porpoise is well adapted to the sea, and many programs across the country are studying these animals to find how man must adapt. The adaptation of the porpoise to the sea can also teach us much about how we might adjust to the hostile environment of space. We're going to demonstrate in the Ocean Science Theatre techniques being used in various laboratories around the world and the discoveries that are being made. For example, we will demonstrate the porpoise's echo-location abilities: we will blindfold the animals and get them to swim through hoops and mazes; we will lower hydrophones into the water and play their echo-ranging sounds back on oscilloscopes and over hi-fi speakers. We will have animals jumping to demonstrate their agility. We will have them count and do other tricks to demonstrate their intelligence. We will reward them with plastic poker chips, which they can later exchange in the "porpoise bank" for fish. And we will have many other educational and technically-oriented demonstrations in this pool.

From this exhibit you will come out onto an Oceanographic Terrace where we will push the sale of cold drinks and other refreshments. We're going to have telescopes and oceano-graphic instruments tied into offshore stations, current meters, and wave recorders. We're going to have a TV camera submerged a half mile off shore in water about 30 feet deep, with a closed circuit monitor to the screens on the Terrace, so that you will be able to stand on the Terrace and look out over all this beautiful ocean and then turn around and look at these instruments and recorders and monitors and see what's happening underneath that area of blue.

From the Oceanographic Terrace you will come down to what is the climax of the Park, our big Whaler's Cove. Here we will dig a hole in the ground, 200 feet long, 90 feet wide, and 25 feet deep, with whales and porpoises and an island in it. We will build a replica of the old Lahaina whaler, the *Essex*, which inspired Melville's *Moby Dick*. Above water it's a 30-ton, 70-foot vessel; below water it will be set on a concrete chamber with underwater view-ing windows. You can ago aboard and see what the old whaling ships looked like, and then go below and watch the whales and porpoise through the portholes below the water line. It will be magnificent. . . . From the whaler you can come around and take a seat in an am-phitheatre and watch a whale chase. We're going to launch a longboat and have a couple of men at the oars chase after the whales. The harpooner will hurl his harpoon at the whale and miss it, and the whale will grab the harpoon and give the men a "Nantucket sleigh ride" around the pool.

We are also going to have spinning porpoises in that tank. Spinning porpoises come up out of the water and spin like tops. It's quite a sight—they'll spin four or five times. In fact, you really can't count the spins, they move so fast. We will train them to respond to an under-water sound from an electronic cue box. You can just walk up to the tank and flip a switch and all of them will hit the air. This will be the climax of the show.

On the island will be a grass shack and some palm trees. And maybe at the end of the whale chase the whale will turn on the boat and sink it, and the whalers will have to swim to the island, there to be met by a Hawaiian maiden, etc., etc. This is more of the "jazz" to balance the science. It'll be fun for photographers as well.

After you leave Whaler's Cove, you will pass a pool for seals, sea birds, and turtles. This will be more landscape and decor than it is exhibit, but it will be authentic and interesting. It's to be located in front of our refreshment and gift centers.

When you come in on the Entrance Dock, you are on a second story looking down on the whole of the Park. If you come up from the Whaler's Cove, you will walk under the Entrance Dock into our gift shop, which we'll call the Sea Chest. There will also be a restaurant there called the Ocean Lanai, a quick-service counter serving hot and cold lunches, hamburgers, salads, sandwiches, Hawaiian dishes, and so forth for the tourists. This will have tables and benches all laid out in a landscaped and terraced area overlooking the Park and the ocean.

That's what the Park will be like when it opens about a year from now. In the central area of the property, between the Park and the Research Institute, there will be two buildings and the training tanks. These tanks will be about 7 to 9 feet deep and 40 to 50 feet long. One building is for the trainers and their equipment, the other will be our office. This general area is reserved for future administrative development and will be shared by the Research Institute and the Oceanics Foundation.

The research area is only jungle now, but we plan to develop it in two parts. First, we will have a series of oceanarium tanks where we will be able to simulate the shallower conditions offshore, the "photic" zone, the depth through which light can penetrate, about 200 feet. You can simulate this zone without adding pressure and you can use tanks similar to those in the exhibit area, providing both visual and electronic observation of the underwater environment. Then there will also be a series of large high-pressure tanks which we will use to simulate the great depths, the "aphotic" zone, down to 10,000-15,000 feet. By simulating offshore underwater conditions in these tanks, we can set up experiments, test equipment, and so forth with fully controlled conditions at low cost and in complete safety. These tanks will have the same great value to marine research that giant wind tunnels have to aeronautical research; in fact, we call them "wet wind tunnels." No such tanks exist anywhere today, and because of their great size and cost, no single company could afford to build them for its own use. We expect firms and institutions from all over the world to come here to carry on the kinds of marine research which these tanks make possible. The laboratories and administrative buildings in back will be shared or occupied by various companies, academic institutions, medical organizations, and the like which come to use the facilities.

There will be no other place in the world where you can do the kind of research which will be possible here. In addition to the large tanks, we have perfect water conditions to support any conceivable exhibit or research requirements. We can save more than $1,000,000 on construction costs because we don't have to have filtration units, or recirculation, or chemical additives. We will save even more because we can use our pumping systems for both the exhibit and research installations. We just take this marvelously clear seawater, run it through or around the exhibit tanks, then on through the research area, and then put it back into the ground at the end of the Park. Besides having this terrific potential for clear seawater capacity, plus all the offshore life at our doorstep, we will also have all the Park's catching and training capabilities available to the research institute.

Within 65 miles of Makapuu Point, there are depths up to 18,000 feet. We can launch and recover deep-diving vehicles right from the shore and go directly down to the great depths, without the usual great expense of using a mother ship hundreds of miles off shore. Off the coast of California, you have to go some 350 to 400 miles before you find such depths. We have them immediately adjacent to our shores. The Navy has allocated us a segment extending over 70 miles into the ocean, which we can monitor with all sorts of buoys, guages, recorders, TV cameras, etc. This way we can obtain a continuous record, on shore, of all that is going on out there—the undersea weather, the currents, the noises, the animal life, everything, and at all depths. Such a thing has never been done before—what we know about the ocean is only the little we have learned by sinking guages at the end of wires. We expect this new facility to produce vast new knowledge and open up many new research opportunities. So we are planning to build our institute around this capability—our abundant sea water, our experience with oceanarium tanks, our catching and training facilities, and the great depths off shore.

The Oceanics Foundation will have a management contract with Sea Life Park. The Foundation will also have a tax-exempt, nonprofit division, the Oceanic Institute, to operate the research facility. It will not do much research itself, but it will make facilities available to other research groups. The arrangement with Sea Life, Inc., will be that Sea Life builds and operates the Park and after four years it starts paying 12 percent of its gross income as rental to the Foundation. The Foundation in turn will use this for promoting the research operation through the Oceanic Institute.

I expect that potential investors will ask, "Why should Sea Life Park pay 12 percent of its gross revenue to the Foundation for the support of the Institute?" The best answer I can give is that there are a great many ways in which the benefits return to Sea Life, and two ways in particular. One is in those areas I already mentioned, in which a research institute alongside the exhibit can lower the overhead, help carry the cost of the staff, and bring new ideas to the exhibit operation. The existing oceanariums are now at about the same point they were when they were built: they have not expanded with ideas; they have not changed their exhibits; they have not had a new staff or new shows or anything else.

All you have to do is watch Disneyland to see the importance of change and addition to a major attraction. Disney has one thing that none of the other exhibit parks have. He's backed up by a "production" outfit. He has the Disney Studios, one of the most creative operations in the world, which has been pumping ideas through Walt himself into Disneyland since it began. I see the Oceanic Institute as providing the same sort of production backup to Sea Life Park. The more the research organization learns about the sea, the more work they do with porpoise and whales for scientific purposes, the more they learn about the great depths, the more this new knowledge can be channeled into Sea Life Park. Because it is channeled in, not from what people might read in the newspapers or elsewhere, but right from an active Institute next door, it will have more meaning to our public. And when people read in the papers about what's happening here in the research area, they will know that in a short period of time they will be able to see it exhibited in the Park.

The other benefit from the Institute seems more significant to me: the opportunity for commercial participation in new oceanographic opportunities by Sea Life. Sea Life, Inc., being in many ways dovetailed into a nonprofit institute which will share government and industrial projects and which will pioneer new research in the marine world, is bound to receive benefits and opportunities in many new areas. There is bound to be some "fallout" with all this research going on and with this close association. And this will inevitably lead to new investment, product, and market opportunities. So the 12 percent rental paid by Sea Life Park will really just be going from one pocket of Sea Life into another.

We have set the admission price at $2.30 for adults and $1.15 for children. This figure was suggested by SRI on the basis of experience in the other oceanariums. We have discussed this with the tour industry and with residents of Hawaii as well, and I get two impressions.

We will pay them a commission of 15 percent on all ticket sales, and they say they wouldn't mind if the price of the ticket were a little bit higher. They just include it on the top of the price of a ten-day tour or similar package, and it doesn't make any difference. The residents, on the other hand, find it high—there is always a kind of a moment of cold silence when I mention the figure. But we are going to have a season pass plan where, for say $4, you can buy a ticket which will admit you as many times as you want during the year. This could be very popular locally, and it could bring in a lot of early cash. I think most of the residents would come on this basis.

We will be highly dependent on the two major bus companies of the island for transporting our customers out to the Park. We have to make it advantageous to these companies to bring the people out here. Actually, more than two companies are involved. We will deal with about 14 tour and travel wholesalers of various sizes in Hawaii, and we will have to bring them all out to the Park regularly when the building begins. They have been very interested so far and have indicated they would advertise in all of their travel folders to be sent out for the 1964 season. It looks like we should be in some 3,000,000 folders. Sea Life is attractive to them because it's 12 miles outside Waikiki, it's the first major attraction in the islands outside of Waikiki Beach, and many of them sell transportation. It's also attractive because of the commission.

We also briefly considered providing transportation ourselves, but we feel that it is much better to concentrate on being a first-rate attraction and let the tour and transportation industry support us. We'll feed them the information and give them a good return on their sales. They have all the contacts. They work with some 3,600 travel agencies in the U.S. and Canada, and, as I indicated, they have agreed to send out notices on their mailing list about what we are doing. They will pay the costs of printing and mailing these folders. It's a marvelous and huge advertising and sales operation out there already in existence for us. We couldn't duplicate it and would not want to compete with it.

We are predicting that 50 percent of the tourist trade and 10 percent of the local trade will come to the Park (based on SRI's figures), and we have budgeted about $50,000 a year for advertising, which will be spent in providing the tour companies with pictures. There are thousands of tour and travel agencies around the country that will do not only our advertising but also our selling for us. Something like 80 percent of the people that come to the islands are already booked for their hotels, tours, meals, and so forth. So the tour industry will do our wholesale job for us.

Exhibit 1. Sea Life Park (A) Excerpts from Visitor Attendance Research Report (Prepared by Sea Life Staff, October 1961, and based on figures from initial SRI study)

CONCLUSIONS

1. The visitor attendance projections presented in the Sea Life Informational Prospectus (August 1961) represent only slightly more than 50 percent of the visitors that go on organized conducted tours on Oahu.

2. Two major operators dominate the tour operations in Hawaii and handle more than 85 percent of the tour passengers. These operators have expressed complete support of the Sea Life proposal and have said that they can sell all of their passengers on the Sea Life Tour.

3. Sales and promotion time and expense can be greatly reduced by allowing the tour operators to sell the Sea Life Tour through their already strongly established wholesaler and travel agent channels. Because 70 percent of the visitors are prebooked

on the mainland, the tour operators have as a virtually captive trade, more booked visitors than the total attendance projection for Sea Life.

4. There is a great potential market for Sea Life in the in-transit visitor arrivals staying less than two days. This potential is equal in size to the two-day or longer visitor potential and can be expected to increase. The prospectus projections did not include this in-transit potential.

5. Sea Life will be a closely integrated part of the Hawaii tour industry from the start of operations and can easily become a major attraction in the Pacific area.

6. Presuming that 85 percent of the tour passengers (i.e., those handled by the two major operators) and 15 percent of the in-transit arrivals would attend Sea Life Park, the corporation can reasonably anticipate 1963 attendance of 505,000 (producing a gross volume of $1,300,000) rather than the projected attendance of 322,000 and gross volume of $837,000 as presented in the prospectus.

7. In summary, it can be stated that the attendance estimates presented in the August 1961 prospectus are ultra-conservative and, by virtue of tour industry support, almost guaranteed. A more realistic appraisal of the potential strongly supports upward revision of the attendance estimates.

PATTERNS OF TOURIST ACTIVITY ON HAWAII

Graph number one and the accompanying data sheet illustrate several important facts about the tour and travel industry in Hawaii as well as the general pattern of tourist activity in Hawaii.

1. Almost all of the visitors staying in Hawaii two days or longer book on some kind of organized conducted tour on Oahu. Several tour operators have indicated that 95 percent is a conservative estimate. Additionally, it is known that many of those not booking on an organized conducted tour rent U-Drive cars and tour the various points of interest independently. As substantiation of this, it is known that there are some 400 U-Drive cars available on Oahu and that the utilization factor for these cars is 75 percent or greater. Therefore, it can be presumed that 300 U-Drive cars are in use every day by some 460 persons. (HVB figures indicate that the average size of travel party is 1.55 persons, not including conventions and tour groups.)

2. Of those visitors booking on tours, 85 percent are handled by two organizations—Gray Line Hawaii and Inter-Island Tradewind Tours. It is clear, therefore, that the tour business in Hawaii is dominated by a very small group of organizations and is, therefore, highly controlled and organized.

3. Further illustrating the high degree of organization and control of the tour industry in Hawaii, it is estimated that 70 percent or more of all visitors staying two days or longer are partially or completely prebooked, prepackaged, and prepaid when they arrive in Hawaii. More important, this prebooking is done almost entirely through ten large worldwide travel organizations known in the trade as "wholesalers." Among these wholesalers are such organizations as American Express, Ask Mr. Foster, Thomas Cook and Son, Cartan Tours, Visitour Happiness Tours, Berry Tours, SITA, and Allied Travel. These "wholesalers" work through some 3500 travel agencies on the mainland U.S., 2000 of which actively sell Hawaii as a destination

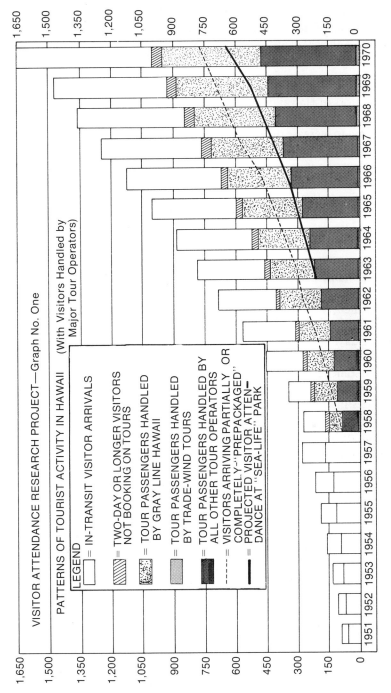

VISITOR ATTENDANCE RESEARCH PROJECT—Graph No. One

PATTERNS OF TOURIST ACTIVITY IN HAWAII   (With Visitors Handled by
Major Tour Operators)

LEGEND

☐ = IN-TRANSIT VISITOR ARRIVALS

▨ = TWO-DAY OR LONGER VISITORS
NOT BOOKING ON TOURS

▦ = TOUR PASSENGERS HANDLED
BY GRAY LINE HAWAII

▦ = TOUR PASSENGERS HANDLED
BY TRADE-WIND TOURS

■ = TOUR PASSENGERS HANDLED BY
ALL OTHER TOUR OPERATORS

- - - = VISITORS ARRIVING PARTIALLY, OR
COMPLETELY-"PREPACKAGED"

── = PROJECTED VISITOR ATTEN-
DANCE AT "SEA-LIFE" PARK

Fig. 1.   Sea Life Park (A) Graph 1.

area. The two major tour companies in Hawaii (Gray Line and Trade Winds) represent almost all of these "wholesalers" and, therefore, dominate the market not only by virtue of their size and equipment, but also by virtue of their close working relationship with the "wholesalers."

ECONOMICS OF THE TOUR INDUSTRY IN HAWAII

The tour operators of Hawaii are basically in the transportation business, supplying transportation to and from the major tourist attractions. As such, they are constantly looking for ways to increase their revenue and their equipment utilization. One of the most promising ways that exists for these operators to increase their revenue and equipment utilization is to increase the traffic on the "Short-Circle-Island Tour" (i.e., over the Pali from Waikiki to Kailua, Kaneohe, then to Waimanolo, Makapuu, the Blowhole, Sandy Beach, Koko Head, Kaiser's Hawaii-Kai, and back to Waikiki) and decrease the traffic on the standard "Circle-Island Tour" (i.e., from Waikiki past Pearl Harbor to Wahiawa Waialua, Kahuku, Panaluu, Kaneohe, Kailua, Waimanalo and back to Waikiki by the same route as the "Short-Circle-Island Tour"). The reason that this is important to the operators is that their equipment can make two "Short-Circle" trips per day versus one "Standard-Circle" trip per day, and the revenue per passenger per trip is only slightly less on the short trip than on the long trip. In effect then, the operators can almost double the revenue per unit per day and the number of passengers that they carry, while running the same number of hours and miles per day.

Because of the relative lack of attractions other than scenery on the short tour, there has been some resistance to the operator's effort to sell the "Short-Circle-Island Tour." However, with Sea Life at Makapuu being a major destination area (in fact, the *only* real destination area outside of Waikiki on Oahu), the sales efforts of the tour operators would be tremendously more effective.

As a result of these economic factors of the tour industry, the tour operators are very strongly in support of the Sea Life proposal. Indicative of their support, they have proposed that they sell the Sea Life Tour "package" through their wholesaler and travel-agent channels as an integral part of their tour operations and that they represent Sea Life at all of their hotel sales outlets. The net result of this tour-operator support is that the long process of establishing contacts in the wholesaler and travel-agent groups would be eliminated and Sea Life Park would be an integral part of the highly controlled tourist industry from the first day of its operations.

HISTORICAL AND FORECASTED VISITOR DATA

Graph number two and the accompanying data sheet showing the specific data from which the graphs were drawn illustrate several basic facts of importance concerning the Hawaii tourist industry.

1. The rate of growth of trade to and through Hawaii to the present time since 1950 can be expected to accelerate in the 1960-1970 period. This is due principally to four factors.

   a. The increasing shift of the American consumer spending pattern away from hardgoods and major capital expenditures toward heavier spending for services—particularly travel.

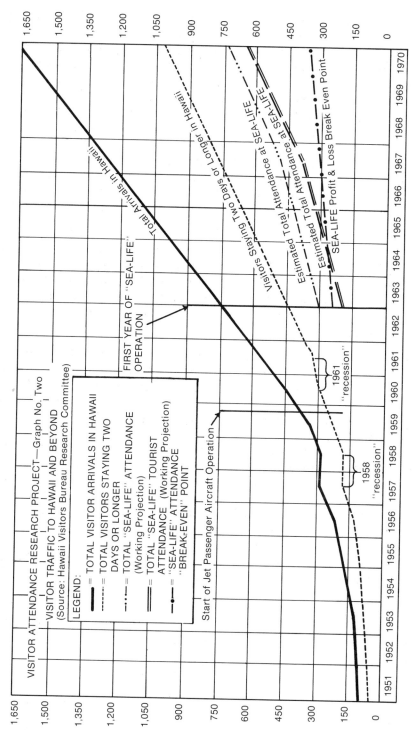

Fig. 2.   Sea Life Park (A) Graph 2.

VISITOR ATTENDANCE RESEARCH PROJECT—Graph No. Two
VISITOR TRAFFIC TO HAWAII AND BEYOND
(Source: Hawaii Visitors Bureau Research Committee)

LEGEND:

= TOTAL VISITOR ARRIVALS IN HAWAII

= TOTAL VISITORS STAYING TWO DAYS OR LONGER

= TOTAL "SEA-LIFE" ATTENDANCE (Working Projection)

= TOTAL "SEA-LIFE" TOURIST ATTENDANCE (Working Projection)

= "SEA-LIFE" ATTENDANCE "BREAK-EVEN" POINT

Start of Jet Passenger Aircraft Operation

FIRST YEAR OF "SEA-LIFE" OPERATION

Total Arrivals in Hawaii

Visitors Staying Two Days or Longer in Hawaii

Estimated Total Attendance at SEA-LIFE

Estimated Total Attendance at SEA-LIFE

SEA-LIFE Profit & Loss Break Even Point

1958 "recession"

1961 "recession"

b. The advent of jet passenger aircraft in the Pacific has greatly shortened the time required to travel from the mainland to Hawaii and beyond, lowered the cost of such travel, and increased passenger comfort for such journeys. It is felt that the full impact of the jet has not yet been felt in Pacific area travel and that great potential lies in foreign travel to the U.S., when and if the countries of the Orient are able to lift currency and travel restrictions for their citizens. It is estimated, for example, that some 500,000 Japanese are ready, willing, and financially able to travel to the U.S. and will do so when the Japanese government lifts currency restrictions on the exportation of yen. Additionally, it is significant to note a large percentage of these potential travelers from Japan will choose Hawaii as their ultimate destination because of relatives in Hawaii and the resulting close ties that Hawaii has with the Orient. Potential Japanese travel to Hawaii and beyond has not been included in the figures presented in this study, but the existence of the potential most certainly should be noted.

c. The wide promotion and advertising that Hawaii has received in the world press and through the promotional efforts of the HVB and the industry as a whole is creating the image of an ideal vacation area. Presuming that the visitors arriving with this image in mind are satisfied, this image will be retained and strengthened, thereby creating greater return travel and all-important word-of-mouth recommendation.

d. The highly unsettled state of political affairs in Germany and the Caribbean does not encourage travelers to visit these areas. With the advent of lower fares and faster air service from the Eastern U.S. to Hawaii and the entire Pacific area, it is reasonable to presume that at least a portion of the European travel market and the Cuban travel market can be diverted to Hawaii.

2. It has been historically taken for granted that the Hawaii travel industry must concentrate on the visitors staying in the state for two days or longer. This is a very valid conclusion as applied to the hotels and visitor attractions presently in existence. However, it is known that an almost equal number of persons pass through Hawaii enroute to the Orient or the U.S. and that this group of travelers stay in Hawaii for a period of from a few hours to two days. It is known that these persons are generally "seasoned" travelers and, as such, are not sufficiently attracted to any of Hawaii's existing tourist attractions (such as Circle-Island Tours, Pearl Harbor, Waikiki Beach, and the Pineapple or Sugar Plantation) to delay their trip to visit these attractions. However, among the leaders of the travel industry, it is the unanimous opinion that a unique attraction such as the proposed Sea Life Park, which offers something which many of these travelers have not seen before, could be of sufficient interest that these through-travelers would make the necessary effort or itinerary alterations to allow a visit to Sea Life. Tour operators enthusiastically support this idea for it would greatly increase their market potential and would be one of the few large areas of new business for them. The carrier companies have indicated a willingness to cooperate by adjusting arrival and departure schedules where possible to allow four to six hours minimum layover time in Hawaii and by assisting the combined Sea Life Tour Company Sales efforts by placing promotional literature on ships and aircraft. A small marine exhibit and Sea Life gift shop at the Honolulu Air Terminal

might assist this promotion. It is also felt that much could be accomplished by locating sales agents in the major airports of the Orient and the U.S.

3. Economic "recessions" on the mainland U.S. are not the disturbing factor that they were once thought to be in terms of their effect on visitor arrivals in Hawaii. In the two most recent recessions (1958 and 1961), the rate of increase of arrivals did not hold up during the period of the actual recession, but, in the following year during the recovery period, arrivals increased sharply from the recession period and, as a result, showed a normal increase over the three-year period straddling the recession year. Additionally, since the advent of jet travel and the greater numbers of foreign (now U.S.) travelers, total arrivals in Hawaii are hardly affected at all by a mainland U.S. recession. This can be clearly seen on the graph in the area of the 1961 recession. This apparent "recession-proof" character of the Hawaii visitor industry provides exceptional stability in Sea Life revenues.

BREAK-EVEN LEVELS OF THE PROPOSED SEA LIFE OPERATION

It should be pointed out that any change in the debt-equity ratio which might partially or completely eliminate current interest expense would appreciably lower the "break-even" points in each of the years. Additionally, any variation in construction costs and resulting annual depreciation expense would have a similar effect on the matter of construction cost. It is anticipated that the projected figure of $1,000,000 (which includes an estimator's built-in safety factor of 20%) will not be exceeded. However, the possibility exists of reducing this $1,000,000 amount through elimination of certain items in the present plan which are desirable but not absolutely essential to complete the exhibits so that they may be opened to the public.

In summary, it can be stated that the break-even points as calculated and plotted in graph number two are maximum points for the years shown and that substantial downward revision of these points could be accomplished through reduction of interest expense, reduction of total construction cost, reduction of total personnel and salaries, and scaling down of the entire project if necessary or advisable.

Exhibit 2. Sea Life Park (A) Early Financial Planning (From Progress Report, April 1962, prepared by Sea Life Staff and based on data from SRI report).

Notes		1964	1966	1968	1970	1972
1.	Gross revenues	$783,000	$928,000	$1,100,000	$1,250,000	$1,400,000
	Estimated visitor attendance	215,000	268,000	329,000	388,000	450,000
	Estimated local attendance	89,000	94,000	98,000	102,000	106,000
2.	Estimated total attendance	304,000	362,000	427,000	490,000	556,000
	Visitor admissions revenue	$348,000	$434,000	$ 533,000	$ 629,000	$ 729,000
	Local admissions revenue	176,000	186,000	194,000	202,000	210,000
3.	Net concessions revenue	58,000	69,000	81,000	93,000	106,000
4.	Other income (net)	25,000	25,000	25,000	25,000	25,000
	Total gross income	$607,000	$714,000	$ 833,000	$ 949,000	$1,070,000

Exhibit 2. *cont'd.*

5. Total operating expenses	$412,000	$442,000	$ 487,000	$ 537,000	$ 590,000
6. Depreciation	20,000	20,000	20,000	20,000	20,000
7. Rental to foundation	130,000	149,000	176,000	200,000	224,000
Total expenses	$562,000	$611,000	$ 683,000	$ 757,000	$ 834,000
Net pre-tax profit	$ 45,000	$103,000	$ 150,000	$ 192,000	$ 236,000
Provision for income taxes	25,000	57,000	82,000	106,000	130,000
Net after-tax earnings	$ 20,000	$ 46,000	$ 68,000	$ 86,000	$ 106,000
Total foundation income	$130,000	$149,000	$ 176,000	$ 200,000	$ 224,000
8. Repayment of long-term debt	$ 66,500	$ 66,500	$ 66,500	$ 66,500	$ 66,500
Interest on long-term debt	48,500	41,200	35,000	28,300	21,700
9. Rental to state of Hawaii	12,000	12,000	13,000	15,000	17,000
foundation operating expenses	1,000	8,300	11,500	15,200	18,800
Total foundation expenses	$128,000	$128,000	$ 126,000	$ 125,000	$ 124,000
Net foundation income	$ 2,000	$ 21,000	$ 50,000	$ 75,000	$ 100,000

Notes to Exhibit 2

1. Gross admissions revenue is based on gate charges of:

$2.20 for adults
$1.10 for children

Presuming 80% adults and 20% children, the average revenue, before commissions, is $1.98.

Presuming an 18% commission to travel agents and tour operators on the visitor attendance, the following admission factors result:

Visitors: $1.62 per attendee
Local: $1.98 per attendee

The 1960 rates at comparable attractions on the Mainland are as follows:

Marineland of the Pacific:	Adults: $2.50
	Children: .90
	(1,400,000 Attendance)
Marineland - Florida:	Adults: $2.20
	Children: 1.10
	(550,000 Attendance)
Seaquarium - Florida:	Adults: $2.25
	Children: 1.10
	(560,000 Attendance)

2. From December, 1960, SRI economic feasibility study.

In October 1961, a second market analysis, by the Sea Life staff (Exhibit 1), included a review of recently up-dated visitor data and discussions with major tour operators, the Hawaii

Notes to Exhibit 2. *cont'd.*

Visitors Bureau and individuals prominent in the Pacific travel industry. This report concluded that an upward revision of attendance estimates was indicated as follows:

	1964	1966	1968
Total Tourists to Oahu	512,000	640,000	760,000
Total Oahu Civilian Residents	460,000	493,000	505,000
Total Outer-Island Residents	145,000	155,000	165,000
Total Military Residents	100,000	100,000	100,000
Percent Tourists Attending	51.0%	53.0%	55.0%
Percent Oahu Residents Attending	10.5%	11.5%	12.5%
Percent Outer-Island Attending	2.5%	3.0%	3.5%
Percent Military Attending	50.0%	50.0%	50.0%
Est. Tourist Attendance	261,100	339,200	420,000
Est. Oahu Residents Attendance	48,300	56,700	64,000
Est. Outer-Island Attendance	3,600	4,700	6,000
Est. Military Attendance	50,000	50,000	50,000
Est. Total Attendance	363,000	450,600	540,000

With either projection the break-even point for attendance in 1964 is estimated to be 260,000 persons.

3. Net concessions revenue is based on 25% of gross at Gift Shop and 20% of gross at Snack Bar providing a total of $0.19 per attendee.*

Gross concession revenue was calculated as follows:

Snack bar: $0.45 per attendee
Gift shop and other: $0.40 per attendee
Total: $0.85 per attendee

4. Net revenue from the operation of three fish-pellet guns at a seal/sea bird pool. Each will gross $25,000 per annum and net, after lease royalties and maintenance expenses, a total of $25,000 per annum.

5. Operating Expenses:*

	1964	1966	1968
Wages and Salaries	$160,000	$170,000	$190,000
Advertising and Promotion	60,000	65,000	70,000
Insurance	25,000	25,000	25,000
Maintenance and Repair	25,000	30,000	35,000
Specimen Collection	10,000	10,000	10,000
Animal Food Cost	24,000	24,000	24,000
Utilities	35,000	35,000	35,000
General and Administrative	25,000	30,000	35,000
Federal Excise Taxes	19,000	20,000	25,000
Property and Misc. Taxes	8,000	8,000	8,000
Hawaii Gross Income Taxes	21,000	25,000	30,000
Total Operating Expenses	$412,000	$442,000	$487,000

---

*Based on December, 1960, SRI study.

Notes to Exhibit 2. *cont'd.*

Wages and Salaries (1964):

Job classification	Number of employees	Total annual cost
Director	1	$ 15,000
Assistant Director	2	18,000
Curator	1	9,000
Accountant	1	7,000
Secretary	2	9,000
Total Administrative Salaries	7	$ 59,000
Chief Whale and Porpoise Trainer	1	$ 7,000
Chief Collector	1	6,000
Whale and Porpoise Trainers	2	10,000
Aquarist Divers	2	10,000
Maintenance Technicians	4	22,000
Ground Keepers	4	12,000
Gate and Ticket Attendants	3	12,000
Total Operating Wages	19	$ 81,000
Part-time Wages	--	20,000
Total Wages and Salaries	24	$160,000

6. Depreciation is based on a straight line amortization, over a period of 15 years, on an investment of $300,000 in concession facilities and pre-opening expenses.

7. Rental to foundation is based on $130,000 per annum or 16% of total gross revenue (including concessionaires' gross revenue), whichever is greater.

8. Represents $1,000,000 of long-term debt repayable over a 15-year term at $66,500 per annum with interest at 5% per annum on the unpaid balance.

9. Rental to the state is established at $12,000 per annum or 1.2% of total gross revenues, whichever is greater.

Exhibit 3. Sea Life Park (A) Marineland, Los Angeles, Operating Results, 1957-1961 (Opened September 1, 1954).

Year	Attendance	Average net admission	Gross income	Gross profit on merchandise sales	Rental from restaurant	Net income after tax
1957	731,620	$1.38	$1,214,045	$ 86,213	$ 68,929	$ 64,765
1958	1,067,474	1.43	1,807,976	160,455	81,459	493,876
1959	1,223,555	1.46	2,137,782	216,026	95,119	403,563
1960	1,378,757	1.64	2,713,943	282,512	109,060	620,668
1961	1,459,954	1.69	2,998,270	364,309	112,895	719,620

Founders purchased 3500 shares in 1954 at $1 per share.

Outside investors purchased "package" in 1954 consisting of:

	Price	Investment	Shares	Total Investment
10 shares common stock	at $ 1.00	$ 10.00	70,000	$ 70,000
1 share preferred stock	at 100.00	100.00	7,000	700,000
1 debenture	at 71.50	71.50	7,000	500,000

In 1961 the common stock was split 7 - 1, preferred split 10 - 1.

In the same year the company issued new common stock to the public at $11.04 per share.

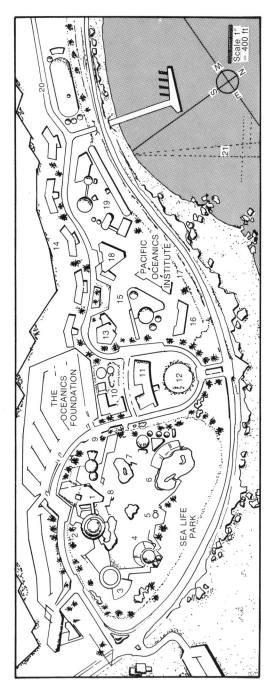

Scale 1" = 400 ft

SEA LIFE PARK

1. Entrance Dock
2. Coral Lagoon
3. Man in the Sea (Future)
4. Glass Porpoise Theater
5. Oceanographic Terrace (Future)
6. Whaler's Cove
7. Pool for Seals, Seabirds and Turtles
8. Sea Chest (gift shop)
9. Ocean Lanai (Restaurant)

JOINT USE

10. Training Pools and Maintenance
11. Administration (Sea Life Park and Oceanic Foundation)
12. Airport for Helicopters

OCEANIC INSTITUTE

13. Administration
14. Laboratory Space for Participating Groups
15. Photic Zone Experimental Complex (without pressure)
16. Offshore Surveillance Center
17. Electronic Library and Data Processing Center
18. Design and Instrumentation Center
19. Aphotic Zone Experimental Tanks (with pressure)
20. Mammal Research Tanks
21. Offshore Surveillance Zone (75 miles, to depths of 18,000 feet)

THE OCEANICS FOUNDATION

PACIFIC OCEANICS INSTITUTE

SEA LIFE PARK

ISLAND OF OAHU

SEA LIFE PARK

Kaupo Park site

Airport
Honolulu
Waikiki

North

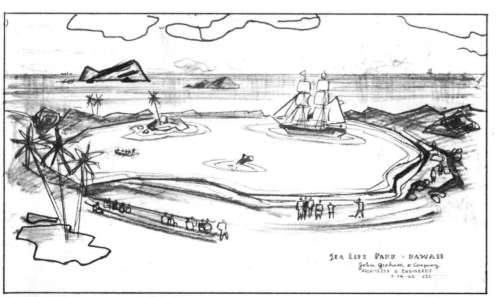

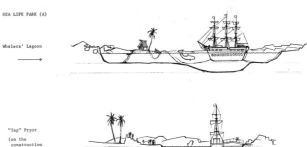

SEA LIFE PARK (A)

Whalers' Lagoon

"Tap" Pryor
(on the
construction
site)

Exhibit 5. Sea Life Park (A).

Exhibit 6. Sea Life Park (A) Artist's Rendition of Proposed Sea Life Park.

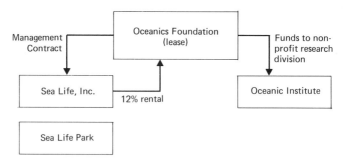

Exhibit 7. Sea Life Park (A) Proposed Organization.

Sea Life Park (B) (Revised)

After Tap Pryor's dream of a marine research facility had jelled into a well-defined concept, Tap turned to the task of financing that concept into a reality. Initially, Sea Life, Inc., had been financed by a small group of stockholders who invested a total of $50,000 early in 1961 at $1 per share. This high-risk money had been invested before there was any lease, land, construction, or porpoise—only the idea, some research data, and a plan. At that same time, the founders had received 50,000 shares in exchange for assets—the research studies, construction and operating plans, the products of four years of Pryor's work.

In order to finance construction and operations, it appeared that about $1.6 million would be required. The following plan for raising that capital was adopted. Additional shares were authorized to be sold as a package with debentures, because Pryor felt that debentures would be difficult to market on their own merits. Thus, subsequent investors purchased 300,000 shares at $2 per share, plus $600,000 worth of 5½ percent 12-year nonconvertible debentures, for a total investment of $1,200,000 by 25 stockholders. Local banks in Hawaii agreed to loan another $400,000 on a five-year note using the exhibit facilities, yet to be built, as collateral.

There were 200,000 additional authorized shares for management options at $2 per share, of which about half had already been granted as options to Tap Pryor. The remaining 100,000 shares were reserved for any new management people that would come in after incorporation. They would have an opportunity to exercise those options over a 10-year period on a contract which would require exceeding the profit projections on which sale of the other stock had been based. In other words, management would have to beat those projections in order to exercise their options at $2 per share. When all options were exercised, the original investors who came in with $50,000, plus the management, would have about 50% of the equity. However, the remaining investors would have majority control until that time, particularly through the underlying indenture to the debentures which contained quite strict provisions with respect to new financing and voting control.

By fall of 1963, the financing was virtually complete. According to Tap:

> The actual financing turned out somewhat differently from that in the original SRI report, which recommended raising $1,000,000 from investors and $700,000 as a loan from the bank. But the bank felt that this was more than they could lend. After all, what did the bank have if this venture failed? They would just have to run an unprofitable oceanarium. If our crowd can't run it successfully, how can a bank do so? Actually, as it's turning out, I have had to ask the bank for an additional $150,000, on top of the $400,000 which we are already borrowing from them, strictly for working capital purposes. The $1,200,000 in equity and debentures and the $400,000 loan were based on the assumption that the restaurant and gift-shop buildings and equipment and working capital for these operations would be put in by concessionaires. Studies in the last six months indicated that, from the standpoint of both control and profit, we should build and operate our own "traps." This requires

additional loans. So the total loan will be up to about $550,000, and as the banks pointed out to me, it's getting close to what they didn't want.

As far as locating investors, I decided to break up the $1,200,000 into 24 units at $50,000 a unit and move ahead on the assumption that I would sell in only $50,000 units, and if anyone should want to buy more than one unit, say one and a half, then I could sell the next unit as two halves, and that's the way it worked. The last two units I sold were for $12,500 each. We did this to keep under 25 investors, since this was a private placement without a Securities and Exchange Commission clearance. Actually, the SEC is a little vague on this question, but the important thing is to place the stock with sophisticated or experienced investors. I'm told you can sell it to a hundred professional brokers, but you are dead if you sell it to two old widows. The Hawaiian law is less reasonable. It specifies 25 investors as the maximum permitted in a new company without registration, and registration is long, involved, and costly.

I located these investors by hammering on a lot of doors. And I was thrown out of a lot of offices. I found out that you don't go to the average investor, but to the small business investment companies, to presidents and board chairmen of large corporations. If you stick to these kinds of people and organizations, and if the project is a sound one, you will be successful. I soon found that I had to get local backing. People want to know right away who in Hawaii has invested, so we got one or two major corporations on the island to buy a unit.

One thing leads to another. Not all of the people you call on will invest themselves, but they will tell you three new names, and you just follow up on these names, and each of them will tell you several others, and sooner or later you find the investors. You just weed out the ones that don't have any interest. If your project is any good, you will find enough people around who have a specific interest in what you're trying to do. We finally ended up with 25 people interested in Hawaii, in marine research, and in oceanarium exhibits.

In January I started placing stock and debentures, and by October, the last dollar of the $1,200,000 financing was committed and then the bank funds, $400,000, came in. The oceanarium is about four-fifths built and will open to the public about the 15th of January.

We have almost finished construction before completing our financing. In getting some early funds in the project—well, going all the way back to when I first got the $12,000 from the broadcasting company, until we got to the point where we could bring in some real venture capital, $1,200,000—it's been my philosophy all along to spend the money as we get it, to keep progressing to the next step in the project, so that we will have something tangible to show and thus help carry on to the next step. For example, when we had about $250,000 of our $1,200,000 committed last January, with the permission of those initial investors, we went ahead and built a porpoise-training facility and went out and collected some porpoise and began to train them one year in advance of the opening date. These training pools were the first construction in the oceanarium. This was perhaps a little risky—we put almost $100,000 into that step with the belief that a good oceanarium should open with a good show; and also with the belief that having a few porpoises might make it look a little more real to attract other investors. And indeed it did.

As I began going around seeing various individuals and companies who might be interested, I had a box full of pictures of these animals, of our collecting, of the location, of the training tanks and so forth, and things began to look more attractive to the investors. As we got in more funds, we graded the area, built the parking lot, cleaned out the exhibit areas, and took some more pictures. And that, in turn, helped us get additional capital to take the next steps.

We decided that when we got three-quarters of our investment requirements subscribed, we would start on the construction of the tanks and exhibits. By May 1963, we had over

$800,000 subscribed and we signed the construction contract for the full $1,200,000 and began the construction of the big tanks and facilities. By mid-summer, we had very much of a going operation. Since then, in the last three months, it has really been no problem at all to sell the remaining stock and debentures, because of all the action and obvious interest and confidence of our original investors. So we are now at a point where we are nearly ready to open the oceanarium.

The Oceanics Foundation was the first organization formed. I had this whole plan fairly well thought out and have not wanted to change it, so it has been important to promote it from a position of strength and to build on it. The Oceanics Foundation obtained the lease of the land from the state. Thus, the Oceanics Foundation was in a position to write the lease contract between itself and Sea Life. We have a very detailed contract which spells out all the interrelationships between the two organizations. It spells out rentals, the quality of the exhibit, the nature of what should be presented, the facilities that can be shared, and so forth. Through the rentals to be received from Sea Life, the Foundation is funded, and at the same time, it has general control over Sea Life Park.

I expect Sea Life, Inc., to develop in two ways. First would be the operation of Sea Life Park. We have the staff fairly well along. I have two assistants, one of whom is operating the plant, the Park itself, and handling public relations. The other is handling marketing and sales. Below them is the Park staff and above them is the corporate staff, that's me and the accountant. I expect someday that Sea Life, Inc. (and this is more of the possible "sex" of this operation) can get into industrial oceanography in some way, through its associations and through the kinds of activities that will be going on in the Oceanic Institute. We already have an Oceanics Division. One of my two assistants in the Park is very much interested in industrial oceanics. He is a graduate of the Stanford Graduate School of Business and is in the process of setting up our gift shop and our restaurant and handling all of our sales to the tour industry, but he is really looking to the oceanic area for his long-run future in the company. The other assistant will be running the Park and handling the relationship between the Park staff and the Institute.

Exhibit 1. Sea Life Park (B) Revised Financial Projections (January 14, 1963).

PEAT, MARWICK, MITCHELL & CO.
CERTIFIED PUBLIC ACCOUNTANTS

TRUSTCO BUILDING

P.O. BOX 3556

HONOLULU 11, HAWAII

Sea Life, Inc.

Introduction and Notes

The accompanying revised projections represent estimated earnings and cash flow arising from the operation of an exhibit of marine life on the Island of Oahu, Hawaii.

The projections are based upon estimates furnished by management as to available financing, capital expenditures, visitor attendance, revenues, costs and expenses, etc. It is our understanding that management has availed themselves of such data as is available in estimating rate of growth of population and tourism as well as a feasibility study by Stanford Research Institute dated October 1962, but such data has not been independently verified by us.

Capitalization

The estimated earnings and cash flow anticipates that in addition to the 100,000 shares of capital stock of $1.00 par value presently outstanding, initial capital will be raised as follows:

Exhibit 1. *cont'd.*

A. Issuance of 300,000 shares of capital stock at $2.00 a share, $1.00 to be credited to capital stock, the remainder, $1.00, to be credited to premium on capital stock, providing additional equity capital of $600,000.

B. Sale of $600,000 of 5 percent debentures, subordinated to the bank loan both as to payment of principal and interest, payable in twelve years, with a sinking fund requirement providing for the deposit of $60,000 annually commencing at the end of the third year until maturity.

C. $400,000 bank loan bearing interest at 6 percent, secured by a mortgage on the leasehold and improvements, repayable in five equal annual installments to be applied first to interest and the remainder to principal.

Additional equity capital aggregating $400,000 is anticipated to be provided during 1968 by the issuance of 100,000 shares of capital stock at $4.00 a share, $1.00 to be credited to capital stock, the remainder, $3.00, to be credited to premium on capital stock.

Construction Costs

Cost of construction of the exhibit area has been based upon an estimate submitted by an independent contractor.

Revenue

A summary of estimated revenue is provided in Schedule 1.

Admissions revenue was computed on gate charges of $2.00 for adults and $1.10 for children presuming that 80% of the attendees would be adults and 20% would be children.

The number of residents and tourists attending the exhibit were obtained from the Stanford Research Institute's feasibility study.

Concession revenue was estimated at an average purchase at the gift and snack shops of $1.00 per attendee. Operating expenses of concessions, excluding rent, were estimated to aggregate 80% of related revenue.

It is estimated that the company will realize $25,000 a year from the operation of fish-pellet guns at a seal/sea bird pool and the sale of souvenir guide books.

Operating Expenses

Operating expenses as detailed on Schedule 1 are in general agreement with the aggregate of operating expenses derived by Stanford Research Institute in its feasibility study.

The company intends to enter into a contract with The Oceanics Foundation (a non-profit organization) under which the company will have the right to operate the exhibit area for a period of twenty years. In consideration therefor, the company will pay the following annual rentals:

First two years	$ 30,000
Second two years	60,000
Fifth year	120,000
Remaining fifteen years	12% of gross revenue or $120,000, whichever is greater

Preoperating and organization expenses estimated to amount to $393,500 (of which $100,000 has been expended prior to September 1, 1962) are being amortized over the first five years of the contract ($78,700 a year) on the accompanying statement of earnings.

Peat, Marwick, Mitchell & Co.

Exhibit 1A. Sea Life Park (B) Estimated Earnings.

	1964	1965	1966	1967	1968	1969	1970	1971	1972	1973
Operating revenue-Schedule 1	$1,124,700	$1,246,900	$1,369,200	$1,497,400	$1,625,600	$1,750,800	$1,876,000	$1,999,700	$2,123,400	$2,245,600
Operating Expenses:										
Rental to the Foundation	30,000	30,000	60,000	60,000	120,000	210,100	225,100	240,000	254,800	269,500
Other operating expenses - Schedule 1	470,200	496,700	523,000	555,100	587,700	619,600	651,900	683,700	716,100	750,400
Concessions (excluding rent)	294,000	328,000	359,000	395,000	428,000	463,000	495,000	529,500	563,000	596,000
Amortization-Schedule 1	144,200	144,200	144,200	144,200	144,200	105,500	105,500	105,500	105,500	105,500
Total operating expenses	938,400	998,900	1,086,200	1,154,300	1,279,900	1,398,200	1,477,500	1,558,700	1,639,400	1,721,400
Earnings from operations	186,300	248,000	283,000	343,100	345,700	352,600	398,500	441,000	484,000	524,200
Interest Expense-Schedule 1	54,000	49,700	42,500	35,100	27,300	19,200	16,500	13,800	11,100	8,400
Earnings before income taxes	132,300	198,300	240,500	308,000	318,400	333,400	382,000	427,200	472,900	515,800
Federal and State Income Taxes	67,600	103,600	126,600	163,400	169,100	176,200	202,600	227,300	252,200	275,600
Net income after income taxes	$ 64,700	$ 94,700	$ 113,900	$ 144,600	$ 149,300	$ 157,200	$ 179,400	$ 199,900	$ 220,700	$ 240,200
Earnings per share:										
400,000 shares	$.16	$.24	$.28	$.36						
500,000 shares					$.30	$.31	$.36	$.40	$.44	$.48
Rate of earnings per share (computed on per share cost to investors of $2.00)	8.0%	12.0%	14.0%	18.0%	15.0%	15.5%	18.0%	20.0%	22.0%	24.0%

Exhibit 1B. Sea Life Park (B) Estimated Cash Flow.

	Sept. 1, 1962 through Dec. 31, 1963	1964	1965	1966	1967	1968	1969	1970	1971	1972	1973	1974	1975	1976
Sources of Cash:														
Earnings from operations		$ 64,700	$ 94,700	$113,900	$144,600	$149,300	$157,200	$179,400	$199,900	$ 220,700	$ 240,200	$ 244,000	$ 246,600	$ 246,600
Add back amortization and depreciation		144,200	144,200	144,200	144,200	144,200	105,500	105,500	105,500	105,500	105,500	100,000	100,000	100,000
Add (deduct) adjustment for income taxes		67,600	57,800	(41,800)	(41,800)	(41,800)								
Sale of debenture bonds	$ 600,000					-								
Sale of capital stock	600,000					400,000								
Proceeds from bank loans	400,000					-								
	1,600,000	276,500	296,700	216,300	247,000	651,700	262,700	284,900	305,400	326,200	345,700	344,000	346,000	346,600
Cash Requirements:														
Direct construction costs of exhibit facilities, parking areas and landscaping	1,200,000					600,000								
Additions to working capital	-	90,000												
Equipment for concessions	55,500		3,000	3,000	3,000	3,000	3,000	3,000	3,000	3,000	3,000	3,000	3,000	3,000
Payment into sinking fund for retirement of debentures				60,000	60,000	60,000	60,000	60,000	60,000	60,000	60,000	60,000		
Repayment of bank loan ($400,000)		71,000	75,300	79,800	84,500	89,600								
Organization and preoperating expenses (including interest of $30,000)	293,000													
	1,549,000	161,000	78,300	142,800	147,500	752,600	63,000	63,000	63,000	63,000	63,000	63,000	63,000	3,000
Cash retention or (deficit)	51,000	115,500	218,400	73,500	99,500	(100,900)	199,700	221,900	242,400	263,200	282,700	281,000	283,600	343,600
Cash balance, beginning of year	-	51,000	166,500	384,900	458,400	557,900	457,000	656,700	878,600	1,121,000	1,384,200	1,666,900	1,947,900	2,231,500
Cash balance, end of year before dividends	$ 51,000	$166,500	$384,900	$458,400	$557,900	$457,000	$656,700	$878,600	$1,121,000	$1,384,200	$1,666,900	$1,947,900	$2,231,500	$2,575,100

Operating Revenue:										
Visitors' admissions	$524,700	$598,900	$673,200	$752,400	$831,600	$910,800	$990,000	$1,069,200	$1,148,400	$1,227,600
Local admissions	206,000	213,000	220,000	226,000	232,000	236,000	240,000	243,000	246,000	248,000
Operations of fish guns and sales of souvenir guide books	25,000	25,000	25,000	25,000	25,000	25,000	25,000	25,000	25,000	25,000
	755,700	836,900	918,200	1,003,400	1,088,600	1,171,800	1,255,000	1,337,200	1,419,400	1,500,600
Concession sales	369,000	410,000	451,000	494,000	537,000	579,000	621,000	662,500	704,000	745,000
Total operating revenue	$1,124,700	$1,246,900	$1,369,200	$1,497,400	$1,625,600	$1,750,800	$1,876,000	$1,999,700	$2,123,400	$2,245,600
Operating Expenses:										
Salaries and wages	$162,000	$167,000	$172,000	$182,000	$192,000	$202,000	$212,000	$222,000	$232,000	$242,000
Advertising and promotion	60,000	62,500	65,000	67,500	70,000	72,500	75,000	77,500	80,000	82,500
Commissions to travel agents	60,700	69,900	78,200	87,400	96,600	105,800	115,000	124,200	133,400	142,600
Insurance	20,000	20,000	20,000	20,000	20,000	20,000	20,000	20,000	20,000	20,000
Maintenance and repairs	17,000	18,300	20,000	21,700	23,300	25,000	26,700	28,300	30,000	31,700
Specimen collection	10,000	10,500	11,000	11,500	12,000	12,500	13,000	13,500	14,000	14,500
Animal food costs	24,000	24,500	25,000	25,500	26,000	26,500	27,000	27,500	28,000	29,000
Utilities	19,000	19,000	19,500	19,500	20,000	20,000	20,500	20,500	21,000	21,000
Federal excise taxes	36,100	40,200	44,200	48,400	52,700	56,800	60,800	64,900	69,000	73,000
State gross income taxes	26,400	29,300	32,100	35,100	38,100	41,000	43,900	46,800	49,700	54,600
Property and other taxes	10,000	10,500	11,000	11,500	12,000	12,500	13,000	13,500	14,000	14,500
Sundry	25,000	25,000	25,000	25,000	25,000	25,000	25,000	25,000	25,000	25,000
Total operating expenses	$470,200	$496,700	$523,000	$555,100	$587,700	$619,600	$651,900	$683,700	$716,100	$750,400
Amortization and Depreciation:										
Leasehold improvements	$60,000	$60,000	$60,000	$60,000	$60,000	$100,000	$100,000	$100,000	$100,000	$100,000
Concession equipment	5,500	5,500	5,500	5,500	5,500	5,500	5,500	5,500	5,500	5,500
Preoperating and organization expenses (Note)	78,700	78,700	78,700	78,700	78,700	–	–	–	–	–
Total amortization and depreciation	$144,200	$144,200	$144,200	$144,200	$144,200	$105,500	$105,500	$105,500	$105,500	$105,500
Interest Expense, net:										
Interest on bank loan at 6%	$24,000	$19,700	$15,200	$10,500	$5,400	–	–	–	–	–
Interest on debentures at 5%	30,000	30,000	30,000	30,000	30,000	30,000	30,000	30,000	30,000	30,000
Interest on sinking fund at 4½%	–	–	(2,700)	(5,400)	(8,100)	(10,800)	(13,500)	(16,200)	(18,900)	(21,600)
Total interest expense	$54,000	$49,700	$42,500	$35,100	$27,300	$19,200	$16,500	$13,800	$11,100	$8,400

Note: Amortization provides for $100,000 of preoperating and organization expenses incurred prior to September 1, 1962.

Exhibit 2. Sea Life Park (B) Estimated Preopening Expenses
(For 16-month period: September 1, 1962-December 31, 1963).

1. Site rental	$ 17,000
2. Salaries and fees	100,300
3. Administrative equipment & expense	15,000
4. Interest	11,600
5. Insurance	8,000
6. Capital equipment	20,000
7. Specimen collecting and training	50,200
8. Consultants' fees and expenses	118,200
9. Public relations	24,000
10. Utilities	12,000
11. Travel and transportation	13,500
12. Construction	1,154,000
Sub-Total	$1,544,300
Contingency	5,700
Estimated working capital, opening date, January 1, 1964	50,000
Total	$1,600,000

Note: These estimates made under assumption that Gift Shop and Restaurant would be built and operated by concessionaires.

Exhibit 3. Sea Life Park (B) Estimated Cash Flow* (Prepared October 6, 1963).

	Sept. 1, 1962 through Sept. 30, 1963 (Actual)	Oct. 1963	Nov. 1963	Dec. 1963	(Opening) Jan. 1, 1964	Feb. 1964	Total
Sources of Cash:							
Sale of Capital Stock	$397,250	$202,750	$	$	$	$	$ 600,000
Sale of Debenture Bonds	397,250	202,750					600,000
Proceeds from Bank Loans			75,000	175,000	109,000	41,000	400,000
Repayment of Performance Bonds		6,000			50,875		56,875
Repayment of Employee Loan					4,500		4,500
Total	794,500	411,500	75,000	175,000	164,375	41,000	1,661,375
Cash Requirements:							
Const. & Capital Equipment	355,557	345,425	206,275	138,650	96,300	40,698	1,182,905
Site Rental & Utilities	18,691	6,700	600	900	509		27,400
Salaries & Fees	71,736	10,200	11,100	10,500	6,600		110,136
General Administrative	13,683	500	500	500	317		15,500
Insurance	7,338	365	365	365			8,433
Specimen Collection/Training	35,060	3,000	3,000	5,000	3,640		49,700
Consultants/Architecture Fees	75,097	5,000	10,000	15,000	12,903		118,000
Public Relations/Promotion	4,658	1,000	1,000	3,000	4,342		14,000
Travel ? Transportation	13,413	800	700	800	400		16,113
Interest		6,000	2,000		1,386		9,386
Performance Bond	56,000						56,000
Employee Loan	8,500						8,500
Total	659,733	378,990	235,540	174,715	126,397	40,698	1,616,073
Cash Retention (deficit)	134,767	32,510	(160,540)	285	37,978	302	45,302
Cash Balance, beginning period	---	134,767	167,277	6,737	7,022	45,000	
Cash Balance, end of period	$134,767	$167,277	$ 6,737	$ 7,022	$ 45,000	$445,302	$ 45,302

*Not including admissions receipts.

Exhibit 4. Sea Life Park (B) Balance Sheet
(For Months Ended September 30 and August 31, 1963).

	Balance at		Increase
Assets	September 30	August 31	(Decrease)
Current Assets			
Cash on hand and in banks	$134,947.24	($324,175.21)	$459,122.45
Advances to employees	3,472.54	3,472.54	---
Accrued interest receivable	145.83	---	145.83
Prepaid expenses	2,778.47	6,778.47	(4,000.00
Deposits	61,710.00	61,700.00	10.00
Total current assets	$203,054.08	($252,224.20)	$455,278.28
Property			
Leasehold improvements	$506,587.07	$331,858.46	$174,728.61
Furniture and fixtures	22,510.78	22,296.48	214.30
Exhibit specimens	894.86	894.66	---
Total property	$529,992.51	$353,968.03	$173,942.91
Less accumulated depreciation	(2,081.57)	(1,081.57)	(1,000.00
Net property	$527,910.94	$353,968.03	$173,942.91
Other Assets			
Employee note & accts. rec.	$ 8,828.98	$ 8,828.98	---
Architects & engineering fees	$ 65,050.35	65,050.35	---
Pre-operating expenses (1962)	63,862.77	63,862.77	---
Organization expense	50,111.14	50,111.14	---
Total other assets	$187,853.24	$187,853.24	$ ---
Total assets	$918,818.26	$289,597.07	$629,221.19
Liabilities and Stockholders' Equity			
Current Liabilities			
Accounts payable	$160,800.00	$ 4,000.00	$156,800.00
Accrued expenses	2,426.74	5,365.23	(2,938.49
Interest payable	6,077.07	---	6,077.07
Total current liabilities	$169,303.81	$ 9,365.23	$159,938.58
5% Debentures payable, due 4/1/75	$397,303.81	$141,000.00	$256,250.00
Total liabilities	$566,553.81	$150,365.23	$416,188.58
Stockholders' Equity			
Capital Stock*	$298,625.00	$170,500.00	$128,125.00
Amount received in excess of capital stock	198,625.00	70,500.00	128,125.00
Less net pre-operating expenses			
(1/63 to 9/63) Exhibit 1B	(144,985.55)	(101,768.16)	(43,217.39
Total stockholders' equity	$352,264.45	$139,231.84	$213,032.61
Total liabilities and stockholders' equity	$918,818.26	$289,597.07	$629,221.19

*Capital Stock - $1.00 par value; authorized 600,000 shares; issued and outstanding, September, 298,625 shares.

Exhibit 5. Sea Life Park (B) Sea Life Park Under Construction (October 1963).

Sea Life Park (C) (Revised)

Sea Life finally opened its doors to the public on February 11, 1964, almost six weeks after the originally planned opening date of January 1. The delayed opening and the higher construction costs seriously upset the Company's financial planning. Construction costs were approximately $40,000 greater than budgeted, and unbudgeted costs resulting from the 41-day delay in opening were $50,288 (the deficit on December 31 was $301,315; on February 10, the day before opening, it was 351,603.) Had it not been for the substantial advance sale of annual passes, the Company would have opened with a negative cash balance. An active publicity campaign, assisted by the local newspapers and radio stations, enabled the Company to sell almost 2000 annual passes, thus generating an unplanned cash income of slightly over $7,500 prior to the opening date.

The Sea Life staff and the construction crew worked overtime throughout the last few weeks before opening. Gradually the Park approached completion. The glass was installed for the second time in the Lagoon Tank and the new seals held. Immediately members of the local skin-diving clubs and the Sea Life collecting crew began to bring in fish. The *Essex* was towed through Honolulu on a truck and out to the Park. It was installed in the Whaler's Lagoon on January 15. As soon as the Lagoon was filled with water the spinning porpoise were moved in from the training tanks. They seemed delighted with their new-found "elbow-room" and after several days were performing well and responding to their electronic cues.

On Sunday, February 9, two days before opening, a preview was held for 550 members of the press corps and their families, 1500 friends of the companies which had designed, built, supplied and financed the Park, and 2000 members of the tour industry. All the shows went well, and were received with great enthusiasm. The animals had not reached the level of training that had been hoped for, but Tap and Karen, Tap's wife, in announcing the shows, told the audience that they were sharing in the Park's "shakedown cruise," and in the training of the animals. They emphasized the importance of research in communicating with these animals and understanding their navigational abilities, relating it to the space and underwater defense programs. Thus the audience was drawn into an emotional involvement with the acts, and short-comings or mistakes in the performance were overlooked.

On opening day, February 11, 600 paying customers, including 408 adults, 19 children, and 23 in a tour group, entered the Park. That they enjoyed the show was indicated by the fact that of those who came, 150 purchased annual passes. Eighty-one more annual passes were sold by mail. The people attending spent an average of $.70 apiece in the restaurant. The gift shop was not yet open. Total revenue was $2,213. This level of attendance was maintained the balance of the week, until Saturday, when attendance jumped to 1304 and total revenue to $4,408 (436 annual passes sold), and Sunday, attendance 2821, total revenue $9,035 (including 917

Reprinted from *Stanford Business Cases 1969* with the permission of the Publishers, Stanford University Graduate School of Business, © 1969 by the Board of Trustees of the Leland Stanford Junior University.

annual passes). Total attendance for the week was 6329, and total revenue was $22,465.

The second week was even better. Attendance climbed to 9313 and total revenue to almost $29,369. If this level could be maintained, it was clear that the Park was an assured success. Late that week the Chairman of the Board of Directors visited the Park and reported to the stockholders that, ". . . our grand new venture is off to a healthy and impressive start" (Exhibit 1). In the third week attendance fell off to 5719, and total revenue dropped to $20,645.

Following the first three weeks, volume dropped precipitously in subsequent weeks to an attendance of slightly over 4000 and total revenue $12,500 during the week before Easter, then climbed in Easter week to an attendance of 8712 and total revenue of $25, 655, including sale of over 2000 annual passes.

The following quotations from memoranda and letters, and the attached exhibits, portray Sea Life's operations during the spring and summer of 1964.

March 6 (Tom)

The key to this in the forthcoming months is going to be our ability to make the transition from substantially *local* attendance to substantially *tourist* attendance. From an average of 87 tourists per day during the second week, we moved up to an average of 142 tourists per day during the third week, so the trend is in the right direction. But there is a lot of work to do working hand in glove with the tour people, as they show remarkably little capacity for solving the smallest of their own internal problems associated with Sea Life Park. Working with them, through them, and around them is quite a game, and the challenge is fun. The results, with time and effort, I am sure will be rewarding.

Of particular interest is the group activity, which is being generated and is very worthwhile going after. Every day during the next thirty operating days we have between two and three groups booked. This gives us a fine base of attendance and it is usually reflected in the restaurant figures.

On the 19th of March the Honolulu Chamber of Commerce will present Sea Life Park with the award for the outstanding accomplishment of this year. We are going to have quite a gathering for this event.

March 11 (Tom)

We are going to give radio and kiddies' TV a few shots here before and during the Easter week to capitalize on that very lucrative holiday.

I am working on a scheme right now to discount our admission to local tour desks that do not qualify for the wholesaler rate. We might sell them a block of tickets less 10 percent for cash with a guaranteed return, or where good credit can be established, handle them as we do the wholesalers. More than anything else, this will act as an impetus to the U-Drive people, who presently are not making any commission on Sea Life Park.

Had a conference this morning with the Honolulu Rapid Transit people to see what it would take for us to provide our own transportation through them. There seems to be no question that we could make out economically and probably make a fine profit on the transportation ourselves. However, we still can't afford the risk of competing with the tour companies, upon whom we will probably always have to count to fill these buses. At the least, I think our negotiations with HRT might cause a little more action with the other companies, and perhaps we can augment the existing transportation without competing too much with the sales organizations.

March 20 (Tap)

Attendance at the Park goes well. Next week Easter should make March look good. April may be a slump. We open again in May and should be able to get big attendance, public relations, etc., all over again, until June. By then summer vacation will be a boost. Meanwhile Tom works 100 percent on the tour industry. We are getting about 20 percent of the visitors to Waikiki today and of course need a great many more. I won't be satisfied until we reach about the 60 percent mark and am considering developing our own bus service at this time.

March 31 (Bob)

Despite torrential rains Tuesday (during which Governor Brown of California stood dowsed but cheering through the Whaler's Cove show), the holiday week just past was a good one.

April 16 (Tom)

Kaena (the new false killer whale) is really a doll. She's as frisky as she can be and I have been hearing stories about how she gives the porpoises in Whaler's Cove rides on her head. Georges is out now looking for a mate for her. She eats about 65 lbs. of mackerel a day. Also, we have two new species of porpoise—*Steno Rostrotus*. Apparently only once in written history has this species ever been spotted and that was a good many years ago off the coast of Africa. They supposedly have the habit of getting up on their tail and skidding for some distance which should be interesting. They are quite unusual looking with a rather thick rostrum and eyebrow type ridges over their eyes. Their eyes are very humanoid.

With the advent of the good news, though, comes some sadness—that is that we lost Mele (our pregnant? porpoise). She got tangled in the net which blocked off the other side of the *Essex* and drowned. Karen dissected her and found she was not pregnant! I think Karen feels a little embarrassed about this since all of Hawaii is "awaiting the birth" so I don't know how far this bit of information should travel.

As for sales, we are making money but we'd like to be making much more. Indications are that we should be getting a substantial portion of the summer tourist trade. We had 7000 at the Park last Sunday, largely due (we think) to the fact that it was the first weekend of the whale's residency.

April 21 (Bob)

Group sales are improving but the tour industry is still dragging its tail. We'll be opening the gift shop this week which should help the revenue picture.

False killer whale "Kaena" is doing fine—giving "Haole" rides on her head.

April 28 (Tap)

The Park continues to be the biggest hit in Honolulu. I'm told at any party one of the first questions asked is, "Have you been to Sea Life Park?" And if the answer is "no," the asker immediately has a cocktail gambit and can spend the next twenty minutes praising the exhibit and all the other aspects of the Park. As a result we have sold over 20,000 passes without any slackening of interest in sight. Sunday, for example, was our largest day yet with about 2000 single admissions sold and around 800 annual passes. In addition, some 1500 pass holders came to the Park and another 1000 or so children. All shows had standing room only during the day on Sunday, so we're now proceeding with adding more seating to the exhibit tanks. The gift shop opens today and the restaurant has been thriving. With my Institute activities the load of the Park has been carried by Tom, Bob, and Karen.

Tom is doing a really superb job here. The sales program seems very sound and productive to me. The number of tourists attending increases all the time and his group-sales program is a real life-saver and will be a large part of our revenue, most of which is unprojected, before the year is out. The restaurant is operating well in the black without any problems that I can see. The food continues to be good and Tom and Bill Johnson have devised ways to relieve the counter of some of the pressure during the heaviest hours. Presently we are working with the architect to put a small food facility down at the Oceanographic Terrace to catch the crowds between the Porpoise Theater and Whaler's Cove, and to relieve some of the pressure at the main counters.

The gift shop looks like it's going to be up to our standards as well. We've divided it into three sections. A little more than half of the front part is the gift area, and the back half is divided into sections for the marine art gallery and book store, which are being filled now. I don't know if the gallery and book store will add much to the revenue, but they certainly add a great deal to the atmosphere and this has carried on into the gift shop in a very strong manner.

Tom's three-part contribution to the Park (sales, restaurant, gift shop) has been marvelously handled, and this is really amazing when you consider that he had no real experience in any of the three areas before starting on this last July. I think what he's done speaks more highly for the value of the graduate business school than anything I've seen so far. He is well trained and he uses his training. Aside from the three areas of his main responsibility, he has also recently helped Bob and Joe set up a "red-flag" system for me so that I can easily analyze the state of our financial affairs on the basis of some fairly simple indicators and graphs.

Bob continues to hold the line on expenses and keeps a firm hand on the operation of the Park. He also has taken over our public relations program, bringing it in effect back from the agency into our house. This is real good use of his experience and I think he's pleased to be back in that business as well. This way when we have some news about the animals, for example, the copy is originated by myself or Karen and is processed by him. Bob and I work together closely on getting it out to the papers. This publicity has been absolutely phenomenal lately and so much so that we think maybe we ought to retire for a while from it and not crowd our luck.

Karen is now full-time curator of exhibits and is doing a fine job at that: She's added more text to the shows. She's developing some narrators to back up Danny and herself in depth. She has three of the trainers able to handle the Glass Porpoise Theater. She has worked with the architect to design ways of putting interpretive material up in the Hawaiian Reef Tank. She has a feeding show going on now after every Whaler's Cove show in the Leeward Island exhibit—the boys get in there and ring a bell and all of the animals, birds, turtles, and what have you, come over to the trainer and most of the people from Whaler's Cove can see this.

Today we are adding a new animal to the Glass Porpoise Theater. This is another tursiops (porpoise) who has, I understand, been trained to go to a numbered card hanging over the tank and select the number depending upon how many whistles have been blown (one whistle, go to number one, two whistles, number two and so forth). Karen added a spinning porpoise to the show to replace Mele, and that animal is already responding along with the other animals on cue. It's been in there about two weeks. The whale is being trained now, and is jumping clear of the water and being fed for the visitors during the Whaler's Cove show. Karen is also working on supervising the training of the porpoise for next summer's research program in the open sea. She had one trainer on that full time now.

I guess the biggest problem is parking now, and we're going to open up a new parking lot under the water tower before June. As I mentioned, there is standing room only at the Sunday shows and this leads us to wonder whether or not we overdid it on the annual passes. By the end of this year we should have a great percentage of the visitors in the Park on an annual pass basis. Still one can't argue with volume and the fact that the sales of passes have allowed us to beat our resident projections by a wide, wide margin. But it does seem likely that we will have to raise the price of the pass next year just to reduce the volume by a certain amount.The big crowds on Sundays of course have a favorable side—the place certainly looks attractive and successful when we see cars lined up all the way over the hill, and can't help but give an impression to the person who hasn't been there that this is something worth going to. We do expect to try some night operations this summer and have some companies begin development on a master lighting plan. The place is terrifically beautiful at night. We had a party for seventy or so people last Friday and they all thought the place was awesome and really quite a different park at night than it is during the day. In fact, at night it seems to be absolutely flawless in appearance and architecturally really exciting. The Hawaiian Reef Tank is a fairyland at night now that we have spotlights rigged for it.

April 29 (Bob)

Although March still includes a substantial reflection of the "start-up" phase of operations, we are continually looking at expenses and April should be better on this score.

May 14 (Tap)

Even with the impact of preopening publicity, our operating results have not been up to the Peat, Marwick and Mitchell projections made January 14, 1963 and based on the Stanford Research Institute attendance projections of 1961.

	PMM Forecast (Jan. 14, 1963 —adjusted)	Actual		
		Feb. 1964	Mar. 1964	April 1964
Admissions	$55,833	$59,545	$66,901*	$51,051
Other (Net)	32,833	7,548	7,231	7,479
Total	$88,666	$67,093*	$74,132*	$58,530*

*Note: Due to accounting method these figures differ slightly from Gross Profit figures shown on monthly profit and loss statements. The difference is in the amount of admissions tax, which in the profit and loss statements is deducted above the line.

In view of these operating results, revenue forecasts for the balance of the year have been revised downward. The new forecast is calculated on a base month computed from the actual results April 20 to May 10. Adjustments are also made for summer and winter months, as follows:

	Base Month	Summer Month	Fall Month
Admissions	$55,034	$76,405	$56,155
Other (Net)	9,773	13,278	9,899
Total	$64,807	$89,683	$66,054

May was a good month at the gate with over 25,000 paid and gross revenue of about $74,000. Looks like we might be in the black on paper for the month.

June 9 (Bob)

Attendance and revenue down for the week, possibly due to competition of graduation week activities at local schools. Kamehameha Day this Thursday should boost current week. Tap and Tom still slugging it out with local tour industry, but tide seems to be turning.

June 16 (Bob)

Here's to bigger and better Hawaiian holidays. Last week was boosted by Kamehameha Day (Thursday), but the really encouraging thing about these figures is the marked pick-up on the normal weekdays (Tuesday, Wednesday, and Friday). May be the beginning of the summer upswing we're looking for.

June 16 (Tap)

The Park is beginning to find its feet in a working manner, and today seems to be the beginning of a really solid summer attendance. We are running over three times the normal daily average today, with the Porpoise Theater filled at every show.

Tom and I have been working for three weeks to set up an Oceanic Tour for next year. We seem to have the support of the tour industry in this and can count on being packaged by most of them. We decided that Sea Life Park should not begin at the gate, but should extend around to Waikiki on both sides. We are devising a presentation of all things marine to and from the Park, including Hawaiian tales of fishing, famous rocks where shark gods lived, Kamehameha's amphibious landing points, as well as the more recent history of whaling. We are going to show Nuuanu Stream, where the whalers filled their water kegs, and the harbor itself. Stops will include the research facilities at Kewalo Basin and a view of Coconut Island Marine Laboratory from the Pali. Tapes on the buses will take the burden off the drivers, and we have assumed the responsibility for providing these tapes. Our final presentation of this tour to the fifteen representatives of the industry is scheduled for June 30th. We have a movie of the Park, pictures of the route, and sample tapes for that occasion. It should sew up our visitor attendance for next year.

June 22 (Bob)

The figures on our May operations are encouraging—income up $7,500 and expenses down $3,500—but not quite good enough to total up in the black.

It looks like expenses will continue to decrease in June (hopefully below $60,000 for the month) but the calendar will rob us somewhat in the total income category despite an increased average daily income.

June 30 (Bob)

After a poor ($11,600) first week, June has given us three $18,000 weeks in a row—an encouraging start to the summer season. We just concluded tour-industry negotiations which lock up into a new Oceanic-Sea Life Park Tour of Oahu starting this Fall. So things look brighter!

July 7 (Bob)

Fourth of July gave us our best week since Easter and an encouraging start on the month. The Tour Industry has brought our Oceanic Tour for 1965 so we should be OK if we can hold out through the rest of '64.

July 15 (Bob)

The 50th State Fair (which claimed 175,000 attendance for the week) ate into us a bit, but not too bad.

The summer to date has been as good on the revenue side as we had looked for so we are now in the process of whacking away at expenses.

July 22 (Bob)

Although June expenses were down almost $2,000, the revenue side of the picture has not been up to expectations. We're taking steps to bolster both present tourist sales and annual pass sales, but it hasn't shown yet. We had been looking for $18-20,000 weekly income for July and August rather than the $16,600 we did last week.

July 24 (Tom)

During the months of June, July, and August the die is being cast for our place in the tourist industry in 1965. As you know, we h ave not been satisfied with the tourists' attendance nor with the way that our product has been presented to the tourists. The remedy for this has been for us to take full responsibility for developing the Oceanic-Sea Life Park Tour and insure a stimulating, high-quality tour from the moment the tourist leaves Waikiki until he returns. With the help of some fine consultants from the Bishop Museum and Department of Education we've put together a wonderful tour. This has already been presented on three separate occasions to over 70 key members of the Oahu tourist industry. All of the wholesalers here have unanimously agreed to include this new tour as part of their program for 1965. This means we will be presold on the mainland, and they will be putting a unified effort behind the promotion of the tour along with some $54,000 of our budget which we are able to devote to the tour.

Still, there are quite a number of significant travel wholesalers on the mainland who make their own decisions independent from the people of Oahu. By the end of August and after covering San Francisco, Los Angeles, Chicago, and New York, I hope to have these wholesalers in our camp as well. What a difference this can make for us next year when we are only getting about 12 percent of the tourists now.

July 27 (Bob)

We had rain on Thursday and Friday which didn't help, but still July continues to disappoint us at the turnstiles.

Charlie Anderson, his family and friends, the Hemphills, toured the Park last week. He was impressed by Sea Life Park and was very encouraging after a brief glance at our figures.

August 5 (Bob)

In the first 25 weeks of operations, Sea Life has grossed $105,354 less than the Peat, Marwick and Mitchell projections of January 14, 1963 and $54,404 less than our own revised forecast of May 14, 1964. Accordingly, we are again making a downward revision in our forecasts.

We have asked for a revision in our bank loan calling for a lump sum interest payment in December and monthly principal and interest payments spread over the remaining 48 months of the loan.

August 14 (Tap—in letter to Stockholders)

For the present, let me say that we feel that we are beginning to run the Park instead of vice versa. Expenses have been reduced every month since we opened, each staff member seems to have control of his own responsibilities, exhibits quite literally improve every day, and the growing community support for the project shows no sign of leveling off. Our relationship with the tour industry for 1965 is excellent. In short, the project is in good health. We feel confident and fortunate.

We aren't meeting our projected totals for revenue and admissions. Far from being disappointing, however, this statement is most encouraging to me. The attendance is largely made up of resident attendance. This is much more than an opening burst of local curiosity. They love the Park and come again and again, often dragging their reluctant friends like missionaries bent on conversion. The friends then return with others and the same intent. We don't think that this is going to stop and happily admit that the resident estimate was wrong.

But where are the tourists? Not here, that's for sure. Not many, anyway. But they're coming next year, and by the thousands. Tom Morrish and I helped to rewrite the "Little Circle Island Tour: this spring," which is now being written into millions of travel folders as the "Oceanic—Sea Life Park Tour: for 1965." Now Tom is on the mainland presenting movies and slides of this tour to travel wholesalers throughout the major cities. He writes that they like the presentation and they are buying the product. With such mainland acceptance and with the marvelous all-out support of the Oahu tour operators, we are capable now of meeting our original tourist projections for 1965. Since this means a great many visitors beyond our present attendance, we expect a good year. One of the happiest facts of the oceanarium business is that costs need not increase with volume. This will give a healthy margin of earnings beginning in January.

Meanwhile, we are about to start a new drive to sell our annual passes this fall. This program has been a success so far. Nearly 35,000 annual passes are outstanding, and we could double that before the end of the year. Most people here think that the cost is remarkably low and we welcome that impression. Actually, because of the cost we may achieve an unheard of membership, perhaps 100,000 residents, which could be renewed, and a restaurant, but many tend to bring tourists with them. A person who purchased an annual pass three years in a row is being admitted six times. This person becomes a friend and a fan.

Personally, I think that our situation here will allow us to become one of the best public exhibits in the world, and easily the best exhibit of marine life. We should continue to grow as the marine world grows around us. With the growth and with more experience we can set a standard here that will be hard to match. It is hard to believe that our idea of a year ago has turned into such a reality today. But it has happened and it suggests that the other ideas that we discussed last year can also happen soon. We do think that Hawaii will become a center of activity in the oceanic world and that our company can be central in that activity. We are surrounded by an unexplored opportunity. Soon, when the Park is strong, we will be able to explore it. I know that I will have your support and your confidence in doing this. I will especially welcome your guidance and participation.

August 24 (Bob)

From a revenue standpoint, the week ending yesterday was our best "nonholiday" week since February. Both the restaurant and gift ship produced record weekly revenues and general admissions showed a strong increase over the preceding week. Gross revenue was $2,000 ahead of the preceding week, which had been $2,400 ahead of the week before that. All in all the trend of current operations is extremely encouraging and it now seems sure that we will exceed our revenue forecast for August ($78,000), perhaps by as much as $5,000.

I now feel confident that we will weather this tight period without having to draw upon the undisbursed $15,000 of our loan commitment.

August 25 (Bob)

Just finished our best "nonholiday" week since February and the current week seems to be holding at the same level. July figures not as good as expected, but they're heavily burdened by nonrecurring expenses. August revenue will exceed forecast, perhaps by $4,000-5,000.

September 2 (Tap)

I'm going back to school full-time (except four half-days at Makapuu) beginning on the 21st. I should be able to finish the Ph.d. degree by June or by August at the latest.

Tom, Bob, Karen, Joe, and Ernie seem to have the Park well in hand. I'll attend staff meetings, read my staff reports, have a weekly inspection, manage the important correspondence, and otherwise forget it.

I'll be taking Biometry, Behavior, Physiology, German, French, Radioisotopic Technique, and Physiologic Basis of Behavior to secure the program, plus finish the thesis and orals. It will be a bit of a load, but it's also a great relief to know that it can be done now and that the team is qualified to do a very good job without me. In fact, backing away a little like this will temper them and strengthen the organization for good. When that's done, and after Tom has built his sales department up, I'll be able to work with him on our commercial potentials, to put Sea Life, Inc. into the industrial oceanics business.

September 2 (Bob)

Attendance and revenue down about $2,500 from last week's record levels, so I guess that was the late summer peak. Total revenue for August was $80,422, up $6,600 from July. I would expect August to be our best month for profitability. Bank approved our proposed revision in loan repayment schedule.

September 9 (Bob)

The chilly winds of autumn began to blow on our attendance as soon as school started. But Labor Day was a good one ($5,600 gross) and we're starting a push on annual pass sales and group sales this week. Tom claims 50,000-75,000 new tourists for '65 from his current mainland trip, so the horizon is bright ahead.

September 15 (Bob)

We have sailed hard into the post-Labor Day doldrums, but today's attendance looks better than last Tuesday so far and we are hopeful. However, cash flow continues to be extremely tight since we have not yet completely overcome the burden of preopening overrun. Long-range outlook still very bright for '65 tours.

September 29 (Bob)

We're in rough shape for September. The seasonal decline has been precipitous and it has hit us particularly hard in our cash position which never really recovered from delayed opening and preoperating overrun. We've taken drastic steps to further reduce operating costs and to try to build attendance in October and November.

October 6 (Tap)

We lost $19,000 in September, which was cash we didn't have. It looks as though it will be another ten gone in October before the upturn can be swung.

To meet this we've made many cuts which will reduce expenses in October by $8,500. Probably many of these are overdue, but I hesitated to chop until the exhibit was entirely satisfactory for this stage. It is now. Really, you would hardly recognize the place. Even the guest book remarks reflect the changes since June. They used to say "wonderful" but now it's "fabulous," or "far, far, far, far better than Marineland," or "worth coming to Hawaii for alone." At least, then, while cutting, we know what to maintain. The product is good and so it's up to sales now and to ingenuity.

Tom is expanding the sales force, going after special areas such as military, groups, pineapple workers, and the like. He is finding people to work on a small base salary plus a percentage of sales, and could develop some quick returns this way. The Sea Life

Association newsletter is going out soon and it will carry a sales message with it which may increase the annual pass sales and will push a guest booklet.

Bob and Ernie are taking the scalpel to operations and may find that they can do more with less now; it's up to them and it's timely to do so anyway. Bob and Joe will also take on some sales assignments. Joe particularly knows the local business and can push the group program there. Now that the exhibit is good, I can give both guys much greater operational and personnel responsibilities without fear of limiting exhibit progress.

Karen is taking care of whatever exhibit progress remains this year. She has turned into the outstanding curator in this country. There are dozens of pictorial interpretations of the exhibit and the marine world around the Park now. The Reef Tank is great. The show animals are performing with precision and discipline. Twenty-two show animals with two full-time trainers (five-day week), two half-time apprentices, two narrators, and two swimmers/feeders—the whole group doesn't earn as much as the training staff alone at a mainland operation and the mainland oceanariums have half the animals and half the performance. In addition, she writes reams of copy as the occasion requires, gives speeches around town, keeps Park VIPs happy, and is deep into the Porpoise research programs. Good girl and powerful support!

This Oceanic - Sea Life Park Tour has captured tour industry imaginations. With it, we'll see 100,000 visitors that weren't here this year. The *National Geographic* magazine will be supporting this by doing a full article on us during that time and *Life* magazine has been sniffing around and is almost certain for a good one, at least Makapuu oriented, in the same period.

October 7 (Bob)

Weekly revenue since Labor Day has been steady at the $8,400 level and we've been scrambling to turn it up. We hope we'll begin to feel the effects this week. We're now revising our cash flow forecast.

October 10 (Tap)

The bottom really dropped out after Labor Day. When our corporate history is written a new chapter will start on September 8, 1964. None of us saw this coming to the severe degree with which it actually hit us and we are taking a number of positive steps to recover.

The first of these is to remake our forecasts on a more realistic basis. Based on our first eight months of actual operating experience, we are making forecasts for 1965.

In these forecasts we have discounted the strong opening effect of the first year. A bad weather contingency factor discounting winter months 10-20 percent has been applied. Projected monthly revenue ranges from a low of about $45,000 in the three winter months to a high of $80-89,000 in the three summer months. Sea Life's share of the Hawaiian tourist market is now projected at 37 percent instead of the 50 percent projected by Stanford Research Institute in their 1961 study. We are projecting expenditures of $ .52 per visitor in the restaurant and $ .30 (not including children) in the gift shop. This compares with $ .45 and $ .40 in the original projection. The renewal rate on annual passes is projected at 60 percent, and new pass sales are projected at $2,500 average per month (half the current rate of $5,000).

We believe that in view of reception of the Oceanic - Sea Life Park Tour by the tour industry and in view of the other steps taken and planned by management to promote tourist, annual pass, school, group and military sales, that these forecasts are conservative and can be realized.

NOW OPEN
YOU'VE NEVER SEEN ANYTHING LIKE
SEA LIFE PARK

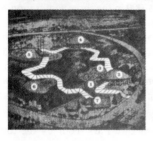

Sea Life Park...the largest marine exhibit in the world...is open. The exhibits are in their first stages, and you'll find them entertaining...educational...exciting. Sea Life Park will never be finished...you'll want to come back again and again. You will always find something new.

(1) Entrance Deck affords a panoramic view of the Park, the blue Pacific, Rabbit Island, Makapuu Point. (2) You make a spiraling descent from sea level to the depths of this 300,000 gallon "ocean." From the glassed-in ramp you have an unobstructed view of the colorful reef life of the Islands. (3) The Shark Pool displays the scavengers of the seas at close range. (4) The Glass Porpoise Theatre, where you witness authentic demonstrations of porpoise behavior—their intelligence, acrobatic and SONAR abilities. (5) This huge sea water pool contains a 70' replica of the famous whaling ship "Essex." You go below decks to view the marine animals through large portholes. Hawaiian spinning porpoises, the only ones in captivity, put on a show of precision and grace. (6) Sea turtles and sea birds inhabit the Leeward Island Pool, where seals will soon be introduced. (7) The Sea Life Park restaurant terrace...a shaded setting under Polynesian roofs that overlooks the Park and the blue Pacific.

Adult admission is $2.30. Children 7 through 12, $1.15. Children under 7, free. ANNUAL PASSES, which admit you to the Park as many times as you wish for 12 months, are $4.30 for adults and $2.15 for children 7 through 12. OPEN DAILY EXCEPT MONDAY, 10 A.M. TO 6 P.M., when the Park closes.

WORLD'S LARGEST & MOST AUTHENTIC MARINE EXHIBIT   MAKAPUU POINT, WAIMANALO, OAHU • PHONE 257-933

Exhibit 1.   Sea Life Park (C).

No mention is made in these quotations about the Oceanics Institute. Tap devoted somewhat more than half his time to promoting the activities of the Institute, which completed a number of significant projects during the year. The two most dramatic were conversion of a decompression chamber to an underwater laboratory for permanent residency by researchers, and the training of a porpoise for offshore testing and research. These tests were the first time a trained porpoise had ever been worked in the open ocean. He responded perfectly to his cues and established a documented speed of almost 25 miles per hour.

A number of additional research proposals had been submitted to Government and other bodies by the Oceanic Institute. In early October it appeared that two or three, including a $350,000 grant for the study of brackish water fish pond culture, and another for the construction of an underwater laboratory and living quarters, where scientists could live and work while conducting research, would be granted.

Exhibit 2. Sea Life Park (C) Letter to the Stockholders of Sea Life, Inc.

WORLD'S LARGEST MARINE EXHIBIT

March 13, 1964

Dear Mr. Wilson:

My family and I have just returned from a visit to Sea Life Park, two weeks after its opening, and wish to report to you, the stockholders, that our grand new venture is off to a healthy and impressive start.

The Hawaiian Reef (Lagoon Tank) still lacks the number and variety of fish, invertebrates, and coral planned for the future; some phases of the porpoise acts are a little ragged about the edges; the Shark Pool has no sharks; the Whale's Cove has no whales; there are bottlenecks in the food operation; the gift shop is not yet opened; and the rigging on the whaling ship is not completed.

But the staff is working long, hard hours to smooth out these details, and they are actually turning many of the shortcomings to advantage and gaining enthusiastic audience participation by sharing with the visitors the excitement of "putting the show on the road."

Even in their not-quite-finished stage, the buildings, scenery, and acts are magnificent, and when completed they will clearly surpass in beauty, imagination, and taste, anything of the kind anywhere in the world. This is evidenced by more than our own biased observation—it is evidenced by the enthusiasm of the visitors to the Park and their appreciative praise of the exhibits. These are happy people, with large families, clearly enjoying their visit, people who feel they have received their money's worth and who openly volunteer their appreciation on leaving. Local publicity has been excellent and word of mouth advertising should be tremendous. Last week the Hawaii State Legislature passed a resolution of appreciation commending Tap and Karen Pryor on the contribution they had made through the Park to Hawaii. Esprit of the staff is very high.

From a business standpoint, the Park was completed with a budget overrun of only three percent. This overrun, which was absorbed by the working capital allowance in the budget, was caused by a six-week delay in opening due mainly to an extended strike last fall in the local concrete industry. A much needed advance cash flow was generated by very successful season ticket sales to Hawaiian residents—$7,544 prior to opening, $9,830 in the first week and $11,246 in the second week.

Largely because of this high level of season ticket sales, the Park was above the break-even level of operations by the end of the second week, even with the food service operating at a fraction of capacity and the gift shop not yet opened. The real test will come during the next few weeks, when the initial excitement wears off and we can guage the success with which tourists can be attracted to the Park, especially during week days. The reaction of current visitors, comments of representatives of the tour industry, promotional plans now in process, and the unprecedented current boom in Hawaiian tourism resulting from the $100 air fare would seem to justify confidence on this score.

Total paid attendance was 6,327 the first week and 9,313 the second week. The ultimate capacity of the Park is probably three to four times the present level of attendance. With a relatively high percentage of fixed costs and low variable costs, the Park should enjoy a high operating leverage and consequent profitability at increased levels of attendance.

The operating and financial problems of the Park are by no means past. But at this point, as Sea Life moves from the construction into the operational stage, it represents a magnificent example of the power of youthful (average age 30!) enthusiasm, energy, and imagination. The stockholders who showed their faith in Tap should take great pride and satisfaction in what has been accomplished. I hope you may all be able to visit Sea Life soon and share in the thrill of seeing this bold and creative dream coming to fruition.

Aloha!

Sincerely,

Wilfred L. Chapin
Chairman of the Board
Sea Life, Inc.

Exhibit 3. Sea Life Park (C) Balance Sheets December 31, 1963 - September 30, 1964.

Assets	December 31, 1963	March 31, 1964	May 31, 1964	July 31, 1964	September 30, 1964
Current Assets:					
Cash	$ 95,565	$ 30,709	$ 15,187	$ 7,318	$ 3,547
Accounts Receivable		4,769	4,897		19,364
Inventories		4,794	11,166	13,757	11,815
Prepaid Expenses	13,632	11,347	7,730	33,884	74,640
Total Current Assets	111,197	51,620	38,979	54,959	59,361
Note Receivable, Employee (5% First Mortgage, due 12/31/68)	8,500	5,000	5,000	5,000	5,000
Property—At cost (subject to Bank Mortgage)	98,370	1,428,736	1,441,969	1,451,653	1,473,312
Leasehold Improvements	98,370	1,428,736	1,441,969	1,451,653	1,473,312
Exhibit Specimens (static value)	7,500	10,000	10,000	10,000	10,000
Furniture and Fixtures	7,749	10,735	12,991	18,656	19,177
Machinery and Equipment	26,199	72,843	15,080	76,751	105,410
Total	139,819	1,522,315	1,540,040	1,557,060	1,558,898
Less Accumulated Depreciation	5,023	17,451	31,257	46,256	60,736
Property - Net	134,796	1,504,864	1,508,783	1,510,804	1,498,163
Construction in Progress—At Cost Subject to Mortgage to Bank)	1,105,905	9,911	4,884		
Other Assets:					
Unamortized Organization Expense	30,233	28,721	27,713	26,706	25,698
Miscellaneous	553	10	10	435	435
Total Other Assets	30,786	28,731	27,723	27,141	26,133
Total Assets	1,391,184	1,600,126	1,585,369	1,597,904	1,588,656

Exhibit 3. *cont'd.*

Liabilities	December 31, 1963	March 31, 1964	May 31, 1964	July 31, 1964	September 30, 1964
Current Liabilities:					
				6,350*	
Accounts Payable	176,745	205,902	89,726	68,524	8,437
Taxes	3,373	22,630	16,239	24,009	22,780
Payroll	4,885	11,561	10,684	10,776	10,266
Interest	7,496	19,862	14,700	24,929	25,279
Total Current Liabilities	192,499	259,955	131,344	134,588	152,696
Long Term Debt:					
First Mortgage, 6% Note, Due 1968	200,000	380,000	510,000	535,000	535,000
Twelve-Year 5% Subordinated Debentures, Due 1975	600,000	600,000	600,000	600,000	600,000
Total Long Term Debt	800,000	980,000	1,100,000	1,135,000	1,135,000
Stockholders' Equity:					
Capital Stock - Authorized 600,000 Shares of $1 Par Value Each, Issued and Outstanding 400,000 Shares	400,000	400,000	400,000	400,000	400,000
Additional Paid-In Capital	300,000	300,000	300,000	300,000	300,000
Total	700,000	700,000	700,000	700,000	700,000
Less Deficit	(301,315)	(339,829)	(355,875)	(371,684)	(399,040)
Stockholders' Equity	398,685	360,171	344,125	328,316	300,960
Total Liabilities	$1,391,184	$1,600,126	$1,585,496	$1,597,904	$1,588,656

*Cash due bank

Exhibit 4. Sea Life Park (C) Comparative Profit and Loss Statements for the Months February 11 to September 30, 1964.

	Feb. 29	March 31	April 30	May 30	June 30	July 31	Aug. 31	Sept. 30	Totals
Income:									
Admissions -Military						752[1]	3,530[1]	614[2]	4,896.00
Adults	24,938.90	34,115.90	27,273.40	29,695.30	31,201.80	32,822	33,952	21,917	235,916.30
Children	1,979.15	3,862.85	2,095.30	2,531.15	3,000.35	3,591	4,677	1,498	23,234.80
Annual Passes-Adults	28,384.30	23,602.70	16,593.70	16,279.80	12,130.30	7,392	7,637	4,678	116,697.80
Children	4,076.40	3,872.15	2,076.90	2,259.65	1,907.65	1,015	1,191	546	16,944.15
Group Sales	355.65	1,801.80	2,968.35	4,662.90	2,400.30	4,434	2,670	312	19,605.00
Less: Admissions Taxes	(5,442.99)	(5,712.66)	(4,341.36)	(4,506.24)	(4,156.72)	(3,890)	(4,367)	(2,258)	(34,674.97)
Commissions	(303.78)	(408.98)	(339.58)	(339.73)	(631.21)	(480)	(403)	(308)	(3,214.28)
Other	135.90	132.13	433.76	205.97	170.58	192	265	222	1,757.34
Food and Beverage Sales	9,257.73	13,583.63	12,082.93	13,135.49	13,438.82	15,384	17,497	10,952	105,331.60
Less Cost of Food/Bev. Sold	(1,974.97)	(6,898.72)	(5,108.41)	(4,751.50)	(5,257.37)	(6,100)	(6,389)	(5,458)	(41,934.97)
Merchandise Sales	890.11	1,009.05	1,486.89	5,474.64	6,487.23	8,257	9,260	6,203	39,067.92
Less Cost of Mdse. Sold	(646.16)	(540.21)	(1,032.73)	(3,170.20)	(4,066.82)	(4,899)	(5,372)	(4,146)	(23,873.12)
Gross Profit	61,650.24	68,419.64	54,189.15	61,477.23	56,624.30	58,469	64,148	34,773	459,753.57
Expenses:									
Advertising Media	6,988.99	6,375.92	4,983.72	4,009.34	5,200.46	5,568	5,643	4,415	43,384.43
Auto Expense	203.05	1,414.72	1,164.55	1,134.98	1,041.40	1,393	1,260	1,187	8,798.70
Collecting Operation Expense	270.13	866.10	1,613.08	1,212.78	651.73	307	324	--	5,244.82
Dues and Subscriptions	120.00	25.00	--	--	--	1,021	20	12	1,198.00
Fish Food	2,521.36	1,397.59	396.57	1,552.41	1,161.41	3,412	3,096	2,664	16,201.34
Insurance	1,333.40	1,674.58	1,724.17	2,137.53	1,058.21	1,818	1,834	1,807	13,386.89
Interest	4,015.84	4,769.96	4,606.37	4,903.34	5,054.11	5,181	5,175	5,179	38,884.62

Exhibit 4. *cont'd.*

	Feb. 29	March 31	April 30	May 30	June 30	July 31	Aug. 31	Sept. 30	Totals
Miscellaneous	1,218.65	1,387.54	1,461.91	1,322.27	1,495.75	1,039	796	1,256	9,977.12
Lost and Damaged Merchandise	--	--	--	88.46	110.42	139	155	113	605.88
Professional Services	1,578.26	1,828.15	3,540.05	1,318.15	1,212.10	984	182	182	10,324.71
Postage and Delivery	177.45	90.01	109.85	141.24	155.62	190	284	218	1,386.17
Rent	1,783.67	2,675.00	2,675.00	2,675.00	2,675.00	2,675	2,675	2,675	20,508.67
Repairs and Maintenance	255.46	2,778.64	2,180.43	1,715.01	1,693.31	6,031	1,670	1,330	17,653.85
Salaries and Wages	21,085.86	28,059.27	27,697.43	26,496.15	24,876.54	26,383	24,814	25,246	204,658.25
Specimens Purchased	--	--	--	227.50	--	38	--	100	365.50
Supplies	3,323.81	2,911.58	2,655.84	2,350.13	2,409.45	1,729	1,443	1,078	17,900.81
Taxes and Licenses	1,174.28	4,452.10	3,357.29	2,913.76	3,627.74	3,410	3,460	2,357	25,252.17
Travel and Entertainment	674.05	496.62	394.62	782.01	729.96	474	1,920	1,311	6,782.26
Utilities	1,706.50	3,579.83	2,826.41	2,730.76	2,640.50	2,825	1,836	2,565	20,710.00
Total Expenses:	48,430.76	64,782.61	61,387.29	57,710.82	55,793.71	64,616	56,588	54,194	463,704.19
Net Profit (Loss) Before Depreciation	13,219.48	3,637.03	(7,198.14)	3,766.41	830.59	(6,147)	7,561	(19,421)	(3,751.63)
Less Depreciation	5,353.24	7,409.28	7,413.98	7,409.44	7,709.14	8,308	7,746	7,750	59,099.08
Net Profit (Loss) for Period	7,866.24	(3,772.25)	(14,612.12)	(3,643.03)	(6,878.55)	(14,455)	(185)	(27,171)	(62,850.71)
Less Capitalized Expenses	4,687.08	2,992.90	1,221.78	887.32	1,079.88	4,545[3]	--	--	15,413.71
Net Profit (or Loss)	12,553.32	(779.35)	(13,390.34)	(2,755.71)	(5,798.67)	(9,910)	--	--	(47,437.00)
Loss, at	351,602.92	339,049.60	339,828.95	353,219.29	355,975.00	361,774	371,684	371,869	351,603.00
Deficit, at end of period	339,049.60	339,828.95	353,219.29	355,975.00	361,773.67	371,684	371,869	399,040	399,040.00

1. Students
2. Military
3. Includes expense of $4,145 incurred in training porpoise for open sea research; will be reimbursed by Oceanic Foundation.

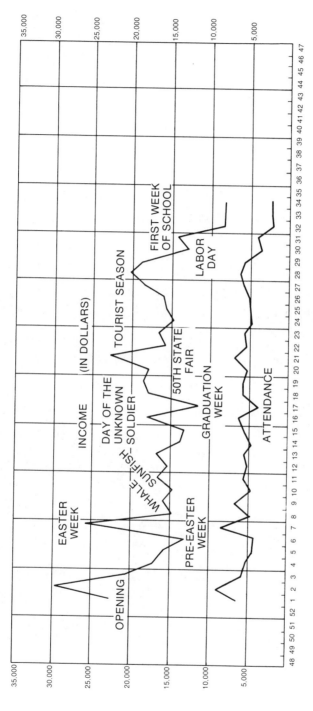

Exhibit 5.   Sea Life Park (C) Weekly Gross Income and Attendance.

Exhibit 6.   Sea Life Park (C) Coral Lagoon.

Exhibit 7.   Sea Life Park (C) Whaler's Cove.

Exhibit 8.   Sea Life Park (C) Oceanic Institute.

Exhibit 9. Sea Life Park (C) Projected Revenues for 1965.

October 5, 1964

	Jan.	Feb.	March	April	May	June	July	Aug.	Sept.	Oct.	Nov.	Dec.
General Admission	$12,600	$13,600	$13,600	$15,300	$17,000	$24,483	$20,506	$21,269	$13,000	$13,500	$13,600	$13,600
Tourist	17,523	19,507	20,499	25,666	28,930	47,941	46,288	53,287	33,063	30,417	24,139	28,423
Annual Pass	11,200	11,997	18,511	13,195	13,120	10,421	7,147	7,310	5,131	3,500	3,500	3,500
School	1,200	1,600	2,000	2,700	3,500	1,000			100	450	400	240
Group	1,600	1,600	1,600	1,800	2,000	2,000	5,000	3,000	500	1,800	1,600	1,600
Military	160	160	160	180	200	300	300	300	5,000	5,000	160	160
Pass Conversions	864	864	864	972	1,080	1,469	1,230	1,276	1,080	972	864	864
Total Admissions	45,147	49,328	57,234	59,813	65,830	87,614	80,471	86,442	57,874	55,639	44,263	48,387
Restaurant	11,360	11,684	12,502	13,528	15,446	19,933	18,693	22,762	15,636	11,900	10,452	9,581
Gift Shop	7,641	7,975	8,498	9,581	10,674	13,988	13,593	14,378	12,127	9,928	7,990	8,474
Total Monthly Revenue	$64,148	$68,987	$78,234	$82,922	$91,950	$121,535	$112,757	$123,582	$85,637	$77,467	$62,705	$66,442

Vermont Tubbs, Inc.

In early August 1971, Mr. C. Baird Morgan, Jr. was reviewing his two years as president of Vermont Tubbs, Inc., a leading manufacturer of snowshoes located in Wallingford, Vermont (population 800). While sales and profit had increased, he knew he had several unresolved problems. In addition, a number of attractive opportunities for expansion and diversification had come up recently and Mr. Morgan thought he should decide which, if any, to pursue. Finally, during the past year, he had rejected an average of one inquiry a week to purchase Vermont Tubbs and he wondered if now was not the time to consider some of the more attractive feelers.

After he received his MBA from the University of Pennsylvania, Wharton School of Business Administration in 1964, Baird Morgan taught mathematics in a small private boys' school near Philadelphia. After three years he found he had lost his zeal for teaching so he moved to Vermont:

I did things backwards. I moved and then looked for a job. Since I enjoyed flying, I helped organize Northern Airways, a regional carrier located in Burlington, Vermont. I was their marketing manager for two years, but all the time I was looking for a company to buy on my own. I was single, independent, not afraid of hard work or long hours and did not want to work for someone else.

Unfortunately, Vermont is a popular place and a lot of other guys also wanted to do what I was doing, so I had a lot of competition. Furthermore, the few people who had businesses to sell all wanted cash in full.

I had met Harold Underwood, the president of Tubbs, shortly after I arrived. He seemed to prefer to fish and hunt rather than own a business so I tried to buy the company. Finally with luck, we agreed. I borrowed $10,000 from my father, borrowed $20,000 on a personal note, mortgaged the rest from Harold Underwood, and Vermont Tubbs was mine.

Morgan owned 2/3 of the stock, Mr. Morgan, Sr. the other 1/3. The Board of Directors consisted of: Mr. Morgan, Mr. Morgan, Sr. and the Corporate Attorney.

COMPANY HISTORY

Vermont Tubbs, Inc, was founded about 100 years ago in Norway, Maine as W. F. Tubbs, Inc. In 1928 it was bought by American Fork and Hoe, Inc. (now True Temper, Inc.) and moved to Wallingford, Vermont and the name changed. During World War II, Tubbs' production of snowshoes reached over 100,000 units (pairs) per year, sold entirely to the U.S. Government for use in Scandinavia, the Alps, and the Himalayas. After the War, production fell drastically and Tubbs was spun off and sold. Thereafter, the company passed through several owners until it went bankrupt in 1958. Mr. Harold Underwood, a local gasoline station owner, was a creditor and received the business in full settlement of his claim (about $250).

Mr. Underwood ran the business successfully. According to Mr. Morgan, production during the last year of Underwood's ownership was approximately 9,000 units (pairs). (Production during 1970–1971 was approximately 15,000 units and 20,000 units were projected for 1971–1972.)

PRODUCT

In one form or another, snowshoes have been used throughout the world for over 2500 years. Snowshoes are devices worn with boots to support the wearer while walking on the surface of snow. They consist of a light, bent-wood frame laced usually with rawhide strips. The wearer's boot is attached to the center section of the snowshoe with a binding which allows the heel to be raised while walking. Expert snowshoers can walk quite fast with them. (See Exhibit 1 for additional information on snowshoes.)

MARKET*

According to Mr. Morgan, snowshoeing has become phenomenally popular in recent years. He attributed this popularity to three causes:

1. Increased emphasis on physical fitness
2. The "Ecology Movement" bringing people back to nature
3. Disenchantment with Alpine (downhill) skiing

Alpine skiing and snowmobiling got people involved in outdoor winter sports. But skiing can cost anywhere from $400–$600 per person per season. At that price the average family of four or five can't afford to ski so they look around for an alternative. Snowshoeing is fun, easy to learn and inexpensive. For as little as $100† you can be in business for a lifetime. Being out alone in the woods and fields is a wonderful experience. Part of our success, of course, has been simply being in the right place at the right time. The market is probably growing at a rate of 30 percent per year. But we know we are also doing better than that. We have recruited a terrific sales network and are putting much more effort into customer orientation. As a result we are knocking the daylights out of competition.

COMPETITION

Mr. Morgan knew of no reliable market survey of the snowshoe industry. There were a few domestic manufacturers and several foreign competitors. Snocraft Division of Garland Industries, located in Saco, Maine, had the reputation of being the largest and best manufacturer. Tubbs, he thought, was considered to produce nearly as good a shoe and would shortly have a large market share. In fact, Mr. Morgan felt Tubbs' shoes were now as high quality as Snocraft's shoes. Other manufacturers were smaller, generally produced a lower quality shoe, and usually used discount store outlets. He believed the total market was $2,500,000 which might be divided as follows:

---

*For background data on recreation in the U.S., see Exhibit 2.

†Includes boots, jacket, cap and gloves, in addition to snowshoes.

	Market share
Snocraft	20.0%
Faber (Canada)	17.0
Tubbs	16.0
Ross Brothers (Canada)	11.0
Bastion Brothers (Canada)	11.0
Snotread (Plastic)	11.0
Swanson & Swanson (Japan)	7.0
Chestnut (Canada)	7.0
	100%

Tubbs' sales in the previous two years had not been analyzed to determine where the company had picked up sales, from whom sales might have been taken, or where competitors might have taken sales from Tubbs. But Mr. Morgan thought he had a good feel for the relative volume of his major customers.

In addition to snowshoes, competitors usually had other product lines. For example, Ross Brothers produced canoes while Snocraft produced childrens' skiis, sleds, toboggans, and some hardware products. They also operated a small sawmill.

DISTRIBUTION

Mr. Morgan believed improved distribution to be the most important improvement made since 1969. Mr. Underwood almost exclusively had sold directly to dealers (i.e., retail sporting goods stores and mail-order houses) primarily in New England. He had had no sales force and used reps and jobbers only infrequently. When he took over, Mr. Morgan recruited an aggressive team of 11 reps outside New England while maintaining the existing network within New England. The reps in turn sold to numerous dealers and 10 jobbers depending on the geographic nature of their territory. Tubbs shoes were now sold nationwide including Alaska. He estimated that next year over 50 percent of his sales would be through jobbers.

Except for a few house accounts which were sold by Mr. Morgan personally, reps received commissions on direct sales to dealers in their areas. The commission was on a sliding scale from 8 percent to 5 percent depending on volume. Exhibits 3 and 4 show dealer and rep price lists and dealers' terms of sale respectively.

PRICING

In previous years, Tubbs snowshoes had been priced slightly below Snocraft. For 1971–1972, factory retail price* had been increased in all shoes to match Snocraft model for model. At the same time, quantity discounts to dealers (see Exhibit 3) had been increased somewhat to provide a slightly larger margin for the Tubbs dealer than Snocraft. Tubbs shoes were not fair traded and no effort was made to set retail prices. Tubbs retailed shoes at the factory for about $40, while dealers usually charged between $30 and $35.

---

*Factory retail prices were not suggested retail, but were set to meet Snocraft and to discourage factory sales in favor of dealer sales.

Typically, the largest and best jobbers and dealers ordered in the late spring (May and June) for delivery commencing in late summer. Smaller firms ordered on a random basis as the snow begins to fall during the late fall and early winter. Almost no orders were received during March and April; few deliveries were made between March and August. Invoices were dated December 10, which was normal practice for winter sporting goods. According to Mr. Morgan, some customers would take the dating whether or not it was offered.

ADVERTISING

Traditionally, snowshoe manufacturers did little or no advertising. Tubbs advertised during the summer months (the buying season for dealers) in *Sporting Goods Dealer*; it did not advertise in any other magazine. However, prior to 1969, Tubbs had been the subject of several feature articles in *Vermont Life, The Boston Globe,* and other publications.

On the other hand, Tubbs had created an 18" x 24" poster for dealers to display. It had also prepared a promotional brochure to show all models sold by Tubbs and to describe the conditions under which each should be used. Exhibit 1 shows *part* of that brochure. Mr. Morgan knew of no competitor who provided these services.

Mr. Morgan felt a booth at a national trade show was too expensive: a 10-foot booth cost $700, while manning and other expenses could cost another $1,300. Rather, he attended the shows himself and tried to contact all his important dealers, reps, and jobbers. He felt he was able to give them personalized attention and to spend more time with them this way and could emphasize the importance of ordering early to avoid shipping delays.

BRAND IMAGE

Since Tubbs was not a registered trademark, Mr. Morgan tried to develop a brand image. He had designed a new logo and written a use and care manual to be provided with each new pair of shoes. Finally, Tubbs shoes were finished with a high-gloss urethane varnish which, Morgan thought, improved their appearance in comparison to competitors. Mr. Morgan felt these steps (particularly the brochure and manual) helped the customer and differentiated Tubbs products from those of competitors:

> Up until a few years ago, we sold primarily to professionals: the Vermont Fish and Game Department, the U.S. Forest Service, etc. These people had lived on snowshoes and knew how to care for them and select the correct model. The newer customer hardly knows what snowshoes are, so we have to teach him. Traditionally, shoes were sold by weight: if you weigh 185 pounds buy this snowshoe; 205, but that snowshoe. We think that is hogwash. We sell based on several factors: usage, terrain, snow conditions, degree of maneuverability. This is a complete break from the Canadian and Snocraft approach.

Tubbs produced nine models, one size each (except Michigans, which had three models). Snocraft produced eight models, five of which had multiple sizes.

BINDINGS

Like skiis, snowshoes required bindings which were sold separately. Tubbs manufactured its own bindings from both leather and neoprene, including one of its own design. Morgan believed that neoprene was superior to leather (it did not stretch when wet) but customers preferred leather:

We're doing ourselves a disservice selling leather, but it is what the customers demand. I think if we doubled the price of leather bindings, they would still sell.

Bindings were sold at retail for between $5 and $8.

PRODUCTION

When Mr. Morgan took over, he only had a skeleton force:

Harold Underwood laid off his workers during the summer, so I essentially had to start from scratch. I remember the exhilarating feeling when we hit 100 units per week. Now we are at 300 aiming for 400. To achieve our production goals, I keep a steady force throughout the year. Even with level production, shipments last winter fell about six weeks behind orders.

The manufacturing process for snowshoes had changed little over the centuries. A piece of wood was bent into either an oval or a racket shape then laced, usually with rawhide thongs (strips).

The bending process put such strain on the wood that the slightest imperfection caused the wood to break, and even the best wood broke occasionally for no apparent reason. Tubbs purchased only the highest quality white ash available: straight grained, absolutely no knots. Mr. Morgan said, "This wood is of such high quality it is above the highest grade in the grading manuals."

Lacing traditionally used untanned cowhide called rawhide. Tubbs purchased hides from tanneries which in turn had purchased from slaughterhouses. The tanneries removed the hair and flesh, soaked them in a lime solution, then stretched and dried them. Tubbs found that only certain hides were suitable and that even in the best hide certain portions did not have adequate strength or consistency.

Mr. Morgan personally handled the purchasing of both wood and rawhide.

There were essentially three steps in this manufacturing process: woodworking, lacing, and finishing. All were performed in a two-story cement-block building just across the railroad tracks from the center of Wallingford. Exhibit 5 shows photographs of the plant and both floors; Exhibit 6 shows a floor plan of the plant.

After a week or two of air drying, white ash boards (approximately 1" x 8" x 84" up to 144")* were planed to 13/16" thickness. They were then rip sawed into 13/16" strips and then cross-cut to the maximum usable length for each board. For example, the strip used in one of Tubbs shoes was 86" long while the next longer was 92" long. A board 89" long would be cut into strips and the strips cross-cut to 86" to fit the smaller shoe. After being cut to length, a shallow scoop or trench was cut on a band saw from what would be the toe of the shoe. This "toeing" process partially relieved the stress of bending.†

After toeing, strips were placed in a steam chamber for at least one hour to soften the fibers and make them more flexible. One at a time strips were removed and bent around a wooden mold (see Exhibit 7 for a photograph of this shaping mold in use). This operation took about one minute per strip. Each model shoe had a unique mold. After a few minutes on the mold, the newly-shaped frames were transferred to a rack

---

*Hardwoods like ash are not normally sold in standardized lengths and widths. Hardwood lumber mills cut logs to get the maximum usable wood rather than standard sized boards.

†The ends of bearpaw models were tapered to facilitate bending and overlapping the heel sections.

(capacity: 28 frames) and dried slowly in a kiln at 120 degrees F. for at least 48 hours. About 10 racks could be filled per day. At the end of the drying operation the wood had a moisture content of about 7 percent. After drying each frame was mortised to accommodate cross bars.

Operations described thus far were performed in the lower floor of the factory. Completed frames were carried upstairs to be sanded (see Exhibit 7), drilled, riveted, and assembled with their cross bars. The tails (i.e., ends) were then trimmed off square to the correct length and sanded smooth. After the logo was placed on the crossbars, the frames were placed in a bath of wood sealer to maintain a constant moisture content.

LACING
Completed frames were then passed to the lacing room where either rawhide or neoprene webs were woven onto the frame. While Tubbs and other manufacturers recommended neoprene as an excellent substitute for natural rawhide, neoprene was requested by 20 percent of Tubbs' customers.

Hides were soaked overnight in a bath to make them pliable and then cut on a machine into laces approximately 1/4" wide. (Neoprene sheets were cut similarly.) Each day's supply of laces was cut by the plant superintendent from about 7:00-10:00 A.M.

Each frame was clamped into place on a "lacing jack."* The center portion was always laced first. As lacing this section required great strength, it usually, but not always, was performed by men, while women usually laced the heels and toe sections (heel and toe lacing was also performed at home by about 15 local women). Fully laced shoes were dried overnight.

Lacing with neoprene was unpopular and many lacers refused to work with it. Neoprene was not as soft and pliable as rawhide and was much harder on the hands of lacers.

FINISHING
Completed frames were dipped in a high gloss urethane varnish and dried. Finished shoes were paired (since the final shape of a shoe varied somewhat depending on vagaries of how the frames cured and the lacing dried) and packaged into bundles of five units. During the off season, bundles were stored both in an adjacent railroad boxcar (which was rented from Vermont Railways for $100 per year) and a nearby warehouse. At its peak, Tubbs inventory was about 5000 units.

SHIPPING
Orders were filled on a first-come, first-serve basis. Commenting on the backlog of orders during the prior winter, Mr. Morgan commented:

> Because production got so far behind orders, we had to be pretty strict. But at the end of each day's production there were usually broken bundles (i.e., bundles less than five units) so we could ship some small orders ahead of other larger orders. The decisions of who gets what are tough: they don't teach you how to do that in an MBA program!

---

*See Exhibit 7.

PRODUCTION ORGANIZATION

Tubbs employed 35 workers of whom, as stated previously, about 15 worked at home. Plant workers were evenly divided over and under 40 years old. There was no union.

The plant superintendent, Hadwin Young, was 41 years old and had 19 years' experience at Tubbs. Mr. Morgan described Mr. Young as "extremely capable," "a hard worker," and "fantastic with people." In addition to his over-all plant duties, he was in charge of the lacing operations.

The downstairs foreman, or manager of wood operations, was Stanley Stewart who had just recently left the GE Rutland plant (which produces aircraft engines) after 18 years, recently as a foreman. He said he "got tired of the big-company politics."

As Mr. Morgan described his philosophy of supervision:

> We are all working supervisors. I don't have enough desk work to keep myself busy, so I fill in wherever I'm needed in the factory. The foremen work alongside everyone else, too.

Recruiting had always been difficult for Tubbs. Rutland, Vermont, was only 10 miles away and a four-lane superhighway connected the two towns. Among others, GE, Howe Richardson Scale, True Temper, and Moore Business Forms had large plants in Rutland. Each had a union and their jobs paid significantly more than Tubbs could afford. In addition, Mr. Morgan said the wood industry was traditionally low paying. Tubbs paid $1.85-$2.75/hour for hourly work while lacers received a piecework rate:

> Bodies: rawhide: $1.00/pair; neoprene: $1.65/pair
> Toe and Heel: rawhide: $0.85/pair; neoprene: $1.10/pair

Mr. Morgan estimated that the best lacers could lace 20 pair per day of either rawhide bodies or toes and heels, while the best neoprene lacers laced 14 bodies or 16 toes and heels.

Foremen received $165/week and $145/week, respectively. Fringe benefits included vacation, normal holidays, and a Blue Cross Major Medical plan. Factory hours were 7:00 A.M. - 4:00 P.M. , one shift, although some personnel set their own hours according to their own requirements. Mr. Morgan had not found reliable personnel to man a second shift.

PRODUCTION CONTROL

Each morning at about 6:30 A.M. Morgan, Young, and Stewart met to plan the day's production. Since some shoes were harder to shape than others and still others were harder to lace, scheduling was best performed daily, Mr. Morgan felt. Based on what orders were due to be shipped and the status of frames in process (which determined the lacing requirements) the models and quantities of shoes to be shaped were determined. According to Mr. Morgan, there were no major bottlenecks in the manufacturing operation although he felt his plant was too crowded for truly efficient operation.

Daily lacing reports* and bending reports were kept to compare output against that for any period desired as far back as a year. There was no formal cost accounting

---

*See Exhibit 8. The bending report was similar.

system in effect and individual models did not have standard costs. Commenting on this situation, Mr. Morgan stated:

> I believe our average cost per unit is around $13.40 for direct costs plus about $4.00 for overhead. Since models vary in how difficult they are to bend and lace, standard costs are hard to pin down. Even more important, since our raw materials vary so much in quality, the waste factor is highly unpredictable. Finally, our raw materials have such wide cost fluctuations, standard costs are meaningless.

Only about two pair of shoes per day were considered to be "seconds": warped or discolored or otherwise imperfect units. Seconds were sold from the factory at $20 per pair.

REPAIRS
Broken lacings on customers' shoes were repaired by one woman at home. Prices ranged from $2.00 for a single lace to $19.50 for a completely new lacing job. Broken frames could not be repaired. Normally repairs were not accepted from September 1 to February 1, although Morgan hoped to be able to accept some the following winter.

CRITICAL PROBLEMS
When asked about his critical problems, Morgan said:

> Well, right now we have only a one-week supply of rawhide. If we don't find any more, I don't know what we'll do. No one knows what makes a good hide: we don't; our suppliers don't. They get hides from dealers who collect them from slaughterhouses. By the time they get to the tanner (our supplier) their origin has long since disappeared.

> The problem with natural raw materials is variety. Each animal is different: where it was raised, what it was fed, its sizes, etc. If the hide is too thick, it is hard to use; if it is too thin or flabby, it stretches and doesn't lace well.

> We simply don't know where to go to get reliable, uniform hides. There are only two tanners in the country from whom we can get acceptable quality hide. Most tanners deal in large volumes and their export business takes most of their volume.

> Even when we can find hides to buy, we have a huge waste factor, anywhere from 25-60 percent because their quality varies so widely. There is virtually no waste with neoprene but there is lower demand for neoprene-laced shoes and we have problems finding lacers willing to work with it.

Finding an adequate supply of wood was also difficult. White ash was being used more and more by furniture manufacturers. Since the ash used by Tubbs was of such extremely high quality, finding a source of supply was extremely difficult. Furthermore, in two years the cost had risen from $250 to $400 per thousand board feet. Mr. Morgan said:

> The $64,000 question is how to reduce waste wood, too. Ash is the only wood we have found which will take the strain of bending and be sturdy enough to stand the punishment of use. Even with ash, we lose between 25 percent and 50 percent. We tried oak but it warps and becomes brittle and breaks. No one has been able to suggest a suitable alternative. We presently haul our waste to the dump.

> One of my bad dreams is synthetics. Eventually, wooden shoes will probably disappear like wooden boats. Chris Craft and Old Towne Canoe both swore they would never change.

But they did. Someone is bound to come up with a synthetic. If we are not first and best, we will get aced.

We have tried alternatives: aluminum is too soft and can't stand the punishment. Laminated wood can't take the compound bending in the toes of our shoes.* I hate to have all our eggs in one basket but I haven't found an alternative.

FINANCE AND CONTROL

Accounting operations were performed by Mrs. Arlene Doty who had been hired about a year earlier. She prepared invoices, handled accounts payable, payroll, accounts receivable and general ledger posting in addition to other routine chores. (Mr. Morgan called her a "good jack-of-all-trades.") She was assisted in peak periods by Mrs. Morgan who was also Mr. Morgan's secretary (Morgan was married in 1969 after he purchased Tubbs). All checks (except payroll) were countersigned by Mr. Underwood, the former owner.†

An outside accountant provided semi-annual financial statements (see Exhibits 9 and 10). He reviewed operations periodically with Mr. Morgan.

Banking relations with a local bank were excellent. Tubbs had a $150,000 line of credit which was used to support the inventory built up during the spring and summer. Typically the loan was paid up by the end of the year. The loan was secured by inventory. Montly statements of models and numbers of units on hand as well as an accounts receivable ageing were provided to the bank.

Mr. Morgan stated:

> Except for my accountant, I really work in a vacuum. I never really know whether I'm doing the right thing or not. I thought of getting someone else in here if we diversify, but my accountant pointed out he would probably want a piece of the action. I'm not willing to give up any yet.

BRISTOL CHEMICAL DIVERSIFICATION OPPORTUNITIES

In order to try to get his "eggs" out of one basket, Mr. Morgan had been looking for some time for diversification opportunities. In the spring of 1971 Mr. Bristol, president of Bristol Chemical Co., had approached him. Mr. Bristol had been forced to move away for medical reasons and wondered if Tubbs could buy out his company. Bristol was located in Burlington, Vermont, 80 miles from Wallingford, and manufactured the varnish Tubbs used on its snowshoes. It also produced "Fall Line Ski Wax"® which was considered by many to be the best ski wax in the world. The U.S. Olympic Ski Team used it exclusively. Other products included "Leath-R-Seal"® a popular boot preservative, as well as specialized coatings for swimming pools and asphalt tennis courts. For the previous year, Bristol had sales of $101,000. Officer salaries and net profit combined were $22,000. The corporation had net assets of approximately $43,000, liabilities of approximately $41,000. Morgan thought that he could bring in Bob Penniman to manage Bristol. Penniman was a tool and die engineer and one of the country's experts in ski waxes.

---

*The toes of certain models are raised like a ski tip. The toe is bent all at once creating a compound bend: the toe and the raising.

†Under the provisions of the mortgage with Mr. Underwood, two signatures were required through 1972. The mortgage contained no other unusual provisions.

To help Mr. Bristol, Tubbs had advanced $50,000 on a short-term basis in late June. While this advance held the purchase option for Tubbs and was revocable, Morgan knew he must decide soon whether to complete the purchase. He felt Bristol would broaden his product line, improve cash flow, and provide needed engineering know-how. But he wondered if the time was appropriate.

CROSS-COUNTRY SKIS

For some time Morgan and Patrick Dule* had discussed the possibility of marketing cross-country skis under the Tubbs label. Dule, one of the nation's foremost skiers (a member of the U.S. Olympic Team), had selected an excellent Scandinavian ski manufacturer who did not have a U.S. distributor. Morgan felt that under Tubbs' name and with Dule's endorsement, sales of $100,000 and a gross profit of $25,000 could be reached the first year. He thought that cross-country skiing was a complementary sport to snowshoeing and attracted somewhat the same kind of customer. It was also one of the fastest growing winter sports. (For background on cross-country skiing see Exhibit 11.)

ANOTHER PLANT

In connection with his concern about the size of his present plant, Mr. Morgan had found a building for sale in Middletown Springs, Vermont, a town about 8 miles (15 minutes drive) away. Located on a two-acre plot, the building contained 6,000 sq. ft., two boilers, and about $5,000 of miscellaneous woodworking equipment. It had an apartment whose rental income completely paid for land taxes. The plant was for sale for $13,700.

SNOWSHOE FURNITURE

While rummaging through some old files, Morgan had found some old plans for a line of "snowshoe furniture" Tubbs had once produced (see Exhibit 12). This furniture had been used by Admiral Byrd at the South Pole and pieces were occasionally returned to Tubbs for relacing. Morgan felt that with a simple advertising campaign in *Yankee* magazine, *Maine Times*, and other similar publications, Tubbs could reintroduce this furniture for indoor or outdoor use. Later he might be able to distribute the line through his existing network of sporting goods dealers and eventually to furniture outlets. Although marketing furniture might be very different from snowshoes, Mr. Morgan felt the line might help reduce waste by using shorter strips and perhaps some sticks broken in the shaping step of making snowshoes. Also, presumably furniture would improve cash flow.

PLASTIC SNOWSHOE

Finally, Mr. Morgan wondered if he should pursue the question of plastic snowshoes:

> One of the advantages of living in Vermont is Yankee ingenuity. I have a friend who has studied snowshoes carefully and has promised to design a die for me to produce plastic frames. It will cost $15,000. I asked my jobbers and dealers about the idea of a plastic shoe to retail for about $20 and they were enthusiastic. But when I asked how many they would order, they only came up to 2,000 shoes.

---

*Disguised name.

SNOWSHOES—
for fun and health

Snowshoes have been used in some form for 2500 years or more, their origin lost in antiquity. There is evidence of a primitive form being used in Asia and Northern Europe and Arctic regions. But only in North America has the snowshoe survived in time. The North American Indians through necessity developed this means of locomotion to such a degree that even today modern technology would be hard put to improve the design. The forest Indians found the short broad shoe best for woods and brush because of easier maneuverability and the plains Indians found the longer narrower shoe best for hunting and tracking the buffalo. Minor variations in these basic designs evolved through the years and this fine heritage of craftsmanship has left us many choices. So your choice of snowshoes will be a matter of personal preference.

SELECTING SNOWSHOES

In selecting the pair of snowshoes which is "right" for you, you should take into consideration several factors:

1. Terrain—flat, open, trails, brush
2. Snow conditions—light powder, deep, crusty
3. Usage—hunting, back packing, forestry, general recreation
4. Weight and height
5. Experience

Rawhide or Neoprene

Rawhide is still a favorite among sportsmen and recreational snowshoers. With the new finish that Tubbs has developed, the rawhide shoe is more abrasion resistant and consequently less prone to wear and sagging. The distinctive Tubbs overlay pattern on the toe and heel, give better all around purchase than the traditional fine weave style or the neoprene.

Neoprene is a synthetic material which represents the first material change in the manufacture of snowshoes in several hundred years. While not as aesthetically appealing as rawhide, neoprene resists snow build-up and consequently is comparatively lighter than rawhide under wet snow conditions. Neoprene is impervious to gasoline, oil, rodents and will generally give better wear. Professional woodsmen prefer the neoprene shoe because of its durability and low maintenance.

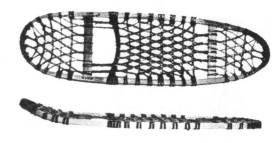

Green Mountain Bear Paw—10 x 36

This shoe, designed by Tubbs, is the most versatile shoe on the market. Its unique design makes it easy for the beginner and is a favorite of the Vermont Fish & Game Department. It is designed for New England snow conditions and is best in the woods and the brush. Very popular with hunters, it will support weights up to 200 lbs.

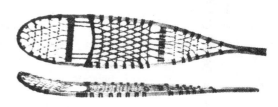

Cross Country—10 x 46

Basically this is the same design as the Green Mountain Bear Paw with the addition of a tail. The tail offers less drag than the Bear Paw models and acts as a stabilizer, much like a fin on a boat. The Cross Country is easy to walk on and is well suited to all conditions. It is popular with professional and recreational snowshoers and will support up to 225 lbs.

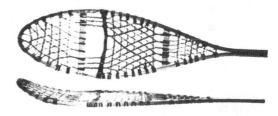

Michigan

The Michigan type is an excellent all-purpose snowshoe. Developed by the Indians, the Michigan was used for both back-packing and hunting. It supports weight better than any other model but is more difficult to master for the beginner. It is suggested for all snow conditions and for all terrain, save for thick brush.
12 x 48 is usually used by women
13 x 48 is for men weighing between 140-200
14 x 48 is for taller men or those weighing over 200

Exhibit 1. Vermont Tubbs, Inc.

Summarizing his feelings, Mr. Morgan said:

Maybe I shouldn't worry: we're making money and I haven't gotten stuck yet. But I still don't know where next week's hides will come from and, as I said before, I hate to have all our eggs in one basket.

A friend came in one day last week scouting for a conglomerate. He told me, "Gee, Baird, we're paying 18-24 times earnings. You should consider coming along." Still, I told him I wasn't ready to sell out. My father did that and grew awfully unhappy working for a conglomerate.

Exhibit 2. Vermont Tubbs, Inc. Selected Data on Recreation in the U.S. 1950-1969.

1. Personal Consumption Expenditure for Recreation

1950	$11.1 Billion
1960	18.3 Billion
1969	36.3 Billion

2. Purchases of Sports Equipment (boats, aircraft, etc.)

1950	$ 869 Million
1960	2106 Million
1969	4219 Million

3. Total Population (incl. Armed Forces abroad)

1950	152.3 Million
1960	180.7 Million
1969	202.6 Million

Source: *Statistical Abstract of the U.S., 1971,* p. 200, 308, 5.

Exhibit 3. Vermont Tubbs, Inc.

Dealer price list effective April 1, 1971

Snowshoes	5-29	30-99	100	Jobber price list	Factory retail price*
10 x 46	$21.60	$20.50	$18.40	$18.40	$40.00
12 x 48	21.60	20.50	18.40	18.40	40.00
13 x 48	21.60	20.50	18.40	18.40	40.00
14 x 48	22.25	21.15	18.60	18.60	41.00
12 x 42	21.60	20.50	18.40	18.40	40.00
10 x 36	21.60	20.50	18.40	18.40	40.00
13 x 33	21.60	20.50	18.40	18.40	40.00
13 x 28	21.60	20.50	18.40	18.40	37.00
14 × 25†	21.10	20.05	18.00	18.00	37.00
10 x 56	23.40	22.20	19.00	19.00	43.50
8 x 40	21.60	20.50	18.00	18.00	40.00

Bindings	1-50	Over 50			
H	$3.60	$3.25	$3.10		$5.95
Howe	5.70	5.10	5.00		7.95
A Mens	3.00	2.50	2.40		4.95
A Womens	3.00	2.50	2.40		4.95
Tubbs	5.70	5.10	4.40		7.95

Varnish $1.15 Minimum 1 Dozen Pints	$1.00 Pint

*Shown for illustrative purposes only. Factory retail prices are not suggested retail prices. Individual dealers set their own prices. (See text).

†Not available in neoprene

Exhibit 4. Vermont Tubbs, Inc. Dealer Information Sheet for 1971–1972.

1971 - 1972 Program

Terms

1 percent 10 Days

Interest at the rate of 1 ½ percent monthly, or 18 percent per year, will be charged on Past Due accounts.

Dating

Winter dating is available for shipment after April 1, 1971 with billing at 1971-1972 prices. Terms are 1 percent December 10, 1971, subject to credit standing. ANTICIPATION is 1 percent per month.

Warranty

VERMONT TUBBS products are guaranteed against defects in material and/or workmanship for one year from date of shipment.

Freight

F.O.B.   Wallingford, Vermont

Dealer Price

The initial order establishes the quantity discount for the year.

Repairs

Repair service will be provided throughout the year. Estimate sheets are available upon request.

Return of Merchandise

No merchandise returns will be accepted without prior written authorization. A 10 percent handling charge will be made on all unauthorized returns. A handling charge equal to 10 percent of the purchase price will be made where the original order was filled correctly and arrived in good condition.

Standard Packs

Snowshoes are packaged throughout the off season in units of five (5). While any quantity of any style of snowshoes is available, initial orders made in units of 5 can be shipped more expeditiously.

Recent photograph of plant

Upstairs: Lacing and inventory

Downstairs: Woodworking operations

Exhibit 5.   Vermont Tubbs, Inc.

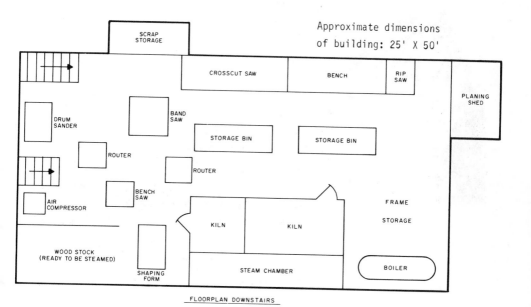

FLOORPLAN DOWNSTAIRS

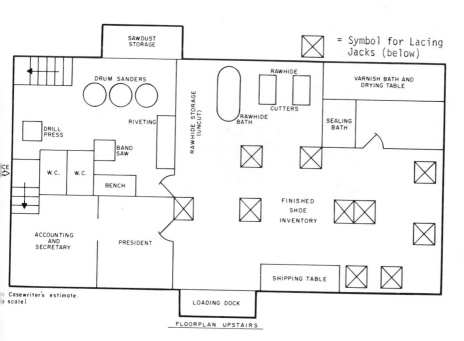

FLOORPLAN UPSTAIRS

Exhibit 6.   Vermont Tubbs, Inc.

Shaping mold in use

Sanding unfinished frame

Lacing jack in use

Exhibit 7.   Vermont Tubbs, Inc.

Exhibit 8. Vermont Tubbs, Inc. Lacing for Week Ending January 30, 1971.

Name					Bodies					
	Cox	Nesbitt	Regimbald	Lerzo	Perry	Tarbell	Day	Senegal	Daily totals	Cumulative
Mon.	14 10x36 5 14x48 3 12x42	9½ 10x36 1 12x43 2½ 10x46		12 pr.	14 10x36	16 10x46	8 10x56 1 10x46	12 10x46 (N)	105	105
Tues.	6 13x29 14 10x36	6 10x46 8 12x48	-	3½ 13x32 2 13x48 4½ 10x46	14½ 10x36	5 10x56 10 10x26	10½ 12x42 2 10x56	-	88½	193½
Wed.	4 13x28 17 10x46	12½ 13x33 2½ 10x46	-	1 13x33 4 10x36	13½ 10x46	14½ 10x46	-	12 10x36	81	274½
Thurs.	3 10x46 9 13x33 10 8x40	11 13x33	9½ 10x56	9 10x36	14 12x42	6 10x46	8 10x56	-	79	349½
Fri.	3 8x40 19 10x46	-	1 10x56 4½ 12x42 5½ 14x48	-	-	16 10x46	7½ 10x56	3 10x36 5 13x30 5 12x42	69½	419
Sat.	12 10x46 6 13x33	15½ 10x36			9 10x46				42½	461
Total										

Exhibit 8. *cont'd.*

Toe & Heel

Name	Perron	Reynolds R.	Kennedy E.	Johnson	Brown	Bullock	Warren	Baker	Stewart	Kennedy D.		
Mon.	14½ 10x46 5½ 10x36	10 10x46	-	11 10x36	9½ 10x36	9 13x28 1 10x56	12 12x46 4½ 10x36	3½ 10x56 6½ 10x46 1 13x48	-	Senegal 12 10x46	106	106
Tues.	-	10 10x46	8½ 10x36	10½ 10x36	8½ 10x36	10 10x56	5½ 8x40 2 10x56 9 12x42	5 10x46 2 13x48 1 13x33 1½ 12x42	-	12 10x46	76	182
Wed.	6½ 10x40 1 10x36 10½ 12x42	10 10x46	10 10x36	10½ 10x36	6½ 10x36	-	1½ 8x4 7 10x46 8 12x48	-	-	2 10x46 1 10x56 3½ 13x33	92	274
Thurs.	18 10x46	10 10x36	10 10x36	10 10x36	8 10x36	10 10x56	4 10x46 4 14x48 8½ 13x33	1 13x33 4 10x36	-	-	87½	361
Fri.	10 12x42 10 8x40	-	-	10½ 13x33	½ 10x36 8½ 13x33	10 10x56	7½ 10x56	-	3 10x36 5 13x33 5 13x42	2½ 13x33	72½	433½
Sat.	-	10 10x46	-	-	-	-	-	5 10x56 3 12x48 ½ 12x42	1½ 10x46 1½ 13x33 1 12x48	-	23½	457
Total										1 14x48		

Exhibit 9. Vermont Tubbs, Inc. Comparative Balance Sheets 6/30/70, 6/30/71.

Assets	1970	1971
Current Assets		
Cash	$ 3,945.69	$ 16,058.28
Accounts Receivable (net)	5,270.34	24,576.64
Inventory	55,869.75	64,369.00
Advance to Bristol Chemical	-0-	50,000.00
Other	349.32	69.86
Total Current Assets	65,435.10	155,073.78
Fixed Assets (net)		
Land	3,000.00	3,000.00
Building & Improvements	50,547.32	49,129.89
Machinery & Equipment	39,553.62	34,303.22
Vehicle	1,833.33	2,907.61
Office Equipment	-0-	187.03
Total Fixed Assets	94,934.27	89,527.75
Other Assets (incl. Goodwill $1,000)	1,211.52	1,159.72
Total Assets	$161,580.89	$245,761.25
Liabilities and Capital		
Current Liabilities		
Accounts Payable	$ 6,710.50	$ 13,795.10
Accrued Taxes	2,592.67	2,396.53
Accrued Wages	-0-	1,013.85
Notes Payable: Bank	10,000.00	50,000.00
Notes Payable: H. Underwood (current portion)	5,572.09	6,430.50
Total Current Liabilities	24,875.26	73,635.98
Long Term Liabilities		
Due Officers & Stockholders	3,395.00	7,394.75
Notes Payable: C. B. Morgan, Sr.	2,000.00	15,000.00
Notes Payable: H. Underwood, Inc.	96,582.77	89,727.37
Total Long Term Liabilities	101,977.77	112,122.12
Total Liabilities	126,853.03	185,758.10
Capital		
Capital Stock	30,000.00	30,000.00
Retained Earnings	4,727.86	30,003.15
Total Capital	34,727.86	60,003.15
Total Liabilities & Capital	$161,580.89	$245.761.25

Prepared from the books without audit.

Exhibit 10. Vermont Tubbs, Inc. Comparative Income Statements F/Y 1970, 1971.

Sales	1970	1971
Snowshoes	$180,436.22	$283,932.13
Bindings	27,669.44	52,912.75
Repairs	1,734.23	2,276.47
Sawdust & Supplies	-0-	2,304.58
Deduct: returns & allowances	(1,378.49)	(3,481.18)
Net Sales	208,461.40	337,944.75
Cost of Sales		
Inventory 7/1/70	37,229.62	55,869.75
Add:		
Lumber	31,499.40	26,293.02
Rawhide, leather, bindings, neoprene	61,531.24	107,099.72
Operating Supplies	10,832.24	14,067.58
Labor	59,691.79	85,767.40
Depreciation	7,728.23	9,321.12
Taxes & Licenses	5,414.83	7,162.57
Heat & Lights	4,464.43	5,196.58
Freight (in)	1,930.26	2,676.03
Other (incl. repairs)	5,354.07	2,435.03
Deduct:		
Inventory 6/30/71	(55,869.75)	(64,369.00)
Total Cost of Sales	169,806.36	251,519.80
Gross Profit	38,655.04	86,424.95
General and Administrative		
Salary: Officer	3,600.00	10,000.00
Salary: Office	3,666.50	5,545.22
Commission	6,293.59	9,277.03
Travel & Promotion	1,741.46	1,033.25
Telephone	1,009.31	2,320.78
Interest	8,488.07	10,407.67
Advertising	2,397.76	1,821.59
Office Expenses	1,465.73	2,936.00
Repairs	-0-	1,606.62
Legal & Audit	2,551.26	1,687.51
Insurance	3,537.18	5,057.09
Bad Debts	-0-	3,653.60
Other	447.07	2,300.84
Total G&A	35,197.93	57,647.20
Profit on Operations	3,457.11	28,777.75
Other Income (cash discounts)	1,270.75	1,225.40
Net Profit	$ 4,727.86	$ 30,003.15

Prepared from the books without audit.

Exhibit 11. Vermont Tubbs, Inc. *Wall Street Journal:* 4/1/71 on Cross-Country Skiing.

"NATURE WALK ON SKIS: 'TOURING' ENTHUSIASTS SPURN DOWNHILL RACING"
by David McLean

SUGARBUSH VALLEY, Vt.—So here you are at one of the country's swingingest ski areas, and what's more fun than clamping on your $155 Head 360s, riding the lift to the top of the slope and schussing downhill at eleventy-seven miles an hour like the real ace you are?

Well, to a growing number of folks, there is something more fun. That's clamping on your $37.50 Bonna skis, walking across the road and trudging at three miles an hour over the snow-blanketed golf course at the foot of the hill like the real plodder you are.

Not for you the fancy gear, the downhill thrills, and the broken legs in casts. You pass up all that because you're in on the newest thing in skiing, a vigorously noncompetitive form of it called ski touring. It caught on in this country last year—partly, its exponents say, because of the crowds and commercialism of downhill, or alpine, skiing. It uses the same kind of equipment as cross-country skiing, but that form of skiing is organized, and competitive.

"Suddenly everyone is tuned in to the newest thing," says *Ski* magazine. Resorts around the country have marked off touring areas and now are renting touring gear. In Stowe, Vt., the famous Trapp family offers a touring area around Mount Mansfield. Here in Sugarbush the Sugarbush Inn has access to 45 miles of touring trails. In the West, touring now is established at such well-known Colorado areas as Steamboat Springs, Vail, and Snowmass.

MODESTY IN ALL THINGS
Fans say there's a lot to be said for ski touring. For one thing, it's inexpensive. You don't need costly arctic wear—blue jeans and a sweater or two will do—because ski touring is hard work that generates a lot of body heat. You don't need skis of space-age materials with sophisticated bindings because you are going slow and rarely risk a serious fall. You don't need a $10 lift ticket because most trails are free.

Touring boots are more like shoes. They don't have to be as sturdy as downhill boots, designed to immobilize the ankle in a viselike grip. A simple toe clamp binds the touring boot to the ski, leaving the heel free. On downhill skis, a more costly and complex heel-and-toe binding is used.

The touring technique probably is the oldest in skiing. It's a sort of sliding walk on long, narrow wooden skis that cut easily through fresh snow. You plant a touring pole into the snow and shift your weight to the foot opposite to slide forward. The "feel" for this step doesn't come naturally to most people, even to experienced downhill skiers, but it doesn't take much time to learn.

To climb hills about all the technique a novice need master is the simple herringbone walk (ski tips pointed outward, ski edges dug in) or a sidestep.

DOWNHILL TECHNIQUE
But when a beginning ski tourer does take a downhill trail, he faces the same problem as an alpine tyro: how to stop. Until you've developed your balance, you simply stop by falling, or preferably, by sitting down. Instructors advise novices to try to slow down by grabbing low-hanging tree branches, or bushes.

Ski-touring enthusiasts liken the activity to other quiet pursuits like ice fishing, hiking, and birdwatching. "It has limitless possibilities," says Janet Nelson, a ski writer who has taken up touring. "You see the birds and the trees, and they're a greater pleasure than you realized. You see things you don't see in summer hiking. I think I like the nature and the quiet best."

Exhibit 11. *cont'd.*

"It's not a hassle," says Suzanne Meister, a novice ski tourer, after her first afternoon of touring here at Sugarbush. "It's a joy to be outside. It's not horribly dangerous. I buy the idea that you can have fun as a beginner, and you can't in alpine skiing."

SALES BOOM

Sporting-goods makers, distributors, and dealers have observed the sharp surge of interest in touring. G.H. Bass & Co., a shoe manufacturer in Wilton, Maine, imported a "couple of hundred" cross-country skis in the winter of 1969–1970 for distribution around the county. In the winter just ended, Bass reports, orders ran into the thousands. "It's fantastic," a spokesman says. "We couldn't keep up with the demand."

Harry Vallin, owner of Scandinavian Ski Shops in New York, expects to have sold about a thousand pairs of touring skis by the end of the current season, double his seasonal sales two years ago.

"I think it will be as popular or more popular than alpine skiing at some point," says Richard Falcone, president of Garcia Ski & Tennis Corp., Teaneck, N.J. Mr. Falcone says his company is in the "throes of negotiating" the import of touring equipment to add to its line of alpine ski gear.

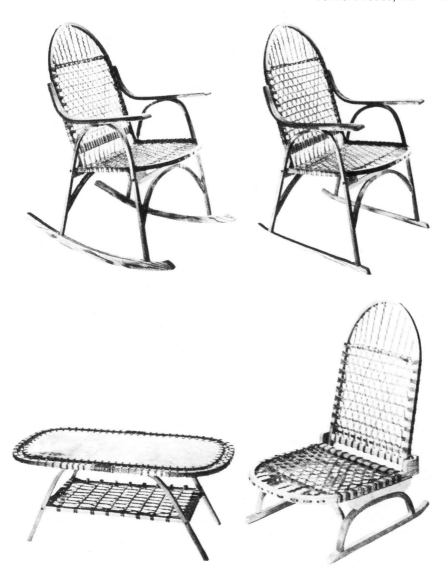

Exhibit 12.   Vermont Tubbs, Inc. Proposed Line of Snowshoe Furniture.

Passport Dinner Club (A)

INTRODUCTION

John Keene and Everett Marshall met for the first time in a number of months at a cocktail party marking the opening of a new ski lodge in Colorado. Their conversation drifted to Keene's recent business activities which included helping his family start the Old South Dinner Club in his Louisiana hometown. In Keene's opinion, these dinner clubs represented virtual "gold mines," for they provided a much-needed service to the restaurants as well as to the restaurants' patrons.

The dinner club concept is based on a membership consisting of dues-paying members who are entitled to one dinner at no cost in each of the participating restaurants when another dinner is purchased at the same time. The member and his guest may select any entrée on the menu, and they need not order the same entrée. The least expensive entrée ordered is the free one. In return for his dues, a member receives a plastic membership card and a directory describing the rules of the club and listing the restaurants participating in the plan and the days of the week on which the cards would be honored. The cards would only be honored one time at each restaurant. Each restaurant would be assigned a number on the membership card. When a member used his card at a restaurant, the cashier would punch out the number of that restaurant on the card, so as to prevent the member from using the card at that same restaurant another time. The term of membership was typically six months or a year depending on the specific plan.

In addition to these attractive savings on meals, the dinner club packages typically offered savings on lodging at selected resort areas. Some dinner clubs also offered two tickets for the price of one to attend certain entertainment and sporting events. These additional benefits were felt to increase greatly the saleability of the dinner club memberships.

These dinner clubs had already been widely accepted in Denver and other Western cities, but John Keene felt that there was a fantastic opportunity for these dinner clubs on the East Coast. Marshall, a reputable young money manager, seemed quite interested in what Keene had to say, and Marshall concluded their conversation by suggesting that Keene give him a call on Monday morning so that they might discuss the dinner club concept further.

BACKGROUND

John Keene, the prospective President of Passport Dinner Club, Inc., was a young 29-year-old businessman with an excellent business background. He received his undergraduate degree from a major Southern university in 1965 and a Master of Business Administration from the same school in 1967. His first job after graduation

This case prepared by John Christie and George Henderson, Graduate Students, under the direction of F. Brown Whittington, Jr., Associate Professor, Graduate School of Business Administration, Emory University. Reprinted with permission.

was involved in the market research field. He later went to a large Western city as Research Director of the largest bank holding company in the state.

The Executive Vice President and other major stockholder of Passport was a 29-year-old businessman, Everett Marshall. Marshall also was a fraternity brother of Keene as an undergraduate. After graduation in 1966, he attended Harvard University, where he received an M.B.A. in 1968. He then went West to manage a hedge fund for a wealthy individual. Eighteen months later he started his own money management firm. Marshall had established an excellent reputation for himself and was considered one of the best young money managers in the West.

After going West, John Keene became a member of one of the two dinner clubs operating in his city. In reading his newsletter, circulated by the dinner club to all members, Keene discovered that he was one of 25,000 members. Keene became deeply interested in these dinner clubs and began talking to the management of several of the participating restaurants to get some feedback on how things were going between the restaurants and the dinner club managements. He also talked to a friend of his who was a banker and who handled the account of one of the dinner clubs. Keene was favorably impressed with everything he learned and his interest in the dinner clubs continued. All of this initial research started in August of 1972.

In December, 1972, Keene was in Louisiana, for a visit with his family. After discussing the concept of a dinner club with them, they felt such a program could work in Baton Rouge, which was about one-fifth the size of the Western city. Both parents were retired and had much time to devote to the project. Keene set up the business plans, and did the design work for the business. By September, 1973, this club had been in operation for about four months and was producing a small profit.

Returning to the West, after the December visit with his parents, Keene saw Marshall at the opening of a ski lodge in Colorado. Later they discussed the figures, possibilities, etc., that Keene had developed. Marshall was impressed and very interested with the concept. They came to the decision to set up a club of a similar type. Keene was very happy with having Marshall, because of his financial knowledge and money management ability.

The initial capitalization of the firm was an investment of $10,000 by each of the two men. This $20,000 amount was felt to be adequate for setting up the organization and to sustain it until sufficient cash inflows were realized. It was also felt that if the situation developed such that more capital were needed, a line of credit was available to the two men from a Denver bank. However, it was felt that, based on the break-even analysis shown as Exhibit 1, the men would have their full $20,000 investment returned to them after 4½ months of operation and sales of 2500 memberships. They believed that their estimates were conservative and that a sales level of 2500 cards was easily attainable in the Atlanta market.

For the next six months the men moved out on the concept, working with the figures and deciding where to initiate the program. Houston and Atlanta were the cities primarily being considered. It was felt that if Houston were chosen, however, Passport would encounter stiff competition from a Dallas dinner club which was planning to expand into the Houston area. Atlanta seemed to be the most viable choice for it was a rapidly growing city which housed many fine restaurants. Keene personally favored the choice of Atlanta, for he had spent many enjoyable weekends there while attending college. He was anxious to return to Atlanta.

A tentative timetable was constructed. The two men wanted to have the membership on the market by October 1, 1973, which was some five months away. It was planned that Keene would go to Atlanta around the first of August to research the area, for Atlanta was known to have an active Chamber of Commerce which would be able to supply any demographics which they needed to know about the Atlanta market.

In July, 1973, Keene resigned from his position at the bank, primarily because he became disenchanted with the holding company's organization. At this time, it was decided Keene himself would go to Atlanta and set up the organization. He would be paid a salary comparable to his past salary out of the operating fund of the business. In other words, he was now on the payroll of Passport Dinner Club.

Keene arrived in Atlanta, August 7, 1973 to set up office. An office location was picked in the southwest part of the city. Through a mutual friend of Marshall, a young man was contacted to help Keene sell the dinner club concept in Atlanta. It was anticipated that this man would become office manager as Keene left to set up plans in other cities.

MARKETING STRATEGY

In this business, John Keene found that he was actually dealing with two distinct markets, each of which needed a different marketing plan. The first market was the restaurants which would participate in the program. The other was the market of prospective members of the club, the actual cardholders.

Before either market could be contacted a name had to be developed. The clubs Keene had seen were "Gourmet" in the West, and "Old South," the one he helped develop for his parents in Louisiana. The name that was decided on was "Passport." It was felt that they could obtain restaurants with different atmospheres and cuisine, so they could develop a promotional strategy based on a theme along the lines of "see the world through the restaurants of Atlanta." The name was also short, two syllables, and hopefully was easy to remember and relate to.

It was proposed each new member would receive a physical package consisting of an embossed plastic card and an informative directory. This directory would explain the rules of the dinner club, and inform the members on which days of the week they were allowed to dine at certain restaurants. In addition, a page was reserved for each restaurant operating hours, the credit cards accepted, the acceptable dress, and the necessity of reservations. The length of the membership period was set at 12 months.

The Restaurants

In choosing the restaurants, John Keene set the following guidelines:

1. No fast-food or convenience take-out restaurants.
2. An average entree price of $4.50 to $5.50.
3. Easy accessibility to the residents of Atlanta.
4. Atmosphere and cuisine consistent with the international mode of Passport.

A list of 90 restaurants meeting this description was compiled. Of these restaurants, some 20 were classified as "most desirable" because of their current popularity among the Atlanta residents. An additional 30 restaurants were labeled as "desirable" because although they were not in the spotlight at the moment, they did enjoy a broad reputation of being fine places to eat. The remaining restaurants on the list were classified as "adequate" because they met the four criteria above, but they did not have the wide-spread reputation for one reason or another. In many cases, these "adequate" restaurants were outstanding new restaurants which had not yet had time to enter the spotlight of popularity.

Keene felt that they should logically begin calling on the "most desirable" restaurants and then work his way down the list. He was quite interested in contracting some of these well-known restaurants because they would greatly increase the appeal of the Dinner Club. At the same time, Keene was aware that his dinner club plan would get the best reception from the "adequate" restaurants because they needed the exposure. As an upper limit, it was felt that 25 restaurants represented a realistic number for two reasons. First of all, it was felt that any restaurants over this number would add little marginal appeal to the dinner club plan. Secondly, it appeared unrealistic that any member would choose to dine out more than 25 times during the period in which their membership was valid (12 months).

Under the dinner club plan, Passport did not compensate the restaurants for their participation. To convince the restaurants of the merits of the dinner club plan, it was necessary that Keene develop an effective personal selling campaign emphasizing the following:

1. The restaurants' increased exposure to the public through Passport's own advertising.

2. Increased business for restaurants on days of the week which have been habitually "slow."

3. The possibility that the restaurants will receive additional patronage in the future from the Passport members after their initial exposure.

4. The entree is the only item on the menu that is given away on a two-for-one basis. Profit can be made on appetizers, cocktails, side-orders, wines, and desserts.

In its personal selling campaign, Passport was at a disadvantage because it was a new firm and it could not sell the restaurants on its past sales performance. As a result, Keene had to base his entire sales presentation on the idea of the dinner club concept alone rather than on any past sales figures. The consenting restaurants were required to sign a contract insuring their compliance to the terms of the dinner club plan for a period of twelve months. No attempt was made to persuade the restaurants to sign for a period for longer than twelve months because Keene wanted to maintain the prerogative to select any restaurants that he wished to participate in next year's plan.

The Consumer Market
After arriving in Atlanta, John Keene became more and more convinced that they had made the correct decision in choosing Atlanta as the city to house their dinner club. Atlanta enjoyed the image of being a "young city" which had in the last ten years

experienced fantastic growth. At this time, the Greater Metropolitan Area (S.M.S.A.) had a population of 1,600,000 people. Atlanta was not an industrial city, but rather its rapid growth had come about because of its central location. Over 400 of the "Fortune 500" largest businesses had established their southeastern offices in Atlanta. The average family income for Atlanta was around $13,000 which was exactly comparable to Denver's average. Atlanta also enjoyed a busy tourist trade, for it seemed to be a favorite as a convention center. To accommodate these conventions, many fine restaurants and restaurant chains were established in Atlanta. Keene was greatly encouraged by all these factors and was confident that Atlanta was the ideal city to house their Passport Dinner Club venture.

Keene decided to adopt the same pricing structure that was used in Denver. The advertised retail price of a membership was $15.00. Special group prices were set at $12.00. Keene also was willing to negotiate a price to follow the Denver dinner clubs in their practice of offering "sweeteners" to their members in the form of weekend travel packages to resorts where they could get reduced rates on meals and lodging. He felt that these "getaways," as he called them, greatly increased the appeal of his product, and they could be set up with a minimum amount of additional time and expense.

PROMOTION
John Keene set the following objectives for his promotional campaign:

1. *Establish credibility in the marketplace*—He felt that he could accomplish this first by using clearly worded ads which could fully explain the dinner club concept. Secondly, he felt that his ads should consistently appear in the same place and at the same time so that the consumer would get the impression that Passport Dinner Club is an established institution which is here to stay.

2. *Generate sales*—Keene wanted wide coverage that would adequately reach his entire target market. He was also working under somewhat severe cost constraints. In view of the amount of paid-in capital, it was felt that only a total of $10,000 to $12,000 could be spent on advertising until substantial cash from membership sales started coming in. In view of the cost constraints, Keene wanted his printed ads to double as sales forms, so he planned to put a membership application in the corner of each ad.

Advertising
Displayed in Exhibit 2 are the costs of the various types of advertising which Keene explored. Keene wanted the best coverage for the money, and he felt that TV ads were much too expensive. He realized that newspaper ads were essential. The "Atlanta Journal and Constitution" offered the widest coverage, but their ad space was too expensive for the Passport Dinner Club ad to appear on a daily basis. Keene faced a problem in that he did not feel that he could legibly display the rules of the club and the names of the restaurants unless the ad was a quarter of a page or larger. In view of these cost and size constraints, Keene felt that they could only afford to place an ad in the "Atlanta Journal and Constitution" weekly. His first thoughts were to place this ad in the weekly TV/Amusements section which is often retained by persons to be used as a TV reference for the entire week. He felt that he would supplement this ad

with ads in the less costly neighborhood newspapers on the north side of Atlanta, ads in various school newspapers, and ads in magazines circulated to apartment dwellers.

Keene planned to conduct his advertising campaign in two stages. The first stage was aimed at general market exposure through the consistent placement of ads in the printed media described above. The objective of this first stage was to make the public familiar with the Passport name and hopefully inquisitive about the dinner club plan itself. The second stage involved an increase in the advertising effort through the use of spot advertising on the radio. The objective of the second stage of the campaign was to generate "gift" sales around Christmas time. Keene felt that the second stage should be started several weeks before Christmas, and the first stage should be in effect two months before the beginning of the second stage. After the holidays, when the Christmas "push" was over, Keene planned to continue to have his ads appear in the chosen printed media for the next several months to insure Passport's credibility in the marketplace.

Point of Purchase Mailers
To supplement the advertising, it was felt that point-of-purchase mailers had huge potential. The mailer would be laid out to contain a brief summary of the dinner club, would list the restaurant within the club, and be designed with the exact Passport logo that had appeared in all the advertising. Keene planned to distribute these mailers to apartments and business offices. The mailer would offer the potential member a membership for the reduced price of $12.00 ($15.00 was regular). The distribution of the mailer would be done by college students to reach the apartments and off-duty airline stewardesses to reach the businesses. Keene had a college friend who was a professor at an Atlanta university who could help him recruit student labor, and he had also made the acquaintance of an airline stewardess who assured him that she and some of her girlfriends could be counted on to distribute these mailers. Between these two sources, Keene felt confident that he would be able to get enough help to distribute all of the return mailers, although Keene really had no idea of how long this distribution might take. The main display vehicle used for the mailers was an easel which also contained the Passport logo and had "Special Group Discount" in bold black letters across its top. These easels containing the return mailers were to be put on bulletin boards and countertops around the city.

Other Promotion
In addition to the advertising and the return mailers, Keene also planned to use a limited direct mail campaign to reach various social clubs and professional organizations which might have a direct interest in purchasing a Passport membership. These memberships would be made available to these solicited groups at a special bulk rate. The actual price would be negotiated and would be directly dependent on the guaranteed volume of cards ordered. For example, Keene would be willing to lower the selling price from $15.00 to $10.00 per card for guaranteed orders of 50 to 100 cards.

Another promotional device that Keene intended to pursue was the use of complimentary memberships as gestures of goodwill to persons with whom he became associated. Keene planned to give these cards away freely because he felt that they would help push the memberships on the marketplace. In Keene's opinion, second-hand, word-of-mouth promotion was essential in the case of a new product such as the Passport memberships. These complimentary cards would help generate some of this word-of-mouth promotion.

The final promotional tool that Keene planned to use was the direct selling of bulk sale contracts to various companies such as banks and Savings and Loan Associations to be used as premiums and incentives to persons opening new accounts. Direct sales were extremely time consuming, and it was felt that it should only be employed later after the Passport operation was established and running smoothly.

PRESENT SITUATION

By October 15, 1973, John Keene was excited because he felt that his venture was finally taking shape. He made an unexpected office move to the north part of town so as to enjoy a more prestigious northside address and to be closer to the majority of the restaurants and prospective members. Two months ago, he found it necessary to replace his office manager with a striking young lady who had just moved to Atlanta from New York, where she had worked for the public relations department of a large bank. Her attractive appearance and her congenial personality had proved to be a definite asset in contracting the restaurants. At this point, twenty restaurants had signed with Passport and the initial response seemed excellent. Keene was confident that he would have his memberships on the market by November 15th.

Although this would mean that the Passport operation was about six weeks behind the original schedule, Keene still felt that they would have ample time to gain the desired general market exposure before making the large Christmas sales push.

Exhibit 1. Passport Dinner Club (A) Financial Data.

Organizational Costs:

Office furniture	$ 300
Typewriter	400
Design work	2500
Plastic credit cards (20,000 @ .06)	1200
Membership directories (5,000 @ .20)	1000
Return mailers and display easels	1100
Miscellaneous	500
	$7000

Projected Funds Flow

	Month 1	Month 2	Month 3	Month 4	Month 5
Organizational Costs	$ 4,000	$3,000	----	----	----
Rent	150	150	150	150	150
Salaries	1,500	1,500	1,500	1,500	1,500
Advertising	4,500	4,500	3,000	3,000	3,000
Miscellaneous	150	150	150	150	150
Total Outflows	$10,300	$9,300	$4,800	$4,800	$4,800
Number of Card Sales	0	300	700	1,000	1,000
Total Inflows*	0	$4,050	$9,450	$13,500	$13,500
Net for Period	(10,300)	($5,250)	$4,650	$8,700	$8,700
Previous Balance	$20,000†	$ 9,700	$4,650	$9,100	$17,800
Ending Balance	$ 9,700	$ 4,450	$9,100	$17,800	$26,500

*The inflows are figured by multiplying the number of cards sold times the average price of the cards. This average price of the $13.50 represents the median between the retail price of $15.00 and the group discount price of 12.00.

† Represents the initial investment of $20,000.

Exhibit 2. Passport Dinner Club (A) Profile on Advertising Media (in the Atlanta area).

I. Newspapers

Name	Frequency	Circulation/audience	Cost Per ½ Page
Atlanta Journal & Constitution	Daily	555,000/general public	$ 1300
Neighborhood Newspapers, Inc.	Weekly	200,000/northside neighborhoods	650
Emory Wheel	Weekly	18,000/students & alumni	100
Ga. Tech Newspaper	Weekly	8,500/students & alumni	70
Ga. State Signal	Weekly	7,000/students & faculty	50
Southern Israelite	Weekly	15,000/Jewish community	130

II. Magazines

Name	Frequency	Circulation/audience	Cost Per ½ Page
Time (Regional)	Weekly	117,000/educated public	$ 700
Sports Illustrated (Regional)	Weekly	110,000/educated public	600
Newsweek (Regional)	Weekly	100,000/educated public	600
Apartment Scene	Monthly	105,000/Apartment Dwellers	300
Atlanta Skier	Monthly	10,000/Ski Crowd	60
Showcase Magazine	Monthly	20,000/Theater Crowd	50
Lifestyle	Monthly	20,000/Apartment Dwellers	115

III. Radio

Station	Program Description		Cost*
WSB	Popular Music, College Sports		$62
WSB (FM)	Easy Listening, Popular Music		16
WQXI	Pop Hits, Young Audience		62
WPCH (FM)	Easy Listening, Adults		40
WKLS (FM)	Easy Listening, Adults		20

IV. Television

Station	Network Affiliation		Cost*
WSB-TV	NBC		$600
WAGA-TV	CBS		600
WXIA-TV	ABC		600
WTGC-TV	Independent		300

V. Outdoor Advertising

One hundred percent traffic coverage of the northside of Atlanta with billboards would cost $1000 per month. Twenty-five percent traffic coverage would cost around $300 per month.

Four Generations

Four Generations, a firm dedicated to producing quality wooden toys and games that would last "four generations," took form in a forest ranger's cabin at Big Sur, California in 1966. The founding partners, Dick Benton and Harry Batlan, designed and produced their earliest products on a part-time basis. In 1968, the firm was relocated in Sebastopol, among the rolling hills and vineyards of the wine country north of San Francisco. Throughout 1968 and 1969, a number of innovative designs were added to the product line. In addition, stemming from the unorthodox outlook of its owners, an unusual system of employer-employee relations evolved. Sales had doubled each year since 1968 and over time the product mix had shifted away from toys and into adult games; yet Four Generations had never earned a profit. Sales for 1972 were projected to exceed $300,000. While management expected to break even at this level, further moves to achieve a more economical production volume and broaden the product mix were being contemplated.

EVOLUTION OF THE COMPANY

The majority owner and president of the firm, Dick Benton, graduated from the University of Colorado in Civil Engineering. His work experience included a stint with Caterpillar Tractor's Export Sales Division, several years as a field engineer for Morrison-Knudsen Construction, and three years as a Special Agent for the FBI. A position in engineering marketing attracted him to Inland Steel where he worked for ten years. His final assignment for that firm brought him to California. "After we moved to California," recalls Benton, "I became interested in efforts to design a construction system that would systemize building. My interest in this problem culminated in a patented design of a flexible steel system—much like an erector set—that was appropriate for schools and other similar institutional construction. While still working at Inland Steel, I founded Design Systems. Stanford University was one of our first contracts; we built the Student Credit Union."

At Inland Steel, Benton relaxed some of the strict regulations. He gave employees responsibility for their jobs and did not require them to punch in and out on the time clock. As a result, morale improved. Employees took shorter coffee breaks, absenteeism decreased, and productivity went up.

> During this same period, I met a forest ranger one weekend at Big Sur. He had four children and I had four children and we became friends. He was educated as an artist and for one reason or another, we both shared an interest in being in business for ourselves. Somehow, our discussion turned to children's toys and Harry had dreams of interesting toy trucks that he thought he could make and sell. So we decided to make children's playthings—toys that

This case was prepared by Assistant Professor Richard T. Johnson and Karen H. Campbell as a basis for class discussion.

Reprinted from *Stanford Business Cases 1972* with the permission of the Publishers, Stanford University Graduate School of Business, © 1972 by the Board of Trustees of the Leland Stanford Junior University.

would last, that were well put together and geometrically "right," designed so a child could play with them by himself and learn about himself and his environment.

Between us we had $6,000 in savings; we bought some used equipment and materials and began making toys in Harry's cabin at Big Sur and selling them at the shop of Nepenthe Restaurant on Highway 1. It was such a shoestring operation that we both kept our regular jobs and did our manufacturing on weekends.

It didn't take long to see that $6,000 wasn't enough to start a company—we needed volume, and volume required dollars to finance inventory and equipment; but getting those dollars meant that neither of us could quit our jobs. However, about this time, Design Systems began to bear fruit and did sufficiently well that by the end of the year I was able to sell my share for $25,000. Thus, by the end of 1967, I really had enough money to make a full-time commitment. Harry had been transferred to Fort Ross so we started looking for a location that was near San Francisco and a major freeway and yet enough in the country to be "real California" . . . like it was when Steinbeck wrote about it. After a while we gave up on rentals . . . industrial sites are so ugly and commonplace. So we ended up buying a sort of small farm with a barn-like shed. In retrospect, it is probably unwise for a starting company to buy anything . . . you don't know what you'll need or how fast you'll grow. But having our own place probably helped us in some ways because it enabled us to do our thing in our own way . . . to come up with a lot of ideas we couldn't have used if we had taken a rented space.

You know there are a lot of things that just happen to you in business . . . it's not always sifting among alternatives and picking the best move. It's the problem of crisis response . . . of selecting among too few alternatives . . . of being constrained by time and space, and money running out. And once you've built an organization of people, your maneuvering room gets even more limited.

About this time, Harry dropped out. He's really a philosophical guy. As matters of money and management began to inject themselves into the venture, he had to excuse himself. Basically, he was unwilling to quit his job with the Forest Service and make the concessions that being in business requires. But with Harry gone, it sure got lonely in that shed . . . me, a few machines . . . and a stack of lumber. Then one day Michael Gonzalez walked down the driveway and asked if he could help. I said I'd split my salary with him if he'd join me. He did. He's had a tremendous influence on all our products and policies ever since.

Throughout 1968, Michael and I developed a whole batch of toys. We lived there, sacking out in sleeping bags, cooking on the pot-bellied stove, working all day in the factory and talking at night about the future. One of the first things Michael asked when he started was about working hours. All I could say was "Let's get the job done." That basic approach to things became our operating philosophy. Why should there be double standards between employer and employee? So as we began to grow and hire other people, they just moved in with us. At one time we had as many as six people living there. Mike and I had worked in factories ourselves; he had felt the boredom of working on one machine all day. We knew that accident rates and low efficiencies were all related to whether a person felt involved with the company he was working for and whether or not he had a way of expressing himself.

We didn't make any money in 1968; in 1969 our sales were $20,000 and we still lost several thousand dollars. At times I just didn't see how we could make it. I tried everything I could think of to make the company work . . . to make people more productive . . . to make it happy, safe, pleasant, and also successful. We paid people when we could . . . and if we couldn't pay them, they moved in and we paid for their food. It's corny but I think we evolved a kind of "do unto others" philosophy. That's how our various payments systems evolved. At first we paid people by the hour. But on some routine jobs people preferred to have a *quota* so they could work like hell and go home. We'd all vote to set the quota based on our production requirements. Then if a guy came in at 7:00 a.m. and left at 12:30, it was better for him and fine for us. Of course, most people can't work like that every day...and besides, it gets boring. So that's where our system of job rotation came from—letting employees pick the machine they wanted to work on each day—depending upon how they felt—and rotating into different jobs throughout the day to keep them alive and creative. We developed other payment systems, too... a *piece rate* (like one cent per cut on the table saw) and a *contract* system so that employees could bid on one whole job and perform that job over a week or two in any manner they wanted. These four payment systems enabled our employees not only to choose what they wanted to do each day but how they wanted to be paid for it. It also contributed to a lot of innovation in the production process. At first employees feared we'd take advantage of them if they found a way to improve productivity. Our solution was to vote the inventor a higher rate of pay depending upon his contribution.

Our payment system gives us a lot of flexibility. For example, in those first years, we'd have no orders and then suddenly an order for 100 units...due *yesterday!* We were always building up our work force and then collapsing it back like an accordion; you couldn't afford to hang on to ten or twelve employees but you hated to lose depth by cutting back to only one or two. So we started looking for odd jobs to keep the factory busy. We got into the business of making trophy plaques and other special order items in wood; we'd under-bid and bank on our ingenuity to improve efficiency. Our contract payment system enabled us to be a broker for our employees' labor. They bid on the job to us; we bid on it to the customer.

Presently, most of the people have elected the hourly rate. They say it was too nerve-wracking to have their earnings tied to production...they wanted to know what next week's pay would be regardless of how they felt or how fast they worked. Some thought the quota system was too demanding and too competitive. The speedy employees would start at 7:00 a.m., go straight through with no breaks, and leave at noon. Others, who maybe lacked the ability to work like that, had a slight uneasiness about it. Still, we are way ahead of competition in terms of productivity. Our cost savings are not very apparent because we're always running out of work or having to design a new jig or interrupt the production process for a crisis order. But there's one unionized woodshop nearby and I'm told their contract specifies an operator limit of 800 cuts on the rip saw per day. We get 2,000 cuts per day on ours without straining. Actually unions periodically come and talk about organizing the factory. The workers listen, but reject unionization because they feel they have better conditions, wages, and benefits now than they would with the union.

The key to our production process is Michael. He and our mechanic, Jeff, have made most of the big production innovations. Michael keeps us all together...He's part school teacher, part fire fighter, part therapist. He's only got an elementary school education but he's a genius. We've never had a conflict. I've never given him a command...we just understand each other.

GROWTH AND THE PRODUCT LINE

Throughout 1968 and 1969, the Four Generations product line grew rapidly. A large proportion of the product designs were contributed by Dick Benton and plant foreman, Michael Gonzalez. In addition, the firm's unusual organization and style of management enabled and encouraged employees to participate in the design process. The factory was open after hours and on weekends for employee use; scrap lumber was made available free of charge. A number of important ideas and projects have resulted from work force involvement with the factory. Employees have created new products and innovative production methods, and have built facilities such as a sauna and shower. At the end of 1969, there were thirty-two items in the product line, ranging from wheeled toys to blocks, easels, toy boats, and geometric puzzles. Every item was made of wood and offered in seven different finishes.

We did nearly all our $20,000 in sales in 1969 in the last four months, said Benton. Michael and I were really deluged. It was just about impossible to handle production and selling too. That's why when Bill Moore approached me and expressed an interest in selling for us, I almost hugged him. I had to play a little coy since he was interested in participating in the ownership as well as helping us sell. But I felt like giving him half the firm in return for a little assistance. Bill joined us early in 1970.

As soon as Bill arrived, he started to push the toys. We made him a wooden display box in the plant, loaded up with toys and he headed off to the toy shows in Chicago and New York. Lots of stores—big stores like Macy's and Bloomingdale's and Marshall Field's—made good opening orders. But it never developed into big volume business. We had also gone after kindergartens and nursery schools but that's a very limited market too. The problem is that parents buy toys as a result of a verbal exchange with the child. The child decides what he wants as a result of what his peers have or what he sees on "Captain Kangaroo." So the parent as an act of self-protection buys the item—even if he knows he'll be lucky to get it home before it breaks. Of course, this is not true for the infant market. In that segment, what the parent buys is sort of a function of "keeping up with the Joneses." For a while, Creative Playthings was "in". . .and that helped our business. But the problem remained that our product line looked like a kindergarten. We opened up a store in Ghirardelli Square during Christmas in 1969 and people came in not to buy things but to *leave their children.* They thought our store was a day care facility provided by the Ghirardelli merchants!

Michael, in addition to developing toys, had come up with some ingenious adult games. As always, we were looking for something to offset the seasonality of production during the post-Christmas slump, so Bill took four of our best games to Skor-Mor—one of the largest adult game manufacturers. They were enthusiastic but they wanted an exclusive. As the negotiations proceeded, they kept lowering the price. We were faced with a tough choice and finally decided to build up a network of jobbers and go it on our own. By the close of 1970, our sales had reached $97,000. . .and 80 percent of it was in games. We discovered we had stumbled into a new field; adult games put us in a brand new ball game.

As 1970 unfolded, we planned to have two separate lines—toys and adult games. But by the end of that year, I decided. . .or maybe the group decided. . .not to make toys any more. It was an agonizing decision. But we had lost $20,000 in 1970 and you come to a point where if you want to survive you've got to do something. By all rights, the company should have been dead a long time ago. Until you reach a certain volume, there is no economical way to buy raw materials, you can't buy efficient equipment or manage time and production effectively. It's all piecemeal and it's hell on our labor force. You get a guy for a rush job, then you find out he's skilled so you try to keep him, and when production slackens overhead goes up; or you let him go and then encounter training and recruiting delays during the next crisis.

I wanted a line that would really grow to a company. I could have made it as a mom and pop operation with one or two items but I didn't want to do it that way. I don't want a mommy-daddy shop. I want a business and an organization with secretaries, a marketing manager, a treasurer. . .with literature and catalogues.

All during 1969 we were getting orders for one tractor, one set of blocks, two rattles; in the factory it was sort of "you do this, I'll do that." What you need is a line where people say "I'll take 100 of these." Then you can buy the automated equipment. We were finally able to purchase an automatic sander this year. I designed it from scratch and it cost $25,000. But at peak capacity of 5,000 units per day it replaces ten people.

I think the climate we've created here is important. We're probably the most innovative company in adult games in the United States. Michael has invented most of the games that we have developed internally. More recently, we have been approached by game designers from the outside who have heard of our reputation. We invite them out here and invariably they like the place. They tour the plant and sense the atmosphere and feel comfortable. What a designer wants is a place that will give his idea love and care. If they go to Parker Brothers or Skor-Mor they get to sit and tremble in a waiting room until some executive summons them to present their prototype. Here they feel safe.

MARKETING
Marketing manager Bill Moore joined Four Generations in early 1970. As one of three major stockholders in the firm, he has watched the sales grow from $20,000 in 1969 to $97,000 in 1970, to $170,000 in 1971, and to an estimated $300,000 in 1972.

I got involved right after the 1969 season [says Moore]. At that time, Dick had been selling strictly to preschool education programs. The real problem was to transform those toys to a volume product once the preschool market was too limited. . .we needed retail sales. I decided to do a market survey. We were making toys of birch. . .but for the retail market, this type of toy didn't really have a lot of appeal. We realized we couldn't make it out of plastic and compete with Mattel. It was clear that our target was the educated parent. So we decided to try to make a toy that would be useful to the child but appeal to the adult. We started making toys out of black walnut and other more decorative woods. We geared our selling to better stores and tried to have our products displayed so they would catch the adult's eyes and appeal to the parent who wanted to give his child a fine, lasting thing of beauty. We went to the toy shows and had reasonable success—we got a few in Marshall Field's catalog, several of the big national chains picked them up, and we sold a number to specialty shops.

Throughout this period, we hadn't done much with the games Michael had invented. I decided to see if I could peddle a few. One of the first of the big game outfits I showed it to—Skor-Mor—offered to buy 10,000 each of three of our games. They wanted an exclusive and their margins were tight. They would be putting their name on it—not ours. So after a lot of sweating, we decided to turn them down and try it on our own. That was a big decision—to turn down an order for 30,000 games. Instead, we went out to build a network of eighteen manufacturers representatives. Fortunately, our product was good and by the fall of 1970, we were deluged with orders of games. As the games began to take off, several things became clear. First, they were twice as profitable as toys. Secondly, they were far easier for us to produce. Toys were slow to build and handle and they took up so much more space. In a small factory like this, big toys with lots of parts and assembly operations really tie everything up. We can manufacture a lot more games under the same roof.

In 1971, we decided to come out with some new games. Once again, virtually all of them were invented by Michael Gonzalez. . .games like Odd Ball, Revolutions, and Sculpture Puzzle. [See Exhibit 2b.] They were good sellers, but with hindsight I think we're encountering many of the same problems with them that we had with toys. They require multiple operations and lots of handwork. Next year we'll be coming out with games with some wood and some plastic parts.

We made tremendous inroads in 1971 with our adult games—we sold them to Sears, Bloomingdale's, Lord & Taylor, Joseph Magnin, Gimbel's, and elsewhere. We did this despite the important disadvantage of being a small firm with a limited line. Skor-Mor or Parker Brothers can walk into a store and offer them a whole game *system*. If the buyer accepts the package, he usually doesn't have much left for extra items like ours.

At the end of the year we took a look and saw that games were just about as seasonal as toys. Our games are good, but they're sold primarily at Christmas time—bought more as gifts than by the end-user himself. We also found a market among big firms that would special order our games for Christmas giveaways. This was good business but it didn't help the seasonal problem.

For a company to grow in a seasonal business you need a lot of cash in a big chunk and you don't get it back until much later. You need the cash to build up inventories for the Christmas season. But ours isn't exactly the kind of inventory you can borrow a lot of money on....A banker looks at us and says, "why do I want to own 10,000 Magic Marbles?" It's not the same as 10,000 gallons of gasoline or similar commodities that are easy to liquidate.

We tried to keep our good games but wanted to add something else to level production. One partial solution was to add a line of classic games in 1971. Presently, we are making poker chips, cribbage boards, and a domino set in a wooden box. These products account for nearly half our sales, and we plan to introduce chess sets in 1973. We're also making cutting boards and spice racks. We sell our spice racks as an exclusive to Spice Islands. At one point, we got into the trophy thing but it didn't fit our factory. Trophies come in jillions of sizes and shapes, they are ordered in small quantities and with lots of specials...and invariably there is an impossible deadline. We found that they had an insidious way of altering our whole production process. We've discontinued them.

Over time I guess we have evolved a product philosophy. We are offered lots of things and we try to select those things which fit our style. Basically, we market products that hit the top of the middle price range; we design our products to be attractive and nicely done...but at a good volume range. We'd make a $30 chess set but not a $100 one; on the other hand, we wouldn't make a $10 chess set either.

One real nightmare for us has been costing. Take the Euclidian Puzzle—it's a $20.00 thing except that our costing wasn't too good and it sold like hot cakes for $5.00 retail. Our rule of thumb around here—if we can figure out what an item costs—is to sell it at two times its variable cost. I think these costing problems are some of the reason why we still lost $40,000 in 1971 despite the fact that our sales doubled to $170,000. Another problem is that you need a large revenue to cover overhead—you need people like Dick and me and Mike and Jeff to run the operation but it takes a lot of sales to cover it.

Our sales projections as a whole have been quite accurate. The aggregate demand projections are right, but projections for individual products are all wrong. Here we are at the end of 1972 and we have stocked out on several items—but we have 5000 of one game I have no idea what to do with.

Reflecting on the overall operation, Marketing Manager Bill Moore made the following comments:

Dick and I handle the external affairs of this company. On the manufacturing side, things are done in a way so that our employees can make a statement. It makes sense to try to run a factory where employees get a feeling of being more than just a number. If someone asks me what I do, I tell them I work for a company which manufactures games and puzzles. I really don't get into the way we operate. Our employees are free, creative-type people who are in an environment that achieves higher rates of production than in a typical factory. They are more willing to change jobs as our production needs change and to get behind things. Everything gets done just like in any factory but we don't make one guy work one machine for a year. But management's job is to make a product—not create a happening.

RECENT PRODUCT IDEAS

One interesting development in 1972 appeared to result from Four Generations' expanding reputation as an innovator in adult games. Game designers began to approach the firm with various ideas. One well-known designer presented five new games, two of which were added to the product line. Both of these games offered the potential of high volume sales but were prohibitively expensive if totally made of wood. As a result, wood and plastic combinations were developed—a first for Four Generations. Even more recently, the firm had been approached by an inventor in Oregon whose mysterious "perpetually spinning top" (see Exhibit 3) captured the imagination of management. This item, made with no wooden parts, was to be manufactured entirely outside Four Generations premises. Four Generations had contributed the product's name and packaging, and had entered into a licensing agreement to distribute the product for the inventor. Originally, the product's name was to have been "Black Magic." But just before the promotional material was sent to press, a member of the Four Generations workforce entered the office, picked up the new product, and dubbed it "Top Secret."

COMPETITION

The adult puzzle game market was highly fragmented and comprised of many small firms—most of them privately held. Skor-Mor, one of the larger firms in this segment, had sales in excess of $2 million in 1972. The total market was estimated to be about $50 million. No published market projections were available; however, major competitors expected continued rapid expansion.

Skor-Mor contracted out production of its product line. The company's 1972 catalog was a 5 x 8 inch brochure featuring descriptions and color photographs of about 35 puzzle games, 15 desk-top accessories, 11 boxed games, and numerous novelty items. The catalog was used in department store advertising. Skor-Mor would supply its brochures (with the store's name on the cover) for inclusion with the store's other mailings—if the store would place a minimum order. Thus Skor-Mor created a competitive advantage in getting shelf and display space.

I've never been sure exactly how much money I've put into the company [said President Benton]. It's probably around $60,000. I sold my house, my car, my stocks, my boat—everything I owned plus all the earnings from Design Systems. But even that wasn't enough. In 1969, we went for three or four months with no income. We had to raise money so I went to friends and raised $1,000 here, another $5,000 there...it's all on a little list somewhere. Someday they'll be stockholders.

When Bill Moore came on board, he invested in the firm. All in all, by early 1970, we had raised an additional $70,000. Our biggest problem is that 80 percent of our sales occur in the last four months of the year. It's hard to borrow on our inventory...and besides, I've never enjoyed doing business with banks. They want a lot of financial information. Financial statements are just not informative.

Under our circumstances, we've got to enter the market gradually. You need time and money to build up big inventories and we certainly lack the latter. I think we're also afraid to have high hopes. Top Secret could be a big seller this season but you can't really intelligently plan for a bonanza. And for too many years we've had too much capacity, too many items so it wouldn't bother me to have $100,000 in unfilled orders.

Maybe some of our financial problems will be ironed out now that John Kellog has come on board as our treasurer and production control man. John became an investor in 1971 and also wanted to be involved in management. With his investment and outside help, we raised another $70,000. Altogether now, we probably have around $200,000 in the firm. John also helped us borrow $75,000 so we could build up a little pre-Christmas inventory. The trouble still remains, however: our games sell about 8,000 units per year and we need a volume of 30,000 to 40,000 per year to really take advantage of volume. With automatic production equipment we could make 8,000 units in six to eight days—but what's the sense of buying automatic equipment for those kinds of runs—and besides, you don't dare ever run off 8,000 because you're never sure you'll sell them. And on top of that, you can't afford to put all the capital into one big piles of boxes...so instead you make 2,000 units which is uneconomical; you can't spread the set-up cost with small batches and you have to use unsophisticated equipment which takes twice as long to do the job.

Perhaps we will find the volume somewhere. We expect 50 percent of our sales this year to come from first-time products—like Top Secret, Impasse, and Tau. But because they are new, all the set-ups will be first—and that means money. It's a real problem for us...generating the cash to build inventories. Maybe Top Secret will do it. But most of the other nonseasonal stuff just hasn't made it. Take the chopping boards—a great idea but they require a whole different distribution network. They're gifts—not games. They just haven't worked for us.

PRODUCTION

In 1971, John Kellog, with a master's degree in history and experience as office manager of a small midwestern printing firm, joined the management team of Four Generations. As part of a package, he took a stock option, lent the firm $50,000, and assumed the responsibilities of production control and bookkeeping:

It's hell just keeping the plant going. If I had known more about manufacturing, I certainly would have thought twice. There's always a crisis. In September, as we were building up for the Christmas rush, we had no increase in productivity but a 40 percent increase in labor. What had happened is that we added people to work on the last of the trophy contracts and there was quite a bit of down time.

We take a month-by-month look at percent of labor; some months it's good and some months it's terrible. It's very hard for us to get cost figures in the plant. We've been very reluctant to ask people to make out detailed time cards. But last month I finally asked one of the secretaries to do it. She asks people how many units they produced and keeps her eye on her watch. We can't tell yet how the employees are taking it; those who resent it she just leaves alone. If we can get some cost figures, I think we can drop some products. Sculpture Puzzle is a likely candidate.

October has been a great month...almost too good to be true. A partial reason is that we're making cribbage boards and poker chip holders and both items lend themselves to smooth production. One requires the saw and gang drill, the other uses the drill press and the router. Between the two, we make good use of the whole shop. I still think it will take sales in excess of $500,000 to get the volumes we need. It's tough competition in the mass-production business and over time we are going to need steadier production and mass-production equipment to keep up.

The big dividend of this labor force is its flexibility. These people can really adjust to changes in mid-stream. Last year we had a fire which destroyed the old plant. Our employees helped us find a new location, pitched in, and moved the machines to the new site. We were back in production in four days. We have virtually no absenteeism. There is more turnover than we'd like but most of it is management-caused. People want to stay but we can't keep production steady. Over time, I think we're getting more employee specialization by department. We're also getting into plastics—but all that work is done by outside contractors.

EMPLOYMENT

The size of the Four Generations staff varies with the seasonal needs of the firm. In November, 1971, Four Generations employed 33 people; in February, 1973, there were 12. The staff normally includes one or two secretaries. If layoffs or shutdowns are necessary, the employees and the management decide who will have to leave. Decisions are made on the basis of the company's needs, the employees' experience, and the employees' needs. As one worker noted, "Obviously an employee who has twelve kids won't get laid off."

A decision affecting employment would normally be made at one of the company meetings. These meetings may be called by anyone who thinks the factory has something to discuss. Meetings are held on company time and may last from five minutes to several hours; discussion centers around topics such as production problems, layoffs, information, new products, or complaints.

OPERATIONS

Michael Gonzalez is the foreman for Four Generations. He joined Benton in early 1968 and has been part of the company ever since. Different people have held the job of foreman—"stage manager"—at different times. In the fall of 1971, at the time of the film, Mike Byers was plant manager. After about a month, Byers decided he did not want to be plant manager. Michael Gonzalez, the head designer (whose paintings were shown in the film), took on the job.

I direct the product [says Gonzalez], I'm not really a manager. In six months people should know all the operations, and I let them do it. If we have to shut down a machine for some reason, I tell the person, "we need to do something else" and they understand that. I try to get people to do the care and feeding of their machines, and to learn to set up the machines themselves. The pace of work around here depends a lot on how big a hurry we're in. It changes every day. We try to set the pace to get the job done. The mood of the day sets the tune, the pace. I don't push it, usually, but I can affect it in one of two ways: (1) by talking to people individually, saying "be careful, but we need the product," or (2) play the role of "foreman" but with a smile—we all laugh at that. Some days it's hard for the group to get into things. Jeff and I normally do the set-ups. We use the blackboard: "today we have to produce so much." As long as everyone knows what has to happen and how to take care of the machines, everything's o.k.

A foreman elsewhere has no feelings at all, it's just the schedule and machine. Most foremen have no sense for the "mood of the day." I was a foreman once for the Forest Service. There was no feeling; if a guy was having a slow day, I'd just get rid of him. It was a strange job, sort of numbing.

Let's face it, workers have problems. I get involved a lot with each person; talk about things like their problems at home. Sometimes I give them advice that has nothing to do with company or job. We're all friends. I suppose in one sense our hiring is super-select. We let our employees walk in off the street, and they tend to weed themselves out. Free-loaders get laid off. And the workers who stay tend to have an interest, commitment; they make friends, and share the same feelings. Of course, everyone isn't the same. One guy likes to work, but he's a loner. When he's far away from other people it makes him happy. He often works at night.

We're all trying to get the product out. If one guy is not working, then why should others? He usually gets bad vibes from the rest and eventually leaves. Sometimes I have to give a freeloader a warning—tell him he's not moving. If the guy is surly, I'm surly. I make the decisions on firing.

Stores send in orders and a summary is sent down to give me an idea of how much is needed. Schedules change weekly, even daily. I'm usually running four projects at a time. We run whatever's on the machine, and when a machine is open, I find something else to use it. Of course, that means having Jeff set it up, and finding someone to operate it. All our games require several operations. I follow through, and move the parts from machine to machine when they are done. I made some carts in which the pieces are stacked and can be easily moved from machine to machine. You've probably noticed the carts have big spray-painted letters on them (Y, Q, Z); maybe someday we'll have a whole alphabet!

People have their own way of expressing themelves. Some make their own products after hours and earn a little extra income. New ideas are welcome here; if someone has a good idea, we'll try it. I also encourage their learning on each machine. Most foremen are on a power trip, they like to control other people.

When there's confusion as to what's happening around here we hold meetings. Some people like them, others don't. I think they're very useful. We hold them during the day—on work time. It doesn't come out of employee time as it might in other companies. Most people are now on the hourly system. Jeff and I are the only salaried production employees.

I suppose we're like a family. I'm sort of an "older brother." When you're tuned into someone they get a direct message. Understanding matters, I try to be "just there" where the other person is at. Where the company will be in two or five years depends on which people stay, and who takes an interest in running the show.

I worry about us growing like other companies. We would have to speed up beyond the mood of the day. If we want to keep a mellow feeling here we have to be human about production. So it takes us one or two years longer to get there. As it is, I think our manufacturing operations could be twice as big without having bad changes in the climate as long as we can find people that work well in this system. But the majority of people can't work in this system. A lot of people don't care. Here we're into learning—machines, wood, other people. Some people hear about that and want to be part of it.

I'm here every day at 8 a.m. and I usually leave at midnight. I work on my own projects from 5 p.m. until midnight and that also helps me keep in contact with the people on the night shift. There are usually other day people here doing their own projects. Just about everyone has a project. We let employees take the scrap lumber. Recently, Dick felt we were giving too much away so lately we've been selling some of the scrap. The rest, people can still use.

I guess the main reason I'm not bored here after four years is that all my friends are here. I can do my own thing—all the machines are available after five. I know that certain things won't happen if I leave. But I will leave in January. I want to do my own thing. I'm into sculpture, and design, and want to set up a kind of studio. Actually, it will be more like a free school, where little kids, adults, and old people can come in and do their own things.

I suppose if we hadn't stopped making toys we wouldn't be alive. Games are easy to produce; they sell, and we grow from that. The toys were complex. They had many more parts and all the parts had to match exactly. We were nonwoodworkers then; we could do it better now. Actually, I'd like to convince Dick to try toys again. Toys were a joy—you'd walk into the finishing room and see a truck and it turned you on. It's energizing to think of kids playing with something you made. Games are less exciting in that respect. I suppose that's why I'm looking forward to my own studio.

There's another really important thing about the place. There's a freedom to leave the company, work for someone else, and be able to come back. There are no hassles from any direction. If someone needs to come back, they can. One of my fears about leaving is that set rules and regimentation might evolve as an alternative to current operations. Sometimes I really don't want to leave this place, for the sake of making sure that doesn't happen. But there's me, which is equally important.

INTERVIEW WITH JEFFERSON RICE, MECHANIC

The place is changing. Michael and I have been here from the beginning. It was different then. With toys you could see it come to life. . .you took a wide plank and made it narrow, shortened it, drilled and shaped it. . .it all went together in stages. There weren't so many people then, either, so you had to switch jobs on the line—and everyone could do everything. It's less and less that way now, people don't switch as much. . .and anyway, there are far fewer operations.

It's not nearly as personal as it used to be making the bus. Take that new game Tau: there are seven pegs for each side and each has two plastic caps which means 28 cappings per game. Now we've got an order for 1000 and that means putting on 28,000 caps: that's a real bummer. Basically, I think it's a lot more fun to play with a toy than trying to get a marble out of a hole.

THE FUTURE

Despite prospects of further change, management looks forward to significant sales growth in 1973. The introduction of traditional games such as Cribbage offers a hedge against seasonality and these products are seen as within Four Generations' established market segment. The new additions among the innovative games (Tau, Impasse, Top Secret) are all projected to have considerable growth potential.

Planning is almost impossible in this business [said President Benton]. I guess I don't live too much in the future because I like the "now" too much. It's too unpredictable a business to think much about projections. . .and I know from history that we can overcome any obstacle. It just depends upon our ability to expend energy and effort. Maybe someday I'll be interested in becoming a publicly held firm. But maybe that will have to wait until I get bored with what I'm doing now.

At the end of the case, no detailed financial information was available although a rough pro forma income statement was used to project cash flow. As of November, 1972, no monthly sales projections had been made for 1973. Monthly projections were believed to be too imprecise to be useful although management expected sales to exceed $500,000 in the coming year.

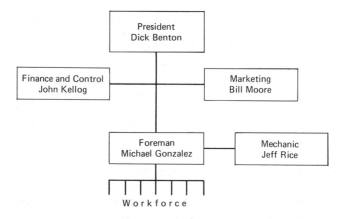

Exhibit 1.   Four Generations Organization Chart.

Exhibit 2(a). Four Generations Current Products.

| **Magic Marble**   Cat. No. 203 | **New Tic Tac Toe**   Cat. No. 205 |

Magic Marble   Cat. No. 203

Drop the marble into the internal maze and then attempt to remove the marble by shaking, tipping or rotating the walnut block. You'll need your sense of touch and hearing with some logic to be successful.

4" x 4" x 1¾"

Plunging Peg   Cat. No. 204

Eight pegs that fit into four holes of different lengths. There are over 2500 ways to replace them, but only two combinations will result in the tops all being level. Six other games are shown on the box.

4" x 4" x 1¼"

New Tic Tac Toe   Cat. No. 205

A beautiful black walnut playing base with an internal storage for the eight black and white playing marbles and instructions on how to play a new way.

4" x 4" x 1¾"

Shrewd Move   Cat. No. 207

A mathematical game for two people that is easy enough for the young, but complex enough for anybody. A solid black walnut base with fifteen solid steel balls.

4" x 4" x 1¼"

African Stone Game   Cat. No. 208

Natural oil finish on black walnut with authentic ocean bottom smooth stones for playing pieces. A classic game from Africa for all ages.

24" x 5" x 1"

Exhibit 2(b). Four Generations Current Products.

Odd Ball Cat. No. 209	**Gravity Trap** Cat. No. 214

Odd Ball   Cat. No. 209

A dexterity, manipulation game. There are nine marbles trapped within a black walnut block. The object of the game is to move the marbles around so that all of one color are in one chamber and all of another color are in the second chamber.

4" x 4" x 1¾"

Gravity Trap   Cat. No. 214

A handsome black walnut block and three steel balls combine to challenge anyone's mental and physical ability. The three balls can be trapped within the block if you put them in just right and if you don't, gravity will get them.

4" x 4" x 1¾"

Revolutions   Cat. No. 210

A black walnut block with a large hole in the center and two internal grooves. The object is to place the two marbles in separate grooves and move the block in such a manner that the marbles rotate around the inside of the block in the grooves in opposite directions.

4" x 4" x 1¾"

Level Learner   Cat. No. 211

The pegs are all different lengths, and the holes in the playing block are all different depths. The large pegs are easy to hold and a child will learn about depth and measuring while playing with this instructional toy.

12" x 3" x 1¾"

Sculpture Puzzle   Cat. No. 212

This is a sculpture for the place where you live and a puzzle to challenge your patience. All you have to do is drop the small sphere on the large sphere until, in one drop, the small sphere will jump into the small hole...and then without moving the block of wood in any manner, retrieve the small sphere.

4" x 4" x 1¾"

Exhibit 2(c). Four Generations Current Products.

Poker Chip Rack, Small   8" x 4" x 2"
120 Chips   Cat. No. 217

Solid American Walnut in a unique design packed with either 240, or 120 quality poker chips. Stores easily and looks handsome on the shelf.

Poker Chip Rack, Large   16" x 4" x 2"
240 Chips   Cat. No. 218

Large Deluxe Cribbage Board
16" x 4" x 2"   Cat. No. 216

A beautiful, sculptured, solid American Walnut traditional cribbage board. Six aluminum and brass pegs included.

Deluxe Cribbage Board
16" x 4" x ¾"   Cat. No. 216A

Sculptured with the same lines as the Large Deluxe board in select dark hardwoods. Six handsome playing pegs included.

Walnut Domino Box   9" x 6" x 2½"
Red   Cat. No. 219
Ivory   Cat. No. 220

A hand crafted, carefully fitted solid Walnut box with traditional beauty. Lined with a soft velvet-like material and containing a full double six set of superb professional dominoes in either red or ivory.

Large Dominoes with Gift Box   8" x 5" x 1"
Red   Cat. No. 221
Ivory   Cat. No. 222

Large size, extra thick, marblelike Dominoes. A double six set in either red or ivory. Packed in an attractive white and silver gift box.

Regular Dominoes with Gift Box
Ivory   7" × 4" × 1"   Cat. No. 223

Regular size, thick, marble-like smooth Dominoes, a double six set packed in an attractive white and black gift box in ivory only.

Exhibit 2(d). Four Generations Current Products.

Tau	12" × 5" × 1"	Cat. No. 213

A new and original game created by Philip Shoptaugh which is simple to play, yet broad enough to inspire deep thought and interesting tactics. The game is for two players who alternate turns in an attempt to place three playing sticks of the same color in a row. The game utilizes the six basic colors on the standard color wheel and players who do not already know the color wheel will learn much about the relationship of colors while enjoying a fascinating game. The base is solid walnut with 14 hardwood playing sticks all finished in natural oil and hand rubbed for a deep finish.

Gomoku (Japanese Five)	14" x 8" x 1½"
	Cat. No. 225

A traditional Japanese Folk game over 4,000 years old. Designed in select hardwoods with 78 playing pieces. A game of skill and logic for two people which can be studied for years, but can be played with ease in a few moments. The object of the game is to be the first player to place 5 pegs in a row.

Adult Game Set No. 2	12" x 4" x 2"
	Cat. No. 215

A gift set which includes Sculpture Puzzle, Odd Ball, and Shrewd Move, in an attractive silver and black gift box. Includes instructions.

Impasse	10" × 8" × 1"
	Cat. No. 224

An original game created by Philip Shoptaugh for those people who like games of skill and action. This new game is played by two people and can be learned in a few minutes. Players attempt to be the first to move their marbles across a movable board. Your oppenent can trap your marble and cause you many extra moves. Strategy and skill are required to win consistently. The playing base is solid walnut with a hand rubbed, penetrating oil finish.

Adult Game Set No. 1	12" x 4" x 2"
	Cat. No. 206

A gift set which includes Magic Marble, Plunging Peg and the New Tic Tac Toe in an attractive silver and black box. Includes instructions.

Exhibit 3. Four Generations.

Introducing "Top Secret"

We know it's late but this promises to be one of the top sellers of the year. Our market testing in the California area shows excellent public acceptance. Its quality is typical of our products. If you display this item near your register it will attract a great deal of attention and increase your sales. Order a dozen or more now! Product is in stock. Immediate delivery is assured.

What Is It?

A deep, rich black base with a concave top surface on which a small Saturn shape spins like a top - well almost like a top - the Saturn spinner is started like a top - with your hand - but then the fun and mystery starts. Watch for a moment and suddenly you will realize that the top is moving faster and faster, until it reaches almost 2500 revolutions per minute - and it moves - it moves all over the top of the base in some strange irregular pattern - and it goes and goes - start it in the morning - it will still be running at night and the next morning and the next. Well for a long, long time. Maybe a month, maybe a year. As long as you own it you can make it work - for ever and that's fascinating, but that's all we can tell you because it's a "TOP SECRET."

Ordering Details

Top Secrets are packed in cases containing 12 pieces and weighing approximately 6 pounds.

No broken cases

Cost Per Case	$60.00
Suggested List Price	$ 9.95

Price F.O.B. Sebastopol, California

Exhibit 4. Four Generations Price List (February 1, 1972).

No.	Product	No. per case	Wt. per case	Case price	Cost each	Sug. List
203	Magic Marble	6	4 lbs.	$12.00	$ 2.00	$ 3.95
204	Plunging Peg	6	4	12.00	2.00	3.95
205	New Tic Tac Toe	6	4	12.00	2.00	3.95
206	Adult Game Set #1	4	9	24.00	6.00	11.95
207	Shrewd Move	6	5	15.00	2.50	4.95
208	African Stone Game	6	15	24.00	4.00	7.95
209	Odd Ball	6	4	15.00	2.50	4.95
210	Revolutions	6	4	12.00	2.00	3.95
211	Level Learner	6	9	15.00	2.50	4.95
212	Sculpture Puzzle	6	5	15.00	2.50	4.95
213	Tau—Available 6/1/72	6	7	24.00	4.00	7.95
214	Gravity Trap	6	4	12.00	2.00	3.95
215	Adult Game Set #2	4	10	30.00	7.50	14.95
216	Lg. Walnut Cribbage Board	6	16	24.00	4.00	7.95
217	Poker Chip Rack/120 Chips	3	5	9.00	3.00	5.95
218	Poker Chip Rack/240 Chips	3	8	16.50	5.50	10.95
219	Walnut Domino Box/Red dbl. 6	1	4	10.00	10.00	19.95
220	Walnut Domino Box/Ivory dbl. 6	1	4	10.00	10.00	19.95
221	Large dbl. 6 Dominoes-Red	3	6	13.50	4.50	8.95
222	Large dbl. 6 Dominoes-Ivory	3	6	13.50	4.50	8.95
223	Regular dbl. 6 Dominoes-Ivory	6	8	15.00	2.50	4.95
224	Impasse - Available 6/1/72	3	12	19.50	6.50	12.95

Minimum Order Case lots only
Freight F.O.B. Factory—Sebastopol, California
Terms 1% 10th Prox. EOM
Advertising Allowance 10% Cumulative from Jan. 1 through Dec. 31 annually, paid upon receipt of tear sheet.

Exhibit 5. Four Generations.

Games People Play Keep Manufacturers Optimistic

Throughout the year—every year, even during a recession—the kids have to play. More and more adults have found that they do, too, and the toy and game market has grown steadfastly through soft and hard economies.

Only twice in the last decade did annual sales drop off from the year before—in 1962 and 1967, by 3 percent and 4 percent respectively. Strong recoveries of 11 and 12 percent were made in the years immediately following the declines.

In 1970s recession, sales increased more than 5 percent and reached $1.35 billion. They should gain another 6 percent this year, says Penton Publishing Co.'s Research Div.

Casually optimistic. Toymakers are almost casually optimistic about their future. They see no end to the 8 to 12 percent annual growth rates they've been experiencing. (The figures provided by Penton do not include dolls or children's vehicles. Total toy industry statistics, which include these fast-growing products, show last year's sales at $2.26 billion, nearly 11 percent ahead of 1969.)

Several factors point to continued growth of the market, not the least of which is rising disposable income, which more than doubled in the sixties, and should grow another 35 percent between 1970 and 1975.

More subtly, a national attitude that favors playthings makes the purchase of these products almost inevitable.

TOYS AND GAMES
FIVE YEAR FORECAST

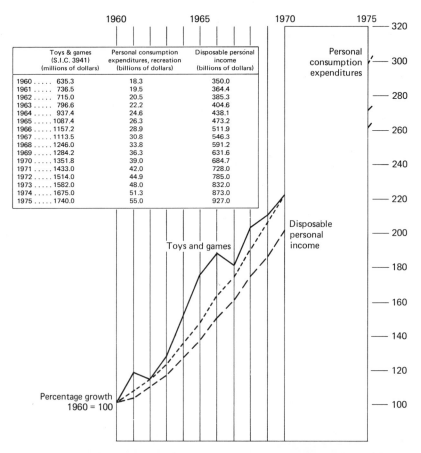

	Toys & games (S.I.C. 3941) (millions of dollars)	Personal consumption expenditures, recreation (billions of dollars)	Disposable personal income (billions of dollars)
1960	635.3	18.3	350.0
1961	736.5	19.5	364.4
1962	715.0	20.5	385.3
1963	796.6	22.2	404.6
1964	937.4	24.6	438.1
1965	1087.4	26.3	473.2
1966	1157.2	28.9	511.9
1967	1113.5	30.8	546.3
1968	1246.0	33.8	591.2
1969	1284.2	36.3	631.6
1970	1351.8	39.0	684.7
1971	1433.0	42.0	728.0
1972	1514.0	44.9	785.0
1973	1582.0	48.0	832.0
1974	1675.0	51.3	873.0
1975	1740.0	55.0	927.0

Exhibit 5. *cont'd.*

Consumer demands. In fact, Fred Ertl, president, Toy Manufacturers of America Inc. (New York), and president, Ertl Co. (Dyersville, Iowa), a subsidiary of Victor Comptometer Corp., maintains that toys and games comprise a new category of consumer products that defy current classification.

"They are not the necessities without which life could not exist," he says. "Nor are they luxuries which consumers are willing to curtail in emergencies. They are quite simply the goods and services people have decided they will not do without."

He cites last year's 10.7 percent sales gain at a time when consumer spending was sharply curtailed. That figure, he says, is "the industry's normal rate of gain—and it is a greater increase than can be accounted for by population growth."

For that reason, he "feels safe in predicting that 1971 will see another industry gain between 8 and 12 percent."

Major manufacturers agree with his forecast wholeheartedly. "Our increases will be the same as they have been—around 10 percent a year," says Don Knutzen, vice president, marketing, Parker Brothers Inc., Salem, Mass.

Monopoly proliferates. Games, he says, have a way of spurting on age. His firm's *Monopoly*, for instance, which is now 36 years old, has been selling better in each recent year than it did the year before. Total sales to date are somewhere around 70 million sets, and the game is played in 16 languages, he says.

Growth of leisure time, the move to the suburbs, and the shooting up of discount stores are all cited as having favorable effects on sales.

The leisure time effect is probably best exemplified in the growth of the hobby industry, where sales grew more than $100 million between 1968 and 1970, reaching about $850 million last year.

The mainstay of that segment of the toy industry is model kits. Last year, plastic models of all types accounted for $230 million of sales, reports the Hobby Industry Assn. of America Inc., New York. Nonplastic model sales of racing cars, railroads, planes, and boats reached $324 million.

"These kits are aimed at all age levels," the association says, "and the sales trend is more stable than the general toy industry because models appeal to all ages and to both sexes, and have an educational appeal."

Not obsolete. Model kits will hardly fade from popularity as do many toys. Manufacturers of games and toys have combated this problem in large measure by diversifying, however. Many maintain a careful balance between those toys with stable year-to-year demand, and those which can be related to fads.

Product obsolescence is becoming less of a problem, as is season. The toy industry, which used to experience extremely heavy seasonal (pre-Christmas) sales, has found the trend evening out in recent years. One spokesman estimates that pre-Christmas business used to account for nearly 75 percent of all sales, but is down now to about 60 percent.

"The nice thing about it," he says, "is that other seasons have not grown at the expense of Christmas business. Sales in the three months before Christmas have steadily increased, but the overall market all year around has increased even more."

RESEARCHER'S NOTE

Of the approximately $1.5 billion spent on toys and games in 1972, around $150 million was spent on adult games. Approximately one-third of this amount—or $50 million—was spent on adult puzzle games of the sort sold by Four Generations.

Casa Madrid, Ltd.

In late May, 1976, Jim Patterson received a telephone call from a close friend, Tom Leary. Tom was obviously excited about a new venture he was helping to put together. After commenting on two other ventures the two of them were participating in, Tom immediately launched into an explanation of the new deal.

The proposition Tom outlined involved a real estate partnership based in Houston. Tom was to be one of the general partners. Jim, if he decided to participate, would be one of the limited partners. The outline of the plan given by Tom sounded interesting enough that Jim asked for more details. Tom said he would send a detailed outline (which follows) as well as the partnership agreements. Further discussion between the two included a dollar figure that Jim felt comfortable with for his share of the partnership. They concluded the conversation with tentative plans to try to get together during the summer.

Jim thought about the deal, sporadically, for the next few days. He trusted Tom's judgment on real estate matters, but had to consider whether he could afford placing more of his capital in a risk venture at this time. Jim had participated in two previous ventures initiated by Tom since they had attended business school together. One had turned out quite well. The other had run into some difficulty.

A few days after the conversation, the following information arrived in the mail. It was the detailed outline promised by Tom.

INTRODUCTION

Casa Madrid, Ltd., a Texas Limited Partnership, is being formed to acquire a twelve-year-old, 124-unit garden apartment complex containing 4.19 acres and .575 acres of fee and leasehold land respectively with two swimming pools known as Casa Madrid, located at 803 East Grand Avenue.

A total of $320,000 will be contributed to the partnership to purchase the units which will be subject to two first notes and deeds of trust totaling approximately $574,199 at closing with annual payments of $98,575 including interest at 7 percent.

CASA MADRID

Casa Madrid is an existing 124-unit garden apartment development containing 16 two-story buildings with 95,604 rentable net square feet. There are 72 one bedroom-one bath, 44 two bedroom-1 ½ bath, and 8 two bedroom studio units. Each apartment has either a patio or balcony. The project has laundry and storage facilities. The exteriors of the buildings are brick veneer and wood shingle with wood trim, and the roofs are built up. Each apartment is equipped with a refrigerator, range and oven, carpet and drapes, and a dishwasher and disposal.

The complex is located on East Grand Avenue approximately ten miles to the south of downtown Houston and near the intersection of the Gulf Freeway (I-45) and Loop 610 (I-610), two of the major freeways in the metropolitan Houston area. East

Prepared by Hugh K. Tirrell with assistance from William Naumes. Case material is prepared for course discussion purpose only. It is not intended to demonstrate either good or bad administrative decisions.

Grand Avenue is a major street with a high traffic count, and Casa Madrid with its lush landscaping has excellent curb appeal and has historically enjoyed a very high occupancy. The complex is only two miles from the Gulfgate shopping center, one of the largest in the Houston area. The immediate neighborhood is middle class.

HOUSTON

Houston is among the most rapidly growing metropolitan areas of the United States. The Houston SMSA (Standard Metropolitan Statistical Area) with an estimated 1975 population of 2,274,000, grew 35.4 percent in the past decade—a gain of 575,100. That was the highest growth rate and the second highest absolute increase among the 15 most populous SMSAs in the nation. In a study put out by "Sales Management Survey of Buying Power" in 1974, it was projected that for the 1974-1979 period, the Houston SMSA will rank first in both categories, with a growth rate two-thirds greater than second-ranking Dallas-Fort Worth. The City of Houston mirrors this growth. Population increased by 269,300—or 25.5 percent—during the last decade and stood at 1,430,000 in 1975, giving Houston the highest absolute increase and the second highest growth rate among nation's ten most populous cities.

Part of this growth rate is explained by the low cost of living in the Houston area. In a 1974 study by the Bureau of Labor Statistics, Houston ranked third lowest in family cost of living among 40 major cities at 89.8 percent of the U.S. Urban Average (San Francisco was seventh highest at 105.5 percent of average).

Another part of the growth is explained by the diversity and strength of the industries in the area. Houston ranks first nationally in total value added by petroleum manufacturing as it does in the petrochemical industry. During the past seven years over 150 companies have moved corporate headquarters, subsidiaries, divisions, or branch offices to Houston, accounting for the 75 percent increase in bank debits since 1971 in terms of constant dollars. Even during the 1974-1975 recession, Houston had a vibrantly expanding economy. From September 1974 to September 1975 it was one of only two major cities in the U.S. where the number of employed increased. The Houston employed increased 40,000 while the Seattle employed increased 2000.

For other interest projections, please refer to the tables which follow.

Houston Apartment Market

The population growth of approximately 1000 people per week, combined with a dramatic decrease in apartment completions during the last two years has turned apartment market into a very tight one. Al Narmore, executive vice president of the Houston Apartment Association, says that Houston can absorb 15,000 to 18,000 new units each year. He estimates that in the last two years only 14,000 have been completed. The rate of construction has picked up markedly, but the rental rates required for these new units to break even are estimated to be more than 20 percent above current market rents.

This tight market condition is prevalent in the Casa Madrid area. In March, 1976, the area was surveyed and of the 1440 units considered there were only 21 vacancies. With the exception of one small complex, all had asking rental rates approximately 20 percent above Casa Madrid's on a per-square-foot basis, indicating an ability to dramatically increase rents on the project.

THE PARTNERSHIP

Casa Madrid, Ltd. will consist of Limited Partners and four General Partners—
Thomas P. Leary, John H. Sears, Pat Day, and Franklin Schuyler. A total of
$320,000 will be contributed as follows:

Purchase of Units	$310,000.00
Closing Costs and Working Capital	10,000.00
Total	$320,000.00

For their services as real estate brokers in this transaction, Messrs. Leary, Sears, and
Day will be paid a $50,000.00 real estate commission. Upon closing, however, they
will lend the partnership this cash for the purposes of initiating the rehabilitation (see
"Rehabilitation"). They will receive an interest rate of 10 percent per annum on this
loan.

The Limited Partners will provide 100 percent of the cash required to close and
will receive a cumulative preferred 8 percent cash on cash return on their investment
after the interest on the above-mentioned note to Leary, Sears, and Day. Any returns
above this amount will be split 32 percent to the Limited Partners, 68 percent to the
General Partners. On the sale or refinancing of the property after paying off the
Leary, Sears, and Day notes the Limited Partners will receive 100 percent of the funds
until such time as they have received their capital back plus any arrearages there may
be in the preferred 8 percent cumulative return. All additional funds, if any, will be
split 32 percent to the Limited Partners and 68 percent to the General Partners. The
Limited Partners will receive 100 percent of the depreciation. If the Limited Partners
have not received their initial cash contribution back within 90 days from the date of
closing, the General Partners' interest in the cash flow and proceeds from sale or
refinancing will be reduced 3 percent per month until such time as the Limited
Partners receive their cash contributions back, this penalty to run for twelve months.
Therefore, should the Limited Partners not receive their initial cash contribution back
within fifteen months from date of closing, the General Partners' subordinated
interest would be reduced by 36 percentage points to 32 percent. The penalty will be
reduced pro rata with the amount returned to the Limited Partners if a full return is
not made within the prescribed 90 day period. Therefore, if the Limited Partners
should receive half of their cash contribution back, the penalty would be 1½ percent
per month for a maximum of twelve months. The General Partners' subordinated
interest would then be reduced 10 percentage points to 50 percent.

Any contribution by any of the General Partners will be treated as though they
had contributed as Limited Partners and will be entitled to the preferred returns
mentioned above.

In addition, the Partnership will hire the General Partners to manage the property. The fee will be 5 percent of the gross proceeds generated by the property. For this
fee the General Partners will perform all of the functions performed by competing
management companies including, but not limited to: personnel hiring and
supervision, accounting, capital improvement budgeting, marketing. The General
Partners have the right to assign all or part of this fee, which takes precedence over the
Limited Partners' preferred return. The General Partners will receive no other fees

except those mentioned above except for Mr. Schuyler who will be paid $5,000.00 to supervise the anticipated rehabilitation program.

The General Partners

Thomas P. Leary is a graduate of Northwestern University and the Stanford University Graduate School of Business. He worked for two years for Loeb, Rhoades & Co., investment bankers in New York, and for three years in corporate finance for the Prudential Insurance Company, making investments in about 15 West Coast companies. In real estate, Mr. Leary is a licensed California Real Estate Broker and the founder of a company which owns six restaurants operated by Victoria Stations, Inc. The company presently has an income of over $400,000.00 per year. In addition, Mr. Leary has worked for Eastdil Realty in New York and Consolidated Capital in Oakland analyzing real estate for possible acquisition.

John Sears is a graduate of U.C. Berkeley and the Stanford University Graduate School of Business. He has worked for various firms as a mechanical engineer and electrical engineer. For the past ten years Mr. Sears has been actively involved in the ownership and management of Houston apartments, having a major interest in eight Houston apartment complexes. He is a licensed Texas Real Estate Broker and a principal in the brokerage firm known as Sears & Day as well as a management company.

Pat Day is a lawyer and licensed Real Estate Broker in the state of Texas and a principal of the brokerage firm Sears & Day. He has had approximately ten years of construction and real estate experience.

Franklin Schuyler is a licensed Real Estate Broker in the state of Texas. He has owned and managed Houston apartments for about ten years. He, in addition to the projects he owns, is managing a 200+ unit complex not far from Casa Madrid for absentee owners.

REHABILITATION

In order to maximize the value of the project and dramatically increase rents, the Limited Partnership anticipates expending approximately $150,000 in capital improvements including reasphalting the driving surfaces, replacing about 50 percent of the carpets, drapes, and dishwashers, covering over the painted wood shingles with long-lasting composition shingles which will require no maintenance. A complete list of the planned improvements and their costs, most of them gotten through bids, accompanies this memorandum. It is anticipated that the rehabilitation will commence immediately and be completed 90 days from date of closing.

Economics and Refinancing

The Partnership is buying the property for $7,129 per unit, $9.25 per square foot and 3.27 times gross rental revenue. This price appears to be substantially under the complex's economic value. An appraisal dated May 20, 1973, done by a large, reputable firm, Real Property Analysts, Inc., showed a value of $1,476,000 vs. our purchase price of approximately $884,000. This same firm has been contracted by Mr. Leary to update the appraisal. Assuming the Partnership's program of rehabilitation was carried out, Real Property Analysts, Inc. has issued a letter stating that in their opinion the complex would be worth $1,584,600. (A copy of this letter is attached.) The full appraisal report will be completed by June 1, 1976.

The General Partners have discussed the possibility of refinancing with a number of lenders and mortgage bankers in Houston, and the indication received was that a number would be very interested in refinancing the property if the Partnership made application once it had legally received title to the project. Most said that they would accept the appraisal of Real Property Analysts, Inc. as an indication of value and would probably lend 75 percent of that value at a rate of around 10 percent for 25 years. There might be a balloon payment in the tenth year. If this loan is available and if they accept the $1,584,600 valuation, this would indicate that a loan might be available for as much as $1,188,450. This would mean that the Partnership would not only receive the $320,000 in initial contributions plus the $150,000 in capital improvements, but as much as $188,000 to be used for working capital and payments to the Partners (Limited and General).

Currently the General Partners plan to file an application for such a loan immediately after closing the purchase. But there can be no guarantee that such loan funds will be available or in the magnitude mentioned above.

The General Partners feel that there is substantial upside potential in increasing the current rental rates. None of the tenants at Casa Madrid has a lease which gives management the utmost in flexibility to increase rents. Furthermore, the last across-the-board increase given the tenants was in August, 1975. Since that time the level of Houston apartment rents has increased about 15 percent. For this reason the General Partners feel that a $10 per month increase could be immediately levied without substantially affecting the turnover on the project. They are convinced, however, that by making the contemplated improvements we can immediately raise all residents to the projected rent roll schedule and have the following new asking rents:

1 Bedroom	$195
2 Bedroom	235
2 Bedroom Studio	250

RISKS

1. Investing in real estate is very risky. High amounts of leverage are used.

2. Cash flow generated by the investment may not be sufficient to pay all expenses and service the debt. In this case the investor is faced with the possibility of losing additional cash.

3. There is no guarantee that the hoped-for refinancing funds will be available.

4. There can be no guarantee that the current tight market conditions will continue.

5. There are always risks associated with any physical structure.

Exhibit 1. Casa Madrid, Ltd. Apartments, 803 East Grand Avenue, Houston, Texas.

Current and Projected Rent Roll

No. of units	Type	Size	Current (3-1-76) Rent	Current (3-1-76) Monthly gross	Project Increase Rent	Project Increase Monthly gross
20	1 Bedroom	638 sq. ft.	$165.	$ 3,300.	$180.	$ 3,600.
16	1 Bedroom	666 sq. ft.	$165.	$ 2,640.	$180.	$ 2,880
8	1 Bedroom	613 sq. ft.	$165.	$ 1,320.	$180.	$ 1,440.
8	1 Bedroom	641 sq. ft.	$165.	$ 1,320.	$180.	$ 1,440.
8	1 Bedroom	650 sq. ft.	$165.	$ 1,320.	$180.	$ 1,440.
8	1 Bedroom	678 sq. ft.	$165.	$ 1,320.	$180.	$ 1,440.
22	2 Bedroom	886 sq. ft.	$200.	$ 4,400	$220.	$ 4,840.
22	2 Bedroom	852 sq. ft.	$200.	$ 4,400.	$220.	$ 4,840.
4	2 Bedroom Studio	933 sq. ft.	$230.	$ 920.	$240.	$ 960.
4	2 Bedroom Studio	981 sq. ft.	$230.	$ 920	$240.	$ 960.
4	1 Bedroom	732 sq. ft.	$165.	$ 660.	$180.	$ 720.
124		95,604 sq. ft.	Average 23.6¢/sq. ft.	$22,520.	Average 25.7¢/sq. ft.	$24,560.

Projected Income

	Annual
Rental Income $24,560.	$294,720.
Less: Vacancy (5%)	14,736.
Net Rental Income	$279,984.
Miscellaneous Income (Furniture, Deposit Forfeitures, Laundry)	7,000.
	$286,984.
Less: Expenses $1.45/sq. ft.	138,626.
Net Operating Income	$148,358.

Note: Owner pays all utilities.

Exhibit 2. Casa Madrid, Ltd. Outline Specifications for the Complete Rehabilitation and Repair of the Casa Madrid Apartments, Houston, Texas.

1. Intent

To correct all existing deficiencies and to generally restore all elements to almost good-as-new condition. After this rehabilitation, we expect that the project will compete on even terms with much newer projects and will experience minimum maintenance costs.

2. Estimated Costs

All estimated costs are based on our experience and knowledge as consulting professional engineers, apartment owners and operators, and from discussions with, and quotations from, appropriate contractors.

3. Mansard Roof

New 250# composition shingles and new 15# felt will be installed over the existing painted wooden shingles. This new roof/siding (top 1/2 of the buildings) will be highly attractive, require minimum maintenance (no painting) and will be guaranteed 15 - 25 years.

Estimated Cost: $17,000.00

4. Built-up Flat Roof

The roofs presently do not cause any undue problems. Certain sections have recently been reroofed. However, the major portion will require reroofing within the next 2 - 3 years. We plan to immediately reroof all of these old areas with a combination of hot and cold processes. The new roofs will be guaranteed as to materials for at least 10 years and will be completely guaranteed for two years. When reroofing all gravel guards, flashing, scuppers, and downspouts not in first-class condition will be repaired. Where experience has shown the advisability of additional gutters and downspouts, they will be added.

Estimated Cost: $42,000.00

5. Concrete and Masonry

Several decorative and nonstructural brick walls have cracked or tilted due to uneven settling of their foundations. This situation has also manifested itself in the cracking of apartment entrance sidewalks when a nearby brick patio wall has shifted. The brick-veneer buildings are not involved. A thorough inside and outside inspection of the buildings indicated well-built and 100 percent-sound foundations and masonry. Remedial work will include releveling of some walls and other brickwork, and removal and replacement of others with new masonry, cedar walls, or landscaping. In addition, cracked concrete sidewalks and entranceways will be repaired by sawing out bad portions and repouring with new concrete.

Estimated Cost: $5,000.00

6. Painting and Caulking

All exterior painted surfaces will be repainted. This work will include proper preparation for painting. Unsound materials will be replaced. All seams and joints will be caulked.

Estimated Cost: $10,000.00

7. Asphalt-Concrete Paving

All defects in the base will be repaired. Then a 1-1/2" asphalt-concrete overlay will be applied over all driving surfaces. To further beautify and protect the driveways, they will be seal coated with an appropriate coal-tar epoxy.

Estimated Cost: $19,000.00

Exhibit 2. *cont'd.*

8. Wooden Fences

All wooden fences will be restored to good condition.

Estimated Cost: $ 1,000.00

9. Swimming Pool

Minor structural repairs of the rear pool will be made.

Estimated Cost: $ 500.00

10. Air Conditioning System

Our inspection of the two-pipe central chilled water and hot water air conditioning and heating system led to the conclusion that this system is in good working order, and that no immediate expenditures are necessary. This judgment has been confirmed by two independent air conditioning firms. The only questionable elements are the forced draft cooling towers that should probably be replaced within the next five years. To insure a conservative estimate and to permit earlier replacement should we so elect, we are including the replacement cost of these towers in the estimate.

Estimated Cost: $12,000.00

11. Carpets and Drapes

About 50 percent of all existing carpets and drapes will be replaced with new.

Estimated Cost of Carpets: $22,000.00

Estimated Cost of Drapes: $ 5,000.00

12. Appliances

Approximately 50 dishwashers, 5 refrigerators, and 5 rusted stove-tops will be replaced with new. The removed appliances will be disassembled to provide a reservoir of spare parts for repairs.

Estimated Cost of Dishwashers: $ 9,000.00

Estimated Cost of Refrigerators: 1,400.00

Estimated Cost of Stove-Tops: 350.00

TOTAL ESTIMATED COST: $144,250.00

+ 10 percent Contingencies   14,425.00

TOTAL $158,675.00

John H. Sears
Professional Engineer
City of Houston Air Conditioning Contractor
Class "A"

Exhibit 3. Casa Madrid, Ltd.

David M. Lewis, Inc. *Affiliate*
4543 Post Oak Place Drive, Suite 240
Houston, Texas 77027 • (713) 627-1800

May 7, 1976

Thomas P. Leary
REI Ltd.
P.O. Box 2031
Burlingame, Cal. 94010

Reference: Casa Madrid Apartments, 803 East Grand Avenue
           Houston, Texas

Dear Mr. Leary:

At your request, we have inspected and reviewed the above referenced property in order to form a preliminary opinion of its market value after a program of remodeling. This program is attached and our conclusion of market value is contingent upon its being carried out completely.

In order to carry out this assignment, we have conducted a market study of real estate activity in the immediate vicinity of the subject property. In this investigation, we have analyzed various sales of similar apartment projects, comparable rents, land sales, and vacancy levels in this particular sub-market. The sources of our data include: the Harris County Deed Records, our own data bank, other real estate appraisers, and interviews with apartment owners, managers, and brokers. This information is in our files and is available to you upon request.

Based on the data obtained through this research, it is our opinion that the subject property, as of May 7, 1976, in fee simple title has a market value as follows:

ONE MILLION FIVE HUNDRED EIGHTY-FOUR THOUSAND
SIX HUNDRED DOLLARS
$1,584,600.00

Exhibit 3. *cont'd.*

It should be noted that a portion of the land containing 25,075 square feet and legally described as being Lot 3, Block 50, Lum Terrace Addition is leased. This portion of the subject is a leasehold estate based on a long-term lease and an option to purchase. This leasehold situation has been taken into consideration in the above estimate of market value.

Market Value, as used in this report, is defined by *Real Estate Appraisal Terminology*, copyright 1975, page 137, by the American Institute of Real Estate Appraisers and the Society of Real Estate Appraisers, as being:

The highest price in terms of money which a property will bring in a competitive and open market under all conditions requisite to a fair sale, the buyer and seller each acting prudently, knowledgeably, and assuming the price is not affected by undue stimulus.

It should be clearly understood that this value estimate letter does not constitute a formal appraisal report. It merely represents one facet of an investment decision on the part of our client and must not be considered as the sole criterion for final judgment.

A complete formal appraisal report is currently being prepared and will be delivered as soon as possible. Because we are familiar with the subject and its neighborhood, we are confident that the value conclusion reached in that report will not vary significantly from the value reported in this letter. We hope that this information has been useful. Should you have any questions regarding this letter, please do not hesitate to contact us.

Sincerely,

_____

David M. Lewis, MAI-SRPA

_____

Albert N. Allen, MAI-SRPA

DML:ANA:ds

Exhibit 4. Casa Madrid, Ltd. Houston Area Economic Data, 1960–1974.

	1960	1965	1966	1967
Total Population (Jan. 1 each year except U.S. Census of April 1, 1960 & 1970)				
Harris County	1,243,158	1,464,000	1,518,000	1,563,000
Houston SMSA*	1,430,374	1,685,000	1,748,000	1,797,000
Total Employment, SMSA* December each year (Thousand employees)	568.1	691.5	737.0	757.4
Unemployed, SMSA, as Percent of Total Work Force[1]				
July	4.9%	3.9%	2.7%	4.1%
December	4.8%	2.4%	1.7%	2.7%
Total Vehicles Registered, Harris Co. (Thousand vehicles)	601.8	811.6	861.7	909.6
Total Bank Debits to Individual Accounts				
Absolute dollars (Billion)	28.1	44.3	49.5	55.2
Constant 1967 dollars (Billion)	31.5	46.7	50.8	55.2
Nonresidential Construction Contracts Awarded, Harris County				
Absolute dollars (Million)	275.1	375.5	407.7	534.1
Constant 1967 dollars (Million)	308.4	396.1	418.1	534.1
Total New Residential Electric Connections, Harris County				
Single Family Units	10,045	12,709	11,504	11,285
Apartment Units	1,936	7,982	5,925	6,769
Nonresidential Electric Current Consumption, Harris County (Billion KWH)	5.6	8.9	10.1	11.4
Nonresidential Natural Gas Consumption, Harris County				
Billion cubic feet	Not	414.4	457.7	474.1
Billion cubic meters	Available	11.6	12.8	13.3
Telephones in Service, Houston District Exchange (Thousand telephones)	536.6	750.1	806.3	870.5
Total Freight Handled by Rail Systems Serving Houston				
Short tons (Million)	15.2	19.0	20.2	19.4
Metric tons (Million)	13.8	17.2	18.3	17.6
Total Cargo Handled by the Port of Houston				
Short tons (Million)	58.0	58.4	60.4	57.6
Metric tons (Million)	52.6	53.0	54.8	52.2
Total Air Passengers Arrivals and Departures (Million passengers)	1.4	2.6	3.0	3.4

*SMSA. Houston Standard Metropolitan Statistical Area consisting of Brazoria, Fort Bend, Harris, Liberty, Montgomery, and Waller Counties.

[1]1967–1974 percentages revised to conform with 1974 estimating procedure.

Exhibit 4. *cont'd.*

1968	1969	1970	1971	1972	1973	1974
1,610,000	1,667,000	1,741,912	1,780,000	1,832,000	1,886,000	1,942,000
1,849,000	1,914,000	1,999,316	2,041,000	2,093,000	2,150,000	2,210,000
785.9	829.1	866.0	882.3	904.9	967.6	1,018.6
3.8%	3.7%	4.8%	5.6%	5.9%	5.2%	4.2%
2.4%	2.5%	3.9%	3.9%	3.5%	3.5%	4.0%
972.3	1,035.3	1,098.9	1,181.2	1,269.9	1,354.0	1,420.9
65.1	73.6	78.9	88.1	105.9	132.7	184.6
62.4	66.3	67.5	73.1	84.8	101.0	126.3
476.1	549.3	587.2	688.1	806.1	949.9	1,068.0
456.5	494.9	502.7	570.5	645.4	722.9	730.1
12,990	12,425	10,897	16,248	18,328	16,747	13,456
8,596	16,319	23,120	22,712	21,497	21,421	15,793
12.7	13.9	15.2	16.8	19.5	21.2	21.8
480.0	490.2	539.8	572.0	550.7	567.1	530.2
13.4	13.7	15.1	16.0	15.4	15.9	14.8
948.3	1,036.9	1,108.0	1,173.1	1,249.8	1,318.7	1,410.1
21.1	20.2	21.1	21.0	21.0	24.0	21.7
19.1	18.3	19.1	19.0	19.0	21.8	19.7
57.4	54.8	62.4	68.4	71.4	86.2	83.9
52.1	49.7	56.6	62.0	64.8	78.2	76.1
4.0	4.5	4.5	4.8	5.5	6.0	6.6

Exhibit 5. Casa Madrid, Ltd. Projected Population, Population Change, and Population Growth Rate: Fifteen Most Populous Standard Metropolitan Statistical Areas of the U.S. (1974–1979).

SMSA	Projected Population 1979	Estimated Population 1974	SMSA	Projected Population Change 1974–1979 Amount	Rank	SMSA	Projected % Population Change 1974–1979 %	Rank
New York	9,880,200	9,885,200	HOUSTON	+210,800	1	HOUSTON	+9.59	1
Chicago	7,151,800	7,089,500	Washington	+166,100	2	Dallas-Fort Worth	+5.75	2
Los Angeles-Long Beach	6,784,400	6,944,400	Dallas-Fort Worth	+143,600	3	Washington	+5.41	3
Philadelphia	4,790,700	4,834,100	Chicago	+62,300	4	Baltimore	+2.46	4
Detroit	4,479,300	4,468,600	San Francisco-Oakland	+60,300	5	Nassau-Suffolk	+1.93	5
Boston	3,440,400	3,421,000	Baltimore	+52,500	6	San Francisco-Oakland	+1.91	6
Washington	3,236,500	3,070,400	Nassau-Suffolk	+50,400	7	Chicago	+0.88	7
San Francisco-Oakland	3,215,700	3,155,400	Boston	+19,400	8	Newark	+0.75	8
Nassau-Suffolk	2,660,500	2,610,100	Newark	+15,500	9	Boston	+0.57	9
Dallas-Fort Worth	2,647,300	2,503,700	Detroit	+10,700	10	Detroit	+0.24	10
HOUSTON	2,408,700	2,197,900	New York	−5,000	11	New York	−0.05	11
St. Louis	2,370,500	2,381,900	St. Louis	−11,400	12	St. Louis	−0.48	12
Pittsburgh	2,329,900	2,380,400	Philadelphia	−43,400	13	Philadelphia	−0.90	13
Baltimore	2,183,400	2,130,900	Pittsburgh	−50,500	14	Pittsburgh	−2.12	14
Newark	2,095,900	2,080,400	Los Angeles-Long Beach	−160,000	15	Los Angeles-Long Beach	−2.30	15

SOURCE: *Sales Management Survey of Buying Power, Part II*, October 28, 1974.

Exhibit 6. Casa Madrid, Ltd. Projected Effective Buying Income—Amount, Change, and Growth Rate: Fifteen Most Populous Standard Metropolitan Statistical Areas of the U.S. (1973–1978).

SMSA	1978 Projections E.B.I. ($000)	Rank*	1973 Estimates E.B.I. ($000)	Rank*	Projected E.B.I. Increase 1973–1978 ($000)	Rank	SMSA	SMSA	Projected E.B.I. Increase 1973–1978 (%)	Rank
New York	$75,458,127	1	$50,404,907	1	$25,053,220	1	New York	Washington	76.7	1
Chicago	56,144,277	2	36,481,890	2	19,662,387	2	Chicago	HOUSTON	73.2	2
Los Angeles-Long Beach	52,699,475	3	34,491,000	3	18,199,475	3	Los Angeles-Long Beach	Detroit	67.6	3
Detroit	38,513,474	4	22,982,445	4	15,531,029	4	Detroit	Baltimore	66.8	4
Philadelphia	33,713,772	5	22,173,291	5	13,244,123	5	Washington	Dallas-Fort Worth	66.2	5
Washington	30,522,194	6	17,278,071	6	11,540,481	6	Philadelphia	San Francisco-Oakland	65.2	6
San Francisco-Oakland	28,094,569	7	17,009,766	7	11,084,803	7	San Francisco-Oakland	Newark	60.7	7
Boston	23,989,802	8	15,708,661	8	8,281,141	8	Boston	St. Louis	55.7	8
Nassau-Suffolk	20,439,103	9	13,718,426	9	7,660,492	9	Dallas-Forth Worth	Chicago	53.9	9
Dallas-Fort Worth	19,235,561	10	11,575,069	10	7,159,342	10	HOUSTON	Los Angeles-Long Beach	52.8	10
Newark	17,728,576	11	11,031,027	11	6,720,677	11	Nassau-Suffolk	Boston	52.7	11
HOUSTON	16,934,812	12	9,775,470	15	6,697,549	12	Newark	Philadelphia	52.0	12
St. Louis	16,346,011	13	10,496,828	12	5,950,617	13	Baltimore	Pittsburgh	51.9	13
Pittsburgh	15,742,519	15	10,364,631	13	5,849,183	14	St. Louis	New York	49.7	14
Baltimore	14,862,412	16	8,911,795	17	5,377,888	15	Pittsburgh	Nassau-Suffolk	49.0	15

*All U.S. SMSA's.

SOURCE: *Sales Management Survey of Buying Power, Parts I & II*, July 8, 1974 and October 28, 1974.

Exhibit 7. Casa Madrid, Ltd. New Capital Expenditures Among the Fifteen Most Populous Standard Metropolitan Statistical Areas of the U.S. (1971).

SMSA	New capital expenditures ($000,000)	Rank	1974 Population rank
Chicago	$972.0	1	2
HOUSTON	600.6	2	13
Detroit	572.6	3	5
Los Angeles-Long Beach	566.2	4	3
Philadelphia	535.4	5	4
New York*	481.2	6	1
Pittsburgh	281.1	7	12
St. Louis	226.0	8	11
Baltimore	221.6	9	14
Newark	211.7	10	15
San Francisco-Oakland	205.4	11	7
Dallas and Fort Worth†	192.8	12	10
Boston	187.5	13	6
Washington	95.7	14	8
Nassau-Suffolk*	92.2	15	9

*The Nassau-Suffolk SMSA was formed from part of the New York SMSA since 1971. Figures shown for current boundaries.

†The Dallas and Fort Worth SMSA's merged in April 1973. Figures shown are combined total for 1971 boundaries.

SOURCE: U.S. Bureau of Census, *Annual Survey of Manufacturers,* 1971.

Exhibit 8. Casa Madrid, Ltd. Total Bank Deposits: Fifteen Most Populous Standard Metropolitan Statistical Areas of the U.S. (June 30, 1973).

SMSA	Total bank deposits ($000)	Deposits rank	Population rank
New York	$91,442,839	1	1
Chicago	36,930,191	2	2
Los Angeles-Long Beach	22,941,482	3	3
San Francisco-Oakland	18,931,909	4	7
Detroit	14,946,521	5	5
Philadelphia	14,418,390	6	4
Dallas and Fort Worth*	9,450,413*	7*	10
Boston	9,354,369	8	6
HOUSTON	8,427,425	9	13
Pittsburgh	8,190,117	10	12
Washington	7,520,068	11	8
St. Louis	6,854,986	12	11
Nassau-Suffolk	5,819,916	13	9
Newark	5,520,214	14	15
Baltimore	3,600,332	15	14

*The Dallas SMSA and the Fort Worth SMSA merged in April 1973. Data shown are combined total for 1971 boundaries.

SOURCE: Federal Deposit Insurance Corporation, *Summary of Deposits in All Commercial and Mutual Savings Banks*, June 30, 1973.

Universal Climate Control Corporation (B)

INTRODUCTION

In early 1974, Al Bono, the CEO of UCC, and Dick Casey, the Vice President and General Manager, were concerned about where the company was going in the years up to 1980. On April 26, 1973, Dick Casey had asked the members of the firm's operating committee to consider the short-and long-term goals of the company and to prepare comments for discussion of these goals. This request was part of a move to introduce more participation into the policy-making process of the firm. However, the results have been disappointing. Only two members of the committee prepared comments on the goals and growth opportunities of the company. As a result of this and the response to some thoughts aired by Bill O'Mally in a recent committee meeting, top management was concerned not only about what the firm's future strategic posture ought to be but also about the organization structure and personnel needed to carry out this strategy. Bill had stated, in the November, 1973, committee meeting, that he was convinced the firm could triple its sales volume by 1980 if it went "all out." The other committee members were aghast at the idea of growing so rapidly. Their comments ranged from doubts that such growth was possible, given current market projections, to visible uneasiness about the change inherent in such growth and the impact of this change on themselves individually and on their organizational units. Messrs. Bono and Casey were further concerned about what business the company should consider itself in. The competitive enviroment was changing, and growth opportunities were far greater in the environmental control business than in the air conditioning business alone.

MARKET AREA

The company's primary market for its products and services is encompassed by the area within a 50-mile radius of Greater New York City. Over 90 percent of the firm's sales come from within this area, although installations have been made as far west as Merced, California, and as far south as Duncan, South Carolina.

Within the primary market, the company's most important product is service. The business rests on personal service in acting as subcontractors to major contractors and in selling maintenance contracts to major facilities (See Appendix).

FACTORS CRITICAL FOR SUCCESS

In discussing what is critical for continued survival and prosperity in the mechanical contracting business, Dick Casey identified three factors of paramount importance. They are management, location, and the marketing concept.

Since the industry is continuously changing, management must be tuned in to the pace and direction of this change and able to adapt the company to the new enviroment. Without this capability, the firm would be left behind. In addition,

George E. Shagory and John Aboud, Babson College. Reprinted with permission.

management must constantly identify and promote creativity within the firm to give it unique advantages by which to remain competitive. This places a premium on conceptual skills in management—the ability to see the so-called "big picture" of the industry and the place of the company within that picture.

Location is important because the market is predominantly a metropolitan/suburban one. In addition, there is a relationship and service base that exists in each market area, and consequently it is very difficult for an outside firm to break into geographically dispersed areas. Typically, the service base of UCC extends out to a 30-50 mile radius from greater New York City.

Within the framework of the marketing concept factor, Dick Casey discussed several items. Primary among these was his viewpoint that a customer orientation based upon an outside-in approach to serving the market is absolutely essential. With this approach, the focus is on customer needs first and then on the ways in which UCC can satisfy these needs. Mr. Casey also emphasized that management had to have a "super sensitivity" to profits. While sales volume was used within the industry as a gross indicator of firm size, the company was in business to make profits. This was translated into an operational philosophy of hustling after business, a tenaciousness in trying to meet potential customer requirements and having this result in contracts (design, installation, service, etc.) for the company, and a determination to be as cost conscious as possible. Of paramount importance in achieving these ends is a reputation for excellence in the sphere of technical skill. If this reputation is lacking, those in need of mechanical contracting services will take their business elsewhere.

MANAGEMENT PHILOSOPHY

The top management of UCC believes that the continued survival and prosperity of the firm rests squarely on the service it can provide to its customers. These customers are regarded as its key resource (see Exhibit 1), and satisfying their needs is heavily emphasized as the primary responsibility of all members of the organization.

Closely related to this emphasis is the requirement that the company possess and maintain a reputation for quick and efficient service on a contract. In the mechanical contracting industry, service excellence means high quality work provided in an expeditious and cost-conscious manner. UCC not only has such a reputation but also is continuously looking for new ways to enhance its service excellence and hence its image.

MANAGEMENT CLIMATE

In the past, UCC was managed in a highly centralized manner by Al Bono with very little broad decision-making authority delegated below the general manager level. Over the years, this has tended to condition the operating managers of the firm to view themselves as "hired hands" rather than as entrepreneurial professionals. One result of this climate has been a lack of dynamism on their part.

Recently, top management has been trying to delegate authority and responsibility to the operating managers in a move to introduce more participation into the strategic decision-making process of the company. However, the operating managers for the most part have been exhibiting an unwillingness to accept this authority and responsibility.

TOP MANAGEMENT VALUES

Al Bono and Dick Casey feel very strongly that the professional staff at UCC must maintain an exemplary level of ethical behavior on the job. This is in line with their conviction that one of the most crucial assets the firm has is its people. Toward this end, a code for the behavior of executives at work has been developed for display in all management offices (see Exhibit 2).

ACQUISITIONS

Like many growing companies, UCC has encountered opportunities to acquire other firms. The management of UCC has not been reluctant to take advantage of these opportunities when it seemed to be in their interest to do so. However, analysis of these acquisitions and their subsequent performance revealed weaknesses in the way acquisition opportunities were investigated and accepted or rejected. This is especially true in the case of those firms which were acquired. Only one remains a wholly owned profitable subsidiary. The others were closed down for lack of managerial talent, sold because of competitive pressures, or merged directly into UCC and experienced a disappearing market (see Exhibits 3, 4, 5, 6, and 7).

Exhibit 1. Universal Climate Control Corporation (B) Ten Commandments of Business.

1. OUR CUSTOMERS are our most valuable asset—and the most important people in our business.

2. OUR CUSTOMERS are *not* dependent upon us—we are dependent on them. They don't owe us any favors.

3. OUR CUSTOMERS are the purpose of our work—without them there would be no jobs.

4. OUR CUSTOMERS are not just names on our books but flesh and blood human beings who have as much right to be satisfied as we ourselves.

5. OUR CUSTOMERS are not "outsiders"—but a very necessary part of our business.

6. OUR CUSTOMERS do us a favor when they buy what we have to sell—and we owe it to them to see that they are completely satisfied.

7. OUR CUSTOMERS are free to take their business wherever they wish—whenever we fail to satisfy them.

8. OUR SATISFIED CUSTOMERS are an army of Ambassadors of Good Will for our company—your company.

9. OUR PROFITS and our jobs depend not only on getting customers—but also on keeping them satisfied with everything we do on their behalf.

10. SATISFIED CUSTOMERS are the Life Blood of our business—and every business in America—for without them there would be no business.

Exhibit 2. Universal Climate Control Corporation (B) Code of Executive Conduct.

ALWAYS GIVE YOUR SUBORDINATES THE CREDIT THAT IS RIGHTFULLY THEIRS. Doing otherwise is not only dishonorable, but it will also destroy good will and seriously hamper your ability to function effectively.

CONTROL YOUR TEMPER. To be an executive, a man must forever give up the right to be angry.

BE COURTEOUS. Have genuine consideration for other people's feelings, wishes, and situations.

BE PROMPT. If you can't keep your appointments on time, you'll soon become a clog in the corporate gears.

NEVER TAMPER WITH THE TRUTH. Every statement you make must be able to withstand the closest scrutiny, and every promise you make must be vigorously fulfilled.

BE CONCISE. In your writing and talking, especially when giving instructions, be succinct.

ENJOY YOUR WORK. Naturally you should have plenty of outside interests. But if, for example, you find it hard to work extra hours when it's necessary, you don't belong in this company.

BE GENEROUS. Remember that it is the productivity of the manual worker that makes possible your executive position.

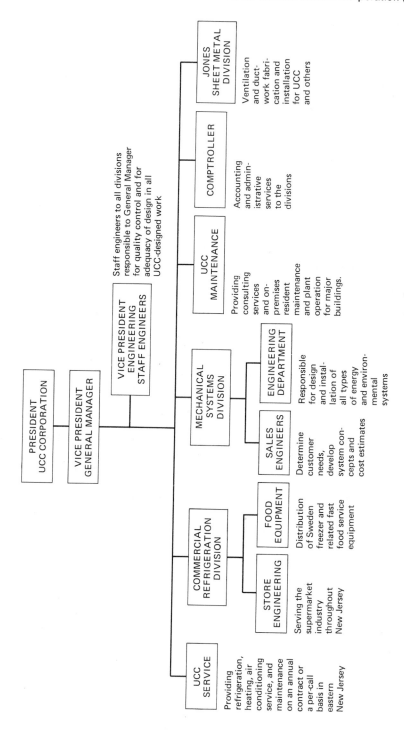

Exhibit 3. Universal Climate Control Corporation (B) The UCC Organization.

Exhibit 4. Universal Climate Control Corporation (B).

Phonex Corporation

Acquired: February 9, 1956.

Business Activity: Originally acquired to distribute a rust preventative called "Galvoplate." When sales in product started declining, UCC used the Phonex Corp. as a wholly owned exclusive agent for the sale or rental of equipment and services by conditional sales contract or lease agreement with or without option on the part of the customer to purchase. All Company vehicles were owned, registered, and insured through Phonex.

Reason for Acquisition: Interest in a product which seemed to have a profitable marketing potential. Transferred into a leasing company for accounting purposes to improve UCC's balance sheet position.

Profitable: Yes.

Final Disposition: Merged with UCC in January, 1967. Market for product dried up.

Exhibit 5. Universal Climate Control Corporation (B).

Atlantic Filters, Inc.

Acquired: Early 1960.

Business Activity: Sales and Service of all types of Air Filters with heavy concentration in industrial, washable, filter service. The Company also began selling and servicing delicatessen and lunch counter/soda fountain equipment.

Reason for Acquisition: To diversify into a profitable field, and at the same time protect UCC's ability to provide an additional service to its customers that would also keep the door open for additional Heating, Ventilating, and Air Conditioning Sales and Service for UCC.

Profitable: Yes.

Final Disposition: Sold in 1962. This type of Filter Service business required relatively low paid and low skilled labor. As the business grew and more men were needed, management felt that it was only a matter of time before the Pipefitter union that the Company had a contract with would intervene. This type of business would not have been able to remain competitive with Union labor. The Company was sold to a man who management felt had the capabilities and the desire to operate the Company and ensure its growth. The Company has grown and is still in business today.

Exhibit 6. Universal Climate Control Corporation (B).

F. A. Hardway Co., Inc.

Acquired: 1969

Business Activity: Engineering, sales, and service of supermarket equipment and store design. Company was located in Flemington, N.J., and conducted its business in western New Jersey and eastern Pennsylvania.

Reason for Acquisition: At the time of acquisition, Hardway Corp. was doing approximately $1,000,000 worth of supermarket business. Its engineers had developed a new refrigeration system for supermarkets that intrigued UCC's management. Management also felt this would diversify UCC's area of activity by capturing some of the work in the western part of the state.

Profitable: No.

Final Disposition: Ceased operations on June 1, 1972. Although this subsidiary was beginning to show a profit in the early months of 1972, the decision to cease operations was made for two reasons: (1) UCC could not find a capable manager to run the company; and (2) the subsidiary's operations were taking up too much of management's time which needed to be spent on UCC's operations. Suit pending against former owner. New refrigeration system not effective.

Exhibit 7. Universal Climate Control Corporation (B).

Jones Sheet Metal Company, Inc.

Acquired: 1969

Business Activity: Ventilation and ductwork fabrication and installation in eastern New Jersey.

Reason for Acquisition: To better serve UCC's customers by ensuring the best possible ductwork at the lowest price. Management was not happy with the work that our sheet metal subcontractors were providing.

Profitable: Yes.

Final Disposition: UCC's only remaining wholly owned subsidiary.

Appendix. Steps Taken for New Construction

---

1. Customer determination is made concerning his needs for a new building (based on Consultant's study).
2. Customer discusses needs with his Plant Engineer and Controller who advise him to what extent his needs can be fulfilled. The decide on a price range for the Project.
3. Customer appoints a committee to select an Architect for the Project.
4. Architect designs the building(s) and puts out feelers (Dodge Report) for General Contractors to bid on the Project.
5. Architect subcontracts to Consulting Engineers to design Mechanical, Electrical, Plumbing, and Structural portions of the building.
6. Plans are drawn up and specs are prepared. Upon customer approval, plans and specs are open for bid amongst General Contractors.
7. Bids are returned to Architect.
8. Architect and customer decide on a General Contractor.
9. General Contractor negotiates final pricing with his subcontractors and then awards contracts to subs.

   Sometimes General Contractor will have to tell subs to reduce their price by a certain percent from the original estimate. In this situation, UCC would reduce the price but then spell out the limitations caused by the reduction.

10. Subs shop equipment called for in specs and submit characteristics to General Contractor who submits them to the Architect. Architect approves them for aesthetic characteristics and then submits them to his Consulting Engineers for approval of engineering characteristics.
11. If approved—approval goes back down the "chain of command." If rejected—rejection goes back down the "chain of command" and the whole process is repeated until the subs find equipment that is satisfactory to all parties.
12. Once all approvals are in, the equipment is ordered. Work on the Project is usually well underway by now.

Changes

As problems on the job occur, the following steps are taken:

1. Problems encountered by the subs are brought to the attention of the General Contractor's job superintendent. He informs his boss (the General Contractor) of the problem. The General Contractor advises the Architect of the problem.

   The problem is usually discussed at the next weekly job meeting. Solutions to the problem are recommended to the Architect by the subs involved.

Note: Architect is usually in contact with the customer during the above steps.

2. The Architect verifies recommendations with his Consulting Engineer and upon a decision for change, a new drawing is issued to the Architect by his Consultant. The Architect submits the new "change" drawing to the General Contractor who sends it to his subcontractor for pricing. (General Contractor's sub may or may not have to further submit plans to his subcontractor.)

3. When a price for the change is arrived at, the subcontractor submits the price to the General Contractor who in turn submits the price to the Architect.

4. The Architect then submits the price to the Consulting Engineer for verification. Once approved, the plans are sent back to the Architect.

5. The Architect then submits plans and price to the customer.

6. Upon customer acceptance, plans are sent back to the Architect, then to the General Contractor, and finally to the subcontractor who implements the change.

Note: Average time for the change from the time the problem occurs to the time the change is implemented is 3-4 weeks, during which time the installation schedule of all subs is disrupted.

Prescription Services, Inc. (A)

"Fine," said Sam Reed, "we will send you our initial order within two weeks, and thank you for your cooperation." Hanging up the phone, Sam turned to his two working partners, John Sachs and Bill Davidson, and said, "Well, it looks like we've got it made! Apex Manufacturing* was the first drug manufacturer we've contacted, and they have agreed to sell their complete line to us. The rest will have to go along."

Almost two years earlier Sam and John had begun discussing a new business venture. The business developed closely along the line initially conceived: buying ethical drugs† from manufacturers and distributing them to doctors who, at prices below those charged at drug stores, would dispense the drugs directly to their patients.

In May, 1966, Sam and his partners had obtained the necessary licenses from the state, financial backing, the word of several doctors that they would be customers, and were presently lining up suppliers. They felt it would be less than two weeks before the company, Prescription Services, Inc., would be in full operation.

THE BEGINNING

In college Sam majored in pre-medicine and obtained a bachelors' degree in liberal arts. After graduation he enlisted in the Air Force, where he became a surgical nurse, gaining varied and practical experience in medicine. Upon discharge Sam decided to go to work rather than continue studying medicine and joined Leading Laboratories, Inc., a manufacturer of fine chemicals and pharmaceuticals. At Leading Labs Sam was employed as a "detail man," a type of salesman peculiar to the drug industry. Detail men called on doctors to introduce and promote their company's products (and thus could be considered missionary salesmen) with the objective that the doctor specify these products in his prescriptions. A doctor could specify either the brand name or the generic name. For example, he could specify the drug Tetracyn, Phizer's brand of tetracycline. The druggist then had to use Tetracyn. Or the doctor could prescribe the generic name, tetracycline, HCL. Then the druggist could use any of the five available brands of tetracycline. The job of the detail man was to convince the doctor to specify his company's product by its brand name. A few companies hired only graduate pharmacists as detail men, but all companies had indoctrinational and continuing training programs to keep the detail men current on new developments.

In carrying out his detailing work, Sam contacted one-third of the doctors in the county. (Two other detail men for Leading Labs covered the remainder of the county.) He developed a knowledge of how much of what medicines were used by the various types of doctors and an understanding of how the distribution system worked.

---

*Apex Manufacturing is the disguised name for a major drug company.

†Drugs or medicines sold only by prescription from a doctor.

Drugs traveled from the manufacturer to the drug retailers either directly or through wholesalers. The point of sale, however, was usually at the doctor's office where the prescription was written. Sam noted that many (he estimated 10 percent) in the physician community were known as "dispensers," who purchased drugs themselves and then gave or sold them to their patients. Most physicians dispensed to a greater or lesser extent. Some limited their dispensing to injectables like penicillin shots, vitamins (some pediatricians provided vitamins "free") etc., while others offered virtually complete drug services. Those with full lines of drugs typically ordered their supplies from mail order houses and sold the drugs to their patients at considerably under the usual price paid at a retail drugstore. As Sam became familiar with the pricing policies of the retail druggists he felt he saw why these physicians went to this trouble:

> In the days when the druggist compounded the prescriptions himself, taking the raw materials and actually manufacturing them at his establishment (each druggist running a sort of job shop operation), the retailers established pricing policies that would fairly compensate them for the skill, the labor, and the risk involved in their trade. Essentially, the pricing technique was to double the cost of the ingredients and add a professional fee. As more and more prescriptions were filled with tablets and capsules already manufactured, the nature of the druggists' work changed, but the druggist maintained the same pricing policy.

Sam felt that retail drug prices were "abnormally" high as a result of several factors in addition to the basic method of pricing. He claimed that the necessity of using registered pharmacists to fill prescriptions, the cost of large drug inventories, and price fixing among pharmacists all contributed to the high retail costs of prescription drugs. He explained that a typical registered pharmacist would cost $1,000 per month, including benefits, and could fill approximately 50 prescriptions per day, amounting to about a $1 cost per prescription for packaging.

Sam pointed out that inventory was a problem for all drug stores:

> Every pharmacy in every town must be ready to handle any M.D.'s drug request. This requires duplication of brands and is a terrific cost. Theoretically, the druggist must carry all the hundreds of thousands of various brands of drugs. In practice, the druggist carries only a small percentage of the products available, the fast movers. In an attempt to still provide service, he often borrows from his pharmacist friend around the block. Even so, he is forced to carry considerable inventory which adds to the overhead and eventually appears in the retail price of the drugs.

The high retail prices of drugs caused discontentment among physicians and patients and led many of them to look for more economical methods of obtaining drugs. Mail-order companies selling directly to physicians appeared and began to grow in size and number. Since many products Leading Labs manufactured could be purchased through the mail-order firms, Sam was particularly cognizant of their activities. Unfortunately, if the demand which Sam generated was satisfied through these channels, he gained no credit toward his commission. While Sam in effect worked in opposition to the mail-order firms, he could not help thinking that they provided a service and fulfilled a real need.

After two years as a detail man, Sam left Leading Labs to enter a midwestern graduate school of business. For one of his first-year courses, he prepared a brief analysis of a new business that had been jelling in his mind—providing drugs manufactured by all the companies to local doctors, who would dispense them to their patients at fair prices. Doctors would maintain a small inventory and could obtain special drugs through immediate delivery. The drugs would be prepackaged to prescription quantities and would have labels with tear strips for inventory control and patient records. Sam felt this concept surpassed the features offered by mail-order houses by providing packages in prescription size, the time-saving label system, and, most of all, fast service. His quick calculations looked promising. Based on serving 100 doctors, who might purchase an average of $500 each per month, with a 20 percent margin to the company, Sam came up with a gross margin of $120,000. This, he felt, was more than adequate to cover costs and substantial salaries. Sam was so enthusiastic that he talked it over with one of his friends, John Sachs, another of the three detail men in the county for Leading Labs. John had had 13 years experience in this position. He confirmed Sam's calculations, and they decided to look seriously into the starting of such a venture. Another friend, Bill Davidson, the third detail man for Leading Labs in the county, with ten years' field experience plus five years in research as a biochemist, joined the group later.

In November 1965, Sam's second year at graduate school, the three decided to proceed with the formation of the company. Since none of the three had sufficient funds to finance the new company's operations, they decided to incorporate and sell stock, hoping to retain control through the issuance of promotional stock and the purchase of such additional stock as necessary.

During the vacation period at Christmas and with the help of his two partners, Sam prepared pro forma cash-flow and income statements, based on the drug needs of a distribution made up of 40 percent general practitioners, 10 percent internists, 10 percent surgeons, 20 percent obstetricians, and 20 percent pediatricians, the actual distribution of doctors found in the county according to the experience of the three. (Exhibits 1 and 2) To keep track of which manufacturer's drugs were being sold by what types of doctors, Leading Labs had required each detail man to tabulate 1,000 prescriptions in each of two drugstores. From that experience the group was able to predict the typical drug needs of each doctor.

On the basis of this data, Sam estimated conservatively that an average doctor would buy around $490 in drugs/month, at prices 20 percent over the known wholesale price. He estimated that ten doctors could easily be added each month and that growth would probably be stopped for existing personnel and projection purposes (by choice) after 12 months. Assuming that no income would be realized until month 3, Sam's cash flow (Exhibit 1) showed that about $35,000 would be needed to carry the venture through the beginning period.

Sam and his partners prepared a prospectus showing these financial projections and an outline of how the business was to operate. Meanwhile, an attorney was retained to handle the incorporation proceedings of the company.

THE SEARCH FOR CAPITAL
Sam and his partners felt that together they could put up $5,000, but would prefer to invest less. They first approached the Bank of Tokyo as Sam had heard "there was a lot of Japanese money looking for investment in this country." The bank was courteous, but was not interested because, as Sam said, "Our own investment was not

sizable enough to guarantee that we were in there pitching.'' Some wheat investors with venture capital available were approached, but were not interested; they had already investigated a similar new venture in Springfield and felt it would never get going.

They next approached a wealthy, local investor-businessman, Mr. Gelt. Mr. Gelt was seeking diversification opportunities, liked the proposed plans, and offered to back the venture. After a week of negotiations, the final financial plan was agreed upon. Sam, John, and Bill each put up $1,000 in cash and each received 20 percent of the stock. Mr. Gelt put up $2,000 cash for 40 percent of the company. Through Mr. Gelt's efforts the company then obtained a $25,000 line of credit from the local bank, with all four acting as cosigners.

The company took the name of Prescription Services, Inc. The plan at that time was to concentrate initially on drugs, the area familiar to the principals, but it was hoped that the group might eventually offer the physician his total office needs such as credit, handling bad debts, records, billing, and accounting. Initially at least, the market was to be limited to the county in which the three knew the doctors. Those doctors currently dispensing drugs to their patients were felt to be the best prospects.

LICENSING
To carry out the business as planned, the group was required to obtain a state license to manufacture (repackaging was considered manufacturing) and a license to wholesale pharmaceuticals. The wholesaling license was obtained with little difficulty. Efforts to obtain the manufacturing license, however, were to no avail until a pharmacist was hired on a part-time basis. The license was finally granted in April 1966.

OPERATING DETAILS
Prescription Services, Inc., planned to contact doctors and sell them the idea of dispensing drugs to their patients. When a doctor had subscribed to the service, Prescription Services would supplement his existing drug inventory, if any, and eventually install ''racks'' in the doctor's office. The rack would be stocked with those drugs desired and used most often by the doctor. Bill, John, and Sam would service the racks, replenishing the supplies automatically whenever the quantity of any drugs dropped below reorder points. The company would subscribe to an answering service which would be adequate to take routine orders phoned to the company between sales-service calls. Deliveries of a routine nature were arranged to be made by United Parcel Service, which would pick up from Prescription Services at 2 P.M. daily and make deliveries to the doctors the next morning. Emergency deliveries would be handled by one of the three managers on a rotational standby basis. Once volume became large, it was anticipated that a truck might be purchased and delivery boys hired to handle both regular and emergency deliveries. Most of the drugs would be prepackaged by the manufacturers in prescription-size quantities. The pharmacist was available evenings and on weekends for additional packaging.

Since practically all the doctors in the county had been contacted routinely before by the three, introductions and entry were not expected to be a problem. John could call on eight doctors a day, while Bill was to spend a half day on calls, using the other half day at the office to fill orders and contact suppliers. Sam was still in school, but

Exhibit 1. Prescription Services, Inc. (A) Cash Flow.

	Month 1	Month 2	Month 3	Month 4	Month 5	Month 6	Month 7	Month 8
Sales Data								
Sales[1]	0	0	$ 4,888	$ 9,776	$14,664	$19,552	$24,440	$29,328
Cost of Drugs[2]	0	0	3,383	6,766	10,149	13,523	16,915	20,298
Cash Flow								
Cash In:								
Balance of receivables paid[3] in 2 months	0	0	0	0	1,711	3,422	5,133	6,844
Loan on Accounts Receivable[3] @ 65% of Sales	0	0	3,177	6,354	9,531	13,708	15,885	19,062
Total Cash In	0	0	3,177	6,354	11,242	16,130	21,018	25,906
Cash Out:								
Payment for Inventory[3]	0	0	3,383	6,766	10,149	13,523	16,915	20,298
Freight & Pck. Expense[4]	0	4,452	527	1,054	1,581	2,108	2,635	3,162
Interest on Receivable Loan[3] @ 7% per annum for 2 months	0	0	37	74	111	148	185	222
Fee for Receivable Loan[3]	0	0	5	5	5	5	5	5
Fixed Expenses[5]	3,100	3,100	3,100	3,100	3,100	3,600	3,600	3,600
Total Cash Out	3,100	7,552	7,052	10,939	14,946	19,384	23,340	27,285
Beginning Cash Balance	(4,595)[6]	(7,695)	(15,247)	(19,122)	(13,707)	(27,411)	(30,665)	(32,987)
Receipts	0	0	3,177	6,354	11,242	16,130	21,018	25,906
Disbursements	3,100	7,552	7,052	10,939	14,946	19,384	23,340	27,285
Excess Receipts/Disbursements	(3,100)	(7,552)	(3,875)	(4,585)	(3,704)	(3,254)	(2,322)	(1,379)
Ending Cash Balance	(7,695)	(15,247)	(19,122)	(13,707)	(17,411)	(30,665)	(32,987)	(34,366)

Exhibit 1. *cont'd.*

	Month 9	Month 10	Month 11	Month 12	Months 13-15	Months 16-18	Months 19-21
Sales Data							
Sales[1]	$34,216	$39,104	$43,992	$48,880	$146,640	$146,640	$146,640
Cost of Drugs[2]	23,681	27,064	30,447	33,830	101,490	101,490	101,490
Cash Flow							
Cash In:							
Balance of receivables paid[3] in 2 months	8,555	10,266	11,977	13,688	49,619	51,330	51,330
Loan on Accounts Receivable[3] @ 65% of Sales	22,239	25,416	28,593	31,770	95,310	95,310	95,310
Total Cash In	30,794	35,682	40,570	45,458	144,929	146,640	146,640
Cash Out:							
Payment for Inventory[3]	23,681	27,064	30,447	33,830	101,490	101,490	101,490
Freight & Pck. Expense[4]	3,689	4,216	4,743	5,270	15,810	15,810	15,810
Interest on Receivable Loan[3] @ 7% per annum for 2 months	259	296	333	370	1,110	1,110	1,110
Fee for Receivable Loan[3]	5	5	5	5	5	15	15
Fixed Expenses[5]	3,600	3,600	3,600	3,600	10,800	10,800	10,800
Total Cash Out	31,234	35,181	39,128	43,075	129,225	129,225	129,225
Beginning Cash Balance	(34,366)	(34,806)	(34,305)	(32,863)	(30,480)	(14,776)	2,639
Receipts	30,794	35,682	30,570	45,458	144,929	146,640	146,640
Disbursements	31,234	35,181	39,128	43,075	129,225	129,225	129,225
Excess Receipts/Disbursements	(440)	501	1,442	2,383	15,704	17,415	17,415
Ending Cash Balance	(34,806)	(34,305)	(32,863)	(30,480)	(14,776)	2,639	20,054

[1] Based on average sales of $488/month/doctor with a distribution of doctors as follows: 4 general practitioners, 1 surgeon, 2 pediatricians, 1 internist, 2 obstetricians. Experience with Leading Labs would indicate an average of 1276 prescriptions/month or monthly sales of $4,888 with a monthly profit of $977.60.

[2] Cost of drugs to Prescription Services, Inc., approximately 69.5 percent of sales. The full cost of goods sold, as considered here includes freight, insurance, and packaging costs, which typically brings COGS to 80 percent of sales.

[3] Consider month 3 as an example. $4,888 worth of drugs are sold. These cost $3,383 and are paid for in the same month. Payment to Prescription Services,

Inc., for the drugs is not expected until month 5, so a loan for 65 percent of the $4,888 ($3,177) is obtained for 2 months at 7 percent/year. Interest on the loan is considered paid in month 3. A nominal fee of $5/month for the loan is considered.

[4] Based on experience. See also note (2) above.

[5] See Exhibit 3. Sam's salary is increased from $500 to $1000/month in month 6.

[6] Preincorporation and capital expenditures.

Note: The initial inventory includes $29,500 worth of drugs received on consignment in month two.

would spend full time on sales after graduation in June. Initial calls were to sell the doctors the service, with later calls to replenish their supplies. Frequency of the service calls was estimated to be once a week to once a month, depending on the particular M.D.

SOURCES OF SUPPLY

Manufacturers of ethical drugs fell into two major classifications: the "specialty" house and the house concentrating on "generic" products. The specialty house developed exclusive and patented items which were heavily promoted to doctors through detail men, direct mail, and journal advertising to build up a brand preference. Specialty items were typically expensive because of their newness, freedom from competition (if only temporary), and (Sam felt) the high cost of promotion. After specialty houses had obtained good market penetration of a new drug, they usually licensed other firms to produce the product. Sam felt they did this "mostly to prevent the government antitrust people from getting on their necks, but also to have other sales forces touting a drug." In addition, Sam believed alternate suppliers helped obtain acceptance of "the old reliable brand" by the cautious doctors.

Generic products had no patent protection and belonged to the public domain. Promotion was negligible, and with no product differentiation and many competitors, the price was low compared to the specialty items. Penicillin, for example, was developed with public funds and thus belonged to the public domain. The original price of penicillin was more than $10 per 10 cc vial, but dropped to $.31 per vial in less than five years.

Sam felt that there were many factors contributing to the high cost of specialty items:

> There are usually several brands of products, not exactly the same chemically, but equally useful in treating the same disorder. Which company's product is sold depends on how successful the sales pitch made to the doctor is. There's magic in the word "new" in this industry and every firm is constantly modifying their product to attempt to have something "new" to offer the doctor. The "new" gimmick helps get the nurse who tends to insulate the doctor from detail men. A lot of molecule shifting goes on, and it is difficult to determine just what is a significant contribution from what is a mere hoax. In the case of the steroids, such as cortisone, changing of the molecule structure has had terrific results in reducing side-effects and improving absorption. However, in the case of the antibiotic tetracycline, the molecular juggling has been aimed at having something "new" to offer, to try to capture greater share of the market.

> Needless to say, the costs of re-educating the medical profession on a change in a product are tremendous and prices of specialty items are accordingly high. The generic producers, however, compete on a price basis, and things like thyroid tablets, some steroids that have reached the public domain, and various antihistamines are relatively inexpensive.

Exhibit 2. Prescription Services, Inc. (A) Pro forma Income Statements.

		Year 1		Year 2
Sales		$268,840[1]		$586,560[1]
Cost of Goods Sold (incl. Var. Costs)		215,050[2]		469,200[2]
		53,790		117,360
Gross Margin				
Expenses:				
Fixed[3]	$40,700		$43,200	
Interest + Charges[4]	2,085		4,500	
Floor Tax[5]	1,500		1,500	
Var. Costs on Inventory not sold[6]	4,425		-	
Total Expenses		48,710		49,200
Net Income		5,080		68,160
Corporate Income Tax		1,524		29,943
Net Income After Taxes		$ 3,556		$ 38,217

[1]Based on cash flow, as shown in Exhibit 1. In year 2, sales have leveled off with 100 doctors each purchasing $488/month.

[2]Approximately 80 percent of sales—includes freight, insurance, and packaging.

[3]See Cash Flow, Exhibit 1, and Expense Breakdown, Exhibit 3.

[4]Interest and charges on accounts receivable loan as shown in Cash Flow, Exhibit 1.

[5]County tax on inventory and furnishings.

[6]Loss on spoilage and return products.

Exhibit 3. Prescription Services, Inc. (A) Outlays Prior to the Initiation of Business.

A. Fees to State and Local Governments:

1.	Filing fee based on $50,000 capitalization		$ 25
2.	Recordation fee		2
3.	Comparing and certifying Articles ($3.00/copy)		15
4.	Minimum annual franchise tax		100
5.	Certificate of filing (County)		3
6.	Filing designation of agent		5
7.	Three exemptions for drug handling, and manufacture exemption (State Board of Pharmacy)		120
		Subtotal	$ 270

B. Licenses:

1.	Wholesale license (State Board of Pharmacy)		$ 50
2.	Manufacturing license (State Board of Pharmacy)		50
		Subtotal	$ 100

C. Incorporating Expenses (Other):

1.	Legal fees		$ 400
2.	Licenses, Stamps, etc.		400
3.	Prospectus		75
		Subtotal	$ 875

D. Capital Expenditures:

1.	Shelves, refrigerator, office equipment		$2,850
2.	Bottling and labeling equipment		500
		Subtotal	$3,350

Total pre-incorporation and capital expenditures $4,595

E. Operating Expenses[1] Prior to Initiation of Sales (Two Months);

1.	Rent	2x$ 150 =	$ 300
2.	Phone	2x 35 =	70
3.	Utilities	2x 30 =	60
4.	Insurance	2x 25 =	50
5.	Truck lease	2x 150 =	300
6.	Refuse	2x 5 =	10
7.	Postage	2x 15 =	30
8.	Office Supplies	2x 15 =	30
9.	Miscellaneous	2x 75 =	150
10.	Salaries[2]	2x 2500 =	5000
	Subtotal		$6000

[1]Fixed expenses are initially $3000–3100/month, increasing to $3500–3600/month when Sam goes to work full time.

[2]Salaries are based on $1000/month for John Sachs and Bill Davidson. Sam is to receive $500/month until graduation when his salary will be raised to $1000/month.

Appendix A | Note on Drug Industry

Today's prescription is one of the biggest bargains in history. The average prescription can be purchased for the equivalent amount of work time that will purchase ten gallons of gas for the family car. The cost of a penicillin prescription represents approximately 45 minutes of necessary work time, while a beauty-shop permanent wave requires 5 hours and 10 minutes; a carton of cigarettes, 1 hour and 3 minutes; a large tube of toothpaste, 24 minutes.

Manufacturer's shipments of all pharmaceutical products in 1965 totaled $6.189 billion, including all domestic drug sales, all consolidated sales by foreign subsidiaries of U.S. companies, and all exports. This total was 15 percent above that of 1964. Approximately 75 percent of industry sales volume was ethical (advertised to physicians and sold on a doctor's prescription), and 25 percent was proprietary (advertised directly to the consumer and sold without prescription).

Industry sales and profits for recent years are given below:

U.S. Pharmaceutical Sales and Profits

| | Factory Shipments, in Millions of Dollars | | | |
| | Sales | | Profit | |
	Department of Commerce[1]	FTC-SEC[2]	FTC-SEC[2]	% of Sales[2]
1965	4,386	6,189	698	11.3
1964	3,921	5,382	577	10.7
1963	3,714	4,868	492	10.1
1962	3,471	4,548	448	9.8
1961	3,238	4,165	410	9.8
1960	3,088	3,913	388	9.9
1959	3,020	3,711	382	10.3
1958	2,855	3,350	343	10.2
1957	2,722	3,165	330	10.4
1956	2,457	2,761	291	10.5
1955	2,137	-	-	-

[1]Excludes sales by foreign subsidiaries of U.S. companies.
[2]Federal Trade Commission—Securities and Exchange Commission.
SOURCE: *Standard & Poor's Industrial Survey*, March, 1966.

Most of the growth of the drug industry has been in the ethical sector, which has benefited from a succession of dramatic new products ranging from antibiotics, steriod hormones, and tranquilizers to vaccines.

Total drug sales by U.S. pharmaceutical producers, estimated at $7.3 billion for 1966, has a projected growth rate of at least 10 percent per annum in the foreseeable future. The greatest growth is expected in domestic ethical volume. Factors favoring such growth are an increasing population, a greater proportion of older age groups, higher health insurance outlays, expansion of Medicare benefits and nursing homes, and expected pharmaceutical breakthroughs resulting from heavier research expenditures by drug companies.

The ethical drug industry is dominated by a few large manufacturers. Of the approximately 600 U.S. producers of ethical pharmaceuticals, 13 accounted for 62 percent of the total U.S. market in 1965. The table below presents 1965 financial data for some of the largest drug manufacturers.

1965 Financial Statistics on Drug Companies

Company	Sales (mil $)	Net profit after tax (mil $)	Earnings per share ($)
Abbott	236.80	24.66	1.87
Baxter	64.64	4.14	.73
Lilly	316.60	41.60	2.59
Merck	331.96	59.60	1.84
Parke Davis	224.60	32.68	2.20
Pfizer	542.60	53.40	2.70
Schering	89.20	14.32	3.64
Searle	88.97	23.20	1.75
Smith, Kline & French	244.00	42.00	2.88
Upjohn	242.43	37.20	2.62

Competition among drug companies is severe because of the nature of the industry. The large firms conduct a large portion of the expensive research and development. While the first company to the market with a new product usually enjoys a distinct competitive advantage for some time, substitutes or variations of those products can quickly erode that position. The result is a highly volatile market for new drugs in which sales and profits can vary widely, depending upon acceptance by physicians and consumers.

RESEARCH
Expenditures for research and development in the past decade increased at a rate nearly three times that of drug industry sales. Outlays for ethical drug research and development totaled $365.1 million in 1965 (10.4 percent of the ethical drug industry's U.S. and export sales). Industry spending for research and development was expected to exceed $400 million in 1966 and to reach $450 million by 1967.

Despite the larger sums being channeled into research, new product introductions had declined. This slackened pace of research productivity arose basically from the complex nature of the remaining diseases to be conquered and the slowdown in the rate with which the Food and Drug Administration (FDA) granted approval to new products.

The 1962 Kefauver-Harris Drug Amendments, which became effective in 1963, gave the FDA control over the advertising of prescription drugs, broadened its authority over manufacturers' quality control, and extended Government supervision to clinical testing. The law extended the time allotted for initial consideration of a new application by the FDA to 180 days, from 60 days. This legislation required the industry to submit extensive evidence to the FDA to establish the efficacy as well as the safety of new drugs including those marketed since 1938 and prior to the 1962 amendments. Some 4000 products were involved in this investigation. This provision generated an enormous amount of paperwork on both sides and considerably lengthened and complicated the FDA review procedure of a new drug application.

New drugs have historically been vital to the profits of drug companies. Rapid obsolescence adds to the urgency of the industry's push for new products. Of all prescriptions written in 1965, seven out of ten were for drugs that were unknown fifteen years ago. The declining trend in new drugs in recent years, however, has prolonged the profitable life of older, established drugs. Closer scrutiny by the FDA of new drug applications has prompted more careful evaluation of research projects and allocation of the research dollar by industry to avoid duplication of effort and assure more lucrative results. Expected research breakthroughs from more aggressive and concentrated research programs will be an important factor in the industry's growth.

DEMAND

The average prescription price rose to an estimated $3.48 in 1965 from $3.19 in 1960. The average number of prescriptions per capita also climbed from 4.07 in 1960 to 4.8 in 1965. In 1965, the average prescription expenditure per person was $16.70, compared with $12.98 in 1960. The trend toward greater outlays for drugs by consumers was expected to continue.

The steadily increasing percentage of persons over 65 years of age was also expected to strongly influence the growth of drug sales. Although persons aged 65 or over represented only 9 percent of the population in 1965, that figure was expected to reach 17 percent by 1975.

The passage in late July, 1965, of the $6 billion Government-sponsored Medicare program was expected to provide a broad program of health insurance to those aged 65 and older and make more money available for drug consumption. The Medicare law, effective July 1, 1966, provides: hospital care for 60 days ($40 deductible), with an additional 30 days of care available under a $10 coinsurance provision (patient pays $10 of hospital per diem charge); up to 100 posthospital home health visits during a one-year period following hospitalization of at least three days (excluding visits by doctors); out-patient hospital diagnostic services, with the patient paying 20 percent coinsurance (20 percent of diagnostic services charge) after $20 deductible for services in a 20-day period in the hospital out-patient clinic. The voluntary supplementary medical insurance plan, also effective July, 1966, covers 80 percent of physicians' and surgeons' fees and various expenses for nonhospital services (after a $50 deductible). Under this plan, the participant pays $3 a month, with matching funds from the Federal Government. Effective January 1, 1967, Medicare also will provide for skilled nursing home care for up to 100 days, after a minimum hospital stay of three days, with the patient paying $5 a day for days in excess of 20.

The drug industry is expected to be a major beneficiary of Medicare. Those eligible for Medicare traditionally spend more than double the national average on drugs (per capita). A study by the U.S. Public Health Service found that 32.7 percent of the total U.S. population in a recent year made no drug purchases of any kind, compared with 24.1 percent for the segment of the population aged 65 and over. The survey also found that 15.5 percent of the total U.S. population spent more than $50 on medication, while 35.4 percent aged 65 and over had expenditures exceeding $50. Medicare provides reimbursement for drugs for those patients aged 65 and in hospitals and extended-care facilities (including nursing homes). A nationwide program for a substantial expansion of these extended-care facilities appears likely as Medicare goes into action. Thus, nursing homes and hospitals are expected to become important sources of increased prescription volume. There are indications that legislation will be introduced calling for an extension of the Medicare program to cover prescription drugs for out-patients under the voluntary insurance programs. This, too, would contribute importantly to increased prescription volume.

The drug industry has indicated some concern about the possibility of future price declines for drugs as a result of increased governmental involvement in health. One form of possible pressure to reduce drug prices would be the increased usage of lower-priced generic (nonbranded) drugs. However, without a reasonable profit potential, drug manufacturers would discontinue expensive research programs required for the discovery and marketing of important new drugs. On balance, the increased volume generated by Medicare for the prescription drug industry is expected to more than offset any foreseeable weakness in drug prices.

MARKETING METHODS
Some companies, such as Lilly, Smith, Kline and French, and Mead Johnson, sell almost exclusively through drug wholesalers. On the other hand, Upjohn sells almost entirely to retailers. Many companies have taken steps designed to increase their direct sales of drugs to retailers. However, in view of the large number of small items which must be readily available, it is expected that wholesalers will continue to play an important role in the drug industry. The only nationwide distributor of drugs in the United States is McKesson & Robbins. Independent pharmacists obtain about 60 percent of their prescription drugs from regional service wholesalers at present.

Pharmaceutical products are distributed through the following groups: physicians, hospitals, drug stores, drug wholesalers, veterinarians, and veterinary hospitals. Ethical drugs reach the ultimate consumer 60 percent through drug stores, 20 percent through hospitals, and 20 percent directly through physicians.

The ethical drug industry's advertising is directed toward the medical profession through detail men. It was estimated that over 15,000 detail men would be employed in the U.S. in a recent year. Samples, trade publication advertising, and direct mail are also used extensively. Promotion, the cost of which generally is about 25 percent of industry sales, emphasizes new drugs and trademarked specialties.

RETAIL DRUG STORE TRENDS
Community pharmacies set new highs in 1965. Total sales for the 2397 stores included in the Lilly Digest for that year climbed to $462,847,459, or an average of $167,647 per store. Total sales per store increased $5,874 or 3.3 percent over the 1964 average reported by the 2400 pharmacies which submitted complete prescription information. Pacing this increase were prescription department revenues, which rose 8.6 percent to $68,587.

The cost of goods sold decreased, yielding a higher gross margin. Total expenses were reduced to 30.4 percent of sales from 1964's 31.0 percent, thus reversing a ten-year trend of growing expenses. Virtually every expense category either held steady or declined in 1965. Net profit climbed to 5.8 percent of total sales. The total income of a pharmacist-owner reached 13.8 percent. On a dollar basis, total income was $23,070—a 9.7 percent increase over 1964 and an all-time high.

Renewed prescriptions showed continuing strength as total prescriptions despensed per pharmacy rose to 19,708. 53.7 percent of total prescription volume was derived from renewals.

Total dollar inventory in the average Lilly Digest pharmacy increased slightly to $28,642, with all of the increase due to ethical drug supplies which averaged $9,928 or

Retail Pharmacy Sales (1956-1965)

Year	Total Rx sales (millions $)	Total non-Rx sales (millions $)	Average Rx price (dollars)	Average sales per store (thousands $)	Percent Rx volume of sales per store (%)
1965	3089	6787	3.48	167.6	40.9
1964	2731	6474	3.41	161.8	39.0
1963	2542	6253	3.39	153.3	38.3
1962	2390	6105	3.32	146.2	36.0
1961	2209	5775	3.25	139.2	35.3
1960	2175	5536	3.19	138.3	34.6
1959	2018	5230	3.09	133.3	34.0
1958	1824	4876	2.96	124.9	32.4
1957	1693	4767	2.85	124.6	30.9
1956	1461	4389	2.62	106.7	29.5

14.5 percent of prescription revenue. Each dollar invested in prescription inventory yielded $6.91 in sales. The return for the other departments was $5.29.

The large independent pharmacies and the prescription departments of drug store chains accounted for most of the increased volume of business from 1960-1965. Large independent pharmacy prescription volume experienced a 61 percent gain and the chain pharmacies more than doubled their business in this period of time. Drug stores in shopping centers and self-service drug stores also accounted for a growing segment of drug store sales.

Multi-line discount houses continued to represent a significant portion of total sales. The increase in discount houses in the late 1950s led to wide availability of drugs at reduced prices for the first time. Discounters first turned to the high margin products normally carried in drug stores and outside of the prescription drug category. Then they began installing prescription departments with registered pharmacists. Concurrently, mail-order operations arose which offered to the public both proprietary and prescription drugs. Most druggists felt that mail-order houses would not last because of the length of time in getting a prescription filled and because their "advertised low rates" were not any lower than those in discount houses. In addition, the possibility of forgery in filling prescriptions by mail raised a legal issue.

Competition from discounters gave retailers much concern. Many felt that their margins would have to be cut to 20 percent, from the usual 33 ⅓ percent to 40 percent. On the other hand, some druggists felt that discounters actually improved their business. One druggist whose store was located one block from a discount drug store stated that his prescription business had increased 10 percent since the competition had announced discount prices. His new customers complained that the discount store advertised aspirin at six cents, and when they saw it was an unknown brand, they would walk out angrily. Some customers felt that if a discounter was promoting off-brands in packaged merchandise, "Who knows what he is using in prescriptions?"

Most drug stores sold many products in addition to drugs although the prescription department was a prime producer of sales. Of the many categories of items sold, only liquor and tobacco products generated a higher sales volume per square foot than ethical drugs. Although the prescription area occupied only 13.1 percent of total floor space, it contributed over 40 percent of the total revenue recorded by the average community pharmacy in 1965. The table above presents comparative pharmacy sales data for 1956-1965.

WHOLESALE DRUGGISTS

According to the operating survey of the National Wholesale Druggists' Association, the sales of all members reached $1,836,000,000. Average sales were $5,144,000. The percentage increase over 1964 sales was 8.05 percent.

Since 1958 there has been a continuous reduction in gross margins. The gross margin for 1965 amounted to 15.54 percent, a decline of 3.5 percent from 1964. This reduction reflects manufacturers' new pricing policies, changing product mix, and the intensification of competition.

During 1965, operating expenses declined from 13.01 percent of net sales to 12.41 percent, representing the fourth consecutive year in which operating expenses declined. Net profit before taxes amounted to 3.13 percent in 1965 as compared to 3.08 percent in 1964. A summary of operations from 1961-1965 appears in the table below.

Summary of Operations for Wholesale Druggists (1961-1965)

	1965	1964	1963	1962	1961
Net Sales	100.00%	100.00%	100.00%	100.00%	100.00%
Net Cost of Goods Sold	84.45	83.91	83.45	83.08	82.84
Gross Profit	15.54	16.10	16.55	16.93	17.16
Operating Expenses	12.41	13.01	13.51	13.81	13.98
a) Administrative	4.95	5.15	5.39	5.53	5.58
b) Occupancy	0.69	0.73	0.77	0.76	0.75
c) Selling	3.13	3.32	3.44	3.47	3.55
d) Warehouse	2.24	2.37	2.44	2.53	2.58
e) Shipping	1.40	1.45	1.47	1.51	1.52
Net Profit Before Taxes	3.13	3.08	3.05	3.12	3.18
Less Federal Income Taxes	1.47	1.49	1.54	1.58	1.64
Net Profit After Taxes	1.66	1.59	1.51	1.54	1.55
Net Profit—% Net Assets	9.82	8.92	8.76	8.72	8.84
Net Profit—% Total Assets	5.12	4.82	4.58	4.73	4.70
Payroll—% Sales	6.81	7.18	7.49	7.70	7.88
Stock Turnover Rate	5.78	5.58	5.48	5.53	5.51
Days Outstanding—Receivables	42.62	43.79	42.57	42.10	42.46
Average Line Extension	$5.08	$4.74	$4.51	$4.33	$4.19
Handling Costs per Invoice Line	62.9¢	61.7¢	60.9¢	59.6¢	58.6¢
Returns, Allowances, Adjustments	3.60	3.60	3.59	3.66	3.73

Prescription Services, Inc. (B)

"It can't be!—this just isn't the way things are in America. They must think this is Nazi Germany," exclaimed Sam Reed as he banged down the telephone. Sam had just spoken to the regional representative of the Pure Chemical Company, manufacturers of prescription drugs. The Pure representative had stated that he would not be able to sell pharmaceuticals to Sam's company, Prescription Services, Inc., because, "Pure feels that the area is already saturated with wholesalers handling Pure products." The same story had been given to Sam by practically all of the other drug manufacturers.

Sam had founded Prescription Services two years earlier as a new service industry: buying drugs from the manufacturers and selling them to doctors who in turn would dispense the drugs at their offices to patients, at prices considerably below prevailing drug store prices. Now it appeared that the company would collapse. Enough doctors were enthusiastic about the idea to support it; however, it appeared that although the new firm met all legal requirements and was licensed by the state as manufacturers and wholesalers of pharmaceuticals, drug manufacturers refused to sell to it.

Sam's description of the events follows:

> The people involved in the pharmaceutical industry are in very close touch with one another by means of a grapevine of salesmen, druggists, and their associations. When my two partners simultaneously quit their jobs at Leading Labs it caused quite a stir. Word spread through the manufacturing companies that we were setting up our own business. About two months before we opened our doors, a firm identical in purpose to ours had opened up in the central part of the state and was the talk of the trade at that time. It was wrongly assumed that we were a northern branch of the same outfit. Naturally any firm that supplied the doctors with prepackaged medication would directly threaten the monopoly of the retail pharmacists in the distribution of these products. The following chain reaction occurred.

> **Difficulties**
> After securing the cooperation of the Apex Manufacturing Co., we approached our former employer, Leading Labs, as a supplier whose products we knew intimately. Leading Labs had received a number of phone calls from various members of the County Pharmaceutical Association—putting pressure on the firm not to sell to us. This is not hearsay but was told to us by close friends of ours in the company. This story was repeated with just about every major firm that manufactured pharmaceuticals. Sure, they had excuses like they already had enough wholesalers, and other answers, but we knew and were told confidentially that it was because of the pressure exerted by the retailer associations. The weapon that the

retailers had was boycott, and the local County Pharmaceutical Association solicited and obtained the cooperation of the associations in the adjoining counties. The manufacturers thus had to choose between a nonentity like Prescription Services and antagonizing the retailers. There was no choice. They didn't contact one firm soon enough, for Apex Manufacturing Co. had already decided to sell to us. However, Apex was subsequently contacted and pressured to stop selling.

Two weeks ago, I contacted the local office of the Anti-Trust Division of the Justice Department, currently engaged in a suit against these very same professional organizations for price fixing. They were very cooperative and gave me several suggestions as to what to look for that would constitute a violation of the Federal Laws. I have summarized for the record what I feel violates the law in a memorandum (Exhibit 1).

We did not feel it was wise to get under way in this new venture until we could carry all lines. Since we were unable to buy from more than one manufacturer, we switched into the area of surgical supplies, and are attempting to learn this end of the business overnight, until our supply position is resolved legally. The Justice Department will go along with us, but it may be years before the case comes up in court.

Exhibit 1. Prescription Services, Inc. (B) Sam Reed's Memo re Anti-trust.

TO: Prescription Services, Inc.

FROM: S.E. Reed

SUBJECT: An inquiry nature of certain suspected activities of the County Pharmaceutical Association as it pertains Prescription Service, Inc. and how these activities may constitute a violation of the Sherman Anti-Trust Act.

On April 13, 1961, I informally contacted the nearest Anti-Trust Division of the Justice Department of the U.S. Government in Chicago. I spoke at length with the attorneys for the Department and briefly with the chief of the Chicago Division.

The purpose of the inquiry was as follows:

a) To ascertain the nature of an action in restraint of trade as it pertains to the right to buy and its denial.

b) To determine the nature of evidence necessary to demonstrate this fact.

c) To determine the extent of the Prescription Services right to purchase from any and all manufacturers in the conduct of our business.

d) To inquire into the nature of the procedure of filing a complaint of a violation of the anti-trust act.

e) To determine as far as possible any actions that may be taken to insure that a violation doesn't take place.

The interview was informal and no action has been taken to date. It was determined that action in restraint of trade exists when two or more individuals conspire to prevent the sale of goods by a competitor. This could be one druggist calling and asking that a manufacturer not sell to us and the manufacturer *on the basis of this call* and not by his own free business judgment deciding to comply. Or if two or more manufacturers decide in concert not to sell to us. Or if a druggist should ask a doctor not to buy from us and he should comply because of this request. Any evidence to this effect, especially written, is useful. Human testimony by witnesses that can be subpoenaed to testify under oath, while less desirable as evidence, is sometimes useful. If a violation is suspected a complaint can be filed with the Justice Department. If they

Exhibit 1. *cont'd.*

feel a violation is possible they then obtain authorization from Washington to investigate. They can at times request authorization to investigate suspected activity in restraint of trade even though there has been no formal complaint. They realize that quite frequently persons wronged in this manner are apprehensive about bringing it to the attention of the Department as they feel it may damage their present business; for this reason the anonymity of the principles is protected as far as possible in any such investigation.

In the event the Justice Department finds a violation and prosecutes the violators in the name of the people of the U.S. and wins the case, this is usually very influential evidence to prove damages insofar as they can be determined. If damages can be proved the violators are liable for triple that amount.

Situation to Date:

Because of the difficulty of Prescription Services, Inc. to obtain suppliers—primarily the major manufacturers of pharmaceuticals—and the evidence that is listed below, we feel that there may be grounds for an investigation into a possible violation of the anti-trust act. The evidence is as follows:

a) A physical therapist, initially contacted by Prescription Services, Inc. as a possible builder of a rack or shelf for our merchandise overheard a pharmacist from the County Society ask for the cooperation of the adjoining County Association, in person, to put pressure on any firm that does business with Prescription Services, Inc. This fact was brought to our attention by the vice president and general manager of a firm primarily owned by the therapist.

b) Various manufacturers' representatives have commented casually about phone calls that their respective firms have received from local pharmacists, about their dealings with Prescription Services, Inc. A specific phone call that was referred to was one from a pharmacist active in the County Association, to Apex Manufacturing Co., inquiring about why they were selling to Prescription Services. The district manager at Apex was concerned that he had erred by selling to us as he was under the impression that the other firms (major) were doing business with us, and stated that he may have gone out on a limb. Many druggists have called and are hopping mad and exerting pressure on the Apex salesmen in the area.

c) An Apex salesman in our area mentioned a conversation by the above-mentioned pharmacist in a bowling alley one evening. The substance of the conversation was that the pharmacist stated that Apex was selling to Prescription Services, and said, "We thought that we had gotten to all the companies and convinced them not to sell to Prescription Services, but that we didn't get to Apex soon enough." Further comments indicated that they were taking action with the State Board of Pharmacy to block the licensing of Prescription Services. This they were not able to do.

d) There have been statements by the local pharmacists that they have figured out a way to stop our activity or rather type of activity by requiring the M.D. to obtain a resale number and charge charge sales tax on the drugs that buy and sell. They are currently working toward this end.

e) A statement by the "representative of the people of Illinois," i.e., a member of the State Board of Pharmacy that "they have figured out a way to shut down" a firm in central Illinois set up to operate the way that Prescription Services planned.

The above reasons indicate to us that there has been activity, primarily on the part of the highly organized State and County Pharmacy groups, directed to hinder the development of Prescription Services. It would also appear that some of the manufacturers have acceded to the pressure from the pharmacists and decided not to sell to Prescription Services.

Social Responsibility:
Who Should Pay?

It was almost midnight when John Esposito, President of Esposito Construction, Inc. received a telephone call from his attorney, James Cary. He held his breath until he heard Mr. Cary say, "Well, John, they turned it down—that should be the end of it." John Esposito heaved a sigh of relief at the news. After a few more comments he hung up the telephone, poured himself a drink, and settled back to think about the past three months.

THE PARK PROPOSAL

The lead story in the November 19, 1967 issue of the *South Shore Post* was the first John knew that he had a serious problem on his hands. The headline had read:

Ocean Park: Considers Second Recreation Area

The lead paragraph stated that the Ocean Park Village Board was considering a two-block square, four-acre site just south of the Southern State Parkway as an additional recreation area for residents of the Village.

His pulse had quickened as he read in the next paragraph the streets which bounded the site (see Exhibit 1). The site under consideration was the heart of John Esposito's housing development, Green Park Homes!

Mayor Michael Anderson was quoted as saying, "This site is the last remaining undeveloped area suitable for recreation within the northern boundaries of the Village. If we delay, the property will be lost to us forever. The owner is prepared to develop the property as home sites immediately." The article noted that a public hearing would be held December 9th to give the Village Board a chance to learn the attitude of the public.

OCEAN PARK

The Incorporated Village of Ocean Park was located on the South Shore of Long Island, in Suffolk County. The Village was about 30 miles from Manhattan, with most of its wage earners commuting to New York City.

Growth had been rapid in the Village in the late 1950s and early 1960s as the postwar housing boom had moved eastward on Long Island. The center of the boom was now somewhat east of the Village where larger tracts of land were available.

Houses in the northern and central areas of the Village were primarily in the medium price range on small plots. Larger and more expensive houses tended to be located on or close to the ocean, along the beach or the canals and waterways leading to the Atlantic Ocean.

The Village was somewhat peculiar in shape, being approximately five miles long on its North-South axis and only one mile or less in width on its East-West axis. The

---

This case was written by Associate Professor Robert J. Pavan, School of Business Administration, Temple University. It is based on field research. Copyright 1975 by the author. Reprinted with permission.

site which Esposito was developing was near the extreme northern boundary. The closest recreation area within the Village was about one a half miles to the south. However, State Park land formed the western boundary of the northern two-thirds of the Village. The land was in a natural state of woods and streams and contained no recreation facilities.

ESPOSITO CONSTRUCTION COMPANY

The Esposito Construction Company was a small builder of residential homes on Long Island. John Esposito had founded the company in the Spring of 1964 when he was 24 years old. In the first year of operations it had built and closed title to six one-family houses in Lakeview in Nassau County. The homes averaged $20,000 in price. The next year the company had sales of $210,000 representing 10 houses built in East Meadow, also in Nassau County. This was followed by a third small development of 14 houses in 1966 producing sales of $300,000. Currently the company was working on a 20-house project which when completed in the Spring of 1968, would represent $400,000 in sales.

John Esposito had been pleased with his progress and felt he had made the right decision in starting his own company. He believed his success to date had been due to hard work, careful supervision of operations, and some good fortune.

He had graduated from Rensselaer Polytechnic Institute in 1963 with a master's in Civil Engineering. Previously he had earned a bachelor's in Civil Engineering (1962) and Management (1961) from the same college. John's attendence at Rensselaer had been made possible by his winning full tuition scholarships and fellowships. These awards had also indirectly led to his starting Esposito Construction.

During his summer vacations he had worked for Vanguard Homes as a laborer, carpenter's helper, and carpenter. Vanguard Homes was a relatively large company which normally built 200-300 houses a year. Mr. Mario Santucci was the sole owner of Vanguard Homes and had taken an interest in John Esposito. Mr. Santucci was particularly proud that the son of an immigrant Italian family had won a college scholarship and often told John he would be glad to help him anytime he could. When John had found himself displeased with his job as structural test engineer at Grumann Aircraft he had gone to see Mr. Santucci.

Mr. Santucci owned six fully improved building plots* in Lakeview, which he offered to sell to John at cost. At the time John had little more than $2,000 in savings. They agreed to form Esposito Construction, Inc. Mr. Santucci transferred title to the plots to the new company and received 25 percent of the stock. When the six houses were delivered to the purchasers, Mr. Santucci would be paid for the land and receive 25 percent of the profit on the houses. John acquired the other 75 percent of the stock for $1,000. The company also borrowed $10,000 from John's father. The arrangement with Mr. Santucci of course reduced the financial resources needed by the new company. Of even more help was the company's ownership of the land without Mr. Santucci holding a mortgage against the land. This meant the company

---

*A fully improved building plot is one which has all offsite improvements already completed, such as paved street, water supply, sewage facility, etc.

would have available the total proceeds from construction loans once the houses were in construction. Having Mr. Santucci known as a partner in the venture also meant John was readily able to purchase building materials on credit, and hire the services of contractors, architect, mortgage broker, etc., on credit as was usual in the construction business. In effect, Mr. Santucci made available to the company his reputation and credit standing in the industry.

John completed his first house and used it as a model house and office. He worked long hours seven days a week. During the week he supervised construction and on weekends acted as salesman. While waiting for prospective buyers he would take care of the administrative tasks and plan the next week's activities. He was particularly pleased to find he was able to produce the same house as Vanguard Homes at a lower cost. At the end of the first year he paid Mr. Santucci for the land, shared the profits as agreed, and acquired Mr. Santucci's shares in the company.

OCEAN PARK DEVELOPMENT

The Ocean Park project was the largest housing development undertaken by John Esposito. The site contained 8.5 acres and would have 50 houses (60 x 100 minimum building plot size). It was in June 1966 that he had acquired the raw land for $170,000 with a down payment of $25,000. The seller took back a 7 percent, three-year mortgage for the balance. Interest was payable quarterly. Principal payments were to be at 125 percent of the mortgage prorated per building plot, and paid when the first installment was taken on the building loan on a particular plot. Two plots were released from the mortgage to be used for the construction of model houses.*

For John the Ocean Park project represented a major break in his past mode of operation. This was the first development he would build starting with raw land rather than improved building plots. This meant there would be a time lag between the acquisition of the land and when construction could start as a subdivision plan was prepared, approved, and filed with the County Clerk. The first step was to have a licensed surveying and engineering firm subdivide the site into building plots in accordance with the zoning laws, determine the grades and layout of the streets and design disposal systems for storm water and sanitary sewage. Inasmuch as Ocean Park was an incorporated village, it maintained its own Zoning Board and Highway Department, each of which had to give formal approval to the proposed subdivision. Following this, approval of the County Planning Commission was necessary. The State Health Department had to approve the sanitary sewage plans. In addition, agreements had to be made with the electric and water companies to provide these utility services before the approved subdivision plan could be filed with the County Clerk.

The Ocean Park site had appealed to John because he felt it would provide a relatively easy opportunity to gain experience in developing raw land. While it was true the site was the last large parcel of land in the area, it was also true that it was small enough so that the subdivision design was essentially fixed by the surrounding

---

*The mortgage of $145,000 was thus divided among 48 building plots, i.e., $3,021 per plot. Payment at 125 percent would thus be $3,776. The mortgage would be fully paid off when a building loan was taken on the 39th house.

pattern of development. He believed this would reduce the chance of delay while alternate subdivision designs were proposed and considered. In fact, there had been no delay of this nature, and little over six months after acquiring the land the subdivision map was filed with the County Clerk.

During the last stages of developing the plan for subdividing the land, John submitted his building plans for the two model houses to the Ocean Park Building Department. The Department had to approve the plans and the material specifications. On January 23, 1967, the day after the County Clerk's office filed the development plan, the Building Department issued the building permits for the two model houses. Construction started the following day.

Negotiations with a lender for building loans and permanent mortgages had begun some months earlier. An informal agreement had been reached and John was assured a formal commitment would be issued by the time the model houses were opened to the public.

The lender would provide both conventional mortgages and FHA insured mortgages. The latter were dependent upon approval by the FHA of the subdivision plans, the house plans, and the material specifications.

Construction of the model houses was pressed through the winter months and opened the weekend after Easter. Here too, for the first time, John had changed his mode of operation. The houses were decorated and furnished under the direction of a professional decorator. The cost for the decorator's services, the decorations, and the furnishings had been $10,000. John believed the furnished models would aid his marketing effort. He included $150 per house as part of his marketing budget to cover this expense. (He assumed he could recover $2,500 from the sale of the furnishings.) The marketing budget also included newspaper advertising (New York City, Long Island, and local newspapers), brochures (on a cooperative basis with a national building material producer), and the services of a large real estate agency which would provide salespersons at the models six days a week and office support for negotiating and preparing purchase agreements. The purchase agreement would not be binding until accepted and signed by John on behalf of Esposito Construction, Inc.

Sales had progressed steadily, if not spectacularly, and by November 19, 1967, purchase agreements had been signed for 30 houses. Five of these had later been cancelled because the purchasers' credit proved unacceptable to the lender. Of the remainder, 18 had been approved for mortgages, and 7 were pending. Upon signing a purchase agreement the average purchaser paid 5 percent of the purchase price. The average purchase price had been $22,500. Upon issuance of a mortgage commitment the purchaser had to pay 50 percent of the cost of any changes specified from the basic models. The average "extras" in a house were about $1,000.

EVENTS FOLLOWING ANNOUNCEMENT
OF THE PROPOSED PARK

The November announcement of the park proposal appeared in the Long Island newspapers as well as in the *South Shore Post*. A number of purchasers had called John Esposito to inquire about what was happening. Most had been reassured that "everything would work out all right," but two had had their attorneys send a letter stating they wanted their money back.

Sales in November and early December dropped to zero. John didn't know if this was related to the newspaper stories or poor weather or Thanksgiving and the approaching holiday season. He did know other developments had sold houses, though at a reduced amount.

The December 12, 1967 *South Shore Post* headlines read:

Villagers React Favorably: Overflow Crowd Jams Rec. Hearing

The Long Island newspapers also carried the story, but not so prominently displayed.

All the articles reported the Village expected to purchase the land for $100,000, and that the land would have to be purchased before detailed plans were drawn up. Purchase of the site would require approval by the voters in a referendum. The referendum would be held, "probably in March."

The *South Shore Post* article reported that objections to the proposed park "were based primarily upon the proximity of the site to homes on the facing and adjacent streets. Most of the objectors agreed that a recreation site was needed in the area, but 'not on my street' appeared to be the theme."

John Esposito became extremely concerned. He felt $100,000 would not compensate him for his actual out-of-pocket costs and opportunity costs. A referendum in March would mean another three months of uncertainty. If the referendum outcome were negative he would have lost considerable time, while his expenses continued. He felt he would never recoup the loss. If the referendum outcome were positive, who knew how long it might be before the Village actually acquired the land. He also feared that the "not on my street" attitude would make it extremely difficult to sell houses on the land which remained.

After consulting with his attorney, James Cary, and reviewing his alternatives he decided to sue the Ocean Park Building Department for refusing to issue him building permits. Esposito Construction had applied for 12 building permits just 10 days before the first announcement of the park proposal. In earlier conversations with the Chief Building Inspector he had been assured that it would take only two or three days for permits to be issued since the houses were the same as the two models. The extras were only items such as additional ceramic tile in the bathrooms, better appliances, wood shingles in place of asbestos shingles, etc., which did not change the structural design, size, or room arrangements. Following the November announcement the company had filed for building permits on all the affected building plots. No permits had been issued and no reason had been given.

The decision to sue was not taken lightly. It appeared obvious the Village Board had instructed the Building Department not to issue permits so as to prevent the cost of acquisition being increased by the value of construction in progress. For this reason, the Village attorney might seek to delay the trial date. Mr. Cary could give no assurance that the Village would not be successful in delaying the trial. He did believe that if the suit came to trial before the Village Board had formally decided to acquire the land, the judge would rule the permits had to be issued.

However, beyond the legal aspects, John Esposito was concerned that even if he was successful in the suit, he had to "live with" the Village until the development was finally completed. The Building Department would have to inspect the construction at various stages. Satisfactory reports were required by the lender before any building loans would be made. Although John personally supervised construction and had never had any difficulty passing inspections, he knew inspections could be delayed and inspectors could become very picayune in their interpretations of the building code. The Building Department also issued the Certificate of Occupancy required before title to a house could be passed to the purchaser. Also, the Village Highway Department had to inspect and approve the construction of the streets, curbs, sidewalks, and storm water sewer system before the insurance company would release John from his personal responsibility under the performance bond. It was conceivable that though both departments were headed by professionals their actions might be politically influenced—as it was the Building Department was delaying the issuance of the building permits—thus a victory in court could be a pyrrhic victory.

On the other hand, John was convinced the publicity about the proposed park was responsible for the severe drop in sales. In the five weeks since the story had first appeared, only one house had been sold. He had also received four more letters from attorneys of previous buyers, plus numerous telephone calls.

After the suit was filed, the Village attorney asked the court to delay the trial date until after a referendum was held. Mr. Cary argued that his client would be seriously harmed by so long a delay. A compromise was agreed upon whereby the trial would be delayed until the Village conducted a post-card survey.

The January 16, 1968, *South Shore Post* headline announced:

Post Card Survey to Gauge Opinion
Board Sets Poll On Village Parks

Following the December public meeting the proposed park site acquisition had generated much controversy in the Village. Mayor Michael Anderson had received two petitions, one with 280 signatures against the acquisition of the four acres, and one with 250 names in favor. In addition, the suggestion that the Village seek to lease five acres of State Park land was also being discussed. The Village Recreation Committee recommended the Esposito property be acquired rather than the State Park land. The Committee argued at the January Village Board meeting that a park was needed and acquisition of a site would be permanent whereas the state would only grant a 10-year lease with an option to renew. Mayor Anderson announced that a post-card survey would be held before the February Village Board meeting. The Mayor did not announce that Esposito Construction had sued the Building Department.

In the last week of January approximately 4500 post-card ballots were mailed. At the February 10th Village Board meeting the results were announced as follows:

1. Acquire site within the Village	199 votes
2. Lease State Park land	384 votes
3. Obtain both sites	229 votes
4. Opposed to any of the above	1,070 votes
	1,882 total replies

The Board announced it would analyze the results before making any decision. Mr. Cary felt certain the threat to John Esposito's land was passed and called to tell him, "Well, John, they turned it down—that should be the end of it."

JOHN ESPOSITO'S VIEW

John Esposito rejoiced in the outcome, which he felt certain would permit him to proceed with construction and remove the uncertainty which had caused sales to drop drastically. However, his initial pleasure receded as he thought about the expenses the whole episode had caused him.

Jim Cary's legal bill covering attendence at Village Board meetings, filing suit, and time in court would probably be about $1,000. The project had been delayed the past three months, which meant some $2,500 for mortgage interest and another $2,500 in real estate taxes. It was likely that sales would not pick up rapidly enough to make up for the loss in sales and put the project on schedule. That would mean more interest and taxes. He was also sure that stretching the job out meant he could expect some contractors to seek price increases, as new labor contracts were negotiated. John wasn't certain how much this would amount to, as most contracts with contractors included both materials and labor. But it was likely some building material prices would be raised also. As a rough estimate, John figured a 5 percent increase on labor and materials for half the houses would amount to $15,000. It would not be possible to pass on any of these costs, as houses were sold under fixed price contracts. He might try to raise prices on the unsold houses but that could slow down sales.

An even more difficult cost to determine but one which John felt was very real, was the cost involved in delaying the acquisition of land for the next development. He couldn't afford the cash to tie up land, nor did he want to take on the additional financial burden of carrying the land and the expenses involved in preparing a development plan. The delay would mean lost profit opportunities—hard to figure, but real nevertheless to John.

No matter how John looked at matters, he felt he was the one paying the most for this exercise in democratic government. In his view, the whole incident was the responsibility of a few politicians who had acted, at best, to alert citizens to a choice which would be lost forever, or at worst, simply to cover themselves from possible political attack. These individuals were not out of pocket, but John had been made to foot the bill. He had acted according to all the rules—the land had been zoned for houses, he hadn't sought any changes, he had obtained all the required approvals—yet he had been interrupted in pursuing his business. It did not seem fair to John Esposito that the private person or company had to pay for the community's opportunity "to act out their hangups." They should pay him!

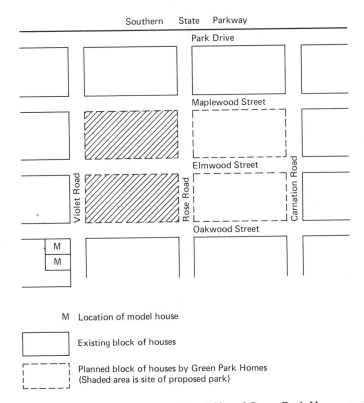

M   Location of model house

Existing block of houses

Planned block of houses by Green Park Homes
(Shaded area is site of proposed park)

Exhibit 1. Social Responsibility: Who Should Pay? Site of Green Park Homes and Proposed Park Site.

Exhibit 2. Social Responsibility: Who Should Pay? Building Permits Issued on Long Island (in dwelling units).*

	Nassau	**Suffolk**	**Queens**	**Brooklyn**	**4 Counties Total**
1950	30,987	9,652	24,336	6,566	71,541
1955	15,388	14,481	7,988	7,776	45,633
1960	7,590	11,008	13,101	10,048	41,747
1961	7,764	11,194	25,876†	13,292†	58,126
1962	5,939	14,316	14,977†	21,333†	56,565
1963	5,726	11,777	17,248	9,864	44,615
1964	5,118	13,105	6,008	4,997	29,228
1965	5,320	13,000	4,907	4,777	28,004
1966	3,869	11,566	5,372	2,512	23,319

*Each one-family house and each apartment is considered a dwelling unit. Dwelling units in Brooklyn and Queens primarily are multiple-family buildings, while those in Nassau and Suffolk are primarily single-family buildings.

†Far above normal authorizations due to builders filing plans for apartment houses to beat expected effective date of more restrictive zoning ordinance in New York City.

Liberty Bell
Furniture Company (A)

George Ross had only been on the job for a little over a year and was now in the midst of the most conflicting situation of his life.

George was a 1973 graduate of Penn. State, where he had majored in Literature and Communications. An active career on campus included editing the literary magazine and serving as President of both his social fraternity and the campus chapter of the journalism fraternity. Inclusion in *Who's Who in American Colleges and Universities* culminated George's goal of success for his collegiate career.

After graduation George set his sights on continuing his success in the business world. After many weeks of looking, George was unsuccessful in obtaining employment. Although he was the independent type and disliked the possibility of using friends and relatives to get a job, George reluctantly agreed to an interview arranged by a family friend, Dick Sweetman. This interview was with the Liberty Bell Furniture Company.

The day before his interview, George obtained copies of the financial statements for the past couple of years. He was impressed by the recent rise in profits after a period of decline (see Exhibit 1).

The Liberty Bell Furniture Company is located in suburban Philadelphia. It is one of the three major manufacturers and suppliers of office furniture in the area. Their customers included several retail outlets and individual businesses. The retailers bought their merchandise at a set wholesale price. Individual businesses could buy individual items at these prices. When a business was opening or remodeling an office they would ask the three to submit bids as to the cost of the entire package of office furniture.

As George discovered in his preinterview preparation, the company has taken a recent turn for the better. The major competition is provided by the Gibbs Furniture Company and Franklin Office Furniture and Supply Company.

The Liberty Bell Company had developed from a small family business into its present size. The company employed about 175 people. The company manufactured and assembled office equipment such as desks, chairs, file equipment, etc.

The structure of the company is illustrated in Exhibit 2. Mr. Bob Reilly, grandson of the now deceased founder, is president and the major stockholder. He likes to run the business completely on his own, although he does have a series of Vice Presidents revolving around him.

The interview turned out to be an interesting experience for George. The interviewer, Scott Murray, was only seven years older than George and possessed an energetic outlook toward his job, the company as a whole, and his future. The two men discovered many similarities between themselves.

Prepared under the supervision of Prof. William Allen, University of Rhode Island. Reprinted with permission.

*This and all the facts of this case have been altered to secure the anonymity of all involved.

The following week George started working for the Liberty Bell as a management trainee. To his great pleasure, Scott Murray was his immediate supervisor. He was to learn the working of the company from the bottom up. The training period was to last for approximately one year, at which time he would be made a manager of a production department or an assistant in an office department, depending upon his performance during the training period.

Throughout his year of internship George demonstrated enormous amounts of interest and enthusiasm for whatever he was doing. Also during this time his respect and admiration for Scott Murray grew. Murray's job was head of the marketing segment of Liberty Bell. He directed the direct mail campaign, supervised the sales force, and organized the trade shows. During his stay in the marketing department, George used his writing skills to their utmost in helping to develop a new advertising campaign. The effort earned him a permanent position in the department at the end of his training.

The interview that had been an obligation to his family turned out to be the beginning of a good job. George felt that a few years under Scott Murray would prepare him for a successful career in marketing and advertising.

Liberty Bell had again shown an increase in profits and George liked to think it was partially because of his efforts in the marketing department. Although he was working in the marketing department, George wanted to gain more knowledge of the total workings of the business. Through Murray, George was invited to attend executive meetings.

Bob Reilly, the President of Liberty Bell, noticed George's ambition and after one meeting asked George if he would like to accompany him to a rather special meeting. George agreed readily and was scheduled to meet with Mr. Reilly in the morning to discuss the forthcoming special conference.

The next morning, George was ushered into the president's office and had a seat while Mr. Reilly finished a telephone conversation. At the conclusion of the call, Mr. Reilly expressed his satisfaction with George's performance and asked him how he felt about Liberty Bell in general. George answered that all was going smoothly and he liked the company as a whole. When Mr. Reilly asked George if he felt he was loyal to the firm, George replied in the affirmative. At the end of the conversation, Mr. Reilly told George to meet him at a country club in a nearby suburban area. George was excited at the prospect of seeing the inside of what was considered the most exclusive club in the entire Philadelphia metropolitan area.

The next day on the way to club, George began to wonder about the loyalty question posed to him the previous morning, but quickly dismissed it and turned his thoughts toward this morning's meeting.

Mr. Reilly met George as he walked in and proceeded to guide him to an outside table near the club's tennis courts. He was then introduced to Mr. Gibbs and Mrs. Dexter, the presidents of the Gibbs and Franklin Furniture Companies respectively. George was extremely surprised but managed to conceal his feelings and conduct himself in a businesslike way.

The meeting was informal and after a half hour of coffee, pastries, and small talk concerning general business and pleasure, George decided that this was just a friendly get-together between the heads of the companies. But, just as George was feeling relaxed, Mrs. Dexter said, "Gentlemen, I believe the cooperation among ourselves has been most beneficial for all of us, I hope that we can agree on a good price for the next contract, since it is my company's turn to submit the low bid." George again tried to retain his composure but felt his surprise must have shown through this time. For the remainder of the meeting George sat silently. The later part of the council was involved with bid arrangements, a proposed across-the-board increase in wholesale prices, and a discussion of a blacklist for employees.

After the weekend and a great deal of soul-searching, George decided to confront Scott Murray concerning the matter. George was disappointed to learn that Murray knew about the arrangement. Scott proceeded to explain his position:

> I learned about the cooperation among the presidents in much the same manner you did, although at that time it was in the planning stages. I told Bob that I didn't approve, but he dismissed me, saying that it would be best for the companies and the customers. I have since put the whole thing out of my mind and removed myself from all responsibility.

George was in a state of great indecision. He wanted to be like Scott and forget but he just couldn't get the whole thing off of his mind. He was slated for a two-week vacation and decided to think things over and make some kind of a decision.

During his vacation George sought the advice of Dick Sweetman. He wanted to know if Mr. Reilly was as inflexible as everyone said he was. Dick reinforced the stories of Bob Reilly's domination of his business; there was no chance of influencing him on a major policy decision from within the company.

George knew he could report the practice to the authorities and action would be taken, but George did not really want to do that to the company or to himself. Somehow he felt that if he did get involved legally he might have trouble getting another job, even though he had taken the side of the law.

Exhibit 1. Liberty Bell Furniture Company (A) Income Statements 1970–1973 ($1,000)

	1970	1971	1972	1973
Liberty Bell				
Net Sales	11,563	10,907	12,598	14,100
Cost of Goods Sold	8,432	7,798	8,694	9,800
Gross Income	3,131	3,109	3,904	4,300
Advertising	100	140	120	120
Other Expenses	2,501	2,489	2,900	3,000
Tax Payments	318	288	530	708
Net Income	212	192	354	472
Franklin Company				
Net Sales	9,010	9,520	10,900	12,120
Cost of Goods Sold	7,007	7,280	7,900	8,610
Gross Income	2,003	2,240	3,000	3,510
Advertising	80	80	110	110
Other Expenses	1,860	1,960	2,400	2,720
Tax Payments	38	120	294	408
Net Income	25	80	196	272
Gibbs Company				
Net Sales	8,440	8,735	10,000	11,370
Cost of Goods Sold	6,111	6,300	7,300	7,900
Gross Income	2,329	2,435	2,700	3,470
Advertising	75	100	110	110
Other Expenses	2,098	2,125	2,200	2,700
Tax Payments	90	126	234	396
Net Income	66	84	156	264

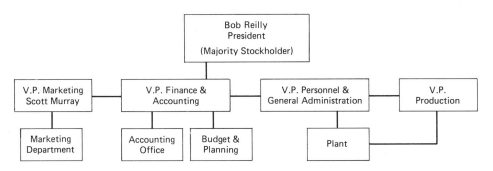

Exhibit 2. Liberty Bell Furniture Company (A) Organization Chart.

Liberty Bell
Furniture Company (B)*

George Ross, a young executive of the Liberty Bell Company, has become aware of the fact that his company is in collusion with its two main competitors.

In total, they virtually monopolize the market. After much thought, George has decided to attempt to coerce the president, Bob Reilly, into getting out of the triumvirate.

The morning following George's decision to change company policy he was in Mr. Reilly's office. He requested an appointment for the middle of the week. In preparing for the meeting, George was diligently putting together an advertising and public relations campaign that he believed would allow his company to retain its position of increasing profits, without any artificial price setting. He was also working on an idea that would help the company to expand its present market.

On Wednesday, George felt he was ready. The meeting went something like this:

George: Good morning sir. I've come to propose to you a new marketing plan that will allow Liberty Bell to get out on its own, so to speak.

Bob Reilly: Oh, so you don't like the idea of our company working with the Gibbs and Franklin Companys? Well, I gave this a great deal of thought before we entered into the arrangement and I think it is in our best interest.

George: Surely, sir, you have more faith in your company than that. Even when things were on the down swing your company was the market leader.

B. Reilly: Well, I had my doubts and, furthermore, I'm not getting any younger and the pressure of us losing ground was becoming too great. In addition, it is my contention that this whole arrangement is better for the three companies and for the customers.

George: The customers! How do you expect higher prices to be better for the customers?

B. Reilly: Well, I should rephrase my last statement. Although it may not be best for the customers, they don't really feel the difference in price. They can afford it. For instance, when we bid, we get a fair price, not one that will underbid the other companies. Since most of these companies are big a few dollars won't hurt. Also, any government agency that we serve is just trying to spend the money that is allotted them. It's better we get the money instead of some foreigners or those lazy s.o.b.'s living on welfare.

George: I totally disagree and the question of big business's wealth or government politics is not the issue. It is against the law to fix prices. All of your rationalizations will not change that.

B. Reilly: Well, son. I'm sorry you don't like the way I run my business. I suppose you don't know that everybody gets together on prices. Therefore, if you are willing

---

Prepared under the supervision of Prof. William Allen, University of Rhode Island. Reprinted with permission.

*This and all the facts of this case have been altered to secure the anonymity of all involved.

to work here, that's fine with me. I think you have a great future with us or any-
place else you might choose to go to, but if you don't get used to the realities of the
business world you may be in trouble anywhere.

George: Well, sir, thank you for your confidence, but I wish you'd listen to my plans
for Liberty to go out on our own.

B. Reilly: (Harshly) I told you, do your job at your level and don't bother me with
your ignorant righteousness.

George: Well, sir, I guess I'm going to have to report this to the proper authorities.
Then you'll see what is right and what's wrong.

At this point, Bob Reilly becomes extremely angry and yells, "Go ahead, if you
can get any proof, and if we were convicted, as a first offense we'd be subject to a fine.
The profits we're making now because of our arrangement more than compensates
for that possibility. Now get out of here before I fire you!"

George left his office and still was undecided as to whether to stay or quit, tell or
not tell.

Bryn Mawr National Bank

In early 1974, President John Fargo of the Bryn Mawr National Bank was attempting
to define the future goals and strategy of his bank. Since its founding in 1965, the Bryn
Mawr National Bank had been moderately successful in terms of asset expansion and
deposit growth. A total deposit target of $20,000,000 had been achieved by the end of
1973. However, President Fargo was concerned about the continued success of his
bank because competitive conditions in the banking industry in the local region were
changing in directions that did not look well for the Bryn Mawr National Bank.

THE LOCAL REGION
Bryn Mawr is a town in eastern Pennsylvania with a population of approximately
27,000. It is located west of Philadelphia and is adjoined by the towns of Wynwood,
Bala, Haverford, and Villanova. The population of Bryn Mawr and its contiguous
towns is about 117,000. Eighty percent of the Bryn Mawr National Bank's deposits
come from the area made up of these towns. Another 15 percent of the bank's deposits
come from an area stretching as far west as Paoli, as far east as Philadelphia, as far
north as the Schuylkill River, and south to Chester. The remaining 5 percent come
from throughout the eastern United States.

Bryn Mawr is an affluent bedroom community. The largest industry in it and the
surrounding towns is education. There are Bryn Mawr College, Haverford College,

George E. Shagory and John Aboud, Babson College. Reprinted with permission.

Woody Knoll, and Villanova University among others. However, neither education nor the educators dominate the Town of Bryn Mawr. Many groups have a voice in the affairs of the town, and none singly is dominant.

The area which the bank serves is predominantly residential, and most of the homes are owner occupied. Average family income was over $23,000 in 1972. The businesses in the area are almost wholly clothing stores, automobile service stations, food chains and small outlets, commercial and residential service establishments, restaurants and other eating establishments, motels, a television station, financial organizations (other than banks), and various department and household goods stores.

COMPETITIVE SITUATION

Throughout the local area, the small suburban country banks are merging with the large county banks. The rationale for this has been the pressure exerted by the stockholders of the country banks for greater and more stable earnings. Small banks have not been able to generate large earnings. While banks in general have not generated high earnings, the city and county banks have achieved higher earnings than their smaller country brethren. Moreover, the "domino" effect has come into play. For example, when an offer was made by the Philadelphia County Bank for the Delaware Valley Security Company in Bryn Mawr, the stockholders of the latter quickly accepted because the offer was thought to be financially beneficial. However, other local banks then became convinced that they had to join larger banks for defensive and other reasons. Within a month the Wynwood National Bank joined the Delaware National Bank. Shortly thereafter, the Commerical Bank of Haverford joined the Citizens' Bank of Philadelphia.

There is also the increasing trend toward bank holding companies. Valley Forge Associates, for example, has gained control over 25 banks. The Delaware National Bank has formed a holding company that was approved by all the regulatory agencies late last year. This holding company is comprised of banks in Pottsboro, Lancaster, Chester, Paoli, Keystone, and Philadelphia. And on January 2, 1974, the Paoli Trust Company, the Wynwood Commercial Bank, and the Commercial Bank of Roxboro joined together in a holding company called the Associated Bank and Trust Group. In two months, the First National Bank of Whitemarsh and the Guaranty Trust Company of Cheltenham will also join this holding company.

In the Town of Bryn Mawr, there are seven commercial banks, one savings bank, and one cooperative bank in addition to the Bryn Mawr National Bank. The level of banking services provided by these institutions is quite sophisticated.

COMPANY HISTORY

The Bryn Mawr National Bank opened its doors on October 1, 1965. It was organized by 17 wealthy town fathers who felt that Bryn Mawr needed to have a bank of its own. Their reasons were several. Five of the men had essentially altruistic reasons for organizing the bank. They wanted to form a bank for the town. Then there were those who were profit motivated. These eight men were after fast money. Another four men felt that being on the Board of Directors of a bank meant power and prestige. These were the status seekers.

The bank is housed in a comfortable rustic building which is conservative and secure in appearance. There is ample room for all of the bank's services and operations. The location is easily accessible and is next to several free off-the-street parking areas. Moreover, there are two conveniently located drive-up windows on the west side of the building. The building is situated in the downtown area of Bryn Mawr on the eastern side. The nearest competition is the co-operative bank located about one-quarter of a mile away.

PHILOSOPHY AND GOALS

According to Mr. Fargo, the primary objective of the Bryn Mawr National Bank is to provide the finest in personal banking services to the people of Bryn Mawr. In line with this, the name Bryn Mawr was included in the corporate name of the bank because it is prestigious and means a great deal to the people who live there.

The bank is interested in two market segments. One is the household accounts of residents of the town and the contiguous area. The second is the small businesses in Bryn Mawr and the surrounding region. Management felt that the bank would be able to provide a full range of services to these groups without overtaxing its resources.

In order to meet the competition of the other banks in the area, the Bryn Mawr National Bank provides a full range of services. These include regular checking accounts ($1 minimum for free checks and no service charge), savings accounts, travelers checks, safe deposit boxes, safe deposit storage of valuables, trust services, drive-in window service, a night depository, banking by mail, certificates of deposit, purchase and sale of securities for customers without a broker, correspondent services, commercial foreign letters of credit, individual foreign letters of credit, and MASTERCHARGE credit cards. Like its competition, the Bryn Mawr National Bank is a member of the Federal Deposit Insurance Corporation.

To meet the needs of its customers, the bank offers three types of loans. One is the installment loan for the purchase of an automobile, boat, trailer, or other consumer durable purchase. These loans varied in length from under one year to four years and were paid back in monthly installments covering interest and principal.

The second type of loan is the real estate loan or mortgage on homes and land. These are usually long term (15, 20, 25 or more years) and are amortized through monthly payments of interest and principal. The total amount of real estate loans depends upon the size of the bank's capital and also on its total time deposits.

The third type of loan involves financing local businesses on a short- or intermediate-term basis that varies from 90 days to two years. The short-term loans are repaid in a single payment on or before a specified date. The intermediate-term loans are usually paid back on an installment basis according to a designated schedule.

By the end of 1973, installment loans totaled over $4.5 million, real estate loans were almost $1 million, and financing to local businesses was up to "several millions." Each type of loan was thought to be profitable.

The literature describing the bank stresses two points primarily:

Service

We believe in money services for people with modern money needs. We believe in maximum privacy and security for your assets. We are Bryn Mawr people dealing person-to-person, in confidence and trust, with Bryn Mawr people.

The Town of Bryn Mawr

The Bryn Mawr National Bank was established by Bryn Mawr people for Bryn Mawr people. It is "our bank." It is based on the conviction that Bryn Mawr should have a bank of its own. A bank that is free to make its own decisions on how best to meet your banking needs.

PROMOTION

In order to get its message to its two market segments, the bank utilized a variety of media. Billboard advertising on heavily traveled highways was thought to be an effective way to reach household accounts. Radio advertising at the beginning of each month was used to reach both markets. Every two months a letter was sent to businessmen. One letter would "sell" payroll accounting. Another letter would "sell" checking accounts. A third letter might "sell" the different types of loans available at the bank. Further, the bank would contribute to or cosponsor local sporting or theatrical events. The bank did not engage in the practice of giving premiums or gifts for opening new accounts or substantially expanding current accounts.

ORGANIZATION

In the bank, there are three officers (see Exhibits 1 and 2). John Fargo, the president, is 52 years old and has been in banking for over a quarter of a century. He had worked for several of the other banks in the area over the years attaining increasingly broader responsibilities in all phases of commercial banking. He was hired to become the Bryn Mawr National Bank's first president in 1965.

The assistant vice-president, Craig Robinson, is 40 years of age and a native son of Bryn Mawr. He has been in banking for just over 15 years, having worked in three other banks in the local area before joining the Bryn Mawr National Bank in 1965.

Arthur Porter, the comptroller, joined the management in 1971. At that time, he resigned from one of the large Philadelphia banks where he was an assistant comptroller. He is 44 years old and has over 22 years of banking experience, mostly in the spheres of accounting, auditing, and bookkeeping.

All three of the officers have bachelor's degrees in business administration and have attended the Stonier School of Banking at Rutgers. In addition, all three have received advanced certificates for completing prescribed banking courses offered by the American Institute of Banking.

Besides the officers, there are 21 clerical/teller personnel in the bank. Four female clerks are in accounting, including a supervisor who has 16 years' experience and is regarded very highly by the officers. Two of the accounting clerks have less than two years of experience, and the third has over five years of experience. There are seven tellers, including a head teller. The tellers are women in their late teens and early to middle twenties. Three are the wives of students at Villanova University. There are also three secretaries who can fill in as tellers when needed. Seven clerks, including a first-line supervisor, comprise the bookkeeping group. They vary in age from late teens to early forties. Their experience varies from one month to twelve years. All seven are women.

Clerical/teller personnel are hired from the local area. Among the younger women, turnover is high. Student wives are generally good workers, but they leave after their husbands' graduation. Some employees leave to get married, others to have children. In the last three years, turnover has averaged 50 percent per year. This is equal to the experience of the other banks in the area.

PERFORMANCE

The Bryn Mawr National Bank has earned profits every month since its eighth month of operation. While the amount of profit in some months was very low, some profit has been steadily achieved since May, 1966.

However, in recent months, the growth in deposits has been less than in previous periods (see Exhibit 3). While the overall target of $20,000,000 in total deposits has been reached, the recent growth rate has management concerned about the impact of changing competitive conditions on the future profitability of the bank.

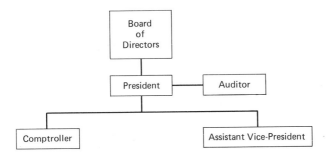

Exhibit 1. Bryn Mawr National Bank Organization Chart.

Exhibit 2. Bryn Mawr National Bank Organizational Manual.

Responsibilities of President

A. Investments

  1. Investment advisory service
  2. Portfolio administration
  3. Money position
  4. Financial planning
  5. Dealer operations
  6. New business
  7. Municipal bids
  8. Customer securities
  9. Reports

B. Lending

  1. Commercial
  2. Real estate
  3. Collateral
  4. Collections
  5. Credit analysis
  6. New business

C. Operations

  1. Overdrafts
  2. Balances
  3. Equipment

Responsibilities of Assistant Vice-President

A. Lending

  1. Installment loans
  2. Credit
  3. Collections
  4. Records
  5. New business

B. Personnel

  1. Employment
  2. Training
  3. Management development
  4. Salary administration
  5. Employee benefits
  6. Organizational planning
  7. Counseling and educational planning
  8. Payroll
  9. Vacations
  10. Substitutions
  11. Blue Cross/Blue Shield

Exhibit 2. *cont'd.*

C. Advertising

1. Public relations
2. Publicity
3. Market analysis
4. Service analysis
5. Branch and office design
6. New business
7. Annual report

D. Business Development

1. Sales planning
2. Customer relations
3. Branch development
4. New business

E. Data Processing

1. Data control
2. Methods and systems

Responsibilities of Comptroller

A. Personnel

1. Records
2. Reports
3. Teller training
4. Proof training
5. Life insurance

B. Operations

1. General services
2. Protection
3. Printing
4. Supply and archives

5. Mail
6. Checkbook order
7. Purchasing
8. Central information file
9. Account maintenance
10. Filing
11. Savings
12. Safe deposit
13. Check collections
14. Proof and transit
15. Clearings

C. Accounting

1. Income and expense
2. Profit analysis
3. Budgeting
4. Bill payments
5. Insurance
6. Taxes
7. Financial and administrative reports
8. Building and maintenance

D. Data Processing

1. Data control
2. Methods and systems
3. Settlement
4. Encoding and control
5. New business
6. Cost analysis
7. Budget and expense
8. Correspondent banking

Exhibit 3. Bryn Mawr National Bank Performance Indicators.

Date	Total number of checking accounts	Total number of savings accounts	Demand deposits	Time deposits	Total deposits
Dec. 31, 1965	105	24	$ 130,366	$ 32,556	$ 162,922
June 30, 1966	549	219	1,159,843	762,479	1,922,322
Dec. 31, 1966	1,758	572	1,728,734	1,391,427	3,120,161
June 30, 1967	3,279	844	2,834,748	1,967,846	4,802,594
Dec. 31, 1967	4,416	1,151	3,777,473	3,135,430	6,912,903
June 30, 1968	5,491	1,473	4,301,007	3,954,471	8,255,478
Dec. 31, 1968	6,521	1,740	4,891,979	3,997,899	8,889,878
June 30, 1969	8,107	2,091	5,673,823	4,697,415	10,371,238
Dec. 31, 1969	9,794	2,738	6,301,347	5,418,644	11,719,991
June 30, 1970	10,781	2,991	6,874,999	6,198,220	13,073,219
Dec. 31, 1970	11,838	3,174	7,499,871	6,904,952	14,404,823
June 30, 1971	13,173	3,583	8,381,792	7,492,119	15,873,911
Dec. 31, 1971	14,598	3,958	9,017,911	8,384,079	17,401,990
June 30, 1972	15,371	4,638	9,483,237	8,696,711	18,179,948
Dec. 31, 1972	16,290	4,927	9,788,279	9,011,620	18,799,899
June 30, 1973	16,956	5,051	10,213,145	9,260,657	19,473,802
Dec. 31, 1973	17,631	5,105	10,798,879	9,305,919	20,104,798

Vail Industries, Inc. (A)

Joseph Becker, president of Vail Industries, seemed to capture his effect on the company with the following quote:

> My basic contribution to the expansion and stability of Vail Industries has been the pioneering, implementation, and extension of the concept of creative selling. Creative selling recognizes the customer's requirements as the prime ingredient in business success, rather than our ability to make the product. This forces us to modify equipment or add equipment or even subcontract work in order to deliver the product which the customer requires. Our current sales force seems to display and utilize the concept very well. With this concept well integrated into the organization, I am currently focusing on the development of a creative, adaptive management team which utilizes modern techniques and modern technology so that we can double our 1973 sales in five years.

HISTORY

Mr. Becker pointed out that Vail Industries has gone through four basic growth stages and is now entering its fifth growth stage. Vail Industries began in 1914 in a pushcart when the Vail brothers purchased merchandise from a large wholesaler and sold to retailers in Baltimore, Maryland. The basic type of merchandise was packaging and paper products, including string, paper bags, etc. In the early 1930s the pushcarts were put into storage and the company became a legitimate paper and paper-related products wholesaling organization. After its initial wholesaling start in the early '30s it maintained a slow, long-term, stable growth pattern. The third phase of development came in 1950 when the company purchased a four-story building containing 85,000 square feet of floor space that was previously used as an automotive repair shop. As a result of an abundance of space, the company began experimenting with paper converting. Paper converting is the process of taking large rolls or quantities of paper and cutting them down to the sizes needed by the individual customers. An example of paper converting products is insert boards used by the textile trades in packaging their products prior to purchase by the customers.

During this period of time, a couple of events set the stage for future developments. The company sales force was basically paid on commission and given very little training. As a consequence, the company had difficulty retaining salesmen. During the mid and late 1950s the company hired its first college graduates and in the span of five years added three or four college graduates to its selling and managerial staff. Partially as a result of the market opportunities seen by these college graduates and the pressure brought by them, the company moved into phase four, which was the creative selling phase. This was materially advanced by the acquisition of four additional large pieces of equipment which allowed the company: (1) to increase its product line, (2) to increase the services which it could provide to its customers, and (3) lower its prices, thus giving the salesman an edge over his competition.

This case was prepared by William Naumes and Robert Schellenberger of Temple University as the basis for class discussion, rather than to illustrate either effective or ineffective handling of an administrative situation.

Creative selling involved a recognition of the consumer needs as the first priority in production and determination of the product line, rather than the particular facilities owned by the company. This may require the addition or modification of existing equipment, or even subcontracting work when the company does not have the facilities, rather than passing by opportunities. Creative selling also involved a training program for new salesmen so that they could operate effectively as salesmen. This training program was approximately one year in duration and required the salesman to rotate jobs throughout the company's capabilities. In addition, the new salesman was involved in role playing, with the sales manager taking the part of the customer and then critiquing the selling job of the salesman. Either because of the company's emphasis on creative selling or because the selling end of the business was the only end with any formal training activities, almost all of the current managers were salesmen at one time.

The fifth and current stage of the company development is the management-team-building stage. This team building is in part necessitated by the dramatic increase in sales which occurred in the last seven years, when the sales went from $2.14 million in 1968 to $4.2 million in 1973, but more important, from a recognition that if the company is to develop and prosper, a strong management team is essential.

MANAGERIAL PERSONNEL

Arthur Wiseman, former president, is chairman of the board. He joined the company in 1931. He and Mr. Becker comprise the only voting stockholders. When not in Florida, or out of town on other business (about one half of the time), Mr. Wiseman spends four to five hours a day in the company offices. He feels that he is basically an experienced resource ready to assist the young management team. He feels that it is usually better to let his subordinates make their own mistakes, however. He added that any mistakes should be new ones. Mr. Wiseman leaves the resolution of conflicts among subordinates to Joe Becker. He added, "If something important happens, or if I don't agree with him, I'll stick my nose in it."

Joseph Becker, age 38, is president and dominant force in the organization. Joe started with the company in 1959, shortly after finishing a BBA degree, advancing through the ranks (primarily in selling areas) to become president and a substantial stockholder in the corporation. Joe assumed the presidency in 1971. He indicated to the casewriters that at the end of four to five years, when the company had attained a sales level of 20 million dollars and the management team had been developed, he expected to take the company public.

The vice-president of administration is Jerry Nicholson, who at 39 is the oldest active manager. Jerry started working with the company in 1954 at the age of 19 and worked at various tasks in the office and plant as needed. These jobs were not primarily supervisory, but they allowed him to see all facets of the business except sales. His second job was in the sales area as a salesman. In 1964, he was promoted to vice-president of administration largely on the basis of his abilities in handling details and negotiating with employees and suppliers. Jerry's duties included managing the office (i.e., all record-keeping activities, all bookkeeping activities, preparation of invoices and approval of credit), purchasing, sales servicing, and preparation of work orders. Sales servicing involved actual selling of some accounts (some of his and Mr. Wiseman's old accounts) and taking orders for accounts credited to other salesmen.

Preparation of work orders involves indicating exactly what raw materials are to be processed, on what equipment, and how.

Robert Green, age 34, is the vice-president of sales, with training in the areas of inventory and production management. Robert began with Vail in 1961 after some college work. His primary responsibility is management of the sales force and the promotion activity. Robert is also responsible for sales service work, order preparation, and some purchasing. He purchases about 10 percent of the raw materials, dealing basically with the l oard mills. In addition to the four top managers who are involved with selling, there are five salesmen whom he supervises.

Mr. Green also takes part in the new product development process. He transmits information from salesmen to the rest of the management group which collectively makes new product decisions. He also assists in the production-planning process for both old and new products.

Ken George is assistant to the president and is being groomed for a future executive position. Ken's primary responsibilities lie in the area of production and purchasing, including the development of production techniques, control of the cost of production, developing primary figures on new equipment purchases, and improvement of shipping and warehousing operations. Ken recently completed an MBA at night at the University of Maryland.

Andy Kramer is responsible for the paper converting and shipping department, and Dan Smith is responsible for the printing and die-cutting departments. These two gentlemen, with the help of Ken George, are responsible for running the production and warehouse operations. The production schedule is made up twice weekly by the president after the executive-committee meeting. The key to Vail's customer service is the ability to adjust production to deliver the goods when needed by the customer. This means frequent changes in the production schedule.

Joe Becker reports that the executive team indeed works as a team. Titles are merely to indicate areas where detailed responsibility and action lie. But the team freely exchanges information on problems as well as discusses the major decisions and policies made by the organization. However, the final decision rests with Mr. Becker, subject to Mr. Wiseman's veto.

Mr. Becker states that "the company is very reflective of my life-style and views." He spend a great deal of time, at least 15 percent of his working day, on outside, charitable projects. Other members of the management team similarly spend time and money on charitable, social, and political efforts.

The atmosphere was extremely informal in the office. Keying on Mr. Becker, dress was casual. Managers would stop in on each other with questions or answers to previous questions with no apparent concern for rank or immediate circumstances.

PRODUCTION

As the casewriters went with Mr. George on a tour of the production, shipping, and warehousing areas, there was a startling change from the cool, quiet, and subdued elegance of the executive offices to the noisy, crowded, and (to the untrained observer) apparently disorganized hustle and bustle of the production area. Equipment is a mixture of new and old. Ken proudly showed the casewriters a new electronically controlled slitting (cutting) machine, pointing out that the machine is faster, uses less personnel, and is more accurate than older versions of the same equipment. Later Ken pointed to a partially assembled piece of equipment which he indicated was acquired "quite used" from a bankrupt organization. Tucked away in one corner of the four-story building is the newly formed printing and lithographing department. Ken points out that the department is basically the acquisition of a small printing and lithographing company, with both the manpower and equipment being moved from its previous location to a location within the plant. Another stop on the tour is at the newly developed paper reclamation press. Almost all waste paper is pressed and sold as waste paper. The development of the press and all facilitating equipment was primarily the work of Vail technicians.

Another stop on the tour is the roll warehouse where great quantities of paper and paper products in roll form are stored. The company acquires damaged rolls of paper and then strips the rolls down to the point where the remainder of the roll is undamaged. The stripped-off portion is used for other legitimate conversion activity. This means wide fluctuations in the volume and size of this type of raw material in the warehouse. These damaged rolls are acquired at great discount from the mills. The willingness of Vail to accept these damaged rolls has led to a great deal of supplier loyalty.

The production workers are members of the United Paper Workers Union. Many of the employees are from minorities, since the plant is located in the inner city. Relations with the union are considered to be neither good nor bad. The current problem is the high incidence of absenteeism on the part of production workers. There are about 65 employees engaged in production and warehousing. Approximately 20 percent of the 85,000 square feet of floor space is devoted to production activities. One half of the total floor space is located on the ground floor, and one-half of the total floor space on the remaining three floors. All production is located on the ground floor. About 70 percent of the total floor space is used for shipping and warehousing. The company recently began renting additional warehouse space. Appendix A shows the equipment owned by the company and its capabilities.

PURCHASING

One of the keys to Vail's success financially has been its ability to effectively utilize odd-sized, odd-lot, and damaged paper and paperboard goods. The company has both the equipment and know-how to derive maximum value from these items.

With the wide range of products handled by the company both as a wholesaler and as a paper converter, it deals with a large number of suppliers. However, there are only a few major suppliers, the most significant of which is the International Paper Company. As paper usage has dramatically increased and environmental considerations and supplies have not, the price of paper has increased and the availability of paper has decreased. During the current paper shortage, Vail Industries is faring better than other paper wholesalers and paper converters in obtaining supplies of paper. Vail attributes this supplier loyalty to: (1) the long history of the company; (2) the fact that the company currently returns scrap paper, i.e., its reclamation project; and (3) the future growth prospects which the suppliers see for Vail, as well as Vail's propensity to purchase odd lots from the paper company.

SALES MANAGEMENT

The pervasiveness of the attention given the customer can be seen in the quote at the beginning of the case by Joe Becker on creative selling. Robert Green claims that "Satisfying the customer is the most important thing we can do," and also says "Never tell a customer 'no'." Arthur Wiseman says that "The customer is the boss providing he pays his bills and is reasonable."

The company is unique because it is the only full-service paper jobber (merchant) and paper converter in Baltimore. Most companies are either jobbers, fine paper converters, or industrial paper converters. Some may perform two of the three functions. Vail is not the largest in any category. Indeed, some companies have total sales in one category exceeding Vail's sales in all three. However, Vail is among the four largest paper converting and jobber companies in Baltimore.

The company relies on personal contact for creating customer interest and informing customers of its presence and capability. From 1971 to 1973 advertising expenditures tripled from $10,000 to $30,000. The bulk of these expenditures were for the development of capability brochures and direct-mail advertising.

Product pricing is a combination of meeting the competition and a target gross margin of 25 percent. Since most work is essentially made to customers' orders, salesmen cannot quote a price unless cleared with Mr. Green in advance. Salesmen are given some leeway to meet competition. They are paid a commission on expected gross profit. This commission varies between 30 percent and 27 percent for items handled by Vail to 35 percent for items sold direct from the mill to the customer. Salesman turnover is very low.

Direct sales are items which are shipped directly from the supplier to the customer. The items include: reinforced and gummed tape, pressure sensitive tape, polybags, shrink wrap film, staples, and occasionally, board and newsprint. The breakdown of direct sales and indirect sales is as follows:

	1973	1972
Direct Sales	1,424,000	945,000
Warehouse Sales	2,735,000	2,195,000
Total Sales	4,159,000	3,140,000

ACCOUNTING AND FINANCE

The plant has a fairly elementary cost-accounting system used for pricing and controlling production costs. Production standards are set from historical records and a knowledge of the business. Salaried and sales personnel participate in a profit-sharing plan. The annual contribution of the company to the plan is established by the board of directors and each employee shares the proceeds of the plan in the proportion his salary is of total salaries.

Almost all stock ownership is vested in the four principals, with Art Wiseman and Joe Becker holding all voting stock. Upon completion of the stock purchase agreement, Joe Becker will hold 37½ percent of the stock, Arthur Wiseman 50 percent, and Robert and Jerry 6¼ percent each. Exhibits 2 and 3 are the income statement and balance sheet for 1970, 1971, 1972, and 1973.

ORGANIZATION AND THE MANAGEMENT TEAM

The casewriters were struck by the frequency with which the term "management team" was mentioned. All three top managers are trained to handle any aspect of the business. All managers engage in purchasing and sales service and work order preparation. This is believed to provide the opportunity to respond to the raw materials market and customer needs rapidly. Further, customer loyalty is enhanced because the customer can deal with whomever he chooses. The casewriters could not identify any conflict or animosity between the principals. The group appears to operate as a team despite overlapping responsibilities. The organization chart is shown in Exhibit 4.

THE PRESENT AND FUTURE OF THE COMPANY AS SEEN BY THE PRINCIPALS

Art Wiseman plans to remain associated with the company as long as he has a contribution to make. He sees the company growing rapidly via market expansion and merger (as the dominant firm). Joe Becker sees retirement five or six years after the company has reached 20 million dollars in sales, and has either gone public or been acquired. This is expected to occur around 1980. Robert Green sees building the company for ten years and then selling it. Jerry sees a doubling of sales volume in ten years to 12 million dollars in sales. He plans to stay with the company as long as he can contribute something to it. If the company is sold, he plans to work elsewhere.

Mr. Becker points out that he has two immediate problems. First, he must cope with crowded conditions in the plant. The plant is already crowded and given a projection of doubling or better of sales in the next five years, conditions can only get worse. The plant was designed as an automotive repair facility and is not ideally laid out nor located for paper and packaging products. Robert Green sees financing, labor, space, and growth as the major problems. Financing is a problem because at 12 percent prime rate of interest, it is essential to keep on top of accounts payable. Labor is a problem because it is always a problem. Space is a problem because of the growth in sales and the limited production and warehouse space. Growth is a problem because at some point management structure must be adjusted to cope with a much higher level of sales. Jerry Nicholson feels that the only immediate problem is space.

The casewriters last visited Mr. Becker on April 12, 1974, when he indicated that first-quarter sales were up 32 percent from the first quarter of last year and he expected that profits would be up 50 percent or more. Further, he predicted that sales for the year might be 50 percent higher than 1973.

Mr. Becker says that:

> The major decision facing the corporation now is related to the question of a new plant, but is much broader than that. It is a question of how we wish to attain growth, whether via more intense competition in existing markets with existing products or via expansion of product line or via geographical expansion. Also we are faced with the question of the company's responsibility and commitment to the city of Baltimore. It currently employs approximately 75 residents of the city of Baltimore, most of which are inner-city residents. Relocation in the city would be expensive because of property costs and limiting because of the location of our customers. Two-thirds of our sales are made to customers outside the Baltimore area. One half of the total sales are made to customers within the state of

Pennsylvania, excluding Philadelphia. About 15 percent of the sales are made to customers in the New Jersey and Philadelphia area. The remaining sales are shipments to customers in Florida, North and South Carolina, western New England, and Puerto Rico.

A possibility is to move to the city of Allentown, Pennsylvania, which would allow us to service our current market. In addition, Allentown would have rail and interstate highway access to the large New York - Philadelphia market. Further, we might find labor costs in Allentown lower than in Baltimore. However, I am a native of Baltimore and I feel some obligation to the city. Indeed, I and my staff spend 10 to 15 percent of our time in community-service activity. A second alternative might be to acquire another company. I own 25 percent stock in another company that might provide a base of operation. The addition of another 30 percent of the stock in that company would allow me to acquire the company and resolve my facilities problem and my dilemma regarding the exact means to be used to acquire the sales growth which I desire.

Exhibit 1. Vail Industries, Inc. (A).

Paper Merchants

cardboard
  chip
  white lined
reinforced gummed tapes
closure systems
kraft paper
pressure-sensitive tapes
tissue paper
plastic film, bags,
  rolls, sheets
plastic strapping
corroflex
corrugated containers
corro bags
corro seal
box liners

bogus paper
cellulose wadding
labels
specialty bags
tape dispensers
  automatic and manual
twines
waterproof papers
special-coated papers
wrapping news
sanitary supplies
garment-industry papers
skid protectors
government-specification
  packaging
shrink packaging

Paper Converting

paperboard and paper
  sheeting
  slitting
  rewinding
  guillotine cutting and trimming

Folding Cartons

printing and lithography
  (paper and board up
  to 58 pt.)
die cutting
scoring
folding and gluing
  (straight, right angle,
  and specialty)
acetate window

Printing and Lithography

our newly formed department
is equipped to handle all
types of printing

Die Cutting

paperboard
  (up to ¼ in. - 250 pt.)
cylinder and platen
  automatic and manual feed

Packaging Design

a complete art design department

Exhibit 2. Vail Industries, Inc. (A) Income Statement (in 000's).

	1970	1971	1972	1973
Net Sales	2704	2830	3103	4159
Cost of Materials	1839	1855	1920	2609
Direct Labor	175	200	260	265
Gross Profit	690	775	923	1285
Selling Expenses	235	260	300	440
Bonuses and Profit Sharing[1]	83	68	68	120
Administrative Expenses	201	220	270	335
Other Income[2]	36	30	25	47
Other Expenses[3]	105	107	160	232
Net Profit (B.T.)	102	150	150	205

1. approximately ½ bonuses and ½ profit sharing
2. primarily purchase discounts and sales of scrap
3. primarily factory overhead, warehousing, and shipping

Exhibit 3. Vail Industries, Inc. (A) Balance Sheet (in 000's).

	1970	1971	1972	1973
Assets				
Cash and Securities	48	28	85	90
Accounts Receivable	280	288	405	420
Inventories	145	170	215	350
Plant and Equipment	355	559	627	720
Accumulated Depreciation	205	215	250	350
Net Plant and Equipment	150	244	377	370
Other Assets	37	47	32	33
Total Assets	650	777	1114	1263
Liabilities				
Accounts Payable	125	84	213	250
Accrued Expenses	72	110	95	170
Short-Term Notes	53	100	135	35
Other Current Liabilities	76	48	75	61
Long-Term Notes	0	37	130	160
Equity				
Stock Outstanding	35	48	61	75
Retained Earnings	299	350	405	512
Total Liabilities and Equity	660	777	1114	1263

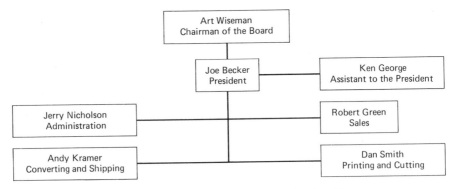

Exhibit 4. **Vail Industries, Inc. (A)** Organization Chart.

Appendix A | Vail Industries, Inc.

Equipment

Converting Department—A. Kramer, Foreman

1   84'' Wide Hamblet Duplex Sheeter
    Capable of sheeting 84'' wide rolls into sheets up to approximately 90' long.
    Runs at maximum speed of 180'/min.
    Tissue, News, Kraft and Board to .040'' thick.

1   72'' Wide Hamblet Sheeter
    Capable of 72'' by 154''—Longer sheet than any of competitors.
    Tissue, News, Kraft and Board to .040'' thick.

2   65'' Slitter and Rewinders
    Slits rolls of paper 65'' wide x up to 40'' diameter to minimum of ¼'' wide
    rolls x any diameter up to 40''. Slits widths less than ¾'' is a specialty not run
    by others in the area.

1   84'' Slitter and Rewinder
    Slits 84'' wide rolls.

1   Lawson Regent Automatic Program Cutter
    Cuts board and paper up to 59'' wide. Can be programmed to cut at
    prespecified distances—up to 24 cuts in each direction. This is highly
    efficient in cutting large quantities of small sizes.

3   Seybold Mechanical Guillotine Cutters
    2 are 51'' maximum width
    1 is 75'' maximum width
    With the 75'' we can trim large sizes, especially for large mill sheets and
    sheeted sizes. With the two smaller ones, provide flexibility for servicing
    customers.

1   Shrink Tunnell
    For shrink wrapping bundles of boards.

Printing Department—D. Smith, Foreman

1   2 Color Press—48" wide. Sheet-fed.

2   1-Color Presses for sheets up to 25" x 38". These presses are primarily not for fine printing. All 4-color work is subcontracted.

Die Cutting Department—D. Smith, Foreman

2   18 x 22 Heidelbergs—Up to .024" Board

1   28 x 41 Thompson—Up to .250" Board

1   65" Wide Miehle—Letterpress printing and/or die cutting. Up to .058" Board.

1   37" x 50½" Isima-Bobst type high speed die cutters. Up to .040" board

1   Round Corner Machine—rounds 2 corners on each cut.

1   Straight Line Gluer for seam gluing folding boxes.

1   Balers/Vacuum Floor Sweeps
        Capable of compacting approximately 12 bales of wastepaper 30" x 36" x 60" or approximately 1200# each per day.

Shipping Department—A. Keller, Foreman

        2 trucks and 3 trailers

Appendix B | Industry Note for Vail Industries

The following industry information is taken from the *Pulp, Paper and Board Quarterly Industry Report*, October 1973 and January 1974, published by U.S. Department of Commerce and *Current Industrial Outlook,* published by U.S. Department of Commerce.

Excerpts from
THE PAPER AND BOARD INDUSTRY OUTLOOK FOR 1974
By Donald W. Butts

Apparent consumption is expected to reach 67.2 million tons in 1973, equal to a 4 percent increase over 1972. Consumption is projected to rise 2 percent higher in 1974 to reach 68.3 million tons.

Bright Sales Dollars and Profits Picture Will Continue

Reflecting a highly favorable product mix coupled with exceptional operating rates and improved pricing, the industry is reaching historic highs in sales and profits. Half-year data available from the Federal Trade Commission revealed paper industry (SIC 26) sales up 14 percent and net profits up 58 percent over the similar period in 1972. The after-tax sales earnings ratio in the second quarter rose to 59 percent and after-tax earnings related to stockholders' equity climbed to 14.6 percent (eclipsing those set in the more recent benchmark year of 1966) to exceed the average of 5.1 percent and 14.0 percent respectively, shown for all manufacturing concerns in the second quarter

Table 1. Paper and Board Industry: Projections 1972–1980¹ (Value of shipments in millions of dollars except as noted)

SIC Code	Industry	1973	Percent Increase 1972–1973	1974	Increase 1973–1974	1980 Low	1980 High	% Increase² 1973–1980 Low	% Increase² 1973–1980 High
2631	Paperboard mills	11,500	8	12,000	4	15,500	16,000	4.4	4.8
2647	Sanitary paper products	1,892	6	2,005	6	2,600	2,800	4.6	5.8

¹Estimated by Bureau of Competitive Assessment and Business Policy.
²Compound annual rate of growth.

Paper and Allied Products: Selected Financial Ratios 1966–1973

	1966	1967	1968	1969	1970	1971¹	Year ending March 31 1972¹	Year ending March 31 1973¹
Net profits (after taxes) as percent of sales	5.4	4.7	4.7	4.8	3.4	2.3	2.4	4.4
Net profits (after taxes) as percent of net worth	10.5	8.8	9.6	9.7	7.0	4.9	5.2	9.9
Annual depreciation as percent of gross fixed assets	4.6	4.7	4.9	4.8	4.9	5.0	5.1	5.1
Sales of net fixed assets (ratio)	2.1	2.0	2.1	2.2	2.2	2.2	2.3	2.4
Current assets to current liabilities (ratio)	2.4	2.4	2.4	2.0	1.8	2.3	2.3	2.3

SOURCE: Federal Trade Commission, Quarterly Financial Reports.

¹Fourth quarter 1971 figures affected by reclassification of some corporations, the net effect of which reduced the reported level of sales, earnings, and assets in the paper industry.

Wholesale Prices and Price Indexes for Woodpulp, Wastepaper, Paper, Paperboard, and Converted Products, 1971–1973

Item	March 1973	March 1972	June 1973	June 1972	September 1973	September 1972	December 1973	December 1972	Average 1971
Indexed (1967 = 100)									
All industrial commodities	122.7	116.9	126.9	117.9	128.8	118.7	119.4	115.1	115.3
Pulp, paper and allied products group	118.3	112.3	112.4	113.5	124.8	114.3	115.1	110.7	110.7
Paper subgroup	119.2	115.7	122.5	116.2	121.7	116.7	117.3	114.7	114.7
Paperboard subgroup	110.7	103.6	116.7	106.0	116.7	106.5	107.1	102.7	102.7
Converted products subgroup	120.0	112.2	121.5	113.5	123.8	114.6	115.8	110.1	110.1

Economic Indicators for the Paper and Board Industry, 1971–1973

Indicator	January-March 1973	1972	January-June 1973	1972	January-September 1973	1972	January-December 1973	1972	Year 1971
General economic indicators by quarters									
Disposable personal income (billions of 1958 dollars, seasonally adjusted quarters at annual rates)	603.9	565.7	604.8	571.6	609.8	579.3		577.9	542.9
Per capita income (1958 dollars)	2,878	2,716	2,877	2,740	2,894	2,771		2,767	2,680
Paper and board production, total (1,000 short tons)	15,421	14,742	31,300	29,796	46,413	44,405		59,310	55,092
Paper and board apparent consumption (1,000 short tons)	16,980	15,294	34,927	32,158	51,363	48,280		54,374	59,680
Value of shipments, paper and allied products (million dollars)	7,626	6,961	16,658	14,115	23,886	21,236		28,413	25,362
Wholesale price index, paper and allied products, end of period (1967 = 100)	118.3	112.3	122.4	113.5	124.8	114.3		115.1	110.7

Production of Paper and Board by Major End Uses, 1971–1973

Type or Grade	January-March 1973	1972	January-June 1973	1972	January-September 1973	1972	January-December 1973	1972	Year 1971
All grades, total	15,421	14,742	31,300	29,796	46,413	44,405		59,310	55,092
Paper, total	6,613	6,368	13,384	12,744	19,839	18,889		25,321	23,838
Printing and writing papers, total	4,125	3,885	8,398	7,775	12,484	11,587		15,578	14,503
Packaging and industrial converting paper, total	1,466	1,450	2,963	2,907	4,385	4,280		5,710	5,468
Tissue and other creped paper, total	1,022	1,033	2,031	2,061	2,979	3,021		4,029	3,876
Paperboard, total	7,429	7,088	15,050	14,392	22,280	21,462		28,636	26,120
Wet machine board	34	33	68	69	100	104		136	138
Construction paper and board, total	1,345	1,253	2,788	2,592	4,184	3,951		5,217	4,995

Estimated Merchant Wholesale Sales and Inventories, Paper and Paper Products, 1971–1973

Item	January-March 1973	1972	January-June 1973	1972	January-September 1973	1972	January-December 1973	1972	Year 1971
Paper, paper products									
Sales	2,206	1,952	4,574	3,981	6,966	6,021		8,186	7,600
Inventories, end of period, at cost	760	682	780	702	793	708		725	683
Inventory-sales ratio (percent)	97	98	97	103	101	193		103	105

1973. This trend is expected to continue through the remainder of 1973 and to carry forward into 1974. Even if the boom demand fades in 1974, it is likely that the anticipated high rate of capacity utilization and the cost-cutting measures employed by the industry in recent years will tend to buoy profitability.

Full Utilization of Capacity and Profit-Oriented Products Anticipated
Demand for printing and writing papers, which trailed the turnabout of the packaging grades in the nation's economic upturn, expanded dramatically in the second half of 1972 and is being maintained through 1973. As with the packaging grades, the other major market area, printing and writing paper mill order backlogs are strong and rising, and tonnage allocations to customers are common. Some supply dislocation has occurred as producers have curtailed or eliminated the production of certain light basis weight papers or lower profit lines.

Capacity utilization is at high levels with paper mills operating at close to 97 percent in 1973 compared with 93 percent in the same period in 1972 and with paperboard mills operating at 101.0 percent of practical maximum capacity compared with 97 percent for the similar period in 1972. Barring unforeseen contingencies, maximization of capacity utilization is also anticipated in 1974.

A REVIEW OF SELECTED PAPER-SUPPLY SITUATIONS
In spite of extremely tight supply situations in some specific grades of paper and board during January-September, and with the crunch approaching actual shortages for individual users for one reason or another, the general situation appears to be one of close balance between capacity and production and demand. Supply problems have surfaced in some paper and board grades even in the face of growing total production—up 4.5 percent (see Table 1). Other problems have resulted from the elimination of some lower grades and less profitable lines, changes in basis weight, the elimination of custom runs or minor specification changes, and the standardization upon fewer grades of paper and board. All of these problems have called for and have generally been solved through grade substitutions, end use or process changes, or conservation practices instituted in paper and board usage.

Developments since September have altered the supply-balance situation, to some extent, with some tightening in supply being attributed to reduced domestic market pulp availability due to increasing exports resulting from the attractiveness of export market prices contrasted with controlled domestic prices.

Paper and Board
A strong upturn in domestic demand, beginning in 1972, coupled with a reduced rate of growth in paper and board production capacity, have resulted in a change in the paper and board supply-demand relationship from one of generally constant oversupply to one of balanced supply-demand; and, for some products, a tight supply. Articles in the business and general press have called attention to the tightening of the paper and board supply and expressed forebodings of a paper shortage.

Demand for paper and board is relatively inelastic. In general, they are raw materials used in the manufacture of other products and represent only a small percentage of the value of the finished commodity. Because substitute materials are not available at competitive prices, consumption is generally unresponsive to price changes.

In contrast, supply of paper and board is normally elastic because of the industry's frequent overcapacity, capital intensive nature, and attendant heavy fixed costs. When, however, a supply-demand balance is reached such as currently exists in some packaging and printing grades, the supply becomes markedly inelastic because it takes around three years to build new capacity.

Boutique des Fleurs

In early December 1971 Dave Moore and Jim Anderson happened to meet while both were attending a prospective shareholders' meeting for a small firm in St. Louis. As the presentation progressed, they both realized that the venture being outlined was not the kind of investment they were interested in. After the meeting, they briefly discussed their investment ideas and were pleased to learn they were very similar.

Dave Moore, 35 years old, was a product manager for a large food processing firm. He had an MBA and over 19 years of experience in retail food merchandising. Jim Anderson, 39, PhD, was an associate professor of finance at a large metropolitan university. He had been located in the St. Louis area only a year, but had 12 years' experience teaching and consulting in the area of finance.

As previously mentioned, both shared similar interests regarding their immediate investment objectives. After their initial meeting they kept in touch and later decided to set a schedule of convenient times when they could get together at a local "watering hole" at the end of the day and exchange ideas. At the first such meeting they outlined the characteristics of the type of investment that would appeal to them.

- Relatively small initial capital outlay.
- Low fixed costs as a percentage of total costs.
- Short time period from concept to cash flow.
- Absentee ownership after developmental stage.
- Dynamic product or service—large market.
- Economies of scale—possible franchising.
- Relatively little connection between selling price and cost of goods sold.
- Good vehicle for building new worth via an "equity play" at the right time.

Over the course of several months, they discussed strategies and ideas and went so far as to look at several firms that were for sale in the local area. Each of these was unattractive for some reason.

Finally at one of their meetings in May 1972, Dave brought up something that he had observed on a trip to the West Coast. He noticed that fresh cut flowers were being

This case was prepared by Associate Professor John J. Andrews of Emory University. Reprinted with permission.

marketed in supermarkets around Los Angeles. Since he was intrigued with the idea, and it seemed that it might be something that could be done by an investor such as himself, he talked with several supermarket managers and customers regarding the feasibility of the idea. Everyone he talked to seemed very enthusiastic about the idea and its possible success.

The more Dave and Jim discussed the idea, the more interested they became. It seemed that the mass marketing of fresh cut flowers in supermarkets and in other high-traffic locations seemed to meet all of their investment criteria. However, in order to get a better perspective they decided to increase the frequency of their meetings, and soon worked up a basic list of positive and negative aspects of the idea.

Positive

- Short time period from concept to positive cash flow.
- Large profit margins in florist business.
- No receivables problems.
- High-traffic areas result in huge potential market.
- Completely new approach to marketing flowers.
- Air transportation makes flowers available year-round.
- Arrangements as well as bunches will be offered.
- Small square-footage area needed for display.
- No skilled labor needed.
- Possible franchising opportunities.

Negative

- Refrigerated cooler needed for each location.
- Flowers are perishable items—refrigerated delivery.
- Demand is normally highly seasonal.
- Spoilage factor (leads to guaranteed sales).
- Source of supply (and price) very important.
- Delivery network must be established.

After thinking over these points, Dave and Jim decided that the basic decision must be predicated on the profitability of such a venture. To analyze the profit potential they investigated four areas:

- Potential market for flower locations.
- Price/cost, structure for products.
- Pro forma cash budget and income statement.
- Possible financing for cash investment.

Dave tackled the first two points. He first determined that the area would support at least 60 locations that would require at least one 55 cubic foot refrigerated unit each (at $800 per unit). This decision was based on the large number of supermarkets doing more than $50,000 in gross sales per week. Expansion into hospitals and other locations would come later.

The price/cost structure for the products turned out to be not only the most important item in the analysis, but also the most difficult to analyze. Jim suggested that prices be determined by carefully assigning full costs to each product based on a very conservative sales forecast, adding an adequate profit margin, spoilage factor, and supermarket discount. The end result would be the sales price and would change from time to time as costs change while the number of flowers and container-style of arrangements would remain the same.

Dave disagreed, arguing that the shopper is very price conscious. Therefore, prices must be established and adhered to. Variations would come in number of flowers and container-style for arrangements. In addition, shoppers are accustomed to certain price patterns and they must be provided. It was then agreed that basic price patterns would be established and when necessary the number of flowers or container varied to maintain margins. Exhibit 1 shows the agreed price pattern. Exhibit 2 relates prices to expected variable costs for three different products.

Using Dave's price/cost patterns and based on a conservative sales forecast, Jim prepared the cash budget shown in Exhibit 3. The assumptions were based on a 30-day lag in both payables and receivables, plus a phase-in of the 60 coolers during October, November, and December. All of the figures were considered reasonable and were extended to the point that the cumulative cash-flow figure turned positive.

Armed with Exhibits 1, 2, and 3 Jim and Dave approached their banker for a loan to allow them to get started. Somewhat to their surprise, their banker was very impressed with their analysis and very quickly accommodated the financing needs by extending an equipment loan (installment) for the equipment and a $20,000 line of credit (endorsed and secured) for working capital.

Dave and Jim now felt they were prepared to move ahead. They split up the remaining tasks and got underway during the late summer to meet their October schedule.

Dave assumed all tasks associated with the marketing effort. One of these was to develop a trade name. A list of 10 names was developed and tested and the one selected was "Boutique des Fleurs." He then developed a logo and point-of-sale literature and was off to contact potential sites for the coolers. Again, the effort was successful with the four largest supermarkets (weekly gross better than $200,000 per store) agreeing to place one cooler per store. Another large chain wanted a cooler in each store regardless of sales size.

While in one of the stores Dave observed a young lady servicing a hosiery display and asked if she could recommend young ladies who would like to consider delivering flowers. This fortunate contact led to the hiring of a young woman for dealing with supermarket delivery techniques.

Jim took care of a location with a refrigeration unit, delivery vehicles, and the corporate charter under the name of Fresh Flowers, Inc.

Since all systems appeared to be go, a letter of credit (cost $100—not budgeted) was sent to the cooler manufacturer for the first shipment of 25 coolers.

Stock ownership was decided with Dave buying 67 shares for $670, and Jim buying 33 shares for $330. No salaries were to be paid to principals until all loans were repaid.

Early in October the first shipment of 25 coolers arrived. It was decided to put 10 of them in locations immediately, service them for several weeks to get the operational logistics working smoothly, and see what the market is interested in purchasing.

The immediate results were better than expected. The flowers were beautiful, priced attractively, and sales projections exceeded the forecast. Many new ideas were now being discussed with regard to such topics as starting design classes (for arrangements), offering special arrangements for pick-up at the supermarket, buying flowers directly from Mexico and South America, and supplying restaurants and industrial customers on a recurring basis.

Things were progressing into the fourth or fifth week of operations with a lot of the start-up details and problems worked out and most of the other 15 coolers ready to be placed in locations, when a bombshell hit the company. Dave's immediate superior at the food-processing firm called him in and said that the president of the firm had heard about a member of the firm who was actively engaged in merchandising a product to supermarkets. The president reiterated a company policy which said that no employee could "actively" pursue outside investments. Dave was given a choice of getting out or giving up his job. He chose to give up the flower business.

Immediately the possible alternatives were discussed:

1. Sell out to Jim.

2. Sell the company to some party.

3. Liquidate.

A balance sheet (Exhibit 4) was drawn up at the end of November. Without closing the books, the trial balance indicated a loss to date of approximately $500.

Three potential outside purchasers were briefed on all aspects of the Boutique des Fleurs operation and its potential. Each of the three were different. One was a whole-sale florist, one a grower with a small retail florist trade, and the third a group of three young persons who just recently had begun selling fresh cut flowers in various street locations in the city.

Exhibit 1. Boutique des Fleurs Product Prices.

.99 Bunch of daisies
$1.59 Carnations, pom poms, or pixie bouquet
$1.99 Roses or small arrangement (carnations)
$2.99 Coffee cup arrangement (carnations)
$3.99 Large arrangement (carnations) with vase

Exhibit 2. Boutique des Fleurs Price/Cost Relationship Examples.

Retail price	.99	$1.99	$2.99
Trade Discount	.20	.40	.60
Gross Income	.79	1.59	2.39
Variable Costs	.40	.76	1.30
Pre-Spoilage Net	.39	.83	1.09
Less Spoilage	.05	.11	.15
Contribution	.34	.72	.94

Exhibit 3. Boutique des Fleurs Cash Budget September 1972–June 1973.

	September	October	November	December	January	February	March	April	May	June
Sales	0	6000	7500	15000	13650	19750	26325	26325	43875	43875
Collection of Receivables	0	0	6000	7500	15000	13650	19750	26325	43875	43875
Cash Outflow:										
Rent and Utilities		350								
Coolers—Freight		3125	3125	1250						
Coolers—Loan Payment @ 10.17%		607	1214	1437	1437	1437	1437	1437	1437	1437
Delivery Vehicles		500	700	900	1000	1000	1000	1000	1000	1000
Labor-Manager	1000	1000	1000	1000	1000	1000	1000	1000	1000	1000
Labor-Other	600	1400	2000	2400	3000	3000	3000	3000	3000	3000
General and Administrative	100	500	500	500	500	500	500	500	500	500
Incorporation and License	300									
Containers and Supplies			500			600				500
Flowers			3300	4125	8250	7508	10863	14479	24131	24131
Total Cash Out	2000	7482	12339	11612	15187	15045	17800	21416	31068	31568
Net Cash In (Out)	(2000)	(7482)	(6339)	(4112)	(187)	1395	(1950)	4909	12807	12307
Cumulative Cash In (Out)	(2000)	(9482)	(15821)	(19,933)	(20120)	(18725)	(20765)	(15766)	(2959)	9348

Exhibit 4. Boutique des Fleurs
Balance Sheet, November 30, 1972

Assets

Cash	$ 1,100
Accounts Receivable	2,600
Inventory	300
Supplies	400
Coolers	20,000
Other Assets	1,200
Furniture and Equipment	1,500
Total Assets	$27,100

Liabilities and Capital

Accounts Payable	2,500
Taxes Payable	100
Bank Loan Payable	24,000
Common Stock	1,000
Retained Earnings	(500)
Total Liabilities and Capital	$27,100

Swane Motors, Inc.

In early June, 1974, the senior management of Swane Motors, Inc. was undecided on how to deal with an explosive situation which had developed among a number of employees in the company. In line with its policy of being a socially responsive and progressive firm, senior management at Swane had hired a young woman for a junior management position in the service department nine months before. While some members of Swane's top management had remained highly enthusiastic about having a female manager in the company, other members had become increasingly skeptical. Now, the company was faced with a crisis because many of its female and male employees felt they were being discriminated against and treated unfairly.

HISTORY AND ORGANIZATION

Swane Motors, Inc. is one of the largest automobile dealerships in the metropolitan Boston area. The company was founded in 1926 by David F. Swane, an aggressive and ambitious man typical of those entering the then-new enterprise of selling and servicing automobiles. From the beginning, Mr. Swane made it his policy to hire the

George E. Shagory, Babson College. Reprinted with permission.

most qualified people he could get for the various jobs in the company. Particular attention was paid to the technical jobs, i.e., the mechanics were made especially attractive offers in order to get and retain the most qualified men available.

In 1961, Mr. Swane died, and the provisions of his will specified that the company was to be offered for sale to Mr. Frank West, Mr. David Harris, and Mr. John Aspen. Other arrangements could be made only in the event that the three men did not pick up their option. However, they decided to pick up the option and undertake the operation of the dealership as a closed corporation. When the new owners took over the firm, a major reorganization was implemented (see Exhibit 1).

Under the new organizational setup, sales and service were run as two separate departments. Mr. Steven Allen was the General Service Manager in charge of service, parts, and the body shop operation. Mr. Arthur Davidson was the manager in charge of sales of new and used cars. The officers of the corporation involved themselves deeply in the day-to-day activities of the business in order to be able to keep abreast of important developments and to make their planning efforts efficient and effective. Mr. Aspen was most involved with the Sales Department, as was Mr. West, while Mr. Harris concerned himself with sales, service, and (being an accountant by education and experience) the financial aspects of the firm's planning efforts.

Swane Motors has long enjoyed an especially good reputation, as automobile dealerships go. Special efforts have been made by Mr. Allen to see that all complaints are followed up and that adjustments are made for every customer who complains. The company has 100 percent service saturation, which means that all the fixed expenses of the company are covered by the revenue from the Service Department. The Sales Department revenues are the "gravy." This rare situation makes the company one of the most financially prosperous dealerships in this area of the country. The management and personnel of Swane Motors pride themselves on the knowledge that Swane is run completely honestly—there is no practice employed to defraud the general public or its automobile manufacturer. (It is well known among the dealers that there are few dealerships that do not play games with claims procedures with the automobile manufacturers, although most dealers are fairly straightforward with their customers.) Swane has taken pride in the fact that its manufacturer has not audited Swane's claims in 20 years (some dealerships are audited twice a year) and that their Service Department has received the Distinguished Service Award every year since its inception.

PERSONNEL POLICIES

There are approximately 30 mechanics, 20 body shop technicians, 10 clerical and secretarial employees, 5 service writers, and 15 salesmen employed at Swane Motors. The payroll arrangements for mechanics and body shop technicians are flat-rate piecework, which have proven satisfactory. All salesmen are on salary plus commission. All other employees are paid by hourly rates. In addition to the above-mentioned categories there are also four or five part-time employees, mostly students who come in after classes. These students are paid $2.00 per hour and perform the "dog work" which accumulates in every organization. Swane is completely integrated; 25 percent of its employees are black. However, all the women in the organization are in clerical positions—in addition, there is an extremely high rate of turnover in these positions, with one or two exceptions.

NEW DEVELOPMENTS IN PERSONNEL POLICIES

In the winter of 1973, Mr. Harris and Mr. Allen, who pride themselves on keeping up with new developments in management, became interested in hiring females with the express intention of putting them in positions of some "responsibility." Although all management positions at Swane have been filled by promotion from within, Mr. Harris and Mr. Allen began looking for promising young business students (female) from local colleges. The young woman would be trained and placed in the Service Department as a service writer. Service writers are often the customer's only contact with the dealership. These writers "write up" the repair orders and do the claims work on each vehicle which is brought in for servicing. Thus, the service writer is, if you will, the image maker in most cases. Mr. Allen was particularly anxious to implement this arrangement because he had heard remarks from customers with respect to the fact that one "never sees a woman at Swane." Being located in Cambridge, near Harvard and MIT, Swane Motors services many members of the academic community. Possibly 60 percent of customers are faculty, students, or staff at one of the above-mentioned institutions.

After several months of searching, Mr. Allen finally located a likely candidate, one of his daughter's friends who attended a business college in the greater Boston area. Carol Dixon was a senior, majoring in management. Miss Dixon had attended a junior college in Boston for two years, and then worked at MIT for two years, first as a secretary, then administrative assistant. Realizing how limited her prospects were at that time, she transferred her credits to Eberle College and was planning to graduate in August of 1973. Mr. Allen and Mr. Harris interviewed Miss Dixon and both were impressed. Mr. Harris said:

> She is not the usual women's lib type. She's bright, industrious, clever, and personable. I'm sure we'll have no problems with her—she'll fit right in.

Miss Dixon began working part-time for Swane Motors during a very slow period (March is very slow for most automobile dealers). In three afternoons per week she wrote perhaps ten customer's orders. One day, after several weeks of this slack period, Miss Dixon asked Mr. Allen if she could have a few words with him. Mr. Allen indicated that he was free that afternoon.

Mr. Allen was surprised to learn from his conversation with Miss Dixon that the service writers working with Miss Dixon were asking her to pull files for them, bring them coffee during the afternoon break, and perform other such clerical duties. Miss Dixon said that while she was not adverse to helping the more experienced writers during periods of heavy traffic, she felt that she should be dealing with customers more during this slack period in order to complete her training requirements. Mr. Allen wholeheartedly agreed and assured Miss Dixon that he would speak to the service writers about the situation.

The reactions of the customers to Miss Dixon were favorable in most cases. Some of the male customers sought out Mr. Allen to tell him that "it's nice to have something pretty to look at around here." Others could not quite trust Miss Dixon to write up their orders. "What could a woman know about servicing an automobile?" was a common remark. Strangely enough, the customers who were least confident of Miss Dixon's ability were the female customers. Nevertheless, Mr. Allen and Mr. Harris felt that Miss Dixon was important for their company image, and they hoped she would stay. Mr. Harris said:

> Eventually, they'll get used to it. As long as the mechanics cooperate it's no real problem. And if it does develop into a problem, Miss Dixon will probably marry and have children in a few years, and that will be the end of it! We can say we tried.

Although the mechanics were cooperating fairly well with Miss Dixon, the other female employees showed resentment. One of them summed up the feelings of most of the others in this way:

> I've been here 15 years, and I guess I know as much about this place as she'll ever know. Why her, why not one of us? This place is always mouthing off about promotion from within. Oh sure, for men, that is.

Mr. Harris and Mr. Allen hoped that these sentiments would die down as people became used to the new situation and better acquainted with Miss Dixon. In early May, 1974, Mr. Allen left for three weeks' vacation.

Miss Dixon had mixed feelings about the situation. She realized that the adjustment would be difficult for everyone:

> The frightening thing is that the greatest opposition to my position is coming from women. This is the kind of reaction I'd expected from the men. Instead I'm meeting resistance from women because I'm a woman, and the male reaction is one of amused indulgence.

> I realized that I would have to be very, very good...much better than a man..in order to get anywhere in this kind of job. That's the reason I went back to school. Perhaps I've picked an industry that will be more especially resistant to women. Perhaps I should have begun in a more female-oriented industry.

> There's really no incentive for people around here to adjust to the situation. There's no affirmative action plan or anything like that—this is a small corporation. There's no government funding, no one threatening to cut off the contracts for noncompliance. The educational level of the people who work here is quite low. Even the managers have worked their ways up as technicians of one kind or another. They have a natural resentment for the college-trained manager in addition to a culture-bred prejudice against women in industry.

Mr. West and Mr. Aspen, who had more or less let things run their course until now, had become concerned about the feelings of the other female employees. Mr. Ryerson, the office manager, had approached Mr. Aspen to discuss what was becoming a serious situation. The clerical workers had been bickering amongst themselves—one had given her notice, not giving a reason, saying it was "personal." Filing and billing had fallen behind, and absenteeism had increased. Mr. Ryerson felt that the presence and position of Miss Dixon were responsible for these difficulties. He expressed exasperation:

> This is a small corporation, John. You can't do anything quietly. These women have their own pecking order, and what's more, they're perfectly aware of your personnel policies. They feel this girl has been made an exception over them. I'm sure that's why Sheryl Andrews is leaving. She's been with us for 15 years, and she's loyal, dependable, hard-working. Why, after 15 years, would she all of a sudden have "personal" reasons for leaving?

At the beginning of June, Mr. Aspen called a meeting to which Mr. West, Mr. Harris, Mr. Ryerson, and Mr. Allen were invited. He began the meeting by stating that the situation concerning Miss Dixon was becoming seriously upsetting to the employees and that he was afraid of the effects it might have on customer relations ultimately:

> We make our money on our sales, but our service is what pays the bills around here. Our service is our fortune and, let's face it, our employees *are* our service. If they're unhappy, dissatisfied, upset, this is going to be communicated to our customers. People have enough problems of their own to cope with without having to deal with the problems of people who are supposed to be making life easier and more cheerful for them.

Mr. Harris and Mr. Allen reaffirmed their commitment to "equal opportunity employment" before the others and asked for their continuing support in hiring women for key positions. They felt that the situation was not really serious. Mr. Harris felt that Mr. Ryerson was using the office staff's general dissatisfaction as an excuse for his actual prejudice against women, although he did not say so. The tone of the meeting was conflict—between Mr. Harris and Mr. Allen, who wished to continue hiring and training women and Mr. Aspen, Mr. West, and Mr. Ryerson, who were concerned with the problem of employee morale and job satisfaction. The meeting ended inconclusively—the men agreed to each consider the other's point of view and to "sleep on it." Another meeting was scheduled for the next week.

Mr. Harris and Mr. Allen left the premises for lunch and met Miss Dixon on the way out to the parking lot. They invited her to join them and she accepted. After lunch, Mr. Harris and Mr. Allen talked in Mr. Allen's office. Mr. Allen was becoming more impressed with Miss Dixon by the day:

> David, we've got to keep her, and get others like her—she's really good. She's picked up the job faster than I've ever seen anybody do it. Furthermore, I think it's our responsibility to be the industry leader in this facet of business as well as the more conventional ones.

Mr. Harris agreed, but he felt more pessimistic than Mr. Allen about their chances of convincing Messrs. Aspen, West, and Ryerson of their convictions.

In the meantime, Scott Matthews, one of the senior service writers, called a general meeting to which all employees were urged to come. Mr. Aspen knew nothing about the meeting until he saw the notices posted around the time clock. He went directly to Mr. Allen's office and angrily demanded to know "what was going on." Mr. Allen was completely ignorant of the meeting himself and both of them went to discuss the matter with Mr. West and Mr. Harris. They decided the best course of action would be not to interfere—Mr. Aspen intended to attend the meeting himself, if possible.

The meeting turned out to be quite noisy, but its intent was quite clear. The service writers and the female clerical workers had decided that they were being expected to bear unfair treatment. They felt that Miss Dixon was being treated preferentially, since no female employee at Swane Motors was ever given an opportunity to train for a staff position or a management position. They also felt that those service writers who had worked their way up from technicians' positions should be considered at a higher level than Miss Dixon was insofar as "status" was concerned.

The meeting was dominated by Mr. Matthews, who made a statement to the effect that the group bore Miss Dixon no personal grudge and that the group's argument was with management. Mr. Aspen said that he would take the comments made at this meeting into serious consideration and communicate them to his colleagues at their impending senior management meeting later that week.

Two days later, at the senior management meeting, Mr. Aspen called everyone to order and summarized the comments of Mr. Matthews and the other employees from the earlier meeting. Mr. Ryerson then discussed the subject of employee dissatisfaction and called for the dismissal of Miss Dixon. Mr. Aspen said he supported dismissal. Mr. Harris and Mr. Allen came out strongly against dismissal. The meeting became heated, and it was eventually halted without a decision being made.

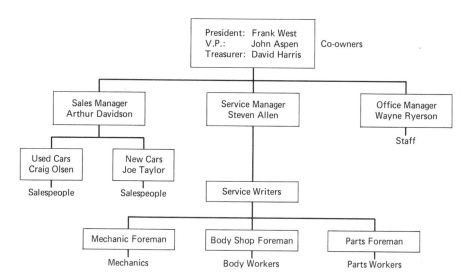

Exhibit 1. Swane Motors, Inc. Organization Chart.

Allen Personnel Agency*

The Allen Personnel Agency, a wholly owned subsidiary of Allen Associates, was fully owned and managed by Richard Allen, President. In addition, Allen Associates owned and managed three other agencies: Eldorado Associates, T.H.E. Secretary Agency, and Harkness Associates. All were located in downtown San Francisco in the same building, but on different floors. Exhibit 1 reveals the structure of Allen Associates, along with salary breakdowns of types of personnel handled by each respective placement agency.

Each company was composed of counselors who, by nature of this highly competitive profession, traditionally were aggressive individuals. Although procedures varied from one company to the next, the fundamental techniques of the personnel agency industry were basically the same. First, each counselor was responsible for finding job orders (openings). This could be done by laboriously phoning companies within a specific field, by following newspaper leads, or by sending numerous cover letters and making one's name "known" to employers. By standard practice, a fee schedule was immediately sent to each employer who indicated any job opening, regardless of whether or not he was willing to pay the fee. Next, qualified applicants had to be found, interviewed by the counselor, carefully screened for strong and weak points, and placed in an applicant pool. After job openings were found and qualified applicants organized by such criteria as appearance, personality, aggressiveness, and general background, the counselor looked for possible match-ups between jobs and job seekers. Once this was done, the counselor approached the applicant with general information about the job and asked if he were willing to interview. If so, the counselor called the employer and presented a brief synopsis of the individual's background. Since Allen agencies' fees were all paid by the employer, it had to be agreed beforehand that if the applicant were hired through the counselor's efforts and remained employed by said company for three months, the employer was fully responsible to pay that fee corresponding to the salary at which the applicant was initially hired. When such an interview was arranged, and the job was offered and accepted, this was termed a "placement." In the event that the employer did not wish to pay the standard fee, no interview was arranged, and the opening was discarded. Counselors worked entirely on commission, with no draw until they had proven their ability to produce. (A sample of Allen Personnel Agency's fee schedule and counselor compensation structure is provided in Exhibit 2.)

The progress of Allen Associates was a series of ups and downs. Begun in 1965 as an engineering placement agency, Allen Associates grew rapidly with the surge of engineering demands by Peninsula electronic and engineering firms, and the willing-

Reprinted from *Stanford Business Cases 1974* with the permission of the Publishers, Stanford University Graduate School of Business, © 1974 by the Board of Trustees of the Leland Stanford Junior University.

This case was prepared as a basis for class discussion by Lawrence E. Lieberman for Assistant Professor Francine E. Gordon.

*All names and locations are disguised.

ness of these firms to consistently pay higher than conventional fees. However, Allen anticipated the decline in demand for such personnel, which came in the late '60s, and wisely branched into different agencies concentrating on different markets. At first capital dwindled rapidly, but by early 1972, T.H.E. Secretary was showing a consistent profit, while Harkness and Eldorado had two or three counselors, each producing extremely well and absorbing the slack created by the inconsistent production of the Allen Personnel Agency.

During the entire year 1972, the production of the Allen Personnel Agency was, for Allen, frustrating and unprofitable. In addition, turnover for the year was much higher than the other three Allen agencies, and higher than average in the industry. Dissention among employees was extremely high, and talk of mass resignation was seriously considered.

ALLEN PERSONNEL AGENCY—SELECTED EMPLOYEES

Richard Allen, President, owner, and manager of Allen Associates, age 38, lawyer, and husband of Margaret Allen, manager of T.H.E. Secretary Agency. Allen entered the industry in 1965 as a counselor with his wife, and rapidly coordinated his capital to own and control four agencies in total. Prior to 1965, Allen practiced law, concentrating primarily on divorce cases. Managers of each agency reported directly to Allen, as often as twice daily. He graduated from San Francisco Law School in 1950.

Jay Wardlow, manager of Allen Personnel Agency, 44 years old, has been with Richard Allen for two years. Wardlow entered the personnel industry in 1966, beginning first as a counselor, and later owner of an engineering placement agency. Following several financial setbacks in the late 1960s, Wardlow came to work for Richard Allen, impressing the owner with his knowledge of new personnel industry techniques. Wardlow was completely responsible for the success or failure of the Allen Personnel Agency, and had been given full management authority by Allen, despite the fact that Allen's executive office was within the physical office space of Allen Personnel (see Exhibit 3). Wardlow's primary responsibility was recruiting and training new counselors. In addition, he was also responsible for coordinating placements, send-outs (applicants being sent on interviews), and job orders on a large bulletin board. He conferred with and reported to Allen daily, and oftentimes traveled to Fresno or Los Angeles to examine Allen operations there. Prior to 1966, Wardlow worked for the State Department. He graduated from Colorado State with a degree in history.

Larry Smothers, counselor, age 22, was a graduate of the University of Michigan, with a degree in economics. He had been employed at Allen Personnel for four months.

Bert Dikes, counselor, age 36, has been in the personnel business for twelve years, concentrating on the field of engineering. Dikes has worked for Allen Personnel for almost two years. He has been the most successful and consistent producer in the agency.

Mark Lessor, age 42, has been in the personnel business for 2½ years, all at Allen Personnel, concentrating on accounting. The second most successful counselor behind Dikes, Lessor has worked for the State of New York and as an independent meat broker.

Tim Johns, age 26, has just entered the personnel business at Allen Personnel. He has been on the job one week. Prior to this position, Johns independently produced nature films.

The following remarks were expressed by or concerning several of the above individuals.

A CONVERSATION WITH THE MANAGER, JAY WARDLOW

Almost all of the employees at Allen Personnel Agency, about twelve or so including the secretary, are originally from out of the Bay Area, and only one counselor has been at Allen Personnel for more than two years. Consequently, not only on the surface, but in reality, our business is in extremely transient one.

Our recruiting system, if you want to refer to it as such, is the following: Basically, in our agency, about half of the counselors have never had any personnel agency experience before. In fact, in all but one of such cases, these people became counselors at Allen Personnel because they came to us originally looking for a job, not even considering personnel work. After screening their appearance, personality, and ability to communicate on the phone, I explain to the individual what agency work entails, and with hard work, what one might expect to make after a few months.

You see, getting started in this type of work is not the easiest thing. The new counselor starts the job working strictly on commission, with no draw until after at least six months at Allen Personnel (this due to extremely high turnover rate of counselors during the first half year). Although it usually takes the beginner six to eight weeks to make his first placement (bringing in for himself generally from $250 to $500), I've seen some make placements their first week, and others go dry for three and four months at a time. Needless to say, the successful counselor must be hard-working, persistent, and self-disciplined. He is essentially his own boss, although I am here to help train and assist whenever necessary. Perhaps the most important trait in the successful counselor, however, is his salesmanship, his ability to sell himself confidently over the phone, and his ability to accept perhaps 20 consecutive negative phone responses before finding a positive one. Unfortunately, what employment agencies call persistence, employer companies consider "hounding" or "pestering," and hostile responses or total avoidance of counselors known by the employer or employer's secretary are none too uncommon. As you can well imagine, one either makes it the first two to five months of the business, or simply quits. Those that make it generally are self-starters, and need little if any motivation from me. It's in the "incubation" stage that we lose so many people.

To counter this common turnover problem in our industry, I've been trying to introduce new training and development procedures, such as the M.B.O. (Management By Objectives), and have been further encouraged by Richard Allen, although he is a self-admitted, rigid authoritarian.

Training the new counselor consists of placing him in the large room with Carst and Stading, two successful and consistent producers, and occupying the desk directly across from mine (refer to Exhibit 3). In this way, the trainee can be exposed to the do's and dont's of the business, while I'm coaching and assisting with his progress. After going through a brief formal meeting with Richard Allen, the trainee is asked to choose a field of business in which he would be most comfortable (sales, marketing, accounting, engineering, data processing, finance, and insurance are currently covered by our agency). The new counselor then gets on the phone and begins calling employers, seeking job information, current status of the market, and who, if anyone, has left that company recently. The successful communicator will extract every possible bit of information from the employer, while of course also verifying that the employer does in fact pay agency fees. This latter point is extremely important, in that many firms do not pay fees and it would be a waste of counselor time to further the contact. Time is valuable in our business and, although it's a dog-eat-dog type of competition, there's plenty of money to be made for the harder worker.

Much of my responsibility lies in acting as an ombudsman between the counselors and Richard Allen. You see, Allen is a peculiar type of individual. He is a true Horatio Alger type from the word go, believing that only through hard work and total dedication to the job can one succeed. Here at Allen Personnel, particularly for the past six or eight months, we have had considerable difficulty motivating our people, and productivity has taken a downward trend of inconsistency.

Allen feels that we should take an iron fist to the problem, watch over our counselors very carefully, and make sure that they are doing the work for which they should be responsible. In addition, he feels that strict punctuality should be enforced along with an acceptable professional dress code.

When I cite the example of Bert Dikes, a veteran counselor and top biller who never wears a tie, keeps inconsistent hours, yet is the most productive and aggressive counselor we have, Allen only responds that, if he wore a tie and kept more "businesslike hours," he would be making that much more money. Unfortunately, although I am not 100 percent certain, I have heard that Dikes and one other counselor are planning to leave in the near future.

This places me in quite an awkward position. I sense a great deal of dissention among the counselors toward the owner, Allen, and fully understand their feeling. Due to the presence of his office in the agency, Allen is frequently walking around, checking on what people are doing. Because I know him fairly well, he doesn't intend to be hawkish or intimidating; he simply comes on that way. When I tell him that, he simply replies that, as owner, he can do as he damn well pleases. At any rate, his presence does in fact bother the counselors, as many have told me. It doesn't help Allen's cause either when he is caught ranting and swearing about an unpaid bill, loud enough for the entire office to overhear. I'd like to have the full confidence of the counselors, but because I'm behind closed doors twice daily with Allen, they feel that I'm on Allen's side. In all honesty, I'm on neither side, trying simply to manage the office as efficiently as I know how. If I were to come out strongly against Allen, this would succeed only in strengthening the undertone of ill feelings currently about the office.

Compensation is a major problem here also. As I mentioned earlier, because all the counselors are on straight commission, those first few months can be pretty tight. Even for the consistent producer, due to the nature of the market, bad months do happen and zero money comes in. Although he has given some draws, Allen is adverse to the practice, since he has in fact been taken; in many instances he's never been repaid. Because of this, Allen and I have decided to introduce a minimum salary plan for trainees, a plan which offers $500 per month for each new counselor who chooses to be on this program. The trainee can stay on salary for up to six months, or if he wishes, at any time move to straight commission.

We feel that the value of this new salary plan is in allowing the struggling trainee to at least eat and live comfortably for those difficult first few months, while also developing a sense of responsibility and/or indebtedness toward the company, a feeling at this time sorely lacking in most counselors. After the counselor gets his feet wet and feels able to consistently earn more than $500 by working straight commission, he simply switches over. However, if while on the salary plan, the counselor makes a phenomenal placement worth a thousand or two in commission, that money stays with the company. We both feel that this is a fair arrangement, an investment in which, depending upon future turnover, we may stand to lose quite a bit of money. At any rate, we are making a sincere effort to help the counselor as much as possible, and by showing him that we do care, we hope to develop a productive and *loyal* employee. We have tried the salary plan confidentially on two new trainees, one of whom has been with us for two months, one for about a week. I cannot as yet say anything about its success or failure.

A CONVERSATION WITH LARRY SMOTHERS

Since I've been working here, about four months or so, I've done fairly well, but not nearly as well as I was led to believe. Jay Wardlow is really a great guy, a friend and usually fair, but when I first came to Allen Personnel looking for a challenging, enjoyable job, he painted the agency business much rosier than it actually is. On the surface, it looked great—be your own boss, carry comfortable hours, work in a nice office in the financial district, and potentially make good money. What he failed to tell me was that it would take countless phone rejections before someone would finally respect and listen to me, and even then, the chances of worthwhile information springing from the contact were very small. True, I quickly discovered the difficult sides (for me) of the business right away—trying to convince someone that I was an expert on something in which I had had only one day's exposure, and being forced to make promises and assurances that I could not always follow through with. Not only that, the business is extremely frustrating, particularly when money coming in is low. For example, last month I had a cosmetics salesman turn down a $15,000 job after he had been carefully screened and chosen out of twelve top people. The fee on that would have been $2250, and I would have made $750. His reason? — Because his wife didn't want to move more than 100 miles away from her parents. Unfortunately, this kind of letdown, particularly when you think you have a sure thing, is not uncommon, and Allen isn't too keen about advancing any cash.

Another drawback that's hitting us hard currently is that this business is quite seasonal. In June, for example, agencies have plenty of qualified college and graduate school applicants, and businesses are looking for sharp people to start during the summer. November and December, on the other hand, are extremely slow months. Due to bookkeeping chores and other end-of-the-year responsibilities, few companies hire until January of the next year. Because I began in mid-August and wasn't aware of the seasonality of the agency business at that time, my feelings are now much more negative than positive.

I guess that the problem which weighs heaviest for me is that Allen doesn't seem to care about what happens to any of his counselors. It's not like we don't ever see him, in fact, we see him too much. By nature of this business, you sometimes relax and converse with other counselors, about what some employer said, or this or that. But if Allen comes in while we're relaxing, his eyes, his scowl, everything about him is critical and intimidating. After all, we are our own bosses, and if we don't produce, we make zero money and it only costs Allen overhead. If we do produce, Allen gets two-thirds of the fee. Ideally, he'd like us to be in from *exactly* 8:30 to 5:00, wear suits or dresses, and do everything as he sees fit. Yet, when we need some help from the company, either a draw or a more professional looking letterhead, our requests are consistently rejected. Then, to add insult to injury, I've found out that Allen has put one or two of the new trainees on salary instead of commission, and can't even offer us a couple of hundred dollars draw when we really need it. You may wonder, but probably the only reason that I'm staying on is that I now finally have some money coming in and leaving would create difficulties in collecting the money due to me. Although I like the idea of being my own boss (when I can), and having no long-range commitments to help a firm that really hasn't much interest in helping me, unless some radical changes take place, I will be gone like a flash when something with more of a future comes along. Here, there's simply nowhere to go.

A CONVERSATION WITH BERT DIKES

I've been in the agency business for twelve years, and if there's one thing I've learned, it's do your own work, and avoid the management at all costs.

I've never had any trouble making money in this business because (1) I'm a self-starter, (2) I really enjoy working over the phone, and (3) I know how much work has to be done to make a placement. But, it hasn't always been easy. It's taken years of pursuing people, letting them know that I can always get the job done well for them, and just getting people to recognize my name and say, "He's a reliable counselor—I'll go to him when we need some people."

From the way I see it, I'm here when I need to work, and when I have some top prospects for placements. Hell, I don't want to go through with this coat and tie and 8:30 to 5:00 stuff; that's just not my style. After all, I'm making money, and my placements are helping to pay the rent. I'm in a great position, because as a consistent biller (producer), I can and will continue to come and go and generally do as I please. You see, by staying in this business for a long time, you gradually build up company contacts that are yours, not the agency's. These companies know *me* and want to deal solely with me because in the past I have come through consistently for them. If Allen fires me, that's no problem, because I'll simply go to another agency and bring my client companies with me. Allen's no fool; he may not like me or my style, but he can't afford to let me go. I'm not blind either. This agency has a lot of problems that Allen is either indirectly or directly responsible for. The way things are now, he needs all the people he can get, and judging by the calibre of the two most recent trainees that he's hired, he's not setting his standards too high.

I guess that the major personal gripe about this agency is that Allen and Wardlow don't seem willing to go out on a limb for anything except the agency. Wardlow's really a nice guy, but by nature of his job as manager, he can only recommend changes to Allen, not implement them. Jay (Wardlow) had some financial problems a few years back, and because he needs the money is forced to convey all policy matters to the counselors. Although we all complain about some things (we need a new photocopy machine and new letterhead, for example), Allen seldom gives any counselor requests serious consideration.

As far as how long I'll remain at Allen Personnel, nobody really knows. As long as Allen keeps his distance, which he has, and my checks are on time, I'm happy.

A CONVERSATION WITH MARK LESSOR

As I see what's going on in this office, there appears to be a basic morale problem. Allen certainly isn't responsible for the dissention within the agency, although I do concede that some of his tactics are a bit unnerving. Nevertheless, demanding that counselors in a professional office environment wear suits or dresses and keep appropriate business hours is not in the least bit unfair or even unusual, for that matter. Take a look at most offices in this building, and nearly all public employment agencies and you'll find people dressing professionally, and keeping professional hours.

As far as compensation is concerned, why should Allen virtually give more to counselors who have not demonstrated an ability to consistently perform, or advance money to a counselor who may be planning to quit the office tomorrow? Sure, it sounds unkind to turn away an employee in need of a few hundred dollars, but this business is plagued with job-hoppers who ask for money, then quit the very next day. This sort of thing seems to happen over and over, and because of this danger, Allen is simply trying to protect himself. Anyway, every new counselor is completely aware of the pay system—if he doesn't like it, he should leave.

Perhaps one major note of disagreement with Allen, however, is his policy in hiring and training almost anyone from off the streets who is willing to "give it a try." Just because the agency needs counselors doesn't mean Allen should bring in bodies. Quite importantly, it's extremely difficult for a young person to do well in the first year or two in the business, if for no other reason than employers are wary of young voices on the phone. Generally, most employers prefer to deal with older individuals, because they are in their forties or fifties themselves. Frankly, if I were Allen, I would simply not hire anyone who hadn't worked for at least several years, or wasn't able to communicate immediately on a mature and professional level. From the turnover that I've seen at Allen Personnel, most counselors have left for reasons of frustration, lack of any money coming in, or simple inability to accept continuous negative responses over the phone. Perhaps this is due to lack of competent or persistent training, but I believe a great deal of the trouble lies in inexperience in a business environment, and inability to professionally communicate with someone sometimes 20 years their elder. Take Johns, for example (confidentially). Here's a sharp young man who I believe is simply wasting his time. I've overheard him on several calls, and he simply doesn't have the communicating skills vital to success in this business. He's from the South, and has a heavy Southern drawl. In fact, *I* sometimes have trouble understanding him. I see certain positive characteristics about this fellow that might easily be developed elsewhere. This is simply not the right place for him, although I have voiced this opinion only to Jay Wardlow, the manager. Jay argued that Johns *did* have what it takes. But, I guess only time will tell.

Turnover for Allen Personnel continued to be a major problem during the year 1973. In January, Chuck Newse, Bert Dikes, and Frank Ford began their own agency; Larry Smothers went to work for a San Francisco brokerage house (a job that came across his desk); Betty Rosen, Gary Shaw, Bill Carst, and Mark Lessor transferred to other agencies apart from Allen Associates; Dave Martin, Tim Johns, and Tony Stading left for positions unknown. (Incidentally, after three slow and frustrating months, Johns became an outstanding counselor, consistently earning four-figure commissions). Finally, at the time of this writing, Jay Wardlow is planning to accept a position as manager of personnel at a large San Francisco insurance company.

Nevertheless, and despite continued inconsistencies, Allen Personnel continued to maintain counselors and show sporadic profits, while also serving as the major drain on funds of Allen Associates. As Jay Wardlow explained, Allen was simply determined to make a profitable operation out of Allen Personnel. Since he'd been successful with the other three agencies, he was sure the same could be done with this.

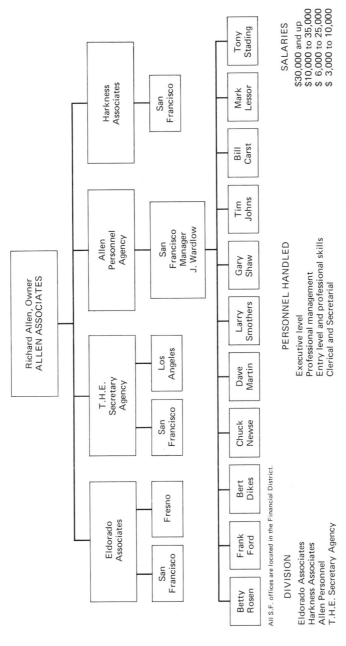

Exhibit 1. Allen Personnel Agency Organization Chart.

All S.F. offices are located in the Financial District.

DIVISION

Eldorado Associates
Harkness Associates
Allen Personnel
T.H.E. Secretary Agency

PERSONNEL HANDLED

Executive level
Professional management
Entry level and professional skills
Clerical and Secretarial

SALARIES

$30,000 and up
$10,000 to 35,000
$ 6,000 to 25,000
$ 3,000 to 10,000

Exhibit 2. Allen Personnel Agency Compensation for Counselors.

Placement Job pays	% Fee	Maximum Fee	Commission 1/3 x Fee
Up to $9,999	9%	$ 900	$ 300
$10,000 to 10,999	10	1,100	367
$11,000 to 11,999	11	1,320	440
$12,000 to 12,999	12	1,560	520
$13,000 to 13,999	13	1,820	607
$14,000 to 14,999	14	2,100	700
$15,000 to 15,999	15	2,400	800
$16,000 to 16,999	16	2,720	907
$17,000 to 17,999	17	3,060	1,020
$18,000 to 18,999	18	3,420	1,140
$19,000 to 19,999	19	3,800	1,267
Over $20,000	20	4,000 and up	1,333 and up

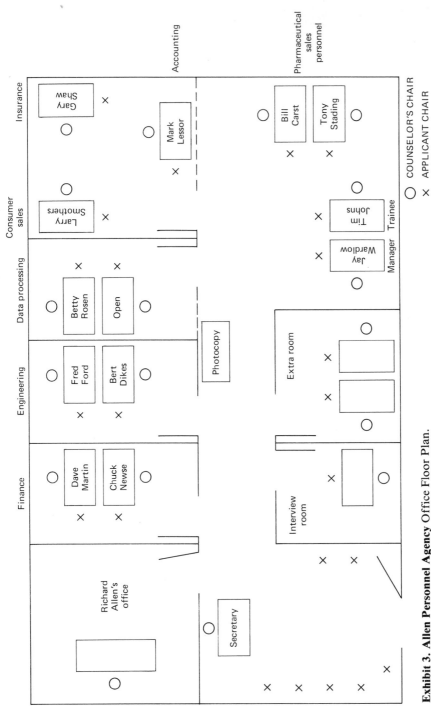

Exhibit 3. Allen Personnel Agency Office Floor Plan.

The Barrett Group (A)*

INTRODUCTION

This is the story of how a small black ownership - management group is struggling to get into the mainstream of the American business system against many handicaps, internal and external. The case tries to delineate the strategies of the formative years of this enterprise, together with the thoughts and actions of its management in determining a basic product - market niche for its operations.

THE PROFILE OF THE ENTREPRENEUR

Tall, congenial, dedicated, dynamic, and with a "big ego," as he readily admits, Frederick E. Barrett, 38, is the founder, sole owner, and architect of the Barrett Group.† Though not holding any office since 1974, he continues to be the leader of the organization.

Born in Jamaica, West Indies, Fred Barrett came to the United States in 1951, and studied engineering at Northeastern and M.I.T. Upon graduating from Northeastern in 1959, where he studied under a work-study cooperative program, he accepted a position with Ampex Corporation in Sunnyvale, California, a manufacturer of audio-video tape recorders. Within two and a half years, he rose to be the Director of Engineering of the company's plant at Bloomfield, New Jersey. In 1962, he resigned and joined Comspace, a producer of electronic audio-video equipment located in Jamaica, New York. In making the change he took a cut in his income, but felt happy that he was where he wanted to be. After about six years with the company, when he became the Vice President of Engineering, he was ready to resign and run his own company that he had organized a little earlier. Though he had yet to secure financial support for it, this fact did not stand in the way of his decision. Also, according to him, "Comspace is not growing any more, nor planning exciting long-range goals; there is no excitement and challenge." The role of "the organizational man" was apparently weighing heavily on him.

Fred Barrett is a man of uncommon views and strong personality traits. Looking back on his employment years he asserts that "a black professional working in a corporation has got to be twice as good to achieve a position and be willing to accept half the compensation."

Of the loneliness of the black businessman, this is what he has to say:

*This case was made possible by the cooperation of the firms of the Barrett Group—Barrett Intercommunication Products Corporation, Quadratech Research Corporation, and The Sequerra Company—and encouragement of Mr. Fredrick E. Barrett, himself. It was prepared by Dr. K.K. Das, Professor of Management, and Dr. Afife N. Sayin, Associate Professor of Management, both of The School of Business and Public Administration, Howard University, with an initial grant from The School's Business Economic Development Research Center funded by The Economic Development Administration, U.S. Department of Commerce, Washington, D.C. and later by The School of Business and Public Administration. It was prepared as a basis for class discussion rather than to illustrate either effective or ineffective handling of an administrative situation.

†The Group consists of: (1) Barrett Intercommunication Products Corporation, formed in 1967 but completely deactivated since 1973; (2) Quadratech Research Corporation, formed in 1972 and the main arm of the Group's activity since then; and (3) 55 percent controlling interest in The Sequerra Company. The Sequerra Company is dealt with in a separate case study.

He does not have the advantage of a relative or close friend who is efficient in his area to render him assistance or help when he needs it. He is very much alone. Professional consultants cannot relate to the subtle nuances of being a black businessman. They are mostly ineffective because their viewpoints—although reflecting sound business practices—are impractical, irrelevant, and fail to consider the overall peculiar ingredient and alien business climate of black businessmen.*

But he is quick to add that the comments of the professional advisers or consultants "must be heard and sifted for certain relevant portions of applicable truth."

Personally, Fred Barrett is at times very unconventional. To cite an example, when he negotiated his loan from the Chemical Bank of New York for $135,000 in 1973, he was wearing his black shirt and dungarees. To the surprised President of the bank, he explained his faith in capability rather than outside veneers. Yet another example, his ideas on the issue of ethnic identity, are rather radical in nature. He thinks it gives "some feeling of pride but not propulsion." He is in favor of deep and constructive social thinking on the needed value system and work ethic to help the economic development of the black world, and strives to make them generally accepted. Socially, he is apt to make the point of the loneliness of a successful black executive.

ATTENTION TO THE BASICS†

As his project of going into business on his own began to firm up, Fred Barrett began to turn his attention to three primary areas: What will be the scope and nature of his operation? Where will the finances come from? How will the management team be set up?

While working with different companies he became increasingly exposed to the extensive field of the electronics industry, more specially to the audio-communication segment of it. Working as the Vice President of Engineering at Comspace he gained considerable insights into problems of production of audio-communication products and components. This expertise, together with his training in electronics, led him to choose the audio-communication segment as the area of operation for his enterprise. Apart from professional considerations, Fred Barrett has always been an enthusiast of products and developments in this area. However, his decision on the broad segment was not enough. Fred Barrett's next unanswered question was: how to make an entry into the field? In view of the highly competitive nature of the industry, and its complex technological orientation, this was a fundamental question to be faced. Much as he was thinking big, Fred Barrett's immediate decision was more modest. He decided to begin as a small defense supplier under the auspices of the Small Business Administration (SBA), apparently for two reasons. One was that this would at once provide supportive finance and allow sheltered operation, giving the young business the opportunity to generate its own funds subsequently. The other was that the management must gain some operational and managerial experience prior to launching its activities in a big way.

---

*All quotations are from notes of interviews with the executives of the company.

†This is based on the notes that the case writers took of a long interview with Mr. Fred Barrett.

How was the task of financing to be faced? At Comspace Fred Barrett saw how loans are negotiated. Once he worked with his superior in getting a loan from a bank, and he formulated the notion of "bankability." According to him bankability is what the banker lends money on. He says:

> The measure of "bankability" is responsibility, dedication to objectives, capability, and collateral resources...presented in a well prepared package...(so) presented, one can receive several fold of his net worth in loans.

Accordingly, the Barrett Group has always relied, almost exclusively, on borrowed finance, as will be explained later. Except for about $10,000.00 in initial equity from the owner, and meager retained earnings over the years, there is no other equity capital in the business.

How about the management group to launch the Barrett Intercomp?* Around 1967, when Fred Barrett was working on the details of his business project, Peter tenBosch, head of a consulting firm, Athena International, called on him and offered his services. This offer was instigated by Capital Formation Incorporation† which was aware of his getting started in business. With his background in consulting, and his willingness to render voluntary service, Peter tenBosch was almost a godsend for him at this time. The two became friends almost immediately, and their friendship endures to this day. At the Barrett Intercomp, Peter tenBosch was made the chairman of the board, though he had no financial interest in the business. When the Quadratech Research Corporation was organized he moved on to the chairmanship of the board again. The official relationship was severed only when he left to settle in Europe.

Another member of the management team has been Fred's brother, Llewellyn (Lew) Barrett, an electronics engineer by training. A man of quiet temperament and analytical mind, Lew Barrett has always been with his brother, often acting as a steadying influence on him. He has filled many roles and is presently the operating head of the Barrett Group.

Around 1972, Barrett brought in more external members, all white. Mr. Sequerra, ‡ a representative from the banking world and an attorney were brought in. Asked about the unique composition of his board, Fred Barrett's reply was clear: "If you are going up a road, and you want to know what to expect, ask someone who has been there. The four whites on the board have already been there."

How did Peter tenBosch and Fred Barrett view their mutual relationship? This is what Peter tenBosch told one of the case writers:

> When I met Mr. Barrett, he needed some one to give him the necessary moral support...My role is to provoke Mr. Barrett to think independently...give him as best as I can the tools to work with and to increase his confidence level...(providing) a sounding board he could throw his ideas at, and expect an impartial, practical reaction.

---

*It stands for Barrett Intercommunication Products Corporation.

†Capital Formation Incorporation, based in New York City, is an organization dedicated to stimulating minority economic development. The corporation has a voluntary service program in recognition of the fact that more than just capital is required for the success of a minority business. It was at the suggestion of the corporation that Peter tenBosch offered his services to the Barrett Group.

‡Mr. Sequerra is the chairman of the Board of the Sequerra Company. The Quadratech Corporation holds a 55% controlling interest in the company.

Fred Barrett echoes similar sentiments, and recalls how he considered the first visit from Peter tenBosch as "god-sent." Asked if he could explain the motivation of his friend, he said that Peter tenBosch was one of the few who would try to live up to the limits of social responsibility even at the personal level. It would also appear that the association must have been a learning process in management for him. Except for the job experience at Ampex and Comspace, which was largely engineering oriented, he had had no opportunity to develop a total managerial dimension of capability required of the top management of a small growing enterprise.*

As for Mr. Sequerra, the other functionally important white member of his team, Fred Barrett viewed his relationship a little differently. His partnership with Mr. Sequerra was intended to provide him with a product line of his own to enable him to establish himself in the marketplace, to be counted as a manufacturer in the real sense of the word.† He felt he needed a product innovator, and one from the white community who hopefully would facilitate his transition from contracting to manufacturing.

The case writers felt that this kind of association, between members of two communities, at the top echelon of an organization, was unique, and perhaps a recent development, indicative of a novel, business strategy on the part of the black businessmen of our time. Also, having seen, in their many visits to the Barrett Group and the Sequerra Company, how closely the members of the team work, the case writers wondered how such a development may help the process of integration of our society.

FORMATION OF BARRETT INTERCOMP

In 1967, while still with Comspace, Barrett formed the Barrett Intercommunication Products Corporation in the basement of his house in Queens, New York. The initial equity capital was only $10,000, part from his personal savings, and part from personal borrowings from a family member and from the mortgage on his house. He subsequently applied for a loan to the Small Business Administration (SBA) in January, 1968. The application was for the standard amount of $25,000, carying 5.5 percent interest, and payable in ten years. In May, 1968, the loan was approved. Under the terms of the loan, about $3,000 was to be set apart for machinery, equipment and inventory; the balance being available for operating expenses. Also, the corporation was required to produce a lease of the business premises prior to disbursement of the approved loan.

With the approval of the SBA loan, the business was entitled to bid for defense contracts earmarked for minority businesses. They were not long in coming. In February, 1969, two U.S. Navy contracts for voltage frequency indicators and amplifiers, amounting to about $75,000, were awarded to Barrett Intercomp.

With this business on hand, the corporation was ready to start operations. But two problems became immediately apparent. One was that the available funds were all too meager. The problem of further financing loomed large. The other was the problem of attaining sizable operating volume. According to the Controller of the Barrett Group, unless individual contracts of similar nature could be dovetailed into

---

*Fred Barrett never had any management education of any kind before embarking on a business career. It is interesting to note that Lew Barrett, his brother, is working for an MBA degree under an evening program.
†More on this later.

one another to provide volume, the cost of operation was bound to be very high, partly because of the problem of overhead, and partly because of failure to realize economies of scale in terms of utilization of personnel and facilities. As he further explained to the case writers, the government enforces standardized cost and margin control on individual contracts; it is only through management of cost of operation that he could show improved operative results.

Confronted with the problem of finances, Barrett Intercomp applied to Bedford-Stuyvesant Corporation for a loan of $107,000 in March, 1969. In June, 1969, the Bed-Sty approved the loan to help Barrett Intercomp "expand its electronics business and create job opportunities in the Bedford-Stuyvesant area of Brooklyn."* It is interesting to note here that in applying for the loan, Fred Barrett had to submit his "bankability" package. Basically, he had to submit a business plan covering the next five years, and a financial projection for the same period, demonstrating ability to pay back the loan.

Under the terms of the loan, the Bedford-Stuyvesant Restoration Corporation† required that Barrett Intercomp be located in its area. Accordingly, Barrett Intercomp finally moved to its present location at St. Marks Avenue, Brooklyn, New York. The plant was actually located on the third floor of a loft there.

On interesting feature of this financing was that the repayment was to be made through training credits. The entire loan could be paid back through such credits. Under the agreement with the Bedford-Stuyvesant Corporation, Barrett Intercomp is obliged to hire only disadvantaged people as certified by the Corporation. For each worker trained, Barrett Intercomp was to get a credit of $2,260.00. This figure was to be raised each year by 5 percent to account for a rise in the cost of living index. The agreement also defined the length of the training period; 1440 hours per trainee was contemplated. Barrett Intercomp was expected to offer the trainees employment even after the training period was over.

It is interesting to note here that according to Barrett Intercomp, earned training credits would wipe out the outstanding loan, though the Corporation has not formally accepted the position yet.

With the major financing in hand, Barrett Intercomp was off to a reasonable start. However, in a few years, for various reasons, Barett Intercomp was to be deactivated, and Quadratech Research Corporation would take over the activities of the Barrett Group.

THE GROUP'S OPERATIONS: 1969 TO 1973
As already indicated, the management decided to turn to defense supplies as the major area of concentration during the first phase of the development of the organization. Because of the engineering specialty of the Barrett brothers, the

---

*Quotation from the company's contract with the lending corporation.

†In May, 1967, the Bedford-Stuyvesant Restoration Corporation and its companion, the Bedford-Stuyvesant Development and Service Corporation initiated a major redevelopment effort to rehabilitate about 400,000 residents, mostly black, of Bedford-Stuyvesant area in Central Brooklyn, New York. Born out of the late Senator Robert F. Kennedy's dream, the objective was to improve the overall quality of life in the area. And Robert Kennedy stated the rationale of such a corporation: "We start then from this truth: if there is to be meaningful revitalization of Bedford-Stuyvesant and places like it, methods must be found to join its human resources with capital resources. No society of people ever thrives without that marriage."

decision would appear to have been further narrowed down to selected items in the field of electronic communications. The items were: voltage frequency indicators; megaphones or public address sets; field telephone sets; amplifiers and tuning drives. Of these, the first three would account for most of the business volume of the period. Exhibit 1 gives a brief description of the nature and volume of some of the major contracts handled during the period. It will be seen that the Navy has been the mainstay of the business.

According to the management, the total dollar value of contracts up to 1973 was about $7.5 million, inclusive of contracts handled by Quadratech Research Corporation, the second arm of the Group.* The annual business volume during the period has been approximately $2.0 million. In 1973, the Barrett Group reported an estimated annual business volume of $3.5 million,† and was given the thirty-second place in the list of 100 largest black enterprises arranged by sales volume.‡ It was, however, the first amongst the three or four such enterprises on the list.

Two other aspects of the operations should be mentioned. One is that the organization has very largely relied on Section 8(a) contracts, earmarked for minority enterprises, particularly on the recommendation of the SBA. However, it has tried to straddle its entire specialized field, albeit slowly. For example, it did work for Sona Labs, Audio Equipment and IBM. The first two transactions related to a supply of megaphones, and the Group was anxious to increase its volume in this line in order to better utilize the tooling costs.

The other aspect of the operation is that, as the business volume increased, the management found it necessary to contract out part of the operation and/or manufacturing of complete products involved. To cite an example, when, in 1971, the U.S. Army contracted for field telephone sets, involving $3.5 million, it was necessary, for various reasons, to contract out a large part of it to Ashtan, Incorporated.§ At the time, despite the facility of progress payments on such contracts, the problem of working funds for such a large volume had to be faced. It was found that to complete the contract within the delivery deadline would require an inordinately large investment in equipment. The financial requirement was then estimated at $400,000. Besides, there was the problem of a considerable expansion of management, organization, and space. Another aspect of the situation arising out of the Army contract was the concern that the large excess capacity which would remain on completion of the contract if there should be no comparable contract volume thereafter. Indeed, it appears that this contingency of excess capacity has been behind the Group's conservative policy in long-term capital investment, even when allowance

---

*To be discussed later in the study.

†According to the Controller of the group, the figure included the sales forecast of the Sequerra Tuner, to be discussed later.

‡See *Black Enterprise*, June, 1974, page 37. In judging its place in the list allowance should be given for the technological orientation of the business. Also, the Barrett Group is not far behind the other enterprises higher up on the list. The estimate includes sales forecast of The Sequerra Company.

§The name is disguised. Ashtan, Incorporated had previously been awarded a similar contract, and had the necessary production facilities and expertise readily available at this time. For the Barrett Group, it was the other way around. So, it was mutually advantageous to set up an arrangement to complete a large part of this contract using the facilities and experience of Ashtan.

is made for the overall financial constraints within which it has been operating from the outset.

The result of this strategy was not altogether satisfactory. After a while, for various reasons, Ashtan began to slow down on deliveries which has resulted in a litigation with the company.

Another strategy to overcome the inadequacy of the operating facility deserves mention here. In 1968, Barrett Intercomp bid for a Navy contract for voltage frequency indicators, and it did not have the plant facility of its own to qualify for the pre-award survey.* Henry Granoff of Henry Products promised that it would put up his facilities in case the Barrett Intercomp should get the contract. In fact, the first meeting with the U.S. Navy representatives took place in the conference room of Granoff's firm.†

What are the highlights of the operating experience of the first five years of the Barrett Group?‡ As specified by the present Chief Executive and the Controller, in discussions with the case writers, they are the problems of: (1) plant and space§ in relation to the growing business volume; (2) the problem of financing operations, despite the facility of progress payments under different contracts;# (3) overhead and cost control; and (4) working with the disadvantaged and hard-core workers, whose productivity was low.

FINANCE

The financing of the activities of the Barrett Group may now be described. Starting with an equity of about $10,000 from the owner, it has relied exclusively on borrowed funds throughout its history. However, later on another $25,000 was injected as the equity of Quadratech. With an initial borrowing of $25,000 from the Small Business Administration (SBA) in 1969, it has borrowed as follows: $107,000 from Bedford-Stuyvesant Restoration Corporation in 1969; $175,000 from PEDCO// in 1973; and $485,000, in two installments, from the Chemical Bank of New York in 1973, amounting to a total of $782,000. Of this, $267,000 was borrowed directly by Barrett

---

*Generally speaking, before awarding the contract to the lowest bidder, the governmental agency concerned must be satisfied about the capability of the firm to be awarded the contract. Therefore, a pre-award survey is conducted by a team from the government, on whose recommendation the contract is finally awarded. The team evaluates four areas: financial capability, technical capability, quality control system, and plant.

†Mr. Henry Granoff was known to the U.S. Navy, having earlier completed contracts on similar products. At the time, Home Products had spare facilities, and Barrett Intercomp was still located in the basement of the house of its owner.

‡As indicated earlier, the operating arms of the Group that the case study is mainly concerned with are (1) Barrett Intercomp until it became defunct; and (2) Quadratech.

§Though largely an assembly operation, at times involving product design, space and equipment continues to be a major problem to this day. Management is presently thinking of moving to a new location.

#Especially weighed under heavy debt burden; see Finances later on.

//Sponsored by the United Presbyterian Church in the United States, PEDCO is a nonprofit corporation under the laws of Delaware state. It gives loans to minority enterprises which have potential for large impact on the economy and employment of the country, and stand in need of large injection of funds. Under its guidelines, it can give loans of as much as $500,000 to a needy enterprise, with a maximum maturity of 15 years. Interest rates are flexible, eligibility does not follow the normal pattern or requirements of most other lending institutions. As of December, 1973, it had lent approximately $6.3 million to 70 minority-owned businesses.

Intercomp and Quadratech. The remaining amount was borrowed by the budding Sequerra Company. But these loans are backed by the explicit or implicit guarantee from the Quadratech Corporation and the executives of the Group. Of the loans from the Chemical Bank, $350,000 carried the guarantee of the SBA. Also, during this period, Quadratech has lent, from out of its resources, around $268,000 to the Sequerra Company, part directly and part in meeting the outside dues of the company.

The task of financing the Group, including the Sequerra Company, is far from being over. By lending funds freely to the other unit of the Group, Quadratech has often experienced shortage of working funds for its own operations. Clearly, if the business volume stays at the high level it has attained, it will be necessary to increase working capital, perhaps also long-term capital. The facility of partial progress payment in governmental work could not fully take care of the situation. As for the Sequerra operation, behind schedule in getting to production, Lew Barrett also takes the view that considerable injection of funds would be necessary.

How about the financial aspect of the Group's performance over the period? The financial statements for the period are given in Exhibits 2* and 3. Asked to explain the unsatisfactory results from governmental work, the Controller made the following points: (1) heavy annual interest obligation; (2) siphoning of funds to Sequerra which has yet to produce; and (3) improper costing in making bids, part due to lack of competent staff, and part due to anxiety to meet deadlines and competition. It should be noted that the interest obligations of the Sequerra Company are perhaps being handled by the Quadratech Corporation. Also, even now, costings for bids are done by Lew Barrett and his controller.† The Controller also felt that the earlier contract bids may well have been motivated by many other considerations than pure cost analysis, more particularly by a desire to get a foothold in the governmental contract field. Anyhow, he felt that for Quadratech that phase was over, and it should be able to report confirming good operating results henceforth. He was more concerned about results from the Sequerra company.

WORK FORCE AND PLANT FACILITIES

With success in acquiring government contracts came the growth of the work force. By 1971 there were 129 workers in the plant. The majority were black Americans and the rest were from the West Indies and Central America. About 80 percent of the workers were women, most of whom had not had a high school education. The average age of the workers was about 30.

In recruiting its work force the organization was constrained by two factors: (1) its location in a disadvantaged area and (2) hiring obligations in terms of the loan from the Bedford-Stuyvesant Corporation. As a result, many personnel problems had to be faced. For example, a worker would be trained to handle test instruments on the basis of certain parameters but would know absolutely nothing of the basic functionality of

---

*In view of the foregoing, all the debts of the Barrett Group, including those of Sequerra, are not reflected in Exhibit 2.

†He is competent in his job, holding an MBA degree from a university on the East Coast. He has considerable work experience to his credit.

the instruments. Next were personal problems arising out of the socioeconomic background of individual workers. These problems were of three kinds: first, alcoholism, anxiety levels, and a persecution complex. Second, there were the problems of absenteeism, turnover, productivity, and poor work habits. Finally, there were often unusual requests made upon the management, such as for a day care center, individual loans, and changes in working hours to suit individual convenience. More important, what often stymied the management was that these problems did not always appear to be plantwide so as to permit any general resolution.

As the case writers could ascertain, management faces these problems in different ways: first, the Barrett brothers maintained an open-door policy toward workers, both on an individual and group basis. Outside agencies such as Job Rehabilitation Center, the Office of Economic Opportunity, and Bedford-Stuyvesant Corporation were all involved in resolving many of the personal problems of the workers. The management also tried to make use of the foremen and group leaders to help individual workers adjust to the work environment.

Since 1972, following a decline in government contracts, there was a layoff of a large number of workers. During this period, Barett Intercomp also persuaded Bedford-Stuyvesant Corporation to allow them to modify its hiring. So the company has developed a judicious mix between trained and untrained workers. Presently, the size of the work force is about 53. It appears that the layoff with the fluctuation in contract volume has helped the company in getting up to this mix by determining on each rehiring phase that it should take only the cream of the top unemployables and/or the previously laid off workers. There is now selective hiring, of course, with acquiescence of the Bedford-Stuyvesant Corporation.

Partly because of its location in a disadvantaged area (Bedford-Stuyvesant) and partly because of obligations under the Bedford-Stuyvesant Corporation contract, Lew Barrett* estimates that the cost of operations in the past five years was perhaps 30 percent higher than it would otherwise have been. It would seem that while training credits, referred to earlier, would partly offset the disadvantage of higher cost of operation it coult not have completely eliminated the disadvantage in competitive bidding for contracts.

Lew Barrett is also of the view that of the disadvantaged workers moving through his operations, only about 10 percent of the total he dealt with may have been fully rehabilitated; 30 percent may have obtained similar jobs elsewhere. He feared that the remaining 60 percent may well have reverted to their old way of drug addiction, alcoholism and the like, and so were lost from the work force.

Turning to plant and equipment, the Group's operating facilities were soon found to be inadequate in relation to the volume of contracts that was coming in.† At some point in 1971 Barrett Group turned to subcontracting. This in its turn brought up two kinds of problems and experience for the management. One was the problem of unionization that threatened the young operation. The organization required the subcontractor, Ashtan, Incorporated to lend some of its skilled workers to train the workers at Barrett Intercomp. Since the subcontractor was unionized, the threats of

---

*Now the Chief Executive Officer of the Group.

†Referred to earlier.

unionization began to appear in the company. The unionization threat was successfully averted, however.

The other problem was the failure on the part of the subcontractor, Ashtan, Incorporated to live up to its commitments. This led to Barrett Intercomp's difficulties with the government as will be mentioned later on.

The company's operations are essentially those of assembling parts and components; though at times it designs or improves upon the contract specifications. Accordingly, the physical facilities of production consist of a large variety of mechanical equipment ranging from presses to transmitters and oscilloscopes. The floor area for the same reason is not very extensive. Initially starting from 10,000 square feet, it has now become 23,000 square feet. But the Group is still struggling with space and intends to move to a new location as soon as possible. As to equipment, the company has from time to time used subcontractors and, whenever possible, has bought used equipment. The company's total investments in physical facilities, located at the present address, originally consisted of about $29,000. Presently the total investment in plant and equipment is around $59,000.*

TURNING TO NEW DIRECTIONS
Even as the organization was strengthening its foothold in the field of governmental contracts, the management was trying to diversify its activities. Mention was made earlier of the effort to generate business in the private sector. The following two sections deal with new trends in the Barrett Group.

SHIFTING TO THE PRIVATE SECTOR
Around 1971, Fred Barrett started to seriously consider other avenues of growth for his organization.† There were various factors behind it. First, he weighed the consequences of a cutback in government spending for small and medium-sized contractors. He feared that the axe might fall very heavily on them. He also observed how firms in the electronics industry were making haste to get into the consumer and industrial markets to ward off the adverse effects of cutback in defense spending. Second, since the SBA 8(a)‡ program contracts are available to a firm normally for two years, it was not clear how much longer the SBA would work with him. It is interesting to note here that the SBA has already served notice that it would not continue helping the organization any longer.§ Finally, as Lew Barrett found, there was more money in the private sector. The government allows only a 10 percent margin; the government continually monitors the operations of the contractors during the period of the contract; and requires maintenance of careful records. These often prove too burdensome for small operations.

Against this background, the management decided to shift to the private sector—seeking contracts from large corporations—while remaining in its chosen line of activity. Until now, the Group has done business in the private sector to the tune of

---

*Mention was made earlier of the struggle to avoid long-term fixed investment as much as possible.

†Fred Barrett's personal ambition has always been, and still is, to grow to be recognized as a member of what he calls the business club of America, as he told one of the case writers in one interview.

‡See Note on SBA and Government Contracts, Appendix.

§The matter is still under negotiation.

only $50,000. Recently, it has bid for a contract for amplifiers by a large corporation for over half a million dollars.

The organization is finding it difficult to get a foothold in this highly competitive sector of the electronics industry. It is learning of the difference between doing business in the public and private sectors. Regarding this, Fred Barrett once said:

> We can sell to the military quite effectively. They have a set of regulations, Armed Services Procurement Regulations (ASPR), which govern their procurement policies. One knows what the regulations are, and how the government would decide on a contract... If one is successful (in price and other criteria already set up), it is mandatory that he be awarded the contract. On the other hand, in the industrial sector, one has to court the buyer and woo his affection. As there are no fixed regulations there are numerous ways in which a close working relationship between a supplier and an industrial buyer can develop...the subtle variations in the buyer's procurement almost always elude us.... Our "bids" are always either "too late" or do not conform to the format that was never established!

Barrett recalls the case of a subsidiary of a large utility company which, upon directives from it headquarters, has for some time been soliciting bids from minority enterprises. He submitted a bid but, to this day, has not heard from the company, which prompted him to make the following point:

> If there is no feedback regarding your bid pattern pointing out where your bid was out of line with the successful bidder, then there is no correction factor that can be employed in future bids. We continue to work in a vacuum.

In addition to no set of well-established rules and no sort of feedback from his efforts, Fred Barrett is disappointed with the industrial market for yet another reason. He thinks that industrial buyers look down upon him because he is black. His complaint is that they are not convinced that the Barrett Group could undertake sophisticated technological work. He states his point thus:

> The buyer, due to lack of confidence in us, often predetermines our incapability to supply goods and services he requires. Unless we can establish the "golf course" or "yacht club" social contact we cannot break through into their purchasing habits.

According to the management, a reasonable foothold in the private sector in the area of electronics, is going to be difficult. But the management continues to work at it.

DEVELOPING A PRODUCT LINE

Faced with the difficulties in shifting to industrial contracts, the management began to consider developing electronic products of its own. It began to look around for a unique, innovative, and quality product, while continuing with the traditional governmental contracts as before.

What further spurred the quest was this. In the fall of 1971, SBA had sponsored a consulting firm to study and to advise them of the kind of products that a company like the Barrett Intercomp could make profitably. The report delineated three major areas for consideration: (1) security electronics and anti-intrusion devices: (2) educational audio-visual equipment, and (3) fixed and mobile communication products.

In consultation with his informal advisors, including Peter tenBosch, the founder of the Barrett Group eliminated the first area for no explicit reason. The second area was, however, ruled out on the ground that it was very largely the domain of big corporations, and it would be almost impossible for a small manufacturer to make its mark. In neither area was there a specific product proposal on hand. It was decided to try to develop products in the third area. Helping in reaching this decision was Barrett's view that the Carter case* had opened up opportunities for small manufacturers like himself to design and develop fixed and mobile communications products, such as radio and television components or units which were previously monopolized by large utility companies.

About this time, Fred Barrett was introduced to Richard Sequerra by a mutual friend. Dick Sequerra and his associate, Sydney Smith, were then well known in the industry as the innovators of the Marantz 10B tuner that came on the market in the "sixties." When Dick Sequerra met Fred Barrett he was no longer with Marantz Corporation. In fact, he was set up as a consulting engineer, and looking for an opportunity to update the tuner concept on the strength of technological advances made in the years following the original tuner. Here was the meeting of minds and a basic product decision, which led to the formation of the Sequerra Company, and the Quadratech Corporation holding a controlling interest in it.† The meeting of minds seems to have been almost complete. Almost immediately the management began to lend money to the new unit of the Barrett Group in large amounts; and by the end of 1973, as much as over $600,000 was made available to it for research and development. More important, except for the initial plan from the innovator, there does not appear to have been any control in the use of funds and management of its actual operations. Oftentimes, funds were made available to the new unit even endangering Quadratech's own operations.‡

It should be added that the tuner was not seen as only one product but as a complex of various component systems. As Dick Sequerra explained to the case writers, the tuner would yield a variety of derivative products, which, in turn, would give opportunities for further product innovation. In short, the tuner development was considered as the foundation for a product line around a common skill and technology.

According to the initial plan, referred to earlier, the developmental work was to be completed by the end of 1973 at the latest, and the company should have been in production early in 1974. However, the developmental work would appear to be far from complete, and, at this writing, the company is producing about three or four tuners a day, and that with difficulty.

A REORGANIZATION

With increasing commitment in product development, Fred Barrett started to think in a big way about his organizational structure. The result was the formation of Quadra-

---

*In 1966 Carter Electronics Corporation brought a successful suit against American Telephone and Telegraph Company for treble damages and injunctive relief for allegedly preventing the company from selling Carterphones by threats to prospective customers that their telephone services would be discontinued if they used the Carter device, thereby substantially lessening competition in the industry. (Thomas Carter and Carter Electronics Corporation vs. American Telephone and Telegraph Company et al, 365 F. DD 486, 5th Circuit, 1966)

†The Sequerra Company constitutes a separate study; see also the section on reorganization later on.

‡In 1973 Quadratech had to borrow $135,000 to cover its own operations. Also, funds to the Sequerra Company were all borrowed from outside on the credit of the Quadratech and the management, explicitly or implicitly. It appears that Fred Barrett jumped into the project more or less on a "gut feel" appraisal of his own. It is not clear who else he consulted before getting into it.

tech Research Corporation in March, 1972. The new member of the group was intended to be a kind of holding unit, owning and controlling Barrett Intercomp and holding the controlling interest (55 percent) of, and providing guidance for, the Sequerra Company.

Now it was time for Fred Barrett to face up to the situation arising out of Ashtan, Incorporated's default on the $3.5 million contract, referred to earlier. In 1972, with only 25 percent of the supplies delivered, Barrett Intercomp became a delinquent supplier. In view of the known arrangement with Ashtan, Incorporated, the company tried to persuade the Army authorities to accept a "novation" and release Barrett Intercomp from all liabilities. While the government agreed, the subcontractor declined to be a party to it. As a result, the government continues to hold the original prime contractor responsible for the default. This has forced Barrett Intercomp to sue Ashtan, Incorporated, and the case is still in court.*

Confronted with a litigation of considerable import, particularly any contingent liability that may arise as a result of adverse judgement, Fred Barrett had to take a hard look at the situation. His major concerns were: (1) how would the litigation affect the reputation of Barrett Intercomp in the business circles? and (2) would it in any way hinder his raising further loans for his operations, including those of the Sequerra Company? The second question was more important since he knew he would be seeking more loans to bring the product development to conclusion.

He elected to completely deactivate Barrett Intercomp† and let the Quadratech Research Corporation, formed in May, 1972, take over the operations of Barrett Intercomp on a *de facto* basis immediately. What was to be the holding company became the operating arm of the Barrett Group; and what was to be the contract and manufacturing division became a defunct member of the organization. Today, Quadratech alone does government and other contracts for the Group, employing the workers and facilities of the Barrett Intercomp. The changeover has been smooth as Quadratech is also located on the same premises at Barrett Intercomp. On the other hand, the Sequerra Company continues to work on the tuner but is now made subject to the general administrative control of the Chief Executive of Quadratech, whose controller also acts as controller for the other company. The present organization structure is shown in Exhibit 4. It will be seen that the Group is now aided by an Advisory Board consisting of members of the white community.

UNEXPECTED DEVELOPMENTS
As of November, 1973, the Quadratech Corporation was continuing its normal operations, though the business volume was not showing as much growth as before; and Lew Barrett, the Vice-President of Production, was in charge of the operating facilities under the general management and control of Fred Barrett, the head of the Barrett Group. Also, the corporation was now responsible, directly or indirectly, for funding as much as $618,000 on account of the Sequerra Company. At the Sequerra Company, the program of product development, though promising, was behind schedule, and was in need of more funds. It was high time that operations there

---

*Novation is an arrangement, legally enforceable, whereby Ashtan, incorporated was to take the place of Barrett Intercomp in the prime contract with the U.S. Army. (It was not made clear to the case writers about the defense that Ashtan, Incorporated may have for their failure on the subcontract.)

†In other words, cease operation but not get into liquidation.

became subject to general managerial control and began to generate funds, but Fred Barrett still continued to give the operation the autonomy that the technologist-manager wanted.

At this juncture, Fred Barrett made an unexpected decision. He decided to move to Washington, D.C. to become the Executive Director of the Consumer Product Safety Commission in the Federal Government. The following month, he put his brother in charge of the Group and departed.

Why did he leave so suddenly, and at this juncture? To the case writers, he offered various explanations. First, he considered the new position as a unique opportunity to serve the country to which he owed so much. Second, he felt that the new position might well be an advantage for the Barrett Group since moving in the upper echelons of the society, he would obviously project the image of where he came from, which might foster social connections for his business that he complained about lacking earlier. Finally, he felt that the Group was settling down to some stability. The "shakedown" period at Sequerra was about to end, and the company was soon to begin regular production. At Quadratech, the business was standardized and he believed his brother could very well manage it. All that was needed for the Group was more financing, and this he could very well work on from outside. There was, therefore, very little challenge for him in the business.

What did the new Chief Executive actually inherit? Based on discussions with various members of the organization at different times, the following may be mentioned. First, how to deal with the problem at Sequerra. According to Lew Barrett, the problems are: how to get the company on to regular production; how to make Dick Sequerra submit to organizational control.* He feels that this is of foremost urgency. Second, the SBA is rather disturbed on the departure of the founder president, Fred Barrett; it has indicated that it would not extend the Section 8(a) support to the Group anymore. It is likely to create an intolerable position, and the management is still negotiating about it. Third, the interest burden of debt is weighing very heavily on the Group's activities, more so as Sequerra delays getting into production;† for the bank loans, the repayment of the principal must also be faced. In addition, more funds must be secured to help Sequerra enlarge its production facilities.‡ Finally, the new management is confronted with the task of shifting to a formal organizational pattern. Under Fred Barrett, the organization was very informal, centered around his own authority, dynamism, restlessness, and entrepreneurial drive. Now that the Group was developing various operating centers, it was time to formalize, at least relatively, the organizational procedures, methods, and interrelationships. He felt the need more as he began to deal with Dick Sequerra alone. Besides, unlike his brother, Lew Barrett is a more methodical man, and believes in clear definition of authority and responsibility within an organizational system.

---

*As may be recalled, Fred Barrett got into the tuner project on a rather general appraisal, and he gave Dick Sequerra complete freedom; there was hardly demand for accountability.

†Fred Barrett admits that the tuner project has not gone according to plan, and a close supervision would perhaps have helped the turn of events. However, he makes the point that the project, as is, could be sold for over $5 million. He already had a negotiating offer of the amount from one of the giants in the electronics industry.

‡Fred Barrett feels that he will have no difficulty in raising equity capital now; though away from office, he is working on it.

Exhibit 1. The Barrett Group (A) Major Contracts Awards Under the U.S. Government.

Job Number	Buyer	Nomenclature	Quantity	$ Value	Award Date
FJ-101	U.S. Navy (Electronics Supply Office)	VFI-a Voltage Frequency Indicator FSN 6625-132-1196 Contract Number N00126-69-C-1577	4,800	$ 47,040.00	26 February 1969
FJ-102	U.S. Navy (E.S.O.)	AM-2631 A.F. Amplifier Contract Number N00126-69-C-1560	215	$ 27,128.70	24 February 1969
FJ-103	A.B.C.	Signal Tally Panel	Misc.	$ 5,000.00	
(8a) FJ-105	U.S. Marine Corps. (Washington, D.C.)	Public Address Set, Hand Held AN/PIQ-5 FSN 5830-688-6633 Contract #M00027-70-C-0105△ SBA-0072-8(a)-70	7,250 AN/PIQ-5 Including Manuals and Spare Parts.	$915,846.00	24 April 1970
FJ-106	U.S. Army (Phil.)	TA-312/PT Telephone Contract #DAAB05-70-C-4104	74036 (17524)	$3.5 million	
(8a) FJ-107	U.S. Navy (Electronics Supply Office)	VFI-3 Voltage Frequency Indicator FSN 6625-132-1196 Contract #N00126-70-C-1182 SBA-0117-8(a)-70	10,000	$ 98,000.00	24 April 1970
FJ-108	IBM Corp. (E. Fishkill, N.Y.)	Calibration Services Contract #KD 3204132	Misc.	n.a.	n.a.
8(a) FJ-111	U.S. Navy (Electronics Supply Office)	VFI-4 Voltage-Frequency Indicator FSN 6625-132-1196	4,500	$ 44,100.00	26 February 1971
8(a) FJ-119	U.S. Navy (Electronics Supply Office)	AN/PIC-2 Megaphones FSN 5830-790-2441 Contract #N00126-71-C-1983 SBA 2108(a)73-C-0009	300	$ 43,221.00	1 August 1972
8(a) FJ-120	U.S. Marine (Washington, D.C.)	Public Address Set, Hand Held AN/PIQ-5 FSN 5830-688-6633 Contract #M00027-72-C-0096 SB2108(a)-72-C-0095	2,580	$319,610.00	24 June 1972

Exhibit 1. *cont'd.*

8(a) FJ-124	U.S. Navy (Electronics Supply Office)	VFI-8 Voltage Frequency Indicator FSN-6625-132-1196 Contract #N00126-72-C-1214 SB2108(a)-72-C-0044	15,157	$243,572.99	27 March 1972
8(a) FJ-128	U.S. Navy (Electronics Supply Office)	VFI-10 Voltage Frequency Indicator FSN 6625-132-1196 Contract #N00126-72-C-1356 SB2108(a)-72-C-0052	4,500	$ 48,600.00	27 March 1972
8(a) FJ-131	U.S. Navy (Electronics Supply Office)	VFI-10 Voltage Frequency Indicator FSN-6625-132-1196 Contract # N00126-73-C-0114 SB2108(a)-73-C-0010	5,000	$ 54,000.00	1 August 1972
8(a) FJ-140	U.S. Marine Corps (Washington, D.C.)	Public Address Set, Hand Held AN/PIQ-5 FSN 5830-688-6633 Contract #M00027-73-C-0074 SB2108(a)-73-C-0125	4,000	$554,868.00	12 April 1973
FJ-157	U.S. Army Electronics (Philadelphia, Pa.)	Tuning Drive FSN 5820-973-3963 Contract #DAAB05-73-C-2433	2,276	$ 82,163.60	23 May 1973

Exhibit 2. The Barrett Group (A) The Barrett Intercommunication Products Corporation Balance Sheet as of:

	Dec. 31, 1969	Dec. 31, 1970	Dec. 31, 1971	Mar. 31, 1973*
Current Assets				
Cash in Bank or on Hand	$ 3,828.88	$ 88,775.24	$ 82,899.31	$ 22,389.69
Accounts Receivable	41,793.34	51,804.31	24,696.27	195,189.92
Inventory	42,976.00	20,327.43	140,825.00	72,734.92
Other Current Assets	1,020.00	2,349.71	8,861.88	27,146.88
Total Current Assets	89,618.22	163,256.69	257,282.46	317,461.41
Fixed Assets				
Machinery and Equipment	24,758.70	34,370.22	45,147.15	34,382.67
Less: Accumulated Depreciation	4,420.33	9,049.95	15,761.94	11,052.46
Net Fixed Assets	20,338.37	25,270.27	29,385.21	23,330.21
Other Assets	1,310.00	1,290.00	4,790.00	102,798.81
Total Assets	111,267.09	189,816.96	291,457.67	443,590.43
Current Liabilities				
Accounts Payable	14,413.91	29,218.71	120,667.81	209,754.46
Taxes		5,041.01	1,508.42	11,230.12
Loans Payable	11,092.20	11,042.20	9,571.67	41,648.00
Unliquidated Progress Payments				16,369.13
Accrued Expenses	3,248.49	17,043.13	36,923.98	17,577.60
Total Current Liabilities	28,754.60	62,445.05	168,671.88	296,574.31
Long Term Liabilities and Stockholders Equity				
Notes Payable	88,813.34	113,642.17	106,472.64	85,499.16
Other Loans Payable				19,334.11
Capital Stock	10,000.00	10,000.00	10,000.00	38,209.60
Retained Earnings (Deficit)	16,350.85	3,729.74	6,323.00	3,973.10
Total Long-Term Liabilities	82,462.49	127,371.91	122,795.64	147,015.97
Total Liabilities	$111,267.09	$189,816.96	$291,457.67	$443,590.43

*Barrett Intercomp and Quadratech consolidated   SOURCE: Company files.

Exhibit 3. The Barrett Group (A) Barrett Intercommunication Products Corporation Income Statement for the Year Ending:

	Dec. 31, 1969	Dec. 31, 1970	Dec. 31, 1971	Mar. 31, 1973*
Sales	$ 72,098.41	$373,871.33	$1,385,091.00	$1,144,685.63
Less: Discounts	-	2,906.77	18,359.32	344.13
Net Sales	72,098.41	370,964.56	1,366,731.18	1,144,341.50
Cost of Goods Sold	66,569.88	311,132.44	1,251,962.56	1,013,350.80
Gross Profit	5,528.53	59,832.12	114,769.12	130,990.70
Less: General and Administration Expenses	22,107.82	56,230,68	111,537.63	110,901.98
Net Operating Income (Loss)	(16,579.29)	3,601.44	3,231.49	20,088.72
Other Income				
Interest Income	228.44	-	-	-
Training Credits	-	21,494.47	-	-
Income Before Other Expenses and Taxes	(16,350.85)	25,095.91	3,231.49	20,088.72
Other Expenses	-	-	-	21,774.30
Income Before Taxes	(16,350.85)	25,095.91	3,231,49	(1,685.62)
Taxes	-	2,298.17	638.23	664.32
Net Income (Loss)	$(16,350.85)	$ 22,797.74	$ 2,593.26	$ 2,349.94

*Barrett Intercomp and Quadratech consolidated

SOURCE: Company files

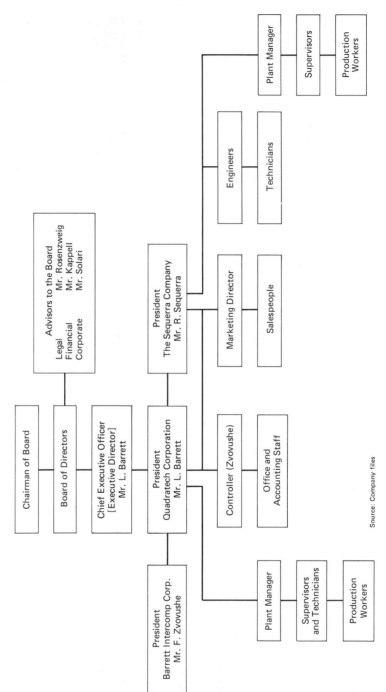

Source: Company files

Exhibit 4. The Barrett Group (A) Barrett Group Organization.

Appendix | A Note on the SBA Financing and Section 8(a) Contracts

The Small Business Administration is an independent, permanent agency established by Congress and the President to serve America's small businesses. The services it provides are authorized by the Small Business Act and the Small Business Investment Act. These direct SBA to help small firms obtain financing, overcome the effects of disasters, sell to or buy from the Federal Government, strengthen their management and production capabilities, and generally grow and prosper.

FINANCIAL ASSISTANCE*

Where borrowing seems necessary, and the businessman's bank (or other commercial sources) cannot provide the needed funds on reasonable terms, SBA often can assist. The agency will consider participating with the bank in a loan to the businessman, or guaranteeing part of a loan made to him by the bank. The SBA may either provide or guarantee up to 90 percent of a loan. If the bank cannot provide any of the funds, SBA will consider lending the entire amount as a "direct" Government loan. However, about two-thirds of the agency's loans are made in participation with banks.

The SBA participates in loans, or makes direct loans, for these purposes:

- Business construction, expansion, or conversion.
- Purchase of machinery, equipment, facilities, supplies, or materials.
- Working capital.

SBA business loans may be for as long as 10 years. The maximum interest rate is 5½ percent. However, a bank may set a higher rate on its share of a participation loan and on SBA's share of a guaranteed loan until the agency actually provides its share. If a bank charges less than 5½ percent on its share, SBA will match the bank's charge down to a minimum of 5 percent.

As a rule, a business qualifies as a small business for purposes of SBIC financing if (a) it meets SBA's regular business loan size standards, or (b) its assets do not exceed $5 million, its net worth is not more than $2.5 million, and its average net income, after Federal income taxes, for the preceding two years did not exceed $250,000.

A business generally qualifies as "small" for SBA loan purposes on the basis of these yardsticks:

- Wholesale—annual sales of not more $5 million.
- Retail or Service—annual sales or receipts of not more than $1 million.
- Manufacturing—small if it has no more than 250 employees, large if it has more than 1000; within these breaking-points are specific size standards for specific industries.

*For a comprehensive account, see SBA Publication No. OPI-6, Small Business Administration, Washington, D.C.

HELPING IN BUSINESS WITH THE GOVERNMENT

Each year the Federal Government does billions of dollars worth of business with private companies, both in buying needed goods and services and in disposing of surplus Goverment property. The SBA helps small businessmen obtain a share of this Government business.

SELLING TO THE GOVERNMENT

The SBA gives several forms of assistance to small firms that want to obtain Government prime contracts and related subcontracts.

Who Buys What and Where. Specialists in SBA field offices counsel small businessmen on prime contracting and subcontracting. They advise them which Government agencies buy the products or services they supply, guide them in having their names placed on bidders' lists, help them obtain drawings and specifications for proposed purchases, and assist in other ways.

The SBA also gives information and guidance by publishing "The U.S. Government Purchasing, Specifications, and Sales Directory." It lists the principal goods and services bought by the military and civilian agencies and the purchasing offices that buy them, tells where to obtain copies of the specifications used in Government purchasing, and provides helpful information on Government sales of property. The directory is sold by the Government Printing Office. Another SBA publication, "Selling to the U.S. Government," explains the Government's buying methods and suggests steps to take in selling to it and to prime contractors. The leaflet is available free from SBA field offices.

Reserving Contracts for Small Business. Officials of SBA and major military and civilian buying offices jointly review proposed purchases, and "set aside" or reserve suitable ones to be made entirely or partially by small business. This is the core of the Section 8(a) program. The objective of the program is to assist eligible firms that are unable to compete effectively in the marketplace toward the goal of self-sufficiency and to achieve self-sustaining independence in the competitive economy.

Small firms that want to sell to the Government should obtain listings on all appropriate bidders' lists, so they will be notified of opportunities to bid on the set-aside purchases. Help in obtaining listing is available from all SBA field offices.

Locating Additional Suppliers. SBA representatives at buying offices are particularly watchful for purchases on which few small firms have bid in the past. If the representatives believe that small firms can perform the contracts, they have SBA offices locate small companies that would be interested in bidding on them. They then ask contracting officials to solicit the firms for bids.

Subcontracting Program. The SBA develops subcontract opportunities for small businesses by maintaining close contact with prime contractors, learning what work they want to subcontract, and referring qualified small firms to them.

In its subcontracting program, SBA works closely with the largest contract-awarding agencies, the Department of Defense and the General Services Administration. Under regulations established by the three agencies, Government prime contractors must give small concerns equal opportunity to compete for their subcontracts.

Facilities Inventory. The SBA maintains an inventory or register of the capabilities of small manufacturers, service firms, research and development concerns, and construction contractors. It uses the inventory to locate additional small firms to bid on Government work, as well as small firms which have special skills and facilities needed by the Government or by private industry. Small firms may register by completing a questionnaire available at any SBA office.

"Contract Opportunity Meetings." In cooperation with local business groups and other Government agencies, SBA sponsors meetings where small businessmen can learn of prime contract and subcontract opportunities. Government contracting agencies and prime contractors present their needs and requirements, and discuss bidding opportunities on a face-to-face basis with businessmen. SBA field offices can provide information about meetings scheduled for their areas.

Certificates of Competency. If a small firm bids low on a contract, and the contracting officer questions its productive or financial ability, he informs SBA of this fact. The SBA then asks the small firm whether it wishes to apply for a "certificate of competency"—an SBA certification that the firm is able to meet the contract requirements.

If the firm applies, SBA specialists make an on-site study of its facilities, management, performance record, and financial status. If SBA concludes that the company has, or can obtain, the necessary credit or productive capacity to perform the contract successfully, it issues a certificate (COC) to this effect. The small business is then awarded the contract.

The following table summarizes the achievement of the SBA to date.

Fiscal years	Number of contracts	Amount of contracts $	Companies awarded contracts
1968	8	10,493,524	7
1969	28	8,857,771	21
1970	199	22,520,209	145
1971	813	68,626,077	509
1972	1720	151,619,093	993
1973	1992	207,953,544	1088
1974	776	106,519,181	562
Totals	5536	576,589,399	

Shalco Corporation (A)

The attached exhibits describe the founding and development of Shalco Corporation.

Exhibit 1. Shalco Corporation (A) Excerpt from Memo to Shalco Employees—December, 1958.

Many of you who have come to Shalco in the past year may be interested in knowing some of the history of the company. All of you will be interested in what we see ahead for the future.

BACKGROUND
We are, of course, in the shell-molding business...

The shell-molding process was developed by Johannes Croning in Germany where it was used in making hand grenades and similar military products during World War II. The process consists of dropping a mixture of sand and thermosetting resin onto a heated metal pattern. The sand-resin mix is left on the pattern for 10-20 seconds, during which time the heat partially cures the resin near the pattern to form a soft sticky layer about ¼'' thick. The uncured sand and resin is then dumped off, and the pattern, with the thin sand-resin layer adhering to it, is put into an oven where the resin is "cured" to form a hard, rigid "shell." After curing, the shell is stripped from the pattern. Two shells are clamped or glued together to form a mold into which molten metal can be poured.

Because the shell exactly duplicates the pattern and because very fine sand can be used, the shell-molding process produces accurate, smooth surfaces on the finished casting. This means better casting and a reduction or elimination of subsequent machining.

Shell molding was brought to this country in 1947 by the United States Government and placed in the public domain. This meant that the process could be used by any American foundry without payment of royalties to the German inventor.

Several larger foundries in the East saw substantial benefits in the new process and began experimental shell-molding operations in their plants. The largest was Ford Motor Company, which built large automatic machines to produce cam shafts, crank shafts, and exhaust valves and claimed to be making savings of over 30 percent. One or two foundry-equipment manufacturers also recognized the potential and developed shell-molding machines for sale to the foundry industry. In general these were large, complex, automatic monstrosities.

THE STANFORD MACHINE
In 1951, a group of Stanford students investigated, as a class project, the extent to which Bay Area foundries were making use of shell molding. They found little use and almost no interest. They received such explanations as:

"It's O.K. for the big production foundry, but no good for the little shop."

"We already have all the business we can handle."

"The equipment is much too elaborate and expensive for us."

"We'll let the big foundries work out the bugs, then we'll take another look at it."

Reprinted from *Stanford Business Cases 1966* with the permission of the Publishers, Stanford University Graduate School of Business, © 1966 by the Board of Trustees of the Leland Stanford Junior University.

Exhibit 1. *cont'd.*

The students thereupon undertook the development of an inexpensive, flexible shell-molding machine designed specifically for the small jobbing foundry. The machine was built, it worked well, and several demonstrations were held for Bay Area foundries.

The machine gained considerable publicity and inquiries were received from all over the country. Several of the foundries whose people saw the demonstrations indicated interest in purchasing the Stanford machine. The University, concerned with potential patent problems, decided not to sell the machine, so the group which developed it decided to form a company to manufacture machines for the foundries which had expressed interest.

The Stanford machine was completely redesigned, adding a second dump box to speed the cycle and incorporating other lessons learned on the first unit. The prototype of the new design was completed in September 1952. This in turn was demonstarted and firm orders were received from McCulloch Motors (Los Angeles), East Bay Brass (Richmond), and Atlas Foundry (San Pablo).

THE HO-4

Again the machine was redesigned, essentially along the lines of the present HO-4. Three were completed in a little jobbing shop in Redwood City and delivered in January 1953. The new company received free newspaper publicity and a spread in *Business Week*, which stated that we had hit a potential jackpot. Actually this article did us more harm than good, for its title, "Schoolboys Show Foundries a Trick," was uncomplimentary to our future customers, and mention of the "jackpot" stirred up interest among potential competitors. But we thought it looked good and hired an engineer, a draftsman, a machinist, and an assemblyman.

We also took a big breath and started a run of ten machines. By the time these were completed, orders for almost all of them had been received, and ten more were started in April. Later in the year we hired a sales manager and a secretary. During this first year, we built 40 HO-4s and the first HO-5, doing all our manufacture and assembly in subcontractors' plants, primarily North Machine Works and Belmetals in Belmont. In March 1954, we moved into our present building at 81 Encina, Palo Alto, bought a lathe and drill press, and started making some of our own parts and doing our own assembly.

Sales came relatively easy in the first few months, but it soon became evident that these orders were coming from the more progressive foundries and that the rest of the foundry industry was not going to "beat a path to our door." We found out, in fact, that the foundry industry is one of the toughest of all to sell a new process to, and that they much prefer to continue doing things the way their grandfathers did.

It was also clear that our largest market was in the East, 2000 miles away. So we made arrangements in early 1953 for manufacture in Pennsylvania, and a new company, Shallway Corporation, was formed to handle both manufacture and sale, under license, in the East. We set up our own distributors in the West and Middle West.

Our first Western showing of the HO-4 was held in Los Angeles in 1953, and our first Eastern showing in Chicago the same year. We made a few sales at each, but among those attending the Chicago demonstration were the executives and engineers of a St. Louis firm, which studied our design, redesigned our machine, and brought out their own cheapened copy, the Tyco, a few months later. Several other firms also copied our machine, one of them even using our sales brochure, retouched, to promote their own machine, which hadn't even yet been built! We had applied for patents on our design, but until they were granted, we could do nothing to stop others from copying.

It didn't take long for us to realize that we were selling not just machines but an entirely new process, and that we would have to provide each new customer with technical advice on patterns, resins, pouring techniques, etc., none of which we knew anything about. But we had

Exhibit 1. *cont'd.*

to do it, and we determined to build for the long pull on a policy of offering top value at a good price and providing with each machine the know-how (what little we had) to use it. Unfortunately, most of those who copied our machine were after the "fast buck," and sold machines whenever and wherever they could. They made so many promises for what shell molding could do, placed so many machines in foundries that had no use for them, and ruined so many patterns by misuse, that they soured the whole foundry industry on shell molding. This did us more damage than their competition did, and 1954 was a rough year for us. We are happy to say that all of these earlier copiers have fallen by the wayside. The competition that has developed in the past couple of years, on the other hand, is competent and tough, and we will have to keep pushing to keep ahead of them.

CORE BLOWERS
In 1954, we began to realize that only a limited number of foundries could profitably use shell molding and then only on special jobs where the volume or precision required justified the high cost of the metal patterns. So we set out to develop a machine to make shell cores which any foundry could use. We were at this time having a few of our own parts made in shell, and had built a machine to extrude shell cores for the oven wheels.

This was a very simple unit, which dumped the sand and resin into a heated metal tube, emptied the uncured mixture and then pushed the finished core from the tube. This machine was demonstrated here and in Seattle, but it could make only straight cores, a small part of the total core requirement. So we redesigned it to handle a split core box to produce more complex cores. The new machine, the MC-4, was finished just in time for air freighting ($900) to the Cleveland Foundry Show in May 1954. It was the first shell core machine offered to the foundry trade and made quite a hit. It was strictly a "dump," rather than "blow" type machine, so it too was somewhat limited in the type of cores it could produce. After building five and selling five, we redesigned it along the basic lines of our present MC-5.

Since that time, our core blower sales have grown, while shell-molding machine sales have declined. Someday we will take a new crack at shell molding, and design a new machine with all the ideas we have learned since the early days. But shell core blowers will probably continue to be our main line, for they offer not only all the precision and casting quality of shell molding, but they also provide substantial cost savings in labor, material, and equipment when compared with the conventional core-making process—blowing solid cores, placing on driers, oven curing, pasting, trimming, shake-out, etc.

Although we have since 1954 concentrated our efforts on shell cores, we have also developed and produced larger shell molding machines, the HOS-5 (18" x 24"), the big HOS-8 (24" x 36"), and several in between. In core blowers, we have added the MC-3, MCM-5, MCM-5S, MCM-7 and more recently Ash's new designs, the U-180 and U-360. We have also built a large number of "specials," including three fully automatic MCM-5S and the world's largest core blower, the Fairmont machine (48" x 52").

In the past two years, customers have been demanding larger and more automatic core blowers and we have tried to design to suit. Our machines today are much more complex, require elaborate automatic electrical and air controls, demand higher quality in their manufacture, and have to be able to stand up under more severe punishment in the foundries.

As our sales have grown, we have added people, space, and products. When we started in 1953 we had 4 employees, today we have 55 full-time and 6 part-time employees.

We dissolved our arrangement with Shallway in 1956 because of differences on sales and service policy and because we now had Wolff handling our sales and could do a better job both for ourselves and the customer through our own sales force. We now have three sales engineers in the East, one in the West, and one in Europe. We use nine distributors in this country and six

Exhibit 1. *cont'd.*

in Europe. Our plant has grown from one room and a garage in 1953 to about 2400 square feet of office space and about 10,000 square feet of shop and storage space. We are adding new tools and equipment as fast as we can afford it and are trying to bring into our own shop all the sub-contract work we can do as well as outsiders.

In addition to our own Shalco machines, we sell supplies, accessories, and spare parts. Six months ago we added the British-built Fordath sand-coating equipment to our line and this month are delivering the first two units. We are now getting under way on a horizontal-parting core and mold blower being made in Wisconsin by one of our customers to blow transmission impeller cores and molds. Ultimately we will probably produce both this unit and the Fordath machine or parts for them in our own shop. Our British licensee, Coleman-Wallwork, is presently producing the MCM-5 and will go into production on the MC-3 and U-180 in 1959.

Shalco core blowers are now being operated in about 15 foreign countries. We once tried to set up a sales program in Japan, but within six months of our introduction of the HO-4, a half dozen copies were being made by Japanese companies.

With the addition of the new lines and increased production of our own products, our sales volume has increased from forty machines in 1953 to more than one hundred and forty in 1958.

1958 has been both a good and bad year for Shalco. The recession hit us in the early months, and we lost heavily, largely because of the costs of developing and putting the U-180 and U-360 into production. But our orders and shipments have been climbing rapidly since August, Norm is getting the procurement and production of the new models shaken down, and we ended the year in the black. Next year we hope to do about twice the 1958 volume.

We have in our short history gone through two serious slumps in the foundry market, have fought some tough battles in design, engineering, sales and patents, and have plowed what earnings we have made into further design, development, promotion, and shop and office equipment.

So far as we can determine, we have outsold all our competitors. Today there are more Shalco machines in operation than all others combined. But our biggest accomplishment is not in the machines we have sold. It is rather in the reputation we have developed in the foundry industry and the organization we have built. The Shalco name is now becoming recognized for quality, service, and value. We still have a long, long way to go in improving the design of our machines, in turning out a top quality product, shipping on schedule, and producing at a cost low enough to offer the customer more of our machines and more service than competition can touch. More and more of our machines are going into the larger production foundries—automobile, appliances, soil pipe, plumbing—all of which demand and deserve reliable equipment, free from breakdowns, able to produce 24 hours a day on a continuous basis day in and day out.

We are faced with new and growing competition from Eastern foundry equipment manufacturers who have lower materials, labor, and transportation costs. They are pushing hard for the markets we have created. This all forces us to do the job that much better than they can to overcome the advantage they have. Thus far we have been able to keep ahead, thanks to the crew we have developed in the shop, in engineering, in sales, and in the office.

We're sure we have some tough battles ahead. Two well-heeled competitors, offering good equipment at lower prices than ours, came into the market in 1958 and several are now producing the large core blowers we pioneered. So there is no doubt that 1959 will be tougher in this respect than we have ever had it before.

We believe that Shalco offers the best equipment any foundry can buy, and we think we have the best organization in the industry to produce and sell it. We intend to keep it that way. For only as we can turn out top grade, low cost equipment and convince the industry that no competitor can offer greater value or quality or service than Shalco can we continue to maintain and increase our volume.

Exhibit 2. Shalco Corporation (A) Collateral Material—(February 8, 1959).

The following provides additional information, expanding on that set forth in the memo to Shalco Employees (Exhibit 1).

ORGANIZATION

The organization at several different stages of the company growth is shown on Exhibit 3.

The Company has always had a strong board of directors. Until recently the original group of students was represented by one member, and other members were chosen from friends who were active in the founding of the Company. Among them were an insurance executive, a professor, an air line pilot, the president of a power tool manufacturing company, and a Lockheed executive. In the last two years, the vice president of a local manufacturing company and Shalco's Vice President and Secretary-Treasurer have been added to the Board.

The Board has been extremely helpful in policy decisions, in obtaining management personnel, in meeting financial problems, in providing sales contacts, etc. They are consulted formally or informally on all major decisions.

The operating organization is divided into sales, engineering, and production-finance. The combination of the production and finance functions is somewhat unusual and arose in 1956. Some months prior to the departure of the President for Australia (August-December) a "Manager of Operations" was employed and given responsibility for all Palo Alto activities other than finance and engineering. Engineering was under the Vice President. Finance was the responsibility of the President and the Secretary-Treasurer, who also was responsible for all purchasing. The Sales Manager was responsible for all sales and service activities. The new Manager of Operations did not work out because of personality difficulties and "big company" ideas, and he resigned in early November. The Secretary-Treasurer took over his responsibilities in the production function. The Executive Committee of the Board assumed responsibility for over-all administration. The President returned in early January. When the Vice President-Engineering resigned in February, the Sales Manager was made Vice-President, and a new Chief Engineer was employed.

Because the President is able to give only limited time to the company, authority is broadly delegated to operating executives. The Vice President has virtual autonomy in the sales function. The President works most closely with the Secretary-Treasurer on financial and production problems and with the Chief Engineer on engineering.

The Vice President is Austrian by birth, sold steel in China and Japan prior to the war, and after the war manufactured drill presses, diesel engines, and other machinery in Japan. He came to Shalco in September 1955. He is an outstanding equipment salesman, and deserves major credit for the growth of Shalco's volume in recent years.

The Secretary-Treasurer graduated from Harvard Business School in 1950, worked for a large department store, and was in charge of purchasing for a small garden equipment manufacturer before coming to Shalco in 1955. He is not a trained engineer, but has an unusually high natural aptitude for shop and technical matters.

The Chief Engineer is a graduate of Stanford, has done machine design work for a food machinery company, a power tool manufacturer, and a calculator and office equipment manufacturer. He is extremely imaginative and creative.

The Accountant graduated from Stanford Business School. After graduation he worked a year for a small manufacturer in San Francisco, then came to Shalco to handle production control. He was transferred to accounting when it was decided that Shalco had outgrown the services of an outside CPA.

All these key personnel are hardworking and deeply interested in the success of the Company. Most work from 8 A.M. to 6 P.M., six days per week, plus occasional Sundays.

Exhibit 2. *cont'd.*

FINANCE

The Company's initial financial needs were met by the President. Stock was given to the students in proportion to the amount of time they had spent on the project and to the President in proportion to his time and money provided. Bonuses in the form of stock were paid in 1953 and 1954 to the directors. In 1954 a modest Christmas stock bonus was paid to employees. In December 1958, 6892 shares were sold to directors, officers, and supervisory personnel, the bulk of it exchanged in cancellation of accrued salaries to officers. In January 1959, 310 shares were sold to supervisory personnel. Original stock was sold at $5.00 per share. In 1958 and 1959, it was sold at $7.50. A stock option and profit-sharing plan for the Vice President, Chief Engineer, and Secretary-Treasurer is presently under consideration.

As the Company's financial requirements grew with expanded operations and early losses, stockholders provided additional funds in the form of loans. Executives contributed through salary accruals. Bank loans were also used, reaching a high of $40,000 in early 1957. Requiring periodic retirement every six months, this type of credit was not well-suited to the Company's continuing financial need. In 1958, the Company started discounting its receivables through Commercial Credit Corporation. Such financing was expensive (10 percent per annum), but was ideally suited to financing the growing sales and resulting receivables. This type of financing is currently continued through the bank (at 7 percent per annum).

Limited capital has been a severe problem for the Company from the start. During many weeks, the most important daily event was opening the mail, hoping for a check to cover pressing obligations. The Company has had to "scrape the bottom of the barrel" and even overdraw on numerous occasions, but it never missed a payroll. Neither has it had to lay off anyone for lack of work.* The Company has depended heavily on supplier credit for working capital, and accounts payable have run as long as 90 days. With increased sales, accumulated earnings, receivable financing, and better planning, financial pressures have been somewhat eased in recent months, and the Company is now able to carry its obligations with "relative" comfort, in spite of the greatly increased level of operations.

The Company now has a full-time accountant and a bookkeeper, and recently acquired a $6000 National Cash Register accounting machine on a term purchase contract. Unfortunately, NCR did not provide proper instructions with the machine, and the accounts for the last three months of 1958 had to be completely reposted because of balances mistakenly left in the machine. The much-delayed program for developing analytical and cost data is only now getting under way.

ENGINEERING

As a pioneer is a new technology, the Company has been forced to make continual improvements to its machines as new techniques or customer needs developed or as field difficulties arose. It has been generally able to keep ahead of its competitors in design and has contributed most of the important technical advances to the industry. It developed the first two-station shell-molding machine, the first production core blower, the largest core blower, the first fully automatic core blower, and it now offers the widest product line of any in its field. In the past year, however, other larger companies have been attracted to the market that Shalco has created, and have developed highly competitive designs. Shalco's future will depend in large part upon its aggressive sales program and the ability of its engineering group to maintain design leadership.

---

*On one occasion in early 1958, the shop was put on a four-day week, but within two weeks they were back on full time and in another month were on overtime.

Exhibit 2. *cont'd.*

With the limited engineering staff available, virtually all efforts have been on machine design, with little time left for research or process development. The Company has on one or two occasions sponsored new designs on its own, but generally new models have been developed to meet specific customer requirements. Thus the customer has in each case in effect financed the development of the new machine. Unfortunately, with such a complex product, and under the time pressure of a promised delivery, new designs inevitably involve engineering errors, and "debugging" of prototype machines in the customer's plants has been very costly. On several occasions, it has been necessary to provide the customer with a later version of the machine at Shalco's expense.

Even production models have given a great deal of trouble in the field. Testing can be done effectively only in actual service, and generally by the time service difficulties develop additional machines are completed and operating in customers' plants. Emergency action is then necessary to make the necessary changes on all units in the field. The new U-180, introduced in mid-1958, is currently giving field troubles—thermostat, hinge, sand feed, controls, valves—and the bulk of the engineering effort in the last two months has been on finding solutions to these problems.

Under customer pressure the machines have become more automatic and much more complex. About one-third of the manufacturing cost goes into automation. The increased complexity increases the likelihood of breakdown, and since foundries are not generally competent to maintain electrical or hydraulic controls, many phone calls, travel, and air shipments result. Thus it has been difficult to give organized, continuous engineering attention to new development work, for when a customer's machine gives trouble, he naturally demands immediate action, and this diverts engineering attention from longer range design projects.

Part of the difficulty stems from inability to find components such as valves, relays, and timers that will stand up under the heavy, dirty conditions prevalent in most foundries. Foundry equipment must be designed for loads, and continuous trouble-free operation under difficult conditions and with minimum care; at the same time, costs must be kept as low as possible. Typical of the component difficulty has been a solenoid valve used on the U-180. The one chosen operated perfectly in all shop tests but has given continued trouble in the field; consequently it may be necessary to exchange almost 200 of them on the U-180s already in operation, at a cost to Shalco of over $3000.

In an attempt to overcome these difficulties, one of the engineers was made Chief of Mechanical Design, with responsibility for the supervision of day-to-day engineering. It was hoped that the Chief Engineer, whose forte is development, might in this way be relieved for work on research and advanced models. Unfortunately the field troubles with the U-180 have been so numerous that he has had little time for such longer term projects. Use has been made of outside engineering help on occasion, but it has usually proven inefficient and costly both in fees and in terms of the time which Shalco's own staff has had to spend in education and supervision.

The Engineering Department presently consists of the Chief Engineer, the Chief of Mechanical Design, one engineer, and two draftsmen. It is hoped that a young graduate engineer may be added in June.

SALES

It was early recognized that in spite of the technical advantages of shell molding Shalco faced a difficult sales problem. The process and equipment was not as yet proven, and the foundry industry was found to be much less progressive with respect to acceptance of new technology than other metal-working industries. Shell molding offered advantages only in large

Exhibit 2. *cont'd.*

production operations or situations where precision or fine finish were important. Shalco was a small, unknown, and undercapitalized company located in an area of high labor and materials costs, 2000 miles from its primary market, at a competitive disadvantage with respect to others who might copy its original design.

The proposal of a friend of the President that he form a new company, Shallway Corporation, in Pennsylvania, to manufacture and sell Shalco equipment in the East appeared to be a solution to some of these problems, for it brought in new funds and personnel and gave immediate market coverage. A contract was signed in late 1953, giving Shallway the right to manufacture and sell in the territory east of Indiana, an area containing about half the foundries in the country. Shalco retained the Midwest, Southwest, and West Coast markets. Shallway paid Shalco a license fee of 10 percent on all machines produced and sold and received a discount ranging from 27½ to 37½ percent on machines built by Shalco.

Shallway set up an aggressive sales organization and invested heavily in promotional activities. Shalco meanwhile had been unable to find a competent sales manager, and Shallway's performance in the East was much better than Shalco's in the West. In early 1955, the entire area east of the Rocky Mountains was turned over to Shallway. However, the quality of machines manufactured by Shallway was so poor that right to manufacture was withdrawn the same year. In October 1955 Shalco hired a new Sales Manager, Herbert Van Wolff, who immediately aggressively set to work to build Shalco's own sales organization.

In 1956, Shallway's President moved West, leaving the Shallway operation in the hands of its Sales Manager. This man's business ethics left much to be desired. His only interest was in immediate commissions, and he completely failed in his obligation to provide proper service and instruction on machines sold. Complaints of idle machines, dissatisfied customers, and "fast buck" deals came back to Shalco. Disagreements arose between Shalco and Shallway over allocation of service and warrantee costs, customer and dealer complaints, inter-company settlements, commission rates, deliveries, and failure of Shallway to provide adequate technical "feed-back" to Shalco's engineering group. In August 1956, the Shallway contract was terminated. To compensate Shallway for its past efforts and investments the termination agreement provided for payment to Shallway of a commission of 5 percent (declining to zero over 5 years) on all sales over $50,000 per month, Shalco's estimated break-even point. In 1957, Shallway violated the contract by representing competitive equipment and royalty payments were stopped.

Under the termination agreement, Shalco took over two of the Shallway salesmen and several Shallway distributors and began to rebuild its poor reputation with distributors and customers in the East. Much of Shalco's effort and expense in late 1956 and early 1957 went into putting idle machines back into operation, replacing defective units, establishing customer confidence. Shalco gradually reestablished its reputation for quality, integrity, and honest, aggressive sales and service.

This reputation suffered a decline again in late 1958 as design defects on the new fully automatic U-180 core blower developed in the field, but the company is currently attempting to remedy all complaints and defects, and to regain the confidence of the industry. This has, of course, been extremely costly, both in direct expense and in sales and engineering time. Design corrections have typically required the substitution of more expensive components or more careful manufacture, and production costs have increased accordingly.

Shalco presently has three salesmen in the East and one in the West, and about 15 foundry supply houses serving as distributors in this country and abroad. Machines are being manufactured under license (10 percent royalty) in England by the Coleman-Wallwork Company, which is just now getting under way on an aggressive manufacturing and promotional program.

Exhibit 2. *cont'd.*

Although the Shalco equipment was originally designed for the smaller foundry, it has gradually become apparent that the costs of educating a new foundry to the use of shell cores or molds is so costly that sales of single units are relatively unprofitable. Therefore emphasis has in the past year been on developing sales to larger foundries which can use multiple units. Substantial markets have been uncovered in the soil pipe, plumbing, and automotive industries. This has in turn necessitated development of large, fully automatic equipment and placed a premium on reliability and continuous, trouble-free operation, with consequent impact on manufacturing standards and engineering. Development of these markets has also attracted competition from larger foundry equipment manufacturers, heretofore uninterested in shell molding and shell cores. It has also created interest in the development of alternative foundry techniques and thereby increased the probability of technological obsolescence both of Shalco equipment and the shell process.

Recent sales have been to Chevrolet, Alabama Pipe, International Harvester, Massey-Harris, and similar large companies. Ford Motor Company has ordered six special fully automatic U-180s at $14,000 apiece for the production of Falcon cylinder cores. Four have been shipped and the remaining two will be delivered in the next two weeks.

In 1958, a muller (for mixing sand and resin), manufactured in England by Fordath Engineering Company, was added to the Shalco line. Mullers will be imported only against firm customer orders; bulky accessory equipment (screen vibrators, control panels, cyclones, gas heaters) will be manufactured in this country. Gross margin is approximately 30 percent of sales.

A new type of shell-molding equipment, the H-300, was recently developed by a Shalco customer for blowing molds, and will be manufactured by this customer for sale by Shalco. Manufacture will be moved this summer to Palo Alto.

Salesmen are paid a base salary and 2 percent commission. Distributors earn a 10 percent commission on all sales except mullers, on which they receive 5 percent. Distributors provide initial contacts and service and in some cases carry customer credit. Most sales are "closed" by Shalco salesmen. The Vice President-Sales Manager travels about two-thirds of the time and closes the majority of the larger orders. A sales office is maintained in Cleveland for salesman headquarters and spare parts warehousing.

PRODUCTION

Initially all manufacturing was subcontracted. Assembly was performed by Shalco employees in the subcontractor's plant. In 1954, when the present office building was leased, small parts machining and assembly were moved into the Quonset hut behind the office building. A new lathe, a used drill press, and a cut-off saw were purchased. Later a welder and small lathe were bought at auction. As volume increased, a second-hand milling machine, tapping machine, two more drill presses, and a new Bridgeport mill were added. Assembly operations were moved out to the carport and driveway. When winter came, a sheet metal building of 2400 square feet, two blocks away, was rented and fitted with power, lights, and heat. This was used for assembly only, and machine work and welding were continued in the Quonset hut. Sheet metal parts, castings, heavy machining, and grinding were subcontracted.

There were problems of coordination and supervision in the divided operation, and in mid-1958 a new building (6000 sq. ft.) was built by the owner of the property next door to the office building and leased to Shalco at $450 per month. About $2500 was invested in painting, lighting, and heating. The building is about evenly divided into machining and assembly, and welding and stores are still in the Quonset. The metal building, formerly used for assembly, is currently used for storage.

Exhibit 2. *cont'd.*

Two new lathes, two vertical mills, two drill presses, a radial drill, a new saw, and other minor equipment have been added to the machine shop in recent months, and a hoist and spray booth have been installed in the assembly area. Considerable work formerly subcontracted has been brought into the machine shop, but grinding, plating, and sheet-metal work are done by outside shops.

The work force presently consists of 18 machinists and 14 assemblymen, approximately twice that of six months ago. Some of the machinists are "moonlighters" from other plants in the area. The machine shop operates two shifts and is currently working a six-day week. The assembly shop is operating on a nine-hour, six-day schedule. Approximately 1800 overtime hours were worked during January 1959.

All nonsupervisory employees are paid on an hourly basis. It is Shalco's policy to pay slightly better than going wages in the area. Currently, the average employee in the assembly or machine shop earns about $2.80 per hour, with beginners as low as $2.00 and a few lead hands about $3.00. A 10 percent premium is paid for work on the swing shift, time-and-a-half for overtime, and double time for Sundays. Wages are thought to be about 20-30 percent above those for similar work in the East where most competitive machines are built. Materials probably average 10-15 percent more than in the East.

Employees are not unionized, although several are union members. In 1956 the local machinists union attempted to organize the shop, but lost the elections 14-1. It was later learned that the union members in the shop drew straws to determine which one would vote for the union so that the union could not determine which had voted against.

The Company provides life insurance and major medical coverage for all employees. Annual vacations of one day for each month worked (except July and August) are provided.

The Assembly Shop Foreman has been with the company since its inception. A former insurance clerk, he is an excellent amateur mechanic and amateur electrician, capable of working closely with the engineers on control circuitry and wiring, and general mechanical design. He has had no previous supervisory experience, and there is some question whether he would be able to handle the responsibility of a shop much larger than the present. He does an adequate, if not outstanding, job supervising the assembly group, and his practical mechanical and electrical ingenuity compensates for his lack of supervisory skills, especially in view of the frequent design changes and the varied product line.

The Machine Shop Foreman is a former journeyman machinist, promoted to his present position about six months ago when the previous foreman proved incapable of handling the increased volume and working effectively with the rest of the organization. The Night Shift Machine Shop Leadman reports to the Day Shift Foreman. The Company has provided no formal training in supervision, planning, or control.

Both Foremen report to the Secretary-Treasurer, who is responsible for production and purchasing as well as financial and office affairs. With the increased volume, it is intended that the Accountant will take over production control as well as supervise the expediting, traffic, and other miscellaneous responsibilities.

Overall production scheduling is done jointly by the President, Vice President, and Secretary-Treasurer, based upon orders received and anticipated. Current schedules call for a production load of about 12 U-180s, 5 MCM-5s, 1 U-360, and 3 MC-3s per month. Machines are scheduled in job lots of 5 to 30 units. Parts are generally made in similar lot sizes, with assembly in groups of 3 to 5 units, scheduled over a 1 to 3 month period.

Until recently the shop frequently failed to meet scheduled delivery commitments, sometimes missing by as much as 2 to 4 weeks. In the past two months, planning has been somewhat more realistic, and production is currently approximately on schedule. Schedules are

Exhibit 2. *cont'd.*

based on roughly estimated man-hours required. There are still occasional delays and emergency overtime due to parts shortages resulting from subcontractor, supplier, or machine shop delays. For example, assembly of U-180s was recently delayed for a week because of a shortage of hinge blocks on which excessive spoilage has occurred in the machine shop. The shortage was reported verbally to the Purchasing agent, but no action was taken to obtain new castings to replace those spoiled. A formal shortage report has not been initiated.

Spare parts shipments are handled by the Store Room Clerk. Since there are several hundred machines in the field and frequent design changes have been made, each time a replacement order is received old job files must be consulted to determine exactly what parts are required. It has been difficult to find a stock clerk sufficiently intelligent and interested to do a good job. The job files frequently do not reflect changes made during production runs. The result has been many frustrated and unhappy customers, whose machines were shut down and whose requests for parts were ignored or to whom the wrong parts were shipped. To remedy this, the employee in charge of Cleveland office was moved to California recently. While there has been improvement, the problem has still not been fully solved.

Only sporadic and inadequate data on production costs is available. Job costs are accumulated and totaled, but not until the job is completed. Since jobs may extend over a period of several months, costs are usually not available until too late to be of value for control purposes. Recently action has been taken to break historical costs down into assembly and machine shop hours, materials, subcontracting and purchased parts, as an aid in setting standards for future production. Past runs are not fully comparable because of design changes, but it is felt this should provide some guidance for scheduling, motivating, and controlling production.

Purchasing is performed by two purchasing agents and a clerk reporting to the Secretary-Treasurer. Raw materials (steel, brass, wire, etc.) components (valves, cylinders, hoses, relays, switches, motors, fasteners), subcontract work (grinding, plating, castings, sheet metal work, machining), and supplies (paint, stationery, crates) are bought for scheduled production runs in quantities and types listed on bills of materials prepared by Engineering. The Secretary-Treasurer personally places orders for most of the steel and major subcontract work. Components are purchased in accordance with brand specifications established by engineering. Subcontract work is placed in Bay Area shops, generally small plants that have served the company in the past. Occasionally very large machines, such as the U-360, are built in their entirety in subcontractor's plants, because of the limited materials handling facilities in Shalco's plant.

Careful make-or-buy analyses are seldom made. The general policy in this respect has been to bring into the machine shop all work which Shalco has the time and equipment to handle. Recently, with the Shalco shop loaded beyond capacity, a large portion of the machine work has been subcontracted.

Competitive bids on outside work are used only rarely. It is felt that now that the Company's purchases are substantial and its credit position is improved, much more favorable prices, terms, delivery and quality can be negotiated, and the purchasing group has been advised to take full advantage of the company's stronger bargaining position.

There has been some discussion recently about the advisability of continuing manufacture on the West Coast, and recently a letter was received from a large Massachusetts manufacturer, Whitin Machine Company, proposing contract manufacture of the Shalco line. It is felt by some that this would not only lead to lower labor, material, and transportation costs, but also provide better customer service and relieve Shalco executives to concentrate on development and sales activities. Others feel that the design has never been frozen for a long enough period to

Exhibit 2. *cont'd.*

make such manufacture practicable, and are concerned that quality may suffer or Shalco "know-how" may fall into potentially competitive hands.

MISCELLANEOUS PROBLEMS

Shalco holds patents on both molding machines and core blowers, but lacks the substantial funds necessary for patent defense. Hence the protection is limited, and imaginative design work by competitors could avoid infringement. Actually Shalco has itself largely obsoleted the concepts on which patents have been granted.

Another area of concern is that of broadening the product line. When a customer purchases a Shalco core blower, he may frequently place orders with his pattern shop for metal core boxes totaling several times the cost of the equipment. Shalco is usually called upon to help design the box but other firms receive the business. Occasionally Shalco accepts orders for core boxes and subcontracts them to outside pattern shops, but this narrows the margin and frequently results in difficulties in quality, design, and delivery. The Vice President believes very strongly that Shalco should establish its own core box making facilities. An investment of about $50,000 would be required, including working capital. Volumes and margins equal to the present Shalco business are probably possible.

An expansion into preparing precoated resin-sand for customers has also been considered. This operation would problably be set up in Cleveland and require an investment of about $30,000, the bulk of which would be for a Fordath muller and auxiliary equipment. This plant would have a capacity of 20 tons per day to be sold at approximately $70 per ton with a gross markup of 40 percent. A joint venture under which Shalco would provide the equipment and the Los Angeles distributor would provide the facilities and sales organization is also under consideration.

There has been some considerable discussion with respect to the variety of machines in the product line. Shalco presently offers:

Model	Size	Price
HOS-5 molding machine	18 x 24	$ 6,950
HOS-8 molding machine (special order only)	24 x 36	17,500
MC-3 core blower	10 x 12	1,795
MCM-5 core blower (mechanized)		3,992
MCM-7 core blower (mechanized)	15 x 30	5,750
U-180 core blower (full automatic)	15 x 30 24 x 15 18 x 18	9,050 9,150 8,850
U-300 core blower (for horizontal boxes)	24 x 24	8,000
U-360 core blower	36 x 36	16,750

Exhibit 2. *cont'd.*

It has been suggested that the MCM-7 be dropped from the line and a mechanized (nonautomatic) version of the U-180 offered in its place. It has also been suggested that only two versions of the U-180 (15 x 30 and 22 x 22) be offered. It is intended that the MC-3 be redesigned to improve performance and reduce manufacturing cost and sales price to compete more effectively with a less expensive unit now being made in Portland, Oregon. The machine made in Portland appears to be infringing the Shalco patents, but Shalco's patent attorney feels that legal action against this firm would be costly and of doubtful outcome. In general, competitive equipment sells at lower prices for equivalent sizes than Shalco equipment.

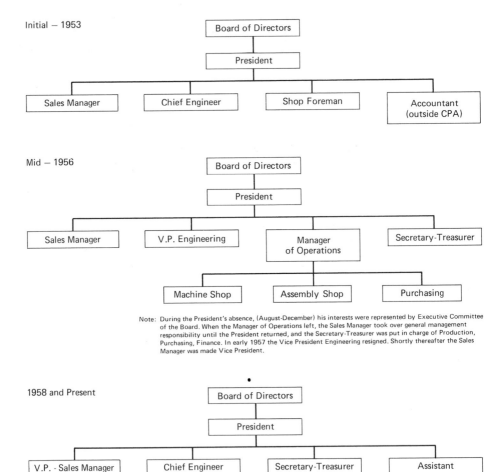

Note: During the President's absence, (August-December) his interests were represented by Executive Committee of the Board. When the Manager of Operations left, the Sales Manager took over general management responsibility until the President returned, and the Secretary-Treasurer was put in charge of Production, Purchasing, Finance. In early 1957 the Vice President Engineering resigned. Shortly thereafter the Sales Manager was made Vice President.

Exhibit 3. Shalco Corporation (A) Shalco Corporation Organization.

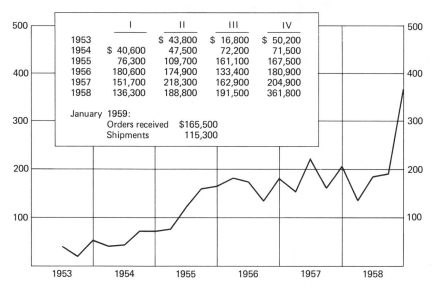

	I	II	III	IV
1953		$ 43,800	$ 16,800	$ 50,200
1954	$ 40,600	47,500	72,200	71,500
1955	76,300	109,700	161,100	167,500
1956	180,600	174,900	133,400	180,900
1957	151,700	218,300	162,900	204,900
1958	136,300	188,800	191,500	361,800

January 1959:
Orders received $165,500
Shipments 115,300

Exhibit 4. Shalco Corporation (A) Shalco Corporation Quarterly Gross Sales (in 000 dollars).

Exhibit 5(a). Shalco Corporation (A) Shipments (1957).

In Stock 12/1/57	Machines	J 1	F 2	M 3	A 4	M 5	J 6	J 7	A 8	S 9	O 10	N 11	D 12	Total
2	HO-4 (14 x 18)						1						1	2
0	HOS-4 (14 x 18)					1								1
2	HO-5 (18 x 24)													0
0	HOS-5 (18 x 24)		1		2		1	1		1	1			7
1	HOS-8 (24 x 36)													0
4	MC-3		1	2	1	3		2	1	1	2		1	14
0	MC-5 (13 x 16)	1		3		3		1			1			9
3	MCM-5 (13 x 16)	4	3	4	8	6	4	2	3	3	5	4	4	50
0	MCM-5S (13 x 30)			1		2	1	4	2	3	5	4	1	23
2	MCM-6 (20 x 25)	1		1	1	1	1		1	1				7
0	MCM-7 (15 x 30)												10	10
0	MCM-8					1								1
1	PF-5 (For HO-4)								2	1		1	1	5
3	PF-6 (For HO-5)	1		1	1		2	1						6

Exhibit 5(b). Shalco Corporation (A) Shipments (1958).

Machines	J 1	F 2	M 3	A 4	M 5	J 6	J 7	A 8	S 9	O 10	N 11	D 12	Value Total	(000)
HO-4		1			1(u)								2	$ 5.7
HOS-4													0	
HO-5													0	
HOS-5							1				2		3	21.7
HOS-8								1(u)				5	1	11.0
MC-3		3	1	2(1u)			2	3			5	5	21	37.4
MC-5						5	3				5	3	3	6.6
MCM-5	2	2	1(u)	3	1(u) 3			1	1(u) 1	1	5		30	127.2
MCA-5	3	1	1				1	1(u)					1	4.8
MCM-5S			1				1		1				7	33.5
MCM-6				2	2				2				6	59.1
MCM-7	3	3	3	2	4	4	1		2	4		3(2u)	29	164.8
MCM-7S				1									1	6.7
U-180							1	2	6	7	8	12	36	252.0
U-360										1			1	16.9
PF-5													0	
PF-6				1				1(u)		1			3	3.6
Shallway														
Muller					1								1	2.9
Shalco-Fordath												2	2	8.3
Spare Parts (000)	$ 7.7	11.1	9.1	7.1	8.9	9.4	7.6	7.3	10.0	11.6	7.6	13.3		111.3
Totals (000)	$48.0	53.0	35.8	62.3	72.8	53.9	47.7	48.7	94.5	107.9	109.3	144.4		878.3

Exhibit 6. Shalco Corporation (A) Profit Margins—Shalco Product Line (March 1, 1957).

Model	Production cost	List price	-10% Average dist. disc.	Net sale before sales commission	Gross margin before sales commission	% Gross margin
MC-3	$ 850.00	$ 1795.00	$ 180.00	$ 1615.00	$ 765.00	47
MC-5	1200.00	2992.00	300.00	2692.00	1492.00	55
MCM-5	1640.00	3992.00	400.00	3592.00	1952.00	54
MCM-5 13 x 30	2050.00	4492.00	450.00	4042.00	1992.00	50
MCM-6	5500.00	9850.00	985.00	8865.00	3365.00	38
MCM-8	7500.00	13,250.00	1325.00	11,925.00	4425.00	37
	(Estimate)					
HO-4	1350.00	3395.00	340.00	3050.00	1700.00	55
HO-5	2100.00	4960.00	496.00	4464.00	2364.00	53
HOS-5	3100.00	6950.00	695.00	6255.00	3155.00	50
HOS-8	9000.000	17,500.00	1750.00	15,750.00	6750.00	43
PF-5	375.00	750.00	75.00	675.00	300.00	45
PF-6	500.00	1250.00	125.00	1125.00	625.00	55
SCM-3	2790.00	3985.00	600.00 (-15)	3385.00	595.00	17

Exhibit 7. Shalco Corporation (A) Summary Profit and Loss Statement.

	1953	1954	1955	1956	1957	1958
Sales						
Shell Molding Machines	n.a.	n.a.	152,640	167,446	75,475	38,495
Core Blowers			303,180	414,558	545,425	713,565
Mixers				8,755	11,955	11,285
Fusers			26,500	19,100	12,875	3,600
Parts, Accessories and Patterns			31,960	56,463	95,135	111,310
Total Sales	110,882	222,084	514,280	666,322	740,865	878,254
Less: Sales Return and Allowance	249		728	11,578	17,763	4,600
Less: Distributers' Commissions			155,436	132,969	49,591	70,555
Royalty Income or Commissions Earned	13,497	21,363	1,078	3,177		2,272
Total	124,580	243,447	359,195	524,952	673,150	805,371
Cost of Sales						
Inventory Beginning		20,165	23,992	34,331	113,349	102,731
Production Expense		51,823	247,851	383,742	339,218	435,110
Pattern and Pattern Accessories		11,454	5,130	4,838	9,157	112
Parts and Accessories		132,778	10,607	27,910	47,957	60,157
Machines Repurchased				22,240	4,650	3,301
Inventory Ending		22,855	34,331	127,405	113,779	100,671
Cost of Sales	58,763	191,080	253,250	373,768	406,242	500,739
Gross Profit	65,817	52,367	105,945	151,184	266,909	304,632

Exhibit 7. *cont'd.*

Operating Expense

Engineering Expense	27,573	16,484	27,995	46,923	27,538	32,572
Tooling	2,783		1,211	1,206	2,118	6,257
Warranty				2,764	4,507	3,954
Sales Expense	20,645	22,723	6,452	64,143	113,467	135,615
Cleveland Expense					12,738	12,505
Purchasing Expense					15,607	21,107
Administrative Expense	19,252	15,223	29,859	46,393	61,081	65,492
Total Operating Expenses	70,253	54,430	65,476	161,429	237,056	277,503
Other Income		1,828	570	1,395	2,771	2,515
Other Expenses and Adjustments	886	1,311	8,479	9,675	12,122	6,325
Bonus to Key Employees						2,250
Income Before Provision for Fed. Inc. Taxes	(5,322)	(1,546)	32,559	(18,524)	20,502	21,129
Less: Provision for Fed. Inc. Taxes			7,860		6,151	6,339
Net Profit or (Loss)	(5,322)	(1,546)	24,700	(18,524)	14,351	14,790

Exhibit 8. Shalco Corporation (A) Summary Balance Sheet.

	1953	Assets 1954	1955	1956	1957	1958
Current Assets						
Cash on Hand and in Bank	6,113	424	10,662	10,974	4,475	5,332
Accounts Receivable	18,721	62,507	79,098	86,756	141,993	203,691
Purchase Contracts Receivable (Provision for					999	5,473
Doubtful Acts)			(3,332)	(5,919)	(5,602)	(810)
A/R Royalty						1,032
Advances to Salesmen				3,724	1,058	1,883
Inventories at Cost	19,017	23,992	34,331	113,399	102,731	104,443
Prepayments	207	199	155	436	2,969	1,794
Total Current Assets	43,851	87,122	120,913	209,319	247,625	322,838
Capital Assets						
Machinery and Equipment	172	254	8,281	11,730	14,441	21,312
Truck and Trailer	1,014	1,014	1,495	1,495	1,495	3,738
Furniture and Office Equipment	1,257	2,740	4,606	5,642	6,033	7,217
Leasehold Improvements			1,480	2,976	1,578	6,161
Total	2,443	4,008	15,863	21,843	23,547	38,428
Less: Provision for Depreciation	278	753	1,105	3,153	5,831	8,893
Net Capital Assets	2,165	3,255	14,758	18,690	17,716	29,535
Other Assets						
Organization Expense	188	188	188	188	188	188
Patents	613	694	694	694	694	694
Deposits	37	37	37	2,050	2,614	2,499
Total Assets	47,061	91,295	136,590	230,941	268,837	355,754

Exhibit 8. *cont'd.*

| | Liabilities and Capital | | | | | |
	1953	1954	1955	1956	1957	1958
Current Liabilities						
Accounts Payable	11,760	11,288	25,772	58,355	65,960	105,925
Accounts Receivable Discounted						9,003
Customer Deposit						13,500
Accounts Payable Officers	10,350	33,915	19,868	16,809	9,322	3,907
Notes Payable—American Trust				34,000	25,000	5,000
Purchase Contracts Payable			2,666			2,151
Sales Tax Payable		240	775	674	1,311	2,766
Commissions Payable		2,610	2,704	146	5,003	15,454
Accrued Salaries		23,200	31,700	33,420	38,938	1,656
Accrued Workmans Comp. Ins.		231	194	419	633	1,154
Accrued Payroll Taxes	2,337	1,994	2,735	3,326	4,513	8,347
Provision for Fed. Inc. Tax-Current			7,860		6,151	6,339
Accrued Bonus Payments						2,250
Provision for Fed. Inc. Tax-Prior Yr.					5,175	
Total Current Liabilities	24,448	73,678	94,273	147,149	162,004	177,451
Notes Payable, Stockholders	5,000			60,000	67,866	67,353
Capital						
Capital Stock Issued 4587 sh ('53), 4897 sh ('54-'57), 11,589 sh ('58-) stated value $5/sh	22,935	24,485	24,485	24,485	24,485	57,945
Paid in Surplus						16,730
Earned Surplus		(5,322)	(6,868)	17,832	(69,236)	21,484
Net Profit or (Loss)	(5,322)	(1,546)	24,700	(18,524)	14,482	14,790
Net Worth	17,613	17,617	42,317	23,793	38,967	100,949
Total Liabilities and Capital	47,061	91,295	136,590	230,941	268,837	355,754

Shalco Corporation (B)

In May 1959 the President of Shalco Corporation asked three of the Company's directors to have dinner and spend the evening with him for the purpose of examining the Company's problems and establishing guidelines for the future.

After dinner the President summarized the problems facing the Company as follows:

We have grown too big too fast. We are standing at the doorstep of either great success or disaster, and it is in our hands to decide which it will be. The Company has become an institution far different from what we had originally intended when we formed it six years ago, and we will have to make further drastic changes if we are to avoid being killed by success. We have developed a far larger market than we can handle. We are now playing ball in the "big leagues," and we have to decide whether we are going to grow up—or get out. We must decide what type of a company we want and then take the necessary action to achieve it.

Shalco began as a hobby, a sideline, a part-time project exploiting a simple piece of equipment developed by a group of Stanford students. It soon became apparent that more money, more people, more time, and more management would be necessary if we were to survive. By the time we realized this, we were too far committed to back out. We put in additional money and struggled along with five years of losses and small profits until the fourth quarter of last year, when, with the introduction of the U-180, we began to "take off." Now our sales have jumped to a level almost three times what they were last year, and the only limit we can see to this explosion is our own ability to engineer and produce and service at a higher level.

We are currently behind on our promised deliveries. We started the year with a backlog and still haven't caught up. We are producing at a rate far beyond our efficient capacity, and shop wastes are robbing us of the profits we should be getting on our increased volume. Our spoilage and production errors are high. Our overtime wages are outrageous. Our engineers are so busy "putting out fires," and correcting troubles in the field, that they have no time left for research and development of new designs, and we are falling behind technologically. Our salesmen find it impossible to handle customers' inquiries, problems, or complaints. Our limited working capital is far overextended, since all our money is tied up in production and accounts receivables. Our accounts payable are running over 90 days. We have already borrowed all we can from the bank and from our stockholders.

This sudden growth has come from a rapid acceptance of shell cores in the past six months and the timely introduction of the U-180. For a long time, people were suspicious of shell cores because they hadn't been proven in production operations, but now that the automobile and pipe and other companies have tested, proven, and adopted the process, everybody else is rushing to adopt it too. Fortunately, when this acceptance came, we were ready with the U-180, specifically designed for high volume core production. Now we have so many inquiries our salesmen can't get around to follow up on them. We don't have

Reprinted from *Stanford Business Cases 1966* with the permission of the Publishers, Stanford University Graduate School of Business, © 1966 by the Board of Trustees of the Leland Stanford Junior University.

enough salesmen and those we do have are too busy installing and servicing the machines we have been shipping into the field to call on new customers.

We might be able to survive these problems and to work our way out if we had time. But we don't have time.

Our friends at Ford, where we have just installed six fully automatic U-180 core blowers for producing cylinder cores for the Falcon engine—an installation totalling almost $100,000—tell us that almost every day visitors come to see these machines in operation. Fortunately most of these are potential customers. But some are salesmen or engineers from other foundry equipment manufacturers, including large firms that have not gone seriously into making shell core machines because they thought the market was too small. Now, Ford tells us, these companies' salesmen see Shalco machines in every large foundry—Chevrolet, Plymouth, General Motors' Foundry Division, pipe, plumbing, and electrical equipment manufacturers, etc.—and they are beginning to realize that the market we have developed is large enough to be very interesting to them.

The Ford people like our machines, even though they have had lots of technical and operating problems, and they like us, but they warn us that we are in for some tough competition when these larger firms enter the market. And, they add, "If SPO, Sutter, or other larger Eastern firms offer new equipment, Ford will have to think twice about placing orders with Shalco." As Ford's foundry superintendent in Cleveland says, "How can I afford to risk my job, how can I risk shutting down the Falcon production lines relying for parts and service on a small, underfinanced company like Shalco, 2000 miles away, if I can buy the same equipment from a large, well-established, reputable manufacturer nearby? We like Shalco equipment and we would like to buy more, but if you want to continue competing in the automobile industry, you'd better manufacture in the East, you'd better add technically trained field service engineers and back them up with substantial part inventories, you'd better get new financing, you'd *better get big*! Otherwise you'll lose it all." We have sensed the same feeling elsewhere.

One or two of the larger, well-established foundry equipment producers are already producing shell core machines, but they have not really entered the market seriously. We have been amazed at how easily we, who really know nothing about the foundry game, have been consistently able to beat them out from an engineering and sales standpoint. They have never designed equipment as good as ours. We think this isn't because they can't do it but because they haven't tried very hard. Our equipment is good, Von Wolff is without question the best shell-molding-equipment salesman in the country, and we have outsold all the others combined. But certainly we don't have a monopoly on good engineering or production or sales. If these other firms really go into the market seriously, with their big engineering departments, their production capability, their reputations, their sales and service organizations, we, a little ten-cent outfit away out on the West Coast, producing low quantities at high cost, wouldn't have a chance.

There is also another threat. Our success with shell cores and that of our customers has generated an interest in other ways of producing precision castings. Processes such as CO_2, "wet mix," urea binders, and plaster and ceramic molds and cores are all receiving new attentions. A breakthrough in any one of these techniques could badly damage the market for Shalco equipment. Yet we don't have the funds or time or people to do the research necessary to keep at the technological forefront in all these areas, so we have no protection against such a breakthrough.

There are, of course, a number of ways we can react to this threat and these problems. One answer would be to raise new equity capital and get big ourselves. Another would be outside manufacture. We have had a series of inquiries from Whitin Machine Company, a large and reputable manufacturer of textile machinery in Massachusetts, who would like to manufacture for us under license. Or we could sell out or merge with a larger company. Or we can stay small, perhaps specializing in a limited portion of the market, and letting the big companies take the rest.

In any case, the Company is becoming something none of us ever intended or desired. It is taking more time, more money, more effort, more worry than we ever planned. A year ago it was a great joy—now it's almost a chore. I used to know all the employees, their families, their children, and their problems—now when I walk through the plant, half of them are strangers to me. Two years ago we beat the union 14 to 1, now there's a new organizing try on in the plant and it looks like the union may get in. I don't object to the union, but I hate to see our people pay high union dues for services they don't need or want or get. And I dislike the feeling of a third party coming between us.

This union matter is just one of the new internal problems that have come with our rapid growth. For example, my own time is limited. I have my other job to do and can't afford to give it up. I am taking time and energy away from it for Shalco. At the same time I am having to delegate too much of the Shalco job to others, and don't have the time to follow up to make sure it is being properly done. So it winds up that I'm not doing either job well. This can't go on.

Our other Shalco people are as overloaded as I am. One of the reasons we have been making money now is that we are understaffed. Take Norm Swanson, for example, our Secretary-Treasurer. He is responsible for all office affairs, purchasing, production, inventories, personnel, finances, accounting, etc. This was OK when we were doing a volume of only $50,000 a month. Then each of these responsibilities was small and he could handle them all. But now we are doing over $150,000 a month, and he simply can't keep up with the load, even though he works nights, Saturdays, and Sundays. So the Company suffers, and he does too. He's unhappy because he knows he isn't doing a good job, and his wife is unhappy because he is never home. Yet he is unwilling to give up any of his responsibilities to anyone else; that would be considered a demotion. And in any case, how can I ask him to do so—it would just mean another man reporting to me.

Wolff, our Vice President and Sales Manager, is also working outrageously long hours. He thrives on it, but I'm afraid he is burning himself out—he gets terribly upset when Engineering or Production can't meet their schedules, or when he has to spend time in the field replacing defective parts or doing work that should have been done in the shop.

The Machine Shop is a madhouse. We are getting the work out, but at very high cost. Our core blowers are much bigger now, and our shop equipment simply isn't large enough to do such work efficiently. We can hardly lift some of the pieces. Yet we don't have money to buy heavier machinery or materials handling equipment, and even if we did, we would not have the space to put it in. So we do the work slowly and inefficiently, or subcontract it to others—either alternative is costly.

Our Machine Shop Foreman is a job shop man, and he doesn't think in terms of volume production. He makes 100 parts the same way he makes one—without jigs, fixtures, or other special tooling—and I don't think he'll change. Somewhat the same is true in Assembly. Our Assembly Foreman was excellent when we were developing and producing equipment in small quantities. His ability to improvise on the job was exactly the skill we needed. But now we have to plan, to organize, to train, to standardize, to take advantage of our volume to obtain the production economies it makes possible. He is intelligent, but I'm not sure he is capable of doing these things. Nor am I sure he wants to—I think he liked it a lot better in the old days, when Shalco was less hectic, when the pressure was less demanding, when we had a small, carefully selected group of men, when every new job was a technical challenge rather than a rush chore.

I'm sure much of our shop inefficiency comes from the influx of new men, who have only been with us for a couple months—they don't know us or the job, and we don't really know them. It's not like the old days, when everybody in the shop had been with us for a couple years or more.

Engineering is another trouble spot. Ash, our Chief Engineer, is a highly creative person. He can come up with more new exciting and promising ideas than anyone I have ever known. But he is not an administrator—he can't plan and organize and supervise the work of others and he shouldn't have to—if he does we lose the benefit of his creativity. He used to be able to dream and plan and innovate, and I could help keep him concentrating on the most practical of his ideas while I watched over the work of the other engineers. Now I can't. I'm too busy elsewhere, and the Engineering Department is so bogged down with customers' complaints and production problems and with debugging the U-180 in the field, that they have no time to devote to new designs or developments. As a result we are making no progress at all on development, and Wolff is angry because we can't turn out the new automatic models he feels are necessary to meet the special demands of big customers like the automobile and cast iron pipe companies. And he has convinced me that if we don't do it someone else will and we will lose these markets.

A special part of this problem is the new emphasis on automation. We started manufacturing simple equipment for the small foundry—now we find ourselves making large automatic equipment for big production foundries. Our engineers are mechanical engineers—they are neither experienced nor trained in the areas where we need strength now—hydraulics, pneumatics, and electronics. So most of our problems in the field come in breakdowns in the complex control circuitry.

Another serious problem is the lack of money. You, the larger stockholders, have together loaned the Company over $60,000 to help us handle this increased load. But you can't lend more, and you shouldn't. We are borrowing all we can from the banks, and are discounting our receivables. Yet we still don't have enough—some of our suppliers haven't received payment for 90 days. Each week we have to scrape to meet the payroll.

We can't afford the equipment we need. We have to produce in inefficient lot sizes because we can't afford the costs of longer runs. And our sales suffer. We can't give the service we should on spare parts because we can't afford to carry the inventory. We can't offer the credit terms to customers that our competitors can. Our credit rating is poor, and a customer paying $10,000 to $20,000 for a piece of equipment hesitates to do business with a manufacturer who has such a weak financial position.

We could sell more equity stock, but the stockholders who have supported the Company through these long, lean years, and the employees who own stock or options, rightfully object to dividing ownership of the Company with others, especially just now when we are beginning to show a nice profit. If we sold stock today, before we have had a chance to demonstrate how much we can earn, we would have to sell it too cheap, we would have to give up too much ownership to obtain the money we need.

There are other problem areas—accounting, purchasing, inventories—and here again the problems have all come from the rapid growth.

What has really happened is that our formula worked too well, our original concept of the Company, our initial policies - top quality, progressive engineering, the most advanced product we could produce, fair pricing, full customer service, honesty, good people, the best we could get - these are what have led us to this volume and the resulting problems. I guess it is the last of these, the "good people," that have really brought us to this point. And Wolff particularly. Our product is good, but so are the competitive machines. Wolff just happens to have an absolutely unbelievable ability to convince customers to convert from conventional sand cores to shell cores, and most importantly, to buy Shalco equipment when they do. He, more than anything else, more even than the increasing "know-how" and interest in shell cores, has expanded our market and the total market as well.

So—what do we do? We want to make money, of course. We want Shalco to survive and prosper. We want our people to have every opportunity for growth and advancement. But we want to run the Company rather than have it run us.

Wolff is delighted with the present situation and frustrated only by the inability of the other functions to keep up with Sales. He gets a bonus of one-half percent of sales, he's making more money than he ever has, and he's anxious to keep pushing the volume up and up and up. Norm and Ash are not so happy. They are working harder than ever but don't make any more, except perhaps through our profit-sharing plan—and then only if the increased volume brings us increased profits. Right now the Company is earning more money than it ever has before, but we will have to invest more in order to keep on earning it, and sometimes I wonder whether it's worth it.

Should we start negotiations with Whitin Machine Company again? Whitin is a large, reliable company. They have beautiful engineering and production facilities, and they are still interested in manufacturing Shalco equipment under license. But the last time I proposed this to Norm, Ash, and Wolff, they blew their tops. They were afraid Whitin would get our designs and know-how and then drop us. For that matter, any company could buy one of our U-180s and be in business manufacturing them within several months. Our patents wouldn't give us much protection. There is not a thing we could do about it, for we couldn't afford the legal action necessary to protect ourselves.

If we had Whitin produce our equipment, how would we get our engineering drawings in shape, so that their shop, 2000 miles away, could use them? What would happen to our shop, our people in Palo Alto? Could we keep them busy doing engineering and development work? Building prototypes? Producing specials that are needed only in small quantity and hence unsuited to Whitin's shop? How would we establish a fair royalty price? Could they, with their large overhead, really produce at lower cost than we can? How would we finance their production? Wouldn't we still require additional working capital to carry receivables? Should we let them sell as well as produce? How can we overcome the objections of Wolff, Norm, and Ash to such a program?

Should we merge or sell out to another company? To whom could we sell? Does selling make sense when we are just beginning to show good profits? Shouldn't we try to continue by ourselves for a while, demonstrate conclusively that we can earn a substantial profit, and then look for a buyer at a much higher price? *We* have confidence in the potential future of shell cores, *we* know that in the hands of a large company with adequate finances and good production facilities Shalco can keep ahead of all the others and earn very good money. But how do we convince another company, which knows nothing about shell cores or of the high potential? How would we find time to locate a buyer and to negotiate? Should we sell for cash, stock, or a share of earnings?

What would become of Wolff, Norm, Ash, the Palo Alto operation? They don't share my concern with Shalco's future. Wolff isn't at all worried—he is confident we can keep our position in the market if we will just improve our engineering and production.

If I became convinced that Shalco's best future and the best interests of Wolff, Norm, and Ash lie in sale or merger, how could I possibly convince them? When we gave them the profit sharing and stock options this year, they asked "What's the gimmick? Is this to replace the Christmas bonuses we have had in the past? Where will get the money to exercise the options? Will the company lend it to us? Won't our options become so valuable that the Company will have to get rid of us?'' Wolff wanted to have his bonus based on sales rather than profits, because he had control over sales, whereas profits were affected by the actions of others over which he had no control. All of them thought the percentages were too low.

If they reacted irrationally to a gift we did not have to give, how would they react to a sale of the Company? Could we convince Wolff that he would have a greater and surer earning opportunity if Shalco were part of a large, well-financed company with an established reputation and modern production facilities? If we couldn't get his cooperation in the merger, what would we have left to sell? Could we persuade Ash and Norm to move East? Or could we persuade the buyer to continue the Palo Alto operation? For what purpose? At what level? The buyer would want to purchase 100 percent of the stock—could we persuade all the stockholders to sell?

Should we sell additional Shalco stock to local investors and ourselves? How much new capital would be needed to guarantee Shalco's future? How much ownership would we have to give up to get it? How would we prove the profit potential to prospective investors? New money would not solve the problems of the high cost of West Coast materials, labor, selling and customer service. Wouldn't we have to move our operations East? Where could we find the people we would need to operate at a higher volume? How should we divide up their responsibilities? Who would manage the new large operation? I can't take on greater responsibilities myself, and I can't move East.

Wolff would be happy to take over the management of the whole company himself and has written me a memo to this effect (Exhibit 1). If we made him General Manager, who would handle the sales function? Could Wolff handle both sales and general management? How can he find time to do any more than he is doing now? Does he have the judgment, the balanced perspective? Would the engineers quit? What would I do? What should be the objectives, the operating policies of such a company? Could we reconcile the personal objectives of the present owners with those of the new investors?

We have one more alternative. Couldn't we remain small, concentrate on limited, specialized markets in which the larger companies are not interested? Couldn't we emphasize advanced engineering, build on Ash's creative abilities, and on being the technological leader of the industry?

But would Wolff be interested in this? He wants Shalco to take every order we can get. He wants us to go into the manufacture of core boxes and resin-coated sand and any other associated venture that can earn us a profit. He could readily get a good job with any of our competitors, or for that matter, with any machinery manufacturer. If we lose him, we lose one of our most important assets—we have no one who could match him in selling. But would he leave? If he did, where would we find another? How would Norm and Ash react to putting a limit on their earning power under the new profit-sharing plan? What would be the reaction of you, our stockholders, to a policy which clearly restricts the growth of the Company?

What should we do? I need your help!

Exhibit 1. Shalco Corporation (B)

November 22, 1958

1. I believe that Shalco has a most promising future, starting as of immediately, ours for the asking.

2. I realize and give full credit to the original founders of Shalco, to wonderful and able persons such as Norm Swanson, Ash Hollingsworth, and several others, without whose ingenuity, aid, and genuine interest Shalco could not have survived.

3. I believe that my person, my work, and my accomplishments have in some measure contributed and helped Shalco into its present position, both technologically and also purely from a business point of view.

4. I believe that my "sales job" as such is finished, and that I have nothing further to contribute unless the company is organized and capable to handle the business volume reliably, efficiently, and profitably, with due consideration toward further development and market trends.

5. I believe that in the face of such rapidly expanding business volume, growing commitments to customers, employees' protection and relations, morale in the organization, and in order to cope with the growing responsibilities of such an expanding organization, concentrated, full-time management is imperative. I think that the President should be relieved from the vastly increasing areas of details and responsibilities.

6. In conclusion: because I believe that it is good for the company, for purely personal reasons and to protect my own interests, and in order to participate in this promising future, and because I believe it is essential, I would like to suggest for due consideration my appointment as General Manager of the Company as from January 1, 1959, retaining my present position as Vice President and Sales Manager.

I believe that I have proven my abilities, my great interest in Shalco, unselfish devotion to this job, and now I would like to have wider fields of responsibility with a view that I may contribute towards Shalco's growth with what I feel I still have to offer.

7. The General Manager and executives are to present to the President, the Board of Directors, and the Stockholders a quarterly, bi-yearly, and yearly overall plan for approval, which the General Manager shall be responsible to carry through and fulfill.

Herbert von Wolff

Exhibit 2. Shalco Corporation (B) Orders and Shipments (January-April 1959).

Machines	J 1	F 2	M 3	A 4	Total	Value (000)
HO-4						
HSO-4						
HO-5						
HOS-5	1		2		3	21.2
HOS-8						
MC-3			5	2	7	12.6
MC-5			2		2	6.0
MCM-5	2		1	5	8	34.3
MCA-5						
MCM-5s						
MCM-6						
MCM-7				2	2	11.5
MCM-7s						
U-180	8	6	14	8	36	356.9
U-360		1		1	2	36.5
H-300						
PF-5			2		2	1.5
PF-6						
#4 Mixer	1	2	1	2	6	26.3
#2 Plant			1	1	2	54.0
#4 Plant	1				1	18.1
Spare Parts	13.4	17.0	24.0	18.0		72.9
Totals	115.2	105.3	242.3	188.0		651.8
Orders Received	165.5	143.7	165.1	162.0		
U Used						
m Mechanized						

Exhibit 3. Shalco Corporation (B) Profit and Loss Statement (January 1 to March 31, 1959).

Sales			
Shell molding machines	$ 21,200.00		
Core blowers	324,262.00		
Pin fusers	1,500.00		
Mixers	63,115.00		
Core boxes	10,003.53		
Spare parts	42,682.31		
Miscellaneous	120.00		
Sales at List Price		$462,882.84	
Less distributor's commission	29,796.60		
Less freight out	1,271.09		
Less cash discounts taken	2,398.22	33,465.91	
		429,416.93	
Miscellaneous Income	431.00		
Royalty Income at 2.80	1,436.51	1,867.51	
Total Income		431,284.44	
Beginning inventory	100,443.20		
Production expense	24,626.12		
Purchases and labor	305,286.83		
Ending inventory	156,064.26		
Cost of goods sold		274,291.89	
Gross margin		156,992.55	
Warranty	2,333.79		
Engineering	11,735.61		
Development and exper.	483.39		
Selling	43,901.05		
Cleveland	3,318.75		
Purchasing	7,942.66		
Core-making expense	900.03		
Total Operating Expense		93,608.00	
Total Net Profit		63,384.55	
Less Accrued Profit Sharing		5,388.68	
Net Profit Before Taxes		57,995.87	
Less Provision for Federal Taxes		24,658.00	
Net Profit After Taxes		33,337.87	

Exhibit 4. Shalco Corporation (B) Balance Sheet (March 31, 1959).

		Assets
Current Assets		
Cash on hand and in bank		$ 31,598.49
Account receivable	$249,318.79	
Less allowance for bad debts	(4,259.21)	245,059.58
A/R employees		972.23
Advance payments		900.00
Royalties receivable		2,468.01
Advances salesmen		2,233.86
Inventories at cost		156,064.26
Prepayments		
Insurance	1,984.55	
Interest	627.12	
Postage	244.50	2,856.17
Purchase contracts		2,823.40
Deposits		2,498.84
Total Current Assets		447,474.84
Other Assets		
Organization expense	187.80	
Patents	694.00	
Total Other Assets		881.80
Fixed Assets		
Machinery and equipment	27,919.91	
Truck-auto-trailer	3,737.59	
Furniture and office equipment	14,668.51	
Leasehold improvements	7,051.99	
Allowance/or depreciation	(10,174.20)	
Total Fixed Assets		43,203.80
Total Assets		491,560.44

Note: In February 1959, a profit-sharing plan was installed, retroactive to January 1. The plan called for division of 15 percent of net profit after taxes between the Vice President, Secretary-Treasurer, and Chief Engineer.

Exhibit 4. *cont'd.*

		Liabilities
Accounts payable		$119,387.10
Sight drafts payable	15,274.00	
A/P officers		4,791.52
Customers deposits		11,050.06
Purchase contracts		7,712.52
Distributor commissions payable		20,980.11
Accrued wages		5,726.98
Employee bonds and payroll taxes		15,830.83
Provision for federal income taxes—prior year		2,695.84
Provision for federal income taxes—current year		24,658.00
Accrued workman compensation insurance		1,965.90
Accrued profit sharing		5,388.68
Discounted accounts receivable		47,382.40
Total Current Liabilities		282,843.94
Notes payable—officers and directors		67,353.44
Capital and Liabilities		
Suspense	616.90	
Corporate expense	(2,055.01)	
Capital stock 11,789 at 5.00 stated value	58,945.00	
Paid in surplus	17,230.00	74,736.89
Earned surplus Dec. 31, 1958	33,288.30	
Profit and (loss) 1959	33,337.87	66,626.17
		491,560.44

On March 27, 1959, Shalco Corporation received a permit to grant to the same key employees options to purchase a total of 2,750 shares of capital stock, and exercisable over a period of 5 years at the rate of not more than 20 percent of the total shares each year. Expiration date of this permit is April 26, 1964. Option price was set at $7.50 per share.

Exhibit 5. Shalco Corporation (B) Summary Profit and Loss Statement.

	1953	1954	1955	1956	1957	1958	1959
Sales							
Shell Molding Machines	n.a.	n.a.	152,640	167,446	75,475	38,495	
Core Blowers			303,180	414,558	545,425	713,565	
Mixers				8,755	11,955	11,285	
Fusers			26,500	19,100	12,875	3,600	
Parts, Accessories, and Patterns			31,960	56,463	95,135	111,310	
Total Sales	110,882	222,084	514,280	666,322	740,865	878,254	
Less: Sales Return and Allowance	249		728	11,578	17,763	4,600	
Less: Distributers' Commissions			155,436	132,969	49,951	70,555	
Royalty Income or Commissions Earned	13,947	21,363	1,078	3,177		2,272	
Total	124,580	243,447	359,195	524,952	673,150	805,371	
Cost of Sales							
Inventory Beginning		20,165	23,992	34,331	113,349	102,731	
Production Expense		51,823	247,851	383,742	339,218	435,110	
Pattern and Pattern Accessories		11,454	5,130	4,838	9,157	112	
Parts and Accessories		132,778	10,607	27,910	47,957	60,157	
Machines Repurchased				22,240	4,650	3,301	
Inventory Ending		22,855	34,331	127,405	113,779	100,671	
Cost of Sales	58,763	191,080	253,250	373,768	406,242	500,739	
Gross Profit	65,817	52,367	105,945	151,184	266,909	304,632	

Exhibit 5. *cont'd.*

	1953	1954	1955	1956	1957	1958	1959
Operating Expense							
Engineering Expense	27,573	16,484	27,995	46,923	27,538	32,572	
Tooling	2,783		1,211	1,206	2,118	6,257	
Warranty				2,764	4,507	3,954	
Sales Expense	20,645	22,723	6,452	64,143	113,467	135,615	
Cleveland Expense					12,738	12,505	
Purchasing Expense					15,607	21,107	
Administrative Expense	19,252	15,223	29,859	46,393	61,081	65,492	
Total Operating Expenses	70,253	54,430	65,476	161,429	237,056	277,503	
Other Income		1,828	570	1,395	2,771	2,515	
Other Expenses and Adjustments	886	1,311	8,479	9,675	12,122	6,325	
Bonus to Key Employees						2,250	
Income Before Provision for Fed. Inc. Taxes	(5,322)	(1,546)	32,559	(18,524)	20,502	21,129	
Less: Provision for Fed. Inc. Taxes			7,860		6,151	6,339	
Net Profit or (Loss)	(5,322)	(1,546)	24,700	(18,524)	14,351	14,790	

Exhibit 6. Shalco Corporation (B) Summary Balance Sheet - Assets.

	1953	1954	1955	1956	1957	1958
Current Assets						
Cash on Hand and in Bank	6,113	424	10,662	10,974	4,475	5,332
Accounts Receivable	18,721	62,507	79,098	86,756	141,993	203,691
Purchase Contracts Receivable					999	5,473
(Provision for Doubtful Acts)			(3,332)	(5,919)	(5,602)	(810)
A/R Royalty						1,032
Advances to Salesmen				3,724	1,058	1,883
Inventories at Cost	19,017	23,992	34,331	113,399	102,731	104,443
Prepayments	207	199	155	436	2,969	1,794
Total Current Assets	43,851	87,122	120,913	209,319	247,625	322,838
Capital Assets						
Machinery and Equipment	172	254	8,281	11,730	14,441	21,312
Truck and Trailer	1,014	1,014	1,495	1,495	1,495	3,738
Furniture and Office Equipment	1,257	2,740	4,606	5,642	6,033	7,217
Leasehold Improvements			1,480	2,976	1,578	6,161
Total	2,443	4,008	15,863	21,843	23,547	38,428
Less: Provision for Depreciation	278	753	1,105	3,153	5,831	8,893
Net Capital Assets	2,165	3,255	14,758	18,690	17,716	29,535
Other Assets						
Organization Expense	188	188	188	188	188	188
Patents	613	694	694	694	694	694
Deposits	37	37	37	2,050	2,614	2,499
Total Assets	47,061	91,295	136,590	230,941	268,837	355,754

Exhibit 7. Shalco Corporation (B) Summary Balance Sheet - Liabilities and Capital.

	1953	1954	1955	1956	1957	1958
Current Liabilities						
Accounts Payable	11,760	11,288	25,772	58,355	65,960	105,925
Accounts Receivable Discounted						9,003
Customer Deposit						13,500
Accounts Payable Officers	10,350	33,915	19,868	16,809	9,322	3,907
Notes Payable—American Trust				34,000	25,000	5,000
Purchase Contracts Payable			2,666			2,151
Sales Tax Payable		240	775	674	1,311	2,766
Commissions Payable		2,610	2,704	146	5,003	15,454
Accrued Salaries		23,200	31,700	33,420	38,938	1,656
Accrued Workmans Comp. Ins.		231	194	419	633	1,154
Accrued Payroll Taxes	2,337	1,994	2,735	3,326	4,513	8,347
Provision for Fed. Inc. Tax—Current			7,860		6,151	6,339
Accrued Bonus Payments						
Provision for Fed. Inc. Tax—Prior Yr.					5,175	2,250
Total Current Liabilities	24,448	73,678	94,273	147,149	162,004	177,451
Notes Payable, Stockholders	5,000			60,000	67,866	67,353
Capital						
Capital Stock Issued	22,935	24,485	24,485	24,485	24,485	57,945
4587 sh ('53), 4897 sh ('54-'57), 11,589 sh ('58) at $5.00/sh						
Paid in Surplus					(69,236)	16,730
Earned Surplus		(5,322)	(6,868)	17,832		21,484
Net Profit or (Loss)	(5,322)	(1,546)	24,700	(18,524)	14,482	14,790
Net Worth	17,613	17,617	42,317	23,793	38,967	100,949
Total Liabilities and Capital	47,061	91,295	136,590	230,941	268,837	355,754

Exhibit 8. Shalco Corporation (B) Balance Sheet (March 31, 1959).

	1/1/59–3/31/59	
Current Assets		
Cash on hand and in bank		$ 31,598.49
Account receivable	$249,318.79	
Less allowance for bad debts	(4,259.21)	245,059.58
A/R employees		972.23
Advance payments		900.00
Royalties receivable		2,468.01
Advances salesmen		2,233.86
Inventories at cost		156,064.26
Prepayments		
Insurance	1,984.55	
Interest	627.12	
Postage	244.50	2,856.17
Purchase contracts		2,823.40
Deposits		2,498.84
Total current assets		447,474.84
Other Assets		
Organization expense	187.80	
Patents	694.00	
Total Other Assets		881.80
Fixed Assets		
Machinery and equipment	27,919.91	
Truck-auto-trailer	2,727.59	
Furniture and office equipment	14,668.51	
Leasehold improvements	7,051.99	
Allowance/or depreciation	(10,174.20)	
Total fixed assets		43,203.80
Total assets		491,560.44

Exhibit 9. Shalco Corporation (B) Profit and Loss (January 1 to March 31, 1959).

Sales		
Shell molding machines	$ 21,200.00	
Core blowers	324,262.00	
Pin fusers	1,500.00	
Mixers	63,115.00	
Core boxes	10,003.53	
Spare parts	42,682.31	
Miscellaneous	120.00	
Sales at list price		
		$462,882.84
Less distributor's commission	29,796.60	
Less freight out	1,271.09	
Less cash discounts taken	2,398.22	33,465.91
		429,416.93
Miscellaneous income	431.00	
Royalty income at 2.80	1,436.51	1,867.51
Total income		431,284.44
Beginning inventory	100,443.20	
Production expense	24,626.12	
Purchases and labor	305,286.83	
Ending inventory	156,064.26	
Cost of goods sold		274,291.89
Gross margin		156,992.55
Warranty	2,333.79	
Engineering	11,735.61	
Development and exper.	483.39	
Selling	43,901.05	
Cleveland	3,318.75	
Purchasing	7,942.66	
Core-making expense	900.03	
Total operating expense		93,608.00
Total net profit		63,384.55
Accrued profit sharing		5,388.68
Net profit B/F taxes		57,995.87
Provision for federal income taxes		24,658.00
Net profit		33,337.87

Exhibit 10. Shalco Corporation (B) Balance Sheet (March 31, 1959).

1/1/59-3/31/59		
Current Liabilities		
Accounts payable		$119,387.10
Sight drafts payable		15,274.00
A/P officers		4,791.52
Customers' deposits		11,050.06
Purchase contracts		7,712.52
Distributor commissions payable		20,980.11
Accrued wages		5,726.98
Employee bonds and payroll taxes		15,830.83
Provision for federal income taxes—prior year		2,695.84
Provision for federal income taxes—current year		24,658.00
Accrued workman compensation insurance		1,965.90
Accrued profit sharing		5,388.68
Discounted accounts receivable		47,382.40
Total current liabilities		282,843.94
Notes payable—officers and directors		67,353.44
Capital and Liabilities		
Suspense	616.90	
Corporate expense	(2,055.01)	
Capital stock 11,789 at 5.00 state value	58,945.00	
Paid in surplus	17,230.00	74,736.89
Earned surplus Dec. 31, 1958	33,288.30	
Profit and (loss) 1959	33,337.87	66,626.17
		491,560.44

Note: On March 27, 1959, Shalco Corporation received permit No. 69304SF to grant key employees options to purchase a total of 2750 shares of capital stock; the option price not to exceed $10.53/share, and exercisable over a period of five years at the rate of not more than 20 percent of the total shares each year. Expiration date of this Permit is April 26, 1964.

Shalco Corporation (C)

At the dinner meeting described in Shalco Corporation (B), one of the directors stated that he felt that the National Acme Company, with which he had had previous business relationships, might be interested in purchasing Shalco. National Acme was a 75-year-old, highly reputable manufacturer of multiple-spindle automatic lathes, die heads, and electrical controls located in Cleveland, Ohio. Through conservative wartime and postwar management, National Acme had accumulated large cash reserves. A new management was now seeking ways to put these idle reserves to work and was considering diversification into new fields through acquisition.

Preliminary discussions between Shalco's President and National Acme executives took place in Cleveland in late May and developed areas of strong mutual interest. For National Acme it offered entrée to a new and growing field, closely related to its present business. For Shalco it offered a solution to all the problems of location (Cleveland is the approximate center of the foundry industry), reputation, production facilities, finance. It appeared that 2 plus 2 might indeed equal 5.

Shalco's President reported his discussions with National Acme to a selected few of Shalco's directors and received their enthusiastic support. He did not discuss the negotiations with Von Wolff, Swanson, and Hollingsworth for he saw little to be gained from arousing their concern until it was clear that a satisfactory agreement might be reached.

Difficulties in the negotiations centered over price and terms of sale and pattern of operation subsequent to sale. Shalco's sales and profits were rising and Shalco was confident that highly profitable operations lay ahead, especially with the financial, engineering, and production resources of National Acme, plus its excellent reputation, behind the Shalco product.

National Acme, on the other hand, knew little about the foundry industry and even less about the shell-molding process or markets. National Acme commissioned Battelle Memorial Institute to evaluate Shalco's potential, but the report was vague and inconclusive. Even Shalco's net worth was indeterminate. The Company's accounting had been quite informal, and an accurate evaluation of its net worth and profit performance would necessitate a professional audit of its books, plant, and inventories.

The Shalco negotiators would have preferred a tax-free exchange of stock, but since National Acme had never before acquired another company and had issued no new stock during the last 30 years, the National Acme executives felt it would be difficult enough to get their elderly board to approve the acquisition without complicating the issue further by issuance of new stock. Besides, National Acme's interest in the acquisition was as a means of investing its idle cash reserves.

Shalco's President was concerned with what might happen to the Shalco employees in the event of a merger. He felt that the three key executives were essential

---

Reprinted from *Stanford Business Cases 1966* with the permission of the Publishers, Stanford University Graduate School of Business, © 1966 by the Board of Trustees of the Leland Stanford Junior University.

to a successful operation of Shalco by National Acme and had to obtain a sales agreement attractive to them. He hoped that others of the Palo Alto staff might also find opportunities with National Acme, although he felt it unlikely that many would be interested in moving to Cleveland. He felt the problem might be solved by continuing the Palo Alto operation on engineering and development work and producing prototypes and specials.

Another problem lay in the profit-sharing and stock options recently granted. Could profit sharing continue after merger? On what basis? The stock options were exercisable over a five-year period. There was no provision in the stock option plan to cover sale of the company.

National Acme was interested only in a total acquisition. Shalco stock was held by 24 stockholders, mostly executives, employees, and directors, all of whom would have to approve the sale of his stock to National Acme, and the options were still outstanding.

Shalco Corporation (D)

General agreement on the terms and conditions of sale of Shalco Corporation to National Acme were reached in June. Shortly thereafter National Acme's Board of Directors gave its executives the "go-ahead" to continue negotiations along the general lines agreed upon.

National Acme's Production Manager scheduled a trip to California in early July to examine the Shalco plant and equipment. In anticipation of his visit, on July 4, Shalco's President called in Von Wolff, Swanson, and Hollingsworth to tell them of the negotiations which had been under way and to explain to them the terms of the proposed sale. The group reacted violently and expressed emphatically their belief that the Company should continue as an independent firm. They pointed out that the Company had come from nothing to a position of leadership in the field, that after all these years it would be foolish to sell out just as the Company was crossing the threshold of big profits, that the sale would negate their new profit-sharing and stock-option rights, that the merger would force them to move East, etc., etc.

They offered to purchase the Company on the same terms offered to National Acme and set out to obtain backing from local financial and corporate interests for such a purchase. They were unsuccessful in obtaining backing but continued their opposition until Wolff, on a sales trip to the East in mid-July, was persuaded to visit National Acme to meet the people and see the plant facilities. He returned to

Reprinted from *Stanford Business Cases 1966* with the permission of the Publishers, Stanford University Graduate School of Business, © 1966 by the Board of Trustees of the Leland Stanford Junior University.

California much impressed by what he had seen and convinced of the wisdom of the sale. The others had little choice but to accept.

To meet the problem of the stock options, the Shalco Board authorized the immediate exercise of the future options so these executives would share in the capital gains to be realized in the sale of the Company. Then Shalco's major stockholders agreed to turn over to these executives a portion of their own receipts from the sale in compensation for termination of the profit-sharing plan, on the condition that the executives would stay with the new company.

During July and August three drafts of the agreement of sale were prepared and modified by the attorneys of both parties. Supporting exhibits evidencing all Shalco's liabilities and assets were prepared and documented. Accountants were called in to audit the Shalco books and prepare them for transfer to National Acme.

In mid-September, the final agreement was completed and copies were sent to all Shalco shareholders for signature. Within a week all but one Shalco shareholder had signed. The one holdout was Shalco's former Machine Shop Foreman, who had come with the company in 1952 and had been discharged in 1958 because of his inability to grow with the Company or to get along with the other executives. Now he decided to block the sale to "get even." After extensive persuasion, and some financial inducement, he signed the agreement to sell.

The actual "closing" took place on October 2, 1959, at which time the initial payment to Shalco stockholders was made, the signed agreements were delivered to the California Commissioner of Corporations, Shalco's Board of Directors resigned, and a new Board composed of National Acme executives was elected.

The next day, Shalco Corporation was dissolved and became the wholly owned subsidiary of the National Acme Company.

Von Wolff and members of the Sales Department moved to Cleveland in September, shortly before the final closing. A new sales office and assembly and demonstration area were set up in Plant 2 of National Acme. During late 1959 and the first half of 1960, production continued in Palo Alto while National Acme prepared for manufacture in Cleveland. The first Cleveland-built U-180 was completed in January 1960, and shortly thereafter Palo Alto terminated production on this model. Present plans call for transfer of all production to Cleveland in July 1960, at which time the Palo Alto plant will be closed.

Engineering has also continued in Palo Alto since the sale of the company. Two new models have been added to the product line; the CTA-18 is a medium-priced, fully automatic core blower, designed to sell for approximately $5,000 and to replace the MCM-5 and MCM-7. The V-200 is more specialized in its application, being designed for blowing "hub" cores used in manufacture of cast iron pipe. Both these machines were introduced at the Philadelphia Foundry Convention in May 1960. Two V-200s have been built in Palo Alto, and the first production run of 10 CTA-18s will be completed in Palo Alto before the plant is closed. Henceforth all machines will be produced in Cleveland.

Design of a third new model, the CT-10, to sell for approximately $2,500, is under way in Palo Alto. Prototyping and production will be done in Cleveland.

At the request of several stockholders and of National Acme, the sales price has been deleted.

This Agreement was drawn by National Acme's attorneys in Cleveland and modified by Shalco's attorneys in San Francisco. It is regarded by those who have studied it as an excellent example of clear, concise, and precise legal language and warrants study as a well-conceived and well-executed model of such a document.

In the Agreement, National Acme, the purchasing company, assures itself that it is protected as to the existence and amount of the assets and liabilities, and that there shall be no changes other than in the normal course of business between the dates of the Agreement to sell and the actual closing several months later.

Shalco, as the selling company, likewise has taken care that all possible liabilities are fully listed and described to protect itself against any future accusation of misrepresentation or breach of warranty. Copies of correspondence and all pertinent documents associated with each item described were furnished to National Acme's attorneys prior to signing of the Agreement, so that they might be fully familiar with all detail behind each item.

Shalco's President, rather than Shalco's stockholders, was required to make personal representations and warranties as to the validity of Shalco's financial statements and other facts regarding the corporation, because he personally negotiated the sale on behalf of the other stockholders and because the other stockholders were not familiar with, and hence unable to warrantee, these facts. Protection against minor errors or oversight is given by clause 9, which limits the liability to amounts in excess of $5,000.

Shalco Corporation (E)

In October 1959, Shalco stockholders sold their stock to the National Acme Company of Cleveland, Ohio. Between that time and July 1960, the Palo Alto plant operated as the Shalco Division of National Acme, carrying on engineering, product development, and production until National Acme could absorb the production of Shalco equipment into their Cleveland plant. In May 1960, it was decided that the transition was sufficiently far along that the Palo Alto operation could be closed down in July.

In order to keep together the nucleus of the Shalco organization, a purchase of the shop and office equipment and assignment of the shop and office leases were negotiated with National Acme and a new company formed. On August 1, the new company began operations under the name of Encina Development Company.

It is the present intention of the new company to carry on job shop machining and assembly on a subcontract basis for other firms. It had originally been intended that engineering services would also be offered and that the new company might develop its own new products. However, both the engineer and draftsman who it was hoped might do such work are considering job opportunities elsewhere and will probably leave. The other engineers are considered competent only to work under supervision and will be released. Outside engineering help is available to the company, and a highly competent engineer with extensive practical manufacturing and machine design experience has expressed some interest in joining the new venture. His personal circumstances, however, are such that he could neither invest nor take a sacrifice in salary if he came with Encina Development Company, and the company is somewhat reluctant to commit itself to his salary of approximately $1,000 per month until more definite plans are made in product development.

With a rush of terminating the former operation and making the final shipments to Cleveland, there has been no opportunity to solicit jobbing work, or to give thorough consideration to the organization and operation of the new company. One project was investigated in some detail (Exhibits 1 and 2). Others have also been considered (Exhibit 3).

The new group has retained from the former Shalco operation the machine shop foreman, assembly foreman, three machinists, two assembly men, and a secretary capable of office management, payroll, accounting, purchasing, and shipping. Shop employees are presently being used to clean and recondition the equipment and to repaint the office building. It is estimated that this work will require about 15 working days. The former Shalco President is available only on a part-time basis. Shalco's production manager will spend August and September with National Acme in Cleveland, after which time he will either join the new company or find other employment. Shalco's Chief Engineer will also spend two months in Cleveland. He has decided to take another position on his return, but will be available on a consulting basis, as would other Shalco engineers. The students who investigated the apricot cutter (Exhibits 1 and 2) will be available if desired for market or sales work. Other management or shop people can be added as needed. Almost all shop employees have indicated a desire to return if an opportunity develops to do so.

Working capital in the amount of approximately $5,000 is immediately available; substantially more may be obtained when and if the prospects warrant additional investment.

Exhibit 1. Shalco Corporation (E) Apricot Cutting Machine.

Two recently graduated MBAs were employed to investigate an apricot cutter developed by engineers of the Agricultural Extension Service of the University of California at Davis, California. The Extension Service provides advisory service to California farmers and employs an engineering division to develop agricultural techniques, chemicals, and equipment. New equipment is patented, and equipment manufacturers are sought to produce it under license to the University, at a standard license fee of five percent of sales value. Among equipment recently developed are a grape harvester, asparagus cutter, tomato harvester, tree shakers, and catching frames.

The apricot cutter was developed four years ago. It was demonstrated on the 1957 crop, and its performance was impressive enough to induce a group of apricot ranchers in Hollister to place firm orders with a small manufacturer of agricultural equipment in Santa Rosa. After accepting advance payments for six machines, this manufacturer decided to concentrate on other equipment he had developed and return the advance payments.

Preliminary investigation indicated that this machine offered exactly the type of potential which the Shalco group sought. It was well within the design and production capabilities of the Shalco organization, the apricot industry was concentrated within 100 miles north and south of

Exhibit 1. *cont'd.*

San Jose and in the Hemit area East of Los Angeles, there appeared to be a trend toward grouping of small apricot growers into associations of corporations whose operations were large enough to justify automatic cutting and drying equipment. The strike of orchard workers in June-July 1960, and consequent loss of many growers' crops, had created a great interest among growers in automation in agricultural equipment. Because of the strike, the growers had not been able to bring in migratory harvesters from Mexico. It appeared likely that the U.S. minimum wage would be increased from $1.00 to $1.25 per hour in the near future, which would be another incentive to mechanization.

It was found that the University prototype machine was in the plant of Sunsweet Growers in San Jose. This organization is a large drier of apricots, prunes, pears, peaches, etc., which are sold under the Sunsweet brand. Apricots are purchased dried from independent growers and are washed, redried, and packaged by Sunsweet. Sunsweet provides various services to assist its suppliers, and in June was rebuilding the University apricot cutter to test and demonstrate on the 1960 crop.

Several Shalco employees visited Sunsweet and studied the dismantled machine. Its design and construction appeared unnecessarily complex, but the basic operating principles were sound. In its present form it was estimated that it could be built and sold profitably for about $5,000. The University was contacted and indicated a willingness to issue a six-year exclusive license if it could be shown that the new company was competent and would be agreeable to a reasonable minimum royalty guarantee. Copies of patents were ordered from the U.S. Patent Office in Washington.

On the University machine the apricots are dumped into a water bath which carries them to a feeder. The feeder drops them individually into shallow rubber cups on a conveyor belt. As they move toward the cutting area, water jets lift them slightly in the cups and orient them so that the "suture" and the pit (seed) lie horizontally. A second set of cups on an overhead drum, driven at the same speed as the conveyor, contact the apricot and hold it as it is drawn between two spring-loaded knives. The knives cut the apricot neatly into two halves around the pit. An ingenious device measures the size variation as the cot approaches the knives and adjusts the spacing between the cups to prevent squeezing the fruit and to center the fruit on the cutting knives.

As the cup on the drum rotates away from the cup on the conveyor, the two top and bottom halves of the apricot follow the drum and conveyor cups, and plungers with five needles about 1/16" in diameter pierce the apricot and knock the pit out. The halves then fall onto a conveyor belt which conveys them to a machine which lays the halves face-up in drying trays on another conveyor belt. Sunsweet engineers stated that a crew of four workers could feed the machine, supervise its operations, and inspect the finished apricots to remove any damaged fruits, remaining pits, and further spread them for drying on the trays.

On the basis of the preliminary investigation, the two students were authorized to investigate the apricot cutter further. They were given a budget of $750 for salary, travel, and miscellaneous expenses. They were at the same time asked to seek other unfilled needs or ideas for agricultural equipment. Salary and expenses which had been paid to date were approximately $125.

The students talked to the president of the Hollister growers' association, who advised them that if the machine could be made to sell for under $4,000 and performed well, he believed about five machines could be sold in his area in the first season. They visited the Agricultural Extension Service in Davis and talked to the economists and engineers who developed the apricot cutting machine. All indicated that there was a great need for such equipment and encouraged the new company to proceed with further development and introduction to the market.

Exhibit 1. *cont'd.*

One of the obvious problems in this project was the short harvest season on apricots—from about June 15 to July 30. Apricots matured first in the northern orchards and about three weeks later in the southern part of the growing area. Apricots had to be cut and dried or canned immediately after harvesting. They could not be stored for more than one or two days. In any given location the harvesting and drying or canning had to be accomplished in a period of about two weeks, so there appeared to be some possibility of moving the cutting machines from one area to another during the season to increase the annual utilization. One of the students was an Australian and suggested the possibility of shipping the machines to Australia during the winter. It was felt that the machines could be sold or leased to growers or could be used to cut apricots on a contract basis, moving the machines from ranch to ranch.

In the process of their investigation, the two students were advised that they should visit the Hemit area, where apricots are cut and dried on a large scale. They were particularly advised to investigate both the Amori machine, used by very large growers in Hemit, and available only on a lease basis ($4,000 per season), and the small hand-fed Burns machine, which is sold for $350.

One week was spent in the Hemit area. The Amori machine was found to be extremely large. It consists primarily of a feeder device and a belt made up of hundreds of "V" shaped rollers, which orient the suture and pit of the apricot by their rotating action. As the apricots are carried along these rollers they pass under the rotating serrated knives, which split the fruit and knock the pit free. Pits and fruit are dropped onto a vibrating plate with holes large enough to allow the pits to fall through. The apricot halves proceed to another conveyor from which they drop in much the same manner as on the University machine to the drying trays.

It was observed that the Amori machine made a somewhat rougher cut than the University machine and could not handle overripe fruit without considerable spoilage. The yield in dried apricots was about 10 percent less than estimated for the University machine. Moreover, the pit removal on the Amori machine was not as efficient, and more girls were required to inspect, remove pits, and orient the fruit on the drying trays. On the other hand, because it could process twelve apricots past the knives at the same time, its production was approximately ten times as great.

Because of the high rental cost of the Amori machine, it was estimated that it was economical for use only by growers who dried over 400 tons of apricots per season. It was estimated that the machine might break even in an operation processing over 50 tons.

The Burns hand-operated machine was also investigated. On this machine the operator orients the fruit and places it in the machine, which splits the apricot. Pits are removed and the halves laid on the drying trays by hand. Two good operators, one cutting and one pitting and laying out, can process about 50 apricots per minute, as against 150 on the University machine and 1500 on the Amori.

Many small ranchers cut apricots by hand. The apricot is held in the left hand and cut by a knife in the right. The pit is flipped out with the thumb and the halves laid on the tray. A good cutter can process about 20 apricots per minute. Hand cutting is frequently done by the entire family.

It was felt that productivity of the University machine might be increased by adding additional conveyors, but this would raise difficulties in designing the mechanism that adjusts the cup spacing to accommodate varying sizes of fruit. This mechanism might be eliminated by presizing the fruit and then processing it through four or more parallel conveyors, all set for different sizes. At the same time it seemed likely that the Amori machine could be produced in smaller sizes to cut 4, 6, 8, or any desired number of appricots at one time. It was rumored that an automatic feeder was being developed for the Burns machine.

There are eight Amori machines in the Hemit area and six elsewhere in California. In general, the growers using the Amori machine are pleased with its operation, although

Exhibit 1. *cont'd.*

admittedly there is no other machine on the market with which it can be compared. The labor situation in Hemit is critical and all large growers are machine-minded.

A visit was made to the only grower in the San Jose area using an Amori machine. He expressed the opinion that mechanized apricot cutting and drying could be done profitably only on a very large scale, primarily because of the large investment in auxiliary equipment—processing and drying shed, water and power installation, sanitary facilities, trays, handling equipment, etc. He estimated that the minimum investment would be about $40,000 plus the cost of the cutting machine. He pointed out that many apricot growers were selling their orchards for tract home developments because of the increasing labor difficulties and costs and the rapidly rising value of land, both in the San Jose and Los Angeles areas. He stated that many of those who were continuing to grow apricots were doing so only to benefit from further appreciation of their land values, and that rather than invest in cutting and drying equipment and other necessary equipment, they would sell their apricots directly to the canneries, even at a substantially lower price than could be obtained for dried fruit. The price of fresh fruit varies from 10¢ to 25¢ per pound, less than for dried fruit, depending mainly on the percentage of the crop dried. About 10-20 percent of the crop is presently dried; the balance is sold to canneries for canning.

Exhibit 2. Shalco Corporation (E) Notes on the Agricultural Equipment Industry.

An investigation into the agriculture and food production equipment industry indicated a total U.S. volume of $2 billion per year, 150,000 employees, about 14,000 manufacturers. Eight firms have approximately 75 percent of the sales. International Harvester Company's agricultural equipment sales are about $500 million. Half the total sales are in tractors. One-fourth of the tractor market is replacement.

Growth has been very great. In 1910 there were 1000 tractors in the U.S.—today there are 5 million (horses and mules on farms have dropped from 24 million in 1910 to 5 million today.) It is estimated that without the equipment produced by this industry, 60 - 70 percent of the U.S. population would be engaged in food production. Today there are only about 10 percent. In 1910, one farmer fed 8 other people. Today he feeds 18. In postwar years the sale of tractors has increased at a lower rate than other farm equipment. Sales of pick-up bailers and field forage equipment have increased over 1000 percent.

In spite of the growth of this industry, profits have fallen off since 1950. This has been attributed to saturation of the market, decline in farm income, and severe competition, most recently from abroad. There are no tariffs, on farm equipment, except in a few special instances. Some American firms are producing abroad for the U.S. market. The export market (20 percent) is decreasing. Smaller manufacturers have suffered more than larger producers, who have built name brands and good will through advertising and parts and repair service.

The demand for farm equipment is highly variable, depending largely on farm net income and weather. The typical farmer thinks carefully before purchasing equipment. The demand for the product of the farmer, food, is inelastic, and a reduction in the price of farm equipment and hence food costs, can do little to increase the volume of food sold.

There appears to be a strong trend toward a higher level of mechanization in farm equipment. The number of farms is declining, and the remaining farms are getting larger and able to use large expensive equipment. Equipment is getting more complex; in some cases a single unit is able to do a complete harvesting and packaging job. The market for general harvesting equipment appears to be saturated, and emphasis is being put upon the automation of such operations as feeding, dairy, and cleaning. Equipment manufacturers have substantially increased their product development budgets.

Exhibit 2. *cont'd.*

Because of the seasonal market, two thirds of the typical argicultural equipment manufacturer's assets are in inventory. Capital investment ranges from $6,000 to $14,000 per employee. Dealers handle equipment on a consignment basis. Costs average about 50 percent raw material, 30 percent labor, 20 percent overhead.

The primary operating problems of the industry appear to be strikes, seasonal demand, competition, level of low mechanization in the farm equipment plants (product variation is great, and with the exception of the large manufacturers, production quantities are low). Smaller companies tend to concentrate in specialized lines of product. Larger firms are diversifying into nonagricultural fields.

Exhibit 3. Shalco Corporation (E) Other Projects Considered.

1. Machine Tools
A nearby pattern shop and foundry has for the last ten years produced and marketed a line of disc sanders, grinders, and saw sharpeners. These are sold through machine-tool dealers, and, although little merchandising effort has been made, volume is about $100,000 per year, most of it on the West Coast. The products enjoy a good reputation for quality and performance and are well liked by those who have used them. The owner of the foundry is elderly and contemplates gradual retirement from his business. A management consulting firm has suggested to him that he license the Shalco group to manufacture the machine tools. Thus far he has not been willing to do so, arguing that he needs the machine shop for his other work, and the tools provide additional profit without additional overhead, as well as a product that can be built for stock when foundry work is low.

2. Engineering and Development
Although the Shalco group has at present no engineers in its employ, it has a continuing interest in engineering and development that could lead to production work. A competent consulting mechanical engineer, who has previously done work for Shalco, has proposed a number of development projects; some of these have been carried through the conceptual state—outdoor toys, equipment for automatic packaging and testing of transistors and other electronic components, farm equipment, simplified digital control devices, etc. His services would be available on a fee basis.

3. Subcontracting Work
Shalco had only moderate success in subcontracting its own production to outside shops. Although some of its suppliers gave good service, many were casual about delivery dates and tolerances, and often charged what Shalco felt were exorbitantly high prices. On a blow valve, for example, Shalco paid $28 to a supplier and later found, when it performed the same work in its own shop, that the cost was only $15, including overhead. With such experiences, it has appeared that the new company, with good organization, proper planning and controls, and a conscientious effort to provide first-class customer service, might find an attractive opportunity in subcontract work for other local firms. The company has no specialized skills, but it could offer a general machining, welding, and assembly service, with engineering if desired. Subcontract rates in the area for such work are $7 - $8 per hour, plus a normal markup of about 10 percent on material. Machinists' wages are about $3 per hour.

Most good jobbing machine shops in the area appear to have plenty of work at the present time. The new company has received one subcontract of $380 for production of machined parts for two prototype units of a new multi-deck tape recorder.

Exhibit 3. *cont'd.*

4. Railroad Journal Box Oiler

The construction of railroad axle bearings is much the same as it was 50 years ago—a bronze bearing lubricated by oil and wicking in the journal box. Roller bearings are used on some passenger cars and on fast freight cars, but the vast majority (approximately 3 million) of freight cars are still equipped with conventional bronze friction bearings.

Lubrication has always been a serious problem on such bearings, and many attempts have been made to solve it, none apparently very successful. Because of the large number of cars involved, and the practice of interchanging cars between railroads, any solution involving conversion of existing equipment could take place only over an extended number of years.

Bearings are ordinarily oiled in the following manner. The freight train (average 50 cars) is stopped in the railroad yard. Two oilers walk along the track, one on each side of the train, opening the journal box doors and filling those which need oil. Filling must be done only to a specified level belore the door lip. If filled too full, oil is wasted and thrown on the track, thus reducing locomotive traction.

Not only is the oiling process time consuming in terms of labor costs, the idle train represents a large investment and the long stops required put the railroads at a serious competitive disadvantage with trucks because of the increased transit time. A typical train might require oiling several times on a trip across the country.

Even more serious is the problem of quality control on this operation. If the oiler carelessly fails to lubricate a bearing which needs it, it may run dry, in which case it develops a "hot box," the train must be stopped, and the car removed and set on a siding for service. If the hot box is not detected, the bearing may be ruined and derailment result.

Through one of its former suppliers of automatic electrical controls, the Shalco group heard of this problem, and have proposed to one of the railroads a joint project to develop an automatic machine which would open the journal box doors, inject oil where necessary, and close the doors, all while the train is in motion at approximately five miles per hour. If successful, the railroad with whom the project was discussed could use about six such units. Railroads compete on the basis of customer service and exchange information and rights on technical developments such as these through the Association of American Railroads. Thus the ultimate market could be very large.

It was felt that the machine to perform the oiling operation would be about 200 feet long and would probably cost over $50,000. Because of the development costs involved, the Shalco group could not undertake such a project except on a development contract financed by the railroad.

The manufacturer of electrical controls, which suggested the project, is frequently asked to develop automatic equipment to meet specialized industrial needs. It is interested only in the electrical control portion of such work and has suggested to the Shalco group that when such projects arise, it be divided, with the Shalco group handling the development and manufacture of the mechanical portion of the project.